P9-DVU-323

Germany
North Sea
DEN
Sylt
Niebüll
To Copenhagen
Flensburg
Husum
SCHLESWIG-HOLSTEIN
Heide
Kiel
Neumünster
Travemünde
Lübeck
Cuxhaven
East Frisian Islands
Norddeich Mole
Wilhelmshaven
Bremerhaven
Elbe
Hamburg
Emden
Worpswede
Leeuwarden
Groningen
Leer
Bremen
Delmenhorst
BERGEN-BELSEN
NETHERLANDS
LOWER SAXONY
Alkmaar
Haarlem
Amsterdam
Schiphol
Bad Bentheim
Celle
Hannover
The Hague
Hengelo
Rheine
Osnabrück
Braunschweig
Delft
Hameln
Arnhem
Bielefeld
Münster
Goslar
Rhine
Nijmegen
Emmerich
Paderborn
HARZ MOUNTAINS
Göttingen
Essen
Duisburg
Dortmund
Ghent
Antwerp
Venlo
Düsseldorf
Kassel
WARTBURG
Brussels
To Bruges
Maastricht
Cologne
Marburg
Bebra
Eisenach
Aachen
Bonn
BELGIUM
Liège
Remagen
Wetzlar
HESSEN
Fulda
Namur
GERM
BURG ELTZ
Koblenz
Cochem
St. Goar
RHINE
Wiesbaden
Frankfurt
MOSEL
Bacharach
Mainz
Hahn
Bingen
Main
Würzburg
LUXEMBOURG
Trier
Nahe
Worms
Luxembourg City
Longwy
Mannheim
Steinach
Saar
Kaiserslautern
Heidelberg
Rothenburg
Thionville
CASTLE ROAD
Metz
Saarbrücken
Karlsruhe
Dinkelsbühl
To Paris
Châlons
LORRAINE
Stuttgart
Nördlingen
Baden-Baden
Schwäbisch Gmünd
Toul
Nancy
Strasbourg
Kehl
BADEN-WÜRTTEMBERG
BLACK FOREST
FRANCE
Tübingen
Ulm
BLACK FOREST OPEN-AIR MUSEUM
ALSACE
LES VOSGES
Colmar
Triberg
Danube
Furtwangen
Freiburg
Meersburg
Ravensburg
To Paris
Culmont
Bad Krozingen
Lake Constance
Kempten
Mulhouse
Staufen
Konstanz
Rhinefalls
Stein
Lindau
Belfort
Basel
APPENZELL
Bregenz
Zürich
Appenzell
Feldkirch
BURGUNDY
Besançon
JURA MTNS.
Dijon
SWITZERLAND
LIECHTENSTEIN

Rick Steves®

BEST OF GERMANY

Contents

LEGEND
Freeway/Autobahn
Major Roads
Major Rail Line
Airport
Museum, Landmark, Other Point of Interest
Castle/Monument/Palace
100 Kilometers
100 Miles
MARK
To Copenhagen
To Trelleborg (Sweden)
Rødby
Puttgarten
Fehmarn
Rügen
Sassnitz
Binz
Stralsund
Baltic Sea
Warnemünde
Rostock
Usedom
Züssow
Świnoujście
MECKLENBURG-VORPOMMERN
Neubrandenburg
Schwerin
Szczecin
Neustrelitz
Szczeciński/Stargard
BRANDENBURG
Lüneburg
Neuruppin
Elbe
Oder
SACHSEN-HAUSEN
Oranienburg
Gorzow Wielkopolski
Uelzen
Berlin
Poznań
To Warsaw
Potsdam
Brandenburg
SANSSOUCI
Rzepin
Wolfsburg
Frankfurt an der Oder
POLAND
Magdeburg
Halberstadt
Wittenberg
Cottbus
Zary
Dessau
Aschersleben
Lubin
Halle
Leipzig
MORITZ-BURG
Bolesławiec
Legnica
Wrocław
THURINGIA
Meissen
Bautzen
Görlitz
Zgorzelec
Naumburg
SAXONY
Dresden
SILESIA
Bad Schandau
To Kraków
Weimar
"SAXON SWITZERLAND"
Zittau
Erfurt
Glauchau
Chemnitz
Seiffen
Děčín
Ustí nad Labem
Litoměřice
TEREZÍN
Suhl
Plauen
Ruzyně
ANY
Karlovy Vary
Prague
Lichkov
Coburg
Marktredwitz
Cheb
Kutná Hora
CZECH REPUBLIC
Bayreuth
Bamberg
KARLŠTEJN
KONOPIŠTĚ
Plzeň
Weiden
BOHEMIA
MORAVIA
Tabor
Český Kubice
Nürnberg
Brno
Telč
Furth
Veseli nad Lužnicí
Slavonice
Břeclav
České Budějovice
Regensburg
Gmund
ROMANTIC ROAD
Ingolstadt
Obertraubling
Český Krumlov
Summerau
Donauwörth
Passau
WACHAU
Krems
Durnstein
Vienna
To Budapest
BAVARIA
Danube
Linz
MAUTHAUSEN
Augsburg
DACHAU
St. Valentin
Melk
SCHÖNBRUNN
Attnang Puchheim
Eisenstadt
Munich
Puchberg
HERREN-CHIEMSEE
Chiemsee
Salzburg
Salzach
Isar
Herrsching
ANDECHS MONASTERY
Sopron
AUSTRIA
Bad Ischl
Hallstatt
Oberammergau
Selzthal
Kufstein
SALZKAMMERGUT
NEUSCHWANSTEIN
Berchtesgaden
Hallein
Bruck an der Mur
Füssen
Garmisch
Leoben
Reutte
Zugspitze
Worgl
Stainach Irdning
TIROL
Hall
Kitzbuhel
Zell am See
Graz
EHRENBERG
Innsbruck
To Italy
To Italy
A-24
A-19
A-11
A-10
A-12
A-2
A-13
A-9
A-15
A-4
A-72
A-70
A-73
A-93
A-6
A-3
A-92
A-95
A-8
A-1
A-2
A-9
E-50
E-65

Introduction

Germany is blessed with some of Europe's most spectacular scenery—the jagged Alps, flower-filled meadows, rolling hills of forests and farms, and rivers such as the raging Rhine and elegant Elbe. It has hundreds of castles, some ruined and mysterious; others stout, crenellated, and imposing; and still others right out of a Disney fairy tale.

And of course there are the cultural clichés, kept alive more by tradition-loving Germans than by tourist demand. The country is dotted with idyllic half-timbered villages where you can enjoy strudel at the bakery or sip a stein of beer while men in lederhosen dance with women in drindls. Peruse a wonderland of chocolates, stock up on Hummels and cuckoo clocks, and learn how to polka.

All of these traditions stand at sharp contrast with the Germany of today. Despite its respect for the past, this truly is a 21st-century country. At the forefront of human progress, Germany is a world of high-tech trains, gleaming cities, social efficiency, and first-class museums celebrating many of history's greatest cultural achievements. Germany was a founding member of the European Union and continues to lead the way in creating a healthy Europe for the future.

With medieval castles, speedy autobahns, old-time beer halls, gleaming skyscrapers, and the best *wurst,* this young country with a long past continues to make history.

THE BEST OF GERMANY

This book focuses on Germany's top destinations—its most fascinating cities and intimate villages—from powerhouse Berlin to sleepy Bacharach. A focused 14-day trip highlights lively Munich, musical Salzburg (just across the Austrian border from Munich, it's too convenient to pass up, even in a book about Germany), the castle-studded countryside of Bavaria, the medieval walled town of Rothenburg, quaint villages along the mighty Rhine, and the fascinating, ever-changing capital, Berlin. And when there are interesting sights or towns near my top destinations, I cover these briefly (as "Near" sights), to help you fill out a free day or a longer stay.

Beyond the major destinations, I cover the Best of the Rest—great destinations that don't quite make my top cut, but are worth seeing if you have more time or specific interests: Würzburg, Nürnberg, Frankfurt, Baden-Baden, Dresden, and Hamburg.

To help you link the best destinations, I've designed a two-week itinerary (see page 26), with tips to help you tailor it to your interests and time.

DEN.
Baltic Sea
North Sea
Hamburg
POLAND
NETHER-
LANDS
100 Kilometers
100 Miles
Berlin
GERMANY
Rhine
Cologne
Dresden
Rhine Valley
BURG
ELTZ
The Rhine
Valley
St. Goar
Bacharach
Frankfurt
CZECH
REPUBLIC
LUX.
Würzburg
Nürnberg
Rothenburg
Rothenburg and
the Romantic Road
Baden-
Baden
FRANCE
Danube
Bavaria
Danube
Rhine
Munich
NEUSCHWAN-
STEIN
Bavaria
Oberammergau
Salzburg
Füssen
Zugspitze
SWITZ.
AUSTRIA

THE BEST OF MUNICH

Lively, livable Munich has a compact, pedestrian-friendly core that welcomes strolling. The city is awash in convivial beer halls, beautiful gardens, stately churches, fancy pastry shops, and fine art museums. The crown jewels at the Residenz and the oompah bands at beer halls remind visitors that Munich has long been equally at ease hosting royalty and commoners alike.

❶ *The towering* ***New Town Hall*** *presides over Munich's main square, Marienplatz.*

❷ *The* ***Viktualienmarkt,*** *a fun open-air market with cheap eateries, sports a Bavarian maypole.*

❸ *A guide proudly introduces visitors to the palatial* ***Residenz,*** *home to Bavarian royalty for centuries.*

❹ *At* ***beer halls,*** *oompah bands play "Roll Out the Barrel!" to crank up the fun.*

❺ *The* ***Chinese Tower*** *in the English Garden is a landmark near a popular beer garden.*

❻ *Ride the rapids at the south end of the* ***English Garden,*** *where the surf's always up.*

❼ *Time to order another!* ***Prost!***

❽ *A statue of Mary and an ornate glockenspiel (with daily shows) overlook* ***Marienplatz****—Mary's Place.*

3

4

5

6

7
HB

8

THE BEST OF SALZBURG

Just across the German border in Austria, Salzburg offers Mozart concerts, Baroque churches, winding cobbled lanes, and *The Sound of Music*. Capped by a sturdy fortress overlooking its charming old town, Salzburg is ringed by hills that are ideal for hiking or lingering at view cafés. At night, there's always music playing, with a beautiful, floodlit backdrop.

Salzburg's charisma and proximity to Munich make it irresistible to tuck into a Germany trip.

❶ *Salzburg's compact* ***Old Town*** *is an inviting maze for visitors to explore on foot.*

❷ *The* ***New Residenz,*** *where prince-archbishops once partied, hosts a glockenspiel and museums today.*

❸ *The* ***Mirabell Gardens*** *anchor a soaring view of Salzburg's old-town spires and hill-capping fortress.*

❹ *Walk or bike along the* ***Salzach River,*** *or just admire the city view from the bridge.*

❺ *Grave sites are lovingly tended at* ***St. Peter's Cemetery.***

❻ ***Fountains*** *add a splash of artistry in this lively city, brimming with music and culture.*

❼ *Festooned with old-time signs, the street called* ***Getreidegasse*** *entices shoppers and photographers.*

THE BEST OF BAVARIA

This alps-strewn region boasts fairy-tale castles, lovely churches, thrilling luge runs, and cozy villages such as Füssen (a handy home base) and adorable Oberammergau. Straddling the border with Austria, the towering Zugspitze offers mountain thrills, with high-altitude lifts, trails, and view cafés.

❶ *Growing up in* ***Hohenschwangau Castle*** *inspired "Mad" King Ludwig to build castles of his own.*

❷ *The ceiling of the* ***Wieskirche*** *opens up to the artist's view of heaven.*

❸ *Visitors admire* ***Linderhof Castle,*** *"Mad" King Ludwig's smallest, most intimate home.*

❹ *Bavaria's* **Lüftlmalarei***—colorful painted scenes on houses—raise the bar for house painters everywhere.*

❺ *To avoid long lines, order* ***timed tickets*** *to tour Neuschwanstein and Hohenschwangau Castles.*

❻ *Swooping downhill on a* ***luge:*** *Wheee!*

❼ **Füssen** *makes a cozy home base for visiting nearby castles and sights.*

❽ *The stunning* ***Neuschwanstein Castle*** *is King Ludwig's masterpiece and swan song.*

THE BEST OF ROTHENBURG AND THE ROMANTIC ROAD

Photogenic Rothenburg, encircled by a medieval wall, has half-timbered buildings and cobbled lanes lined with tempting bakeries, pubs, shops, and museums. It's my favorite stop on the Romantic Road, a route linking cute towns and divinely beautiful churches in the serene, green countryside.

❶ *Vineyards and forests blanket the hill topped by* ***Rothenburg,*** *Germany's best walled town.*

❷ *Half-timbered buildings, arches, and towers contribute to the* ***picturesque charm*** *of Rothenburg.*

❸ *Rothenburg's* ***main square*** *draws locals and tourists alike.*

❹ *In this Middle Ages* ***altarpiece,*** *the master wood-carver, Tilman Riemenschneider, brought wood to life.*

❺ *Walk the narrow,* ***roofed wall*** *of Rothenburg early or late for maximum medievalism.*

❻ *If you go for Baroque, visit the gardens of* ***Weikersheim Palace,*** *along the Romantic Road.*

THE BEST OF THE RHINE VALLEY

The mighty Rhine River is steeped in legend, where storybook villages (including the quaint home-base towns Bacharach and St. Goar) cluster under imposing castles. Tour the Rhine by boat, train, or bike, passing vineyard-draped hillsides, vintage castles, slow barges, and the massive cliff of the Loreley along the way.

1

2

3

4

❶ *Costumed soldiers evoke* ***feudal times,*** *when lords and robber barons vied for control of the Rhine.*

❷ *The village of* ***Bacharach,*** *nestled on the Rhine, is delightful for a stroll.*

❸ *Ferries* ***cruise*** *up and down the Rhine, taking passengers on a joyride.*

❹ *Visitors can clamber up and down the ruins of* ***Rheinfels Castle,*** *enjoying Rhine views.*

❺ ***Cologne****'s grand Gothic cathedral is impressive day or night.*

❻ *The Rhine Valley produces* ***fine wine,*** *which can be sampled in tastings at wine bars.*

❼ *Castles have built-in chapels, ranging from plain stone to decorative, with fine* ***stained glass.***

❽ ***Burg Eltz,*** *in the Mosel Valley, wins Europe's best-furnished castle award.*

THE BEST OF BERLIN

The most happening place in the country—from avant-garde architecture to vibrant nightlife—is Berlin. Germany's capital also features evocative monuments and memories of the Wall that once divided the city and country. The modern dome topping the old Reichstag exemplifies how the city has melded its complicated past with its exciting future.

❶ *Along the* ***Spree River,*** *crowds come out with the sun.*

❷ *Dating from 575 B.C., the* ***Ishtar Gate*** *(detail shown) from Babylon graces the Pergamon Museum.*

❸ *Sunset highlights the dome topping the* ***Reichstag,*** *Germany's historic parliament building.*

❹ *Berlin's stocky* ***cathedral*** *is just over a century old, built under the reign of Kaiser Wilhelm.*

❺ *The* ***Brandenburg Gate,*** *once separating East and West Berlin, is now a powerful symbol of freedom.*

❻ *Segments of the former* ***Berlin Wall*** *are decorated with graffiti.*

❼ *The* ***Hackescher Markt*** *neighborhood is appealing to explore day or night.*

❽ *The quirky little green man on the stoplight is a nostalgic reminder of communism.*

THE BEST OF THE REST

With extra time, splice any of these destinations into your trip. **Nürnberg**'s Old Town invites browsers while its Nazi sites fascinate historians. Walkable **Würzburg** has a palace fit for a prince-bishop, while **Baden-Baden**'s baths are just right for spa lovers. Amid a forest of skyscrapers, **Frankfurt** has a pleasant old-time square and popular riverfront park. **Dresden**'s art museums and rebuilt church are worth a visit. Germany's largest port, **Hamburg,** offers a harbor tour that shows off the city's stunning new architecture.

❶ ***Hamburg,*** *Germany's most important port, has a huge harbor that even landlubbers enjoy touring.*

❷ *In* ***Dresden,*** *a cyclist joins the Parade of Nobles, a mural made with 24,000 porcelain tiles.*

❸ *In* ***Baden-Baden,*** *it's fun to make waves at the Baths of Caracalla.*

❹ ***Nürnberg,*** *largely rebuilt after World War II, has a sweet Old Town but powerful Nazi sites.*

❺ *Modern* ***Frankfurt*** *has skyscraping towers and down-to-earth parks.*

❻ *Guarding* ***Dresden****'s treasures*

❼ *The Residenz Palace is just one reason to visit* ***Würzburg,*** *a town dotted with atmospheric wine bars.*

3

4

5

6

7

TRAVEL SMART

Approach Germany like a veteran traveler, even if it's your first trip. Design your itinerary, get a handle on your budget, line up your documents, and follow my travel strategies on the road. For my best advice on sightseeing, accommodations, restaurants, and transportation, see the Practicalities chapter.

Designing Your Itinerary

Decide when to go. Peak season (roughly May through September) offers the best weather, long days (light until after 21:00), and the busiest schedule of tourist fun. Late spring and fall generally have decent weather and lighter crowds. Winter can be cold and dreary, but Germany's famous Christmas markets brighten main squares from late November until Christmas.

Choose your top destinations. My itinerary (on page 26) gives you an idea of how much you can reasonably see in 14 days, but you can adapt it to fit your timeframe and choice of destinations.

Fun-loving Munich is a must for anyone, with its engaging mix of beer gardens and world-class art. If castles spark your imagination, linger in Bavaria and on the Rhine. Historians appreciate Nürnberg, Dresden, and Berlin. For music and Mozart, settle in Salzburg (Austria). If you like medieval walled towns, make tracks for Rothenburg. To feel the pulse of 21st-century Germany, head to Berlin. Hedonists luxuriate in the baths at Baden-Baden. Hikers love to go a'wandering in Bavaria, and photographers want to go everywhere.

Draft a rough itinerary. Figure out how many destinations you can comfortably fit in the time you have. Don't overdo it—few travelers wish they'd hurried more. Allow enough days per stop: Figure on at least two or three days for major destinations.

Staying in a home base (such as Munich) and making day trips can be more time-efficient than changing locations and hotels. Minimize one-night stands, especially consecutive ones; it can be worth taking a late-afternoon train ride or drive to get settled into a town for two nights.

Connect the dots. Link your destinations into a logical route. Determine which cities in Europe you'll fly into and out of; begin your search for transatlantic flights at Kayak.com. If you fly into Frankfurt (a popular arrival point), note that the airport has its own train station to easily get you to your first destination (the Rhine villages are just an hour away).

Decide if you'll travel by car or public transportation, or a combination. Trains connect major cities easily and frequently. Trains in Germany are either fast and pricey (book ahead for discounts, or use a railpass), or they're slow and cheap (even cheaper with one of several day passes). The long-distance buses are inexpensive, though it's wise to book several days in advance.

A car is useless in big cities, but it's helpful for exploring countryside regions such as Bavaria, where train and bus connections are relatively infrequent and time-consuming.

Some travelers rent a car on site for a day or two, and use public transportation for the rest of their trip. Also, keep in mind that minibus or bus tours (available at most destinations) help day-trippers reach regional sights efficiently without a car.

Allot sufficient time for transportation in your itinerary. Whether you travel by train, bus, or car, it'll take a half-day to get between most destinations.

To determine approximate transportation times, study the driving chart (on page 408) or train schedules (Germany's Deutsche Bahn, www.bahn.com). Compare the cost of any long train ride with a budget flight; check Skyscanner.com for cheap flights within Europe.

Plan your days. Finetune your itinerary; write out a day-by-day plan of where you'll be and what you want to be sure to see. To help you make the most of your time, I've suggested day plans for destinations. But check the opening hours of sights; avoid visiting a town on the one day a week that your must-see sight is closed. Also look into whether any holidays or festivals will fall during your trip—these attract crowds and can close sights (for the latest, visit Germany's national tourism website, www.cometogermany.com).

Give yourself some slack. Nonstop sightseeing can turn a vacation into a blur. Every trip, and every traveler, needs downtime for doing laundry, picnic shopping, relaxing, people-watching, and so on. Pace yourself. Assume you will return.

Ready, set... You've designed the perfect itinerary for the trip of a lifetime.

Trip Costs per Person

Run a reality check on your dream trip. You'll have major transportation costs in addition to daily expenses.

Airfare: Frankfurt has the most convenient, cheapest flights from the US, though Munich is affordable and makes a better starting point. A basic round-trip flight from the US to Germany can cost about $1,000 to $2,000, depending on where you fly from and when.

Car Rental: Allow roughly $250 per week, not including tolls, gas, parking, and insurance. Rentals and leases (an economical way to go if you need a car for at least three weeks) are cheaper if arranged from the US.

Public Transportation: For my suggested two-week trip, allow $350 per person; it'd be worthwhile to buy a German Flexipass with five train days (to use for longer trips between major destinations) and purchase point-to-point tickets for short, cheap, regional trips (e.g., between villages on the Rhine). German rail passes are sold at most train stations in Germany.

If you rent a car for part of the trip, you won't need a rail pass. You could pay ahead of time for the one long train trip you'll need (Rhine to Berlin), to take advantage of the advance-purchase discount (order online at www.bahn.com).

Budget Tips: You can cut my suggested average daily expenses by taking advantage of the deals you'll find throughout Germany and mentioned in this book.

Average Daily Expenses Per Person: $150

Cost	Category	Notes
$40	Meals	$15 for lunch, and $25 for dinner
$65	Lodging	Based on two people splitting the cost of a $130 double room (includes breakfast)
$30	Sights and Entertainment	This daily average works for most people.
$10	City Transit	Buses, subways
$145	**Total**	Applies to cities, figure on less for towns

THE BEST OF GERMANY IN 14 DAYS

This unforgettable trip will show you the very best Germany has to offer, with a little help from Austria.

DAY	PLAN	SLEEP IN
	Arrive in Munich	Munich
1	Sightsee Munich	Munich
2	Munich, half-day trip to Dachau in morning	Munich
3	Munich, late afternoon to Salzburg (1.5 hours by train)	Salzburg
4	Salzburg	Salzburg
5	Leave early for Bavaria (4 hours by train). Visit Neuschwanstein Castle (make reservations for later in the day or tomorrow morning)	Füssen
6	Choose among these Bavarian sights (easiest by car): Wieskirche, Linderhof Castle, Oberammergau, Zugspitze	Füssen
7	Travel to Rothenburg (5 hours by train)	Rothenburg
8	Rothenburg	Rothenburg
9	To Bacharach (4.5 hours by train)	Bacharach
10	Short Rhine cruise to St. Goar, return by train	Bacharach
11	Travel to Berlin (5.5 hours by train)	Berlin
12	Berlin	Berlin
13	Berlin	Berlin
14	Berlin	Berlin
	Fly home	

This trip can work by train or car. Or use trains to connect major cities and rent a car for the countryside. For example, following this itinerary, rent a car in Füssen on the morning of Day 6, explore Bavaria, drive the Romantic Road to Rothenburg, then visit the Rhine (including Burg Eltz); you could drop the car in Frankfurt (or Cologne) on the morning of Day 11, then take the train to Berlin.

Here are other options: You could stay longer in Munich, using it as a home base for day trips to Bavaria (by bus tour or public transit) and even to Salzburg (by train). Or you could fly into Salzburg, start your trip there, then continue to Munich, Bavaria, Rothenburg, the Rhine, and Berlin.

Join a walking tour to learn from a local expert.

City transit passes (for multiple rides or all-day usage) decrease your cost per ride.

If using trains, opt for the cheaper slow trains, and use day passes for further savings (most cost-effective for groups of 2-5; see Practicalities for more info).

Avid sightseers buy combo-tickets or passes that cover multiple museums. If a town doesn't offer deals, visit only the sights you most want to see, and seek out free sights and experiences (people-watching counts).

Some businesses—especially hotels and walking-tour companies—offer discounts to my readers (look for the RS% symbol in the listings in this book).

Book your rooms directly with the hotel. Many hotels offer a discount if you pay in cash and/or stay three or more nights (check online or ask). Rooms cost less outside of peak season (May-Sept). And even seniors can sleep cheap in hostels (some have double rooms) for about $30 per person. Or check Airbnb-type sites for deals.

It's easy to eat cheap in Germany. Restaurants offer among the most reasonable prices in Europe. You can get tasty, inexpensive meals at bakeries (many sell sandwiches), department-store cafeterias, and fast-food stands. Cultivate the art of picnicking in atmospheric settings.

When you splurge, choose an experience you'll always remember, such as a concert, spa visit, or alpine lift. Minimize souvenir shopping—how will you get it all home? Focus instead on collecting wonderful stories, vivid memories, and new friends.

Before You Go

You'll have a smoother trip if you tackle a few things ahead of time. For more information on these topics, see the Practicalities chapter (and www.ricksteves.com, which has helpful tips and travel talks).

Make sure your passport is valid. If it's due to expire within six months of your ticketed date of return, you need to renew it. Allow up to six weeks to renew or get a passport (www.travel.state.gov).

Arrange your transportation. Book your international flights. Figure out your main form of transportation within Germany. It's worth thinking about buying train tickets online in advance, getting a rail pass there, renting a car, or booking cheap European flights. (You can wing it once you're there, but it may cost more.)

Book rooms well in advance, especially if your trip falls during peak season or any major holidays or festivals.

Reserve or buy tickets ahead for major sights, saving you from long ticket-buying lines. Reserve ahead for Neuschwanstein Castle. For a Munich BMW factory tour, sign up at least two months in advance. To visit the Reichstag dome in Berlin, reserve a free entry slot online a week or two in advance. To see Dresden's Historic Green Vault, book your tickets online well in advance, or take your chances and line up early for same-day tickets. Tickets for the music-packed Salzburg Festival (mid-July through August) go fast; buy tickets far in advance (on sale in January). Details are in the chapters.

Consider travel insurance. Compare the cost of the insurance to the cost of your potential loss. Check whether your existing insurance (health, homeowners, or renters) covers you and your possessions overseas.

Call your bank. Alert your bank that you'll be using your debit and credit cards in Europe. Ask about transaction fees, and get the PIN number for your credit card. You don't need to bring euros for your trip; you'll withdraw euros from cash machines in Europe.

Use your smartphone smartly. Sign up for an international service plan to reduce your costs, or rely on Wi-Fi in Europe instead. Download any apps you'll want on the road, such as maps, translation, transit schedules, and Rick Steves Audio Europe (see sidebar).

Pack light. You'll walk with your luggage more than you think. Bring a single carry-on bag and a daypack. Use the packing checklist in Practicalities as a guide.

Travel Strategies on the Road

If you have a positive attitude, equip yourself with good information (this book), and expect to travel smart, you will.

Read—and reread—this book. To have an "A" trip, be an "A" student. Note opening hours of sights, closed days, crowd-beating tips, and whether reservations are required or advisable. Check the latest at www.ricksteves.com/update.

Be your own tour guide. As you travel, get up-to-date info on sights, reserve tickets and tours, reconfirm hotels and travel arrangements, and check transit connections. Visit local tourist information offices (TIs). Upon arrival in a new town, lay the groundwork for a smooth departure; confirm the train, bus, or road you'll take when you leave.

Give local tours a spin. Your appreciation of a city or region and its history can increase dramatically if you take a walking tour in any big city or even hire a private guide. If you want to learn more about any aspect of Germany, you're in the right place with experts happy to teach you.

Stick This Guidebook in Your Ear!

My free Rick Steves Audio Europe app makes it easy for you to download my audio tours of many of Europe's top attractions and listen to them offline during your travels. For Germany, these include major sights and neighborhoods in Munich, Rothenburg, the Rhine Valley, and Berlin, plus Salzburg in Austria. Sights covered by audio tours are marked in this book with this symbol: 🎧. The app also offers insightful travel interviews from my public radio show with experts from Germany and around the globe. It's all free! You can download the app via Apple's App Store, Google Play, or Amazon's Appstore. For more info, see www.ricksteves.com/audioeurope.

Outsmart thieves. Be alert for pickpockets in bigger cities in crowded places where tourists congregate (at sights, on buses, getting on and off trains). Treat commotions—such as people bumping into you—as smokescreens for theft. Keep your cash, cards, and passport secure in a money belt tucked under your clothes; carry only a day's spending money in your front pocket. Don't set valuable items down on counters or café tabletops, where they can be quickly stolen or easily forgotten. In case of theft or loss, see page 384.

To minimize potential loss, keep your expensive gear to a minimum. Bring photocopies or take photos of important documents (passport and cards) to aid in replacement if they're lost or stolen.

Guard your time and energy. Taking a taxi can be a good value if it saves you a long wait for a cheap bus or an exhausting walk across town. To avoid long lines at sights, follow my crowd-beating tips, such as making advance reservations, or sightseeing early or late.

Be flexible. Even if you have a well-planned itinerary, expect changes, closures, sore feet, bad weather, and so on. Your Plan B could turn out to be even better. And when problems arise (e.g., miscommunication, a confusing restaurant bill, or a noisy hotel room), keep things in perspective. You're on vacation...and you're in Germany!

Attempt the language. Most Germans—especially in the tourist trade and in cities—speak English, but if you learn some German, even just a few phrases, you'll get more smiles and make more friends. Practice the survival phrases near the end of this book, and even better, bring a phrase book.

Connect with the culture. Interacting with locals carbonates your trip. Enjoy the friendliness of the German people. Ask questions—many locals are as interested in you as you are in them. Slow down, step out of your comfort zone, and be open to unexpected experiences. When an opportunity pops up, say "yes."

Hear the beer hall band playing? See that hilltop castle? Your next stop... Germany!

Welcome to Rick Steves' Europe

Travel is intensified living—maximum thrills per minute and one of the last great sources of legal adventure. Travel is freedom. It's recess, and we need it.

I discovered a passion for European travel as a teen and have been sharing it ever since—through my tours, public television and radio shows, and travel guidebooks. Over the years, I've taught thousands of travelers how to best enjoy Europe's blockbuster sights—and experience "Back Door" discoveries that most tourists miss.

This book offers a balanced mix of Germany's cities and villages. I've also included Salzburg, just over the border in Austria. The book is selective—rather than covering dozens of castles along the Rhine, I focus on the best: Rheinfels and Marksburg. My self-guided museum tours and city walks give insight into Germany's vibrant history and today's living, breathing culture.

I advocate traveling simply and smartly. Take advantage of my money- and time-saving tips on sightseeing, transportation, and more. Try local, characteristic alternatives to expensive hotels and restaurants. In many ways, spending more money only builds a thicker wall between you and what you traveled so far to see.

We visit Germany to experience it—to become temporary locals. Thoughtful travel engages us with the world, as we learn to appreciate other cultures and new ways to measure quality of life.

Judging from the positive feedback I receive from readers, this book will help you enjoy a fun, affordable, and rewarding vacation—whether it's your first trip or your tenth.

Gute Reise! Happy travels!

Rick Steves

Munich

Munich ("München" in German) is one of Germany's most historic, artistic, and entertaining cities. Until 1871, it was the capital of an independent Bavaria. Its imperial palaces and grand boulevards constantly remind visitors that Munich has long been a political and cultural powerhouse.

Walking through Munich, you'll understand why it is consistently voted one of Germany's most livable cities. It's safe, clean, cultured, built on a human scale, and close to the beauties of nature. Though Munich is a major metropolis, its low-key atmosphere has led Germans to dub it "Millionendorf"—the "village of a million people."

Orient yourself in Munich's old center, with its colorful pedestrian zones. Immerse yourself in the city's art and history—crown jewels, Baroque theater, royal palaces, great paintings, and beautiful parks. Spend time in a frothy beer hall or outdoor *Biergarten*, prying big pretzels from no-nonsense beer maids amidst an oompah atmosphere.

MUNICH IN 3 DAYS

Day 1: Follow the "Munich City Walk" laid out in this chapter, visiting sights along the way. After lunch, tour the Residenz.

On any evening: Try a beer hall one night and a beer garden on another. Stroll through Marienplatz and the core pedestrian streets. Have a dinner picnic at the English Garden.

Day 2: Visit the Dachau Memorial in the morning. Later, if the weather's fine, rent a bike to enjoy the English Garden. Or tour the top art museum, the Alte Pinakothek.

Day 3: Take your pick of these fine sights: Egyptian Museum, Deutsches Museum, Neue Pinakothek, Munich City Museum, and—away from the center—the Nymphenburg Palace and BMW-Welt and Museum.

With extra time: Day-trip options include a day-long bus tour to see "Mad" King Ludwig's Castles (covered in the Bavaria chapter) or even a visit to Salzburg (1.5 hours one-way by train).

ORIENTATION

The tourist's Munich is circled by a ring road (site of the old town wall) marked by four old gates: Karlstor (near the main train station—the Hauptbahnhof), Sendlinger Tor, Isartor (near the river), and Odeonsplatz (no surviving gate, near the palace). Marienplatz marks the city's center. A great pedestrian-only zone (Kaufingerstrasse and Neuhauser Strasse) cuts this circle in half, running neatly from the Karlstor and the train station through Marienplatz to the Isartor. Orient yourself along this east-west axis. Ninety percent of the sights and hotels I recommend are within a 20-minute walk of Marienplatz and each other.

Tourist Information

Munich has two helpful city-run TIs (www.muenchen.de). One is in front of the **main train station** (Mon-Sat 9:00-20:00, Sun 10:00-18:00, with your back to the tracks, walk through the central hall, step outside, and turn right). The other TI is on Munich's main square, **Marienplatz,** below the glockenspiel (Mon-Fri 9:00-19:00, Sat 9:00-16:00, Sun 10:00-14:00).

Private Munich Ticket offices inside the TIs sell concert and event tickets (www.muenchenticket.de). The free magazine *In München* lists all movies and entertainment in town (in German, organized by date).

At counter #1 in the train station's main *Reisezentrum* (travel center, opposite track 21), the hardworking, eager-to-help **EurAide desk** is a godsend for Eurailers and budget travelers. Paid by the German rail company to help you design your train travels (including day trips), EurAide makes reservations and sells train tickets, *couchettes,* and sleepers for the same price you'd pay at the other counters (open May-Oct Mon-Fri 8:30-20:00, Sat 8:30-14:00, closed Sun; off-season Mon-Fri 10:00-19:00, closed Sat-Sun and Jan-Feb, www.euraide.com). As EurAide helps about 500 visitors per day in the summer, a line can build up; do your homework and have a list of questions ready.

Tours

Munich's two largest tour companies, Radius Tours and Munich Walk, run comparable tours in Munich as well as day trips to Dachau, Neuschwanstein Castle, and other places. Both offer discounts to Rick Steves readers.

Munich Walk uses Marienplatz as its meeting point (tel. 089/2423-1767, www.munichwalktours.de). Consider a walking tour (€12-15, daily year-round, 2-2.5 hours), "Beer and Brewery" tour (€28, May-mid-Sept on Mon, Wed, and Fri-Sat at 18:15, fewer tours off-season, 3.5 hours), Bavarian food-tasting tour with lunch at Viktualienmarkt (€24 includes food), or bike tour (€25, April-Oct Sat-Sun only).

Radius Tours has a convenient office and meeting point in the main train station, in front of track 32 (tel. 089/543-487-7730, www.radiustours.com). Consider a walking tour (€13-15, daily at 10:00, 2-2.5 hours), "Bavarian Beer and Food" tour with samples and a visit to the Beer and Oktoberfest Museum (€30, April-mid-Oct Mon-Sat 18:00, 3.5 hours, reserve well in advance), or a 3.5-hour bike tour (€25, April-mid-Oct daily at 10:00).

Gray Line Tours has hop-on, hop-off city bus tours that leave from in front of the Karstadt department store at Bahnhofplatz, directly across from the train station (buses run 9:40-18:00). Choose the basic, 1-hour "Express Circle," or the more extensive 2.5-hour "Grand Circle," which includes Nymphenburg Palace and BMW-Welt and Museum and is an efficient way to see both. Just show up and pay the driver (€17 Express tour—valid all day, €22 Grand tour—valid 24 hours, daily in season, tel. 089/5490-7560, www.sightseeing-munich.com).

Rick's Tip: *If you're interested in a* **Gray Line bus tour** *of the city or to nearby castles,* **get discounted tickets at EurAide** *(cash only). They also sell* **Munich Walk** *tour tickets.*

While you can do many **day trips from Munich** on your own by train, going as part of an organized group can be convenient. All-day tours to **Neuschwanstein** are offered by **Radius,** using **public transit** (€42, €35 with rail pass, does not include castle admission; daily April-Dec;

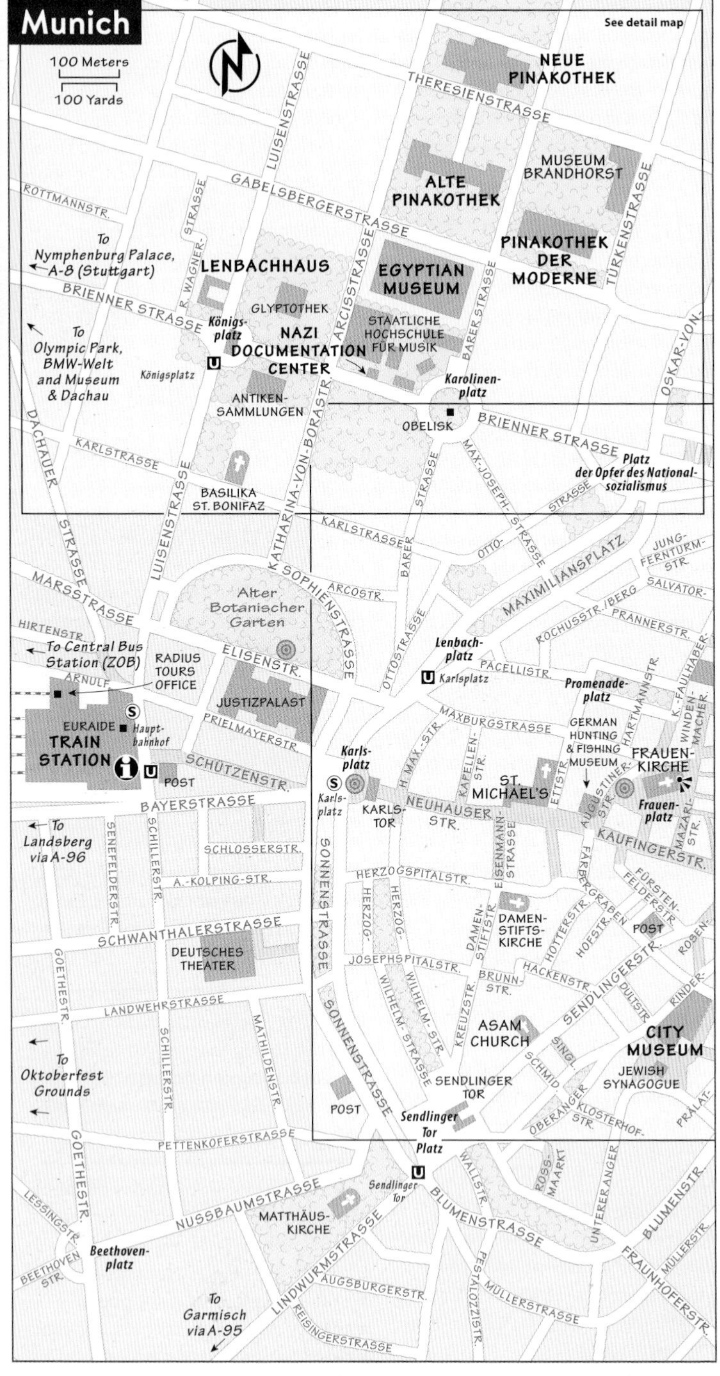
Munich
See detail map
100 Meters
100 Yards
NEUE PINAKOTHEK
THERESIENSTRASSE
MUSEUM BRANDHORST
ALTE PINAKOTHEK
PINAKOTHEK DER MODERNE
TÜRKENSTRASSE
LUISENSTRASSE
GABELSBERGERSTRASSE
ROTTMANNSTR.
WAGNER-STRASSE
To Nymphenburg Palace, A-8 (Stuttgart)
LENBACHHAUS
EGYPTIAN MUSEUM
ARCISSTRASSE
BARER STRASSE
BRIENNER STRASSE
GLYPTOTHEK
Königsplatz
NAZI DOCUMENTATION CENTER
STAATLICHE HOCHSCHULE FÜR MUSIK
OSKAR-VON-
To Olympic Park, BMW-Welt and Museum & Dachau
Königsplatz
Karolinenplatz
ANTIKEN-SAMMLUNGEN
OBELISK
DACHAUER STRASSE
KARLSTRASSE
MAX-JOSEPH-STRASSE
Platz der Opfer des Nationalsozialismus
BASILIKA ST. BONIFAZ
KATHARINA-VON-BORA-STR.
OTTOSTRASSE
JUNGFERNTURM-STR.
MAXIMILIANSPLATZ
SOPHIENSTRASSE
ARCOSTR.
SALVATOR-
MARSSTRASSE
Alter Botanischer Garten
ROCHUSSTR./BERG
PRANNERSTR.
HIRTENSTR.
To Central Bus Station (ZOB)
RADIUS TOURS OFFICE
ELISENSTR.
Lenbachplatz
PACELLISTR.
ARNULF-
Karlsplatz
Promenadeplatz
JUSTIZPALAST
K.-FAULHABER-
EURAIDE
Hauptbahnhof
TRAIN STATION
PRIELMAYERSTR.
MAXBURGSTRASSE
GERMAN HUNTING & FISHING MUSEUM
HARTMANNSTR.
WINDENMACHER
SCHÜTZENSTR.
POST
Karlsplatz
H. MAX-STR.
KAPELLENSTR.
ST. MICHAEL'S
ETTSTR.
FRAUENKIRCHE
AUGUSTINERSTR.
Frauenplatz
BAYERSTRASSE
KARLSTOR
NEUHAUSER STR.
MAZARISTR.
To Landsberg via A-96
SENEFELDERSTR.
SCHILLERSTR.
SCHLOSSERSTR.
SONNENSTRASSE
EISENMANNSTRASSE
KAUFINGERSTR.
HERZOGSPITALSTR.
FÜRSTENFELDERSTR.
A.-KOLPING-STR.
HERZOG-WILHELM-STR.
DAMENSTIFTSTR.
DAMENSTIFTSKIRCHE
FÄRBERGRABEN
HOTTERSTR.
HOFSTR.
POST
SCHWANTHALERSTRASSE
DEUTSCHES THEATER
ROSEN-
GOETHESTR.
JOSEPHSPITALSTR.
BRUNNSTR.
HACKENSTR.
SENDLINGERSTR.
DULTSTR.
RINDER-
LANDWEHRSTRASSE
ASAM CHURCH
WILHELM-STRASSE
KREUZSTR.
CITY MUSEUM
SINGL.
SCHMID.
To Oktoberfest Grounds
MATHILDENSTR.
SENDLINGER TOR
JEWISH SYNAGOGUE
POST
Sendlinger Tor Platz
OBERANGER
KLOSTERHOF-
PRÄLAT-
PETTENKOFERSTRASSE
WALLSTR.
ROSSMARKT
UNTERER ANGER
NUSSBAUMSTRASSE
Sendlinger Tor
BLUMENSTRASSE
BLUMENSTR.
LESSINGSTR.
MATTHÄUSKIRCHE
Beethovenplatz
BEETHOVENSTR.
LINDWURMSTRASSE
PESTALOZZISTR.
FRAUNHOFERSTR.
MÜLLERSTR.
AUGSBURGERSTR.
MÜLLERSTRASSE
To Garmisch via A-95
REISINGERSTRASSE

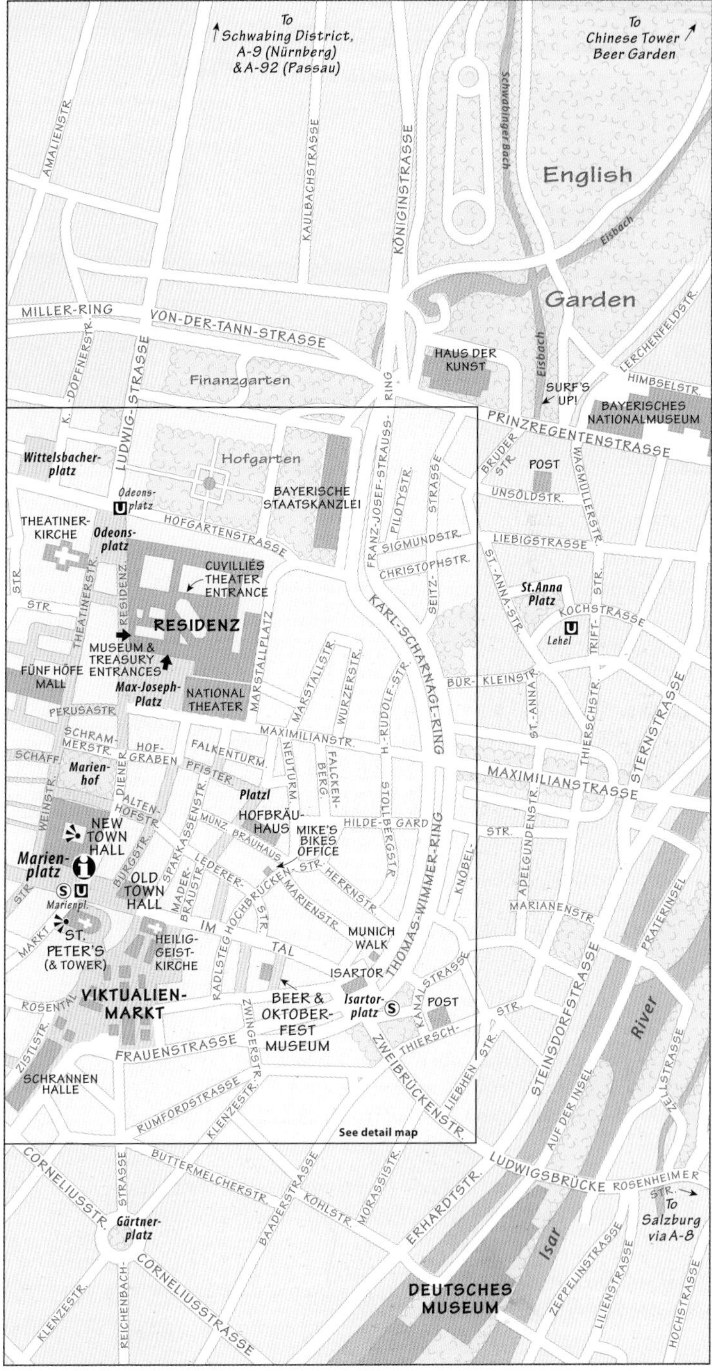
To Schwabing District, A-9 (Nürnberg) & A-92 (Passau)
To Chinese Tower Beer Garden
English Garden
Schwabinger Bach
Eisbach
AMALIENSTR.
KAULBACHSTRASSE
KÖNIGINSTRASSE
MILLER-RING
VON-DER-TANN-STRASSE
Finanzgarten
HAUS DER KUNST
SURF'S UP!
LERCHENFELDSTR.
HIMBSELSTR.
BAYERISCHES NATIONALMUSEUM
PRINZREGENTENSTRASSE
K.-DÖPFNERSTR.
LUDWIG-STRASSE
Wittelsbacher-platz
Hofgarten
BAYERISCHE STAATSKANZLEI
Odeonsplatz
THEATINER-KIRCHE
Odeons-platz
HOFGARTENSTRASSE
CUVILLIÉS THEATER ENTRANCE
RESIDENZ
MUSEUM & TREASURY ENTRANCES
FÜNF HÖFE MALL
Max-Joseph-Platz
NATIONAL THEATER
MARSTALLPLATZ
FRANZ-JOSEF-STRAUSS-RING
PILOTYSTR.
SIGMUNDSTR.
CHRISTOPHSTR.
BRUDERSTR.
POST
UNSÖLDSTR.
WAGMÜLLERSTR.
LIEBIGSTRASSE
St.Anna Platz
KOCHSTRASSE
Lehel
KARL-SCHARNAGL-RING
PERUSASTR.
SCHRAMMERSTR.
HOFGRABEN
Marienhof
FALKENTURM.
PFISTER.
MAXIMILIANSTR.
Platzl
HOFBRÄUHAUS
MIKE'S BIKES OFFICE
HILDEGARD STR.
NEW TOWN HALL
Marienplatz
Marienpl.
OLD TOWN HALL
ST. PETER'S (& TOWER)
HEILIG-GEIST-KIRCHE
IM TAL
MUNICH WALK
ISARTOR
VIKTUALIENMARKT
BEER & OKTOBERFEST MUSEUM
Isartorplatz
POST
THOMAS-WIMMER-RING
MAXIMILIANSTRASSE
STERNSTRASSE
MARIANENSTR.
STEINSDORFSTRASSE
PRATERINSEL
River
FRAUENSTRASSE
SCHRANNENHALLE
RUMFORDSTRASSE
ZWEIBRÜCKENSTR.
See detail map
CORNELIUSSTR.
BUTTERMELCHERSTR.
Gärtnerplatz
KOHLSTR.
ERHARDTSTR.
LUDWIGSBRÜCKE
ROSENHEIMER STR.
To Salzburg via A-8
Isar
DEUTSCHES MUSEUM
CORNELIUSSTRASSE
ZEPPELINSTRASSE
LILIENSTRASSE
HOCHSTRASSE

MUNICH AT A GLANCE

In the Center

▲▲**Marienplatz** Munich's main square, at the heart of a lively pedestrian zone, watched over by New Town Hall and its glockenspiel show. **Hours:** Always open; glockenspiel jousts daily at 11:00 and 12:00, plus 17:00 May-Oct. See page 40.

▲▲**Viktualienmarkt** Munich's "small-town" open-air market, perfect for a quick snack or meal. **Hours:** Closed Sun; beer garden open daily 10:00-22:00 (weather permitting). See page 45.

▲▲**Hofbräuhaus** World-famous beer hall, worth a visit even if you're not chugging. **Hours:** Daily 9:00-23:30. See page 53.

▲▲**Residenz Complex** Elegant palace awash in Bavarian opulence. Complex includes the Residenz Museum (private apartments), Residenz Treasury (housing royal crowns and knickknacks), and the impressive, heavily restored Cuvilliés Theater. **Hours:** Museum and treasury—daily April-mid-Oct 9:00-18:00, mid-Oct-March 10:00-17:00; theater keeps shorter hours. See page 56.

▲▲**Alte Pinakothek** Bavaria's best painting gallery, with a wonderful collection of European masters from the 14th through 19th century. **Hours:** Tue 10:00-20:00, Wed-Sun 10:00-18:00, closed Mon. See page 66.

▲▲**Egyptian Museum** Easy-to-enjoy collection of ancient Egyptian treasures. **Hours:** Tue 10:00-20:00, Wed-Sun 10:00-18:00, closed Mon. See page 70.

▲**Asam Church** Small church dripping with Baroque. **Hours:** Sat-Thu 9:00-18:00, Fri 13:00-18:00. See page 49.

▲**Munich City Museum** The city's history in five floors. **Hours:** Tue-Sun 10:00-18:00, closed Mon. See page 64.

▲**Neue Pinakothek** The Alte's twin sister, with paintings from 1800 to 1920. **Hours:** Wed 10:00-20:00, Thu-Mon 10:00-18:00, closed Tue. See page 69.

▲**English Garden** The largest city park on the Continent, packed with locals, tourists, surfers, and nude sunbathers. (On a bike, I'd rate this ▲▲.) **Hours:** Always open. See page 70.

▲**Deutsches Museum** Germany's version of our Smithsonian Institution, with 10 miles of science and technology exhibits. **Hours:** Daily 9:00-17:00. See page 72.

Outside the City Center

▲▲**Nymphenburg Palace Complex** Impressive summer palace, featuring a hunting lodge, coach museum, fine royal porcelain collection, and vast park. **Hours:** Park—daily 6:00-dusk, palace buildings—daily April-mid-Oct 9:00-18:00, mid-Oct-March 10:00-16:00. See page 73.

▲▲**BMW-Welt and Museum** The carmaker's futuristic museum and floating-cloud showroom, highlighting BMW past, present, and future. **Hours:** BMW-Welt building—exhibits daily 9:00-18:00; museum—Tue-Sun 10:00-18:00, closed Mon. See page 78.

▲▲**Dachau Memorial** Notorious Nazi concentration camp, now a powerful museum and memorial. **Hours:** Daily 9:00-17:00. See page 98.

Jan-March tours run Mon, Wed, and Fri-Sun; reserve ahead, www.radiustours.com), and by **Gray Line Tours** via **private bus** (€51, does not include castle admission, daily all year, www.sightseeing-munich.com). Although they're a little more expensive, I prefer the guided private bus tours because you're guaranteed a seat (public transportation in summer is routinely standing-room only).

For organized tours to **Dachau,** see page 98.

Six people splitting the cost can make a **private guide** affordable. I've had great days with **Georg Reichlmayr** (€165/3 hours, tel. 08131/86800, mobile 0170-341-6384, www.muenchen-stadtfuehrung.de, info@muenchen-stadtfuehrung.de) and **Monika Hank** (€120/2 hours, €140/3 hours, tel. 089/311-4819, mobile 0172-547-8123, monika.hank@web.de).

Rick's Tip: *Supposedly* **"free" walking tours are advertised all over town.** *Tipping is expected, and the guides actually have to pay the company for each person who takes the tour—so unless you tip more than they owe the company, they don't make a penny. Expect a sales pitch for the company's other, paid tours.*

Helpful Hints

Museum Tips: Museums closed on Monday include the Alte Pinakothek, Munich City Museum, the BMW Museum, and the Beer and Oktoberfest Museum (also closed Sun). The Neue Pinakothek closes on Tuesday. The art museums are generally open late one night a week.

Taxi: Call 089/21610.

Private Driver: Johann Fayoumi is reliable and speaks English (€70/hour, mobile 0174-183-8473, www.firstclasslimousines.de).

Car Rental: Several car-rental agencies are located upstairs at the train station, opposite track 21 (open daily, hours vary).

MUNICH CITY WALK

With its pedestrian-friendly historic core, big, modern Munich feels like an easy-going Bavarian town. On this self-guided walk, rated ▲▲▲, we'll start in the central square, see its famous glockenspiel, stroll through a thriving open-air market, and visit historic churches with lavish Baroque decor. We'll sample chocolates and take a spin through the world's most famous beer hall.

Length of This Tour: It takes two or three hours to walk through a thousand years of Munich's history; allow extra time if you want to take a break to tour the museums (details under "Sights").

🎧 Download my free Munich City Walk audio tour.

➲ Self-Guided Walk

• *Begin at the heart of the old city, with a stroll through...*

❶ *Marienplatz*

Riding the escalator out of the subway into sunlit Marienplatz (mah-REE-en-platz, "Mary's Square," rated ▲▲) gives you a fine first look at the glory of Munich: great buildings, outdoor cafés, and people bustling and lingering like the birds and breeze with which they share this square.

The square is both old and new: For a thousand years, it's been the center of Munich. It was the town's marketplace and public forum, standing at a crossroads along the Salt Road, which ran between Salzburg and Augsburg.

Lining one entire side of the square is the impressive facade of the **New Town Hall** (Neues Rathaus), with its soaring 280-foot spire. The structure looks medieval, but it was actually built in the late 1800s (1867-1908). The style is "Neo"-Gothic—pointed arches over the doorways and a roofline bristling with prickly spires. The 40 statues look like medieval saints, but they're from around 1900, depicting more recent Bavarian kings and nobles. This medieval-looking style was all the rage in the 19th century as Germans were rediscovering their historical roots and uniting as a modern nation.

The New Town Hall is famous for its **glockenspiel.** A carillon in the tower chimes a tune while colorful figurines come out on the balcony to spin and dance. It happens daily at 11:00 and 12:00 all year (also at 17:00 May-Oct). The *Spiel* of the glockenspiel tells the story of a noble wedding that actually took place on the market square in 1568. You see the wedding procession and the friendly joust of knights on horseback. The duke and his bride watch the action as the groom's family (in Bavarian white and blue) joyfully jousts with the bride's French family (in red and white). Below, the barrel-makers—famous for being the first to dance in the streets after a deadly plague lifted—do their popular jig. Finally, the solitary cock crows.

At the very top of the New Town Hall is a statue of a child with outstretched arms, dressed in monk's garb and holding a book in its left hand. This is the **Münchner Kindl,** the symbol of Munich. The town got its name from the people who first settled here: the monks *(Mönchen).* You'll spot this mini monk all over town, on everything from the city's coat of arms to souvenir shot glasses to ad campaigns (often holding not a book, but maybe a beer or a smartphone). The city symbol was originally depicted as a grown man, wearing a gold-lined black cloak and red shoes. By the 19th century, artists were representing him as a young boy, then a gender-neutral child, and, more recently, a young girl. These days, a teenage girl dressed as the *Kindl* kicks off the annual Oktoberfest by leading the opening parade on horseback, and then serves as the mascot throughout the festivities.

For great **views** of the city, you can ride an elevator to the top of the New Town Hall tower (€2.50, May-Sept daily 10:00-19:00; Oct-April Mon-Fri 10:00-17:00, closed Sat-Sun, elevator located under glockenspiel).

The **golden statue** at the top of the column in the center of Marienplatz honors the square's namesake, the Virgin Mary. Sculpted in 1590, it was a rallying point in the religious wars of the Reformation. Back then, Munich was a bastion of southern-German Catholicism against the heresies of Martin Luther to the north.

New Town Hall

Glockenspiel

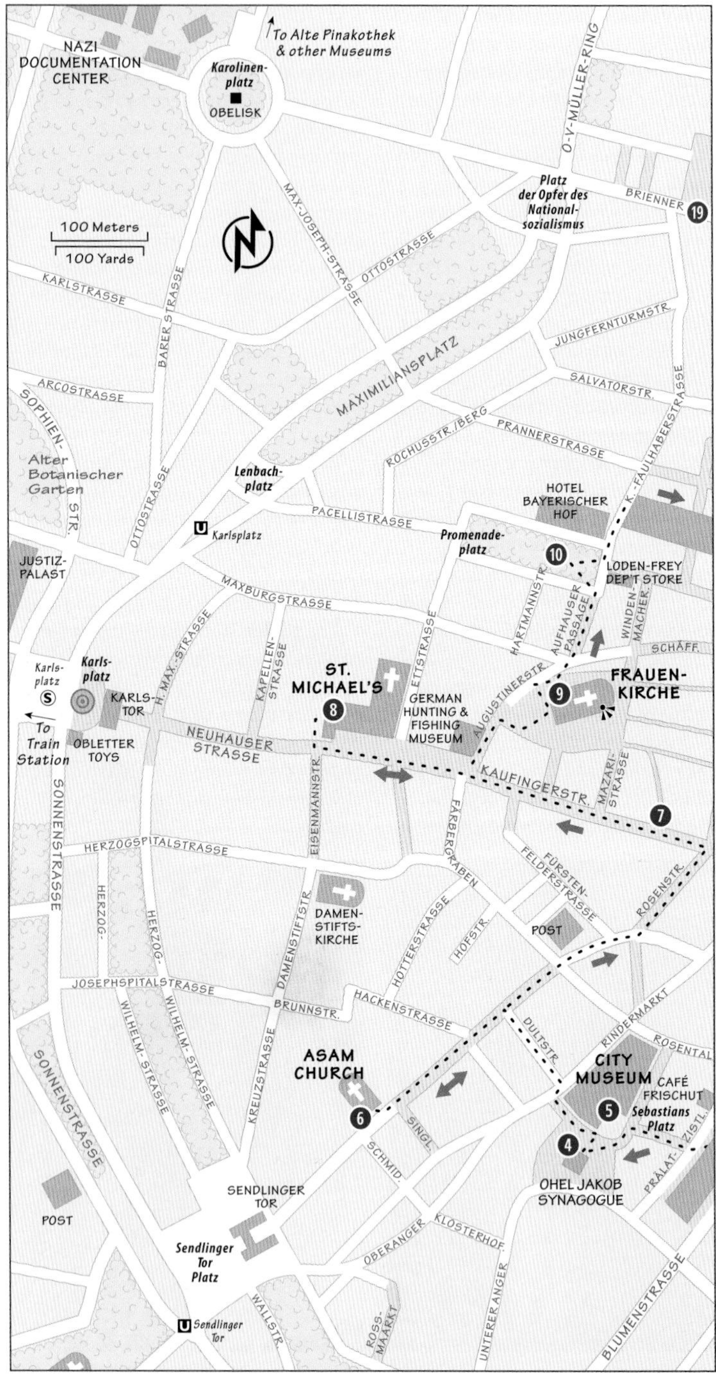
To Alte Pinakothek & other Museums
NAZI DOCUMENTATION CENTER
Karolinen-platz
OBELISK
O-V-MÜLLER-RING
Platz der Opfer des National-sozialismus
BRIENNER
19
100 Meters
100 Yards
KARLSTRASSE
BARER STRASSE
MAX-JOSEPH-STRASSE
OTTOSTRASSE
JUNGFERNTURMSTR.
MAXIMILIANSPLATZ
SALVATORSTR.
ARCOSTRASSE
SOPHIEN-STR.
Alter Botanischer Garten
ROCHUSSTR./BERG
PRANNERSTRASSE
K.-FAULHABERSTRASSE
OTTOSTRASSE
Lenbach-platz
HOTEL BAYERISCHER HOF
PACELLISTRASSE
Karlsplatz
Promenade-platz
10
LODEN-FREY DEP'T STORE
JUSTIZ-PALAST
MAXBURGSTRASSE
HARTMANNSTR.
AUFHAUSER PASSAGE
WINDEN-MACHER.
KAPELLEN-STRASSE
ETTSTRASSE
SCHÄFF.
Karls-platz
Karls-platz
H. MAX.-STRASSE
ST. MICHAEL'S
AUGUSTINERSTR.
FRAUEN-KIRCHE
9
KARLS-TOR
8
GERMAN HUNTING & FISHING MUSEUM
To Train Station
OBLETTER TOYS
NEUHAUSER STRASSE
MAZARI-STRASSE
KAUFINGERSTR.
SONNENSTRASSE
EISENMANNSTR.
7
FÄRBERGRABEN
HERZOGSPITALSTRASSE
FÜRSTEN-FELDERSTRASSE
ROSENSTR.
HERZOG-
DAMENSTIFTSTR.
DAMEN-STIFTS-KIRCHE
HOTTERSTRASSE
HOFSTR.
POST
HERZOG-
JOSEPHSPITALSTRASSE
BRUNNSTR.
HACKENSTRASSE
RINDERMARKT
WILHELM-STRASSE
WILHELM-STRASSE
DULTSTR.
ROSENTAL
SONNENSTRASSE
KREUZSTRASSE
ASAM CHURCH
CITY MUSEUM
CAFÉ FRISCHUT
5
Sebastians Platz
6
SINGL.
ZISTL.
4
SCHMID.
PRÄLAT.
POST
SENDLINGER TOR
OHEL JAKOB SYNAGOGUE
OBERANGER
KLOSTERHOF
Sendlinger Tor Platz
WALLSTR.
ROSS-MARKT
UNTERER ANGER
BLUMENSTRASSE
Sendlinger Tor

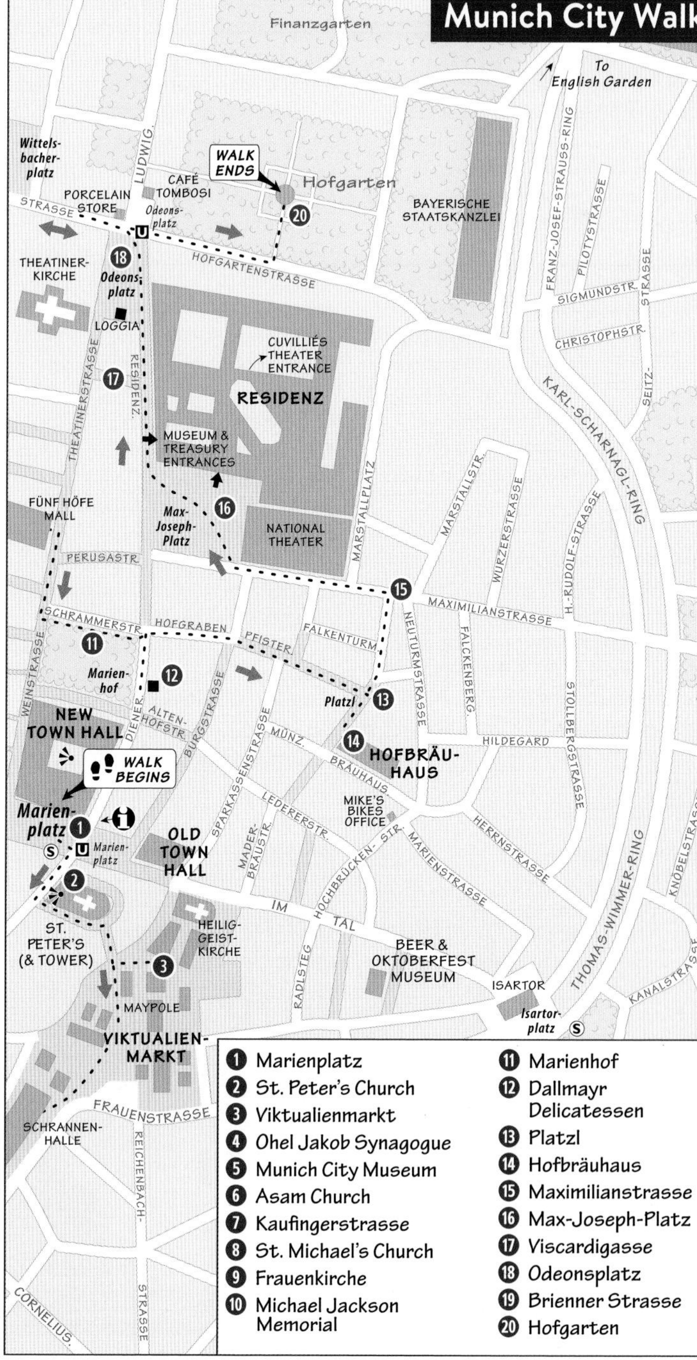
Munich City Walk
1 Marienplatz
2 St. Peter's Church
3 Viktualienmarkt
4 Ohel Jakob Synagogue
5 Munich City Museum
6 Asam Church
7 Kaufingerstrasse
8 St. Michael's Church
9 Frauenkirche
10 Michael Jackson Memorial
11 Marienhof
12 Dallmayr Delicatessen
13 Platzl
14 Hofbräuhaus
15 Maximilianstrasse
16 Max-Joseph-Platz
17 Viscardigasse
18 Odeonsplatz
19 Brienner Strasse
20 Hofgarten
WALK BEGINS
WALK ENDS
To English Garden
Finanzgarten
Hofgarten
Wittelsbacherplatz
PORCELAIN STORE
CAFÉ TOMBOSI
Odeonsplatz
THEATINERKIRCHE
LOGGIA
CUVILLIÉS THEATER ENTRANCE
RESIDENZ
MUSEUM & TREASURY ENTRANCES
Max-Joseph-Platz
NATIONAL THEATER
BAYERISCHE STAATSKANZLEI
FÜNF HÖFE MALL
Marienhof
NEW TOWN HALL
Marienplatz
OLD TOWN HALL
HOFBRÄUHAUS
Platzl
MIKE'S BIKES OFFICE
ST. PETER'S (& TOWER)
HEILIG-GEIST-KIRCHE
MAYPOLE
VIKTUALIENMARKT
BEER & OKTOBERFEST MUSEUM
ISARTOR
Isartorplatz
SCHRANNENHALLE
BRIENNER STRASSE
LUDWIG
HOFGARTENSTRASSE
RESIDENZ
THEATINERSTRASSE
PERUSASTR.
SCHRAMMERSTR.
HOFGRABEN
PFISTER
FALKENTURM
WEINSTRASSE
DIENER
ALTEN-HOFSTR.
BURGSTRASSE
SPARKASSENSTRASSE
MÜNZ.
BRÄUHAUS
LEDERERSTR.
MADER-BRÄUSTR.
HOCHBRÜCKEN-STR.
MARIENSTRASSE
HERRNSTRASSE
IM TAL
RADLSTEG
FRAUENSTRASSE
REICHENBACHSTRASSE
CORNELIUS
MARSTALLPLATZ
MARSTALLSTR.
WURZERSTRASSE
MAXIMILIANSTRASSE
NEUTURMSTRASSE
FALCKENBERG.
HILDEGARD
STOLLBERGSTRASSE
H.-RUDOLF-STRASSE
KARL-SCHARNAGL-RING
THOMAS-WIMMER-RING
FRANZ-JOSEF-STRAUSS-RING
PILOTYSTRASSE
SIGMUNDSTR.
CHRISTOPHSTR.
SEITZSTRASSE
KNÖBELSTRASSE
KANALSTRASSE

Notice how, at the four corners of the statue, cherubs fight the four great biblical enemies of civilization: the dragon of war, the lion of hunger, the rooster-headed monster of plague and disease, and the serpent. The serpent represents heresy—namely, Protestants. Bavaria is still Catholic country, and Protestants weren't allowed to worship openly here until about 1800.

To the right of the New Town Hall, the gray pointy building with the green spires is the **Old Town Hall** (Altes Rathaus). On its adjoining bell tower, find the city seal. It has the Münchner Kindl (symbolizing the first monks), a castle (representing the first fortifications), and a lion (representing the first ruler—Henry the Lion, who built them).

As you look around, keep in mind that the Allies bombed Marienplatz and much of Munich during World War II. Most of the buildings had to be rebuilt. The Old Town Hall looks newer now because it was completely destroyed by bombs and had to be rebuilt after the war. The New Town Hall survived the bombs, and it served as the US military headquarters after the Americans occupied Munich in 1945.

Before moving on, face the New Town Hall one more time and get oriented. Straight ahead is north. To the left is the pedestrian shopping street called Kaufingerstrasse, which leads to the old gate called Karlstor and the train station. To the right, the street leads to the Isartor gate and the Deutsches Museum. This east-west axis cuts through the historic core of Munich.

• *Turn around to the right to find Rindermarkt, the street leading from the southeast corner of Marienplatz. Head to St. Peter's Church, just beyond the square, with its steeple poking up above a row of buildings.*

❷ *St. Peter's Church*

The oldest church in town, St. Peter's stands on the hill where Munich's original monks probably settled—perhaps as far back as the ninth century (though the city marks its official birthday as 1158). Today's church (from 1368) replaced the original monastery church.

St. Peter's ("Old Peter" to locals) is part of the soul of the city. There's even a popular song about it that goes, "Munich is not Munich without St. Peter's."

Cost and Hours: Church-free, tower-€2, Mon-Fri 9:00-18:30, Sat-Sun 10:00-

Old Town Hall

Climb the tower of St. Peter's Church for great views.

18:30, off-season until 17:30.

Visiting the Church: On the outside of the church, notice the 16th- and 17th-century tombstones plastered onto the wall. Originally, people were buried in the holy ground around the church. But in the Napoleonic age, the cemeteries were dug up and relocated outside the city walls for hygienic and space reasons. They kept a few tombstones here as a reminder.

Step inside. (If there's a Mass in progress, visitors are welcome, but stay in the back. If there's no Mass, feel free to explore.) Typical of so many Bavarian churches, it's whitewashed and light-filled, with highlights in pastel pinks and blues framed by gold curlicues. The ceiling painting opens up to the heavens, where Peter is crucified upside down.

Some photos (on a pillar near the entrance) show how St. Peter's was badly damaged in World War II—the roof caved in, and the altar was damaged. But the beloved church was rebuilt and restored, thanks to donations—half from the Augustiner brewery, the rest from private donors. The accuracy of the restoration was possible thanks to Nazi catalog photos. For decades after World War II, the bells played a popular tune that stopped before the last note, reminding locals that the church still needed money to rebuild.

Explore further. The nave is lined with bronze statues of the apostles, and the altar shows a statue of St. Peter being adored by four Church fathers. The finely crafted, gray iron fences that line the nave were donated after World War II by the local blacksmiths of the national railway. The precious and fragile sandstone Gothic chapel altar (to the left of the main altar) survived the war only because it was buried in sandbags.

Find the second chapel on the left side. Now there's something you don't see every day: a skeleton in a box. As the red Latin inscription says, this is St. Munditia. In the fourth century, she was beheaded by the Romans for her Christian faith. Munich has more relics of saints than any city outside Rome. That's because it was the Pope's Catholic bastion against the rising tide of Protestantism in northern Europe during the Reformation. In 1675, St. Munditia's remains were given to Munich by the Pope as thanks for the city's devoted service. It was also a vivid reminder to the faithful that those who die for the cause of the Roman Church go directly to heaven without waiting for Judgment Day.

It's a long climb to the top of the **spire** (306 steps, no elevator)—much of it with two-way traffic on a one-lane staircase—but the view is dynamite. Try to be two flights from the top when the bells ring at the top of the hour. Then, when your friends back home ask you about your trip, you'll say, "What?"

• *Just beyond St. Peter's, join the busy commotion of the...*

❸ *Viktualienmarkt*

The market (rated ▲▲, closed Sun) is a lively world of produce stands and budget eateries. Browse your way through

Viktualienmarkt

The History of Munich

Born from Salt and Beer (1100-1500)
Munich began in the 12th century, when Henry the Lion (Heinrich der Löwe) established a lucrative salt trade near a monastery of "monks"—München. After Henry's death, an ambitious merchant family, the Wittelsbachs, took over. By the 1400s, Munich's market bustled with trade in salt and beer, the twin-domed Frauenkirche drew pilgrims, and the Wittelsbachs made their home in the Residenz. When the various regions of Bavaria united in 1506, Munich became the capital.

Religious Wars, Plagues, Decline (1500-1800)
While Martin Luther and the Protestant Reformation raged in northern Germany, Munich became the Catholic heart of the Counter-Reformation, decorated in the ornate Baroque and Rococo style of its Italian allies. Religious wars and periodic plagues left the city weakened. While the rest of Europe modernized, Munich remained behind the times.

The Golden Age of Kings (1806-1886)
When Napoleon invaded, the Wittelsbach duke surrendered and was rewarded with a grander title: King of Bavaria. Munich boomed. **Maximilian I** (r. 1806-1825), a.k.a. Max Joseph, rebuilt in Neoclassical style—grand columned buildings connected by broad boulevards. **Ludwig I** (r. 1825-1848) turned Munich into a modern railroad hub and budding industrial city. His son **Maximilian II** (r. 1848-1864) continued the modernization program. **Ludwig II** (r. 1864-1886) didn't much like Munich, preferring to build castles in the Bavarian countryside (for his story, see page 169).

the stalls and pavilions, as you make your way to the market's main landmark, the blue-and-white striped maypole. Early in the morning, you can still feel small-town Munich here. Remember, Munich has been a market town since its earliest days as a stop on the salt-trade crossroads. By the 1400s, the market bustled, most likely beneath a traditional maypole, just like you see today.

Besides salt, Munich gained a reputation for beer. By the 15th century, more than 30 breweries pumped out the golden liquid, brewed by monks who were licensed to sell it. They stored their beer in cellars under courtyards kept cool by the shade of bushy chestnut trees—a tradition Munich's breweries still stick to.

The market's centerpiece seems to be its **beer garden** (daily 10:00-22:00, weather permitting). Its picnic tables are filled with hungry and thirsty locals, all in the shade of the traditional chestnut trees. Shoppers pause here for a late-morning snack of *Weisswurst*—white sausage—served with mustard, a pretzel, and a beer. Here, you can order just a half-liter—unlike at other *Biergartens* that only sell by the full liter. As is the tradition at all of the city's beer gardens, some tables (those without tablecloths) are set aside for patrons who bring their own

End of the Wittelsbachs (1886-1918)

When Bavaria became part of the newly united Germany, Berlin overtook Munich as Germany's power center. Then World War I devastated Munich. After the war, mobs of poor, angry Münchners roamed the streets. In 1918, they drove out the last Bavarian king, ending 700 years of Wittelsbach rule.

Nazis and World War II (1918-1945)

In the power vacuum, a fringe group emerged—the Nazi party, headed by Adolf Hitler. Hitler rallied the Nazis in a Munich beer hall, leading a failed coup d'état known as the Beer Hall Putsch (1923). When the Nazis eventually took power in Berlin, they remembered their roots, dubbing Munich "Capital of the Movement." In World War II, nearly half the city was leveled by Allied air raids.

Munich Rebuilds (1945-Present)

After the war, with generous American aid, Münchners rebuilt. Nazi authorities had created a photographic archive of historic sights, which now came in handy. Munich chose to preserve its low-rise, medieval feel, but with a modern infrastructure. For the 1972 Olympic Games, they built a futuristic stadium, a sleek new subway system, and one of Europe's first pedestrian-only zones—Kaufingerstrasse. In 1990, when Germany reunited, Berlin once again became the country's focal point, relegating Munich to a backseat role.

Today's Munich is home to more banks and financial firms than any German city besides Frankfurt. With a population of 1.5 million, Munich is Germany's third-largest city, after Berlin and Hamburg. A center for book publishing, Munich also hosts universities, two TV networks, the electronics giant Siemens, the German branch of Microsoft, and BMW, maker of world-famous cars ("Bayerische Motoren Werke"—Bavarian Motor Works). Safe, clean, cultured, and productive, Munich is a success story.

food; they're welcome here as long as they buy a drink. The Viktualienmarkt is ideal for a light meal (see page 85).

Now make your way to the towering **maypole.** Throughout Bavaria, colorfully ornamented maypoles decorate town squares. Many are painted, like this one, in Bavaria's colors, white and blue. The decorations are festively replaced every year on the first of May. Traditionally, rival communities try to steal each other's maypole. Locals guard their new pole day and night as May Day approaches. Stolen poles are ransomed only with lots of beer for the clever thieves.

The decorations that line each side of the pole explain which merchants are doing business in the market. Munich's maypole gives prominence (on the

The market's maypole

bottom level) to a horse-drawn wagon bringing in beer barrels. And you can't have a kegger without coopers—find the merry barrelmakers, the four cute guys dancing. Today, traditional barrel making is enjoying a comeback as top breweries like to have real wooden kegs.

The bottom of the pole celebrates the world's oldest food law. The German Beer Purity Law *(Reinheitsgebot)* of 1487 actually originated here in Bavaria. It stipulated that beer could consist only of three ingredients: barley, hops, and water. (Later they realized that a fourth ingredient, yeast, is always present in fermentation.) Why was beer so treasured? Back in the Middle Ages, it was considered liquid food.

From the maypole, take in the bustling scene around you. The market was modernized in the 1800s as the city grew. Old buildings were torn down, replaced with stalls and modern market halls. Now, in the 21st century, it's a wonder such a traditional place survives—especially because it sits on the most expensive real estate in town. But locals love their market, so the city protects these old-time shops, charging them only a small percentage of their gross income, enabling them to carry on.

• *At the bottom end of the Viktualienmarkt, spot* ***Café Frischhut,*** *with its colorful old-time sign hanging out front (at Prälat-Zistl-Strasse 8). This is Munich's favorite place to stop for a fresh* Schmalznudel*—a traditional fried-dough treat (best enjoyed warm with a sprinkling of sugar).*

Across the street, you'll pass the Pschorr beer hall. Continue just past it to a modern glass-and-iron building, the ***Schrannenhalle.*** *This 1800s grain exchange has been renovated into a high-end mall of deli shops. Chocoholics could detour downstairs here into* ***Milka Coco World*** *for tasty samples (and a good WC).*

When you're ready to move on, exit the Schrannenhalle midway down on the right-hand side (or if it's closed, walk around the top of the building to Prälat-Zistl-Strasse and turn left). You'll spill out into Sebastiansplatz, a small square lined with healthy eateries. Continue through Sebastiansplatz and veer left, where you'll see a cube-shaped building, the...

❹ *Ohel Jakob Synagogue*

This modern synagogue anchors a revitalized Jewish quarter. In the 1930s, about 10,000 Jews lived in Munich, and the main synagogue stood near here. Then, in 1938, Hitler demanded that the synagogue be torn down. By the end of World War II, Munich's Jewish community was gone. But thanks to Germany's acceptance of religious refugees from former Soviet states, the Jewish population has now reached its prewar size. The new synagogue was built in 2006. There's also a kindergarten and day school, playground, fine kosher restaurant (at #18), and bookstore. Standing in the middle of the square, notice the low-key but efficient security.

While the synagogue is shut tight to nonworshippers, its architecture is striking from the outside. Lower stones of travertine evoke the Wailing Wall in Jerusalem, while an upper section represents the tent that held important religious wares during the 40 years of wandering through the desert. The synagogue's door features the first 10 letters of the Hebrew alphabet, symbolizing the Ten Commandments.

The cube-shaped **Jewish History Museum** (behind the cube-shaped synagogue) is stark and windowless. The

Ohel Jakob Synagogue

museum's small permanent collection focuses on Munich's Jewish history; good temporary exhibits might justify the entry fee (€6, ticket gets you half-price admission to Munich City Museum, Tue-Sun 10:00-18:00, closed Mon, St.-Jakobs-Platz 16, tel. 089/2339-6096, www.juedisches-museum-muenchen.de).

• *Facing the synagogue, on the same square, is the...*

❺ *Munich City Museum (Münchner Stadtmuseum)*

The highs and lows of Munich's history are covered in this surprisingly honest municipal museum (rated ▲). It covers the cultural upheavals of the early 1900s, Munich's role as the birthplace of the Nazis, and the city's renaissance during Germany's postwar "economic miracle." There's scant information posted in English, but an included audioguide can fill in the gaps.

• *You can stop and tour the museum now* *(see page 64)**. Otherwise, continue through the synagogue's square, past the fountain, across the street, and one block farther to the pedestrianized Sendlinger Strasse. Down the street 100 yards to the left, the fancy facade (at #62) marks the...*

❻ *Asam Church (Asamkirche)*

This tiny church (rated ▲) is a slice of heaven on earth—a gooey, drippy Baroque masterpiece by Bavaria's top two Rococonuts—the Asam brothers. Just 30 feet wide, it was built in 1740 to fit within this row of homes. Originally, it was a private chapel where these two brother-architects could show off their work (on their own land, next to their home and business headquarters—to the left), but it's now a public place of worship.

Asam Church

Cost and Hours: Free, Sat-Thu 9:00-18:00, Fri 13:00-18:00, tel. 089/2368-7989. The church is small, so visitors are asked not to enter during Mass (held Tue and Thu-Fri 17:00-18:00, Wed 8:30-9:30, and Sun 10:00-11:00).

Visiting the Church: This place of worship served as a promotional brochure to woo clients, and is packed with every architectural trick in the book. Imagine approaching the church not as a worshipper, but as a shopper representing your church's building committee. First stand outside: Hmmm, the look of those foundation stones really packs a punch. And the legs hanging over the portico... nice effect. Those starbursts on the door would be a hit back home, too.

Then step inside: I'll take a set of those over-the-top golden capitals, please. We'd also like to order the gilded garlands draping the church in jubilation, and the twin cupids capping the confessional. And how about some fancy stucco work, too? (Molded-and-painted plaster was clearly an Asam brothers specialty.) Check out the illusion of a dome painted on the flat ceiling—that'll save us lots of money. The yellow glass above the altar has the effect of the thin-sliced alabaster at St. Peter's in Rome, but it's within our budget! And, tapping the "marble" pilasters to determine that they are just painted fakes, we decide to take that, too. Crammed between two buildings, light inside this narrow church is limited, so there's a big, clear window in the back for maximum illumination—we'll order one to cut back on our electricity bill.

On the way out, say good-bye to the gilded grim reaper in the narthex (left side as you're leaving) as he cuts the thread of life—reminding all who visit of our mortality...and, by the way, that shrouds have no pockets.

• *Leaving the church, look to your right, noticing the Sendlinger Tor at the end of the street—part of the fortified town wall that circled Munich in the 14th century. Then turn left and walk straight up Sendlinger Strasse. Walk toward the Münchner Kindl, still capping the spire of the New Town Hall in the distance, and then up (pedestrian-only) Rosenstrasse, until you hit Marienplatz and the big, busy...*

❼ *Kaufingerstrasse*

This car-free street leads you through a great shopping district, past cheap department stores, carnivals of street entertainers, and good old-fashioned slicers and dicers. As far back as the 12th century, this was the town's main commercial street. Traders from Salzburg and Augsburg would enter the town through the fortified Karlstor. This street led past the Augustiner beer hall (opposite St. Michael's Church to this day), right to the main square and cathedral.

Up until the 1970s, the street was jammed with car traffic. Then, for the 1972 Olympics, it was turned into one of Europe's first pedestrian zones. At first, shopkeepers were afraid that would ruin business. Now it's Munich's living room. Nearly 9,000 shoppers pass through it each hour. Merchants nearby are begging for their streets to become traffic-free, too.

The 1972 Olympics transformed this part of Munich—the whole area around Marienplatz was pedestrianized and the transit system expanded. Since then, Munich has become one of the globe's greenest cities. Skyscrapers have been banished to the suburbs, and the nearby Frauenkirche is still the tallest building in the center.

• *Stroll a few blocks away from Marienplatz toward the Karlstor, until you arrive at the big church on the right.*

❽ *St. Michael's Church (Michaelskirche)*

This is one of the first great Renaissance buildings north of the Alps. The ornate facade, with its sloped roofline, was inspired by the Gesù Church in Rome—home of the Jesuit order. Jesuits saw themselves as the intellectual defenders of Catholicism. St. Michael's was built in the late 1500s—at the height of the Protestant Reformation—to serve as the northern outpost of the Jesuits. Appropriately, the facade features a statue of Michael fighting a Protestant demon.

Cost and Hours: Church—free, open daily generally 8:00-19:00, stays open later on Sun and summer evenings; crypt—€2, Mon-Fri 9:30-16:30, Sat until 14:30, closed Sun; frequent concerts—check the schedule outside; tel. 089/231-7060.

Visiting the Church: Inside, admire the ornate Baroque interior, topped with a barrel vault, the largest of its day. Stroll up the nave to the ornate pulpit, where Jesuit priests would hammer away at Reformation heresy. The church's acoustics are spectacular, and the choir—famous in

St. Michael's Church

Munich—sounds heavenly singing from the organ loft high in the rear.

The **crypt** (*Fürstengruft*, down the stairs by the altar) contains 40 stark, somewhat forlorn tombs of Bavaria's ruling family, the Wittelsbachs. There's the tomb of Wilhelm V, who built this church, and Maximilian I, who saved Munich from Swedish invaders during the Thirty Years' War. Finally, there's Otto, who went insane and was deposed in 1916, virtually bringing the Wittelsbachs' seven-century reign to an end.

The most ornate tomb holds the illustrious Ludwig II, known for his fairy-tale castle at Neuschwanstein. Ludwig didn't care much for Munich. He escaped to the Bavarian countryside, where he spent his days building castles, listening to music, and dreaming about knights of old. His excesses earned him the nickname "Mad" King Ludwig. But of all the Wittelsbachs, it's his tomb that's decorated with flowers—placed here by romantics still mad about their "mad" king.

• *Our next stop, the Frauenkirche, is a few hundred yards away. Backtrack a couple of blocks up Kaufingerstrasse to the wild boar statue, which marks the* ***German Hunting and Fishing Museum.*** *This place has outdoorsy regalia, kid-friendly exhibits, and the infamous* Wolpertinger*—a German "jackalope" invented by creative local taxidermists. At the boar statue, turn left on Augustinerstrasse, which leads to Munich's towering, twin-domed cathedral, the...*

❾ *Frauenkirche*

These twin onion domes are the symbol of the city. They're unusual in that most Gothic churches have either pointed steeples or square towers. Some say Crusaders, inspired by the Dome of the Rock in Jerusalem, brought home the idea. Or it may be that, due to money problems, the towers weren't completed until Renaissance times, when domes were popular. Whatever the reason, the Frauenkirche's domes may be the inspiration for the characteristic domed church spires that mark villages all over Bavaria.

Cost and Hours: Free, open daily generally 7:00-19:00, tel. 089/290-0820.

Rick's Tip: *If the* **Frauenkirche** *towers are closed for renovation during your visit, you can enjoy great* **city views** *from* **New Town Hall** *(elevator) or the towers of* **St. Peter's Church** *(stairs only).*

Visiting the Church: The church was built in just 22 years, from 1466 to 1488. It's made of brick—easy to make locally, and cheaper and faster to build with than stone. Construction was partly funded by the sale of indulgences (which let sinners bypass purgatory on the way to heaven). It's dedicated to the Virgin—Our Lady (*Frau*)—and has been the city's cathedral since 1821.

Step inside, and remember that much of this church was destroyed during World War II. The towers survived, and the rest was rebuilt essentially from scratch.

Near the entrance is a big, black, ornate monument honoring Ludwig IV the Bavarian (1282-1347), who was elected Holy Roman Emperor—a big deal. The

Frauenkirche

Frauenkirche was built a century later with the express purpose of honoring his memory. His monument was originally situated in front at the high altar, right near Christ. Those Wittelsbachs—always trying to be associated with God. This alliance was instilled in people through the prayers they were forced to recite: "Virgin Mary, mother of our duke, please protect us."

Nearby, a relief (over the back pew on the left) honors one of Munich's more recent citizens. Joseph Ratzinger was born in Bavaria in 1927, became archbishop of the Frauenkirche (1977-1982), then moved to the Vatican, where he later served as Pope Benedict XVI (2005-2013).

Now walk slowly up the main aisle, enjoying stained glass right and left. This glass is obviously modern, having replaced the original glass that was shattered in World War II. Ahead is the high altar, under a huge hanging crucifix. Find the throne—the ceremonial seat of the local bishop. From here, look up to the tops of the columns, and notice the tiny painted portraits. They're the craftsmen from five centuries ago who helped build the church.

Now walk behind the altar to the apse, where there are three tall windows. These still have their original 15th-century glass. To survive the bombs of 1944, each pane had to be lovingly removed and stored safely away.

• *Our next stop is at Promenadeplatz, about 400 yards north of here. Facing the altar, take the left side exit and walk straight 50 yards until you see a tiny but well-signed passageway (to the left) called the Aufhauser Passage. Follow it through a modern building, where you'll emerge at a park (surrounded by concrete) called Promenadeplatz. Detour a few steps left into the park, where you'll find a colorful modern memorial.*

⑩ *Michael Jackson Memorial*

When Michael Jackson was in town, he'd stay at the Hotel Bayerischer Hof, like many VIPs. Fans would gather in the park waiting for him to appear at his window. He'd sometimes oblige (but his infamous baby-dangling incident happened in Berlin, not here). When he died in 2009, devotees created this memorial by taking over a statue of Renaissance composer Orlando di Lasso. They still visit daily, leave a memento, and keep it tidy.

• *Now backtrack and turn left, up Kardinal-Faulhaber-Strasse. The street is lined with former 18th-century mansions that have since become offices and bank buildings. At #11, turn right and enter a modern shopping mall called the* **Fünf Höfe Passage.** *The place tries to take your basic shopping mall and give it more class. It's divided into five connecting courtyards (the* "fünf Höfe"*), spruced up with bubbling fountains, exotic plants, and a hanging garden.*

Emerging on a busy pedestrian street, turn right, and head down the street (noticing the Münchner Kindl again high above), to a big green square: Marienhof, with the most aristocratic grocery store in all of Germany.

⑪ *Marienhof*

This square, tucked behind the New Town Hall, was left as a green island after the wartime bombings. If you find that the square's all dug up, it's because Munich has finally started building an additional subway tunnel here. With virtually the entire underground system converging on nearby Marienplatz, this new tunnel will provide a huge relief to the city's con-

Marienhof

gested subterranean infrastructure.

On the far side of Marienhof is ⓬ **Dallmayr Delicatessen.** When the king called out for dinner, he called Alois Dallmayr. This place became famous for its exotic and luxurious food items: tropical fruits, seafood, chocolates, fine wines, and coffee (there are meat and cheese counters, too). As you enter, read the black plaque with the royal seal by the door: *Königlich Bayerischer Hof-Lieferant* ("Deliverer for the King of Bavaria and his Court"). Catering to royal and aristocratic tastes (and budgets), it's still the choice of Munich's old rich (closed Sun, www.dallmayr.com).

• *Leaving Dallmayr, turn right and then right again to continue along Hofgraben. Walk three blocks gently downhill to Platzl—"small square." (If you get turned around, just ask any local to point you toward the Hofbräuhaus.)*

⓭ *Platzl*

As you stand here—admiring classic facades in the heart of medieval Munich—recall that everything around you was flattened in World War II. Here on Platzl, the reconstruction happened in stages: From 1945 to 1950, they removed 12 million tons of bricks and replaced roofs to make buildings weather-tight. From 1950 to 1972, they redid the exteriors. From 1972 to 2000, they refurbished the interiors. Today, the rebuilt Platzl sports new—but old-looking—facades.

Officials estimate that hundreds of unexploded bombs still lie buried under Munich. As recently as 2012, they found a 550-pound bomb in Schwabing, a neighborhood just north of the old city center. They had to evacuate the neighborhood and detonate the bomb.

Today's Platzl hosts a lively mix of places to eat and drink—pop-culture chains like Starbucks and Hard Rock Café alongside top-end restaurants like the recommended Wirtshaus Ayingers and Schuhbecks (Schuhbecks Eis is a favorite for ice cream; Pfisterstrasse 9-11).

• *At the bottom of the square (#9), you can experience the venerable...*

⓮ *Hofbräuhaus*

The world's most famous beer hall (rated ▲▲) is a trip. Whether or not you slide your lederhosen on its polished benches, it's a great experience just to walk through the place in all its rowdy glory (with its own gift shop).

Before going in, check out the huge arches at the entrance and the crown logo. The original brewery was built here in 1583. As the crown suggests, it was the Wittelsbachs' personal brewery to make the "court brew" *(Hof Brau)*. In 1880, the brewery moved out, and this 5,000-seat food-and-beer palace was built in its place. After being bombed in World War II, the Hofbräuhaus was one of the first places to be rebuilt (German priorities).

Now, take a deep breath and go on in. Dive headlong into the sudsy Hofbräu mosh pit. Don't be shy. Everyone's drunk anyway. The atmosphere is thick with the sounds of oompah music, played here every night of the year.

You'll see locals stuffed into lederhosen and dirndls, giant gingerbread cookies that sport romantic messages, and kiosks selling postcards of the German (and apparently beer-drinking) ex-pope. Notice the quirky 1950s-style painted ceiling, with Bavarian colors, grapes, chestnuts, and fun "eat, drink, and be merry" themes. You'll see signs on some tables reading

Hofbräuhaus

Stammtisch, meaning they're reserved for regulars, and their racks of old beer steins made of pottery and pewter. Beer halls like the Hofbräuhaus sell beer only by the liter mug, called a *Mass* (mahs). You can get it light *(helles)* or dark *(dunkles).* A slogan on the ceiling above the band reads, *Durst ist schlimmer als Heimweh*—"Thirst is worse than homesickness" (daily 9:00-23:30, live oompah music during lunch and dinner; for details on eating here, see page 82).

• *Leaving the Hofbräuhaus, turn right and walk two blocks, then turn left when you reach the street called...*

⓯ *Maximilianstrasse*

This broad east-west boulevard, lined with grand buildings and exclusive shops, introduces us to Munich's Golden Age of the 1800s. In that period, Bavaria was ruled by three important kings: Max Joseph, Ludwig I, and Ludwig II. They transformed Munich from a cluster of medieval lanes to a modern city of spacious squares, Neoclassical monuments, and wide boulevards. At the east end of this boulevard is the palatial home of the Bavarian parliament.

The street was purposely designed for people and for shopping, not military parades. And to this day, Maximilianstrasse is busy with shoppers browsing Munich's most exclusive shops.

• *Maximilianstrasse leads to a big square—Max-Joseph-Platz.*

⓰ *Max-Joseph-Platz*

The square is fronted by two big buildings: the National Theater (with its columns) and the Residenz (with its intimidating stone facade).

The **Residenz,** the former "residence" of the royal Wittelsbach family, started as a crude castle (c. 1385). Over the centuries, it evolved into one of Europe's most opulent palaces (see page 56).

The centerpiece of the square is a grand statue of **Maximilian I**—a.k.a. Max Joseph. In 1806, Max was serving in the long tradition of his Wittelsbach family as the city's duke...until Napoleon invaded and deposed him. But then Napoleon—eager to marry into the aristocracy—agreed to reinstate Max, with one condition: that his daughter marry Napoleon's stepson. Max Joseph agreed, and was quickly crowned not duke but king of Bavaria.

Max Joseph and his heirs ruled as constitutional monarchs. Now a king, Max Joseph was popular; he emancipated Protestants and Jews, revamped the Viktualienmarkt, and graced Munich with grand buildings like the **National Theater.** This Neoclassical building, opened in 1818, celebrated Bavaria's strong culture, deep roots, and legitimacy as a nation; four of Richard Wagner's operas were first performed here. It's now where the Bavarian State Opera and the Bavarian State Orchestra perform. (The Roman numerals MCMLXIII in the frieze mark the year the theater reopened after the WWII bombing restoration—1963.)

• *Leave Max-Joseph-Platz opposite where you entered, walking alongside the Residenz on Residenzstrasse for about 100 yards to the next grand square. But before you get to Odeonsplatz, pause at the first corner on the left and look down Viscardigasse at the gold-cobbled swoosh in the pavement.*

⓱ *Viscardigasse*

The cobbles in Viscardigasse recall one of Munich's most dramatic moments: It

Max-Joseph-Platz

was 1923, and Munich was in chaos. World War I had left Germany in shambles. Angry mobs roamed the streets. Out of the fury rose a new and frightening movement—Adolf Hitler and the Nazi Party. On November 8, Hitler launched a coup, later known as the Beer Hall Putsch, to try to topple the German government. It started with a fiery speech by Hitler in a beer hall a few blocks from here (which no longer exists). The next day, Hitler and his mob of 3,000 Nazis marched up Residenzstrasse. A block ahead, where Residenzstrasse spills into Odeonsplatz, stood a hundred government police waiting for the Nazi mob. Shots were fired. Hitler was injured, and 16 Nazis were killed, along with four policemen. The coup was put down, and Hitler was sent to a prison outside Munich. During his nine months there, he wrote down his twisted ideas in his book *Mein Kampf.*

Ten years later, when Hitler finally came to power, he made a memorial at Odeonsplatz to honor the "first martyrs of the Third Reich." Germans were required to raise their arms in a *Sieg Heil* salute as they entered the square. The only way to avoid the indignity of saluting Nazism was to turn left down Viscardigasse instead. That stream of shiny cobbles marks the detour taken by those brave dissenters.

• *But now that Hitler's odious memorial is long gone, you can continue to...*

⓲ *Odeonsplatz*

This square links Munich's illustrious past with the Munich of today. It was laid out by the Wittelsbach kings in the 1800s. They incorporated the much older (yellow) church that was already on the square, the Theatinerkirche. This church contains about half of the Wittelsbach tombs. The church's twin towers and 230-foot-high dome are classic Italian Baroque, reflecting Munich's strong Catholic bent in the 1600s.

Nearby, overlooking the square from the south, is an arcaded loggia filled with statues. In the 1800s, the Wittelsbachs commissioned this Hall of Heroes to honor Bavarian generals. It was modeled after the famous Renaissance loggia in Florence. Odeonsplatz was part of the Wittelsbachs' grand vision of modern urban planning.

At the far end of the square, several wide boulevards lead away from here.

Odeonsplatz and Theatinerkirche

First, face west (left) down ⓳ **Brienner Strasse** (watch out for bikes). In the distance, and just out of sight, a black obelisk commemorates the 30,000 Bavarians who marched with Napoleon to Moscow and never returned. Beyond the obelisk is the grand Königsplatz, or "King's Square," with its Neoclassical buildings. Back in the 1930s, Königsplatz was the center of the Nazi party. Remember, Munich was the cradle of Nazism. Today, the Nazi shadow has largely lifted from that square (only two buildings from that era remain) and Königsplatz is home to Munich's cluster of great art museums. A few miles beyond Königsplatz is the Wittelsbachs' impressive summer home, Nymphenburg Palace.

Now turn your attention 90 degrees to the right. The boulevard heading north from Odeonsplatz is Ludwigstrasse. It stretches a full mile, flanked by an impressive line of uniform 60-foot-tall buildings in the Neo-Gothic style. In the far distance is the city's Triumphal Arch, capped with a figure of Bavaria, a goddess riding a lion-drawn chariot. The street is named for the great Wittelsbach builder-king, Ludwig I, who truly made Munich into a grand capital. ("I won't rest," he famously swore, "until Munich looks like Athens.") Ludwigstrasse was used for big parades and processions, as it leads to that Roman-style arch.

Beyond the arch—and beyond what you can see—lie the suburbs of modern Munich, including the city's modern skyscrapers and the famous BMW headquarters. Yes, Munich is a major metropolis, but you'd hardly know it by walking through its pleasant streets and parks.

• *We'll finish our walk in the enjoyable Hofgarten. Its formal gate is to your right as you're facing up Ludwigstrasse. Step through the gate and enter the...*

⓴ *Hofgarten*

This elegant "garden of the royal court" is a delight. Built by the Wittelsbachs as their own private backyard to the Residenz palace, it's now open to everyone. Just inside the gate is an arcade decorated with murals commissioned by Ludwig I in the early 1800s. While faded, they still tell the glorious story of Bavaria from 1155 until 1688. The garden's 400-year-old centerpiece is a Renaissance-style temple with great acoustics. (There's often a musician performing here for tips.) It's decorated with the same shell decor as was popular inside the Residenz.

Take some time to enjoy the garden as the royals did. If you're ready to eat, you have several choices, including Café Luitpold (best for coffee and cake) and the elegant Spatenhaus beer hall, both nearby.

• *This walk is done. Where to go next? You're near the English Garden (just a few blocks away—see the map; people surf in the rapids created as the small river tumbles underground beneath the bridge east of Haus der Kunst), the Residenz complex, and the Odeonsplatz U-Bahn stop for points elsewhere.*

SIGHTS

Most of the top sights in the city center are covered on my self-guided walk. But there's much more to see in this city.

Rick's Tip: *If you're unsure about which of Munich's top two palaces to visit, the* **Residenz** *is more central and has the best interior, while* **Nymphenburg** *has the finest garden and outdoor views.*

▲▲Residenz Complex

For 500 years, this was the palatial "residence" and seat of power of the ruling Wittelsbach family. It began (1385) as a crude castle with a moat around it. The main building was built from 1550 to 1650, and decorated in Rococo style during the 18th century. The final touch was the grand south facade modeled after Florence's Pitti Palace. In March 1944, Allied air raids left the Residenz in shambles, so much of what we see today is reconstructed.

The vast Residenz complex is divided into three sections, each with its own admission ticket: The **Residenz Museum** is a long hike through 90 lavishly decorated rooms. The **Residenz Treasury** shows off the Wittelsbach crown jewels. The **Cuvilliés Theater** is an ornate Rococo opera house. You can see the three sights individually or get a combo-ticket to see them all. I consider the museum and treasury to be the essential Residenz visit, with the Cuvilliés Theater as extra credit.

Rick's Tip: *The Bavarian Palace Department offers a* **14-day ticket** *(called the* ***Mehrtagesticket****) that covers admission to Munich's Residenz and Nymphenburg Palace complexes, as well as the Neuschwanstein and Linderhof castles in Bavaria. If you're planning to visit at least three of these sights within a two-week period, the pass will likely pay for itself (€24, €44 family/partner pass, purchase at participating sights or online at www.schloesser.bayern.de).*

Planning Your Time: Start your visit with the Residenz Treasury because it's small and you can easily manage your time there. Then visit the sprawling Residenz Museum, where you can wander until you say "Enough." The Cuvilliés Theater doesn't take long to see and is easy to fit in at the start or end. If you run out of time or energy, you can reenter on the same ticket to visit anything you missed. The entrances on Max-Joseph-Platz and Residenzstrasse both lead to the ticket office, gift shop, and start of the treasury and museum tours.

Cost and Hours: Residenz Museum-€7, Residenz Treasury-€7 (both include audioguides), Cuvilliés Theater-€3.50; €11 combo-ticket covers museum and treasury; €13 version covers all three; treasury and museum open daily April-mid-Oct 9:00-18:00, mid-Oct-March 10:00-17:00; theater open April-mid-Sept Mon-Sat 14:00-18:00, Sun 9:00-18:00; mid-Sept-March Mon-Sat 14:00-17:00, Sun 10:00-17:00; for all three sights, last entry is one hour before closing, tel. 089/290-671, www.residenz-muenchen.de.

The Residenz—the "residence" of Bavaria's rulers

RESIDENZ TREASURY (SCHATZKAMMER)

The treasury shows off a thousand years of Wittelsbach crowns and knickknacks. You'll see the regalia used in Bavaria's coronation ceremonies, valuable liturgical objects and relics, and miscellaneous wonders that dazzled the Wittelsbachs' European relatives. It's the best treasury in Bavaria, with fine 13th- and 14th-century crowns and delicately carved ivory and glass.

➲ **Self-Guided Tour:** In **Room 1,** the oldest jewels are 200 years older than Munich itself. The gem-studded 11th-century Crown of Kunigunde (on the left) is associated with the saintly Bavarian queen, who was crowned Holy Roman Empress in 1014 in St. Peter's Basilica in Rome. The pearl-studded prayer book of Charles the Bald (Charlemagne's grandson) allowed the book's owner to claim royal roots dating all the way back to that first Holy Roman Emperor crowned in 800. The spiky Crown of an English Queen (c. 1370) is actually England's oldest crown, brought to Munich by an English princess who married a Wittelsbach duke. The lily-shaped Crown of Henry II (c. 1270-1280) dates from Munich's roots, when the town was emerging as a regional capital.

Along the right side of the room are religious objects such as reliquaries and portable altars. The tiny mobile altar allowed a Carolingian king to pack light in 890—and still have a little Mass while on the road. Many of the precious objects in this room were confiscated from the collections of various prince-bishops when their realms came under Bavarian rule in the Napoleonic era (c. 1800).

Room 3: Study the reliquary with St. George killing the dragon—sparkling with more than 2,000 precious stones. Get up close (it's OK to walk around the rope posts)...you can almost hear the dragon hissing. A gold-armored St. George, seated atop a ruby-studded ivory horse, tramples an emerald-green dragon. The golden box below contained the supposed relics of St. George, who was the patron saint of the Wittelsbachs. If you could lift the minuscule visor, you'd see that the carved ivory face of St. George is actually the Wittelsbach Duke Wilhelm V—the great champion of the Catholic Counter-Reformation—slaying the dragon of Protestantism.

Room 4: The incredibly realistic carved ivory crucifixes from 1630 were done by local artist Georg Petel. Look at the flesh of Jesus' wrist pulling around the nails. In the center of the room is the intricate portable altarpiece (1573-74) of Duke Albrecht V, the Wittelsbach ruler who (as we'll see in the Residenz Museum) made a big mark on the Residenz.

Room 5: The freestanding glass case (#245) holds the impressive royal regalia of the 19th-century Wittelsbach kings—the crown, scepter, orb, and sword that were given to the king during the cor-

Crown of Henry II

St. George reliquary

onation ceremony. (The smaller pearl crown was for the queen.) They date from the early 1800s when Bavaria had been conquered by Napoleon. The Wittelsbachs struck a deal that allowed them to stay in power under the elevated title of "king" (not just "duke" or "elector" or "prince-archbishop"). These objects were made in France by the same craftsmen who created Napoleon's crown.

Rooms 6-10: The rest of the treasury has objects that are more beautiful than historic. Admire the dinnerware made of rock crystal (Room 6), stone (Room 7), and gold and enamel (Room 8). Room 9 has a silver-gilt-and-marble replica of Trajan's Column. Finally, explore the "Exotica" of Room 10, including a green Olmec figure, knives from Turkey, and a Chinese rhino-horn bowl with a teeny-tiny Neptune inside.

• *From the micro-detail of the treasury, it's time to visit the expansive Residenz Museum. Cross the hall, exchange your treasury audioguide for the museum audioguide, and enter the...*

RESIDENZ MUSEUM (RESIDENZMUSEUM)

Though called a "museum," what's really on display here are the 90 rooms of the Residenz itself: the palace's spectacular banquet and reception halls, and the Wittelsbachs' lavish private apartments. The rooms are decorated with period (but generally not original) furniture: chandeliers, canopied beds, Louis XIV-style chairs, old clocks, tapestries, and dinnerware of porcelain and silver. It's the best place to glimpse the opulent lifestyle of Bavaria's late, great royal family. (Whatever happened to the Wittelsbachs, the longest continuously ruling family in European history? They're still around, but they're no longer royalty, so most of them have real jobs now—you may well have just passed one on the street.)

➲ **Self-Guided Tour:** The place is big. Follow the museum's prescribed route, using this section to hit the highlights and supplementing it with the audioguide. Grab a free museum floor plan to help locate room numbers mentioned here. The route can vary because rooms are occasionally closed off.

• *One of the first "rooms" you encounter (it's actually part of an outdoor courtyard) is the...*

❶ **Shell Grotto** (Room 6): This artificial grotto is made of volcanic tuff and covered completely in Bavarian freshwater shells. In its day, it was an exercise in man controlling nature—a celebration of the Renaissance humanism that flourished in the 1550s. Mercury—the pre-Christian god of trade and business—oversees the action. Check out the statue in the courtyard—in the Wittelsbachs' heyday, red wine would have flowed from the mermaid's breasts and dripped from Medusa's severed head.

• *Before moving on, note the door marked OO, leading to handy WCs. Now continue into the next room, the...*

❷ **Antiquarium** (Room 7): This low, arched hall stretches 220 feet end to end. It's the oldest room in the Residenz, built around 1550. The room was, and still is, a festival banquet hall. The ruler presided from the raised dais at the near end (warmed by the fireplace). Two hundred dignitaries can dine here, surrounded by allegories of the goodness of just rule on the ceiling.

The hall is lined with busts of Roman emperors. In the mid-16th century, Europe's royal families (such as the Wittelsbachs) collected and displayed such busts, implying a connection between themselves and the enlightened ancient Roman rulers. There was such huge demand for these classical statues in the courts of Europe that many of the "ancient busts" were fakes cranked out by crooked Romans. Still, a third of the statuary you see here is original.

The small paintings around the room show 120 Bavarian villages as they looked in 1550. Even today, when a Bavarian historian wants a record of how his village once looked, he comes here. Notice the town of Dachau in 1550 (in the archway closest to the entrance door).

• *Keep going through a few more rooms, then up a stairway to the upper floor. Pause in the* ***Black Hall*** *(Room 13) to admire the head-spinning trompe l'oeil ceiling, which makes the nearly flat roof appear to be a much grander arched vault. From here, the prescribed route winds through a number of rooms surrounding a large courtyard.*

❸ **Upper Floor Apartments** (Rooms 14-45): In this series of rooms we get the first glimpse of the Residenz Museum's forte: chandeliered rooms decorated with ceiling paintings, stucco work, tapestries, parquet floors, and period furniture.

Rooms to the left of the Black Hall are the **Electoral Apartments** (Rooms 22-31), the private apartments of the monarch and his consort.

In the long **All Saints Corridor** (Room 32), you can glance into the adjoining All Saints' Chapel. This early-19th-century chapel, commissioned by Ludwig I, was severely damaged in World War II, didn't reopen until 2003, and is still being refurbished.

From the All Saints Corridor you can reach the **Charlotte Chambers/ Court-Garden Rooms,** a long row of impressive rooms across the courtyard from the Electoral Apartments, first used to house visiting rulers. Some of them later served as the private rooms of Princess Charlotte, Max Joseph's daughter.

• *Your visit eventually reaches a hallway—* ❹ ***Room 45****—where you have a choice: to the left is the "short" route that heads directly to the stunning Ornate Rooms (described later). But we'll take the "long" route to the right (starting in Room 47) that adds a dozen-plus rooms to your visit.*

❺ **The "Long" Route:** Use your Residenz-issued map to find some of the following highlights. The large **Imperial Hall** is in Room 111; the **Stone Rooms** (104-109) are so-called for their colorful marble—both real and fake. Then come several small rooms, where the centerpiece painting on the ceiling is just blank black, as no copy of the original survived World War II.

The **Reliquary Room** (Room 95) harbors a collection of gruesome Christian relics (bones, skulls, and even several mummified hands) in ornate golden cases.

The Antiquarium, the palace's banquet hall

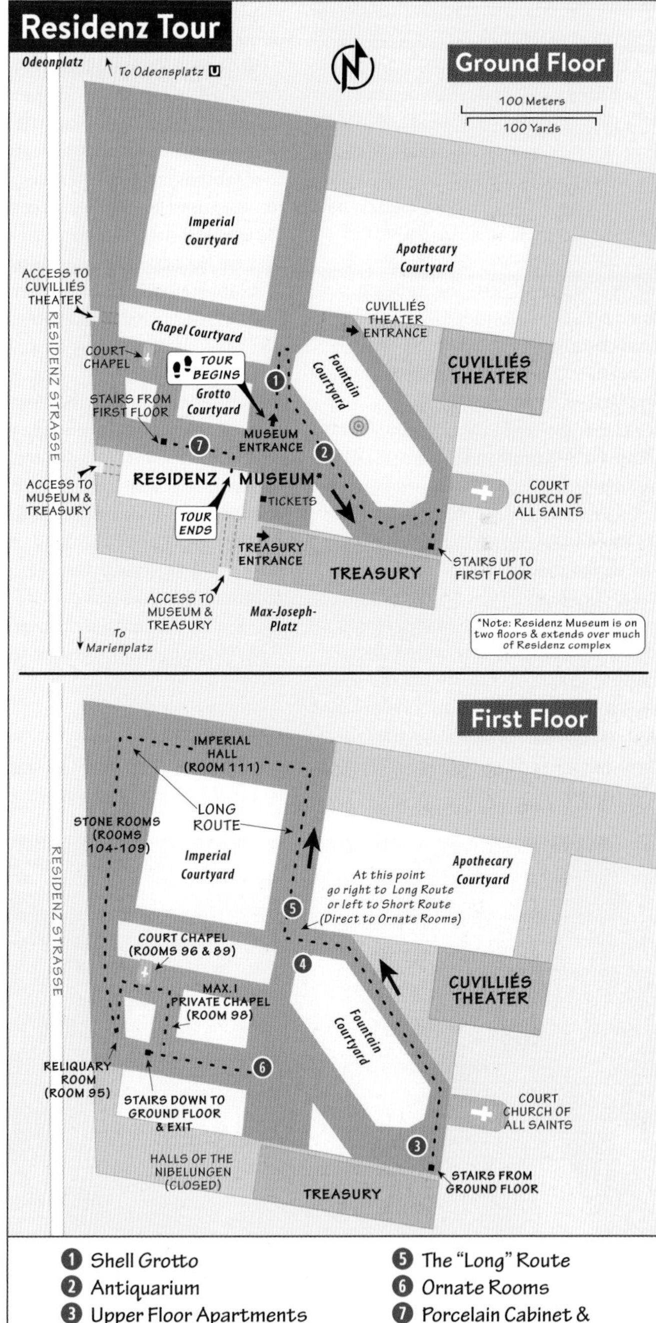
Residenz Tour
Odeonplatz
To Odeonsplatz U
Ground Floor
100 Meters
100 Yards
Imperial Courtyard
Apothecary Courtyard
ACCESS TO CUVILLIÉS THEATER
Chapel Courtyard
CUVILLIÉS THEATER ENTRANCE
CUVILLIÉS THEATER
Fountain Courtyard
COURT CHAPEL
TOUR BEGINS
Grotto Courtyard
STAIRS FROM FIRST FLOOR
MUSEUM ENTRANCE
RESIDENZ STRASSE
ACCESS TO MUSEUM & TREASURY
RESIDENZ MUSEUM*
TICKETS
COURT CHURCH OF ALL SAINTS
TOUR ENDS
TREASURY ENTRANCE
TREASURY
STAIRS UP TO FIRST FLOOR
ACCESS TO MUSEUM & TREASURY
Max-Joseph-Platz
To Marienplatz
*Note: Residenz Museum is on two floors & extends over much of Residenz complex
First Floor
IMPERIAL HALL (ROOM 111)
LONG ROUTE
STONE ROOMS (ROOMS 104-109)
Imperial Courtyard
Apothecary Courtyard
At this point go right to Long Route or left to Short Route (Direct to Ornate Rooms)
COURT CHAPEL (ROOMS 96 & 89)
CUVILLIÉS THEATER
MAX. I PRIVATE CHAPEL (ROOM 98)
Fountain Courtyard
RELIQUARY ROOM (ROOM 95)
STAIRS DOWN TO GROUND FLOOR & EXIT
COURT CHURCH OF ALL SAINTS
HALLS OF THE NIBELUNGEN (CLOSED)
TREASURY
STAIRS FROM GROUND FLOOR
1 Shell Grotto
2 Antiquarium
3 Upper Floor Apartments
4 Room 45
5 The "Long" Route
6 Ornate Rooms
7 Porcelain Cabinet & Ancestral Gallery

• *A few more steps brings you to the balcony of the...*

Court Chapel (Rooms 96/89): Dedicated to Mary, this late-Renaissance/early-Baroque gem was the site of "Mad" King Ludwig's funeral after his mysterious murder—or suicide—in 1886. (He's buried in St. Michael's Church, described on page 50.) About 75 years earlier, in 1810, his grandfather and namesake (Ludwig I) was married here. After the wedding ceremony, carriages rolled his guests to a rollicking reception, which turned out to be such a hit that it became an annual tradition—Oktoberfest.

A couple of rooms ahead is the **Private Chapel of Maximilian I** (Room 98). Duke Maximilian I, the dominant Bavarian figure in the Thirty Years' War, built one of the most precious rooms in the palace. The miniature pipe organ (from about 1600) still works. The room is sumptuous, from the gold leaf and the fancy hinges to the miniature dome and the walls made of stucco "marble." Note the post-Renaissance perspective tricks decorating the walls; they were popular in the 17th century.

• *Whichever route you take—long or short—you'll eventually reach a set of rooms known as the...*

❻ **Ornate Rooms** (Rooms 55-62): As the name implies, these are some of the richest rooms in the palace. The Wittelsbachs were always trying to keep up with the Habsburgs, and these ceremonial rooms—used for official business—were designed to impress. The decor and furniture are Rococo—over-the-top Baroque. The family art collection, now in the Alte Pinakothek, once decorated these walls.

The rooms were designed in the 1730s by François de Cuvilliés, a Belgian who first attracted notice as the clever court dwarf for the Bavarian ruler. He was sent to Paris to study art and returned to become the court architect. Besides the Residenz, he designed the Cuvilliés Theater and the Amalienburg lodge at Nymphenburg Palace. Cuvilliés' style, featuring incredibly intricate stucco tracery twisted into unusual shapes, defined Bavarian Rococo. As you glide through this section of the palace, be sure to appreciate the gilded stucco ceilings above you.

Each room is unique. The **Green Gallery** (Room 58)—named for its green silk

Every Residenz room is unique and ornate.

damask wallpaper—was the ballroom. Imagine the parties they had here—aristocrats in powdered wigs, a string quartet playing Baroque tunes, a card game going on, while everyone admired the paintings on the walls or themselves reflected in the mirrors. The **State Bedroom** (Room 60), though furnished with a canopy bed, wasn't an actual bedroom—it was just for show. Rulers invited their subjects to come at morning and evening to stand at the railing and watch their boss ceremonially rise from his slumber to symbolically start and end the working day.

Perhaps the most ornate of these Ornate Rooms is the **Cabinet of Mirrors** (Room 61) and the adjoining **Cabinet of Miniatures** (Room 62) from 1740. In the Cabinet of Mirrors, notice the fun visual effects of the mirrors around you—the corner mirrors make things go on forever. Then peek inside the coral red room (the most royal of colors in Germany) and imagine visiting the duke and having him take you here to ogle miniature copies of the most famous paintings of the day, composed with one-haired brushes.

• *After exploring the Ornate Rooms (and the many, many other elaborate rooms here on the upper floor), find the staircase (near Room 65) that heads back downstairs. On the ground floor, you emerge in the long Ancestral Gallery (Room 4). Before walking down it, detour to the right, into Room 5.*

❼ **Porcelain Cabinet** (Room 5) and **Ancestral Gallery** (Room 4): In the 18th century, the royal family bolstered their status with an in-house porcelain works. See how the mirrors enhance the porcelain vases, creating the effect of infinite pedestals. If this inspires you to acquire some pieces of your own, head to the Nymphenburg Porcelain Store at Odeonsplatz (see page 81).

The Ancestral Gallery (Room 4) was built in the 1740s to display portraits of the Wittelsbachs. All official guests had to pass through here to meet the duke (and his 100 Wittelsbach relatives). The room's symbolism reinforced the Wittelsbachs' claims to being as powerful as the Habsburgs of Vienna.

Midway down the hall, find the family tree labeled (in Latin) "genealogy of an imperial family." The tree is shown being planted by Hercules to boost their royal street cred. Opposite the tree are two notable portraits: Charlemagne, the first Holy Roman Emperor, and to his right, Louis IV (wearing the same crown), the first Wittelsbach H.R.E., crowned in 1328. For the next 500 years, this lineage was used to substantiate the family's claim to power as they competed with the Habsburgs. (After failing to sort out their differences through strategic weddings, the two families eventually went to war.)

Allied bombs took their toll on this hall. The central ceiling painting has been restored, but since there were no photos documenting the other two ceiling paintings, those spots remain empty. Looking carefully at the walls, you can see how each painting was hastily cut from its frame. That's because—though most of Munich's museums were closed during World War II to prevent damage—the Residenz remained open to instill confidence in local people. It wasn't until 1944, when bombs were imminent, that the last-minute order was given to hide the paintings away.

• *Your Residenz Museum tour is over. The doorway at the end of the hall leads back to the museum entrance. If you're visiting the Cuvilliés Theater, from the exit walk straight through the courtyard to Residenzstrasse. Take a right and pass by the two green lions standing guard just ahead. Walk to the far end of the lane until you reach a fountain. Just above a doorway to the left you'll see a nondescript sign that says* Cuvilliés Theater.

CUVILLIÉS THEATER

In 1751, this was Germany's ultimate Rococo theater. Mozart conducted here several times. Designed by the same brilliant architect who designed the Ornate Rooms in the palace, this theater is dazzling enough to send you back to the days of divine monarchs.

It's an intimate, horseshoe-shaped performance venue, seating fewer than 400. The four tiers of box seats were for the four classes of society: city burghers on bottom, royalty next up (in the most elaborate seats), and lesser courtiers in the two highest tiers. The ruler occupied the large royal box directly opposite the stage. "Mad" King Ludwig II occasionally bought out the entire theater to watch performances here by himself.

François Cuvilliés' interior is exquisite. Red, white, and gold hues dominate. Most of the decoration is painted wood, even parts that look like marble. Even the proscenium above the stage—seemingly draped with a red-velvet "curtain"—is actually made of carved wood. Also above the stage is an elaborate Wittelsbach coat of arms. The balconies seem to be supported by statues of the four seasons and are adorned with gold garlands. Cuvilliés achieved the Rococo ideal of giving theater-goers a multimedia experience—uniting the beauty of his creation with the beautiful performance on stage. It's still a working theater.

WWII bombs completely obliterated the old Cuvilliés Theater, which originally stood at a different location a short distance from here. Fortunately, much of the carved wooden interior had been removed from the walls and stored away for safekeeping. After the war, they built this entirely new building near the ruins of the old theater and paneled it with the original decor.

Near the Residenz

▲MUNICH CITY MUSEUM (MÜNCHNER STADTMUSEUM)

The museum's permanent exhibit on Munich's history is interesting, but it's exhaustive, and there's no posted English information. I'd use the following mini tour for an overview, then supplement it with the audioguide and English booklet.

Cost and Hours: €4 includes good audioguide, more for special (skippable) exhibits, Tue-Sun 10:00-18:00, closed Mon, ticket gets you half-price admission to Jewish History Museum, St.-Jakobs-Platz 1, tel. 089/2332-2370, www.muenchner-stadtmuseum.de. The

Cuvilliés Theater

humorous Servus Heimat souvenir shop in the courtyard is worth a stop.

Eating: The museum's recommended Stadt Café is handy for a good meal (see page 85).

Visiting the Museum: Start in the ticketing hall with the wooden model showing Munich today. Find the Frauenkirche, Isar River, New Town Hall, Residenz...and no skyscrapers. The city looks remarkably similar in scale to the model (in the next room) from 1570.

Ground Floor—Medieval: A big gray statue of Henry the Lion introduces us to the city's 12th-century founder. The eight statues of Morris dancers (1480) became a symbol of the vibrant market town (and the tradition continued with the New Town Hall glockenspiel's dancing coopers). On the rest of the ground floor, paintings, armor, and swords capture more medieval ambience.

First Floor—1800s: The "New Munich" was created when the city was expanded beyond the old medieval walls (see the illuminated view of the city from 1761 in the "Canaletto-Blick," opposite the top of the stairs). The city was prosperous, as evidenced by the furniture and paintings on display. In the center of the room, find big paintings ("Effigies") of the century's magnificent kings—Maximilian I, Maximilian II, and Ludwig I.

Second Floor—Munich 1900: As Munich approached its 700th birthday, it was becoming aware of itself as a major capital. The Münchner Kindl logo was born. It was a city of artists (Wagner operas, Lenbach portraits, Von Stuck soirées), *Jugendstil* furniture, beer, and a cosmopolitan outlook (see the "emperor panorama," the big barrel-shaped 3-D peep show of African/Asian peoples). But after the destruction of World War I, Munich became a hotbed of discontent. The "revue" room shows the city's clash of ideas: communists, capitalists, Nazis, and the anarchic theater of comedian Karl Valentin and early works by playwright Bertolt Brecht. A nearby display gives some background on Munich's role as the birthplace of Nazism (much more thoroughly covered in the museum's National Socialism wing).

From here, you can detour upstairs to the **third floor puppet theater** to see an extensive collection of marionettes, Punch-and-Judy hand puppets, and paper cutouts of this unique Bavarian art form with a long cabaret tradition.

Back on the second floor, finish with a kaleidoscope of images capturing the contemporary Munich scene—rock music, World Cup triumphs, beer gardens, and other things that are..."typically Munich."

National Socialism Wing: This small but worthwhile exhibit of photos and uniforms takes you chronologically through the Nazi years, focused on Munich: the post-WWI struggles, Hitler's 1923 Beer Hall Putsch, his writing of *Mein Kampf*, the mass rallies in Königsplatz and Odeonsplatz, establishment of the Dachau concentration camp, and the destruction rained on Munich in World War II.

Munich City Museum

Museum Quarter (Kunstareal)

This quarter's cluster of blockbuster museums displays art spanning from 3000 B.C. right up to the present. Of the seven museums in the quarter, we'll focus on the top three: Egyptian Museum, Alte Pinakothek, and Neue Pinakothek. Most people don't come to Munich for the art,

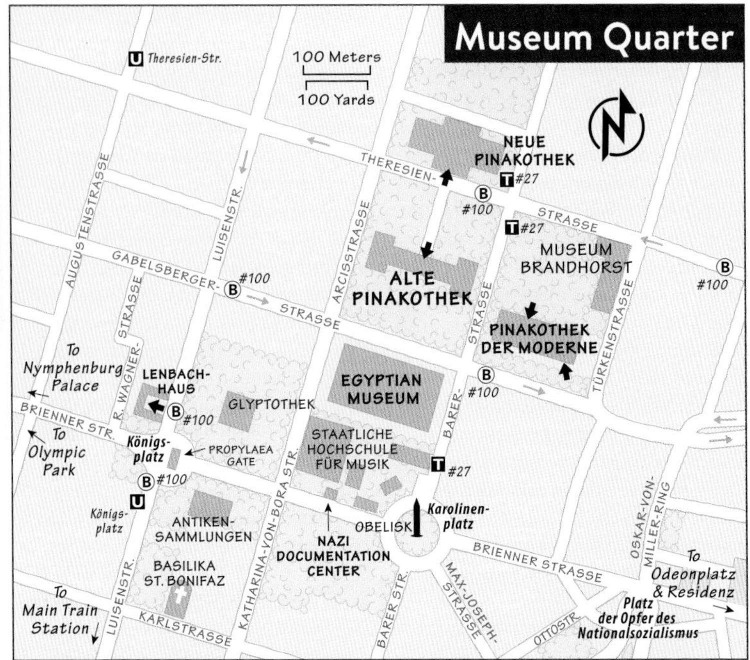

but this group makes a case for the city's world-class status.

Getting There: Handy tram #27 whisks you right to the Pinakothek stop from Karlsplatz (between the train station and Marienplatz). You can also take bus #100 from the train station, or walk 10 minutes from the Theresienstrasse or Königsplatz stops on the U-2 line.

▲▲ALTE PINAKOTHEK

Bavaria's best painting gallery (the "Old Art Gallery," pronounced ALL-teh pee-nah-koh-TEHK) shows off a world-class collection of European masterpieces from the 14th to 19th century, starring the two tumultuous centuries (1450-1650) when Europe went from medieval to modern. See paintings from the Italian Renaissance (Raphael, Leonardo, Botticelli, Titian) and the German Renaissance it inspired (Albrecht Dürer). The Reformation of Martin Luther eventually split Europe into two subcultures—Protestants and Catholics—with their two distinct art styles (exemplified by Rembrandt and Rubens, respectively). Because of a major renovation project, expect some galleries to be closed when you visit.

Cost and Hours: €4 during renovation (otherwise €7), €1 on Sun, open Tue 10:00-20:00, Wed-Sun until 18:00, closed Mon, free and excellent audioguide (€4.50 on Sun), pleasant Café Klenze; U-2: Theresienstrasse, tram #27, or bus #100; Barer Strasse 27, tel. 089/2380-5216, www.pinakothek.de/alte-pinakothek.

➲ **Self-Guided Tour:** All the paintings we'll see are on the upper floor, which is laid out like a barbell. This tour starts at one fat end and works its way through the "handle" to the other end. From the ticket counter, head up the stairway to the left to reach the first rooms.

German Renaissance (Room II): Albrecht Altdorfer's *The Battle of Issus (Schlacht bei Issus)* shows a world at war. Masses of soldiers are swept along in the currents and tides of a battle completely

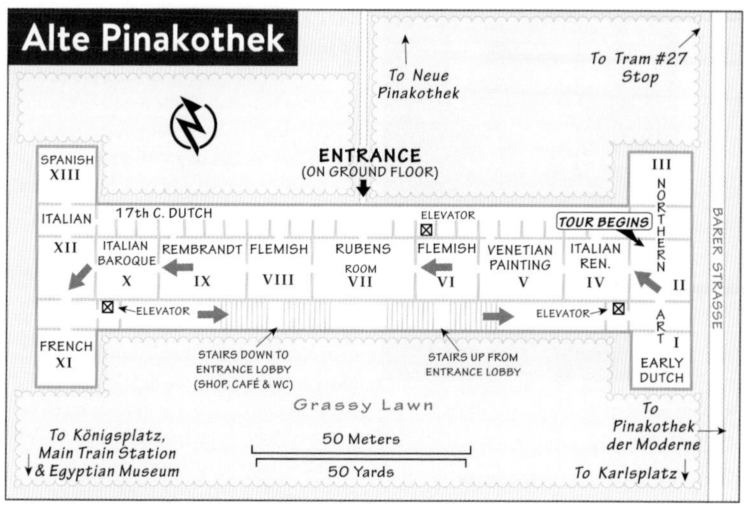

beyond their control, their confused motion reflected in the swirling sky. Though the painting depicts Alexander the Great's history-changing victory over the Persians (find the Persian king Darius turning and fleeing), it could as easily have been Germany in the 1520s. Christians were fighting Muslims, peasants battled masters, and Catholics and Protestants were squaring off for a century of conflict. The armies melt into a huge landscape, leaving the impression that the battle goes on forever.

Dürer, Self-Portrait in Fur Coat

Albrecht Dürer's larger-than-life *Four Apostles (Johannes und Petrus* and *Paulus und Marcus*) are saints of a radical new religion: Martin Luther's Protestantism. Just as Luther challenged Church authority, Dürer—a friend of Luther's—strips these saints of any rich clothes, halos, or trappings of power and gives them down-to-earth human features: receding hairlines, wrinkles, and suspicious eyes. The inscription warns German rulers to follow the Bible rather than Catholic Church leaders. The figure of Mark—a Bible in one hand and a sword in the other—is a fitting symbol of the dangerous times.

Dürer's *Self-Portrait in Fur Coat (Selbstbildnis im Pelzrock)* looks like Jesus Christ but is actually 28-year-old Dürer himself, gazing out, with his right hand solemnly giving a blessing. This is the ultimate image of humanism: the artist as an instrument of God's continued creation.

Italian Renaissance (Room IV): With the Italian Renaissance—the "rebirth" of interest in the art and learning of ancient Greece and Rome—artists captured the realism, three-dimensionality, and symmetry found in classical statues. Twenty-one-year-old Leonardo da Vinci's *Virgin*

Ⓐ *Leonardo da Vinci,* Virgin and Child

Ⓑ *Raphael,* Canigiani Holy Family

Ⓒ *Rubens,* Rubens and Isabella Brant

and Child (Maria mit dem Kinde) need no halos—they radiate purity. Mary is a solid pyramid of maternal love, flanked by Renaissance-arch windows that look out on the hazy distance. Baby Jesus reaches out to play innocently with a carnation, the blood-colored symbol of his eventual death.

Raphael's *Canigiani Holy Family (Die hl. Familie aus dem Hause Canigiani)* takes Leonardo's pyramid form and runs with it. Father Joseph forms the peak, with his staff as the strong central axis. Mary and Jesus (on the right) form a pyramid-within-the-pyramid, as do Elizabeth and baby John the Baptist on the left.

In Botticelli's *Lamentation over Christ (Die Beweinung Christi),* the Renaissance "pyramid" implodes, as the weight of the dead Christ drags everyone down, and the tomb grins darkly behind them.

Venetian Painting (Room V): In Titian's *Christ Crowned with Thorns (Die Dornenkrönung),* a powerfully built Christ sits, silently enduring torture by prison guards. The painting is by Venice's greatest Renaissance painter, but there's no symmetry, no pyramid form, and the brushwork is intentionally messy and Impressionistic. By the way, this is the first painting we've seen that is done on canvas rather than wood, as artists experimented with vegetable-oil-based paints.

Rubens and Baroque (Room VII): Europe's religious wars split the Continent in two—Protestants in the northern countries, Catholics in the south. (Germany itself was divided, with Bavaria remaining Catholic.) The Baroque style, popular in Catholic countries, featured large canvases, bright colors, lots of flesh, rippling motion, wild emotions, grand themes... and pudgy winged babies, the sure sign of Baroque. This room holds several canvases by the great Flemish painter Peter Paul Rubens.

In Rubens' 300-square-foot *Great Last Judgment (Das Grosse Jüngste Gericht),* Christ raises the righteous up to heaven (left side) and damns the sinners to hell (on the right). This swirling cycle of nudes was considered risqué and kept under wraps by the very monks who'd commissioned it.

Rubens and Isabella Brant shows the artist with his first wife, both of them the picture of health, wealth, and success. They lean together unconsciously, as people in love will do, with their hands clasped in mutual affection. When his first wife died, 53-year-old Rubens found a replacement—16-year-old Hélène Fourment, shown in an adjacent painting (just to the left) in her wedding dress. You may recognize Hélène's face in other Rubens paintings.

The Rape of the Daughters of Leucippus (Der Raub der Töchter des Leukippos) has many of Rubens' most typical elements—fleshy, emotional, rippling motion; bright colors; and a classical subject. The legendary twins Castor and Pollux crash a wedding and steal the brides as their own. The chaos of flailing limbs and rearing horses is all held together in a subtle X-shaped composition. Like the weaving counterpoint in a Baroque fugue, Rubens balances opposites.

Rembrandt and Dutch (Room IX): From Holland, Rembrandt van Rijn's *Six Paintings from the Life of Christ* are a down-to-earth look at supernatural events. The *Adoration (Die Anbetung der Hirten)* of Baby Jesus takes place in a 17th-century Dutch barn with ordinary folk as models. The canvases are dark brown, lit by strong light. The Adoration's light source is the Baby Jesus himself—literally the "light of the world." In the *Deposition (Kreuzabnahme)*, the light bounces off Christ's pale body onto his mother, Mary, who has fainted in the shadows, showing how his death also hurts her. The drama is underplayed, with subdued emotions. In the *Raising of the Cross (Kreuzaufrichtung)*, a man dressed in blue is looking on—a self-portrait of Rembrandt.

▲NEUE PINAKOTHEK

The Alte Pinakothek's younger sister is an easy-to-like collection located just across the street, showing paintings from 1800 to 1920. Breeze through a smattering of Romantics on your way to the museum's highlight: some world-class Impressionist paintings, and one of Van Gogh's *Sunflowers*.

Cost and Hours: €7, €1 on Sun, open Wed 10:00-20:00, Thu-Mon until 18:00, closed Tue, well-done audioguide is usually free but €4.50 on Sun, classy Café Hunsinger in basement spills into park; U-2: Theresienstrasse, tram #27, or bus #100; Barer Strasse 29, but enter on Theresienstrasse, tel. 089/2380-5195, www.pinakothek.de/neue-pinakothek.

Visiting the Museum: Pick up the audioguide and floor plan, and follow their prescribed route. Along the way, be sure to hit these highlights.

Rooms 1-3: In Room 1, Jacques-Louis David's curly-haired *Comtesse de Sorcy* shows the French noblewoman dressed in the ancient-Greek-style fashions popular during the Revolution. Room 3 features English painters—Turner's stormy seascapes and Gainsborough's contemplative *Mrs. Thomas Hibbert*. Nearby, you'll see other less-famous works by other major European artists.

Rooms 4-18: These rooms—the bulk of the museum—feature colorful, pretty, realistic (and mostly forgettable) paintings

Stieler, King Ludwig I in Coronation Robes *(detail)*

by German Romantics. In the remarkable *King Ludwig I in Coronation Robes* (Room 8), the young playboy king is both regal and rakish. (You can learn more on the king, the artist, and their Gallery of Beauties at Nymphenburg Palace; see page 76.) Caspar David Friedrich (Room 9) is Germany's best-known chronicler of the awe-inspiring power of nature (though these small canvases aren't his best). Carl Spitzweg's tiny *The Poor Poet* (Room 12) is often reproduced. Room 13 has huge (hard-to-miss) canvases: *The Destruction of Jerusalem by Titus* and the nationalist-themed *Thusnelda Led in Germanicus' Triumph*, showing a German noblewoman and her son, captured by the Romans, being paraded before the emperor.

Rooms 19-22: In these rooms, you'll find classic examples of all the Impressionist and Post-Impressionist masters: Degas' snapshots of women at work, Monet's sunny landscapes and water lilies, Manet's bourgeois Realism, Cézanne's still lifes, and Gauguin's languid Tahitian ladies. Van Gogh's *Sunflowers* is one of 11 such canvases he did.

In the final rooms, see works by Gustav Klimt and Munich's answer to Klimt, Franz von Stuck.

▲▲EGYPTIAN MUSEUM (STAATLICHES MUSEUM ÄGYPTISCHER KUNST)

To enjoy this museum, you don't need a strong interest in ancient Egypt (but you may have one by the time you leave). This new space was custom-made to evoke the feeling of being deep in an ancient tomb, from the wide staircase outside that descends to the narrow entry, to the twisty interior rooms that grow narrower and more catacomb-like as you progress. The museum's clever design creates a low-stress visit—just follow the one-way route marked by brass arrows in the floor.

Cost and Hours: €12, €6 on Sun, open Tue 10:00-20:00, Wed-Sun until 18:00, closed Mon; U-2 or U-8 to Königsplatz, tram #27 to Karolinenplatz, or bus #100 to Pinakothek stop; 10-minute walk from main train station, Gabelsbergerstrasse 35, tel. 089/2892-7630, www.smaek.de.

Near the River

▲ENGLISH GARDEN (ENGLISCHER GARTEN)

Munich's "Central Park," the largest urban park on the Continent, was laid out in 1789 by an American, Benjamin Thompson (who left New England when the American Revolution broke out). More than 100,000 locals commune with nature here on sunny summer days. The park stretches three miles from the center, past the university and the trendy Schwabing quarter. For the best quick visit, take bus #100 or tram #18 to the Nationalmuseum/Haus der Kunst stop. Under the bridge, you may see surfers. Follow the path, to the right of the surfing spot, downstream until you reach the big lawn. The Chinese Tower beer garden is just beyond the tree-covered hill to the right. Follow the oompah music and walk to the hilltop temple, with a postcard view of the city on your way. Afterward, instead of

Chinese Tower beer garden

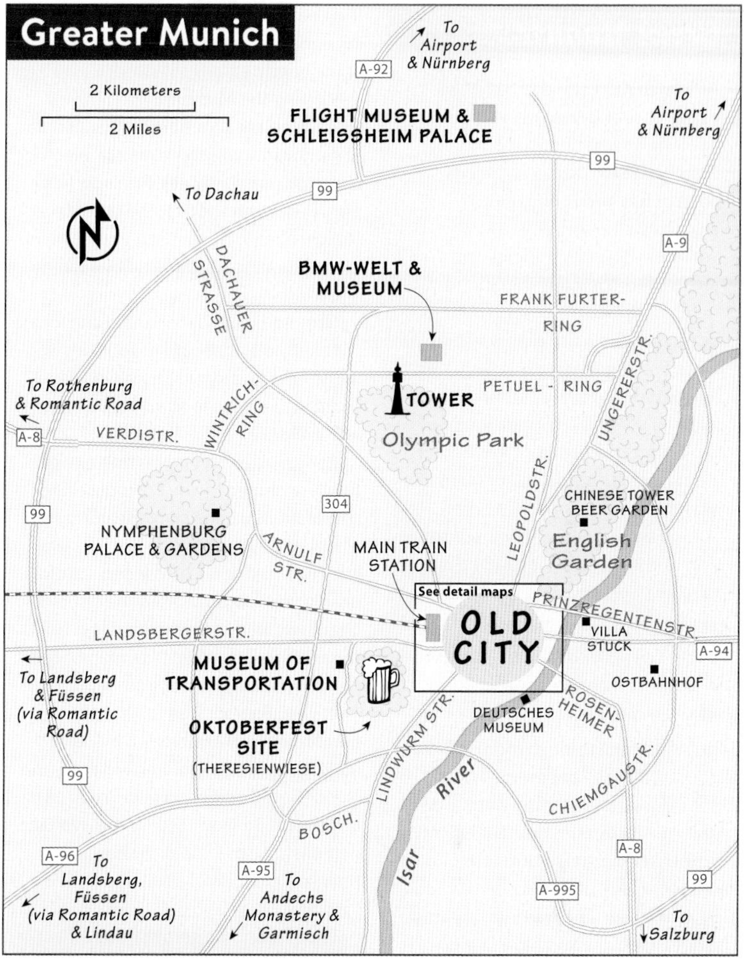

Greater Munich

2 Kilometers
2 Miles
To Airport & Nürnberg
A-92
FLIGHT MUSEUM & SCHLEISSHEIM PALACE
To Airport & Nürnberg
99
To Dachau
99
A-9
DACHAUER STRASSE
BMW-WELT & MUSEUM
FRANKFURTER-RING
UNGERERSTR.
TOWER
PETUEL - RING
To Rothenburg & Romantic Road
A-8
VERDISTR.
WINTRICH-RING
Olympic Park
LEOPOLDSTR.
CHINESE TOWER BEER GARDEN
English Garden
99
304
NYMPHENBURG PALACE & GARDENS
ARNULF STR.
MAIN TRAIN STATION
See detail maps
OLD CITY
PRINZREGENTENSTR.
VILLA STUCK
LANDSBERGERSTR.
A-94
To Landsberg & Füssen (via Romantic Road)
MUSEUM OF TRANSPORTATION
OSTBAHNHOF
OKTOBERFEST SITE (THERESIENWIESE)
DEUTSCHES MUSEUM
ROSENHEIMER
LINDWURMSTR.
99
Isar River
CHIEMGAUSTR.
BOSCH.
A-96
To Landsberg, Füssen (via Romantic Road) & Lindau
A-95
To Andechs Monastery & Garmisch
A-8
A-995
99
To Salzburg

English Garden

retracing your steps, you can walk (or take bus #54 a couple of stops) to the Giselastrasse U-Bahn station and return to town on the U-3 or U-6.

A rewarding respite from the city, the park is especially fun—and worth ▲▲—on a bike under the summer sun and on warm evenings (to rent some wheels, see page 96). Caution: While local law requires sun worshippers to wear clothes on the tram, the park is sprinkled with buck-naked sunbathers—quite a shock to prudish Americans (they're the ones riding their bikes into the river and trees).

Green Munich

Although the capital of a conservative part of Germany, Munich has long been a liberal stronghold. For nearly two decades, the city council has been controlled by a Social Democrat/Green Party coalition. The city policies are pedestrian-friendly—you'll find much of the town center closed to normal traffic, with plenty of bike lanes and green spaces. As you talk softly and hear birds rather than motors, it's easy to forget you're in the center of a big city. On summer Mondays, the peace and quiet make way for "blade Monday"—when streets in the center are closed to cars and as many as 30,000 inline skaters swarm around town in a giant rolling party.

▲DEUTSCHES MUSEUM

Enjoy wandering through rooms of historic airplanes, spaceships, mining, the harnessing of wind and water power, hydraulics, musical instruments, printing, chemistry, computers, astronomy, and nanotechnology...it's the Louvre of technical know-how. The museum is dated, and not all the displays have English descriptions—but major renovations are under way. About a third of the collection will likely be closed during your visit, but with 11 acres of floor space and 10 miles of exhibits, even those on roller skates will still need to be selective. Use my mini tour to get oriented, then study the floor plan and choose which departments interest you.

Cost and Hours: €11, daily 9:00-17:00, worthwhile €7 English guidebook, tel. 089/21791, www.deutsches-museum.de.

Getting There: Take tram #16 to the Deutsches Museum stop. Alternatively, take the S-Bahn or tram #18 to Isartor, then walk 300 yards over the river, following signs. (The entrance is near the far end of the building along the river.)

Visiting the Museum: After buying your ticket, ask about the day's schedule of demonstrations (for example, electric power or glass-blowing). Pick up a floor plan, then continue past the ticket taker, straight ahead, into a vast high-ceilinged room (Room 10) dominated by a tall-masted ship.

Ground Floor: Get oriented and locate the handy elevator behind you—it's one of the few elevators in this labyrinthine building that goes to all six floors. Now, let's explore.

Room 10's exhibit on **marine navigation** is anchored by the 60-foot sailing ship *Maria*. Take the staircase down, where you can look inside her cut-away hull and imagine life below decks. Before heading back upstairs, find the bisected U1 submarine (on the wall farthest from the entrance)—the first German *U-Boot* (undersea boat), dating from 1906.

Now make your way to several new technology exhibits—DNA and nano-technology. Children will enjoy the "Kinderreich" (downstairs in Room 24) and the exciting twice-daily high-voltage demonstrations (Room 9) showing the noisy creation of a five-foot bolt of lightning.

First Floor: The **aeronautics** collection occupies virtually the entire floor (Room 33). You'll see early attempts at flight—gliders, hot-air balloons, and a model of the airship pioneered by Germany's Count Zeppelin. The highlight is a Wright Brothers double-decker airplane from 1909—six years after their famous first flight, when they began to manufacture multiple copies of their prototype. By World War I, airplanes were becoming a formidable force. The Fokker tri-plane was made famous by Germany's war ace the Red Baron (Manfred von Richthofen, whose exploits, I've heard, prompted enemies to drop the f-bomb). The exhibit continues into WWII-era Junkers and Messerschmitts and postwar passenger planes.

Second Floor: Gathered together near the main elevator, you'll find a replica of prehistoric **cave paintings** (Room 39) and daily **glass-blowing** demonstrations (Room 40).

Third Floor: The third floor traces the **history of measurement,** including time (from a 16th-century sundial and an 18th-century clock to a scary Black Forest wall clock complete with grim reaper), weights, and geodesy (surveying and mapping). In the computer section (Rooms 52-53), you go from the ancient abacus to a 1956 Univac computer—as big as a room, with a million components, costing a million dollars, and with less computing power than your smartphone.

Floors 4-6: If you have trouble finding your way to these floors, there's always that main elevator. The focus here is on **astronomy.** A light-show exhibit (Room 62) traces the evolution of the universe. The recently renovated planetarium (Room 63) requires a €2 extra ticket (purchase at the info desk beforehand)—but the lecture is in German. Finally, you emerge on the museum rooftop—the "sundial garden" (Room 64)—with great views. On a clear day, you can see the Alps.

▲▲Nymphenburg Palace Complex

For 200 years, this oasis of palaces and gardens just outside Munich was the Wittelsbach rulers' summer vacation home, a getaway from the sniping politics of court life in the city. Their kids could play, picnic, ride horses, and frolic in the ponds and gardens, while the adults played cards, listened to music, and sipped coffee on the veranda. It was at Nymphenburg that a 7-year-old Mozart gave a widely heralded concert, 60-year-old Ludwig I courted the femme fatale Lola Montez, and "Mad" King Ludwig II (Ludwig I's grandson) was born and baptized.

Today, Nymphenburg Palace and the surrounding one-square-mile park are a great place for a royal stroll or discreet picnic. Indoors, you can tour the Bavarian royal family's summer quarters and visit the Royal Stables Museum (carriages, sleighs, and porcelain). If you have time, check out playful extras, such as a hunting lodge (Amalienburg), bathhouse (Badenburg), pagoda (Pagodenburg), and fake ruins (Magdalenenklause). The complex also houses a humble natural history museum and Baroque chapel. Allow at least three hours (including travel time) to see the palace complex at a leisurely pace.

Cost and Hours: Palace-€6; combo-ticket-€11.50 (€8.50 off-season) covers the palace, Royal Stables Museum, and outlying sights open in summer. All of these sights are open daily April-mid-Oct 9:00-18:00, mid-Oct-March 10:00-16:00—except for Amalienburg and the other small palaces in the park, which are closed mid-Oct-March. The park is open daily 6:00-dusk and free to enter. Tel. 089/179-080, www.schloss-nymphenburg.de.

Getting There: The palace is three miles northwest of central Munich. Take tram #17 (direction: Amalienburgstrasse) from the north side of the train station (or catch it at Karlsplatz). In 15 minutes you reach the Schloss Nymphenburg stop. From the bridge by the tram stop, you'll see the palace—a 10-minute walk away. The palace is a pleasant 30-minute bike ride from the main train station (either follow Arnulfstrasse all the way to Nymphenburg, or turn up Landshuter Allee—at Donersburgerbrücke—then follow Nymphenburger Strasse until you hit the canal that stretches to the palace). Biking in the palace grounds is not permitted.

Eating: A café serves lunches in the former palm house, behind and to the right of the palace (open year-round). More eating options are near the tram stop.

NYMPHENBURG PALACE

In 1662, after 10 years of trying, the Bavarian ruler Ferdinand Maria and his wife, Henriette Adelaide of Savoy, finally had a son, Max Emanuel. In gratitude for a male heir, Ferdinand gave this land to his Italian wife, who proceeded to build an Italian-style Baroque palace. Their son expanded the palace to today's size. (Today's Wittelsbachs, who still refer to themselves as "princes" or "dukes," live in one wing of the palace.)

The palace interior, while interesting, is much less extensive than Munich's Residenz—you can visit only 16 rooms. The place is stingy on free information; you'll need the serviceable audioguide if you'd like more info than what I've provided below.

➲ **Self-Guided Tour:** Your visit starts in the **Great Hall** (a.k.a. **Stone Hall**). As the central room of the palace, this light and airy space was the dining hall, site of big Wittelsbach family festivals. One of the grandest and best-preserved Rococo rooms in Bavaria (from about 1758), it sports elaborate stucco work and a ceiling fresco by Johann Baptist Zimmermann (of Wieskirche fame).

Zimmerman's fresco opens a sunroof to the heavens, where Greek gods cavort. In the sunny center, Apollo drives his chariot to bring the dawn, while bearded Zeus (astride an eagle) and peacock-carrying Juno look on. The rainbow symbolizes the peace brought by the enlightened Wittelsbachs. Around the borders of the painting, notice the fun optical illusions: For example, a painted dog holds a stucco bird in its mouth. The painting's natural setting and joie de vivre reflect the pastoral pleasures enjoyed here at the Wittelsbachs' summer home. At one end of the fresco (away from the windows) lounges a lovely maiden with flowers in her hair: it's Flora, the eponymous nymph who inspired this "nymph's castle"—Nymphenburg.

From here, two wings stretch to the left and right. They're mirror images of one another: antechamber, audience chamber, bedchamber, and private living quarters. Guests would arrive here in the Great Hall for an awe-inspiring first impression, then make their way through a series of (also-impressive) waiting rooms for their date with the Wittelsbach nobility.

Nymphenburg Palace

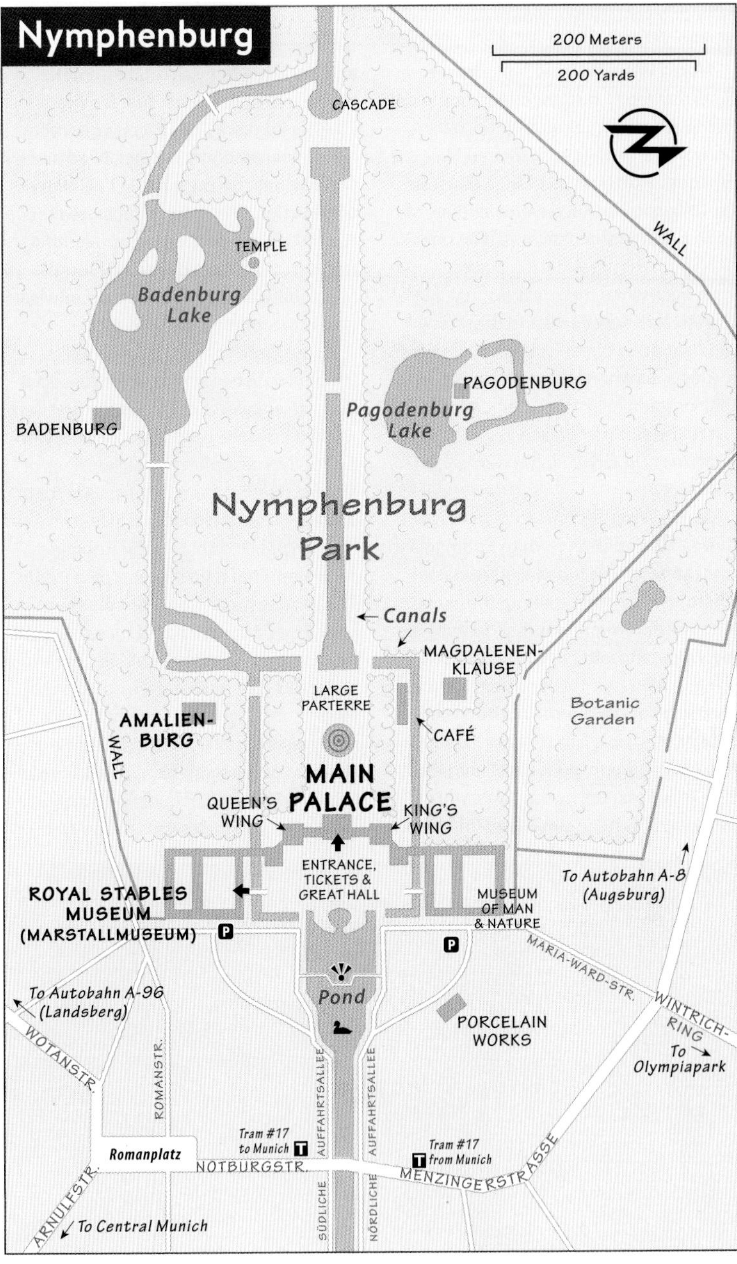
Nymphenburg
200 Meters
200 Yards
CASCADE
WALL
TEMPLE
Badenburg Lake
PAGODENBURG
Pagodenburg Lake
BADENBURG
Nymphenburg Park
Canals
MAGDALENEN-KLAUSE
LARGE PARTERRE
AMALIEN-BURG
WALL
CAFÉ
Botanic Garden
MAIN PALACE
QUEEN'S WING
KING'S WING
ENTRANCE, TICKETS & GREAT HALL
ROYAL STABLES MUSEUM (MARSTALLMUSEUM)
MUSEUM OF MAN & NATURE
To Autobahn A-8 (Augsburg)
MARIA-WARD-STR.
WINTRICH-RING
To Olympiapark
Pond
PORCELAIN WORKS
To Autobahn A-96 (Landsberg)
WOTANSTR.
ROMANSTR.
AUFFAHRTSALLEE
AUFFAHRTSALLEE
Tram #17 to Munich
Tram #17 from Munich
Romanplatz
NOTBURGSTR.
MENZINGERSTRASSE
ARNULFSTR.
To Central Munich
SÜDLICHE
NÖRDLICHE

• *The tour continues to the left (as you look out the big windows).*

North Wing (Rooms 2-9): Breeze quickly through this less interesting wing, filled with tapestries and Wittelsbach portraits (including curly-haired Max Emanuel, who built this wing). Pause in the long corridor lined with paintings of various Wittelsbach palaces. The ones of Nymphenburg show the place around 1720, back when there was nothing but countryside between it and downtown (and gondolas plied the canals). Imagine the logistics when the royal family—with their entourage of 200—decided to move out to the summer palace.

• *Return to the Great Hall and enter the other wing.*

South Wing (Rooms 10-20): Pass through the gold-and-white Room 10 and turn right into the red-walled Audience Chamber. The room calls up the exuberant time of Nymphenburg's founding couple, Ferdinand and Henriette. A portrait on the wall shows them posing together in their rich courtly dress. Another painting depicts them in a Greek myth: Henriette (as the moon-goddess Diana) leads little Max Emanuel by the hand, while Ferdinand (as her mortal lover Endymion) receives the gift of a sword. The ceiling painting (of the earth goddess Cybele) and the inlaid table also date from the time of Nymphenburg's first family.

After admiring the Queen's Bedroom and Chinese lacquer cabinet, head down the long hall to **King Ludwig I's Gallery of Beauties.** The room is decorated top to bottom with portraits of 36 beautiful women (all of them painted by Joseph Stieler between 1827 and 1850). Ludwig I was a consummate girl-watcher.

Ludwig prided himself on his ability to appreciate beauty regardless of social rank. He enjoyed picking out the prettiest women from the general public and, with one of the most effective pickup lines of all time, inviting them to the palace for a portrait. Who could refuse? The portraits were on public display in the Residenz, and catapulted their subjects to stardom. The women range from commoners to princesses, but notice that they share one physical trait—Ludwig obviously preferred brunettes. The portraits are done in the modest and slightly sentimental Biedermeier style popular in central Europe, as opposed to the more flamboyant Romanticism (so beloved of Ludwig's "mad" grandson) also thriving at that time.

The Great Hall has remained unchanged since 1758.

Most of these portraits have rich stories behind them, none more than the portrait of Lola Montez, the king's most notorious mistress. The portrait shows her the year she met Ludwig (she was 29, he was 60), wearing the black-lace mantilla and red flowers of a Spanish dancer. (And where in the "gallery of beauties" is the portrait of Ludwig's wife, Queen Therese? She's not here...you'll have to duck into the elegant, green Queen's Study to see her portrait.)

Pass through the blue Audience Room (with elaborate curtain rods and mahogany furniture in the French-inspired Empire style) and into the (other) **Queen's Bedroom.** The room has much the same furniture it had on August 25, 1845, when Princess Marie gave birth to the future King Ludwig II. Little Ludwig (see his bust, next to brother Otto's) was greatly inspired by Nymphenburg—riding horses in summer, taking sleigh rides in winter, reading poetry at Amalienburg. The love of nature and solitude he absorbed at Nymphenburg eventually led Ludwig to abandon Munich for his castles in the remote Bavarian countryside. By the way, note the mirror in this bedroom. Royal births were carefully witnessed, and the mirror allowed for a better view. While Ludwig's birth was well-documented, his death was shrouded in mystery (see page 169).

Stieler, Lola Montez *(detail)*

PALACE GROUNDS

The wooded grounds extend far back beyond the formal gardens and are popular with joggers and walkers (biking is not allowed). Find a bench for a low-profile picnic. The park is laced with canals and small lakes, where court guests once rode on Venetian-style gondolas.

ROYAL STABLES MUSEUM (MARSTALLMUSEUM)

These former stables (to the left of the main palace as you approach the complex) are full of gilded coaches that will make you think of Cinderella's journey to the king's ball. Upstairs, a porcelain exhibit shows off some of the famous Nymphenburg finery. If you don't want to visit the main palace, you can buy a €4.50 ticket just for this museum (no audioguide available).

Visiting the Museum: Wandering through the collection, you can trace the evolution of **300 years of coaches**—getting lighter and with better suspension as they were harnessed to faster horses. In the big entrance hall is a golden carriage drawn by eight fake white horses. In 1742, it carried Karl Albrecht Wittelsbach to Frankfurt to be crowned Holy Roman Emperor. As emperor, he got eight horses—kings got only six. The event is depicted in a frieze on the museum wall; Karl's carriage is #159.

Other objects bear witness to the good times of the relaxed Nymphenburg lifestyle. You'll see the sleigh of Max Emanuel, decorated with a carved Hercules. The carousel (not always on display) was for the royal kids.

Next up are things owned by Ludwig II—several sleighs, golden carriages, and (in the glass cases) harnesses. Ludwig's over-the-top coaches were Baroque. But this was 1870. The coaches, like the king, were in the wrong century.

Head upstairs to a collection of

Nymphenburg porcelain. Historically, royal families such as the Wittelsbachs liked to have their own porcelain factories to make fit-for-a-king plates, vases, and so on. The Nymphenburg Palace porcelain works is still in operation (their factory store on Odeonsplatz is happy to see you). Find the large room with copies of 17th-century Old Masters' paintings from the Wittelsbach art collection (now at the Alte Pinakothek). Ludwig I had these paintings copied onto porcelain for safekeeping into the distant future. Take a close look—they're exquisite.

AMALIENBURG

Three hundred yards from Nymphenburg Palace, hiding in the park (head into the sculpted garden and veer to the left, following signs), you'll find a fine little Rococo hunting lodge, which takes just a few minutes to tour. In 1734, Elector Karl Albrecht had it built for his wife, Maria Amalia. Amalienburg was designed by François de Cuvilliés (of Residenz fame) and decorated by Johann Baptist Zimmermann. It's the most worthwhile of the four small "extra" palaces buried in the park that are included on the combo-ticket. The others are the Pagodenburg, a Chinese-inspired pavilion; Badenburg, an opulent bathing house and banquet hall; and the Magdalenenklause, a mini palace that looks like a ruin from the outside but has an elaborate altar and woody apartments inside.

Visiting Amalienburg: As you approach, circle to the front and notice the facade. Above the pink-and-white grand entryway, Diana, goddess of the chase, is surrounded by themes of the hunt and flanked by busts of satyrs. The queen would shoot from the perch atop the roof. Behind a wall in the garden, dogs would scare nonflying pheasants. When they jumped up in the air above the wall, the sporting queen—as if shooting skeet—would pick the birds off.

Tourists now enter this tiny getaway through the back door. Doghouses under gun cupboards fill the first room. In the fine yellow-and-silver bedroom, the bed is flanked by portraits of Karl Albrecht and Maria Amalia—decked out in hunting attire. She liked her dogs. The door under the portrait leads to stairs to the rooftop pheasant-shooting perch.

The mini Hall of Mirrors is a blue-and-silver commotion of Rococo nymphs designed by Cuvilliés. In the next room, paintings depict court festivities, formal hunting parties, and no-contest kills (where the animal is put at an impossible disadvantage—like shooting fish in a barrel). Finally, the kitchen is decorated with Chinese-style drawings on Dutch tile.

Outside the Center

▲▲BMW-WELT AND MUSEUM

At the headquarters of BMW ("beh-em-VEH" to Germans), Beamer dreamers can visit two space-age buildings to learn more about this brand's storied heritage.

Royal Stables Museum

Amalienburg

The renowned *Autos* and *Motorräder* are beautifully displayed (perhaps even fetishized), but visitors who aren't car enthusiasts might find them less impressive. This vast complex—built on the site of Munich's first airstrip and home to the BMW factory since 1920—has four components: the headquarters (in the building nicknamed "the Four Cylinders"—not open to the public), the factory (tourable with advance reservations), the showroom (called BMW-Welt—"BMW World"), and the BMW Museum.

Cost and Hours: Museum—€10, Tue-Sun 10:00-18:00, closed Mon; BMW-Welt showroom—free, daily 9:00-18:00, tel. 089/125-016-001, www.bmw-welt.com/en.

Tours: English tours are offered of both the museum (€13, 1.5 hours, call ahead for times) and BMW-Welt (€7, daily at 14:00, 80 minutes). Factory tours must be booked at least two months in advance (€8, 2.5 hours, Mon-Fri only, ages 7 and up, book by calling 089/125-016-001, more info at www.bmw-werk-muenchen.de; ask at the BMW-Welt building about cancellations—open spots are released to the public 15 minutes before each tour).

Getting There: It's easy: Ride the U-3 to Olympia-Zentrum; the stop faces the BMW-Welt entry. To reach the museum, walk through BMW-Welt and over the swoopy bridge. This area also makes for a pleasant destination by bike, and is easily reached, and well-signed, from the English Garden.

Visiting the BMW-Welt: The futuristic, bowl-shaped **BMW Museum** encloses a world of floating walkways linking exhibits highlighting BMW motorcycle and car design and technology through the years. The museum traces the Bavarian Motor Works' history since 1917, when the company began making airplane engines. Motorcycles came next, followed by the first BMW sedan in 1929. You'll see how design was celebrated here from the start. Exhibits showcase motorsports, roadsters, and luxury cars. Stand on an *E* for English to hear the chief designer talk about his favorite cars in the "treasury." And the 1956 BMW 507 is enough to rev almost anyone's engine.

The futuristic BMW-Welt is a one-of-a-kind auto showroom.

The **BMW-Welt** building itself—a cloud-shaped, glass-and-steel architectural masterpiece—is reason enough to visit. It's free and filled with exhibits designed to enthuse car lovers so they'll find a way to afford a Beamer. While the adjacent museum reviews the BMW past, BMW-Welt shows you the present and gives you a breathtaking look at the future. This is where customers come to pick up their new Beamers (stand on the sky bridge to watch in envy), and where hopeful customers-to-be come to nurture their automotive dreams.

EXPERIENCES

Oktoberfest

A carnival of beer, pretzels, and wurst that draws visitors from all over the globe, Oktoberfest lasts just over two weeks, usually starting on the third Saturday in September and ending on the first Sunday in October (www.oktoberfest.de). It's held at the Theresienwiese fairground south of the main train station, in a meadow known as the "Wies'n" (VEE-zen), where about 15 huge tents can each seat several thousand beer drinkers. The festivities kick off with an opening parade, followed by a two-week frenzy of drinking, dancing, music, and food. A million gallons of beer later, they roast the last ox.

If you'll be here during the festivities, reserve a room early. During the fair, the city functions even better than normal, but is admittedly more expensive and crowded. It's a good time to sightsee, even if beer-hall rowdiness isn't your cup of tea.

The enormous beer tents are often full, especially on weekends—if possible, avoid going on a Friday or Saturday night. For some cultural background, hire a local guide (see page 40) or go with a group (Radius Tours, for example, offers a €110 tour that includes two beers, half a chicken, and guaranteed seating, Sun-Fri at 10:00, no tours on Sat, reserve ahead, www.radiustours.com; Size Matters Beer Tour runs one for €120, includes breakfast, lunch, four beers, and reserved seating, www.sizemattersbeertour.de).

In the city center, the humble **Beer and Oktoberfest Museum** (Bier- und Oktoberfestmuseum), offers exhibits

and artifacts on the origins of the celebration and the centuries-old quest for the perfect beer (apparently achieved in Munich). The oldest house in the city center, the museum's home is noteworthy in itself (€4, Tue-Sat 13:00-18:00, closed Sun-Mon, between the Isartor and Viktualienmarkt at Sterneckerstrasse 2, tel. 089/2423-1607, www.bier-und-oktoberfestmuseum.de).

Rick's Tip: *The Theresienwiese fairground also hosts a* **Spring Festival** *(*Frühlingsfestival*, two weeks in late April-early May, www.fruehlingsfest-muenchen.de), and* **Tollwood,** *an artsy, multicultural event held twice a year—once in summer (late June-July) and in winter (alternative Christmas market, late Nov-Dec, www.tollwood.de).*

Shopping

The most glamorous shopping area is around Marienplatz. It's fun to window shop, even if you have no plans to buy.

The upscale **Ludwig Beck** department store, with six floors of designer clothing, has been a local institution since 1861 (Mon-Sat 9:30-20:00, closed Sun, Marienplatz).

The third floor of department store **Loden-Frey Verkaufshaus** is dedicated to classic Bavarian wear *(Trachten)* for men and women (Mon-Sat 10:00-20:00, closed Sun, a block west of Marienplatz at Maffeistrasse 7, tel. 089/210-390, www.loden-frey.com).

The **Nymphenburg Porcelain Store** carries contemporary and classic dinnerware and figurines (Mon-Sat 10:00-18:00, closed Sun, Odeonsplatz 1, tel. 089/282-428, www.nymphenburg.com).

The **Hugendubel bookstore** on Karlsplatz has some English offerings (Mon-Sat 10:00-20:00, closed Sun, Karlsplatz 12, tel. 089-3075-7575, www.hugendubel.de).

Nightlife

Here are a few nightlife alternatives to the beer hall scene. Ballet and opera fans can check the schedule at the **Bayerisch Staatsoper,** centrally located next door to the Residenz. Book at least two months ahead—seats range from €13 to pricey (Max-Joseph-Platz 2, tel. 089/2185-1920, www.bayerische.staatsoper.de). The **Hotel Bayerischerhof's** posh nightclub hosts major jazz acts plus pop/soul/disco (Promenadeplatz 2, tel. 089/212-0994, www.bayerischerhof.de). For Broadway-style musicals (most in German), try the **Deutsches Theatre,** located near the train station (Schwanthalerstrasse 13, tel. 089/5523-4444, www.deutsches-theater.de).

EATING

Munich's cuisine is traditionally seasoned with beer. In beer halls, beer gardens, or at the Viktualienmarkt, try the most typical meal in town: *Weisswurst* (white-colored veal sausage—peel off the skin before eating, often available only until noon) with *süsser Senf* (sweet mustard), a salty *Brezel* (pretzel), and *Weissbier* ("white" wheat beer). Another traditional favorite is *Obatzda* (a.k.a. *Obatzter*), a mix of soft cheeses, butter, paprika, and often garlic or onions that's spread on bread. *Brotzeit,* literally "bread time," gets you a wooden platter of cold cuts, cheese, and pickles and is a good option for a light dinner.

Beer Halls and Gardens

For those in search of the boisterous, clichéd image of the beer hall, nothing beats the Hofbräuhaus (the only beer hall in town where you'll find oompah music). Locals prefer the innumerable beer gardens. On a warm day, when you're looking for the authentic outdoor beer-garden experience, your best options are the Augustiner (near the train station), the small beer garden at the Viktualienmarkt (near Marienplatz), or the sea of tables in the English Garden.

Rick's Tip: *By law,* **any place serving beer** *must admit the public (whether or not they're customers) to* **use the bathrooms.**

Near Marienplatz

The **$$ Hofbräuhaus** (HOAF-broy-howz) is the world's most famous beer hall. While it's grotesquely touristy, it's a Munich must. Drop by anytime for a large or light meal or just for a drink. Choose from four zones: the rowdy main hall on the ground floor, a quieter courtyard under the stars, a dainty restaurant with mellow music one floor up, or the giant festival hall under a big barrel vault on the top floor. They sell beer by the *Mass* (one-liter mug, €8)—and they claim to sell 10,000 of these liters every day. Live oompah music plays at lunch and dinner (daily 9:00-23:30, 5-minute walk from Marienplatz at Platzl 9, tel. 089/2901-3610, www.hofbraeuhaus.de).

$$$ Wirtshaus Ayingers, just across the street from the Hofbräuhaus, is less chaotic. It serves quality Bavarian food—especially the schnitzels—and beer from Aying, a village south of Munich. There's lively outside seating on the cobbles facing the tourist chaos or a simple woody interior (€14-18 main courses, daily 11:00-24:00, Platzl 1a, tel. 089/2370-3666, www.ayingers.de).

$$ Andechser am Dom, at the rear of the twin-domed Frauenkirche on a breezy square, is a local staple serving Andechs beer and great food to appreciative regulars. Münchners favor the dark beer (ask for *dunkles*), but I love the light *(helles)*. The *Gourmetteller* is a great sampler of

Munich's Beer Scene

In Munich's beer halls *(Brauhäuser)* and beer gardens *(Biergartens),* meals are inexpensive, white radishes are salted and cut in delicate spirals, and surly beer maids pull mustard packets from their cleavage. Beer is truly a people's drink—and the best is in Munich. The big question among connoisseurs is "Which brew today?"

Huge liter beers (*ein Mass* or "*ein* pitcher") cost about €8. You can order your beer *helles* (light), *dunkles* (dark), or ask for a *Weiss* or *Weizen* ("white" or wheat-based beer—cloudy and sweet) or a *Radler* (half lemon soda, half beer).

Beer-hall food is usually *selbstdienst* (self-service)—a sign may say *Bitte bedienen Sie sich selbst* (please serve yourself). If two prices are listed, *Schank* is for self-service, while *Bedienung* is for table service. At a large *Biergarten,* assemble your dream feast by visiting various counters, marked by type of food (*Bier* or *Bierschänke* for beer, *Bratwürste* for sausages, *Brotzeiten* for lighter fare served cold, and so on). Look for these specialties:

Fleischpfanzerl (or *Fleischklösse* or *Frikadellen*): Meatballs
Grosse Brez'n: Gigantic pretzel
Hendl (or *Brathähnchen*): Roasted chicken
Radi: Radish thinly spiral-cut and salted
Schweinrollbraten: Pork belly
Schweinshax'n (or *Hax'n*): Pork knuckle
Spareribs: Spareribs
Steckerlfisch: A whole fish (usually mackerel) herbed and grilled on a stick

their specialties, but you can't go wrong with *Rostbratwurst* with kraut (€8-20 main courses, daily 10:00-24:00, Weinstrasse 7a, reserve during peak times, tel. 089/2429-2920, www.andechser-am-dom.de).

$$ Nürnberger Bratwurst Glöckl am Dom, around the corner from Andechser am Dom, offers a more traditional, fiercely Bavarian evening. Dine outside under the trees or in the dark, medieval interior. Enjoy the tasty little *Nürnberger* sausages with kraut (€10-20 main courses, daily 10:00-24:00, Frauenplatz 9, tel. 089/291-9450, www.bratwurst-gloeckl.de).

$$$ Altes Hackerhaus serves its traditional Bavarian fare with a slightly fancier feel in one of the oldest buildings in town. It offers a small courtyard and a fun forest of characteristic nooks. This place is greatly appreciated for its Hacker-Pschorr beer (€8-10 wurst dishes, €9-25 main courses, daily 10:30-24:00, Sendlinger Strasse 14, tel. 089/260-5026, www.hackerhaus.de).

Munich's **$$$ Ratskeller** fills the City Hall's vast cellar and also has some tables in the courtyard with 360-degree views. While it's hectic and touristy, locals still enjoy the timeless atmosphere (€14-24 main courses, daily 10:00-24:00, Marienplatz 8, tel. 089/219-9890, www.ratskeller.com).

$$$ Der Pschorr, an upscale beer hall occupying a former slaughterhouse, has a terrace overlooking the Viktualienmarkt and serves what many consider Munich's finest beer. With organic "slow food" and chilled glasses, this place mixes modern with classic dishes. The sound of the hammer tapping wooden kegs every few minutes lets patrons know their beer is good and fresh (€15-25 main courses, daily 10:00-24:00, Viktualienmarkt 15, at end of Schrannenhalle, tel. 089/442-383-940, www.der-pschorr.de).

The small **$ beer garden** at the center of the Viktualienmarkt has just about the best budget eating in town; it's just steps from Marienplatz. There's table service wherever you see a tablecloth; to picnic, choose a table without one—but you must buy a drink from the counter (daily 10:00-22:00). Countless stalls surround the beer garden and sell wurst, sandwiches, and produce.

Rick's Tip: *Most beer gardens have a* **€1 deposit *(Pfand)* for their big glass steins.** *When you're finished drinking, take the mug and your deposit token* (Pfandmarke) *to the return man* (Pfandrückgabe) *for your refund. If you buy a bottled beer, pour it into the glass before you check out; otherwise you'll pay two deposits (one for the glass, the other for the bottle).*

$$$ Spatenhaus has served elegant food in a woody setting since 1896—maybe it's not even right to call its almost refined restaurant a "beer hall." You can also eat outside, on the square facing the opera and palace. It's pricey, but you won't find better Bavarian cuisine. The upstairs restaurant is a more formal dining room—reservations are advised (€15-30 main courses, daily 9:30-24:00, on Max-Joseph-Platz opposite opera, Residenzstrasse 12, tel. 089/290-7050, www.spatenhaus.de).

Near the Train Station

$$ Augustiner Beer Garden, a true under-the-leaves beer garden packed with Münchners, is a delight. In fact, most Münchners consider Augustiner the best beer garden in town—which may be why it has 5,000 seats. There's no music, it's away from the tourist hordes, and it serves up great beer, good traditional food, huge portions, reasonable prices, and perfect conviviality. The outdoor self-service ambience is best, making this place ideal on a nice summer evening (figure €15 for a main course and a drink). Parents with kids can sit at tables adjoining a sizable playground. There's also indoor and outdoor seating at a more expensive restaurant with table service (daily 11:00-24:00, Arnulfstrasse 52, 3 looooong blocks from station going away from the center—or take tram #16/#17 one stop to Hopfenstrasse, tel. 089/594-393, www.augustinerkeller.de).

$$ Park Café is a nice hideaway, tucked inside the Alter Botanischer Garden, just north of the train station. When it's hot, the prime spot is the beer garden out back, where you can also order Bavarian food from self-service counters or classy cocktails and cuisine from an international menu (€9-20 main courses). The indoor section is modern and cozy and features DJs or live music in the late evening (daily 10:00-24:00, beer garden opens at 11:30, Sophienstrasse 7, tel. 089/5161-7980, www.parkcafe089.de).

In the English Garden

For outdoor ambience and a cheap meal, spend an evening at **$$ Chinese Tower beer garden** *(Chinesischer Turm Biergarten).* You're welcome to B.Y.O. food and grab one of the 6,000 seats, or buy from the food stalls. This is a fine opportunity to try a *Steckerlfisch*, sold at a separate kiosk (daily, long hours in good weather, usually live music, playground, tel. 089/383-8730, www.chinaturm.de; take tram #18 from main train station or Sendlinger Tor to Tivolistrasse, or U-3 or U-6 to Giselastrasse and then bus #54 or #154 two stops).

Restaurants

Man does not live by beer alone. Well, maybe some do. But here are some alternatives for the rest of us.

On and near Marienplatz

$$$ Glockenspiel Café is good for a coffee or a meal with a bird's-eye view down on the Marienplatz action—I'd come for the view more than the food (€12-24 main courses, Mon-Sat 9:00-24:00, Sun 10:00-19:00, ride elevator from Rosenstrasse entrance, opposite glockenspiel at Marienplatz 28, tel. 089/264-256).

$$ Blatt Salate is a self-serve salad bar on a side street between the Frauenkirche and the New Town Hall; it's a great little hideaway for a healthy, quick lunch (€12-14 vegetarian and meat salads and soups, Mon-Fri 11:00-21:30, Sat until 18:00, closed Sun, Schäfflerstrasse 7, tel. 089/2102-0281).

Around the Viktualienmarkt

$$ Restaurant Opatija, in the Viktualienmarkt passage a few steps from Marienplatz, is homey and efficient, with an eclectic mix of Italian, Balkan, and German favorites. Choose between the comfortable indoor section and the outdoor seating in a quiet courtyard. It's family-friendly, and they do takeout (good €7-8 pizzas, €8-13 main courses, daily 11:30-21:30, enter the passage at Viktualienmarkt 6 or Rindermarkt 2, tel. 089/2323-1995).

$ Die Münchner Suppenküche ("Munich Soup Kitchen"), a self-service soup joint at the Viktualienmarkt, is fine for a small, cozy sit-down lunch at picnic tables under a closed-in awning. The maroon chalkboard lists the soups of the day—I go for the goulash or the carrot soup (€4-6 soup meals, Mon-Sat 10:00-18:00, closed Sun, near corner of Reichenbachstrasse and Frauenstrasse, tel. 089/260-9599).

Stadt Café is a lively café serving healthy fare with an inventive mix of Italian, German, vegetarian, salads, and a big selection of cakes by the slice. This no-frills restaurant draws newspaper readers, stroller moms, and locals meeting for a drink. Dine in the quiet cobbled courtyard, inside, or outside facing the new synagogue (daily specials for €7-12, daily 10:00-24:00, in same building as Munich City Museum, St.-Jakobs-Platz 1, tel. 089/266-949).

$$$ Prinz Myshkin Vegetarian Restaurant is an upscale vegetarian eatery in the old center. The seasonal menu is clever and appetizing, the arched ceilings are cool, and the outside seating is on a quiet street. They also have vegetarian sushi, pastas, Indian dishes, and their own baker, so they're proud of their sweets (€14-20 main courses, daily 11:00-23:00, Hackenstrasse 2, tel. 089/265-596).

Sebastiansplatz is a long, pedestrianized square between the Viktualienmarkt and the synagogue, lined with **$$** bistros handy for a quick lunch. All serve €10 main courses on the busy cobbled square or inside—just survey the scene and choose. The **Schrannenhalle,** the former grain exchange overlooking the square, is busy with creative, modern eateries and gourmet delis (Mon-Sat 10:00-20:00, closed Sun).

Near Odeonsplatz

Café Luitpold is where Munich's high society comes to sip its coffee and nibble on exquisite cakes. The café is proudly home to the original *Luitpoldtorte*—sponge cake with layers of marzipan and buttercream, covered in dark chocolate (Tue-Sat 8:00-23:00, Sun-Mon 9:00-19:00, Brienner Strasse 11, tel. 089/242-8750).

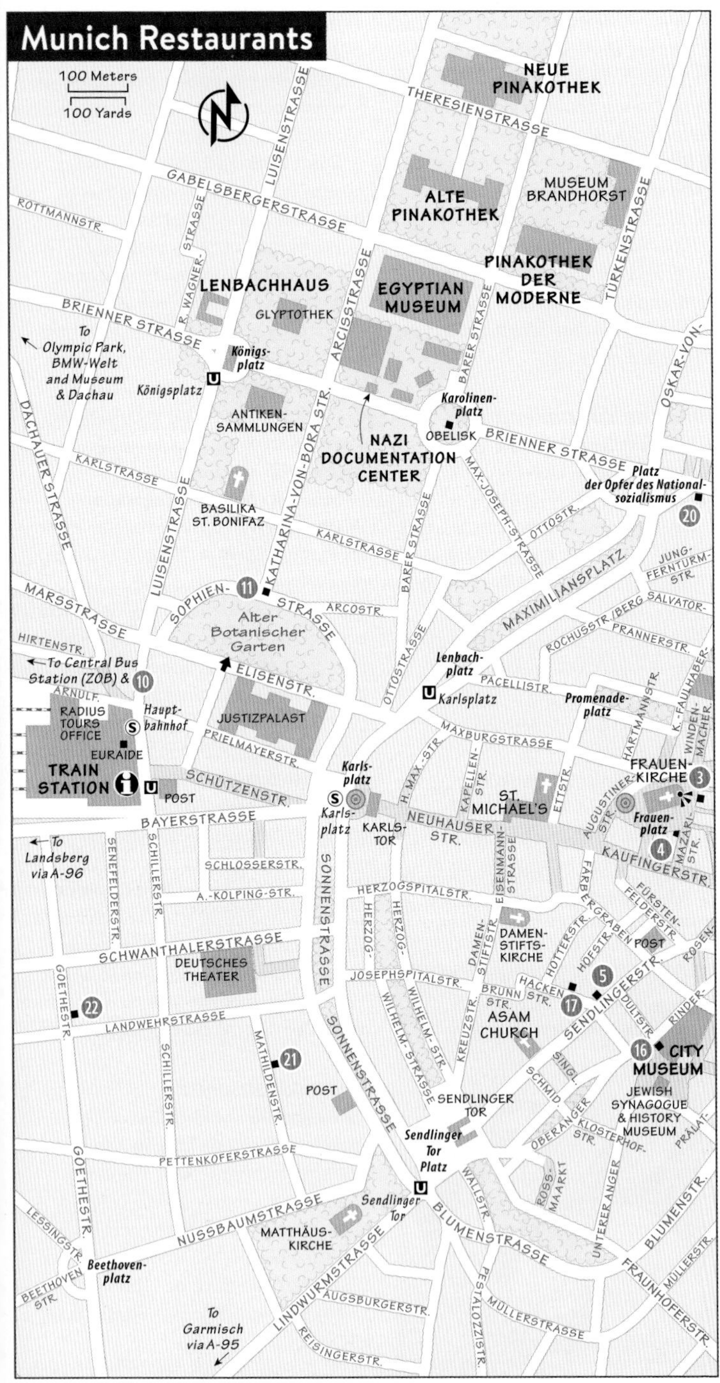

Munich Restaurants
100 Meters
100 Yards
NEUE PINAKOTHEK
THERESIENSTRASSE
MUSEUM BRANDHORST
ALTE PINAKOTHEK
PINAKOTHEK DER MODERNE
TÜRKENSTRASSE
GABELSBERGERSTRASSE
LUISENSTRASSE
ROTTMANNSTR.
R. WAGNER-STRASSE
LENBACHHAUS
EGYPTIAN MUSEUM
GLYPTOTHEK
ARCISSTRASSE
BARER STRASSE
BRIENNER STRASSE
To Olympic Park, BMW-Welt and Museum & Dachau
Königsplatz
Königs-platz
ANTIKEN-SAMMLUNGEN
Karolinen-platz
OBELISK
NAZI DOCUMENTATION CENTER
OSKAR-VON-
Platz der Opfer des National-sozialismus
DACHAUER STRASSE
KARLSTRASSE
BASILIKA ST. BONIFAZ
KATHARINA-VON-BORA-STR.
MAX-JOSEPH-STRASSE
OTTOSTR.
MAXIMILIANSPLATZ
JUNG-FERNTURM-STR.
SALVATOR-
MARSSTRASSE
SOPHIEN-STRASSE
ARCOSTR.
Alter Botanischer Garten
ROCHUSSTR./BERG
PRANNERSTR.
HIRTENSTR.
To Central Bus Station (ZOB) &
ELISENSTR.
OTTOSTRASSE
Lenbach-platz
PACELLISTR.
Promenade-platz
ARNULF.
RADIUS TOURS OFFICE
Haupt-bahnhof
JUSTIZPALAST
Karlsplatz
MAXBURGSTRASSE
EURAIDE
TRAIN STATION
PRIELMAYERSTR.
H. MAX.-STR.
KAPELLEN-STR.
HARTMANNSTR.
K.-FAULHABER-
WINDEN-MACHER-
FRAUEN-KIRCHE
POST
SCHÜTZENSTR.
Karls-platz
ST. MICHAEL'S
ETTSTR.
AUGUSTINER-STR.
Frauen-platz
MAZARI-STR.
BAYERSTRASSE
KARLS-TOR
NEUHAUSER STR.
EISENMANN-STRASSE
KAUFINGERSTR.
To Landsberg via A-96
SENEFELDERSTR.
SCHILLERSTR.
SCHLOSSERSTR.
A.-KOLPING-STR.
SONNENSTRASSE
HERZOGSPITALSTR.
HERZOG-WILHELM-STR.
FÄRBERGRABEN
FÜRSTEN-FELDERSTR.
DAMEN-STIFTSTR.
DAMEN-STIFTS-KIRCHE
HOTTERSTR.
HOFSTR.
SCHWANTHALERSTRASSE
DEUTSCHES THEATER
JOSEPHSPITALSTR.
HACKENSTR.
BRUNNSTR.
SENDLINGERSTR.
ROSEN-
GOETHESTR.
LANDWEHRSTRASSE
ASAM CHURCH
DULTSTR.
RINDER-
MATHILDENSTR.
KREUZSTR.
WILHELM-STRASSE
SINGL.
CITY MUSEUM
POST
SCHMID
JEWISH SYNAGOGUE & HISTORY MUSEUM
SENDLINGER TOR
OBERANGER
KLOSTERHOF-STR.
PRÄLAT-
Sendlinger Tor Platz
PETTENKOFERSTRASSE
ROSS-MARKT
WALLSTR.
UNTERERANGER
BLUMENSTR.
LESSINGSTR.
NUSSBAUMSTRASSE
Sendlinger Tor
MATTHÄUS-KIRCHE
BLUMENSTRASSE
Beethoven-platz
BEETHOVENSTR.
LINDWURMSTRASSE
FRAUNHOFERSTR.
MÜLLERSTR.
AUGSBURGERSTR.
To Garmisch via A-95
REISINGERSTR.
PESTALOZZISTR.
MÜLLERSTRASSE
3
4
5
10
11
16
17
20
21
22

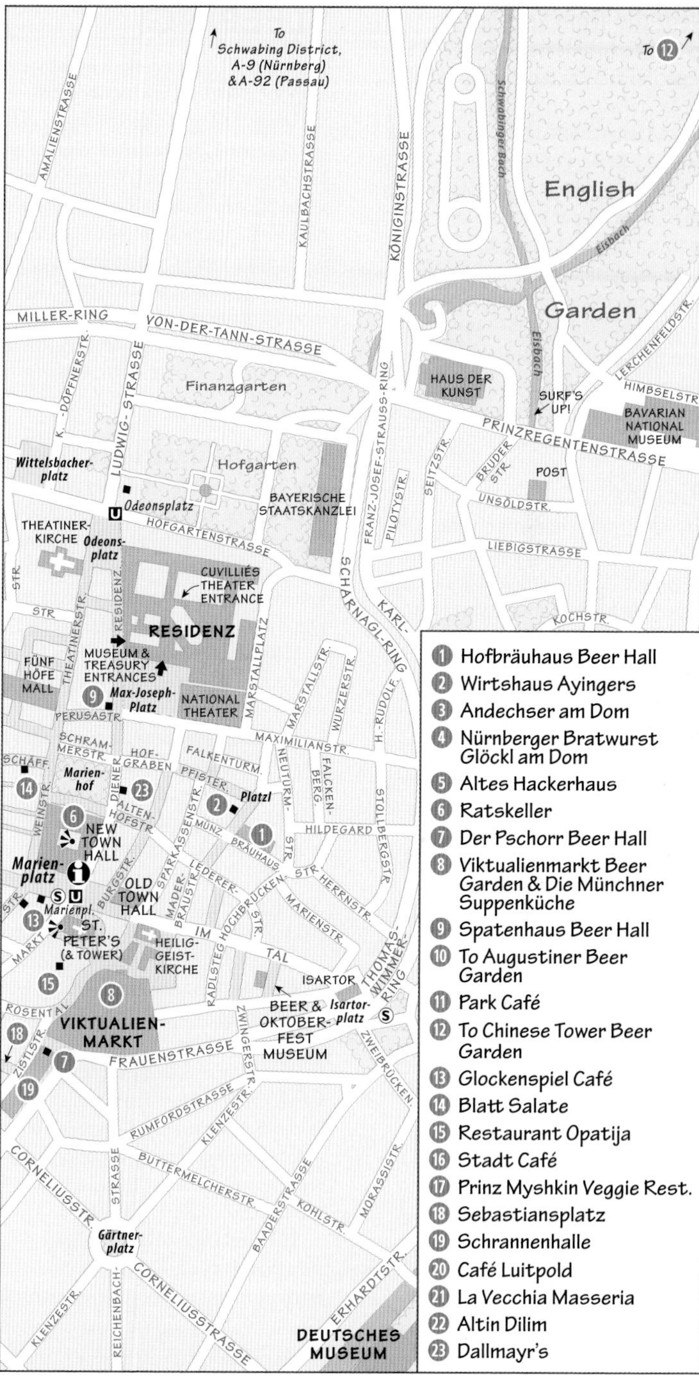
To Schwabing District, A-9 (Nürnberg) & A-92 (Passau)
To 12
English Garden
Schwabinger Bach
Eisbach
AMALIENSTRASSE
KAULBACHSTRASSE
KÖNIGINSTRASSE
MILLER-RING
VON-DER-TANN-STRASSE
LUDWIG-STRASSE
K.-DÖPFNERSTR.
Finanzgarten
HAUS DER KUNST
SURF'S UP!
LERCHENFELDSTR.
HIMBSELSTR.
BAVARIAN NATIONAL MUSEUM
PRINZREGENTENSTRASSE
FRANZ-JOSEF-STRAUSS-RING
BRUDER STR.
POST
Wittelsbacherplatz
Hofgarten
BAYERISCHE STAATSKANZLEI
PILOTYSTR.
SEITZSTR.
UNSÖLDSTR.
Odeonsplatz
HOFGARTENSTRASSE
LIEBIGSTRASSE
THEATINERKIRCHE
CUVILLIÉS THEATER ENTRANCE
KARL-SCHARNAGL-RING
KOCHSTR.
RESIDENZ
RESIDENZSTR.
THEATINERSTR.
FÜNF HÖFE MALL
MUSEUM & TREASURY ENTRANCES
Max-Joseph-Platz
NATIONAL THEATER
MARSTALLPLATZ
MARSTALLSTR.
WURZERSTR.
H.-RUDOLF-
PERUSASTR.
SCHRAMMERSTR.
MAXIMILIANSTR.
SCHÄFF.
HOFGRABEN
FALKENTURM.
NEUTURM-STR.
FALCKENBERG.
STOLLBERGSTR.
Marienhof
DIENER
PFISTER.
Platzl
ALTEN-HOFSTR.
MÜNZ
BRAUHAUS
HILDEGARD
WEINSTR.
NEW TOWN HALL
SPARKASSENSTR.
Marienplatz
OLD TOWN HALL
BURGSTR.
LEDERER-
HOCHBRÜCKEN-
STR.
HERRNSTR.
MADER-BRÄUSTR.
Marienpl.
MARIENSTR.
ST. PETER'S (& TOWER)
HEILIG-GEIST-KIRCHE
IM TAL
THOMAS-WIMMER-RING
MARKT
RADLSTEG
ISARTOR
ROSENTAL
VIKTUALIEN-MARKT
BEER & OKTOBERFEST MUSEUM
Isartorplatz
ZWINGERSTR.
ZWEIBRÜCKEN.
FRAUENSTRASSE
ZISTLSTR.
RUMFORDSTRASSE
KLENZESTR.
CORNELIUSSTR.
STRASSE
BUTTERMELCHERSTR.
BAADERSTRASSE
KOHLSTR.
MORASSISTR.
Gärtnerplatz
ERHARDTSTR.
CORNELIUSSTRASSE
REICHENBACH-
KLENZESTR.
DEUTSCHES MUSEUM
1 Hofbräuhaus Beer Hall
2 Wirtshaus Ayingers
3 Andechser am Dom
4 Nürnberger Bratwurst Glöckl am Dom
5 Altes Hackerhaus
6 Ratskeller
7 Der Pschorr Beer Hall
8 Viktualienmarkt Beer Garden & Die Münchner Suppenküche
9 Spatenhaus Beer Hall
10 To Augustiner Beer Garden
11 Park Café
12 To Chinese Tower Beer Garden
13 Glockenspiel Café
14 Blatt Salate
15 Restaurant Opatija
16 Stadt Café
17 Prinz Myshkin Veggie Rest.
18 Sebastiansplatz
19 Schrannenhalle
20 Café Luitpold
21 La Vecchia Masseria
22 Altin Dilim
23 Dallmayr's

Near the Train Station

$$ La Vecchia Masseria, between Sendlinger Tor and the train station hotels, serves Italian food inside amid cozy Tuscan farmhouse decor, or outside in a beautiful flowery courtyard (€6-8 pizza or pasta, €14-16 main courses, daily 11:30-23:30, reservations smart, Mathildenstrasse 3, tel. 089/550-9090).

$$ Altin Dilim, a cafeteria-style Turkish restaurant, is a standout among the many hole-in-the-wall Middle Eastern places near the station. A handy pictorial menu helps you order (€5 *Döner Kebab,* €8-13 main courses, daily 10:00-24:00, Goethestrasse 17, tel. 089/9734-0869).

Picnics

The crown in **Dallmayr's** emblem reflects that even the royal family assembled its picnics at this historic delicatessen. Assemble a royal (pricey) spread to munch in the nearby Hofgarten or visit the classy cafés that serve light meals on the ground and first floors (Mon-Sat 9:30-19:00, closed Sun, behind New Town Hall, Dienerstrasse 13-15, tel. 089/213-5110).

The **supermarkets** that hide in the basements of department stores are on the upscale side, such as the **Galeria Kaufhof** stores at Marienplatz and Karlsplatz, and the **Karstadt** across from the train station. Cheaper options include the **REWE** in the basement at Fünf Höfe (entrance is in Viscardihof) or the **Lidl** at Schwantaler Strasse 31, near the train-station hotels. They're generally open daily (until 20:00) except closed on Sunday.

SLEEPING

I've listed accommodations in two neighborhoods: within a few blocks of the central train station (Hauptbahnhof), and in the old center, between Marienplatz and Sendlinger Tor. Although I give the approximate price for a double room, hotels also have singles (which can be double rooms offered at a lower price), triples, and sometimes quads (which I term "family rooms" in listings). During major conventions and events, prices can increase 20 to 300 percent (worst at Oktoberfest; reserve well in advance).

Near the Train Station

Good-value hotels cluster in the multicultural area immediately south of the station. Some find it colorful; for others it feels seedy after dark (with erotic cinemas and men loitering in the shadows). It's sketchy only for those in search of trouble.

$$$ Marc München—polished, modern, and with 80 newly renovated rooms—is a good option if you need more luxury than the other listings here. It's just a half-block from the station on a relatively tame street, and has a nice lobby and classy breakfast spread. The cheaper "superior king" rooms are the best value (Db-€147-221, ask about Rick Steves discount, pay parking, air-con, Senefelderstrasse 12, tel. 089/559-820, www.hotel-marc.de, info@hotel-marc.de).

$$ Hotel Monaco is a delightful hideaway, tucked inside the fifth floor of a giant, nondescript building two blocks from the station (D-€75, Db-€79-99, family rooms, breakfast-€9, cash preferred, Schillerstrasse 9, entrance on Adolf-Kolping-Strasse, tel. 089/545-9940, www.hotel-monaco.de, info@hotel-monaco.de).

$$ Hotel Uhland is a stately mansion that rents 29 rooms with modern bathrooms in a genteel, residential neighborhood a slightly longer walk from the station (toward the Theresienwiese

Oktoberfest grounds). It's been in the Hauzenberger and Reim families for 60 years (small Db-€95, big Db-€105-118, family rooms, limited free parking, Uhlandstrasse 1, tel. 089/543-350, www.hotel-uhland.de, info@hotel-uhland.de). From the station, take bus #58 (direction: Silberhornstrasse) to Georg-Hirth-Platz, or walk 15 minutes: Out the station's south exit, cross Bayerstrasse, take Paul-Heyse-Strasse three blocks to Georg-Hirth-Platz, then take a soft right on Uhlandstrasse.

$$ Hotel Belle Blue, three blocks from the station, has 30 rooms and is a great value if you are looking for modern furnishings and air-conditioning (Db-€96, Schillerstrasse 21, tel. 089/550-6260, www.hotel-belleblue.de, info@hotel-belleblue.com, Irmgard). Their two apartments are perfect for families (7-night minimum in summer).

$$ Hotel Bristol is efficient, with 57 business-like rooms. It's located across the street from the Sendlinger Tor U-Bahn station (Db-€97, breakfast-€9.50, air-con in lobby, pay parking, Pettenkoferstrasse 2, tel. 089/5434-8880, www.bristol-munich.de, info@bristol-munich.de).

$$ Hotel Deutsches Theater, filled with brass and marble, has 27 three-star rooms. The back rooms face the courtyard of a neighboring theater, so there can be some noise (Db-€90-100, family rooms, pricier suites, breakfast-€9, Landwehrstrasse 18, tel. 089/545-8525, www.hoteldeutschestheater.de, info@hoteldeutschestheater.de).

$$ Hotel Europäischer Hof, across the street from the station, is a huge, impersonal hotel with 150 decent rooms. During cool weather, when you can keep the windows shut, the street-facing rooms are an acceptable option. Courtyard-facing rooms are quieter—and more expensive, except for a few cheap rooms with shared bath (streetside Db-€100; courtyard D with head-to-toe twin beds-€60; ask about Rick Steves discount, pay parking, Bayerstrasse 31, tel. 089/551-510, www.heh.de, info@heh.de).

Sleep Code

$$$$ Splurge: Over €170
$$$ Pricier: €130-170
$$ Moderate: €90-130
$ Budget: €50-90
¢ Backpacker: Under €50

Hotels are classified based on the average price of a standard double room with bath in high season. Unless otherwise noted, credit cards are accepted, breakfast is included, hotel staff speak English, and Wi-Fi is available.

$ Hotel Royal is one of the best values in the neighborhood (as long as you can look past the strip joints flanking the entry). While institutional, it's clean and plenty comfortable. Most important, it's energetically run by Pasha and Christiane. Each of its 40 rooms is fresh and bright (Db-€74-94, family rooms, comfort rooms on quiet side cost €10 extra—worth it in summer when you'll want the window open, ask about Rick Steves discount, Schillerstrasse 11a, tel. 089/5998-8160, www.hotel-royal.de, info@hotel-royal.de).

$ Litty's Hotel is a basic hotel offering 37 small rooms with little personality (D-€72-€78, Db-€88, Wi-Fi at reception reaches lower floors, near Schillerstrasse at Landwehrstrasse 32c, tel. 089/5434-4211, www.littyshotel.de, info@littys hotel.de).

¢ The **CVJM (YMCA),** open to all ages, rents 85 beds in clean, slightly worn rooms with sinks in the rooms and showers and toilets down the hall. Doubles are head-to-head; triples are like doubles with a bunk over one of the beds (D-€64; only €10/night more per person during Oktoberfest—reserve 6-12 months ahead; includes linens and

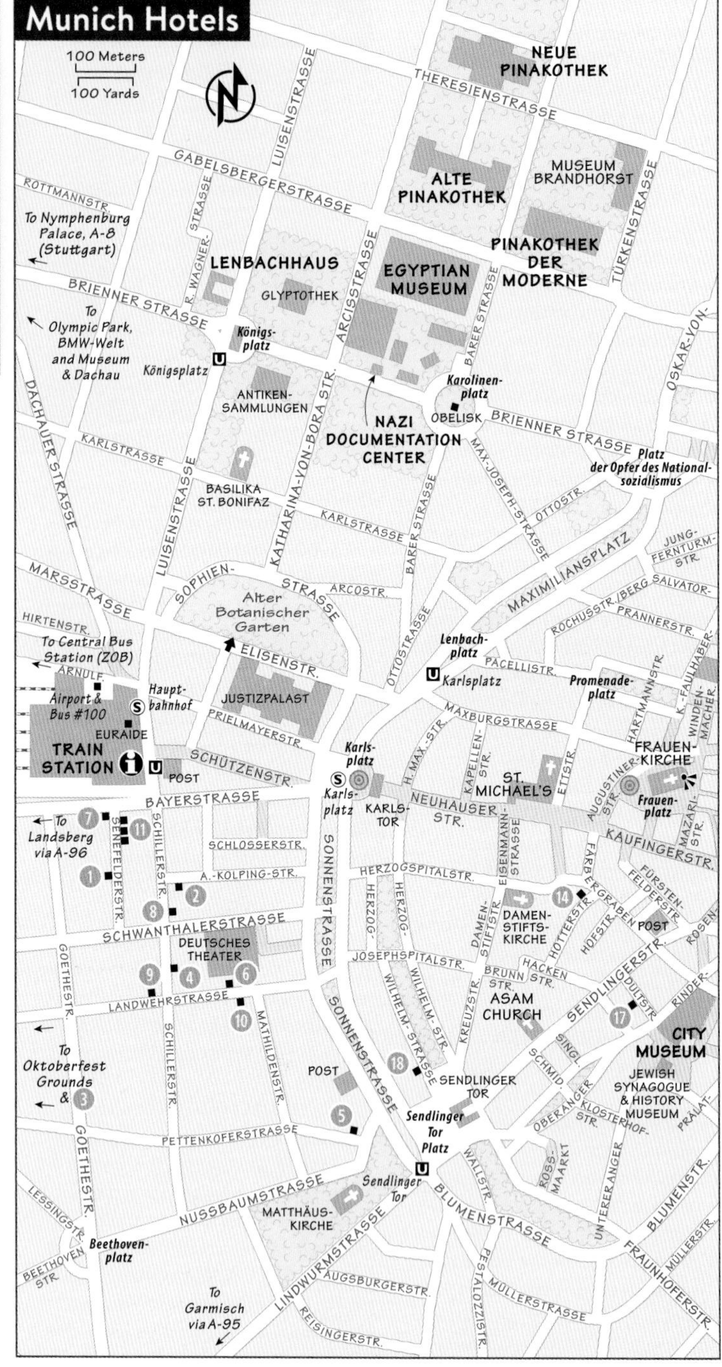
Munich Hotels
100 Meters
100 Yards
NEUE PINAKOTHEK
ALTE PINAKOTHEK
MUSEUM BRANDHORST
PINAKOTHEK DER MODERNE
LENBACHHAUS
GLYPTOTHEK
EGYPTIAN MUSEUM
ANTIKEN-SAMMLUNGEN
NAZI DOCUMENTATION CENTER
BASILIKA ST. BONIFAZ
Alter Botanischer Garten
JUSTIZPALAST
TRAIN STATION
EURAIDE
POST
ST. MICHAEL'S
FRAUEN-KIRCHE
DAMEN-STIFTS-KIRCHE
DEUTSCHES THEATER
ASAM CHURCH
CITY MUSEUM
JEWISH SYNAGOGUE & HISTORY MUSEUM
MATTHÄUS-KIRCHE
SENDLINGER TOR
KARLS-TOR
OBELISK
To Nymphenburg Palace, A-8 (Stuttgart)
To Olympic Park, BMW-Welt and Museum & Dachau
To Central Bus Station (ZOB)
Airport & Bus #100
To Landsberg via A-96
To Oktoberfest Grounds & 3
To Garmisch via A-95
Königsplatz
Karolinenplatz
Platz der Opfer des Nationalsozialismus
Lenbachplatz
Karlsplatz
Promenadeplatz
Hauptbahnhof
Frauenplatz
Sendlinger Tor Platz
Sendlinger Tor
Beethovenplatz
THERESIENSTRASSE
GABELSBERGERSTRASSE
ROTTMANNSTR.
BRIENNER STRASSE
KARLSTRASSE
MARSSTRASSE
HIRTENSTR.
ARNULF.
ELISENSTR.
PRIELMAYERSTR.
SCHÜTZENSTR.
BAYERSTRASSE
SCHLOSSERSTR.
A.-KOLPING-STR.
SCHWANTHALERSTRASSE
LANDWEHRSTRASSE
PETTENKOFERSTRASSE
NUSSBAUMSTRASSE
LESSINGSTR.
BEETHOVEN STR.
LUISENSTRASSE
ARCISSTRASSE
KATHARINA-VON-BORA STR.
BARER STRASSE
TÜRKENSTRASSE
OSKAR-VON-
DACHAUER STRASSE
SOPHIENSTRASSE
ARCOSTR.
OTTOSTRASSE
OTTOSTR.
MAX-JOSEPH-STRASSE
MAXIMILIANSPLATZ
JUNGFERNTURM-STR.
SALVATOR-
ROCHUSSTR.
PRANNERSTR.
PACELLISTR.
MAXBURGSTRASSE
H. MAX-STR.
KAPELLEN-STR.
ETTSTR.
HARTMANNSTR.
K.-FAULHABER-
WINDEN-MACHER-
AUGUSTINER-STR.
NEUHAUSER STR.
KAUFINGERSTR.
MAZARI-STR.
EISENMANN-STRASSE
HERZOGSPITALSTR.
FÄRBERGRABEN
HOTTERSTR.
HOFSTR.
FÜRSTEN-FELDERSTR.
ROSEN-
SENEFELDERSTR.
SCHILLERSTR.
SONNENSTRASSE
HERZOG-
JOSEPHSPITALSTR.
WILHELM-STRASSE
WILHELM-STR.
DAMEN-STIFTSTR.
HACKEN STR.
BRUNN STR.
KREUZSTR.
SENDLINGERSTR.
DULTSTR.
RINDER-
SINGL.
SCHMID.
OBERANGER
KLOSTERHOF-
PRÄLAT-
GOETHESTR.
MATHILDENSTR.
ROSS-MAARKT
UNTERER ANGER
WALLSTR.
BLUMENSTRASSE
BLUMENSTR.
FRAUNHOFERSTR.
MÜLLERSTR.
MÜLLERSTRASSE
PESTALOZZISTR.
LINDWURMSTRASSE
AUGSBURGERSTR.
REISINGERSTR.
R. WAGNER-STRASSE
1
2
3
4
5
6
7
8
9
10
11
14
17
18

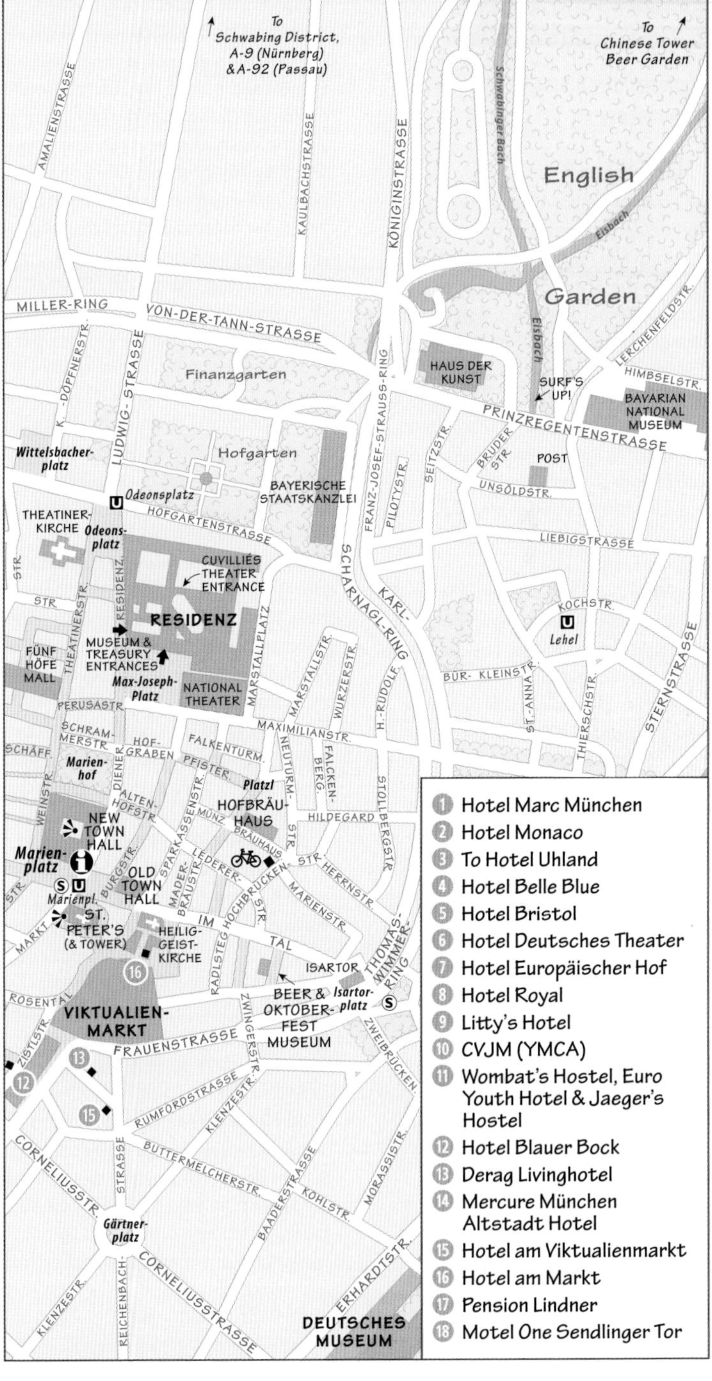
To Schwabing District, A-9 (Nürnberg) & A-92 (Passau)
To Chinese Tower Beer Garden
AMALIENSTRASSE
KAULBACHSTRASSE
KÖNIGINSTRASSE
Schwabinger Bach
English Garden
Eisbach
MILLER-RING
VON-DER-TANN-STRASSE
LERCHENFELDSTR.
HIMBSELSTR.
K.-DÖPFNERSTR.
LUDWIG-STRASSE
Finanzgarten
HAUS DER KUNST
SURF'S UP!
BAVARIAN NATIONAL MUSEUM
FRANZ-JOSEF-STRAUSS-RING
PRINZREGENTENSTRASSE
Wittelsbacher-platz
Hofgarten
SEITZSTR.
BRUDERSTR.
POST
PILOTYSTR.
UNSÖLDSTR.
Odeonsplatz
BAYERISCHE STAATSKANZLEI
THEATINER-KIRCHE
Odeons-platz
HOFGARTENSTRASSE
LIEBIGSTRASSE
CUVILLIÉS THEATER ENTRANCE
SCHARNAGL-RING
KARL-
RESIDENZ
KOCHSTR.
Lehel
FÜNF HÖFE MALL
THEATINERSTR.
MUSEUM & TREASURY ENTRANCES
MARSTALLPLATZ
MARSTALLSTR.
WURZERSTR.
H.-RUDOLF-
BÜR- KLEINSTR.
Max-Joseph-Platz
NATIONAL THEATER
ST.-ANNA-
THIERSCHSTR.
STERNSTRASSE
PERUSASTR.
SCHRAM-MERSTR.
MAXIMILIANSTR.
HOF-GRABEN
FALKENTURM-
SCHÄFF-
Marien-hof
DIENER-
PFISTER-
NEUTURM-
FALCKEN-BERG-
STOLLBERGSTR.
Platzl
HOFBRÄU-HAUS
ALTEN-HOFSTR.
WEINSTR.
NEW TOWN HALL
SPARKASSENSTR.
MÜNZ-
BRÄUHAUS-
HILDEGARD-
Marien-platz
BURGSTR.
OLD TOWN HALL
LEDERER-
MADER-BRÄUSTR.
HOCHBRÜCKEN-STR.
HERRNSTR.
MARIENSTR.
Marienpl.
ST. PETER'S (& TOWER)
HEILIG-GEIST-KIRCHE
IM TAL
MARKT
THOMAS-WIMMER-RING
ISARTOR
RADLSTEG
ROSENTAL
VIKTUALIEN-MARKT
BEER & OKTOBER-FEST MUSEUM
Isartor-platz
ZWINGERSTR.
FRAUENSTRASSE
ZWEIBRÜCKEN-
ZISTLSTR.
RUMFORDSTRASSE
KLENZESTR.
CORNELIUSSTR.
STRASSE
BUTTERMELCHERSTR.
BAADERSTRASSE
KOHLSTR.
MORASSISTR.
Gärtner-platz
ERHARDTSTR.
KLENZESTR.
REICHENBACH-
CORNELIUSSTRASSE
DEUTSCHES MUSEUM
1 Hotel Marc München
2 Hotel Monaco
3 To Hotel Uhland
4 Hotel Belle Blue
5 Hotel Bristol
6 Hotel Deutsches Theater
7 Hotel Europäischer Hof
8 Hotel Royal
9 Litty's Hotel
10 CVJM (YMCA)
11 Wombat's Hostel, Euro Youth Hotel & Jaeger's Hostel
12 Hotel Blauer Bock
13 Derag Livinghotel
14 Mercure München Altstadt Hotel
15 Hotel am Viktualienmarkt
16 Hotel am Markt
17 Pension Lindner
18 Motel One Sendlinger Tor

breakfast but no lockers; cheap Wi-Fi by reception, Landwehrstrasse 13, tel. 089/552-1410, www.cvjm-muenchen.org/hotel/jugendhotel, hotel@cvjm-muenchen.org).

"Hostel Row"

All three of the following hostels on Senefelderstrasse are casual and well-run, with friendly management, and all cater to the needs of young beer-drinking backpackers enjoying Munich on a shoestring. With 900 cheap dorm beds, this is a spirited street. There's no curfew, and each place has a lively bar that rages until the wee hours. All have 24-hour receptions, Wi-Fi, laundry facilities, lockers, and included linens. None has a kitchen, but each offers a buffet breakfast. Sleep cheap in big dorms, or spend more for a 2- to 4-bed room.

¢ Wombat's Hostel, perhaps the most hip and colorful, rents cheap doubles and dorm beds with lockers. The dorms are fresh and modern, and there's a relaxing and peaceful winter garden (dorm bed-€23-32, Db-€84, Senefelderstrasse 1, tel. 089/5998-9180, www.wombats.eu, office@wombats-munich.de).

¢ Euro Youth Hotel fills a rare pre-WWII building (dorm bed-€22-33, D-€70-85, includes breakfast for private rooms, Senefelderstrasse 5, tel. 089/5990-8811, www.euro-youth-hotel.de, info@euro-youth-hotel.de).

¢ Jaeger's Hostel, with 300 cheap beds, has fun and efficiency—plus the only air-conditioning on the street. This seems to be the quietest hostel of the group (dorm bed-€19-32, hotel-quality Db-€79-84, Senefelderstrasse 3, tel. 089/555-281, www.jaegershostel.de, office@jaegershostel.de).

In the Old Center

A few good deals remain in the area south of Marienplatz, going toward the Sendlinger Tor. This neighborhood is more genteel and is convenient for sightseeing.

$$$ Hotel Blauer Bock, formerly a dormitory for Benedictine monks, has been on the same corner near the Munich City Museum since 1841. Its 70 remodeled rooms are classy, if spartan for the price, but the location is great (D-€70-100, Db-€135-165, premium Db-€190-220, pay parking, Sebastiansplatz 9, tel. 089/231-780, www.hotelblauerbock.de, info@hotelblauerbock.de).

$$$$ Derag Livinghotel's 83 sleek, tech-savvy rooms are located right off the Viktualienmarkt. Half the rooms are less modern and have kitchenette suites. If you can nab a double room for less than €180, it's a good deal (Db-€165-250 though official rates much higher, breakfast-€19.50, air-con, pay parking, Frauenstrasse 4, tel. 089/885-6560, www.deraghotels.de, vitualienmarkt@derag.de).

$$$$ Mercure München Altstadt Hotel is reliable, with all the modern comforts in its 75 business-class rooms, and is located on a quiet street close to the Marienplatz action. A few newer but less expensive rooms are available on the first floor (Db-€186, air-con, block south of the pedestrian zone at Hotterstrasse 4, tel. 089/232-590, www.mercure-muenchen-altstadt.de, h3709@accor.com).

$$$ At **Hotel am Viktualienmarkt,** everything about this 27-room hotel is small but well-designed, including the elevator and three good-value, tiny single rooms. It's on a small side street a couple of blocks from the Viktualienmarkt (Db-€135, family rooms, Utzschneiderstrasse 14, tel. 089/231-1090, www.hotel-am-viktualienmarkt.de, reservierung@hotel-am-viktualienmarkt.de).

$$ Hotel am Markt, right next to the Viktualienmarkt, has 32 decent rooms; it's a better deal if you skip the expensive breakfast (Db-€112-124, breakfast-€12, Heiliggeiststrasse 6, tel. 089/225-014, www.hotel-am-markt.eu, service@hotel-am-markt.eu).

$$ Pension Lindner is clean and quiet, with nine pleasant, pastel-bouquet rooms off a bare stairway. Frau Sinzinger offers a warm welcome and good buffet breakfasts, but she rarely has room for last-minute bookings (D-€75, Db-€100, cash discount on doubles and triples, Dultstrasse 1, tel. 089/263-413, www.pension-lindner.com, info@pension-lindner.com, Marion Sinzinger).

$$ Motel One Sendlinger Tor is a busy, inexpensive, 241-room chain hotel with rushed-but-pleasant staff in a fine location around the corner from the Sendlinger Tor tram and U-Bahn stop. The stylish, modern rooms are fairly tight but are a good value—and sell out a few weeks in advance. Streetside rooms on upper floors have great views. When booking on their website, make sure to choose the Sendlinger Tor location—they have six other hotels in Munich (Db-€94, breakfast-€9.50, air-con, pay parking, Herzog-Wilhelm-Strasse 28, tel. 089/5177-7250, www.motel-one.com, muenchen-sendlingertor@motel-one.com).

TRANSPORTATION

Getting Around Munich

Much of Munich is walkable. But given that the city is laced by many trams, buses, and subways, it's worth learning the system and considering getting a day pass. Public transit also makes it super-easy to access sights outside the historic core, such as Dachau or Nymphenburg Palace. Cabbies are honest and professional, but taxis are expensive (about €12 between the Hauptbahnhof and Marienplatz) and generally unnecessary.

By Subway, Tram, and Bus

Subways are called U-Bahns and S-Bahns. (S-Bahns are actually commuter railways that run underground through the city and are covered by rail passes—but it's smarter to save your limited number of pass days for long-distance trips.) These transit lines are numbered (for example, S-3 or U-5). The U-Bahn lines mainly run north-south, while the S-Bahn lines are generally east-west. For more info, visit the transit customer-service center underground at the main train station or Marienplatz (closed Sun), call 0800-344-226-600 (Mon-Fri only), or visit www.mvv-muenchen.de.

TICKETS

The entire transit system (subway/bus/tram) works on the same tickets. There are four concentric zones—white, green, yellow, and orange. Almost everything described in this chapter is within the white/inner zone, except for Dachau (green zone) and the airport (orange zone).

Transit tickets are sold at booths in the subway and at ticket machines with the MVV logo. Machines take coins and €5-50 bills; newer ones take PIN-enabled credit cards, too. Start the transaction by choosing "English," then press "Transit Association-MVV," which displays the array of tickets and passes available.

A one-zone **regular ticket** (*Einzelfahrkarte*, €2.70) is good for three hours in one direction, including changes and stops. For short rides (four stops max, only two of which can be on the subway lines), buy the **short-stretch ticket** (*Kurzstrecke*, €1.40). The **all-day pass** (*Single-Tageskarte*, €6.20) for the white/inner zone is a great deal for a single traveler.

All-day small-group passes (*Partner-Tageskarte*) are an even better deal—they cover all public transportation for up to five adults (two kids count as one adult, so two adults and six kids can travel with this ticket). A *Partner-Tageskarte* for the white/inner zone costs €11.70 (the €14.80 ***XXL*** version includes Dachau; the €22.30 ***Gesamtnetz*** version includes the airport). These partner tickets are a real steal—the only catch is that you've got to stay together.

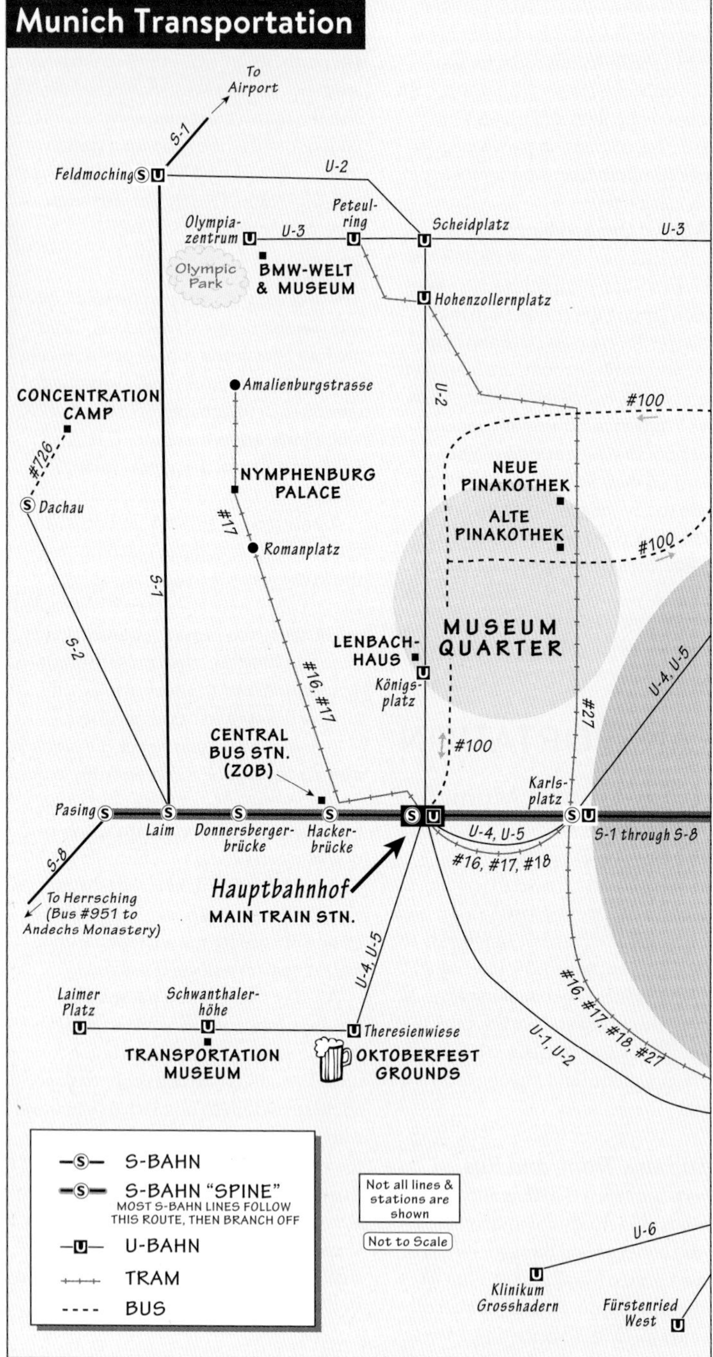
Munich Transportation
To Airport
S-1
Feldmoching
U-2
Olympiazentrum
U-3
Peteulring
Scheidplatz
U-3
Olympic Park
BMW-WELT & MUSEUM
Hohenzollernplatz
Amalienburgstrasse
CONCENTRATION CAMP
#726
Dachau
NYMPHENBURG PALACE
#17
Romanplatz
S-1
S-2
U-2
#100
NEUE PINAKOTHEK
ALTE PINAKOTHEK
#100
MUSEUM QUARTER
LENBACHHAUS
Königsplatz
#16, #17
#27
U-4, U-5
CENTRAL BUS STN. (ZOB)
#100
Karlsplatz
Pasing
Laim
Donnersbergerbrücke
Hackerbrücke
U-4, U-5
S-1 through S-8
#16, #17, #18
S-8
To Herrsching (Bus #951 to Andechs Monastery)
Hauptbahnhof
MAIN TRAIN STN.
U-4, U-5
#16, #17, #18, #27
U-1, U-2
Laimer Platz
Schwanthalerhöhe
Theresienwiese
TRANSPORTATION MUSEUM
OKTOBERFEST GROUNDS
S-BAHN
S-BAHN "SPINE"
MOST S-BAHN LINES FOLLOW THIS ROUTE, THEN BRANCH OFF
U-BAHN
TRAM
BUS
Not all lines & stations are shown
Not to Scale
U-6
Klinikum Grosshadern
Fürstenried West

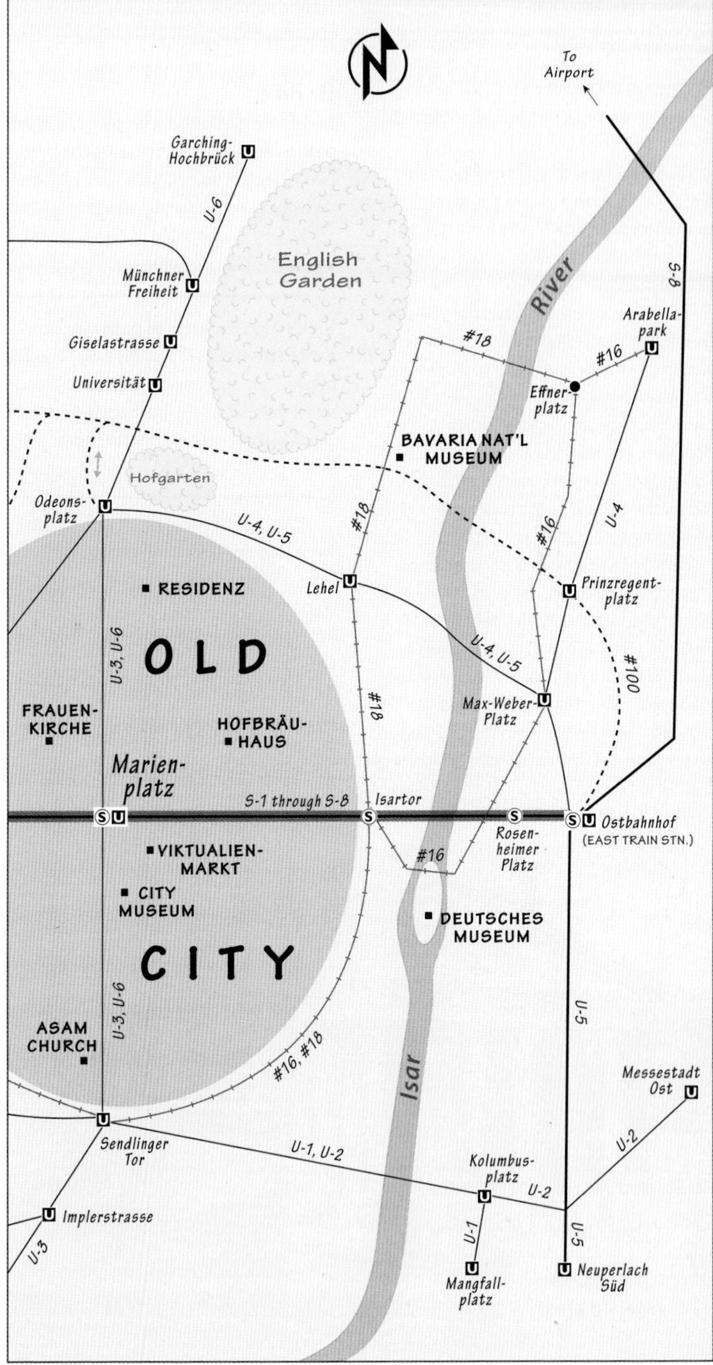
To Airport
Garching-Hochbrück
U-6
English Garden
River
S-8
Münchner Freiheit
Giselastrasse
Universität
#18
Arabella-park
#16
Effner-platz
BAVARIA NAT'L MUSEUM
Hofgarten
Odeons-platz
U-4, U-5
#18
#16
U-4
Lehel
Prinzregent-platz
RESIDENZ
U-3, U-6
OLD
U-4, U-5
#100
FRAUEN-KIRCHE
HOFBRÄU-HAUS
#18
Max-Weber-Platz
Marien-platz
S-1 through S-8
Isartor
Rosen-heimer Platz
Ostbahnhof
(EAST TRAIN STN.)
VIKTUALIEN-MARKT
#16
CITY MUSEUM
DEUTSCHES MUSEUM
CITY
U-5
U-3, U-6
ASAM CHURCH
#16, #18
Isar
Messestadt Ost
Sendlinger Tor
U-1, U-2
U-2
Kolumbus-platz
U-2
Implerstrasse
U-1
U-5
U-3
Mangfall-platz
Neuperlach Süd

USING THE SYSTEM

To find the right platform, look for the name of the last station in the direction *(Richtung)* you want to travel. For example, a sign saying *Richtung: Marienplatz* means that the subway, bus, or tram is traveling in the direction of Marienplatz. Know where you're going relative to Marienplatz, the Hauptbahnhof, and Ostbahnhof, as these are often referred to as end points.

You must stamp tickets prior to using them (for an all-day or multiday pass, stamp it only the first time you use it). For the subway, punch your ticket in the blue machine *before* going down to the platform. For buses and trams, stamp your ticket once on board. Plainclothes ticket checkers enforce this honor system, rewarding freeloaders with stiff €60 fines.

Handy Lines: Several subway lines, trams, and buses are especially convenient for tourists. All the main S-Bahn lines (S-1 through S-8) run east-west along the main tourist axis between the Hauptbahnhof, Marienplatz, and the Ostbahnhof. For travel within the city center, just find the platform for lines S-1 through S-8. One track *(Gleis)* will be headed east to the Ostbahnhof, the other west to the Hauptbahnhof. Hop on any train going your direction.

By Bike

Level, compact, and with plenty of bike paths, Munich feels made for those on two wheels. You can take your bike on the subway, but not during rush hour (Mon-Fri 6:00-9:00 & 16:00-18:00) and only if you buy a bike day pass.

Rick's Tip: *The* **strip of pathway closest to the street is usually reserved for bikes.** *Signs painted on the sidewalk or blue-and-white street signs show which part of the sidewalk is designated for pedestrians and which is for cyclists.*

You can **rent bikes** quickly and easily from **Radius Tours** in the train station in front of track 32 (daily April-Oct 8:30-19:00, May-Aug until 20:00; closed Nov-March, tel. 089/543-487-7730, www.radiustours.com).

Arriving and Departing

By Plane

Munich's airport (code: MUC) is an easy 40-minute ride on the S-1 or S-8 **subway**

(every 20 minutes from 4:00 in the morning until almost 2:00 in the morning). The S-8 is a bit quicker and easier; the S-1 line has two branches and some trains split—if you ride the S-1 to the airport, be certain your train is going to the *Flughafen* (airport). The Munich *Gesamtnetz* day pass ("Airport-City-Day-Ticket") is worth getting if you'll be making even one more public transport trip that day. The trip is free with a validated and dated rail pass.

The **Lufthansa airport bus** links the airport with the main train station (€10.50, €17 round-trip, 3/hour, 45 minutes, buses depart train station 5:15-19:55, buy tickets on bus; from inside the station, exit near track 26 and look for yellow *Airport Bus* signs; www.airportbus-muenchen.de). Avoid taking a **taxi** from the airport—it's a long, expensive drive (roughly €65). Airport info: tel. 089/97500, www.munich-airport.de.

By Train

For quick help at the main train station (München Hauptbahnhof), stop by the service counter in front of track 18. For better English and more patience, drop by the EurAide desk at counter #1 in the *Reisezentrum* (see page 35). Train info: toll tel. 0180-699-6633, www.bahn.com.

You'll find a city-run **TI** (out front of station and to the right) and **lockers** (opposite track 26). Up the stairs opposite track 21 are **car-rental agencies** (overlooking track 22).

Subway lines, trams, and buses connect the station to the rest of the city (though some of my recommended hotels are within walking distance of the station). If you get lost in the underground maze of subway corridors while you're trying to get to the train station, follow the signs for *DB* (Deutsche Bahn) to surface successfully. Watch out for the hallways with blue ticket-stamping machines in the middle—these lead to the subway, where you could be fined if nabbed without a validated ticket.

From Munich by Train to: Füssen (hourly, 2 hours), **Oberammergau** (nearly hourly, 2 hours, change in Murnau), **Salzburg,** Austria (2/hour, 1.5 hours on fast trains, 2 hours on slower trains eligible for regional day ticket), **Cologne** (2/hour, 4.5 hours, some with 1 change), **Würzburg** (1-2/hour, 2 hours), **Rothenburg** (hourly, 2.5-4 hours, 2-3 changes), **Frankfurt** (hourly, 3.5 hours), **Dresden** (every 2 hours, 6 hours, change in Leipzig or Nürnberg), **Hamburg** (hourly direct, 6.5 hours), **Berlin** (1-2/hour, 6.5 hours).

By Bus

Munich's central bus station (ZOB) is by the Hackerbrücke S-Bahn station (from the train station, it's one S-Bahn stop; www.muenchen-zob.de). The Romantic Road bus leaves from here (see page 166).

NEAR MUNICH

DACHAU MEMORIAL

Established in 1933, Dachau was the first Nazi concentration camp. In its 12 dismal years of operation, more than 200,000 prisoners from across Europe were incarcerated here—and at least 41,500 died, many of them murdered. The memorial on the grounds today, rated ▲▲, is an effective voice from our modern but grisly past, pleading "Never again."

Planning Your Time: Allow about five hours, giving you at least 2.5 hours at the camp, and including round-trip travel from central Munich.

Cost and Hours: Free, daily 9:00-17:00. Note that the museum discourages parents from bringing children under age 12.

Getting There on Your Own: The camp is a 45-minute trip from downtown Munich. The **Munich XXL day pass** covers the entire journey, both ways (€8.30/person, €14.80/partner ticket for up to 5 adults).

Take the S-2 (direction: Petershausen) from any of the central S-Bahn stops in Munich to Dachau (3/hour, 20-minute trip from Hauptbahnhof). Then, at Dachau station, go down the stairs and follow the crowds out to the bus platforms; find the one marked *KZ-Gedenkstätte-Concentration Camp Memorial Sight*. Here, catch bus #726 and ride it seven minutes to the KZ-Gedenkstätte stop (3/hour). Before you leave this bus stop, be sure to note the return times back to the station.

Drivers follow Dachauer Strasse from downtown Munich to Dachau-Ost, then follow *KZ-Gedenkstätte* signs.

Getting There by Guided Tour: Two companies offer good-value tours to Dachau from Munich for about the same price (€24, includes public transportation, €2 Rick Steves discount). It's smart to reserve the day before, especially for morning tours. Choose between **Radius** (April-mid-Oct daily at 9:15 and 12:15, mid-Oct-March daily at 10:00, tel. 089/543-487-7730, www.radiustours.

Dachau today

Near Munich

To Nürnberg
GERMANY
Augsburg
CONCENTRATION CAMP
DACHAU
Munich Strauss
FLIGHT MUSEUM & SCHLEISSHEIM PALACE
Braunau
Inn River
Munich
A-96
BAVARIA
Salzach
To Vienna
Herrsching
Landsberg
Ammersee
Starnberg
A-8
Chiemsee
HERRENCHIEMSEE
Freilassing
ANDECHS MONASTERY
Starnberger-see
Rosenheim
Prien
A-8
Salzburg
A-95
Bad Reichenhall
Hallein
WIES
Murnau
Isar
NEUSCHWANSTEIN
Oberammergau
Berchtesgaden
KEHLSTEIN (HITLER'S EAGLE'S NEST)
Kufstein
LINDERHOF
Füssen
Reutte
Garmisch-Partenkirchen
Kitzbühel
A-12
EHRENBERG
Zugspitze
TIROL
Inn
AUSTRIA
Hall
A-12
Innsbruck
Zell
25 Kilometers
25 Miles
To Switzerland
To Italy

com) and **Munich Walk** (April-Oct daily at 10:15 and 13:15, Nov-March daily at 10:15, tel. 089/2423-1767, www.munichwalktours.de).

Visitors Center: The visitors center, outside the camp wall, lacks exhibits, but has a bookstore with English-language books on Holocaust themes, a small cafeteria, and a WC (more WCs inside the camp).

At the center's information desk, you can rent an audioguide or sign up for a tour. The €3.50 **audioguide** covers the grounds and museum in 1.5 hours. **Guided walks** in English start from the visitors center (€3, daily at 11:00 and 13:00, 2.5 hours, limited to 30 people, so show up early—especially in summer, tel. 08131/669-970, www.kz-gedenkstaette-dachau.de).

➲ *Self-Guided Tour*

You enter the camp, like the prisoners did, through the infamous **iron gate** that held the taunting slogan *Arbeit macht frei* ("Work makes you free"). Inside are these key stops: the museum, the bunker behind the museum, the restored barracks, and a pensive walk across the huge but now-empty camp to the memorials and crematorium at the far end.

Museum: Before touring the rooms, check show times for the museum's powerful 22-minute documentary film, a sobering, graphic, and sometimes grisly account of the rise of Hitler and the atrocities committed at the camp (usually shown 5 times/day in English). The

Iron gate with "Work makes you free" slogan

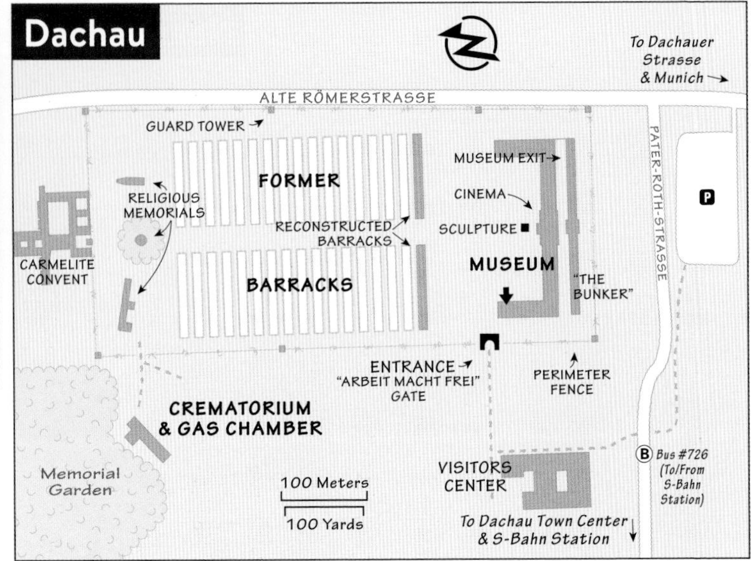

museum is organized chronologically, everything is thoughtfully described in English, and computer touch-screens let you watch early newsreels.

Rooms 1-2 cover the founding of the camp and give an overview of the Nazi camp system. Some were concentration camps, like Dachau, and others were extermination camps, built with the express purpose of executing people on a mass scale. Photos and posters chronicle the rise of Hitler in the 1920s.

Rooms 3-7 are devoted to the early years of the camp. Besides political activists, prisoners included homosexuals, Jehovah's Witnesses, Roma, and Jews. The camp was run by the SS (Schutzstaffel), the organization charged with Germany's internal security. Dachau was a strictly regimented work camp: a wake-up call at 4:00, an 11-hour workday, roll call at 5:15 and 19:00, lights out at 21:00. The labor was hard, whether quarrying or hauling loads or constructing the very buildings you see today. The rations were meager, rule-breakers were punished severely, and all manner of torture took place here.

The Bunker (camp prison)

Rooms 8-15 document the war years and their immediate aftermath. After Germany invaded Poland on September 1, 1939, conditions at Dachau deteriorated. The original camp had been designed to hold just under 3,000 inmates. In 1937 and 1938, the camp was expanded, with barracks intended to hold 6,000 prisoners. During the war, the prisoner population swelled, and the Nazis found other purposes for the camp. It was less a concentration camp for German dissidents and more a dumping ground for foreigners and POWs. It was used as a special prison for 2,000 Catholic priests. From Dachau, Jewish prisoners were sent east to the gas chambers. Inmates were put to use as slave labor for the German war machine—many were shipped to nearby camps to make armaments. Prisoners were used as human guinea pigs for war-related medical experiments of human tolerance for air pressure, hypothermia, and biological agents like malaria.

As the Allies closed in on both fronts, Dachau was bursting with more than 30,000 prisoners jammed into its 34 barracks. Disease broke out, and food ran short in the winter of 1944-1945. With coal for the crematorium running low, the corpses of those who died were buried in mass graves outside the camp site. The Allies arrived on April 29. After 12 years of existence, Dachau was finally liberated.

Bunker: This was a cellblock for prominent "special prisoners," such as failed Hitler assassins, German religious leaders, and politicians who challenged Nazism. Exhibits profile the inmates and the SS guards who worked at Dachau, and allow you to listen to some inmates' testimonies. Cell #2 was the interrogation room. Cell #9 was a "standing cell"—inmates were tortured here by being forced to stay on their feet for days at a time.

Barracks: Take a look inside to get an idea of what sleeping and living conditions were like in the terribly overcrowded camp. When the camp was at its fullest, there was only about one square yard of living space per inmate.

Religious Remembrance Sights: At the far end of the camp, in space that once housed the camp vegetable garden, there are now several places of meditation and worship (Jewish to your right, Catholic straight ahead, and Protestant to your left). Beyond them, just outside the camp, is a Carmelite convent. In the garden near the crematoria is a Russian Orthodox shrine.

Camp Crematoria: These facilities were used to dispose of the bodies of prisoners. The larger concrete crematorium was built to replace the smaller wooden one. One of its rooms is a gas chamber, which worked on the same principles as the much larger one at Auschwitz, and was originally disguised as a shower room (the fittings are gone now). It was never put to use at Dachau for mass murder, but some historians suspect that a few people were killed in it experimentally. The memorial garden that now surrounds the crematoria is the main place of remembrance at Dachau.

Memorials throughout Dachau remind visitors: Never Again.

Salzburg

Just over the Austrian border, lively Salzburg is irresistably close to Munich (1.5 hours by direct train). Thanks to its charming Old Town, splendid gardens, Baroque churches, and one of Europe's largest intact medieval fortresses, the city feels made for tourism. Its huge annual music festival and constant concerts have made it a musical mecca. Salzburgers are forever smiling to the tunes of Mozart and *The Sound of Music.*

SALZBURG IN 1 DAY

While Salzburg's museums are mediocre, the town itself is a Baroque showpiece of cobbled streets and elegant buildings—simply a stroller's delight by day or floodlit night.

With one day, start with my Salzburg Old Town Walk, seeing sights (such as the cathedral) along the way. In the afternoon, choose what appeals to you most: Consider taking *The Sound of Music* tour; you'll get a city overview, *S.O.M.* sights, and a fine drive by the lakes. Other good options (which could easily fill another day) are the Hohensalzburg Fortress, Salzburg Museum, Mozart's Birthplace, and outside of town, the Hellbrunn Palace with its trick fountains. You can also bike along the riverside paths and hike across the Mönchsberg.

If you have the time, spend at least two

The Mirabell Gardens are filled with Baroque statuary and fountains.

nights in Salzburg—nights are important for lingering in atmospheric beer gardens and attending concerts in Baroque halls and chapels. Seriously consider one of Salzburg's many evening musical events.

ORIENTATION

Salzburg, a city of 150,000 (Austria's fourth-largest), is divided into old and new. The Old Town (Altstadt), between the Salzach River and Salzburg's mini mountain (Mönchsberg), holds nearly all the charm and most of the tourists. The New Town (Neustadt), across the river, has the train station, a few sights and museums, and some good accommodations.

Rick's Tip: **Welcome to Austria**, *which uses the same* **euro currency** *as Germany, but* **postage stamps** *and* **phone cards** *work only in the country where you buy them. To* **telephone** *from a German number to an Austrian one, dial 00-43 and then the number (omitting the initial zero). To call from an Austrian phone to a German one, dial 00-49 and then the number (again, omitting the initial zero).*

Tourist Information

Salzburg has three helpful TIs (main tel. 0662/889-870, www.salzburg.info): at the **train station** (daily generally 9:00-18:00, until 19:00 or 20:00 in summer; tel. 0662/8898-7340); on **Mozartplatz** in the old center (daily 9:00-18:00, July-Aug often until 19:00, closed Sun mid-Oct-March; tel. 0662/8898-7330); and at the **Salzburg Süd park-and-ride** (shorter hours, closed Sun and off-season; tel. 0662/8898-7360).

At any TI, you can pick up a free city-center map (though the cheap map you can buy has broader coverage and more information on sights, and is particularly worthwhile if biking out of town), the free bus map (*Liniennetz;* shows bus stop names not on the city map), the Salzburg Card brochure (listing sights with current hours and prices), and a bimonthly events guide. The TIs also book rooms (for a small fee and a 12 percent deposit). Inside the Mozartplatz TI is the privately run Salzburg Ticket Service counter, where you can book concert tickets.

Sightseeing Pass

The TIs sell **the Salzburg Card,** which covers all your public transportation (including the Mönchsberg elevator and funicular to the fortress) and admission to all the city sights (including Hellbrunn Palace and a river cruise). The card is pricey, but if you want to pop into all the sights, it can save money and enhance your experience (€27/24 hours, €36/48 hours, €42/72 hours, www.salzburg.info). To analyze your potential savings, here are the major sights and what you'd pay without the card: Hohensalzburg Fortress and funicular-€11.30; Mozart's Birthplace and Residence-€17; Hellbrunn Palace-€10.50; 24-hour transit pass-€4. Busy sightseers can save plenty. Get this card, feel the financial pain once, and the city will be all yours.

Tours

▲▲*THE SOUND OF MUSIC* TOURS

Salzburg is the joyful setting of *The Sound of Music*. The Broadway musical and 1965 movie tell the story of a stern captain who hires a governess for his unruly children and ends up marrying her. Though the movie took plenty of Hollywood liberties, it's based on the actual Von Trapp family, who really did come from Salzburg. Maria really was a governess who became the captain's wife. They did sing in the Festival Hall, they did escape from the Nazis, and after the war they ended up in Vermont, where Maria passed away in 1987.

Salzburg today has a number of *Sound of Music* sights—mostly locations where the movie was shot, but also some actual

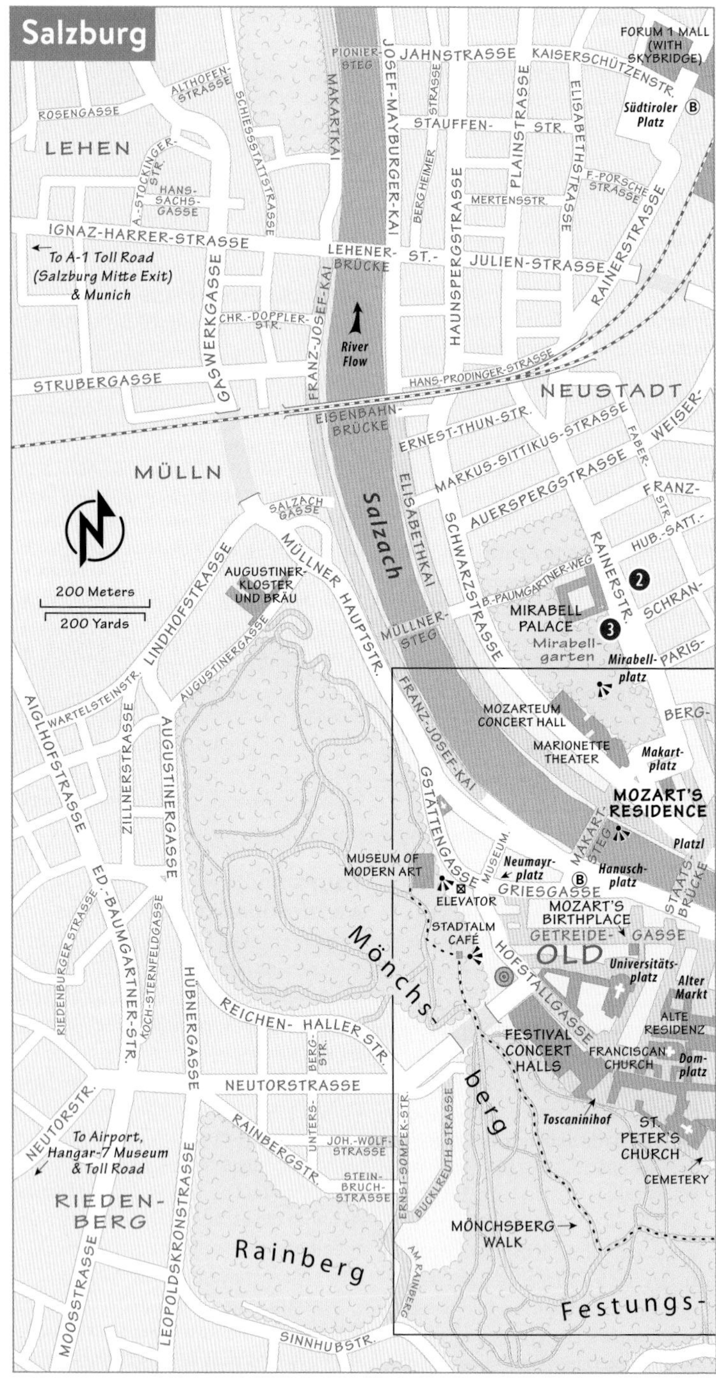
Salzburg
FORUM 1 MALL (WITH SKYBRIDGE)
Südtiroler Platz
JAHNSTRASSE
KAISERSCHÜTZENSTR.
PIONIER-STEG
JOSEF-MAYBURGER-KAI
MAKARTKAI
STAUFFEN- STR.
PLAINSTRASSE
ELISABETHSTRASSE
MERTENSSTR.
F.-PORSCHE-STRASSE
RAINERSTRASSE
HAUNSPERGSTRASSE
BERGHEIMER
ALTHOFEN-STRASSE
ROSENGASSE
LEHEN
SCHIESSSTATTSTRASSE
A.-STOCKINGER-STR.
HANS-SACHS-GASSE
IGNAZ-HARRER-STRASSE
To A-1 Toll Road (Salzburg Mitte Exit) & Munich
LEHENER- BRÜCKE
ST.- JULIEN-STRASSE
GASWERKGASSE
CHR.-DOPPLER-STR.
FRANZ-JOSEF-KAI
River Flow
STRUBERGASSE
HANS-PRODINGER-STRASSE
NEUSTADT
EISENBAHN-BRÜCKE
ERNEST-THUN-STR.
MARKUS-SITTIKUS-STRASSE
FABER-
WEISER-
AUERSPERGSTRASSE
FRANZ-
STR.
HUB.-SATT.-
MÜLLN
Salzach
ELISABETHKAI
SCHWARZSTRASSE
SALZACHGASSE
MÜLLNER HAUPTSTR.
200 Meters
200 Yards
AUGUSTINER-KLOSTER UND BRÄU
LINDHOFSTRASSE
AUGUSTINERGASSE
B.-PAUMGARTNER-WEG
MIRABELL PALACE
Mirabell-garten
RAINERSTR.
SCHRAN-
MÜLLNER-STEG
Mirabell-platz
PARIS-
WARTELSTEINSTR.
AIGLHOFSTRASSE
ZILLNERSTRASSE
AUGUSTINERGASSE
MOZARTEUM CONCERT HALL
BERG-
MARIONETTE THEATER
Makart-platz
GSTÄTTENGASSE
MOZART'S RESIDENCE
MAKART-STEG
Platzl
MUSEUM OF MODERN ART
MUSEUM.
Neumayr-platz
Hanusch-platz
STAATS-BRÜCKE
ELEVATOR
GRIESGASSE
MOZART'S BIRTHPLACE
ED.-BAUMGARTNER-STR.
RIEDENBURGER STRASSE
KOCH-STERNFELDGASSE
STADTALM CAFÉ
GETREIDE- GASSE
OLD
Universitäts-platz
Alter Markt
HOFSTALLGASSE
Mönchs-berg
HÜBNERGASSE
REICHEN- HALLER STR.
BERG-STR.
FESTIVAL CONCERT HALLS
ALTE RESIDENZ
FRANCISCAN CHURCH
Dom-platz
NEUTORSTRASSE
NEUTORSTR.
To Airport, Hangar-7 Museum & Toll Road
RAINBERGSTR.
UNTERS-
JOH.-WOLF-STRASSE
STEIN-BRUCH-STRASSE
ERNST-SOMPEK-STR.
BUCKLREUTH STRASSE
Toscaninihof
ST. PETER'S CHURCH
CEMETERY
RIEDEN-BERG
LEOPOLDSKRONSTRASSE
MOOSSTRASSE
Rainberg
AM RAINBERG
MÖNCHSBERG WALK
Festungs-
SINNHUBSTR.

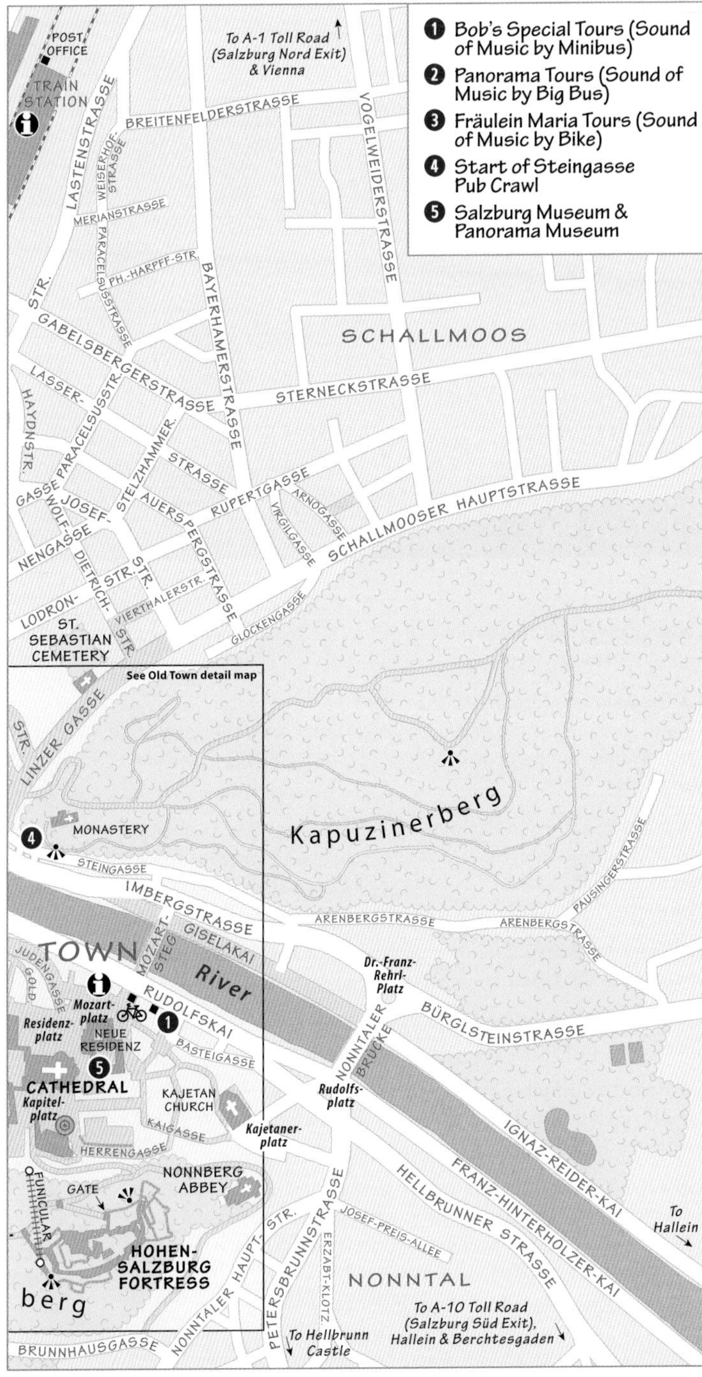
1 Bob's Special Tours (Sound of Music by Minibus)
2 Panorama Tours (Sound of Music by Big Bus)
3 Fräulein Maria Tours (Sound of Music by Bike)
4 Start of Steingasse Pub Crawl
5 Salzburg Museum & Panorama Museum
POST OFFICE
TRAIN STATION
To A-1 Toll Road (Salzburg Nord Exit) & Vienna
BREITENFELDERSTRASSE
LASTENSTRASSE
WEISERHOFSTRASSE
VOGELWEIDERSTRASSE
MERIANSTRASSE
PARACELSUSSTRASSE
PH.-HARPFF-STR.
BAYERHAMERSTRASSE
SCHALLMOOS
GABELSBERGERSTRASSE
STR.
LASSER-
HAYDNSTR.
PARACELSUSSTR.
STERNECKSTRASSE
STELZHAMMER-
STRASSE
GASSE
WOLF-
JOSEF-
AUERSPERGSTRASSE
RUPERTGASSE
ARNOGASSE
VIRGILGASSE
SCHALLMOOSER HAUPTSTRASSE
NENGASSE
DIETRICH-
STR.
STR.
LODRON-
VIERTHALERSTR.
GLOCKENGASSE
ST. SEBASTIAN CEMETERY
See Old Town detail map
LINZER GASSE
STR.
MONASTERY
Kapuzinerberg
STEINGASSE
IMBERGSTRASSE
ARENBERGSTRASSE
ARENBERGSTRASSE
PAUSINGERSTRASSE
GISELAKAI
MOZART-STEG
TOWN
River
JUDENGASSE
GOLDGASSE
Mozart-platz
RUDOLFSKAI
Residenz-platz
NEUE RESIDENZ
BASTEIGASSE
Dr.-Franz-Rehrl-Platz
BÜRGLSTEINSTRASSE
NONNTALER BRÜCKE
CATHEDRAL
Kapitel-platz
KAJETAN CHURCH
Rudolfs-platz
KAIGASSE
Kajetaner-platz
HERRENGASSE
IGNAZ-REIDER-KAI
FRANZ-HINTERHOLZER-KAI
HELLBRUNNER STRASSE
FUNICULAR
GATE
NONNBERG ABBEY
PETERSBRUNNSTRASSE
JOSEF-PREIS-ALLEE
To Hallein
HOHEN-SALZBURG FORTRESS
NONNTALER HAUPT-STR.
ERZABT-KLOTZ-STR.
NONNTAL
berg
To A-10 Toll Road (Salzburg Süd Exit), Hallein & Berchtesgaden
To Hellbrunn Castle
BRUNNHAUSGASSE

SALZBURG AT A GLANCE

▲▲▲**Salzburg Old Town Walk** Old Town's best sights in handy orientation walk. **Hours:** Always open. See page 113.

▲▲***The Sound of Music* Tours** Cheesy but fun tour through the *S.O.M.* sights of Salzburg and the surrounding lake district, by minibus, big bus, or bike. **Hours:** Various options daily at 9:00, 9:15, 9:30, 14:00, and 16:30. See page 105.

▲▲**Salzburg Cathedral** Glorious, harmonious Baroque main church of Salzburg. **Hours:** May-Sept Mon-Sat 8:00-19:00, Sun 13:00-19:00; March-April, Oct, and Dec until 18:00; Jan-Feb and Nov until 17:00. See page 116.

▲▲**Getreidegasse** Picturesque old shopping lane with characteristic wrought-iron signs. **Hours:** Always open. See page 121.

▲▲**Salzburg Museum** Best place to learn more about the city's history. **Hours:** Tue-Sun 9:00-17:00, closed Mon. See page 123.

▲▲**Mozart's Birthplace** House where Mozart was born in 1756, featuring his instruments and other exhibits. **Hours:** Daily July-Aug 8:30-19:00, Sept-June 9:00-17:30. See page 124.

▲▲**Hohensalzburg Fortress** Imposing castle capping the mountain overlooking town, with tourable grounds, several small museums, commanding views, and good evening concerts. **Hours:** Fortress museums open daily May-Sept 9:00-19:00, Oct-April 9:30-17:00. Concerts nearly nightly. See page 125.

▲▲Hellbrunn Palace and Gardens Lavish palace on the outskirts of town featuring gardens with trick fountains. **Hours:** Daily May-Sept 9:00-17:30, July-Aug until 21:00, April and Oct 9:00-16:30, closed Nov-March. See page 133.

▲Mirabell Gardens and Palace Beautiful palace complex with fine views, Salzburg's best concert venue, and *Sound of Music* memories. **Hours:** Gardens—always open; concerts—free in the park May-Aug Sun at 10:30 and Wed at 20:30, in the palace nearly nightly. See page 131.

▲Mozart's Residence Restored house where the composer lived. **Hours:** Daily July-Aug 8:30-19:00, Sept-June 9:00-17:30. See page 132.

▲St. Sebastian Cemetery Baroque cemetery with graves of Mozart's wife and father, and other Salzburg VIPs. **Hours:** Daily April-Oct 9:00-18:00, Nov-March 9:00-16:00. See page 133.

St. Peter's Cemetery Atmospheric old cemetery with mini gardens at the base of a cliff with monks' caves. **Hours:** Daily May-Aug 6:30-21:30, off-season until 18:00 or 19:00. See page 118.

St. Peter's Church Romanesque church with Rococo decor. **Hours:** Daily April-Oct 8:00-21:00, Nov-March 8:00-19:00. See page 119.

The Sound of Music *Debunked*

Rather than visit the real-life sights from the life of the Von Trapp family, most tourists want to see the places where Hollywood chose to film this fanciful story. Local guides are happy not to burst any *S.O.M.* pilgrim's bubble, but keep these points in mind:

•"Edelweiss" is not a cherished Austrian folk tune or national anthem. Like all the "Austrian" music in *The S.O.M.,* it was composed for Broadway by Rodgers and Hammerstein. It was the last composition that the famed team wrote together, as Hammerstein died in 1960—nine months after the musical opened.

•*The S.O.M.* implies that Maria was devoutly religious throughout her life, but Maria's foster parents raised her as a socialist and atheist. Maria discovered her religious calling while studying to be a teacher. After completing school, she joined the convent not as a nun, but as a novitiate (that is, she hadn't taken her vows yet).

•Maria's position was not as governess to all the children, but specifically as governess and teacher for the Captain's second-oldest daughter, also called Maria, who was bedridden with rheumatic fever.

•The Captain didn't run a tight domestic ship. His seven children were as unruly as most. But he did use a whistle to call them—each kid was trained to respond to a certain pitch.

•Though the Von Trapp family did have seven children, the show changed all their names and even their genders. As an adult, Rupert, the eldest child, responded to the often-asked question, "Which one are you?" with "I'm Liesl!" Maria and the Captain later had three more children together.

•The family didn't escape by hiking to Switzerland (which is a five-hour drive away). Rather, they pretended to go on one of their frequent mountain hikes.

places associated with the Von Trapps. Some of the main ones are:

•**The Mirabell Gardens,** with its arbor and Pegasus statue, where the kids in the movie sing "Do-Re-Mi."

•**Festival Hall,** where the real-life Von Trapps performed, and where (in the movie) they sing "Edelweiss."

•**St. Peter's Cemetery,** the inspiration for the scene where the family hides from Nazi guards (actually filmed on a Hollywood set).

•**Nonnberg Abbey,** where the nuns sing "How Do You Solve a Problem like Maria?"

•**Leopoldskron Palace,** which serves as the Von Trapps' lakeside home in the movie (though it wasn't their actual home).

•**Hellbrunn Palace gardens,** now home to the gazebo where Liesl, the Von Trapp's oldest daughter, sings, "I am sixteen going on seventeen."

There are many more sights—the horse pond, the wedding church, the fountain in Residenzplatz. Since they're scattered throughout greater Salzburg, taking a tour is the best way to see them efficiently.

Rick's Tip: *Virtually all* **hotels make tour recommendations** *based on their* **potential kickback,** *not what's best for you. Take any tour advice with a grain of salt.*

I took a *S.O.M.* tour skeptically—and had a great time. The bus tour includes

With only the possessions in their backpacks, they "hiked" all the way to the train station (it was at the edge of their estate) and took a train to Italy. The movie scene showing them climbing into Switzerland was actually filmed near Berchtesgaden, Germany...home to Hitler's Eagle's Nest, and certainly not a smart place to flee to.

• The actual Von Trapp family house exists...but it's not the one in the film. The mansion in the movie is actually two different buildings—one used for the front, the other for the back. The interiors were all Hollywood sets.

• For the film, Boris Levin designed a reproduction of the Nonnberg Abbey courtyard so faithful to the original (down to its cobblestones and stained-glass windows) that many still believe the cloister scenes were really shot at the abbey. And no matter what you hear in Salzburg, the graveyard scene (in which the Von Trapps hide from the Nazis) was also filmed on the Fox lot.

• In 1956, a German film producer offered Maria $10,000 for the rights to her book. She asked for royalties, too, and a share of the profits. The agent claimed that German law forbids paying royalties to foreigners (Maria was by then a US citizen). She agreed to the contract and unknowingly signed away all film rights to her story. Only a few weeks later, he offered to pay immediately if she would accept $9,000 in cash. Because it was more money than the family had seen in all their years of singing, she accepted the deal. Later, she discovered the agent had swindled them—no such law existed.

Rodgers, Hammerstein, and other producers gave the Von Trapps a percentage of the royalties, even though they weren't required to—but it was a fraction of what they otherwise would have earned. But Maria wasn't bitter. She said, "The great good the film and the play are doing to individual lives is far beyond money."

a quick but good general city tour, hits the *S.O.M.* spots, and shows you a lovely stretch of the lake district. Warning: Many think rolling through the Austrian countryside with 30 Americans singing "Doe, a deer..." is pretty schmaltzy. Austrians don't understand all the commotion; many have never heard of the movie.

Two companies (Bob's and Panorama) offer *S.O.M.* tours by bus, while a third company does a bike version. Reserve ahead. Your hotel will be eager to reserve for you—to get their commission—but you won't get the discount I've negotiated. Both Bob's and Panorama also offer day trips from Salzburg.

Minibus Option: Most of **Bob's Special Tours** use an 8-seat minibus (and occasionally a 20-seat bus) and have good access to Old Town sights, promote a more casual feel, and spend less time waiting to load and unload. Online bookings close three days prior to the tour date—after that, email, call, or stop by the office to reserve (€48 for adults—get a €6 discount with this book if you pay cash and book direct, €42 for kids ages 7-15 and students with ID, €36 for kids 6 and under—includes required car seat but must reserve in advance; daily at 9:00 and 14:00 year-round, tours leave from Bob's office along the river just east of Mozartplatz at Rudolfskai 38, tel. 0662/849-511, mobile 0664-541-7492, www.bobstours.com, office@bobstours.com). Nearly all of Bob's tours stop for a fun luge ride in

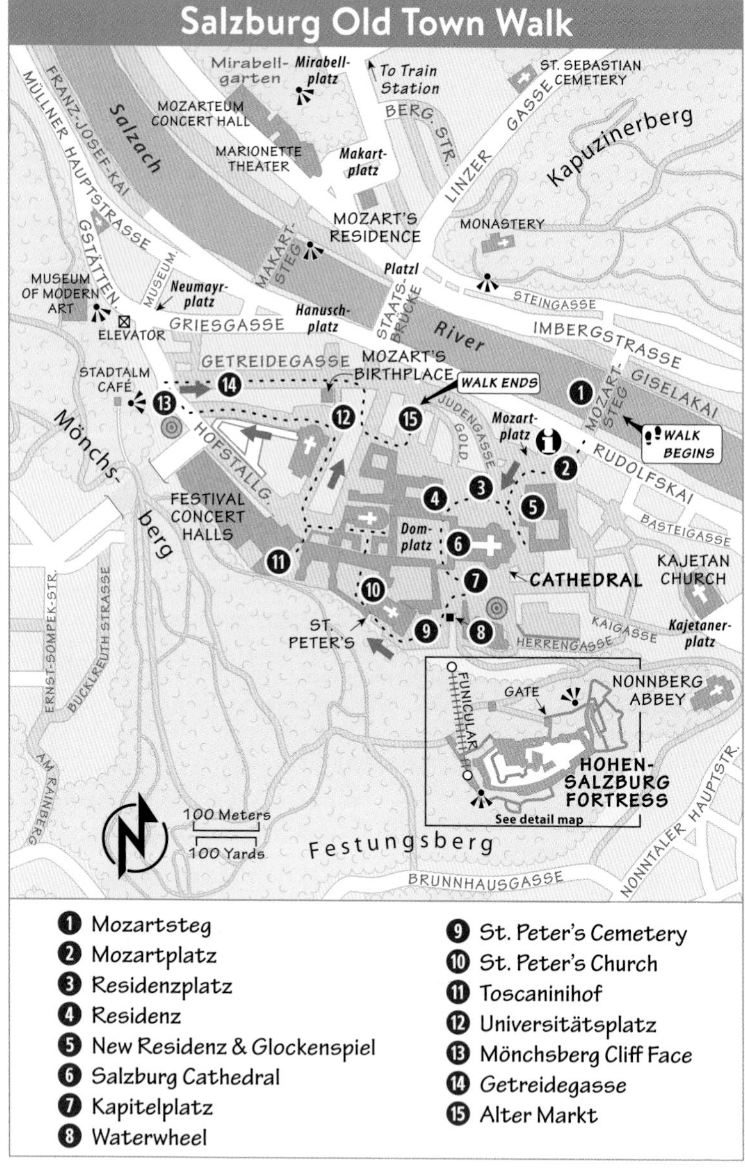

Fuschl am See when the weather is dry (mountain bobsled-€4.50 extra, generally April-Oct, confirm beforehand).

Big-Bus Option: Many travelers appreciate **Panorama Tours'** roomier buses, higher vantage point, and business-like feel (€40, €5 discount for *S.O.M.* tours with this book if you pay in cash and don't need hotel pickup, daily at 9:15 and 14:00 year-round, tours leave from their kiosk at Mirabellplatz, book by calling 0662/874-029 or 0662/883-2110, discount not valid for online reservations, www.panoramatours.com).

Bike Tours by "Fräulein Maria": For some exercise with your *S.O.M.* tour, you can meet your guide (likely a man) at the Mirabell Gardens (at Mirabellplatz 4, 50 yards to the left of palace entry). The tour is family-friendly and includes stops for goofy photo ops (€30 includes bike, €18 for kids ages 13-18, €12 for kids under age 13, €2 discount for adults and kids with this book, daily April-Oct at 9:30, June-Aug also at 16:30, allow 3.5 hours, reservations required, mobile 0650-342-6297, www.mariasbicycletours.com). For €8 extra (€20 per family), you can keep the bike all day.

WALKING TOUR

Any day of the week, you can take an informative **one-hour guided walk** of the Old Town without a reservation—just show up at the TI on Mozartplatz and pay the guide. They're generally in English only, but on slow days you may be listening to everything in both German and English (€9, daily at 12:15, Mon-Sat also at 14:00, tel. 0662/8898-7330).

PRIVATE GUIDES

Salzburg has many good guides, including **Sabine Rath** (€160/2 hours, €220/4 hours, €330/8 hours, mobile 0664-201-6492, www.tourguide-salzburg.com, info@tourguide-salzburg.com) and **Christiana Schneeweiss** (on foot: €150/2 hours, €195/3 hours; full-day tours with minibus: €750/10 hours, mobile 0664-340-1757, www.kultur-tourismus.com, info@kultur-tourismus.com). For a longer list, see www.salzburgguides.at.

SALZBURG OLD TOWN WALK

I've linked the best sights in the Old Town into this handy orientation walk (rated ▲▲▲).

🎧 Download my free Salzburg Town Walk audio tour.

➲Self-Guided Walk

• *Begin at the Mozartsteg, the pedestrian bridge over the Salzach River.*

❶ *Mozartsteg*

Get your bearings: Face the sprawling fortress atop the hill—it overlooks the Old Town. Behind you is the New Town, across the river.

Take in the charming, well-preserved, historic core of Salzburg's Old Town. The

The Mozartsteg pedestrian bridge connects the New Town with the Old Town.

skyline bristles with Baroque steeples and green, copper domes. Salzburg has 38 Catholic churches, plus two Protestant churches and a synagogue. The biggest green dome is the cathedral, which we'll visit shortly. Overlooking it all is the castle called the Hohensalzburg Fortress. Far to the right of the fortress, find the Museum of Modern Art—it looks like a minicastle, but that's actually a water reservoir alongside the modern building.

The milky-green Salzach River thunders under your feet. It's called "salt river" not because it's salty, but because of the precious cargo it once carried. The salt mines of Hallein are just nine miles upstream. For 2,000 years, barges carried salt from here to the wider world—to the Danube, the Black Sea, and on to the Mediterranean. As barges passed through here, they had to pay a toll on their salt. The city was born from the trading of salt (*Salz*) defended by a castle (*Burg*)—"Salz-burg."

• *Now let's plunge into Salzburg's Old Town. From the bridge, walk one block toward the hill-capping castle into the Old Town. Pass the traffic barriers (that keep this quiet town free of too much traffic) and turn right into a big square, called...*

❷ *Mozartplatz*

All the tourists around you probably wouldn't be here if not for the man honored by this statue—Wolfgang Amadeus Mozart. The great composer spent most of his first 25 years (1756-1781) in Salzburg. He was born just a few blocks from here. He and his father both served Salzburg's rulers before Wolfgang went on to seek his fortune in Vienna. The statue (considered a poor likeness) was erected in 1842, just after the 50th anniversary of Mozart's death. The music festival of that year planted the seed for what would become the now world-renowned Salzburg Festival.

Mozartplatz

Mozart stands atop the spot where the first Salzburgers settled. Two thousand years ago, the Romans had a salt-trading town here called Juvavum. In the year 800, Salzburg—by then Christian and home to an important abbey—joined Charlemagne's Holy Roman Empire as an independent city. The Church of St. Michael (whose tower overlooks the square) dates from that time. It's Salzburg's oldest, if not biggest, church.

• *Before moving on, note the TI (which also sells concert tickets). The entrance to the Salzburg Museum is also on this square (described on page 123). Also, looking back past Mozart's statue, you may catch a glimpse of a TV tower. This stands atop the 4,220-foot-high Gaisberg hill. The summit is a favorite destination for local nature lovers and strong bikers. Now walk toward the cathedral and into the big square with the huge fountain.*

❸ *Residenzplatz*

As Salzburg's governing center, this square has long been ringed with important buildings. The cathedral borders the south side. The Residenz—the former palace of Salzburg's rulers—is to the right (as you face the cathedral). To the left is the New (Neue) Residenz, with its bell tower.

In the 1600s, this square got a makeover in the then-fashionable Italian Baroque style. The rebuilding started under energetic Prince-Archbishop Wolf Dietrich, who ruled from 1587 to 1612. Dietrich had been raised in Rome. He counted the Medicis as his cousins, and had grandiose Italian ambitions for Salzburg. Fortunately for him, the cathedral conveniently burned down in 1598. Dietrich set about rebuilding it as part of his grand vision to make Salzburg the "Rome of the North."

The fountain is as Italian as can be, an over-the-top version of Bernini's famous Triton Fountain in Rome. It shows Triton on top blowing his conch-shell horn. The water cascades down the basins and sprays playfully in the wind.

Notice that Salzburg's buildings are made from three distinctly different types of stone. Most common is the chunky gray conglomerate (like the cathedral's side walls) quarried from the nearby cliffs. There's also white marble (like the cathedral's towers and windows) and red marble (best seen in monuments inside buildings), both from the Alps.

You'll likely see horse buggies (*Fiaker*) congregating at this square; they charge €40 for a 25-minute trot around the Old Town.

• *Turn your attention to the...*

❹ Residenz

This was the palace of Salzburg's powerful ruler, the prince-archbishop—that is, a ruler with both the political powers of a prince and the religious authority of an archbishop. The ornate Baroque entrance attests to the connections these rulers had with Rome. You can step inside the Residenz courtyard to get a glimpse of the impressive digs. Going inside to see the chandeliered state rooms and paintings is not worth it for most (€12 for DomQuartier ticket, includes audioguide, Wed-Mon 10:00-17:00, closed Tue except in July-Aug, Residenzplatz 1, tel. 0662/8042-2109, www.domquartier.at).

Notice that the Residenz has a white-stone structure (called the Cathedral Terrace) connecting it with the cathedral. This skyway gave the prince-archbishops an easy commute to church and a chance to worship while avoiding the public.

• *At the opposite end of Residenzplatz from the Residenz is the...*

❺ New (Neue) Residenz

In the days of the prince-archbishops, this building hosted parties in its lavish rooms. These days, the New Residenz houses both the Salzburg Museum (entrance on Mozartplatz) and the Panorama Museum. It's also home to the Heimatwerk, a fine shop showing off locally made products ranging from jelly to dirndls.

The New Residenz bell tower has a famous glockenspiel. This 17th-century carillon has 35 bells (cast in Antwerp) and chimes daily at 7:00, 11:00, and 18:00. It also plays little tunes appropriate to the season. The mechanism is a big barrel with adjustable tabs that turns like a giant music box, pulling the right bells in the right rhythm. (Twice-weekly tours let you get up close to watch the glockenspiel action: €3, April-Oct Thu at 17:30 and Fri at 10:30, no tours Nov-March, meet at Panorama Museum, no reservations needed—but get your tickets at least a few minutes ahead of time around the corner at the Salzburg Museum.)

Notice the tower's ornamental top: an upside-down heart in flames surrounds the solar system, representing how God loves all of creation.

Residenzplatz sets the tone for the whole town. From here, a series of inter-

Residenzplatz and the New Residenz

connecting squares—like you'll see nowhere else—make a grand procession through the Old Town. Everywhere you go, you'll see similar Italian architecture. As you walk from square to square, notice how easily you slip from noisy and commercial to peaceful and reflective.

• *Exit the square by walking under the prince-archbishop's skyway. You'll step into Domplatz (Cathedral Square). A good place to view the cathedral facade is from the far end of the square.*

❻ *Salzburg Cathedral (Salzburger Dom)*

Salzburg's cathedral (rated ▲▲) was one of the first Italian Baroque buildings north of the Alps. The dome stands 230 feet high. Two domed towers flank the entrance. Between them is a false-front roofline. The windows are flanked with classical half-columns and topped with heavy pediments. The facade is ringed with a Baroque balustrade, decorated with garlands and masks, and studded with statues. The whole look reminded visitors that Salzburg was the "Rome of the North."

The church, rebuilt under Wolf Dietrich, was consecrated in 1628. Experts differ on what motivated the builders. As it dates from the years of Catholic-Protestant warfare, it may have been meant to emphasize Salzburg's commitment to the Roman Catholic cause. Or it may have represented a peaceful alternative to the religious strife. Regardless, Salzburg's archbishop was the top papal official north of the Alps, and the city was the pope's northern outpost. With its rich salt production, Salzburg had enough money to stay out of the conflict and earn the nickname "The Fortified Island of Peace."

Cost and Hours: Free, but donation prominently requested; May-Sept Mon-Sat 8:00-19:00, Sun 13:00-19:00; March-April, Oct, and Dec until 18:00; Jan-Feb and Nov until 17:00; www.salzburger-dom.at. If the Jedermann theater production is underway (July and August), enter the church through the back (via Residenzplatz; entrance across from post office).

Salzburg Cathedral, where Mozart was baptized

Visiting the Cathedral: As you approach the church, pause at the iron entrance doors. The dates on the doors are milestones in the church's history. In the year 774, the first church was consecrated by St. Virgil (see his statue), an Irish monk who became Salzburg's bishop. In 1598, the original church burned. It was replaced in 1628 by the one you see today. The year 1959 marks a modern milestone: The cathedral had been severely damaged by a WWII bomb that blew through the dome. In 1959, the renovation was complete.

The interior is clean and white, without excess decoration. Because it was built in just 14 years (from 1614 to 1628), the church boasts harmonious architecture. And it's big—330 feet long, 230 feet tall—built with sturdy pillars and broad arches. When Pope John Paul II visited in 1998, some 5,000 people packed the place.

At the back pew, black-and-white photos show the bomb damage of October 16, 1944, which left a gaping hole where the dome once was. In the first chapel on the left is a dark bronze baptismal font. It dates from 1320—a rare survivor from the medieval cathedral. In 1756, little Wolfgang Amadeus Mozart was baptized here. For the next 25 years, this would be his home church. Amadeus, by the way, means "beloved by God."

As you make your way slowly up the nave, notice how you're drawn toward the light. Imagine being part of a sacred procession, passing from the relatively dim entrance to the bright altar with its painting of Christ's resurrection, bathed in light from the dome overhead. The church never had stained glass, just clear windows to let light power the message.

Under the soaring dome, look up and admire the exceptional stucco work by an artist from Milan. It's molded into elaborate garlands, angels, and picture frames, some of it brightly painted. You're surrounded by the tombs (and portraits) of 10 archbishops.

You're also surrounded by four organs. (Actually, five. Don't forget the biggest organ, over the entrance.) Mozart served as organist here for two years, and he composed several Masses still played today. Salzburg's prince-archbishops were great patrons of music, with a personal orchestra that played religious music in the cathedral and dinner music in the Residenz. The tradition of music continues today. Sunday Mass here can be a musical spectacle—all five organs playing, balconies filled with singers and musicians, creating glorious surround-sound. Think of the altar in Baroque terms, as the center of a stage, with sunrays serving as spotlights in this dramatic and sacred theater.

Other Cathedral Sights: Skip the underwhelming **crypt,** which has more tombs and a prayer chapel (free, downstairs from the left transept). In summer, the **Cathedral Excavations Museum** (Domgrabungsmuseum) shows off the church's medieval foundations and a few Roman mosaics—worthwhile only for Roman-iacs (€2.50, July-Aug daily 9:00-17:00, closed Sept-June, outside the church on Residenzplatz and down the stairs, www.salzburgmuseum.at).

• *As you leave the cathedral, check out the concert and Mass schedules posted near the entrance. Exiting the cathedral, turn left, heading in the direction of the distant fortress on the hill. You'll soon reach a spacious square with a golden orb.*

❼ *Kapitelplatz*

The playful modern sculpture in the square shows a man atop a golden orb. Every year, a foundation commissions a different artist to create a new work of public art somewhere in the city; this one's from 2007. Kapitelplatz is a pleasant square—notice the giant chessboard that often draws a crowd.

Follow the orb-man's gaze up the hill to **Hohensalzburg Fortress.** (I think he's trying to decide whether to shell out for the funicular or save money by hiking up.) Construction of the fortress began in 1077. Over the centuries, the small castle grew into a mighty, whitewashed fortress—so formidable that no army even tried attacking for over 800 years. These days, you can tour the castle grounds, visit some interior rooms and museums, and enjoy incredible views. You can walk up (Festungsgasse leads up from Kapitelplatz) or, for a few euros more, take the funicular (for details, see page 127). The funicular's rails actually date from as far back as the 1500s, when animals pulled cargo up to the fortress. Today's electric-powered funicular is from 1910.

Now walk across the square to the pond surrounded by a balustrade and adorned with a Trevi-fountain-like statue of Neptune. It looks fancy, but the pond was built as a horse bath, the 18th-century equivalent of a car wash. Notice the gold lettering above Neptune. It reads, "Leopold the Prince Built Me." But the artist added a clever twist. The inscription uses the letters "LLDVI," and so on. Those are also Roman numerals—add 'em up: L is 50, D is 500, and so on. It all adds up to 1732—the year the pond was built.

• *With your back to the cathedral, leave the square, exiting through the right corner. You'll pass by a sign on a building that reads* zum Peterskeller—*to St. Peter's Cemetery. But first, you reach a waterwheel.*

❽ *Waterwheel*

The waterwheel—overlooked by a statue of St. Peter—is part of a clever canal system that brings water to Salzburg from the foothills of the Alps, 10 miles away. The canal was built in the 13th century and is still used today. When the stream reached Salzburg, it was divided into five smaller canals for the citizens' use. The rushing water was harnessed to waterwheels, which powered factories. There were more than 100 watermill-powered firms as late as the 19th century. The water also was used to fight fires, and every Thursday morning they flushed the streets. Hygienic Salzburg never suffered from a plague...it's probably the only major town in Austria with no plague monument.

This particular waterwheel (actually, it's a modern replacement) once ground grain into flour to make bread for the monks of St. Peter's Abbey. Nowadays, you can pop into the adjacent **bakery**—fragrant and traditional—and buy a fresh-baked roll for about a euro (closed Wed and Sun).

• *You've entered the borders of the former St. Peter's Abbey, a monastic complex of churches, courtyards, businesses (like the bakery), and a cemetery. Find the* Katakomben *sign and step through the wrought-iron gates into...*

❾ *St. Peter's Cemetery*

This collection of lovingly tended graves abuts the sheer rock face of the Mönchsberg (free, silence requested; open daily

Fountain in Kapitelplatz

Waterwheel

May-Aug 6:30-21:30, off-season until 18:00 or 19:00; www.stift-stpeter.at). Walk in about 30 yards to the middle of the cemetery. You're surrounded by three churches, each founded in the early Middle Ages atop a pagan Celtic holy site. The biggest church, St. Peter's, sticks its big Romanesque apse into the cemetery.

The graves surrounding you are tended by descendants of the deceased. In Austria (and many other European countries), gravesites are rented, not owned. Rent bills are sent out every 10 years. If no one cares enough to make the payment, your tombstone is removed. The well in the center is used to fill the watering cans for the family members who keep these flowery graves so pretty.

The cemetery plays a role in *The Sound of Music*. The Captain and his large family were well-known in Salzburg for their musical talents. But when Nazi Germany annexed Austria in 1938, the Von Trapps decided to flee so that the father would not be pressed into service again. In the movie, they hid here as they made their daring escape. The scene was actually filmed on a Hollywood set, inspired by St. Peter's Cemetery.

Look up the cliff, which has a few buildings attached—called (not quite accurately) "catacombs." Legendary medieval hermit monks are said to have lived in the hillside here. For a small fee, you can enter the *Katakomben* and climb lots of steps to see a few old caves, a chapel, and some fine city views (daily 10:00-18:00, Oct-April until 17:00, visit takes 10 minutes, entrance at the base of the cliff, under the arcade).

St. Peter's Cemetery

Explore the arcade at the base of the cliff with its various burial chapels. Alcove #XXI has the tomb of the cathedral architect—forever facing his creation. #LIV (which is also the catacombs entry) has two interesting tombs marked by plaques on the floor. "Marianne" is Mozart's sister, nicknamed "Nannerl." As children, Mozart and his sister performed together on grand tours of Europe's palaces. Michael Haydn was the brother of Joseph Haydn. He succeeded Mozart as church cathedral organist.

• *Exit the cemetery at the opposite end. Just outside, you enter a large courtyard anchored by...*

⑩ St. Peter's Church (Stiftskirche St. Peter)

You're standing at the birthplace of Christianity in Salzburg. St. Peter's Abbey—the monastery that surrounds this courtyard—was founded in 696, barely two centuries after the fall of Rome. The recommended Stiftskeller St. Peter restaurant in the courtyard (known these days for its Mozart Dinner Concert) brags that Charlemagne ate here in the year 803, making it (perhaps) the oldest restaurant in Europe. St. Peter's Church dates from 1147.

Cost and Hours: Free, daily April-Oct 8:00-21:00, Nov-March 8:00-19:00, www.stift-stpeter.at.

Visiting the Church: Enter the church, pausing in the atrium to admire the Romanesque tympanum (from 1250) over the inner doorway. Jesus sits on a rainbow, flanked by Peter and Paul. Beneath them is a stylized Tree of Life, and overhead, a Latin inscription reading, "I am the door to life, and only through me can you find eternal life."

Enter the nave. The once purely Romanesque interior (you may find a few surviving bits of faded 13th-century frescoes) now lies hidden under a sugary Rococo finish. It's Salzburg's only Rococo interior—all whitewashed, with highlights of pastel green, gold, and red. If it feels Bavarian, it's because it was done by Bavarian artists. The ceiling paintings feature St. Peter receiving the keys from Christ (center painting), walking on water, and joining the angels in heaven.

The monastery was founded by St. Rupert (c. 650-718). Find his statue at the main altar—he's the second gold statue from the left. Rupert arrived as a Christian missionary in what was then a largely pagan land. He preached the gospel, reopened the Roman salt mines, and established the city. It was he who named it "Salzburg."

Rupert's tomb is midway up the right aisle. It's adorned with a painting of him praying for his city. Beneath him is a depiction of Salzburg circa 1750 (when this was painted): one bridge, salt ships sailing the river, and angels hoisting barrels of salt to heaven.

• *Exit the courtyard at the opposite side from where you entered, through the arch under the blue-and-yellow sundial. The passageway takes you past dorms still used for student monks. At the T-intersection (where you bump into the Franciscan Church), turn right for a quick detour to appreciate another view of Domplatz.*

St. Peter's Church

The Baroque style was all about putting on a show, and that's wonderfully illustrated by the **statue of Mary** (1771) that welcomes visitors on this square. As you approach her from the center of this lane, walking between the brass railings in the cobblestones, keep an eye on the golden crown above and far behind her on the cathedral's facade. Just as you get to the middle arch, watch as she's crowned Queen of Heaven by the two angels on the church facade. Bravo!

• *Do a U-turn and head back down Franziskanergasse. Pass beneath the archway painted with a modern Lamentation scene (1926) to enter a square called Max-Reinhardt-Platz. Pause here to admire the line of impressive Salzburg Festival concert halls ahead of you. Then turn left, through a square archway, into a small square called...*

⓫ *Toscaninihof*

In this small courtyard, you get a peek at the back end of the large Festival Hall complex. The Festival Hall, built in 1925, has three theaters and seats 5,000 people. It's busy during the Salzburg Music Festival each summer. As the festival was started in the 1920s (an austere time after World War I), Salzburg couldn't afford a new concert hall, so they remodeled what were once the prince-archbishop's stables and riding school.

The tunnel you see (behind the *Felsenkeller* sign) leads to the actual concert hall. It's generally closed, but you might be able to look through nearby doorways and see carpenters building stage sets for an upcoming show.

The Von Trapp family performed in the Festival Hall. In the movie, this courtyard is where Captain von Trapp nervously waited before walking onstage to sing "Edelweiss." Then the family slipped away to begin their escape from the Nazis.

The Toscaninihof also has the entrance to the city's huge, 1,500-space, inside-the-mountain parking lot. The stone stairway in the courtyard leads a few flights up to a panoramic view. Continuing up farther you reach the recommended Stadtalm Café.

• *Return to Max-Reinhardt-Platz. Continue straight along the right side of the big church, passing popular sausage stands and a public toilet, then enter...*

⓬ *Universitätsplatz*

This square, home to the huge Baroque Kollegienkirche (University Church), also hosts Salzburg's liveliest open-air produce market. It generally runs mornings, Monday through Saturday. It's at its best early Saturday mornings, when the farmers are in town. The fancy yellow facade overlooking the square marks the back end of Mozart's Birthplace, which we'll see shortly.

Find the fountain—it's about 30 yards along. As with public marketplaces elsewhere, it's for washing fruit and vegetables. This fountain—though modern in design—is still part of a medieval-era water system. The water plummets down a hole and on to the river. The sundial over the water hole shows both the time (easy to decipher) and the date (less obvious).

• *Continue toward the end of the square. Along the way, you'll pass several nicely arcaded medieval passageways (on the right), which lead to Salzburg's old main*

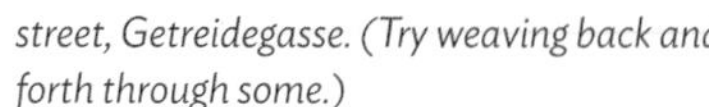

street, Getreidegasse. (Try weaving back and forth through some.)

⓭ *Mönchsberg Cliff Face*

Rising 200 feet above you is the Mönchsberg, Salzburg's mountain. Today you see the remains of an aborted attempt in the 1600s to cut through the Mönchsberg. It proved too big a job, and when new tunneling technology arrived, the project was abandoned. The stones cut did serve as a quarry for the city's 17th-century growth spurt—the bulk of the cathedral, for example, is built of this economical and local conglomerate stone.

Early one morning in 1669, a huge landslide killed more than 200 townspeople who lived close to where the elevator is now (to the right). Since then, the cliffs have been carefully checked each spring and fall. Even today, you might see crews on the cliff, monitoring its stability.

At the base of the cliff are giant horse troughs, for the prince-archbishops' former stables. Paintings show the various breeds and temperaments of horses in the stable. Like Vienna, Salzburg had a passion for the equestrian arts.

• *Before turning right onto the long pedestrian street, take note of the elevator up the Mönchsberg, which leaves from the cliffside just ahead. Now turn right onto...*

⓮ *Getreidegasse*

Old Salzburg's colorful main drag, Getreidegasse (rated ▲▲) has been a center

Market at Universitätsplatz

Horse troughs at the base of the Mönchsberg cliff

of trade since Roman times. Check out all the old wrought-iron signs that advertise what's sold inside. This was the Salzburg of prosperous medieval businessmen. These days it bustles with the tourist trade. The buildings date mainly from the 15th century. They're tall and narrow, because this neighborhood was prime real estate, and there was nowhere to build but up. Space was always tight, as the town was squeezed between the river and the mountain, and lots of land was set aside for the church. The architecture still looks much as it did in Mozart's day—though many of the buildings themselves are now inhabited by chain outlets.

Enjoy the traditional signs, and try to guess what they sold. There are signs advertising spirits, a book maker, and a horn indicating a place for the postal coach. A brewery has a star for the name of the beer, "Sternbräu." There's a window maker, a key maker, a pastry shop, a tailor, a pretzel maker, a pharmacy, a hat maker, and...ye olde hamburger shoppe, McDonald's.

On the right at #39, **Sporer** serves up homemade spirits (about €2/shot, Mon-Fri 9:30-19:00, Sat 8:30-17:00, closed Sun). This has been a family-run show for a century—fun-loving, proud, and English-speaking. *Nuss* is nut, *Marille* is apricot (typical of Austria), the *Kletzen* cocktail is like a super-thick Baileys with pear, and *Edle Brande* are the stronger schnapps. The many homemade firewaters are in jugs at the end of the bar.

After noticing the building's old doorbells—one per floor—continue down Getreidegasse. At #40, **Eisgrotte** serves good ice cream. Across from Eisgrotte, a tunnel leads to the recommended **Balkan Grill** (signed as *Bosna Grill*), the local choice for the best wurst in town. At #28 (a blacksmith shop since the 1400s), Herr Wieber, the ironworker and locksmith, welcomes the curious. Farther along, you'll pass McDonald's (required to keep its arches Baroque and low-key).

At Getreidegasse #9, the knot of excited tourists marks the home of Salzburg's most famous resident. Mozart

Getreidegasse is Salzburg's main shopping street.

was born here in 1756. It was here that he composed most of his boy-genius works. Inside you see paintings of his family, letters, personal items (a lock of his hair, a clavichord he may have played), all trying to bring life to the Mozart story (see the description on page 124).

• *At Getreidegasse #3, turn right, into the passageway. You'll walk under a whale bone (likely symbolizing the wares of an exotic import shop) and reach the Old World time-capsule café called* ***Schatz Konditorei*** *(worth a stop for coffee and pastry). At Schatz, turn left through the passage. When you reach Sigmund-Haffner-Gasse, glance to the left (for a nice view of the City Hall tower), then turn right. Walk along Sigmund-Haffner-Gasse and take your first left, to reach a square called...*

⓯ *Alter Markt*

This is Salzburg's old marketplace. Here you'll find a sausage stand, the venerable and recommended Café Tomaselli, and a fun candy shop at #7. Next door is the beautifully old-fashioned Alte F. E. Hofapotheke pharmacy—duck in discreetly to peek at the Baroque shelves and containers (be polite—the people in line are here for medicine; no photography allowed).

• *Our walk is over. If you're up for more sightseeing, most everything's a short walk from here. The Old Town has several museums, or you can head up to the Hohensalzburg Fortress. To visit sights across the river in the New Town, cross the pedestrian bridge nearby.*

Hofapotheke pharmacy at Alter Markt

SIGHTS

In the Old Town

▲▲SALZBURG MUSEUM

This is your best look at Salzburg's history. As the building was once the prince-archbishop's New Residence, many exhibits are in the lavish rooms where Salzburg's rulers entertained.

Cost and Hours: €7, includes so-so audioguide, open Tue-Sun 9:00-17:00, closed Mon; tel. 0662/620-8080, www.salzburgmuseum.at.

Visiting the Museum: The centerpiece of the museum is the permanent exhibit called **The Salzburg Myth,** on the second floor. You'll learn how the town's physical beauty—nestled among the Alps, near a river—attracted 19th-century Romantics who made it one of Europe's first tourist destinations, an "Alpine Arcadia." When the music festival began in the 1920s, Salzburg's status grew still more, drawing high-class visitors from across the globe.

After that prelude, the exhibit focuses on the glory days of the prince-archbishops (1500-1800), with displays housed in the impressive ceremonial rooms. Portraits of the prince-archbishops (in Room 2.07) show them to be cultured men, with sensitive eyes, soft hands, and carrying books. But they were also powerful secular rulers of an independent state that extended far beyond today's Salzburg (see the map in Room 2.08).

Room 2.09 holds a remarkable painting, titled *View of the City of Salzburg from Kapuzinerberg,* showing just how well preserved the city is. Even though the painting is from 1635, most everything shown in it is still fully recognizable.

The heart of the exhibit is Room 2.11—a **big, colorful hall** where the Salzburg Diet (the legislature) met. The elaborate painted ceiling depicts heroic Romans who sacrificed for their country. Spend some time here with the grab-bag of interesting displays, including old guns, rock crystals, and medallions. A portrait shows the prince-archbishop who sums up Salzburg's Golden Age—Wolf Dietrich von Raitenau (1559-1617). Here he is at age 28, having just assumed power. Educated, well-traveled, a military strategist, and fluent in several languages, Wolf Dietrich epitomized the kind of Renaissance Man who could lead both church and state. He largely created the city we see today—the rebuilt cathedral, Residenz, Residenzplatz, and Mirabell Palace—done in the Italian Baroque style. Nearby exhibits flesh out Wolf Dietrich the man (his shoes and gloves) and the city he created with Italian architect Vincenzo Scamozzi. That city inspired visits and depictions by countless artists, who helped to create what the museum calls the "Salzburg Myth."

The first floor and the *Kunsthalle* in the basement house temporary exhibits.

▲▲MOZART'S BIRTHPLACE (GEBURTSHAUS)

In 1747, Leopold Mozart—a musician in the prince-archbishop's band—moved into this small rental unit with his new bride. Soon they had a baby girl (Nannerl) and, in 1756, a little boy was born—Wolfgang Amadeus Mozart. It was here that Mozart learned to play piano and violin and composed his first boy-genius works. Even after the family gained fame, touring Europe's palaces and becoming the toast of Salzburg, they continued living in this rather cramped apartment.

Today this is the most popular Mozart sight in town—for fans, it's almost a pilgrimage. Shuffling through with the crowds, you'll peruse three floors of rooms with exhibits displaying paintings, letters, personal items, and lots of facsimiles, all attempting to bring life to the Mozart story. There's no audioguide, but everything's described in English.

Both Mozart sights in Salzburg—the Birthplace and the Residence—are equally good. If I had to choose, I'd go with the Birthplace as the best overall introduction (though it's more crowded),

Mozart's Salzburg

Salzburg was Mozart's home for the first 25 years of his brief, 35-year life. He was born on Getreidegasse and baptized in the cathedral. He played his first big concert, at age six, at the Residenz. He was the organist for the cathedral, conducted the prince-archbishop's orchestra, and dined at what's now called Café Tomaselli. It was from Salzburg that he gained Europe-wide fame, touring the continent with his talented performing family. At age 17, Mozart and his family moved into lavish digs at Wohnhaus (see Mozart's Residence on page 132).

As his fame and ambitions grew, Mozart eventually left Salzburg to pursue his dreams in Vienna. His departure from Salzburg's royal court in 1781 is the stuff of legend. Mozart, full of himself, announced that he was quitting. The prince-archbishop essentially said, "You can't quit; you're fired!" and as Mozart walked out, he was literally kicked in the ass.

Mozart's Birthplace

and consider the Residence extra credit. If you're truly interested in Mozart and his times, take advantage of the combo-ticket and see both. If Mozart isn't important to you, skip both museums and concentrate on the city's other sights and glorious natural surroundings.

Cost and Hours: €10, €17 combo-ticket with Mozart's Residence in New Town, daily July-Aug 8:30-19:00, Sept-June 9:00-17:30, Getreidegasse 9, tel. 0662/844-313, www.mozarteum.at. Avoid the shoulder-to-shoulder crowds by visiting right when it opens or late in the day.

Visiting Mozart's Birthplace: You'll begin on the top floor in the actual apartment—five small rooms, including the bedroom where Mozart was born. The rooms are bare of any furnishings. Instead, you see portraits of the famous family and some memorabilia: Mozart's small-size childhood violin, some (possible) locks of his hair, buttons from his jacket, and a letter to his wife, whom he calls his "little rascal, pussy-pussy."

After leaving the actual apartments, you'll enter the museum portion. First up is an exhibition on Mozart's life after he left Salzburg and moved to Vienna: He jams with Haydn and wows the Viennese with electrifying concerts and new compositions (see a "square piano," which may have been his). Despite his fame, Mozart fell on hard times and died young and poor. But, as the museum shows, his legacy lived on. Computer terminals let you hear his music while following along on his handwritten scores.

Downstairs, the focus is on the operas he wrote (*Don Giovanni, The Magic Flute, The Marriage of Figaro*), with stage sets and video clips. The finale is an old clavichord on which Mozart supposedly composed his final work—the *Requiem*, which was played for his own funeral. (A predecessor of the more complicated piano, the clavichord's keys hit the strings with a simple teeter-totter motion that allows you to play softly—ideal for composers living in tight apartment quarters.)

The lower-floor exhibit takes you on the road with the child prodigy, and gives a slice-of-life portrait of Salzburg during Mozart's time, including a bourgeois living room furnished much as the Mozart family's would have been.

Atop the Cliffs Above the Old Town

Atop the Mönchsberg—the mini mountain that rises behind the Old Town—is a tangle of paved walking paths with great views, a hostel with a pleasant café/restaurant, a modern art museum, a neighborhood of fancy homes, and one major sight (the Hohensalzburg Fortress, perched on the Festungsberg, the Mönchsberg's southern arm). You can walk up from several points in town, including Festungsgasse (near the cathedral), Toscaninihof, and the recommended Augustiner Bräustübl beer garden. At the west end of the Old Town, the Mönchsberg elevator whisks you up to the top for a couple of euros. The funicular directly up to the fortress is expensive during the day, and worthwhile only if you plan to visit the fortress, which is included in the funicular ticket.

▲▲HOHENSALZBURG FORTRESS (FESTUNG)

Construction of Hohensalzburg Fortress was begun by Archbishop Gebhard of Salzburg as a show of the Catholic Church's power (see sidebar on page 126). Built on a rock (called Festungsberg) 400 feet above the Salzach River, this fortress was never really used. That was the idea. It was a good investment—so foreboding, nobody attacked the town for over 800 years. The city was never taken by force, but when Napoleon stopped by, Salzburg wisely surrendered. After a stint as a military barracks, the fortress was opened to the public in the 1860s by Habsburg Emperor Franz Josef. Today, it remains one of Europe's mightiest castles, dom-

Battlefield Salzburg: Popes vs. Emperors

Salzburg is architecturally fortified today in large part because of the Roman Catholic Church. This town was on the frontline of a centuries-long power struggle between Church and emperor. The town's mighty Hohensalzburg Fortress—a symbol of the Church's determination to assert its power here—was built around 1100, just as the conflict was heating up.

The medieval church-state argument, called the "Lay Investiture Controversy," was a classic tug-of-war between a series of popes and Holy Roman Emperors. The prize: the right to appoint church officials in the Holy Roman Emperor's domain. (Although called "Holy," the empire was headed not by priests, but by secular rulers.)

The Church impinged on the power of secular leaders in several ways. Their subjects' generous tithes went to Rome, leaving less for the emperor to tax. The Church was the biggest landowner (people willed their land to the Church in return for prayers for their salvation). And the pope's appointees weren't subject to secular local laws. Holy Roman Emperors were plenty powerful, but not as powerful as the Church.

In 1075, Emperor Henry IV bucked the system, appointing his own church officials and boldly renouncing Gregory VII as pope. In retaliation, Gregory excommunicated both Henry and the bishops he'd appointed. One of Henry's chief detractors was Salzburg's pope-appointed archbishop, Gebhard, who started construction of Hohensalzburg Fortress in a face-off with the defiant emperor.

The German nobility saw the conflict as an opportunity to rebel, seizing royal property and threatening to elect a new emperor. To placate the nobles, Henry sought to regain the Church's favor. In January 1077, Henry traveled south to Canossa, Italy, where the pope was holed up. The emperor knelt in the snow outside the castle gate for three days, begging the pope's forgiveness.

But the German princes continued their revolt, electing their own king (Henry's brother-in-law, Rudolf of Rheinfelden). Henry's reconciliation with the Church was brief: In short order he named an antipope (Clement III), killed Rudolf in battle, and invaded Rome. Archbishop Gebhard was forced out of Salzburg and spent a decade in exile, raising forces against Henry in an attempt to reclaim the Salzburg archdiocese.

The back-and-forth continued until 1122, when a power-sharing accord was finally reached between Henry's son, Emperor Henry V, and Pope Calistus II.

inating Salzburg's skyline and offering incredible views, cafés, and a handful of mediocre museums. It's a pleasant place to grab an ice-cream cone and wander the whitewashed maze of buildings while soaking up some medieval ambience.

Cost and Hours: Your cost to enter the fortress and its museums depends on whether you take the funicular or walk (easier than it looks—described later, under "Getting There"). Either way, your ticket includes all the interior sights at the fortress: the Regency Rooms with an audioguide (Tour A), the Fortress and Rainer Regiments museums (Tour B), the Marionette Exhibit, and a few minor sights. The museums are open daily May-Sept 9:00-19:00, Oct-April 9:30-17:00.

Most visitors opt for the one-minute trip on the **funicular** *(Festungsbahn).* The round-trip funicular ticket is €11.30 (family ticket-€26.20). If you board the funicular going up within one hour of the museums' closing time (i.e., May-Sept after 18:00 or Oct-April after 16:00), you pay only €8.30, or €6.70 if you don't want to take the funicular down.

After the museums have closed, the fortress grounds stay open and the funicular continues to run until about 21:30 or 22:00 (later if there's a concert—300 nights a year) and costs €4.30 round-trip, or €2.70 one-way.

For **walkers,** it's €8 to enter at the fortress gate; this includes all the fortress sights plus the funicular ride down—whether you want it or not. Within one hour of the museums' closing time, the entry price is reduced to €4. For a little while after the museums close, you can usually enter the grounds for free (explained later).

Avoiding Crowds: Avoid waits for the funicular ascent with the Salzburg Card (which lets you skip to the head of the line) or by walking up. In summer, there are often long waits to get into Tour A (only 60 people are admitted at a time). To avoid crowds in general, visit early in the morning or late in the day.

Rick's Tip: *Since the view is more exciting than the museums,* **save money by visiting the fortress in the evening.** *After the museums close, you can usually walk up (free) or ride the funicular (small fee). After a certain time (about 20:30 in summer, 17:30 off-season), you won't be able to enter on foot, but you can still exit (the door will lock behind you). Enjoy the scenery over dinner or a drink at the café, then walk or ride back down in the dark (the path is well lit).*

Getting There: On foot, it's a steep but quick **walk** from Kapitelplatz (next to the cathedral), up Festungsgasse. The **funicular** starts from Festungsgasse (just off Kapitelplatz, by the cathedral) and comes up inside the fortress complex.

Information: Tel. 0662/8424-3011, www.salzburg-burgen.at.

Concerts: The fortress serves as a venue for evening concerts (the Festungskonzerte), which are held in the old banquet rooms on the upper floor of the palace museum. A concert is a good way

The mighty Hohensalzburg Fortress dominates the city's skyline.

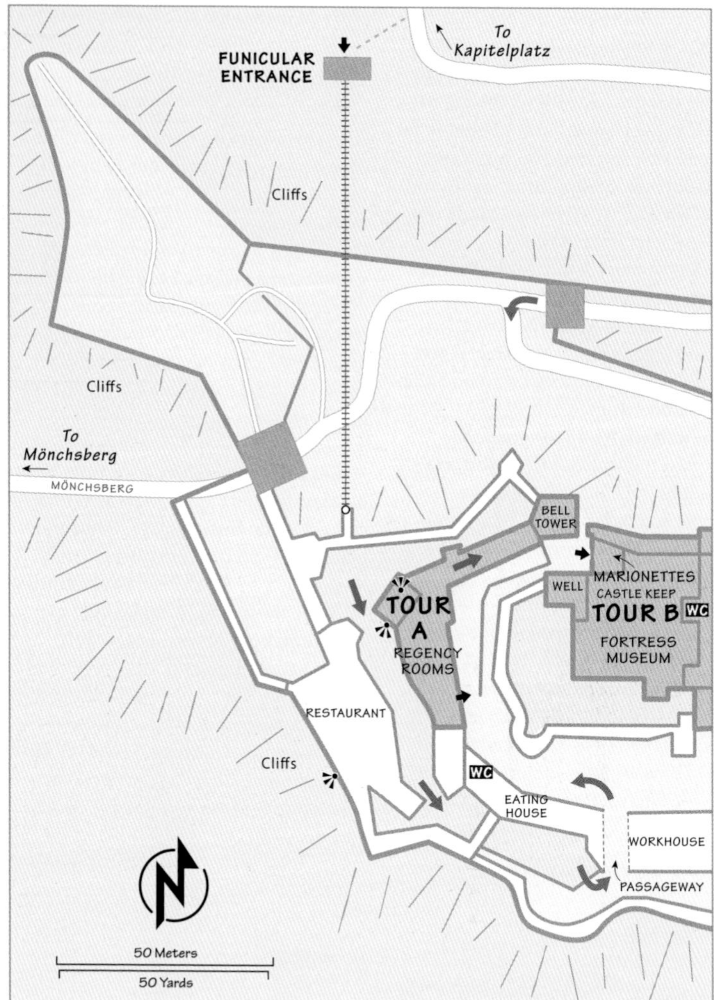

to see the fortress without noisy crowds. For concert details, see page 135.

Eating: The cafés to either side of the upper funicular station are a great place to linger over an open-air dinner or nibble on apple strudel while taking in the jaw-dropping view (reasonable prices, daily 11:30-22:00, food served until about 20:30, closed Jan-Feb).

➲ **Self-Guided Tour:** The fortress is an eight-acre complex of some 50 buildings, with multiple courtyards and multiple rings of protective walls.

• *At the top of the funicular, turn right, and bask in the* ***view*** *to the south (away from town) toward the Alps. Continue up through the fortress gates—two defensive rings for double protection. Emerging into the light, go left (uphill) to find the entrance to....*

Tour A—The Regency Rooms: Here you see a few (mostly bare) rooms, following an audioguide included with your ticket. The Stable Rooms highlight various prince-archbishops and models

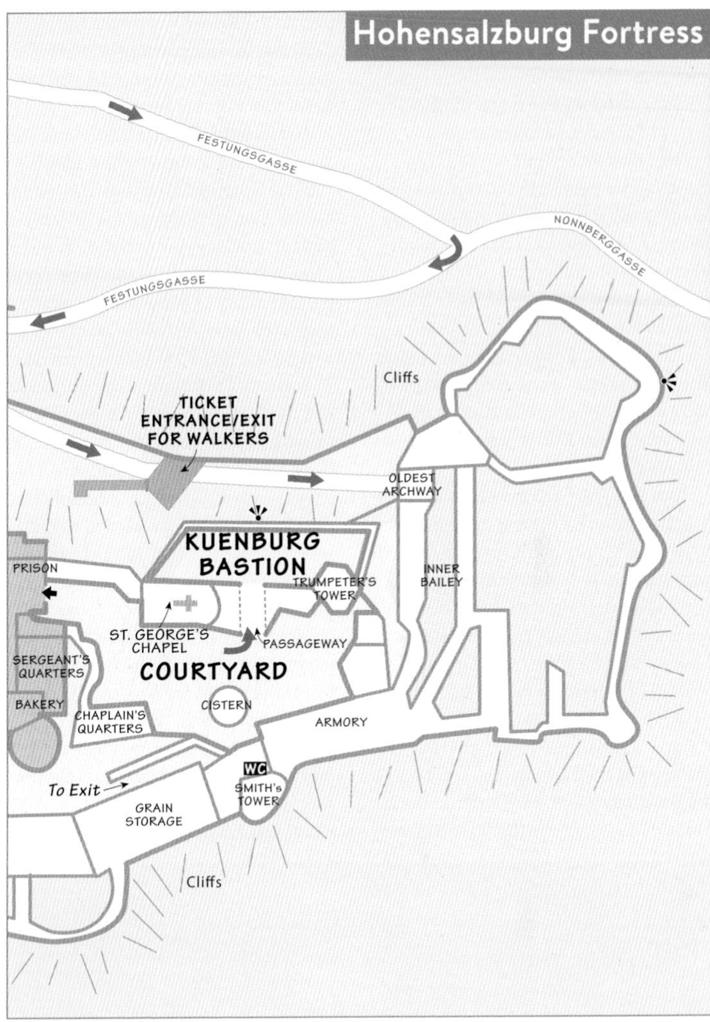

showing the fortress' growth, starting in 1077. The last model (1810) shows it at its peak. The fortress was never overthrown, but officials did make a negotiated surrender with Napoleon, and the fortress never saw action again. Your tour includes a room dedicated to the art of "enhanced interrogation" (to use American military jargon)—filled with tools of that gruesome trade.

One of the most esteemed prisoners held here was Prince-Archbishop Wolf Dietrich, who lost favor with the pope, was captured by a Bavarian duke, and spent his last seven years in Hohensalzburg. It's a complicated story—basically, the pope counted on Salzburg to hold the line against the Protestants for several generations following the Reformation. Wolf Dietrich was a good Catholic, as were most Salzburgers. But the town's important businessmen and the region's salt miners were Protestant, and for Salzburg's financial good, Wolf Dietrich dealt with them in a tolerant and pragmatic way. Eventually the pope—who allowed zero tolerance for Protestants in those heady Counter-Reformation days—had Wolf Dietrich locked up and replaced.

The highlight of Tour A is the commanding city view from the top of a tower. To the north is the city. To the south are Salzburg's suburbs in a flat valley, from which rises the majestic 6,000-foot Untersberg massif of the Berchtesgaden Alps. To the east, you can look down into the castle complex to see the palace where the prince-archbishops lived. As you exit, pause at the "Salzburger Bull," a mechanical barrel organ used to wake the citizens every morning.

Tour B—The Fortress Museum (Festungsmuseum): This extensive museum covers the history of the fortress (including models of how it was constructed), everyday objects (dishes, beds, ovens), weapons (pikes, swords, pistols, cannons), old musical instruments, and more torture devices (including a chastity belt).

On the top floor are three pretty ceremonial rooms, including the one where the evening concerts are held. (Check out the colorfully painted tile stove in the far room.) The rest of the top floor is given over to the Rainer Regiments Museum, dedicated to the Salzburg soldiers who fought mountain-to-mountain on the Italian front during World War I.

Marionette Exhibit: Marionette shows are a Salzburg tradition (think of the "Lonely Goatherd" scene in *The Sound of Music*). Two fun rooms show off various puppets and scenery backdrops. Videos show glimpses of the Marionette Theater performances of Mozart classics (see page 136). Give the hands-on marionette a whirl, and find Wolf Dietrich in a Box.

Fortress Courtyard: The courtyard was the main square for the medieval fortress's 1,000-some residents, who could be self-sufficient when necessary. The square was ringed by the shops of craftsmen, blacksmiths, bakers, and so on. The well dipped into a rain-fed cistern. The church is dedicated to St. George, the protector of horses (logical for an army church) and decorated by fine red marble reliefs (1512). Behind the church is the top of the old lift (still in use) that helped supply the fortress. Under the archway next to it are the steps that lead back into the city, or to the paths across the Mönchsberg.

• *Just downhill from the chapel, find an*

Marionette display at Hohensalzburg Fortress

opening in the wall that leads to a balcony with a view of Salzburg—the Kuenburg Bastion.

Kuenburg Bastion: Survey Salzburg from here and think about fortifying an important city by using nature. The fortress sits atop a ridgeline with sheer cliffs on three sides, giving it a huge defensive advantage. Meanwhile, the town of Salzburg sits between the natural defenses of the Salzach River and the ridge. (The ridgeline consists of the Mönchsberg, the cliffs to the left, and Festungsberg, the little mountain you're on.) The fortress itself has three concentric rings of defense: the original keep in the center (where Tour B is located), the vast whitewashed walls (near you), and still more beefed-up fortifications (on the hillside below you, added against an expected Ottoman invasion). With all these defenses, the city only required a few more touches: the New Town across the river needed a wall arcing from the river to its hill. Back then, only one bridge crossed the Salzach into town, and it had a fortified gate. Cradled amid the security of its defenses—both natural and man-made—independent Salzburg thrived for nearly a thousand years.

• *Our tour is over. To* ***walk****—either down to Salzburg or across the Mönchsberg—you'll want to take the exit at the east end of the complex. Get out your fortress-issued map and locate the route that leads to that exit.*

To reach the ***funicular,*** *just backtrack. If you take the funicular down, check out (at the bottom of the lift) the...*

Alm River Canal Exhibit: At the base of the funicular, below the fortress, is this fine little exhibit (included with your funicular ticket) on how the river was broken into five smaller streams—powering the city until steam took up the energy-supply baton. Pretend it's the year 1200 and follow (by video) the flow of the water from the river through the canals, into the mills, and as it's finally dumped into the Salzach River.

In the New Town, North of the River

The following sights are across the river from the Old Town. Cross the Makartsteg pedestrian bridge, walk two blocks inland, and take a left past the heroic statues into the Mirabell Gardens. From the gardens, it's a long block southeast to Makartplatz, where you'll find Mozart's residence.

▲MIRABELL GARDENS AND PALACE

These bubbly gardens, laid out in 1730 for the prince-archbishop, have been open to the public since 1850 (thanks to Emperor Franz Josef, who was rattled by the popular revolutions of 1848). The gardens are free and open until dusk. The palace is open only as a concert venue (explained later). The statues and the arbor (far left) were featured in *The Sound of Music.*

Walk through the gardens to the palace and find the statue of the horse (on the river side of the palace). Look back, enjoy the garden/cathedral/castle view, and imagine how the prince-archbishop must have reveled in a vista that reminded him of all his secular and religious power.

The rearing **Pegasus statue** (rare and well-balanced) is the site of a famous *Sound of Music* scene where the kids all danced before lining up on the stairs with Maria (30 yards farther along). The steps lead to a small mound in the park (made of rubble from a former theater).

Nearest the horse, stairs lead between two lions to a pair of tough dwarves (early

Mirabell Gardens and Palace

volleyball players with spiked mittens) welcoming you to Salzburg's **Dwarf Park.** Cross the elevated walk (noticing the city's fortified walls) to meet statues of a dozen dwarves who served the prince-archbishop—modeled after real people with real fashions in about 1600. This was Mannerist art, from the hyper-realistic age that followed the Renaissance.

There's plenty of **music** here, both in the park and in the palace. A brass band plays free park concerts (May-Aug Sun at 10:30 and Wed at 20:30). To properly enjoy the lavish Mirabell Palace—once the prince-archbishop's summer palace and now the seat of the mayor—get a ticket to a Schlosskonzerte (my favorite venue for a classical concert—see page 135).

▲MOZART'S RESIDENCE (WOHNHAUS)

In the fall of 1773, when Wolfgang was 17—and his family was flush with money from years of touring—the Mozarts moved here from their cramped apartment on Getreidegasse. The exhibits are aimed more toward the Mozart connoisseur than those at Mozart's Birthplace, but the place comes with a good introductory video, is less crowded, and includes an informative audioguide. The building itself, bombed in World War II, is a reconstruction.

Cost and Hours: €10, €17 combo-ticket with Mozart's Birthplace in Old Town, daily July-Aug 8:30-19:00, Sept-June 9:00-17:30, allow an hour to visit, Makartplatz 8, tel. 0662/8742-2740, www.mozarteum.at. Behind the ticket desk is the free Mozart Sound and Film Collection, an archive of historic concerts on video (Mon-Tue and Fri 9:00-13:00, Wed-Thu 13:00-17:00, closed Sat-Sun).

Visiting Mozart's Residence: The exhibit—seven rooms on one floor—starts in the main hall, which was used by the Mozarts to entertain Salzburg's high society. Here, you can see the museum's prize possession—Mozart's very own piano, as well as his violin. The family portrait on the wall (from around 1780) shows Mozart with his sister Nannerl at the piano, their father on violin, and their mother—who'd died two years earlier in Paris. Before moving on, consider spending time with the fine introductory video in this room.

Room 2 trumpets the successes the Mozart family enjoyed while living here: portraits of Salzburg bigwigs they hung out with, letters from Mozart bragging about his musical successes, and the publication of Leopold's treatise on playing violin.

Room 3 is dedicated to father Leopold—*Kapellmeister* of the prince—a member of the archbishop's orchestra, a musician, and a composer in his own right. Was Leopold a loving nurturer of young Wolfgang or an exploiting Svengali?

Room 4 stars "Nannerl" (Maria Anna), Mozart's sister, who was five years older than Mozart. Though both were child prodigies, playing four-hand show-pieces for Europe's crowned heads, Nannerl went on to lead a stable life as a wife and mother.

Room 5 boasts letters and music books from the nearby Mozarteum library. Room 6 shows many portraits of Mozart, some authentic, some not, but all a testament to his long legacy. By the time Mozart was 25, he'd grown tired of his father, this house, and Salzburg, and he went on to Vienna—to more triumphs, but ultimately, a sad end.

Mozart's Residence

▲ST. SEBASTIAN CEMETERY

Wander through this quiet oasis. Mozart is buried in Vienna, his mom in Paris, and his sister is in Salzburg's Old Town (St. Peter's)—but Wolfgang's wife Constanze ("Constantia") and his father, Leopold, are buried here (from the black iron gate entrance on Linzer Gasse, walk 19 paces and look left). When Prince-Archbishop Wolf Dietrich had the cemetery moved from around the cathedral and put here, across the river, people didn't like it. To help popularize it, he had his own mausoleum built as its centerpiece. Continue straight past the Mozart tomb to this circular building (English description at door). In the corner to the left of the entrance is the tomb of the Renaissance scientist and physician Paracelsus, best known for developing laudanum as a painkiller.

Cost and Hours: Free, daily April-Oct 9:00-18:00, Nov-March 9:00-16:00, entry at Linzer Gasse 43 in summer; in winter go around the corner to the right, through the arch at #37, and around the building to the doorway under the blue seal.

Near Salzburg

▲▲HELLBRUNN PALACE AND GARDENS

In about 1610, Prince-Archbishop Sittikus decided he needed a lavish palace with a vast and ornate garden purely for pleasure (I imagine after meditating on stewardship and Christ-like values). He built this summer palace and hunting lodge, and just loved inviting his VIP guests from throughout Europe to have some fun with his trick fountains. Today, Hellbrunn is a popular sight for its formal garden (one of the oldest in Europe, with a gazebo made famous by *The Sound of Music*), amazing fountains, palace exhibits, and the excuse it offers to simply get out of the city.

Cost and Hours: €10.50 ticket includes fountain tour and palace audioguide, daily May-Sept 9:00-17:30, July-Aug until 21:00—but tours from 18:00 on don't include the castle (which closes in the evening), April and Oct 9:00-16:30, these are last tour times, closed Nov-March, tel. 0662/820-3720, www.hellbrunn.at.

Getting There: Hellbrunn is nearly four miles south of Salzburg. Take **bus #25** from the train station or the Rathaus stop by the Staatsbrücke bridge, and get off at the Schloss Hellbrunn stop (2-3/hour, 20 minutes). Or, in good weather, the trip out to Hellbrunn makes for a pleasant 30-minute **bike** excursion (see "Riverside or Meadow Bike Ride" next, and ask for a map when you rent your bike).

Visiting the Palace: Upon arrival, buy your **fountain tour** ticket and get a tour time (generally on the half-hour). The 40-minute English/German tours take you laughing and scrambling through a series of amazing 17th-century garden settings with lots of splashy fun and a guide who seems almost sadistic in the joy he has in soaking his group. (Hint: When you see a wet place, cover your camera.) If there's a wait until your tour, you can see the palace first.

With the help of the included audioguide, wander through the modest **palace** exhibit to the sounds of shrieking, fountain-taunted tourists below. The palace was built in a style inspired by the Venetian architect Palladio, who was particularly popular around 1600, and it quickly became a cultural destination. This was the era when the aristocratic ritual was to go hunting in the morning (hence the wildlife-themed decor) and enjoy

Hellbrunn Palace Garden

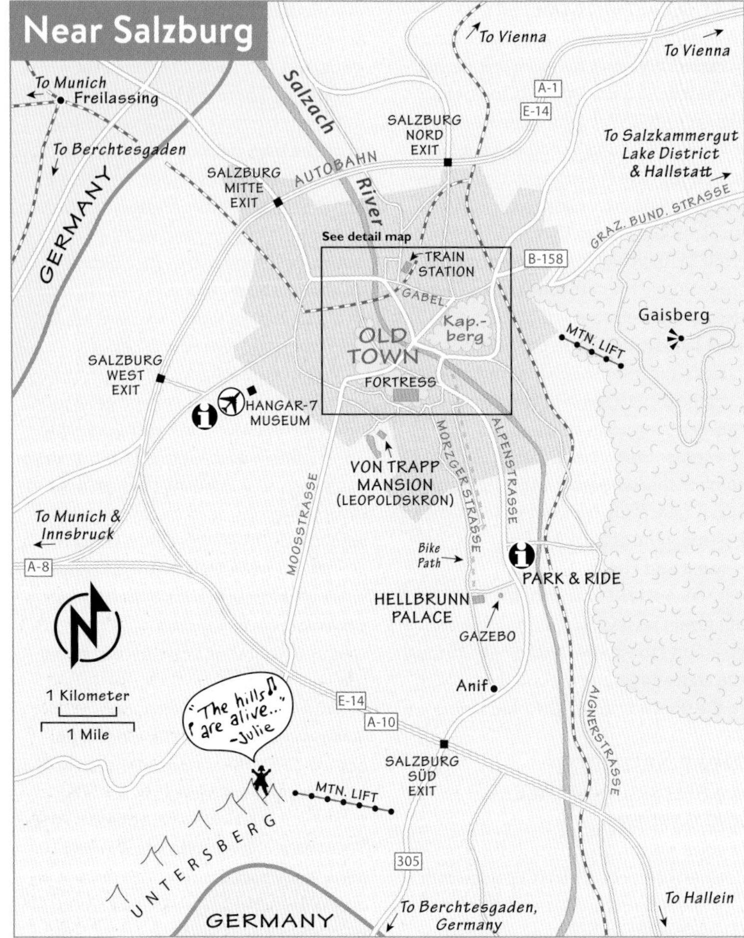

an opera in the evening. The first opera north of the Alps, imported from Italy, was performed here. The decor is Mannerist (between Renaissance and Baroque), with faux antiquities and lots of surprising moments—intentional irregularities were in vogue after the strict logic, balance, and Greek-inspired symmetry of the Renaissance. (For example, the main hall is not in the palace's center, but at the far end.) The palace exhibit also explains the 17th-century hydraulic engineering that let gravity power the intricate fountains.

After the fountain tour, you're also free to wander the delightful **garden.** Pop out to see the **gazebo** made famous by the "Sixteen Going On Seventeen" song from *The Sound of Music* (relocated here in the 1990s; look for *Sound-of-Music Pavilion* signs).

▲▲RIVERSIDE OR MEADOW BIKE RIDE

The Salzach River has smooth, flat, and scenic bike lanes along each side (thanks to medieval tow paths—cargo boats would float downstream and be dragged back up by horses). On a sunny day, I can think of no more shout-worthy escape from the city. You can rent bikes at **A'Velo Radladen,** just outside the TI on Mozartplatz in the Old Town (for more info, see page 148).

Perhaps the most pristine, meadow-filled, farm-country route is the nearly four-mile path along Hellbrunner Allee to Hellbrunn Palace. It's an easy ride with a worthy destination: From the middle of town, head along the river on Rudolfskai, with the river on your left and the fortress on your right. After passing the last bridge at the edge of the Old Town (Nonntaler Brücke), cut inland along Petersbrunnstrasse, until you reach the university and Akademiestrasse. Beyond it, find the start of Freisaalweg, which becomes the delightful Hellbrunner Allee bike path... which parallels Morzgerstrasse and leads directly to Hellbrunn Palace.

MUSIC

Music lovers come to Salzburg from mid-July through August for the Salzburg Festival, but you can enjoy concerts all year long. Pick up the events calendar brochure at the TI (free, bimonthly) or check www.salzburg.info (under "Art & Culture," click on "Music"). I've never planned in advance, and I've enjoyed great concerts with every visit.

Rick's Tip: *Virtually all* **hotels make concert recommendations based on their potential kickback,** *not what's best for you. If you book a concert through your hotel, you're probably paying too much.*

Daily Events

The following concerts are mostly geared to tourists and can have a crank-'em-out feel, but they still provide good value, especially outside festival times.

CONCERTS AT HOHENSALZBURG FORTRESS

Nearly nightly fortress concerts (Festungskonzerte) are held atop the hill in the "prince's chamber," featuring small chamber groups playing Mozart's greatest hits for beginners. The medieval-feeling chamber has windows overlooking the city, and the concert gives you a chance to enjoy the grand city view and a stroll through the castle courtyard (€34-42 plus €4.30 for the funicular, open seating after the first six more expensive rows; at 19:30, 20:00, or 20:30; doors open 30 minutes early, reserve at tel. 0662/825-858 or via www.salzburghighlights.at, pick up tickets at the door). For €54, you can combine the concert with a four-course dinner (starts 2 hours before concert).

CONCERTS AT THE MIRABELL PALACE

The nearly nightly palace concerts (Schlosskonzerte) are performed in a lavish Baroque setting. They offer more sophisticated chamber music and better musicians than the fortress concerts...and Baroque music flying around a Baroque hall is a happy bird in the right cage (open seating after the first five pricier rows, €31-37, usually at 20:00—but check flier for times, doors open one hour ahead, tel. 0662-828-695, www.salzburg-palace-concerts.com).

MOZART DINNER CONCERT
For those who'd like some classical music but would rather not sit through a concert, the elegant **Stiftskeller St. Peter restaurant** offers a traditional candlelit meal with Mozart's greatest hits performed by a string quartet and singers in historic costumes gavotting among the tables. Tourists clap between movements and get three courses of food (from Mozart-era recipes) mixed with three 20-minute courses of crowd-pleasing music—structured much as such evenings were in the Baroque era (€56, €9 discount for Mozart lovers who reserve directly by phone or email and mention this book, music starts nightly at 19:30, arrive 30 minutes before that, dress is "smart casual," next to St. Peter's Church at foot of Mönchsberg, tel. 0662/828-695, www.mozart-dinner-concert-salzburg.com, office@skg.co.at).

RESIDENZKONZERTE
On virtually any afternoon, you can catch a 45-minute concert of 16th-century music ("from Baroque through Mozart") played on Renaissance instruments at the Residenz (€18, discount with Salzburg Card, daily at 15:00, tickets available at 14:30, tel. 0664/423-5645, www.agenturorpheus.at).

MARIONETTE THEATER
A troupe of 10 puppeteers brings to life artfully created puppets who star in operas performed to recorded music. The 180 performances a year alternate between *The Sound of Music* and various German-language operas (with handy superscripts in English). While the 300-plus-seat venue is forgettable, the art of the marionettes enchants adults and children alike (€20-35, kids-€15, May-Sept nearly nightly at 19:30 plus matinees on some days, also a few shows during Christmas season, no shows Oct-Nov or Jan-April, near Mozart's Residence at Schwarzstrasse 24, tel. 0662/872-406, www.marionetten.at).

Weekly Events

FRIDAY AND SATURDAY: MOZART PIANO SONATAS
These fairly inexpensive 45-minute concerts in St. Peter's Abbey are ideal for families (€22, €11 for kids, €55 for a family of four, almost every Fri and Sat at 19:00 year-round, in the abbey's Romanesque Hall—a.k.a. Romanischer Saal, enter from inner courtyard 20 yards left of St. Peter's Church, mobile 0664-423-5645, www.agenturorpheus.at, then click on "Konzerte" and "Salzburg—Mozart Klaviersonaten").

SUNDAY MORNING: MUSIC AT MASS
Each Sunday morning, three great churches offer a Mass, generally with glorious music. The **Salzburg Cathedral** is likely your best bet for fine music for worship. The 10:00 service generally features a Mass written by a well-known composer performed by choir, organist, or other musicians. The worship service is often followed at 11:30 by a free organ concert (music program at www.kirchen.net/dommusik). Nearby (just outside Domplatz, with the pointy green spire), the **Franciscan Church** is the locals' choice (at 9:00, www.franziskanerkirche-salzburg.at—click on "Programm"). **St. Peter's Church** also sometimes has music (often at 10:15, www.stift-stpeter.at—click on "Kirchenmusik," then "Jahresprogramm").

SUNDAY AND WEDNESDAY: FREE BRASS BAND CONCERTS
Traditional brass bands play in the Mirabell Gardens (May-Aug Sun at 10:30 and Wed at 20:30).

Annual Events

Each summer, from mid-July to the end of August, is the famous **Salzburg Festival** (Salzburger Festspiele), founded in 1920 to employ Vienna's musicians in the summer. A total of 200,000 tickets are sold to festival events annually—but there are usually plenty of beds (except for a few August weekends). Events take place primarily in three big halls: the Opera and Orchestra venues in the Festival House, and the Landestheater, where German-language plays are performed. Tickets for the big festival events are generally expensive (€50-600) and sell out well in advance (bookable from January). But many "go to the Salzburg Festival" by seeing smaller, nonfestival events that run during the same weeks. For these unofficial events, same-day tickets are normally available—ask at the TI for details. For specifics on this year's festival schedule and tickets, visit www.salzburgfestival.at.

Music lovers who don't have tickets (or money) can still enjoy **Festival Nights,** a free series of previously filmed festival performances, projected on a big screen on Kapitelplatz (behind the cathedral). It's a fun scene, with plenty of folding chairs and a food circus of temporary eateries. For info and schedules, go to www.salzburg.info and search for "Festival Nights."

Other annual musical events include **Mozart Week** (January), the **Easter Music Festival, Whitsun Festival,** and **October's Culture Days.** In mid-September, the **St. Rupert's Fair** (Ruperti-Kirtag) fills the sky with fireworks and Old Town with music (www.rupertikirtag.at). Throughout Advent, Salzburg boasts three **Christmas markets.**

EATING

In the Old Town

Restaurants

$$ Gasthaus Wilder Mann is *the* place if the weather's bad and you're in the mood for a hearty, cheap meal at a shared table in one well-antlered (and nonsmoking) room. For a quick lunch, get the *Bauernschmaus*, a mountain of dumplings, kraut, and peasant's meats (€13). While they have a few outdoor tables, the atmosphere is all indoors, and the menu is more geared to cold weather (€10-14 main courses, specials posted on the wall, kitchen open Mon-Sat 11:00-21:00, closed Sun, 2 minutes from Mozart's Birthplace, enter from Getreidegasse 22 or Griesgasse 17, tel. 0662/841-787, www.wildermann.co.at).

$$ St. Paul's Stub'n Beer Garden is tucked away under the fortress with a decidedly untouristy atmosphere. The food is better than at beer halls. A bohemian-chic clientele fills its two troll-like rooms and idyllic garden. *Kasnock'n* is a tasty dish of *Spätzle* with cheese served in an iron pan—it's enough food for two, and includes a side salad. Reservations are smart (€9-17 main courses, Mon-Sat 17:00-22:00, open later for drinks only, closed Sun, Herrengasse 16, tel. 0662/843-220, www.paul-stube.at).

$ Zirkelwirt serves reasonably priced Austrian standards (schnitzel, goulash, *Spätzle* with kraut) and big salads in an updated *Gasthaus* dining room and terrace. While it's just a block off Mozartplatz, the authentic atmosphere is a world away from the tourism of Old Town (€9-13 main courses, daily 11:00-22:00, Pfeifergasse 14, tel. 0662/842-796, www.zumzirkelwirt.at).

$ Saran Essbar, in the middle of Old Town, casts a rich orange glow under medieval vaults. Its fun menu is small, mixing South Asian and Austrian cuisine (€12-17 main courses, vegetarian options, daily 11:00-15:00 & 17:00-22:00, longer hours during festival and in December, cash only, no reservations, a block off Mozartplatz at Judengasse 10, tel. 0662/846-628).

$ Café Tomaselli has long been Salzburg's top place to see and be seen. It serves light meals and lots of drinks, keeps long hours, and has fine seating on the square, a view terrace upstairs, and indoor tables. Despite its fancy inlaid wood paneling, 19th-century portraits, and chandeliers, it's surprisingly low-key (€4-8 light meals, daily 7:00-20:00, until 22:00 during festival, Alter Markt 9, tel. 0662/844-488, www.tomaselli.at).

$$$ Stiftskeller St. Peter has been in business for more than 1,000 years—it was mentioned in the biography of Charlemagne. These days it's high-end touristy, serving uninspired traditional Austrian cuisine (€17-30 main courses, kitchen open daily 11:30-21:00 or later, indoor/outdoor seating, next to St. Peter's Church at foot of Mönchsberg, tel. 0662/841-268, www.haslauer.at). They host the Mozart Dinner Concert described on page 136.

Rick's Tip: *Austria has been slow to embrace the smoke-free movement. By law,* **big restaurants must offer smoke-free zones** *(and smoking zones, if they choose). Smaller places choose to be either smoking or nonsmoking, indicated by stickers on the door: red for smoking, or green for nonsmoking.*

Cafés at the West End of the Old Town

$$ Bar Club Café Republic, a hip hangout for young locals opposite the base of the Mönchsberg elevator, is mod, untouristy, and un-wursty. It serves good Asian and international food both outdoors and in—with both smoking and nonsmoking rooms inside (€10-16 main courses, inexpensive weekday lunches, lots of hard drinks, food served daily 8:00-22:00, drinks served till much later, trendy breakfasts served 8:00-18:00, live music Sun 10:00-13:00, music with a DJ Fri and Sat from 23:00, salsa dance club Tue night from 21:00—no cover, Wi-Fi, Anton-Neumayr-Platz 2, tel. 0662/841-613, www.republiccafe.at).

$$$$ Carpe Diem is a project of Red Bull tycoon Dietrich Mateschitz. Salzburg's beautiful people, fueled by Red Bull, present themselves here in the chic ground-floor café and "lifestyle bar" (smoking allowed), which serves quality cocktails and finger food (café open daily 8:30-24:00). Upstairs is an expensive, nonsmoking restaurant boasting a Michelin star (€26-37 main courses, €4.50 cover charge, €19.50 weekday lunch special, restaurant open Mon-Sat 12:00-14:00 & 18:30-22:00, closed Sun; Getreidegasse 50, tel. 0662/848-800, www.carpediemfinestfingerfood.com).

On the Cliffs Above the Old Town

Riding the Mönchsberg elevator from the west end of the Old Town up to the clifftop deposits you near two very different eateries.

$$$$ Mönchsberg 32 is a sleek, modern café/bar/restaurant at the modern art museum, overlooking Salzburg from the top of the Mönchsberg elevator. Even if you're not hiking anywhere, this makes for a great place to enjoy a drink and the view (€5 coffee, €20-35 main courses, €3 cover charge for meals, €14 weekday lunch special, Tue-Sun 9:00-24:00, closed Mon except during festival, popular breakfasts served until 12:00, buy a one-way elevator ticket—they give customers a free pass to descend, tel. 0662/841-000, www.m32.at).

$ Stadtalm Café is a funky old mountaineers' hut on the edge of the cliff, with great views, cheap prices, and good traditional food. Nearby are the remnants of the old city wall. If you're hiking across the Mönchsberg, make this a stop (€10-12 main dishes, cliff-side garden seating or cozy-mountain-hut indoor seating, May-Aug Mon-Sat 11:30-20:00 or later, Sun 11:30-18:00; closes earlier off-season, hours are weather- and whim-dependent, 5 minutes from top of Mönchsberg elevator, also reachable by stairs from Toscaninihof, Mönchsberg 19C, tel. 0662/841-729, www.stadtalm.at).

Eating Cheaply in the Old Town

$ Fisch Krieg Restaurant, on the river, serves fast, fresh, and inexpensive fish in a casual dining room—where trees grow through the ceiling—and also has great riverside seating (cheap fishwiches to go, €8-9 self-serve main courses, salad bar, Mon-Fri 8:30-18:30, Sat 8:30-13:00, closed Sun, Hanuschplatz 4, tel. 0662/843-732).

Sausage stands (*Würstelstände*) serve the town's favorite "fast food." The 66-year-old **Balkan Grill** is a Salzburg institution with a steady and sturdy local crowd, selling just one type of spicy sausage—*Bosna*—with your choice of toppings. Survey the five options—described in English—and choose a number (€3.50, takeout only, Mon-Fri 11:00-19:00, Sat until 18:00, Sun 15:00-19:00, hours vary with demand, Jan-Feb closed Sun, hiding down the tunnel at Getreidegasse 33 across from Eisgrotte).

Picnic supplies can be found at the well-stocked **Billa supermarket** next to the Hanuschplatz bus stop (Mon-Fri 7:40-20:00, Sat until 18:00, Sun 11:00-15:00, Griesgasse 19a). The smaller **Spar supermarket** in the train station is open long hours daily. The bustling morning **produce market** on Universitätsplatz, behind Mozart's Birthplace, isn't cheap, but it's fun (daily except Sun, best on Sat).

Rick's Tip: *Popular* **farmers markets** *pop up on Saturdays at Universitätsplatz in the Old Town, and on Thursdays around the Andräkirche in the New Town. On summer weekends, a string of craft booths with fun goodies for sale stretches along the river.*

Away from the Center

$$ Augustiner Bräustübl, a huge 1,000-seat beer garden within a monk-run brewery in the Kloster Mülln, is rustic and raw. On busy nights, it's like a Munich beer hall with no music but the volume turned up. When it's cool outside, enjoy a historic indoor setting in any of several beer-sloshed and smoke-stained halls (one of which is still for smokers). On balmy evenings, it's like a Renoir painting—but with beer breath and cigarette smoke—outdoors under chestnut trees. Students mix with tourists eating hearty slabs of grilled meat with their fingers or cold meals from the self-serve picnic counter, while children frolic on the playground kegs. For your beer: Pick up a half-liter or full-liter mug, pay the lady (*Schank* means self-serve price, *Bedienung* is the price with waiter service), wash your mug, give Mr. Keg your receipt and empty mug, and you will be made happy. Waiters only bring beer; they don't bring food—instead, go up the stairs, survey the hallway of deli counters, grab a tray, and assemble your own meal. Stick with the freshly cooked meat dishes. Or, as long as you buy a drink, you can bring in a picnic—many do (daily 15:00-23:00, Augustinergasse 4, tel. 0662/431-246, www.augustinerbier.at).

Getting There: It's about a 15-minute walk along the river (with the river on your right) from the Old Town side of the Staatsbrücke bridge. After passing the Müllnersteg pedestrian bridge, just after Café am Kai, follow the stairs up

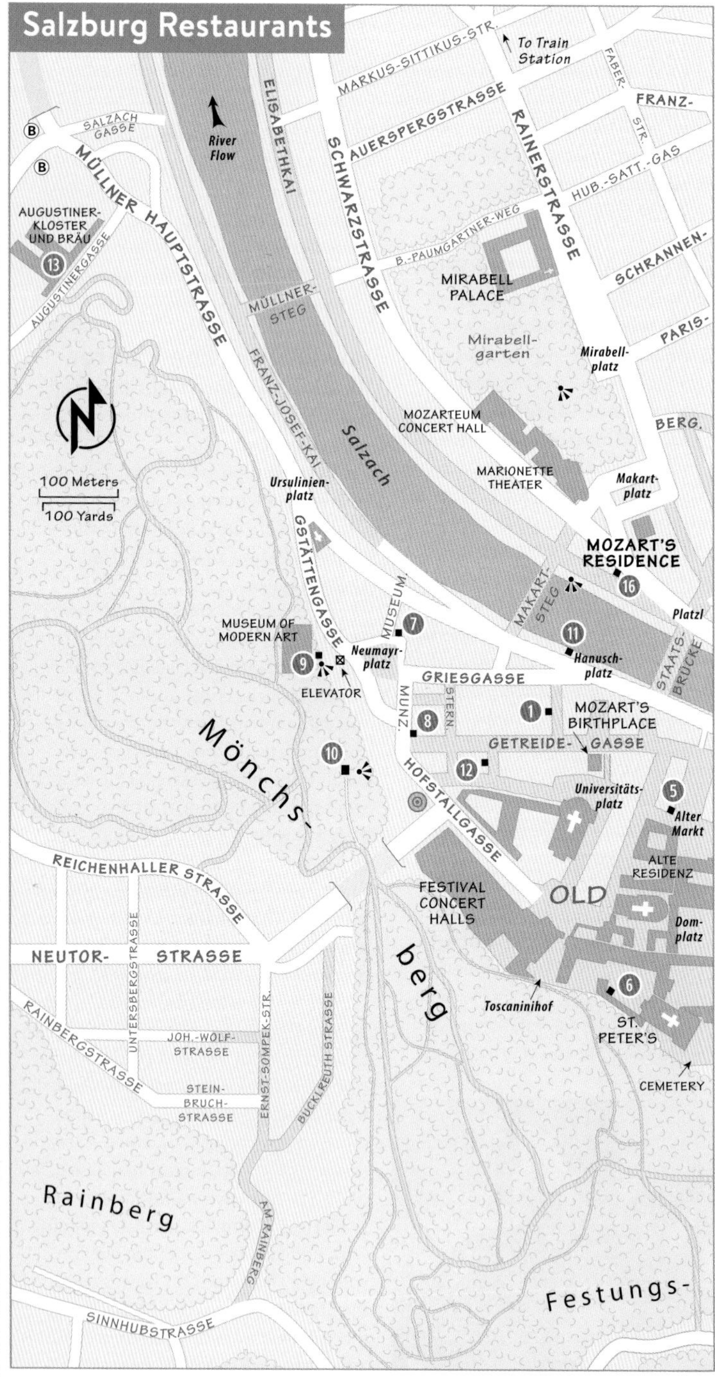
Salzburg Restaurants
To Train Station
MARKUS-SITTIKUS-STR.
FABER-STR.
FRANZ-
AUERSPERGSTRASSE
RAINERSTRASSE
HUB.-SATT.-GAS
SALZACH GASSE
River Flow
ELISABETHKAI
SCHWARZSTRASSE
MÜLLNER HAUPTSTRASSE
AUGUSTINER-KLOSTER UND BRÄU
AUGUSTINERGASSE
B.-PAUMGARTNER-WEG
SCHRANNEN-
MIRABELL PALACE
MÜLLNER-STEG
Mirabell-garten
PARIS-
Mirabell-platz
FRANZ-JOSEF-KAI
Salzach
MOZARTEUM CONCERT HALL
BERG.
100 Meters
100 Yards
MARIONETTE THEATER
Makart-platz
Ursulinien-platz
GSTÄTTENGASSE
MOZART'S RESIDENCE
MUSEUM
MAKART-STEG
Platzl
MUSEUM OF MODERN ART
Neumayr-platz
Hanusch-platz
STAATS-BRÜCKE
ELEVATOR
GRIESGASSE
MUNZ.
STERN.
MOZART'S BIRTHPLACE
GETREIDE-GASSE
Mönchs-
HOFSTALLGASSE
Universitäts-platz
Alter Markt
ALTE RESIDENZ
REICHENHALLER STRASSE
FESTIVAL CONCERT HALLS
OLD
Dom-platz
NEUTOR-STRASSE
UNTERSBERGSTRASSE
berg
Toscaninihof
RAINBERGSTRASSE
JOH.-WOLF-STRASSE
ERNST-SOMPEK-STR.
BUCKLREUTH STRASSE
ST. PETER'S
CEMETERY
STEIN-BRUCH-STRASSE
Rainberg
AM RAINBERG
Festungs-
SINNHUBSTRASSE

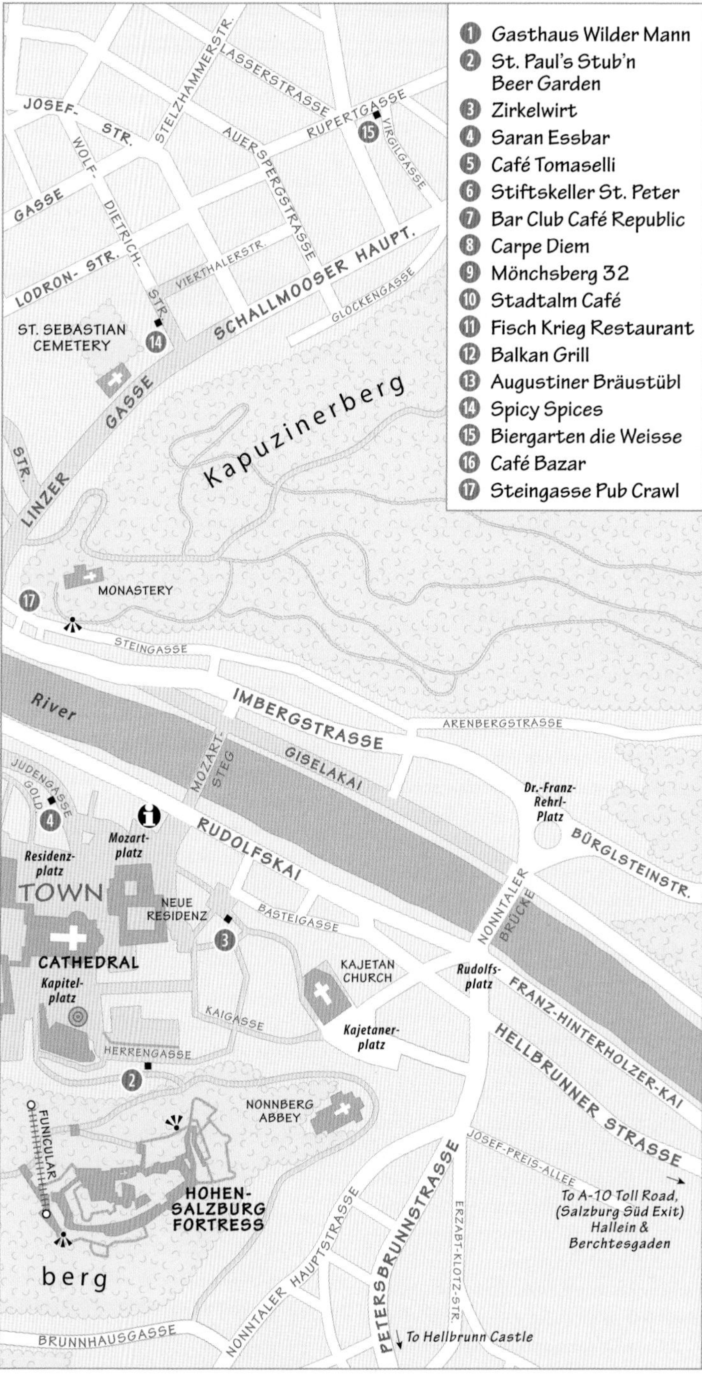
1 Gasthaus Wilder Mann
2 St. Paul's Stub'n Beer Garden
3 Zirkelwirt
4 Saran Essbar
5 Café Tomaselli
6 Stiftskeller St. Peter
7 Bar Club Café Republic
8 Carpe Diem
9 Mönchsberg 32
10 Stadtalm Café
11 Fisch Krieg Restaurant
12 Balkan Grill
13 Augustiner Bräustübl
14 Spicy Spices
15 Biergarten die Weisse
16 Café Bazar
17 Steingasse Pub Crawl
JOSEF-STR.
WOLF-DIETRICH-STR.
STELZHAMMERSTR.
LASSERSTRASSE
RUPERTGASSE
VIRGILGASSE
AUERSPERGSTRASSE
GASSE
LODRON-STR.
VIERTHALERSTR.
SCHALLMOOSER HAUPT.
GLOCKENGASSE
ST. SEBASTIAN CEMETERY
GASSE
LINZER
STR.
Kapuzinerberg
MONASTERY
STEINGASSE
River
IMBERGSTRASSE
ARENBERGSTRASSE
GISELAKAI
MOZART-STEG
JUDENGASSE
GOLD.
Mozart-platz
Residenz-platz
TOWN
RUDOLFSKAI
Dr.-Franz-Rehrl-Platz
BÜRGLSTEINSTR.
NEUE RESIDENZ
BASTEIGASSE
NONNTALER BRÜCKE
CATHEDRAL
Kapitel-platz
KAJETAN CHURCH
Rudolfs-platz
FRANZ-HINTERHOLZER-KAI
KAIGASSE
Kajetaner-platz
HERRENGASSE
HELLBRUNNER STRASSE
NONNBERG ABBEY
FUNICULAR
JOSEF-PREIS-ALLEE
HOHEN-SALZBURG FORTRESS
To A-10 Toll Road, (Salzburg Süd Exit) Hallein & Berchtesgaden
NONNTALER HAUPTSTRASSE
PETERSBRUNNSTRASSE
ERZABT-KLOTZ-STR.
berg
BRUNNHAUSGASSE
To Hellbrunn Castle

to a busy street, and cross it. From here, either continue up more stairs into the trees and around the small church (for a scenic approach to the monastery), or stick to the sidewalk as it curves around to Augustinergasse. Either way, your goal is the huge yellow building. Don't be fooled by second-rate gardens serving the same beer nearby. You can also take a bus from Hanuschplatz (#7, #8, #21, #24, #27, or #28) two stops to the Landeskrankenhaus stop, right in front of the beer garden.

Rick's Tip: *Visit the* **strudel kiosk at Augustiner Bräustübl** *and enjoy your dessert alongside the incomparable flood-lit* **views from the nearby Müllnersteg pedestrian bridge.**

North of the River

Restaurants near Linzer Gasse Hotels

$ Spicy Spices is a trippy vegetarian Indian restaurant serving tasty curry and rice, samosas, and vegan soups. It's a *namaste* kind of place, where everything's proudly organic (€7.50 specials served all day, €9.50 with soup or salad, €0.50 extra for takeout—refunded if you return the container, Mon-Fri 10:30-21:30, Sat-Sun 12:00-21:00, Wolf-Dietrich-Strasse 1, tel. 0662/870-712).

$ Biergarten die Weisse, close to the hotels on Rupertgasse, is a longtime local hit. If a beer hall can be happening, this one—modern yet with antlers—is it. Enjoy their famous beers, including fizzy wheat beer (Die Weisse Original) and seasonal offerings, alongside good, cheap traditional food in the great garden seating or in the wide variety of indoor rooms (€10-14 main courses, Mon-Sat 10:00-24:00, closed Sun, Rupertgasse 10, bus #2 to Bayerhamerstrasse or #4 to Grillparzerstrasse, tel. 0662/872-246, www.dieweisse.at).

$ Café Bazar, overlooking the river between the Mirabell Gardens and the Staatsbrücke bridge, is as close as you'll get to a Vienna coffee house in Salzburg. Their outdoor terrace is a venerable spot for a classy drink with a castle view (reasonable prices, light meals, generally Mon-Sat 7:30-19:30, Sun 9:00-18:00, July-Aug daily until 23:00 or later, Schwarzstrasse 3, tel. 0662/874-278).

Steingasse Pub Crawl

For a fun evening (post-concert?) activity, drop in on a couple of atmospheric bars along medieval Steingasse. This tranquil, tourist-free, cobbled lane is a hip local scene. The dark, trendy bars are filled with well-dressed Salzburgers lazily smoking cigarettes and talking philosophy as laid-back tunes play. Yet it's accessible to older tourists.

The following places are within about 100 yards of each other. Start at the Linzer Gasse end of Steingasse. Survey the choices before choosing the spot that's right for you (all are open until the wee hours). Most don't serve food but **Reyna** does; it's a convenient four-table pizzeria and Döner Kebab shop at #3.

Pepe Cocktail Bar, with Mexican decor and Latin music, serves cocktails and nachos (Tue-Sat 19:00-until late, closed Sun-Mon, live DJs on Sat, Steingasse 3, tel. 0662/873-662).

Saiten Sprung wins the "Best Atmosphere" award. The door is kept closed to keep out the crude and rowdy. Just ring the bell and enter its hellish interior—lots of stone and red decor, mountains of melted wax beneath age-old candlesticks, and classic '70s and '80s music. It serves cocktails and fine wine, though no food (Mon-Sat 21:00-until late, closed Sun except in Dec, Steingasse 11, tel. 0662/881-377).

Fridrich, two doors down, is an intimate little bar under an 11th-century vault, with lots of mirrors, a silver ceiling fan, and a tattered collection of vinyl determined to keep the 1970s alive. Little dishes are designed to complement drinking and socializing, though their €15 "little of everything dish" can be a meal for two (€7-15 appetizers, Thu-Tue from 18:00, closed Wed except during festival and Dec, Steingasse 15, tel. 0662/876-218).

SLEEPING

I've listed the rates you'll typically find in May, June, the first half of July, September, and October. Rates rise significantly (20-30 percent) during the music festival (mid-July-Aug), during Advent (the four weeks leading up to Christmas, when street markets are at full blast), and around Easter. Many places charge 10 percent extra for a one-night stay. Salzburg also levies a hotel tax of €1 per person per night. Remember, to call an Austrian number from a German one, dial 00-43 and then the number (minus the initial zero).

In the New Town, North of the River

Near Linzer Gasse

These listings cluster around Linzer Gasse, a lively pedestrian shopping street that's a 15-minute walk or quick bus ride from the train station and a 10-minute walk to the Old Town. If you're coming from the Old Town, simply cross the main bridge (Staatsbrücke). Linzer Gasse is straight ahead. If driving, exit the highway at Salzburg-Nord, follow Vogelweiderstrasse straight to its end, and turn right. Parking is easy at the nearby Mirabell-Congress garage on Mirabellplatz; your hotelier may be able to get you a small discount off their daily rate (about €18/day).

$$$ Altstadthotel Wolf-Dietrich, around the corner from Linzer Gasse on pedestrians-only Wolf-Dietrich-Strasse, has 40 plush rooms (half of them overlook St. Sebastian Cemetery; a third are in an annex across the street). Prices include a huge breakfast spread and an afternoon *Kaffee-und-Kuchen* snack (Db-€150-170, family deals, ask for Rick Steves discount if you book direct; nonsmoking, elevator, annex rooms have air-con, pool with loaner swimsuits, sauna, free DVD library, Wolf-Dietrich-Strasse 7, tel. 0662/871-275, www.wolf-dietrich.at, office@wolf-dietrich.at).

$$ Cityhotel Trumer Stube, three blocks from the river just off Linzer Gasse, has 20 small, attractive rooms (Db-€116-176, family rooms, ask for Rick Steves discount if you book direct and pay cash, pay less if you skip breakfast; nonsmoking, elevator, look for the flower boxes at Bergstrasse 6, tel. 0662/874-776, www.trumer-stube.at, info@trumer-stube.at).

$$ Hotel Krone 1512, about five blocks from the river, offers 23 simply furnished rooms in a building that dates to medi-

Sleep Code

$$$$ Splurge: Over €170
$$$ Pricier: €130-170
$$ Moderate: €90-130
$ Budget: €50-90
¢ Backpacker: Under €50

Hotels are classified based on the average price of a standard double room with bath in high season. Unless otherwise noted, credit cards are accepted, breakfast is included, hotel staff speak English, and Wi-Fi is available.

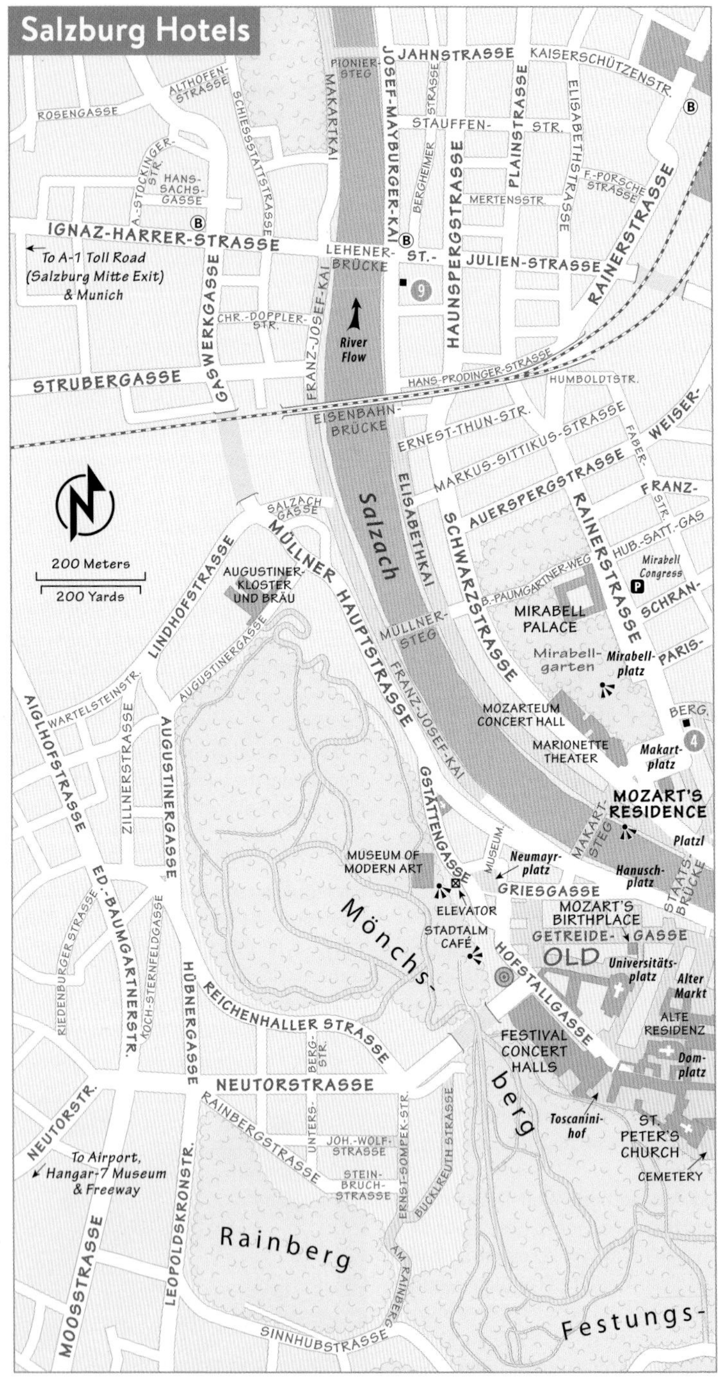
Salzburg Hotels
JAHNSTRASSE
KAISERSCHÜTZENSTR.
PIONIER-STEG
MAKARTKAI
JOSEF-MAYBURGER-KAI
PLAINSTRASSE
ELISABETHSTRASSE
STAUFFEN- STR.
ALTHOFEN-STRASSE
ROSENGASSE
SCHIESSSTATTSTRASSE
A.-STOCKINGER-STR.
HANS-SACHS-GASSE
BERGHEIMER STRASSE
HAUNSPERGSTRASSE
MERTENSSTR.
F.-PORSCHE STRASSE
RAINERSTRASSE
IGNAZ-HARRER-STRASSE
LEHENER-BRÜCKE
ST.-JULIEN-STRASSE
To A-1 Toll Road (Salzburg Mitte Exit) & Munich
GASWERKGASSE
CHR.-DOPPLER-STR.
FRANZ-JOSEF-KAI
River Flow
STRUBERGASSE
HANS-PRODINGER-STRASSE
HUMBOLDTSTR.
EISENBAHN-BRÜCKE
ERNEST-THUN-STR.
MARKUS-SITTIKUS-STRASSE
FABER-STR.
WEISER-
AUERSPERGSTRASSE
FRANZ-
Salzach
ELISABETHKAI
SCHWARZSTRASSE
SALZACH GASSE
200 Meters
200 Yards
MÜLLNER HAUPTSTRASSE
LINDHOFSTRASSE
AUGUSTINER-KLOSTER UND BRÄU
HUB.-SATT.-GAS
Mirabell Congress
B.-PAUMGARTNER-WEG
MIRABELL PALACE
SCHRAN-
MÜLLNER-STEG
Mirabell-garten
Mirabell-platz
PARIS-
AUGUSTINERGASSE
WARTELSTEINSTR.
MOZARTEUM CONCERT HALL
BERG.
MARIONETTE THEATER
Makart-platz
AIGLHOFSTRASSE
ZILLNERSTRASSE
GSTÄTTENGASSE
MOZART'S RESIDENCE
Platzl
MAKART-STEG
MUSEUM.
Neumayr-platz
MUSEUM OF MODERN ART
Hanusch-platz
STAATS-BRÜCKE
GRIESGASSE
ED.-BAUMGARTNERSTR.
ELEVATOR
MOZART'S BIRTHPLACE
Mönchs-berg
STADTALM CAFÉ
GETREIDE-GASSE
OLD
RIEDENBURGER STRASSE
KOCH-STERNFELDGASSE
HÜBNERGASSE
HOFSTALLGASSE
Universitäts-platz
Alter Markt
REICHENHALLER STRASSE
ALTE RESIDENZ
FESTIVAL CONCERT HALLS
BERG-STR.
Dom-platz
NEUTORSTRASSE
NEUTORSTR.
Toscanini-hof
ST. PETER'S CHURCH
UNTERS.
JOH.-WOLF-STRASSE
RAINBERGSTRASSE
To Airport, Hangar-7 Museum & Freeway
STEIN-BRUCH-STRASSE
CEMETERY
ERNST-SOMPEK-STR.
BUCKLREUTH STRASSE
LEOPOLDSKRONSTR.
MOOSSTRASSE
Rainberg
AM RAINBERG
Festungs-
SINNHUBSTRASSE

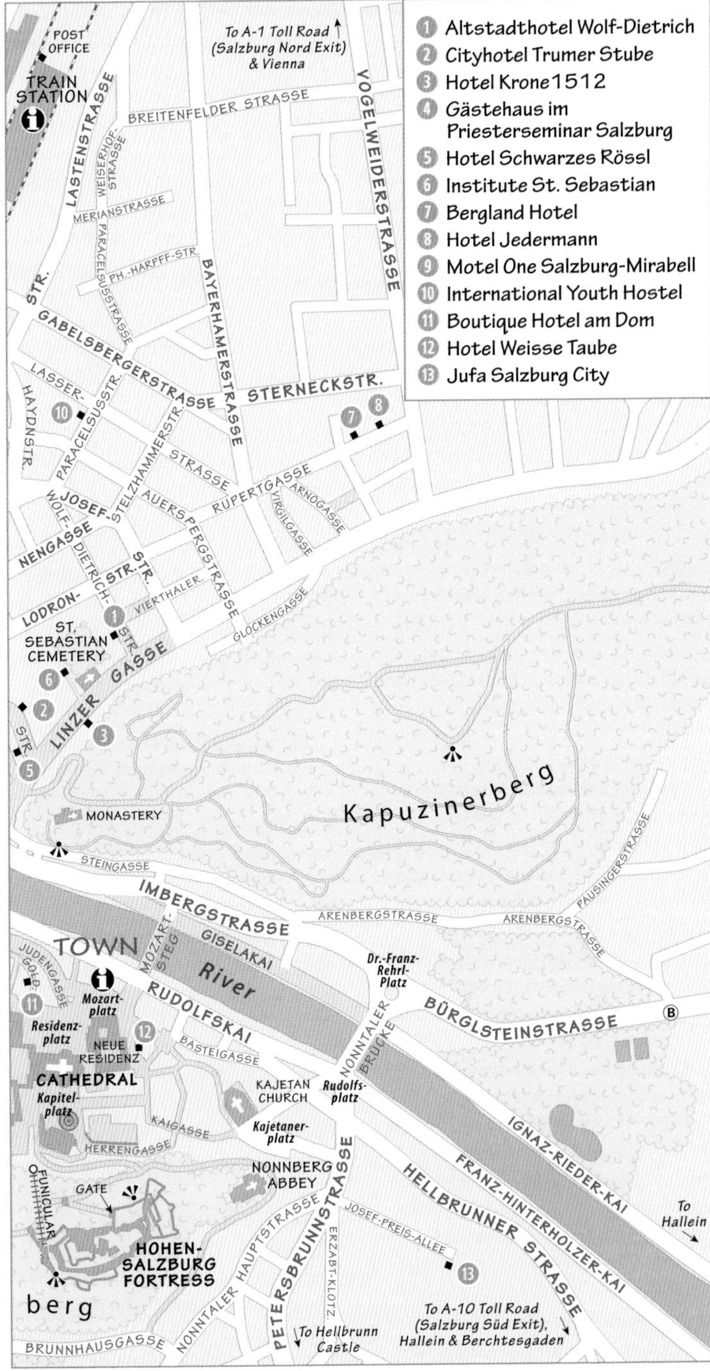

1 Altstadthotel Wolf-Dietrich
2 Cityhotel Trumer Stube
3 Hotel Krone1512
4 Gästehaus im Priesterseminar Salzburg
5 Hotel Schwarzes Rössl
6 Institute St. Sebastian
7 Bergland Hotel
8 Hotel Jedermann
9 Motel One Salzburg-Mirabell
10 International Youth Hostel
11 Boutique Hotel am Dom
12 Hotel Weisse Taube
13 Jufa Salzburg City
POST OFFICE
TRAIN STATION
To A-1 Toll Road (Salzburg Nord Exit) & Vienna
BREITENFELDER STRASSE
VOGELWEIDERSTRASSE
LASTENSTRASSE
WEISERHOF-STRASSE
MERIANSTRASSE
PARACELSUSSTRASSE
PH.-HARPFF-STR.
BAYERHAMERSTRASSE
GABELSBERGERSTRASSE
STERNECKSTR.
LASSER-
HAYDNSTR.
PARACELSUSSTR.
STELZHAMMERSTR.
STRASSE
RUPERTGASSE
ARNOGASSE
VIRGILGASSE
JOSEF-
AUERSPERGSTRASSE
NENGASSE
WOLF-DIETRICH-STR.
LODRON-
STR.
VIERTHALER-
GLOCKENGASSE
ST. SEBASTIAN CEMETERY
LINZER GASSE
MONASTERY
Kapuzinerberg
STEINGASSE
IMBERGSTRASSE
ARENBERGSTRASSE
PAUSINGERSTRASSE
TOWN
MOZART-STEG
GISELAKAI
River
JUDENGASSE
GOLD-
Mozart-platz
Residenz-platz
NEUE RESIDENZ
RUDOLFSKAI
BASTEIGASSE
Dr.-Franz-Rehrl-Platz
BÜRGLSTEINSTRASSE
NONNTALER BRÜCKE
CATHEDRAL
Kapitel-platz
KAJETAN CHURCH
Rudolfs-platz
Kajetaner-platz
KAIGASSE
HERRENGASSE
NONNBERG ABBEY
FUNICULAR
GATE
HOHEN-SALZBURG FORTRESS
berg
IGNAZ-RIEDER-KAI
FRANZ-HINTERHOLZER-KAI
HELLBRUNNER STRASSE
To Hallein
PETERSBRUNNSTRASSE
NONNTALER HAUPTSTRASSE
JOSEF-PREIS-ALLEE
ERZABT-KLOTZ-
BRUNNHAUSGASSE
To Hellbrunn Castle
To A-10 Toll Road (Salzburg Süd Exit), Hallein & Berchtesgaden

eval times. Back-facing rooms are quieter than the streetside ones. Stay awhile in their pleasant cliffside garden (Db-€98-158, family rooms and deals, ask for Rick Steves discount if you book direct and pay with cash at check-in, pay even less if you skip breakfast—bakeries and cafés nearby; elevator, loaner iPad, Linzer Gasse 48, tel. 0662/872-300, www.krone1512.at, hotel@krone1512.at).

$$ Gästehaus im Priesterseminar Salzburg occupies two floors of a dormitory for theological students that have been turned into a hotel. The 54 high-ceilinged rooms ring the stately Baroque courtyard of a grand building. Each room has a Bible and a cross, but guests need not be religious (Db-€116-128, also suites, discount if staying four or more nights, email or call when booking for July-Aug, elevator, Wi-Fi—but must borrow router and leave deposit, kitchen, laundry facilities, reception closes Mon-Sat at 18:00 or 19:00 in summer, Sun at 15:00—arrange ahead if arriving later; Dreifaltigkeitsgasse 14, tel. 0662/8774-9510, www.gaestehaus-priesterseminar-salzburg.at, gaestehaus@priesterseminar.kirchen.net).

$$ Hotel Schwarzes Rössl is a university dorm that becomes a student-run hotel each July-September. Its 56 rooms are spartan but comfortable (D-€88, Db-€106, ask for Rick Steves discount, good breakfast, no rooms rented Oct-June, just off Linzer Gasse at Priesterhausgasse 6, tel. 0662/874-426, www.academiahotels.at, salzburg@academiahotels.at).

$$ Institute St. Sebastian is in a sterile historic building next to St. Sebastian Cemetery. From October through June, the institute houses female students from various colleges and also rents 40 beds for travelers (men and women). From July through September, the students are gone, and they rent all 118 beds (including 20 twin rooms) to travelers. The building has spacious public areas, a roof garden, and a piano. The immaculate doubles come with modern baths and head-to-toe twin beds (D-€72, Db-€90, family rooms, one-night stay-€5/person extra; elevator, nonsmoking, self-service laundry-€4/load; reception closes at 21:00 or in the afternoon off-season; Linzer Gasse 41, enter through arch at #37, tel. 0662/871-386, www.st-sebastian-salzburg.at, office@st-sebastian-salzburg.at). Students like the €28 bunks in dorm rooms (free lockers). Self-service kitchens are on each floor (fridge space is free; request a key). If you need parking, request it when you book.

On Rupertgasse

These two similar hotels are about five blocks farther from the river—a breeze for drivers—but with more street noise than the places on Linzer Gasse. They're good values if you don't mind being a 15- to 20-minute walk or quick bus ride from the Old Town. From the station, take bus #2 to the Vogelweiderstrasse stop; from Hanuschplatz, take #4 to Grillparzerstrasse.

$$ Bergland Hotel is charming and classy, with 18 comfortable neo-rustic rooms (Db-€95-120, also suites, nonsmoking, elevator, pay guest computer, free parking, Rupertgasse 15, tel. 0662/872-318, www.berglandhotel.at, office@berglandhotel.at).

$$ Hotel Jedermann is tasteful and comfortable, with an artsy painted-concrete ambience, a backyard garden, and 30 rooms (Db-€119-174, family rooms, save money if you skip breakfast, nonsmoking, elevator, pay guest computer, pay parking, Rupertgasse 25, tel. 0662/873-2410, www.hotel-jedermann.com, office@hotel-jedermann.com).

Near the Train Station

$$ Motel One Salzburg-Mirabell is right along the river. Its 119 cookie-cutter rooms are small, but the staff is helpful, the decor is fun, and the lounge is inviting. It's six blocks (or a two-stop bus ride) from the train station, and a 15-minute riverside walk or short bus ride from the Old Town (Db-€103, cheaper if you skip breakfast, €20-50 more during events, elevator, guest iPad at front desk, pay parking, Elisabethkai 58, bus #1 or #2 from platform D at station to St.-Julien-Strasse—use underpass to cross road safely, tel. 0662/885-200, www.motel-one.com, salzburg-mirabell@motel-one.com).

¢ International Youth Hostel, a.k.a. the "Yo-Ho," is the most lively, handy, and American of Salzburg's backpacker havens. Welcoming anyone of any age, it offers 186 beds, cheap meals, lockers, tour discounts, and no curfew; the noise can make it hard to sleep (€18-22/person in dorms, D-€65, D with shower only-€75, family rooms, includes sheets, cheap breakfast, pay guest computer, laundry-€4/load, 6 blocks from station toward Linzer Gasse and 6 blocks from river at Paracelsusstrasse 9, tel. 0662/879-649, www.yoho.at, office@yoho.at).

In the Old Town

These first two hotels are nicely located near Mozartplatz. While cars are restricted in this area, your hotel can give you a code (punch the code into the gate near Mozartplatz) that lets you drive in to unload, pick up a map and parking instructions, and then head for the huge, €18-per-day Altstadtgarage in the mountain. You can't actually drive into the narrow Goldgasse, but you can park to unload at the end of the street.

$$$ Boutique Hotel am Dom, on the narrow Goldgasse pedestrian street, offers 15 chic, upscale rooms, some with their original wood-beam ceilings. Manager Josef promises his best rates to readers of this book who reserve directly and pay cash. The categories for double rooms are defined only by size (standard Db-€130-190, "superior" and "deluxe" doubles cost more, air-con, nonsmoking, elevator, Goldgasse 17, tel. 0662/842-765, www.hotelamdom.at, office@hotelamdom.at).

$$$ Hotel Weisse Taube has 30 comfortable rooms in a quiet, dark-wood, 14th-century building, well-located about a block off Mozartplatz (D with shower-€129-149, Db-€159-169, ask for Rick Steves discount if you reserve directly and pay cash, discount can't be combined with other deals; elevator, tel. 0662/842-404, Kaigasse 9, www.weissetaube.at, hotel@weissetaube.at).

$$ Jufa Salzburg City is a short walk from the Old Town, quietly set amidst modern university buildings. It has 132 spartan rooms, a cheap cafeteria, pleasant public spaces, and games such as ping-pong and foosball. *The Sound of Music* movie plays daily at 20:00 (Db-€100-110, family rooms, Wi-Fi in common areas, elevator, laundry-€5/load, limited pay parking, just around the east side of the castle hill at Josef-Preis-Allee 18; tel. 05/708-3613, www.jufa.eu/en, salzburg@jufa.eu). To get there from train station, take bus #3, #5, #6, or #25 to the Justizgebäude stop, then continue one block past the bushy wall, and cross Petersbrunnstrasse. Find Josef-Preis-Allee and walk a few minutes to the end—the hotel is the orange-and-green building on the right.

TRANSPORTATION

Getting Around Salzburg

By Bus

Most visitors take at least a couple of rides on Salzburg's extensive bus system. Everything in this chapter is within the *Kernzone* (core zone). Basic single-ride tickets are €2.50 from the driver, or €2 if bought at a *Tabak/Trafik* shop or (scarce) ticket machine. For midday rides, you can save with a *09/17 Kernzone* ticket (€1.40, good Mon-Sat between 9:00 and 17:00, not valid Sun or holidays, not sold on bus). For short rides, get a *Kurzstrecke* ticket (€1.30, maximum two stops in one direction, no changes, buy from driver). A *24-Stunden-Karte* day pass is good for 24 hours (€5.50 from driver, cheaper from machines and shops). Validate your ticket after purchase (insert it in the machines on board).

Get oriented using the free bus map *(Liniennetz),* available at the TI. Many lines converge at Hanuschplatz, on the Old Town side of the river, in front of the recommended Fisch Krieg Restaurant.

To get from the Old Town to the train station, catch bus #1 from the inland side of Hanuschplatz. From the other side of the river, find the Makartplatz/Theatergasse stop and catch bus #1, #3, #5, or #6.

Busy stops like Hanuschplatz and Mirabellplatz have several bus shelters; look for your bus number to double-check where you should wait.

For more info, visit www.svv-info.at, call 0662/632-900 (open 24 hours), or visit the transit-info office downstairs from bus platform C in front of the train station (Mon-Fri 6:00-19:00, Sat 7:30-15:00, closed Sun).

By Bike

Salzburg is great fun for cyclists. **A'Velo Radladen** rents bikes in the Old Town, just outside the TI on Mozartplatz, and offers 10 percent off to anyone with this book if you ask (€12/4 hours, €18/24 hours, more for electric or mountain bikes; daily 9:00-18:00, July-Aug until 19:00 but hours unreliable, shorter hours off-season and in bad weather; passport number for security deposit, mobile 0676-435-5950). Some of my recommended hotels also rent or loan bikes to guests.

By Funicular and Elevator

The Old Town is connected to the top of the Mönchsberg mountain (and great views) via funicular and elevator. The **funicular** *(Festungsbahn)* whisks you up into the imposing Hohensalzburg Fortress (included in castle admission, goes every few minutes—for details, see page 127). The **elevator** *(Mönchsberg Aufzug)* on the west side of the Old Town lifts you to the recommended Stadtalm Café, the modern art museum and its chic café, wooded paths, and more great views (see page 138 for details).

Arriving and Departing

By Plane

Salzburg's airport is easily reached by regular city buses #2, #10, and #27 (airport code: SZG, tel. 0662/85800, www.salzburg-airport.com).

By Train

The gleaming train station has all the services you need: train info, tourist info, luggage lockers and a pay WC (by platform 5), and a handy Spar supermarket (long hours daily). Ticket counters for both the Austrian and German railways are off the main hall (long hours daily). If you're looking for the TI, follow the green-and-white information signs (the blue-and-white ones lead to a railway "InfoPoint"). Next to the train station is Forum 1, a sizable shopping mall.

Getting downtown from the station is a snap. Simply step outside, find **bus platform C** (labeled *Zentrum-Altstadt*), buy a ticket from the machine, and hop on the next bus. Buses #1, #3, #5, #6, and #25 all do the same route into the city center before diverging. For most sights and Old Town hotels, get off just after the bridge, at the fifth stop (either Rathaus or Hanuschplatz, depending on the bus). For my recommended New Town hotels, get off at Makartplatz (the fourth stop), just before the bridge.

Taking a **taxi** from the train station into town doesn't make much sense as it's expensive (€2.50 drop charge, about €8 for most rides in town).

To **walk** downtown (15 minutes), turn left as you leave the station, and walk straight down Rainerstrasse, which leads under the tracks past Mirabellplatz, turning into Dreifaltigkeitsgasse. From here, you can turn left onto Linzer Gasse for some of my recommended hotels, or cross the river to the Old Town.

TRAIN CONNECTIONS

By train, Salzburg is the first stop over the German-Austrian border. This means that if Salzburg is your only stop in Austria, and you're using a rail pass that covers Germany (including the regional day ticket) but not Austria, you don't have to pay extra or add Austria to your pass to get here. Deutsche Bahn (German Railway) ticket machines at the Salzburg train station make it easy to buy tickets to German destinations. German train info: Tel. 0180-699-6633; from Austrian phone, call 00-49-180-599-6633; www.bahn.com. Austrian train info: Tel. 051-717 (to get an operator, dial 2, then 2); from German phone, call 00-43-51-717; www.oebb.at.

From Salzburg by Train to: Füssen (roughly hourly, 4 hours on fast trains, 5 hours on slow trains eligible for regional day ticket, change in Munich and sometimes in Buchloe), **Nürnberg** (hourly with change in Munich, 3 hours), **Innsbruck** (hourly, 2 hours), **Vienna** (3/hour, 2.5-3 hours), **Munich** (2/hour, 1.5 hours on fast trains, 2 hours on slower trains eligible for regional day ticket), **Frankfurt** (4/day direct, 6 hours), **Prague** (4/day, 6.5 hours with change in Linz or 7.5 hours with change in Landshut), **Venice** (5/day, 6-8 hours, change in Innsbruck or Villach, short night train option).

By Car

Mozart never drove in Salzburg's Old Town, and neither should you. The best place to park is the **park-and-ride** lot at the Alpensiedlung bus stop, near the Salzburg Süd autobahn exit. Coming on A-8 from Munich, cross the border into Austria. Take A-10 toward Hallein, and then take the next exit (Salzburg Süd) in the direction of Anif. Stay on the Alpenstrasse (road 150) for a little over 2.5 miles, following P+R signs to arrive at the park-and-ride (€5/24 hours). From the parking lot, catch bus #3 or #8 into town. The TI, in a small building next to the lot, sells bus tickets for less than bus drivers do. Alternatively, groups of 2-5 people can buy a combo-ticket from the parking lot attendant, which includes the 24-hour parking fee and a 24-hour transit pass for the whole group (€14, group must stay together).

Rick's Tip: *To drive on expressways in Austria, you need a* **toll sticker** *called a* Vignette *(€8.70/10 days, buy at the border, gas stations, car-rental agencies, or* Tabak *shops). You won't need the sticker if you* **avoid toll roads:** *To bypass the A-1 toll road between the German border and Salzburg, exit the A-8 autobahn at Bad Reichenall while you're still in Germany, take B-20, and then B-21, which becomes B-1 as it crosses the border into Austria.*

If you prefer parking lots to park-and-rides, head to the easiest, cheapest, most central parking lot—the 1,500-car Altstadtgarage, in the tunnel under the Mönchsberg (€18/day, note your slot number and which of the twin lots you're in, tel. 0662/809-900); your hotel may provide discounted parking passes. If staying in Salzburg's New Town, park at the Mirabell-Congress garage on Mirabellplatz.

Bavaria

In this picturesque corner of the Alps bordering Germany and Austria, you'll find a timeless land of fairy-tale castles, painted houses, and locals who still dress in dirndls and lederhosen. They even yodel when they're happy.

You can tour "Mad" King Ludwig II's ornate Neuschwanstein Castle, stop by the Wieskirche, a lavishly decorated Baroque church that puts the faithful in a heavenly mood, and browse through Oberammergau, Germany's woodcarving capital. A cozy castle (Linderhof) and a sky-high viewpoint (the Zugspitze) round out Bavaria's top attractions.

The region is best traveled by car, and the sights can be seen within an easy 60-mile loop. Even if you're doing the rest of your trip by train, consider renting a car for your time here (for rental offices, see page 158).

The best home base is Füssen, near the region's biggest attraction, the "King's Castles" (Neuschwanstein and Hohenschwangau). It's also the easiest option for train travelers, offering frequent connections with Munich and beyond.

Drivers could also consider cute, little, touristy Oberammergau as a home base. World-famous for its once-per-decade Passion Play, it's much sleepier the other nine years.

You could do this region as a day trip from Munich by blitzing the top sights on a bus tour (see page 35) or coming independently by train to see just the King's Castles (see page 167). But many travelers enjoy the magic of settling into this lovely region.

BAVARIA IN 2 DAYS

Reserve ahead for Neuschwanstein and Hohenschwangau to avoid wasting your time in line.

By Car: On the first day, visit Neuschwanstein and Hohenschwangau. Then choose among the sights that cluster nearby: the Tegelberg Gondola, Tegelberg Luge, Royal Crystal Baths, and a stroll in Füssen.

On the second day, drive a loop that includes the rugged Zugspitze, Oberammergau, and Linderhof Castle. If the glorious Wieskirche appeals, you could fit it in on either day, or when you're departing (or arriving in) the region.

Note that the first day's activities could

be done by public transit; you could put off renting a car until the morning of the second day.

Without a Car: Using Füssen as a base, bus or bike to Neuschwanstein, Hohenschwangau, and the Tegelberg Gondola and Luge. Fill out the day by exploring Füssen.

For the second day, I'd suggest taking a bus tour or hiring a driver guide to take you to other sights in the area. Otherwise, you could day-trip by bus to the Wieskirche or Oberammergau.

FÜSSEN

Dramatically situated under a renovated castle on the lively Lech River, Füssen (FEW-sehn) has been a strategic stop since ancient times. Its main street was once part of the Via Claudia Augusta, which crossed the Alps in Roman times. Going north, early travelers could follow the Lech River downstream to the Danube, and then cross over to the Main and Rhine valleys—a route now known to modern travelers as the "Romantic Road." Today, while Füssen is overrun by tourists in the summer, few venture to the back streets...which is where you'll find its real charm. Apart from my self-guided walk and the Füssen Heritage Museum, there's little to do here—but it's a fine base for visiting the King's Castles.

Orientation

Füssen's roughly circular old town huddles around its castle and monastery, along the Lech River. The train station, TI, and many shops are at the north end of town, and my recommended hotels and eateries are within easy walking distance. Roads spin off in all directions (to the lake, to Neuschwanstein, to Austria). Halfway between Füssen and the German border (as you drive, or a nice woodsy walk from town) is the **Lechfall,** a thunderous waterfall (with a handy WC).

Tourist Information: The TI is in the center of town (Mon-Fri 9:00-18:00, Sat 10:00-14:00, Sun 10:00-12:00 but closed Sun mid-Sept-June, 3 blocks from station at Kaiser-Maximilian-Platz 1, tel. 08362/93850, www.fuessen.de). The TI can help you find a room, and after hours, the little self-service info pavilion near the front of the TI features an automated room-finding service with a phone to call hotels.

Hotel Card: Your hotel tax entitles

The charming riverside town of Füssen

BAVARIA AT A GLANCE

Near Füssen

▲▲▲**Neuschwanstein Castle** The ultimate fairy-tale castle, dreamed up by "Mad" King Ludwig. **Hours:** Ticket center open daily April-Sept 8:00-17:30, Oct-March 9:00-15:30. The first tour of the day departs an hour after the ticket office opens and the last normally departs 30 minutes after it closes: April-Sept at 9:00 and 18:00, Oct-March at 10:00 and 16:00. See page 172.

▲▲▲**Hohenschwangau Castle** King Ludwig's boyhood home, a less famous but more historic castle than nearby Neuschwanstein. **Hours:** Same hours as Neuschwanstein. See page 170.

▲▲**Mary's Bridge** Pedestrian bridge overlooking Neuschwanstein, offering the best view of the castle. **Hours:** Always open. See page 174.

▲**Royal Crystal Baths** A pool/sauna complex outside Füssen, made for relaxing. **Hours:** Daily 9:00-22:00, Fri-Sat until 23:00; nude swimming everywhere Tue and Fri after 19:00. See page 163.

▲**Pöllat Gorge** An uncrowded hiking trail down from Neuschwanstein, a pleasant alternative to the road. **Hours:** Closed in winter. See page 174.

▲**Tegelberg Gondola** A scenic ride to the mountain's 5,500-foot summit, popular with view-seekers and paragliders. **Hours:** First ascent daily at 9:00; last descent April-Oct at 17:00, mid-Dec-March at 16:00, closed Nov-mid-Dec. See page 175.

▲**Tegelberg Luge** A fun summer luge course, next to the gondola's valley station. **Hours:** Typically April-June Mon-Fri 13:00-17:00, Sat-Sun 10:00-17:00; July-Sept daily 10:00-18:00. See page 176.

Beyond Füssen

▲▲**Wieskirche** Germany's greatest Rococo-style church with a divinely decorated interior. **Hours:** Daily April-Oct 8:00-20:00, Nov-March 8:00-17:00; interior closed to sightseers during services: Sun 8:00-13:00; Tue, Wed, and Sat 10:00-12:00; and Fri 17:00-20:00. See page 176.

▲▲**Linderhof Castle** Exquisite, likeable mini Versailles, another creation of "Mad" King Ludwig. **Hours:** Daily April-mid-Oct 9:00-18:00, mid-Oct-March 10:00-16:00 (grotto closed mid-Oct-mid-April). See page 182.

▲▲**Zugspitze** Germany's tallest mountain at 9,700 feet, accessible by lifts or cogwheel train, with summit restaurants, shops, telescopes, and on a clear day, far-reaching views. **Hours:** Cable car departs at least every 30 minutes; daily 8:00-16:15. See page 184.

▲**Oberammergau** Adorable town well-known for woodcarving, frescoed buildings, and the Passion Play that it puts on every decade. See page 178.

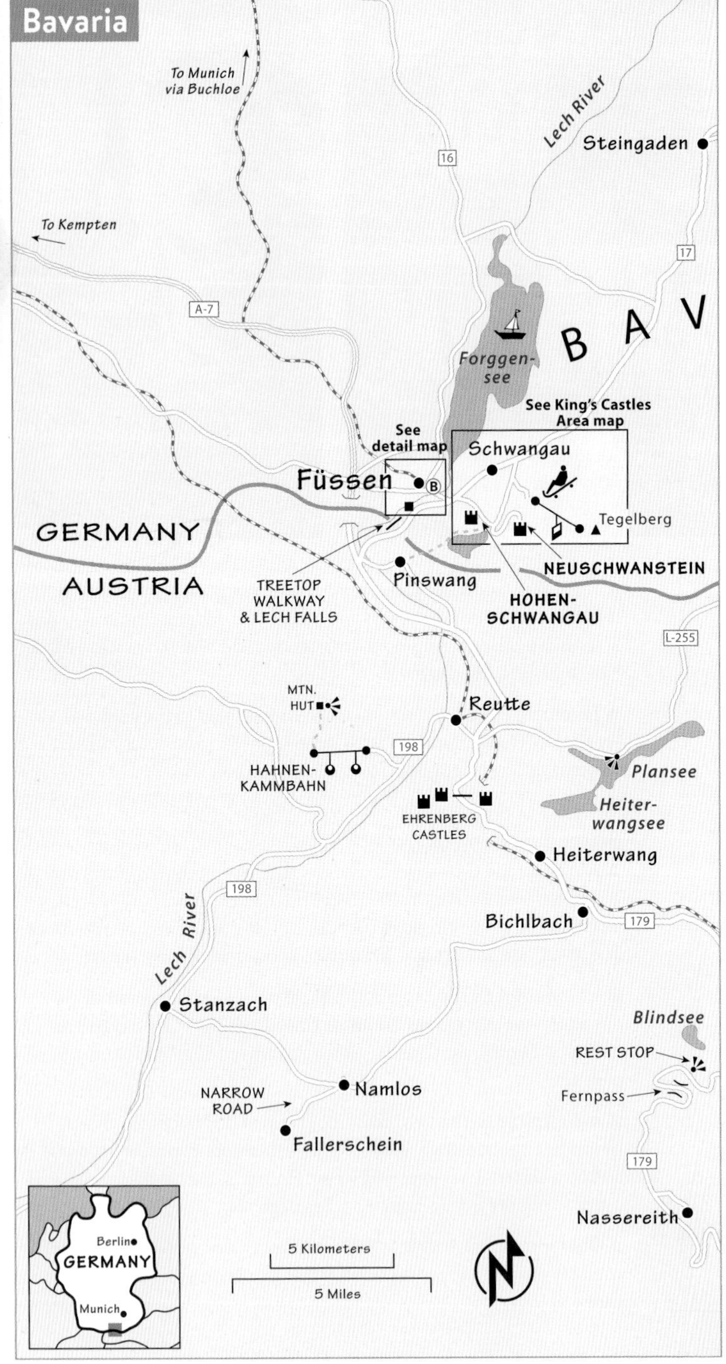
Bavaria
To Munich via Buchloe
To Kempten
Lech River
Steingaden
16
17
A-7
BAV
Forggen-see
See King's Castles Area map
See detail map
Schwangau
Füssen
B
GERMANY
AUSTRIA
Tegelberg
NEUSCHWANSTEIN
HOHEN-SCHWANGAU
Pinswang
TREETOP WALKWAY & LECH FALLS
L-255
MTN. HUT
Reutte
198
HAHNEN-KAMMBAHN
Plansee
Heiter-wangsee
EHRENBERG CASTLES
Heiterwang
198
Bichlbach
179
Lech River
Stanzach
Blindsee
REST STOP
Fernpass
NARROW ROAD
Namlos
Fallerschein
179
Nassereith
Berlin
GERMANY
Munich
5 Kilometers
5 Miles

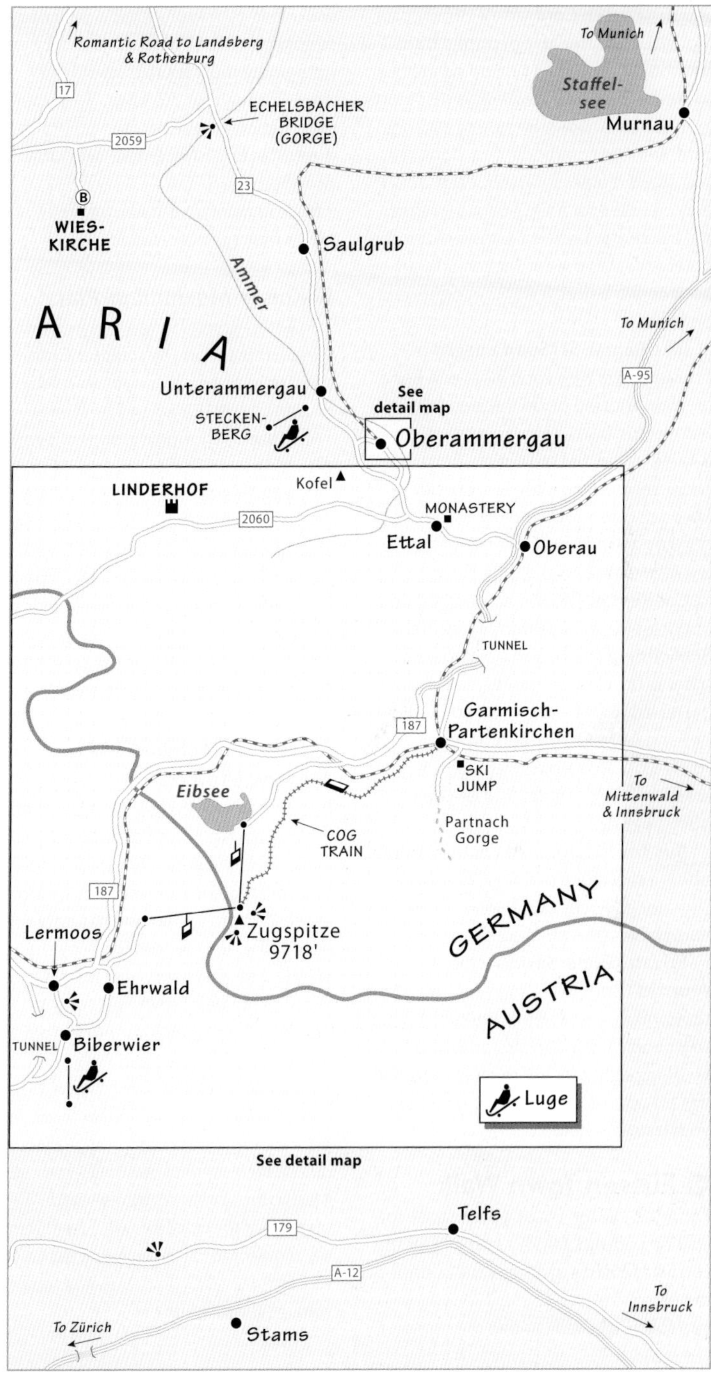

Romantic Road to Landsberg & Rothenburg
17
2059
ECHELSBACHER BRIDGE (GORGE)
23
WIES-KIRCHE
Ammer
Saulgrub
A R I A
To Munich
Staffel-see
Murnau
To Munich
A-95
Unterammergau
STECKEN-BERG
See detail map
Oberammergau
Kofel
LINDERHOF
2060
MONASTERY
Ettal
Oberau
TUNNEL
Garmisch-Partenkirchen
187
SKI JUMP
To Mittenwald & Innsbruck
Eibsee
COG TRAIN
Partnach Gorge
187
Zugspitze 9718'
GERMANY
AUSTRIA
Lermoos
Ehrwald
TUNNEL
Biberwier
Luge
See detail map
179
Telfs
A-12
To Innsbruck
To Zürich
Stams

you to a **Füssen Card,** an electronic pass that gives you **free use of public transit** in the immediate region (including the bus to Neuschwanstein), as well as **discounts** at major attractions. Be sure to ask for a card; some accommodations won't tell you about it unless you request it. You may be asked for a €3-5 deposit; return the card before you leave town. After the hotel activates the card, it can take an hour or two before it works at sights and on buses.

Bike Rental: Ski Sport Luggi outfits sightseers with good bikes and tips on two-wheeled fun in the area (also has electric bikes, Mon-Fri 9:00-12:00 & 14:00-18:00, Sat until 13:00, Sun until 12:00; shorter hours off-season, call ahead to reserve; Luitpoldstrasse 11, tel. 08362/505-9155, mobile 0176-2205-3080, www.ski-sport-luggi.de).

Car Rental: Two rental agencies are about an €8 taxi ride from the center: **Schlichtling** (Mon-Fri 8:00-18:00, Sat 9:00-12:00, closed Sun, Hiebeler Strasse 49, tel. 08362/922-122, www.schlichtling.de) and **Auto Osterried/Europcar** (daily 8:00-19:00, past waterfall on road to Austria, Tiroler Strasse 65, tel. 08362/6381).

Bus Tours: European Castles Tours offers a six-hour Bavarian Highlights Tour (but not daily, check schedule, http://europeancastlestours.com).

Private Guide: Silvia Skelac, an American born to German parents, offers tours, hikes, and walks (€80/half-day, up to 4 people). She can also drive you to far-flung sights (figure roughly €120/half-day for up to 4; mobile 0664-978-7488, yodel4silvia@yahoo.com).

➔ Füssen Town Walk

For most, Füssen is just a home base for visiting Ludwig's famous castles. But the town has a rich history and hides some evocative corners, as you'll see when you follow this self-guided orientation walk. This 45-minute stroll is designed to get you out of the cutesy old cobbled core where most tourists spend their time. Throughout the town, "City Tour" information plaques explain points of interest in English (in more detail than I've provided).

• *Begin at the square in front of the TI, three blocks from the train station.*

Ⓐ *Kaiser-Maximilian-Platz*

The entertaining "Seven Stones" fountain on this square, by sculptor Christian Tobin, was built in 1995 to celebrate Füssen's 700th birthday. The stones symbolize community, groups of people gathering, conviviality...each is different, with "heads" nodding and talking. It's granite on granite. The moving heads are not connected, and nod only with waterpower. It's frozen in winter, but is a popular and splashy play zone for kids on hot summer days.

• *Walk along the pedestrian street towards the glass building. You'll soon see...*

Ⓑ *Hotel Hirsch and Medieval Towers*

Recent renovations have restored some of the original Art Nouveau flavor to Hotel Hirsch, which opened in 1904. In those days, aristocratic tourists came here to appreciate the castles and natural wonders of the Alps. Across the busy street stands one of two surviving towers from Füssen's medieval town wall (c. 1515), and next to it is a passageway into the old town.

• *Cross the street and walk 50 yards farther down the busy street to another tower. Just before it, you'll see an information plaque and an archway where a small street called Klosterstrasse emerges through a surviving piece of the old town wall. Step through the smaller pedestrian archway, walk along Klosterstrasse for a few yards, and turn left through the gate into the...*

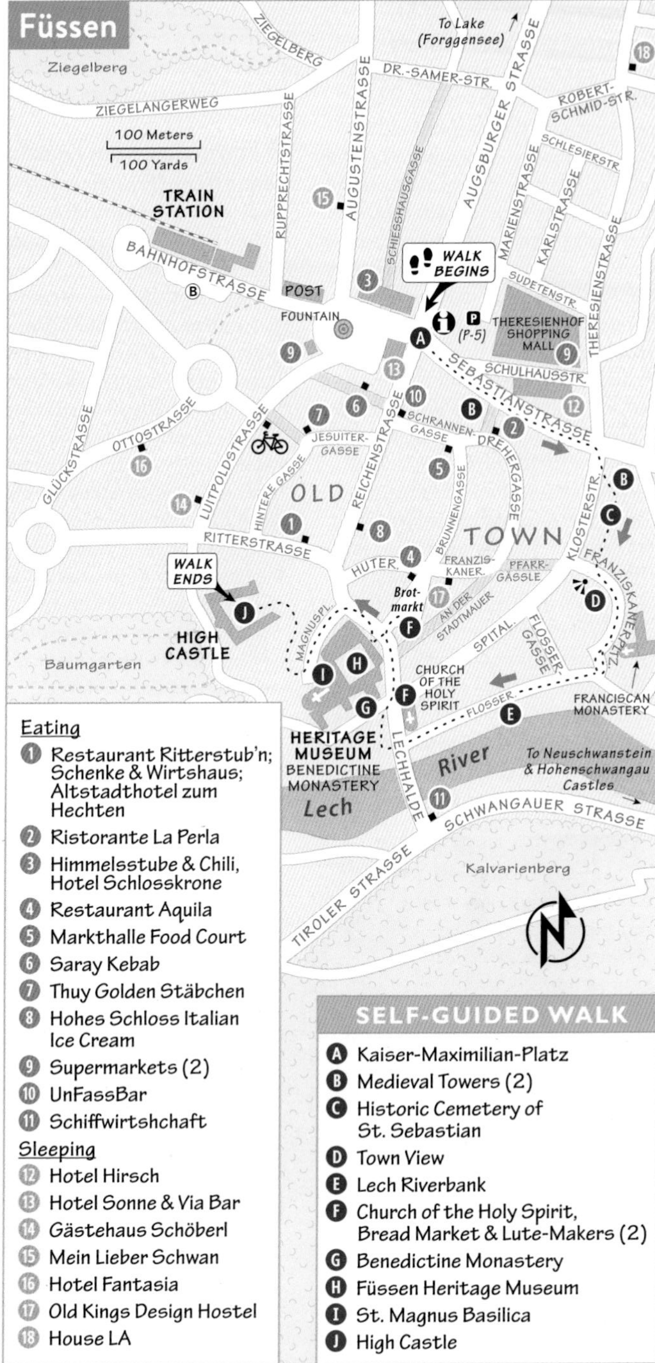
Füssen
Ziegelberg
ZIEGELANGERWEG
ZIEGELBERG
100 Meters
100 Yards
TRAIN STATION
BAHNHOFSTRASSE
POST
FOUNTAIN
To Lake (Forggensee)
DR.-SAMER-STR.
AUGSBURGER STRASSE
AUGUSTENSTRASSE
RUPPRECHTSTRASSE
SCHIESSHAUSGASSE
ROBERT-SCHMID-STR.
SCHLESIERSTR.
MARIENSTRASSE
KARLSTRASSE
THERESIENSTRASSE
SUDETENSTR.
WALK BEGINS
(P-5)
THERESIENHOF SHOPPING MALL
SCHULHAUSSTR.
SEBASTIANSTRASSE
OTTOSTRASSE
GLÜCKSTRASSE
LUITPOLDSTRASSE
JESUITER-GASSE
HINTERE GASSE
REICHENSTRASSE
SCHRANNEN-GASSE
DREHERGASSE
BRUNNENGASSE
OLD TOWN
KLOSTERSTR.
FRANZISKANERPLTZ.
RITTERSTRASSE
HUTER
FRANZIS-KANER.
PFARR-GASSLE
Brot-markt
AN DER STADTMAUER
WALK ENDS
HIGH CASTLE
Baumgarten
MAGNUSPL.
SPITAL
FLOSSER-GASSE
CHURCH OF THE HOLY SPIRIT
FRANCISCAN MONASTERY
FLOSSER
HERITAGE MUSEUM
BENEDICTINE MONASTERY
LECHHALDE
Lech River
To Neuschwanstein & Hohenschwangau Castles
SCHWANGAUER STRASSE
TIROLER STRASSE
Kalvarienberg
Eating
1 Restaurant Ritterstub'n; Schenke & Wirtshaus; Altstadthotel zum Hechten
2 Ristorante La Perla
3 Himmelsstube & Chili, Hotel Schlosskrone
4 Restaurant Aquila
5 Markthalle Food Court
6 Saray Kebab
7 Thuy Golden Stäbchen
8 Hohes Schloss Italian Ice Cream
9 Supermarkets (2)
10 UnFassBar
11 Schiffwirtshchaft
Sleeping
12 Hotel Hirsch
13 Hotel Sonne & Via Bar
14 Gästehaus Schöberl
15 Mein Lieber Schwan
16 Hotel Fantasia
17 Old Kings Design Hostel
18 House LA
SELF-GUIDED WALK
A Kaiser-Maximilian-Platz
B Medieval Towers (2)
C Historic Cemetery of St. Sebastian
D Town View
E Lech Riverbank
F Church of the Holy Spirit, Bread Market & Lute-Makers (2)
G Benedictine Monastery
H Füssen Heritage Museum
I St. Magnus Basilica
J High Castle

C Historic Cemetery of St. Sebastian (Alter Friedhof)

This peaceful oasis of Füssen history, established in the 16th century, fills a corner between the town wall and the Franciscan monastery. It's technically full, and only members of great and venerable Füssen families—who already own plots here—can join those who are buried (free, daily 8:00-19:00, off-season until 17:00).

Immediately inside the gate and on the right is the tomb of Domenico Quaglio, who painted the Romantic scenes decorating the walls of Hohenschwangau Castle in 1835. Across the cemetery, on the old city wall (beyond the church), is the World War I memorial, listing all the names of men from this small town killed in that devastating conflict (along with each one's rank and place of death). A bit to the right, also along the old wall, is a statue of the hand of God holding a fetus—a place to remember babies who died before being born. And in the corner, farther to the right, is a gated area with the simple wooden crosses of Franciscans who lived just over the wall in the monastery. Strolling the rest of the grounds, note the fine tomb art from many ages collected here, and the loving care this community gives its cemetery.

• *Exit on the far side, just past the dead Franciscans, and turn right just outside the gate.*

D Town View from Franciscan Monastery (Franziskaner-kloster)

Enjoy a fine view over the medieval town with an alpine backdrop. In the distance you'll see the Church of St. Magnus and the High Castle (the former summer residence of the Bishops of Augsburg), where this walk ends. The tall, skinny smokestack (c. 1886) is a reminder that when Ludwig built Neuschwanstein the textile industry (linen and flax) was very big here. Retrace your steps and follow the wall of the Franciscan Monastery, which still has big responsibilities but only a handful of monks in residence. Walk all the way to the far end of the monastery chapel and peek inside to see if it's open.

• *Go around the corner, down the stairway, and turn left through the medieval "Bleachers' Gate" (marked 5½) to the...*

E Lech Riverbank

This low end of town, the flood zone, was the home of those whose work depended

Walking in Füssen's old town

Bavarian Craftsmanship

The scenes you'll see painted on the sides of houses in Bavaria are called *Lüftlmalerei.* The term came from the name of the house ("Zum Lüftl") owned by a man from Oberammergau who pioneered the practice in the 18th century. As the paintings became popular during the Counter-Reformation Baroque age, their themes focused on Christian symbols, saints, and stories that reinforced the Catholic Church's authority. Some scenes also depicted an important historical event that took place in that house or town.

Especially in the northern part of this region, you'll see *Fachwerkhäuser*—half-timbered houses. A timber frame outlines the wall, which was traditionally filled in with a mixture of wicker and clay. These are most often found inside fortified cities (such as Rothenburg) that were once strong and semi-independent. Farther south, you'll see sturdy, white-walled masonry houses with woodwork on the upper stories and an overhanging roof. Many Bavarian homes and hotels have elaborate wooden paneling and furniture, often beautifully carved or made from special sweet-smelling wood.

on the river—bleachers, rafters, and fishermen. In its heyday, the Lech River was an expressway to Augsburg (about 70 miles to the north). Around the year 1500, the rafters established the first professional guild in Füssen. Cargo from Italy passed here en route to big German cities farther north. Rafters would assemble rafts and pile them high with wine, olive oil, and other goods—or with people needing a lift. If the water was high, they could float all the way to Augsburg in as little as one day. There they'd disassemble their raft and sell off the lumber along with the goods they'd carried, then make their way home to raft again. Today you'll see no modern-day rafters here, as there's a hydroelectric plant just downstream.

• *Walk upstream a bit, appreciating the river's milky color, and turn right to head inland immediately after crossing under the bridge.*

F ***Church of the Holy Spirit, Bread Market, and Lute-Makers***

Climbing uphill, you pass the colorful Church of the Holy Spirit (Heilig-Geist-Spitalkirche) on the right. As this was the church of the rafters, their patron, St. Christopher (with the Baby Jesus on his shoulder), is prominent on the facade.

Church of the Holy Spirit

Today it's the church of Füssen's old folks' home (it's adjacent—notice the easy-access skyway).

Farther up the hill on the right is Bread Market Square *(Brotmarkt)*, with a fountain honoring a famous 16th-century lute-making family, the Tieffenbruckers. In its day, Füssen (surrounded by forests) was a huge center of violin- and lute-making, with about 200 workshops. Today only three survive.

• *Backtrack and go through the archway into the courtyard of the former...*

G Benedictine Monastery (Kloster St. Mang)

From 1717 until secularization in 1802, the monastery was the power center of town. Today, the courtyard is popular for concerts, and the building houses the City Hall and Füssen Heritage Museum.

H Füssen Heritage Museum

This is Füssen's one must-see sight (€6, €7 combo-ticket includes painting gallery and castle tower; April-Oct Tue-Sun 11:00-17:00, closed Mon; shorter hours and closed Mon-Thu Nov-March; tel. 08362/903-146, www.museum.fuessen.de).

Füssen Heritage Museum

Pick up the loaner English translations and follow the one-way route. In the St. Anna Chapel, you'll see the famous *Dance of Death*. This was painted shortly after a plague devastated the community in 1590. It shows 20 social classes, each dancing with the Grim Reaper—starting with the pope and the emperor. The words above say, essentially, "You can say yes or you can say no, but you must ultimately dance with death." Leaving the chapel, you walk over the metal lid of the crypt. Upstairs, exhibits illustrate the rafting trade, and violin- and lute-making (with a complete workshop). The museum also includes an exquisite *Kaisersaal* (main festival hall), an old library, an exhibition on textile production, and a King Ludwig-style "castle dream room."

• *Leaving the courtyard, hook left around the old monastery, and go uphill. The square tower marks...*

I St. Magnus Basilica (Basilika St. Mang)

St. Mang (or Magnus) is Füssen's favorite saint. In the eighth century, he worked miracles all over the area with his holy rod. For centuries, pilgrims came from far and wide to enjoy art depicting the great works of St. Magnus. Above the altar dangles a glass cross containing his relics (including that holy stick). Just inside the door is a chapel remembering a much more modern saint—Franz Seelos (1819-1867), the local boy who went to America (Pittsburgh and New Orleans) and lived such a righteous life that in 2000 he was beatified by Pope John Paul II.

• *From the church, turn right and walk uphill towards the castle entrance (or you can continue straight for a little break in the shady Baumgarten).*

J High Castle (Hohes Schloss)

This castle, long the summer residence of the Bishop of Augsburg, houses a painting gallery (the upper floor is labeled in English) and a tower with a view over the town and lake (included in Füssen Heritage Museum combo-ticket, same hours as museum). The courtyard is worth even a few minutes to admire the striking perspective tricks painted onto its flat walls.

• *From below the castle, the city's main drag (once the Roman Via Claudia, and now Reichenstrasse) leads from a grand statue of St. Magnus past lots of shops, cafés, and strolling people to Kaiser-Maximilian-Platz and the TI...where you began.*

Sights

▲ROYAL CRYSTAL BATHS (KÖNIGLICHE KRISTALL-THERME)

This pool/sauna complex just outside Füssen is the perfect way to relax on a rainy day, or to cool off on a hot one. The main part of the complex (downstairs), called the *Therme*, contains two heated indoor pools and a café; outside, you'll find a shallow kiddie pool, a lap pool, a heated *Kristallbad* with massage jets and a whirlpool, and a salty mineral bath. The extensive saunas upstairs are well worth the few extra euros, as long as you're OK with nudity. (Swimsuits are required in the downstairs pools, but *verboten* in the upstairs saunas.) You'll see pool and sauna rules in German all over, but don't worry—just follow the locals' lead.

To enter the baths, first choose the length of your visit and your focus (big outdoor pool only, all ground-floor pools but not the saunas, or the whole enchilada—a flier explains all the prices in English). You'll get a wristband and a credit-card-sized ticket with a bar code. Insert that ticket into the entry gate, and keep it—you'll need it to get out. Enter through the yellow changing stalls—where you'll change into your bathing suit—then choose a storage locker (€1 coin deposit). When it's time to leave, reinsert your ticket in the gate—if you've gone over the time limit, feed extra euros into the machine.

Cost and Hours: Baths only-€12/2 hours, €19/4 hours, €24/all day; saunas-about €5-6 extra; they rent towels and bathrobes and sell swimsuits; daily 9:00-22:00, Fri-Sat until 23:00; nude swimming everywhere Tue and Fri after 19:00; tel. 08362/819-630, www.kristalltherme-schwangau.de.

Getting There: From Füssen, drive, bike, or walk across the river, turn left toward Schwangau, and then, about a mile later, turn left at signs for *Kristall-Therme*. It's at Am Ehberg 16.

Eating

$ Restaurant Ritterstub'n offers delicious, reasonably priced German grub, fish, salads, veggie plates, gluten-free options, and a fun kids' menu. They have three eating zones: modern decor in front, traditional Bavarian in back, and a courtyard (€8-16 main courses, smaller portions available for less, €6.50 lunch specials, €19 three-course fixed-price dinners, Tue-Sun 11:30-14:00 & 17:30-22:00, closed Mon, Ritterstrasse 4, tel. 08362/7759, www.restaurant-ritterstuben.de).

$ Schenke & Wirtshaus, inside Altstadthotel zum Hechten, dishes up hearty Bavarian dishes in a cozy setting, specializing in pike *(Hecht)* pulled from the Lech River (€8-16 main courses, salad bar, daily 11:00-21:00, Ritterstrasse 6, tel. 0836/91600, www.hotel-hechten.com).

$ Ristorante La Perla is an Italian restaurant with a classic rosy interior, streetside tables, and a hidden courtyard out back (€8-12 pizzas and pastas, €12-22 meat and fish dishes, seasonal specials, daily 11:00-22:00, Nov-Jan closed 14:30-17:30 and all day Mon, Drehergasse 44, tel. 08362/7155).

$ Himmelsstube, inside Hotel Schlosskrone right on Füssen's main traffic circle, has a traditional dining room and a winter garden. They serve daily breakfast including a huge €17 Sunday brunch buffet, a €10 weekday lunch buffet, and dinner—with live zither music most Fridays and Saturdays (€10-25 main course, Mon-Sat

7:30-10:30 & 11:30-14:30 & 18:00-22:00, Sun 7:30-13:00 & 18:00-22:00, Prinzregentenplatz 2, tel. 08362/930-180, www.schlosskrone.de). The hotel's second restaurant, **Chili,** serves Mediterranean dishes.

$$ Restaurant Aquila serves modern German and Italian-influenced dishes in a simple indoor setting and at outdoor tables on little Brotmarkt square (€10-18 main courses, serious €10 salads, Wed-Mon 11:30-21:30, closed Tue, Brotmarkt 9, tel. 08362/6253, www.aquila-fuessen.de).

The fun **Markthalle food court** offers a wide selection of affordable wurst-free food. Located in an old warehouse from 1483, it's now home to a fishmonger, deli counters, a fruit stand, a bakery, and a wine bar. Buy your food from one of the vendors, park yourself at any one of the tables, then look up and admire the Renaissance ceiling (Mon-Fri 8:00-18:30, sometimes later, Sat 8:00-15:00, closed Sun, corner of Schrannengasse and Brunnengasse).

$ Saray Kebab, at the outer end of the Luitpold-Passage, is the town's favorite Middle Eastern takeaway joint (Mon-Sat 11:00-23:00, Luitpoldstrasse 1, tel. 08362/2847). **$ Thuy Golden Stäbchen** serves a mix of Vietnamese, Chinese, and Thai food on a deserted back street with outdoor tables and a castle view (daily 10:00-22:00, Hinteregasse 29, tel. 08362/939-7714).

Hohes Schloss Italian Ice Cream is a popular *gelateria* on the main drag (Reichenstrasse 14).

For **picnic supplies,** try bakeries and butcher shops *(Metzger),* which frequently have ready-made sandwiches. Other options are the discount **Netto** supermarket, at the roundabout across from Hotel Schlosskrone, or the mid-range **REWE** in the Theresienhof shopping complex (both open Mon-Sat 7:00-20:00, closed Sun).

After dark, locals gather at the **UnFass-Bar,** on Füssen's main drag, for drinks and small bites (Tue-Sat 10:00-22:00, closed Sun-Mon, Reichenstrasse 32, tel. 08362/929-6688). The **Via Bar,** in Hotel Sonne, has an inviting patio. **Schiffwirtschaft,** just across the river, attracts a younger crowd with live music and late nights (Tue-Sat 17:00-24:00, closed Sun-Mon).

Sleeping

All recommended accommodations are within a few handy blocks of the train station and the town center. Parking is easy; some hotels also have their own lot or garage. Prices listed are for one-night stays in high season (mid-June-Sept). Most hotels give about 5-10 percent off for two-night stays and prices drop by 10-20 percent off-season. Competition is fierce, so shop around.

Rick's Tip: *Ask your hotelier for a* **Füssen Card,** *which gives you* **free use of public transit** *in the immediate region (including the bus to Neuschwanstein), as well as* **discounts** *at major attractions.*

Big Hotels in the Center of Town

$$$ Hotel Schlosskrone is a formal hotel with 62 rooms and all the amenities. It also runs two recommended restaurants and a fine pastry shop (standard Db-€155, bigger Db-€179, Db with balcony-€189, family rooms, pricey suites, air-con in some rooms, elevator, free sauna and fitness center, spa, playroom, parking-€10/day, Prinzregentenplatz 2, tel. 08362/930-180, www.schlosskrone.de, rezeption@schlosskrone.de).

$$$ Hotel Hirsch is an old-style, family-run, 53-room hotel that takes pride in tradition. Rooms with historical and landscape themes are a fun splurge (standard Db-€140-155, theme Db-€180-190, book direct on their website for best prices, family rooms, elevator, nice rooftop terrace, free parking, Kaiser-Maximilian-Platz 7, tel. 08362/93980, www.hotelfuessen.de, info@hotelhirsch.de).

$$$ Hotel Sonne has a modern flair in its 50 stylish and unique rooms (Db-€135, fancier Db-€145-195, family rooms, 5 percent discount if you book on their website, air-con in some rooms, elevator, free laundry machine, free sauna and fitness center, pay parking, kitty-corner from TI at Prinzregentenplatz 1, on GPS you may need to enter Reichenstrasse 37, tel. 08362/9080, www.hotel-sonne.de, info@hotel-sonne.de).

Mid-Priced Hotels and Pensions

$$ Altstadthotel zum Hechten offers 34 modern rooms in a friendly, family-run hotel with borderline-kitschy decor. Extras include a travel-resource/game room, borrowable hiking gear, miniature bowling alley in basement, and a recommended restaurant (Db-€108, bigger Db-€125, family rooms, often less if you stay 3 nights, ask when you reserve for discount with this book, tall people ask for longer beds, lots of stairs, pay parking, positioned right under Füssen Castle in the old-town pedestrian zone at Ritterstrasse 6, on GPS you may need to enter Hinteregasse 2, tel. 08362/91600, www.hotel-hechten.com, info@hotel-hechten.com).

$ Gästehaus Schöberl rents six attentively furnished and spacious rooms on a quiet street just off the main drag. One room is in the owners' house, and the rest are in the building next door (Db-€85, family rooms, cash only, free parking, Luitpoldstrasse 14-16, tel. 08362/922-411, www.schoeberl-fuessen.de, info@schoeberl-fuessen.de).

$$ Mein Lieber Schwan, a block from the train station, has four superbly outfitted apartments, each with a double bed, sofa bed, kitchen, and antique furnishings. The catch is the three-night minimum stay in high season (Sb-€77-88, Db-€89-100, Tb-€107-116, Qb-€124-133, cash or PayPal only, no breakfast, free parking, laundry facilities, garden, from station turn left at traffic circle to Augustenstrasse 3, tel. 08362/509-980, www.meinlieberschwan.de, fewo@meinlieberschwan.de).

$$ Hotel Fantasia has 16 trendy rooms adorned with violet paint and pictures of King Ludwig that might make the nuns who once lived here blush (Db-€99-129, family rooms, small discount if you book on their website, breakfast-€8, pay parking, peaceful garden, trampoline,

Sleep Code

$$$$ Splurge: Over €170
$$$ Pricier: €130-170
$$ Moderate: €90-130
$ Budget: €50-90
¢ Backpacker: Under €50

Hotels are classified based on the average price of a standard double room with bath in high season. Unless otherwise noted, credit cards are accepted, breakfast is included, hotel staff speak English, and Wi-Fi is available.

Ottostrasse 1, tel. 08362/9080, www.hotel-fantasia.de, info@hotel-fantasia.de).

Budget Beds

¢ Old Kings Design Hostel shoehorns two eight-person dorms and three doubles into an old townhouse. While the quarters are tight (all the rooms share two bathrooms), the central location, creative decor, and reasonable prices are enticing (dorm bed-€24, D-€60, breakfast-€5, kitchen, laundry-€5/load, reception open daily 7:30-12:00 & 16:00-21:00, buried deep in the pedestrian zone at Franziskanergasse 2, tel. 08362/883-7385, www.oldkingshostel.com, info@oldkingshostel.com).

¢ House LA has two branches. The backpacker house has 11 basic, clean, mostly four-bed dorm rooms about a 10-minute walk from the station (dorm bed-€18, D-€49, breakfast-€3, free parking, Wachsbleiche 2). A second building has five family apartments with kitchen and bath, each sleeping 4 to 6 people (apartment-€60-90, depends on number of people and season—mention Rick Steves for best price, breakfast-€3, free parking, 6-minute walk back along tracks from station to von Freybergstrasse 26; contact info for both: tel. 08362/607-366, mobile 0170-624-8610, www.housela.de, info@housela.de). Both branches rent bikes (€9/day) and have laundry facilities (€8/load).

Transportation

Arriving and Departing

BY CAR

Füssen is known for its traffic jams, and you can't drive into the old town. The most convenient lots (follow signs) are the underground P-5 (near the TI) and the aboveground P-3 (off Kemptener Strasse).

BY TRAIN

The train station is two blocks from the center of town and the TI. Train info: toll tel. 0180-699-6633, www.bahn.com.

From Füssen to: Munich (hourly, 2 hours, some change in Buchloe); **Salzburg** (roughly hourly, 4 hours on fast trains, 5 hours on slow trains eligible for Bayern-Ticket, change in Munich and sometimes in Buchloe); **Rothenburg ob der Tauber** (hourly, 5-6 hours, look for connections with only 3 changes—often in Augsburg, Treuchtlingen, and Steinach); **Frankfurt** (hourly, 5-6 hours, 1-2 changes).

BY BUS

Buses to Neuschwanstein and elsewhere leave from a parking lot next to the station.

From Füssen to: Neuschwanstein (bus #73 or #78, most continue to Tegelberg lift station after castles, at least hourly, 10 minutes, buses #9606 and #9651 may also make the trip); **Wieskirche** (bus #73, #9606, or #9651; 4-6 buses/day, 45-60 minutes); **Oberammergau** (bus #9606, 4-5/day, 1.5 hours, bus sometimes starts as #73 and changes number to #9606 en route—confirm with driver that bus is bound for Oberammergau); **Zugspitze** (possible as day trip via bus #74 to Reutte, then train to Ehrwald or Garmisch-Partenkirchen, allow up to 3.5 hours total to reach the top).

BY ROMANTIC ROAD BUS

The northbound Romantic Road bus departs Füssen at 8:00 (and arrives in Munich at 10:40 and Rothenburg at 16:20); the southbound bus arrives in Füssen at 20:30 (daily, mid-April-late Oct only, bus stop is at train station, www.romanticroadcoach.de). A rail pass gets you a 20 percent discount on the bus (without using up a day of a flexipass). The bus is much slower than the train, especially to Rothenburg; the only reason to take the bus is that the northbound bus gives you a brief stop at the Wieskirche and other sights along the way, and requires no changes. (The southbound bus stops at the Wieskirche, but after the church has closed.) For more info, see page 216.

THE KING'S CASTLES

Two miles from Füssen, you'll find the otherworldly "King's Castles" of Neuschwanstein and Hohenschwangau. With fairy-tale turrets in a fairy-tale alpine setting built by a fairy-tale king, these castles are understandably a huge hit. The older Hohenschwangau, King Ludwig's boyhood home, is less famous but more historic. The more dramatic Neuschwanstein, which inspired Walt Disney, is the one everyone visits. I recommend visiting both and hiking above Neuschwanstein to Mary's Bridge. Reservations are a magic wand that smooths out your visit.

Getting There

If arriving by **car,** note that road signs in the region refer to the sight as *Königsschlösser,* not Neuschwanstein. There's plenty of parking (all lots-€6). The first lots require more walking. The most convenient lot, by the lake (#4, *Parkplatz am Alpsee*), is up the small road past the souvenir shops and ticket center.

From Füssen: Those without cars can catch **bus** #73 or #78 (generally departs Füssen's train station at :05 past the hour, 10 minutes; a few departures of #9606 and #9651 also make this trip). A regional day ticket (see "Rick's Tip," this page) or the guest card available from your hotel (see page 153) lets you ride for free. The bus drops you at the TI (note return times); it's a one-minute walk from there to the castle ticket office. When returning, note that buses #73 and #78 pointing left (with your back to the TI) are headed to Füssen, while the same numbers pointing right are going elsewhere.

Other ways to get from Füssen to the castles: Take a **taxi** (€11 one-way), ride a rental **bike** (it's a level two miles), or—if you're in a pinch—**walk** (less than an hour).

Day-Tripping from Munich: If coming by train, make a castle tour reservation and take a train leaving at least four hours before your reserved castle entry. (The train to Füssen takes over two hours, getting from Füssen to the castle ticket office by bus takes another half-hour, and you must be there an hour before your tour.) Trains from Munich leave hourly at :53 past the hour. So, if you take the 9:53 train, you can make a 14:00 castle tour. If you reserve a castle tour for 11:00, you'll need to pack breakfast and take the 6:53 train (confirm train times in advance).

Rick's Tip: *Rather than buy point-to-point train tickets,* **day-trippers from Munich should buy the regional day ticket for Bavaria,** *which covers buses and slower regional trains, including the bus between Füssen and the castles at a low price (€23/day for the first person plus €5 for each additional person). The only catch is that on weekdays, the pass isn't valid before 9:00.*

Orientation

Cost: Neuschwanstein and Hohenschwangau cost €12 apiece. A "Königsticket" combo-ticket for both castles costs €23. Children under age 18 (accompanied by an adult) are admitted free.

Rick's Tip: *Don't confuse the* ***Mehrtagesticket*** **pass** *with the* **pointless combination ticket** *for "Mad" Ludwig's castles, which costs the same (€24) but covers only three castles—Neuschwanstein, Linderhof, and Herrencheimsee (farther east and not covered in this book).*

Sightseeing Pass: The Bavarian Palace Department offers a **14-day ticket** (called the ***Mehrtagesticket***) that covers admission to Neuschwanstein (but not Hohenschwangau) and Linderhof; the Residenz and Nymphenburg Palace in Munich; as well as other castles and palaces in Bavaria (€24, €44 family/partner pass,

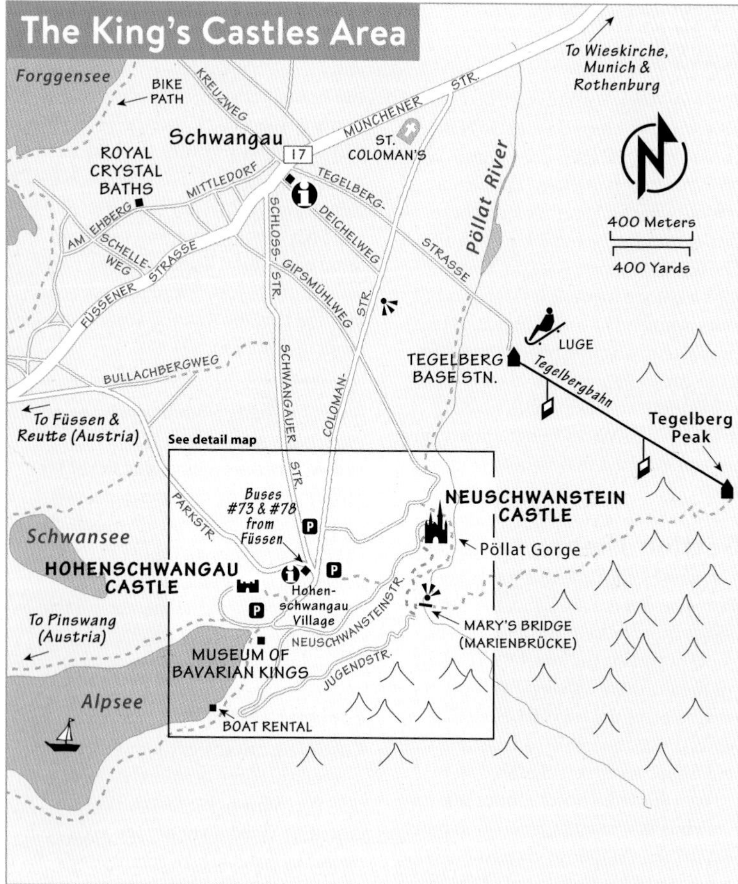

purchase at participating sights or online at www.schloesser.bayern.de). If you are planning to visit at least three of these sights within a two-week period, the pass will likely pay for itself.

Hours: The ticket center, located at street level between the two castles, is open daily April-Sept 8:00-17:30, Oct-March 9:00-15:30. The first castle tour of the day departs an hour after the ticket office opens and the last normally departs 30 minutes after it closes: April-Sept at 9:00 and 18:00, Oct-March at 10:00 and 16:00.

Reservations: Reserve ahead, particularly for holidays and weekends in peak season (June-Oct—especially in July-Aug, when slots can book up several days in advance). Reservations cost €1.80 per person per castle, and must be made online at least two days in advance (no later than 15:00 local time, www.hohenschwangau.de). A few hotels can book these tickets for you with enough notice. Pick up your reserved tickets an hour before the appointed entry time, as it takes a while to walk up to the castles. Show up late and they may have given your slot to someone else (but will likely help you make another reservation). If you know a few hours in advance that you're running late, call the office (tel.

"Mad" King Ludwig (1845-1886)

Tragic Ludwig II (a.k.a. "Mad" King Ludwig) ruled Bavaria for 22 years until his death in 1886 at the age of 40. Bavaria was weak. Ludwig's only political options were to "rule" either as a pawn of Prussia or a pawn of Austria. Rather than deal with politics in Bavaria's capital, Munich, Ludwig frittered away his time at his family's hunting palace, Hohenschwangau. He spent much of his adult life constructing his fanciful Neuschwanstein Castle—like a kid builds a tree house—on a neighboring hill upon the scant ruins of a medieval castle. Here and in his other projects (such as Linderhof Castle), he strove to evoke medieval grandeur while embracing the state-of-the-art technology of the Industrial Age in which he lived. Neuschwanstein had electricity, running water, and a telephone (but no Wi-Fi).

Ludwig was a true romantic. His best friends were artists, poets, and composers such as Richard Wagner. His palaces are wallpapered with misty medieval themes—especially those from Wagnerian operas.

Although Ludwig spent 17 years building Neuschwanstein, he lived in it only 172 days. Soon after he moved in (and before his vision for the castle was completed), Ludwig was declared mentally unfit to rule Bavaria and taken away. Two days after this eviction, Ludwig was found dead in a lake. To this day, people debate whether the king committed suicide or was murdered.

08362/930-830); they may rebook you at no charge.

Ticket Times: Tickets, whether reserved in advance or bought on the spot, come with admission times. If you miss your appointed tour time, you can't get in. To tour both castles, you must do Hohenschwangau first (logical, since this gives a better introduction to King Ludwig's short life). You'll get two tour times: Hohenschwangau and then, two hours later, Neuschwanstein.

Arrival: Make the **ticket center** your first stop. If you have a reservation, stand in the short line for picking up tickets. If you don't have a reservation...welcome to the very long line. Arrive by 8:00 in summer, and you'll likely be touring at 9:00. During August, the busiest month, tickets for English tours can run out by around noon. If you don't have a reservation, get here by 11:00 to beat day-trippers from Munich, who tend to take the morning train—with a bus connection arriving at the castles by about 11:15.

Getting Up to the Castles: From the ticket booth, Hohenschwangau is an easy 10-minute **walk** up the paved path past the bus parking, or for a quicker ascent just zigzag up to the big yellow castle using the ramp/stairs behind Hotel Müller. Neuschwanstein is a moderately steep, 30-minute hike in the other direction (also well-signed—the most direct and least steep approach begins across the street from the ticket center).

A **shuttle bus** departs every few minutes from the parking lot just below

Hohenschwangau (occasionally full or on break) and drops you off near Mary's Bridge (Marienbrucke), leaving you a steep, 10-minute downhill walk to the castle—so be sure to see the view from Mary's Bridge before hiking down (€1.80 one-way, €2.60 round-trip not worth it since you have to hike uphill to the bus stop for your return trip).

Horse-drawn carriages, which leave from in front of Hotel Muller, are slower than walking and stop below Neuschwanstein, leaving you a five-minute uphill hike (€6 up, €3 down). Be warned that both these options can have long lines; you might wait up to 45 minutes, making it slower than walking. With time, here's the most economical and least strenuous plan: Ride the bus to Mary's Bridge for the view, hike down to Neuschwanstein, and then catch the horse carriage from below the castle back down to the parking lot (round-trip cost: €4.80). If you're on a tight schedule, consider taking the bus back down, as carriages can be unpredictable. Carriages also run to Hohenschwangau (€4.50 up, €2 down).

Entry Procedure: For each castle, wait in the courtyard for your ticket number to light up on the board. When it does, power through the mob and go to the turnstile. Warning: You must use your ticket while your number is still on the board. If you space out, you'll miss your entry window and won't get in.

Services: A TI, bus stop, ATM, pay WC, lockers, pay computer, and post machine cluster around the main intersection a couple hundred yards before you get to the ticket office (TI open daily April-Sept 10:00-17:30, Oct-March 10:00-16:00, tel. 08362/819-765, www.schwangau.de).

While the tiny bathrooms inside the castles themselves are free, you'll pay to use the WCs elsewhere.

Eating: For the best value, bring a packed lunch. The park by the Alpsee (the nearby lake) is ideal for a picnic, although you're not allowed to sit on the grass—only on the benches. You can also eat out on the lake in one of the old-fashioned rowboats (rented by the hour in summer).

The restaurants in the "village" at the foot of Neuschwanstein are mediocre and overpriced. There are no grocery stores nearby, but you'll find plenty of German fare at the stand next to Hotel Alpenstuben (between the TI and ticket center), as well as sandwiches and hot dogs across from the TI. For a sit-down meal, the yellow **Bräustüberl restaurant** serves the cheapest grub (€6-11 gut-bomb grill meals, daily 11:00-17:00, next to the maypole). Up near Neuschwanstein itself (near the horse carriage drop-off) is another cluster of overpriced eateries.

The Castles

The two castles complement each other perfectly. But if you have to choose one, Neuschwanstein's wow factor—inside and out—is undeniable.

▲▲▲HOHENSCHWANGAU CASTLE

Standing quietly below Neuschwanstein, the big, yellow Hohenschwangau Castle is where Ludwig spent his summers as a young boy. Originally built in the 12th century, it was ruined by Napoleon. Ludwig's father, King Maximilian II, rebuilt it in 1830. Hohenschwangau (hoh-en-SHVAHN-gow, loosely translated as "High Swan-land") was used by the royal family as a summer hunting lodge until 1912. The Wittelsbach family, which ruled Bavaria for nearly seven centuries, still owns the place (and lived in the annex—today's shop—until the 1970s).

The interior decor (mostly Neo-Gothic, like the castle itself) is harmonious, cohesive, and original—all done in 1835, with paintings inspired by Romantic themes. As you tour the castle, imagine how the paintings must have inspired young Ludwig. For 17 years, he lived here at his dad's place and followed the construction of his dream castle across the way—you'll see the telescope still set up—

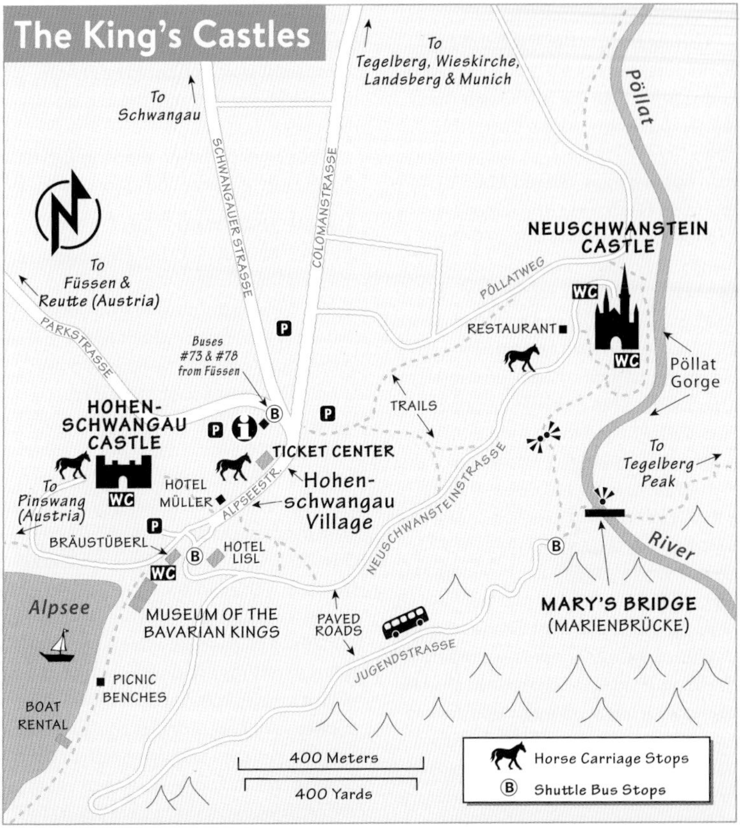

The King's Castles

To Schwangau
To Tegelberg, Wieskirche, Landsberg & Munich
Pöllat
SCHWANGAUER STRASSE
COLOMANSTRASSE
NEUSCHWANSTEIN CASTLE
To Füssen & Reutte (Austria)
PÖLLATWEG
WC
RESTAURANT
PARKSTRASSE
P
Buses #73 & #78 from Füssen
WC
Pöllat Gorge
HOHENSCHWANGAU CASTLE
B
P
TRAILS
TICKET CENTER
To Tegelberg Peak
To Pinswang (Austria)
WC
HOTEL MÜLLER
ALPSEESTR.
Hohenschwangau Village
NEUSCHWANSTEINSTRASSE
P
BRÄUSTÜBERL
B
HOTEL LISL
B
River
WC
Alpsee
MUSEUM OF THE BAVARIAN KINGS
PAVED ROADS
MARY'S BRIDGE (MARIENBRÜCKE)
JUGENDSTRASSE
PICNIC BENCHES
BOAT RENTAL
400 Meters
400 Yards
Horse Carriage Stops
B Shuttle Bus Stops

Hohenschwangau Castle

and directed at Neuschwanstein.

Visiting the Castle: The excellent 30-minute tours give a better glimpse of Ludwig's life than the more-visited and famous Neuschwanstein Castle tour. Tours here are smaller (35 people rather than 60) and more relaxed. You'll explore rooms on two floors—the queen's rooms, and then, upstairs, the king's. (Conveniently, their bedrooms were connected by a secret passage.) You'll see photos and busts of Ludwig and his little brother, Otto; some Turkish-style flourishes (to please the king, who had been impressed after a visit to the Orient); countless swans—try to find them (honoring the Knights of Schwangau, whose legacy the Wittelsbachs inherited); over-the-top gifts the Wittelsbachs received from their adoring subjects; and paintings of VIGs (very important Germans, including Martin Luther—who may or may not have visited here—and an infant Charlemagne).

One of the most impressive rooms is the Banquet Hall (also known as the Hall of Heroes); one vivid wall mural depicts a savage, yet bloodless, fifth-century barbarian battle. Just as the castle itself had running water and electricity despite its historic appearance, its Romantic decor presents a sanitized version of the medieval past, glossing over inconvenient details. You'll also see Ludwig's bedroom, which he inherited from his father. He kept most of the decor (including the nude nymphs frolicking over his bed), but painted the ceiling black and installed transparent stars that could be lit from the floor above to create the illusion of a night sky.

Banquet Hall

After the tour is over, wind through the castle gardens where Ludwig once played.

▲▲▲NEUSCHWANSTEIN CASTLE

Imagine "Mad" King Ludwig as a boy, climbing the hills above his dad's castle, Hohenschwangau, dreaming up the ultimate fairy-tale castle. Inheriting the throne at the young age of 18, he had the power to make his dream concrete and stucco. Neuschwanstein (noy-SHVAHN-shtine, roughly "New Swanstone") was designed first by a theater-set designer...then by an architect. While it was built upon the ruins of an old castle and looks medieval, Neuschwanstein is modern iron-and-brick construction with a sandstone veneer—only about as old as the Eiffel Tower. It feels like something you'd see at a home show for 19th-century royalty. Built from 1869 to 1886, it's the epitome of the Romanticism popular in 19th-century Europe. Construction stopped with Ludwig's death (only a third of the interior was finished), and within six weeks, tourists were paying to go through it.

During World War II, the castle took on a sinister role. The Nazis used Neuschwanstein as one of their primary secret storehouses for stolen art. After the war, Allied authorities spent a year sorting through and redistributing the art, which filled 49 rail cars from this one location alone. It was the only time the unfinished rooms were put to use.

Visiting the Castle: Today, guides herd groups of 60 through the castle, giving an interesting—if rushed—30-minute tour. (While you're waiting for your tour time to pop up on the board, climb the stairs up to the upper courtyard to see more of the exterior, which isn't covered on your tour.) Once inside, you'll go up and down more than 300 steps, visiting 15 lavish rooms with their original furnishings and fanciful wall paintings—mostly based on Wagnerian opera themes.

Rick's Tip: *In the morning, your initial* **view of Neuschwanstein** *may be hazy and disappointing. Later in the day, the sun drops down into the pasture, lighting up Neuschwanstein magnificently. Regardless of the time of day, the* **best accessible view is from Mary's Bridge,** *an easy 10-minute hike from the castle.*

Ludwig's extravagant throne room, modeled in a Neo-Byzantine style to emphasize his royal status, celebrates six valiant Christian kings (whose mantle Ludwig clearly believed he had donned) under a huge gilded-bronze chandelier. The exquisite two-million-stone mosaic floor is a visual encyclopedia of animals and plant life. The most memorable stop may be the king's gilded-lily bedroom, with his elaborately carved canopy bed (with a forest of Gothic church spires on top), washstand (filled with water piped in from the Alps), and personal chapel. After passing through Ludwig's living room and a faux grotto, you'll climb to the fourth floor for the grand finale: the Singers' Hall, an ornately decorated space filled with murals depicting the story of Parzival, the legendary medieval figure with whom Ludwig identified.

After the tour, wedge yourself through the crowded gift shop and past the WCs and a café to see the 13-minute video (runs continuously, English subtitles). This uses historical drawings and modern digital modeling to tell the story of how the castle was built, and illustrates all the unfinished parts of Ludwig's vision (more prickly towers, a central chapel, a fancy view terrace, an ornate bathhouse, and more). Finally, you'll see a digital model of Falkenstein—a whimsical, over-the-top, never-built castle that makes Neuschwanstein look stubby. Falkenstein occupied Ludwig's fantasies the year he died.

Then head downstairs to the kitchen (state of the art in its day for this high-tech king). You'll see a room lined with fascinating drawings (described in English) of the castle plans, as well as a large castle model.

After the tour ends, you could go up to Mary's Bridge for the view, or take the Pöllat Gorge trail down.

Storybook Neuschwanstein Castle

Sights near the Castles

▲▲MARY'S BRIDGE (MARIENBRÜCKE)

Before or after the Neuschwanstein tour, climb up to Mary's Bridge to marvel at Ludwig's castle, just as Ludwig did. Jockey with a United Nations of tourists for the best angle. This bridge was quite an engineering accomplishment 100 years ago. (Access to the bridge is closed in bad winter weather, but many travelers walk around the barriers to get there—at their own risk, of course.)

For an even more glorious castle view, the courageous can hike even higher: After crossing the bridge, you'll see very rough, steep, unofficial trails crisscrossing the hillside on your left. If you're willing to ignore the *Lebensgefahr* (danger of death) signs, you can scamper up to the bluff just over the bridge.

The trail connecting Neuschwanstein to Mary's Bridge is also scenic, with views back on Neuschwanstein's facade in one direction, and classic views of Hohenschwangau—perched on its little hill between lakes, with cut-glass peaks on the horizon—in the other.

▲PÖLLAT GORGE (PÖLLATSCHLUCHT)

If it is open, the river gorge that slices into the rock just behind Neuschwanstein's lofty perch is a more scenic—and less crowded—alternative to shuffling back down the main road. While it takes an extra 15 minutes or so, it's well worth it. You'll find the trailhead just above the Neuschwanstein exit, on the path toward Mary's Bridge (look for *Pöllatschlucht* signs; gorge trail slippery when wet and closed in winter).

You'll begin by walking down a steep, well-maintained set of concrete stairs, with Germany's finest castle looming through the trees. Then you'll pop out along the river, passing a little beach (with neatly stacked stones) offering a view up at the grand waterfall that gushes beneath Mary's Bridge. From here, follow the river as it goes over several smaller waterfalls—and stroll for a while along steel walkways and railings that help make this slippery area safer. After passing an old wooden channel used to harness the power of all that water, you'll hit level ground; turn left and walk through a pleasantly untouristy residential settlement back toward the TI.

Mary's Bridge straddles the Pöllat Gorge.

Luge Lesson

Taking a wild ride on a summer luge (pronounced "loozh") is a quintessential alpine experience. In German, it's called a *Sommerrodelbahn* ("summer toboggan run"). To try one of Europe's great accessible thrills (€3-8), take the lift up to the top of a mountain, grab a wheeled, sled-like go-cart, and scream back down the mountainside on a banked course. Then take the lift back up and start all over again.

Luge courses are highly weather-dependent, and can close at the slightest hint of rain. If the weather's questionable, call ahead to confirm that your preferred luge is open. Stainless-steel courses are more likely than concrete ones to stay open in drizzly weather.

Operating the sled is simple: Push the stick forward to go faster, pull back to apply brakes. Be cautious on your first run; even a novice can go very, very fast. To avoid a bumper-to-bumper traffic jam, let the person in front of you get as far ahead as possible before you start. You'll emerge from the course with a windblown hairdo and a smile-creased face.

Along with the Tegelberg Luge near Neuschwanstein Castle, there's a luge course near Oberammergau (double seats—good for kids—at Unterammergau, www.steckenberg.de; see page 180) and another across the border in Austria (near the Zugspitze, at Biberwier, www.bergbahnen-langes.at).

▲TEGELBERG GONDOLA (TEGELBERGBAHN)

Just north of Neuschwanstein is a fun play zone around the mighty Tegelberg Gondola, a scenic ride to the mountain's 5,500-foot summit. At the top on a clear day, you get great views of the Alps and Bavaria and the vicarious thrill of watching hang gliders and paragliders. Weather permitting, scores of adventurous Germans line up and leap from the launch ramp at the top of the lift. From the top of Tegelberg, it's a steep and demanding 2.5-hour hike down to Ludwig's castle. (Avoid the treacherous trail directly below the gondola.) Around the gondola's valley station, you'll find a playground, a cheery eatery, the stubby remains of an ancient Roman villa, and a summer luge ride.

Cost and Hours: €19.40 round-trip, €12.40 one-way; first ascent daily at 9:00; last descent April-Oct at 17:00, mid-Dec-March at 16:00, closed Nov-mid-Dec; 4/hour, 5-minute ride to the top,

Tegelberg Gondola

Zipping downhill on a luge

in bad weather call first to confirm, tel. 08362/98360, www.tegelbergbahn.de.

Getting There: From the castles, most #73 and #78 buses from Füssen continue to the Tegelbergbahn valley station (5-minute ride). It's a 30-minute walk or 10-minute bike ride from the castles.

▲TEGELBERG LUGE

Next to the gondola's valley station is a summer luge course (*Sommerrodelbahn*). A summer luge is like a bobsled on wheels. This course's stainless-steel track is heated, so it's often dry and open even when drizzly weather shuts down the concrete luges. A funky cable system pulls riders (in their sleds) to the top without a ski lift.

Cost and Hours: €3.60/ride, shareable 6-ride card-€15.30; hours vary but typically April-June Mon-Fri 13:00-17:00, Sat-Sun 10:00-17:00; July-Sept daily 10:00-18:00; may open for season earlier in spring or stay open later in fall if weather is good; in bad weather call first to confirm, waits can be long in good weather; no children under age 3, ages 3-8 may ride with an adult, tel. 08362/98360, www.tegelbergbahn.de.

WIESKIRCHE

Germany's greatest Rococo-style church, this "Church in the Meadow"—worth ▲▲—looks as brilliant now as the day it floated down from heaven. Overripe with decoration but bright and bursting with beauty, this church is a divine droplet, a curly curlicue, the final flowering of the Baroque movement.

Orientation

Cost and Hours: Donation requested, daily April-Oct 8:00-20:00, Nov-March 8:00-17:00. The interior is closed to sightseers during services: Sun 8:00-13:00; Tue, Wed, and Sat 10:00-12:00; and Fri 17:00-20:00. Tel. 08862/932-930, www.wieskirche.de.

Getting There: By **car,** the Wieskirche is a 30-minute drive north of Neuschwanstein or Füssen. Head north, turn right at Steingaden, and follow the brown signs (pay parking). With careful attention to schedules, you can day-trip here from Füssen by **bus** (#73, #9606, or #9651; 4-6/day, 45-60 minutes), but it's a long round-trip for a church that most see in 15 minutes.

Trinket shops and snack stands (one sells freshly made doughnuts—look for *Wiesküchert* sign) clog the parking area in front of the church; take a commune-with-nature-and-smell-the-farm detour back through the meadow to the parking lot.

The **Romantic Road bus tour** stops here for 20 minutes on the northbound route to Frankfurt. Southbound buses stop here for 15 minutes, but it's after the church has closed for the day.

Visiting the Church

This pilgrimage church is built around the much-venerated statue of a scourged (or whipped) Christ, which supposedly wept in 1738. The carving—too graphic to be accepted by that generation's Church—was the focus of worship in a peasant's barn. Miraculously, it shed tears—empathizing with all those who suffer. Pilgrims came from all around. A tiny and humble chapel was built to house the statue in 1739. (You can see it where the lane to the church leaves the parking lot.) Bigger and bigger crowds came. Two of Bavaria's top Rococo architects, the Zimmermann

Wieskirche

brothers (Johann Baptist and Dominikus), were commissioned to build the Wieskirche that stands here today.

Follow the theological sweep from the altar to the ceiling: Jesus whipped, chained, and then killed (notice the pelican above the altar—recalling a pre-Christian story of a bird that opened its breast to feed its young with its own blood); the painting of Baby Jesus posed as if on the cross; the golden sacrificial lamb; and finally, high on the ceiling, the resurrected Christ before the Last Judgment. This is the most positive depiction of the Last Judgment around. Jesus, rather than sitting on the throne to judge, rides high on a rainbow—a symbol of forgiveness—giving any sinner the feeling that there is still time to repent, with plenty of mercy on hand. In the back, above the pipe organ, notice the closed door to paradise, and at the opposite end (above the main altar), the empty throne—waiting for Judgment Day.

Above the doors flanking the altar are murky glass cases with 18th-century handkerchiefs. People wept, came here, were healed, and no longer needed their hankies. Walk through either of these doors and up an aisle flanking the high altar to see votives—requests and thanks to God (for happy, healthy babies and so on). Notice how the kneelers are positioned so that worshippers can meditate on scenes of biblical miracles painted high on the ceiling and visible through the ornate tunnel frames. A priest here once told me that faith, architecture, light, and music all combine to create the harmony of the Wieskirche.

Rick's Tip: *If you'd like* **to attend a church service,** *look for the* ***Gottesdienst*** **schedule.** *In every small German town in the very Catholic south, when you pass the big town church, look for a sign that says* Heilige Messe. *This is the schedule for holy Mass, usually on Saturday* (Sa.) *or Sunday* (So.).

Two paintings flank the door at the rear of the church. The one on the right shows the ceremonial parade in 1749 when the white-clad monks of Steingaden carried the carved statue of Christ from the tiny church to its new big one. The second painting (on the left), from 1757, is a votive

The Wieskirche's decor is Rococo to the max.

from one of the Zimmermann brothers, the artists and architects who built this church. He is giving thanks for the successful construction of the new church.

If you can't visit the Wieskirche, visit one of the other churches that came out of the same heavenly spray can: Oberammergau's church, Munich's Asamkirche, and, on a lesser scale, Füssen's basilica.

OBERAMMERGAU

Exploited to the hilt by the tourist trade, Oberammergau wears too much makeup. During its famous Passion Play (every 10 years, next in 2020), the crush is unbearable—and the prices at the hotels and restaurants can be as well. The village has about 1,200 beds for the 5,000 playgoers coming daily. But the rest of the time, Oberammergau is a pleasant, and at times even sleepy, Bavarian village.

If you're passing through, Oberammergau is a ▲ sight—worth a wander among the half-timbered, frescoed *Lüftlmalerei* houses. For drivers partial to villages, it makes a cozy home base. Train travelers would do better to stay in well-connected Füssen.

Orientation

This village of about 5,000 feels even smaller, thanks to its remote location. The downtown core, huddled around the onion-domed church, is compact and invites strolling; all of my recommended sights, hotels, and restaurants are within about a 10-minute walk of each other. While the town's name sounds like a mouthful, it's based on the name of the local river (the Ammer) and means, roughly, "Upper Ammerland."

Tourist Information: The helpful, well-organized TI provides English information on area hikes and will store your bags for free during opening hours (mid-July-mid-Sept Mon-Fri 9:00-18:00, Sat-Sun 9:00-13:00; mid-Sept-mid-July same hours but closed Sun; Nov-Dec also closed Sat; Eugen-Papst-Strasse 9A, tel. 08822/922-740, www.ammergauer-alpen.de).

Hotel Card: If you are staying in the Oberammergau area, you are entitled to a **Gäste-Karte**—ask your hotel for one. The TI has a sheet explaining all the benefits of this card, including free travel on local buses and discounts on admission to Linderhof Castle.

Sights

▲OBERAMMERGAU MUSEUM

This museum showcases local woodcarving, with good English explanations. The ground floor has a small exhibit of nativity scenes (*Krippe*—mostly made of wood, but some of paper or wax). In the back, find the small theater, where you can watch an interesting film in English about the 2010 Passion Play. Upstairs is a much more extensive collection of the wood carvings that helped put Oberammergau on the map, including a room of old woodcarving tools, plus a small exhibit on Roman archaeological finds in the region. Your ticket also lets you into the lobby of the Passion Play Theater, described next.

Cost and Hours: €6, includes museum and theater lobby; Easter-Oct and Dec-mid-Jan Tue-Sun 10:00-17:00, closed Mon; also closed Nov and mid-Jan-Easter; Dorfstrasse 8, tel. 08822/94136, www.oberammergaumuseum.de.

PASSION PLAY THEATER (FESTSPIELHAUS)

Back in 1633, in the midst of the bloody Thirty Years' War and with horrifying plagues devastating entire cities, the people of Oberammergau promised God that if they were spared from extinction, they'd "perform a play depicting the suffering, death, and resurrection of our Lord Jesus Christ" every decade thereafter. The town survived, and, heading into its 41st decade, the people of Oberammergau are still making good on the deal. For 100 days every 10 years (most recently in

Oberammergau

To Munich
OBERLANDSTR.
BUS & TRAIN STATION
PASSION PLAY THEATER
FELDIGL.
IN DER FURCH
ROTTSTRASSE
SCHMÄDIG.
DEUTINGERSTR.
PASSIONSWIESE
THEATER STR.
OBERAMMERGAU MUSEUM
ST.-LUKAS-STR.
BAHNHOFSTRASSE
To Unterammergau & Wieskirche
DORFSTR.
To Laber Bergbahn (lift), WellenBerg (pool) & 4
WELFENG.
FRANZOSENG.
FREIKORP.
EUGEN.
DEDLERSTR.
DAISEN.
Ammer River
VERLEGER.
PILATUS HOUSE
PAPST-STR.
DORFSTR.
CHURCH
To Wieskirche & Kolbensattel (chairlift)
TIROLER.
KÖNIG-LUDWIG STR.
HANSEL & GRETEL HOUSE
LITTLE RED RIDING HOOD HOUSE
KOFELAU WEG
MALENSTEINWEG
ETTALER STR.
200 Meters
200 Yards
To Ettal, Linderhof, Reutte, Garmisch & Munich

Eating

1. Ammergauer Maxbräu
2. Gasthof zur Rose & Gästehaus Magold
3. El Puente
4. To Café Hochenleitner
5. Eis Café Paradiso

Sleeping

6. Hotel Fux
7. Oberammergau Youth Hostel

The Passion Play has been performed in Oberammergau every 10 years since 1634.

2010), about half of the town's population (a cast of 2,000) are involved in the production of this extravagant five-hour Passion Play—telling the story of Jesus' entry into Jerusalem, the Crucifixion, and the Resurrection.

Until the next show in 2020, you'll have to settle for reading the book, seeing Nicodemus tool around town in his VW, or taking a quick look at the theater, a block from the center of town.

Visiting the Theater: With a ticket for the Oberammergau Museum (described earlier), you can enter the theater lobby, where there's a modest exhibit on the history of the performances. A long wall of photographs of past performers shows the many generations of Oberammergauers who have participated in this tradition. Climb the stairs and peek into the theater itself, which has an unusual indoor/outdoor design and a real-life alpine backdrop.

To learn more, you can take a 45-minute guided tour of the theater, organized by the museum (€6, or €8 if you also want to visit the museum; tours run Easter-Oct only, Tue-Sun at 11:00 in English, at 10:00 and 14:00 in German; tel. 08822/94136, www.oberammergaumuseum.de).

Near Oberammergau

These attractions are a long walk from town, but easy to reach by car or bike.

MOUNTAIN LIFTS

Oberammergau has two mountain lifts of its own. At the east end of town is the **Laber Bergbahn,** a gondola that lifts you up to fine views over the town. For an easy hike take the lift up and walk down in about 2.5 hours (www.laber-bergbahn.de). Across town to the west is the **Kolbensattel** chairlift—popular for skiers in winter and hikers in summer (www.kolbensattel.de). Also at Kolbensattel is the 1.5-mile-long Alpine Coaster (similar to a luge), a mountain playground, and a climbing paradise perfect for families.

Woodcarving in Oberammergau

The Ammergau region is relatively poor, with no appreciable industry and no agriculture, save for some dairy farming. What they *do* have is wood. Carving religious and secular themes became a lucrative way for the locals to make some money, especially when confined to the house during the long, cold winter. Carvers from Oberammergau peddled their wares across Europe, carrying them on their backs (on distinctive wooden backpack-racks called *Kraxe*) as far away as Rome.

Today, the Oberammergau Carving School (founded in 1887) is a famous institution that takes only 20 students per year out of 450 applicants. Their graduates do important restoration work throughout Europe.

WELLENBERG SWIMMING POOL

Near the Laber Bergbahn lift is this sprawling complex of indoor and outdoor pools and saunas (€7/3 hours, €12/day, extra for sauna, daily 10:00-21:00, Himmelreich 52, tel. 08822/92360, www.wellenberg-oberammergau.de).

SOMMERRODELBAHN STECKENBERG

The next town over, Unterammergau, hosts a stainless-steel summer luge track that's faster than the Tegelberg luge. This one has double seats (allowing a parent to accompany kids) and two sticks—one for each hand; be careful of your elbows. Unlike other luges, children under age three are allowed, and you only pay one fare when a parent and child ride together.

Cost and Hours: €3.50/ride, €15/6 rides; May-late Oct daily 10:00-17:00, Sat-Sun until 18:00, closed off-season and when wet; Liftweg 1 in Unterammergau, tel. 08822/4027, www.steckenberg.de.

Shopping

▲LOCAL ARTS AND CRAFTS

Browse through Oberammergau's woodcarving shops *(Holzschnitzerei)*, small art galleries filled with very expensive whittled works. The beautifully frescoed **Pilatus House** has an open workshop where you can watch woodcarvers and painters at work on summer afternoons (free, late May-mid-Oct Tue-Sun 13:00-17:00, closed Mon, open weekends in Dec, closed rest of year, Ludwig-Thoma-Strasse 10, tel. 08822/949-511). Upstairs is a small exhibit of "reverse glass" paintings *(verre églomisé)* that's worth a quick glance.

Eating

$$ Ammergauer Maxbräu, in Hotel Maximilian on the edge of downtown, serves high-quality Bavarian fare with an international twist. The rustic-yet-mod interior—with big copper vats where they brew their own beer—is cozy on a rainy day. In nice weather, locals fill the beer garden out front (€12-19 main courses, daily 11:00-22:00, right behind the church, Ettaler Strasse 5, tel. 08822/948-740, www.maximilian-oberammergau.de).

$ Gasthof zur Rose, a couple of blocks off the main drag, serves Bavarian food in its dining room and at a few outdoor tables (€10-15 main courses, Tue-Sun 12:00-14:00 & 18:00-21:00, closed Mon, Dedlerstrasse 9, tel. 08822/4706, www.rose-oberammergau.de).

$$ El Puente may vex Mexican-food purists, but it's the most hopping place in town, with €7.50 cocktails attracting young locals and tourists alike. Come not for the burritos and enchiladas, but for the bustling energy (€10-15 burgers and Mexican standards, €15-24 steaks, Mon-Sat 18:00-23:30, closed Sun, Daisenbergerstrasse 3, tel. 08822/945-777, www.elpuente-oberammergau.de).

$ Café Hochenleitner, just a few minutes from the center, is a quiet café with nice outdoor seating that's winning awards for its creative confections (Tue-Sun 12:00-18:00, closed Mon, Faistenmantlgasse 7, tel. 08822/1312).

$ Eis Café Paradiso serves up good gelato along the main street. Enjoy a big €5 sundae on the patio (daily 9:00-22:00 in summer, Dorfstrasse 4, tel. 08822/6279).

Sleeping

Accommodations in Oberammergau are friendly and cheaper than in Füssen. All offer free parking. Prices listed are for summer (generally May-Oct).

$$ Hotel Fux—quiet and romantic—rents eight large rooms decorated in the Bavarian *Landhaus* style (Db-€93, free sauna, indoor playground, Mannagasse 2a, tel. 08822/93093, www.hotel-in-oberammergau.de, info@firmafux.de). They also have six apartments for stays of at least 3-4 days.

$ Gasthof zur Rose is big and centrally located, with 19 mostly small but comfortable rooms run by the friendly Frank family. At the reception desk, see photos showing the family performing in the Passion Play (Db-€84, family rooms, Dedlerstrasse 9, tel. 08822/4706, www.rose-oberammergau.de, info@rose-oberammergau.de).

$ Gästehaus Magold, homey and family-friendly, has three bright and spacious rooms and two apartments—twice as nice as the cheap hotel rooms in town, and for much less (Db-€64, family rooms, cash only, cable Internet, minimum stay in summer, immediately behind Gasthof zur Rose at Kleppergasse 1, tel. 08822/4340, www.gaestehaus-magold.de, info@gaestehaus-magold.de).

¢ Oberammergau Youth Hostel, on the river, is just a short walk from the center (€23/bed, includes breakfast and sheets; small extra fees for nonmembers, one-night stays, and those over age 26; reception open 8:00-10:00 & 17:00-19:00, closed mid-Nov-Dec, Malensteinweg

10, tel. 08822/4114, www.oberammergau.jugendherberge.de, oberammergau@jugendherberge.de).

Transportation

Arriving and Departing

BY CAR

Drivers can get to Oberammergau from Füssen or Munich in about an hour. There are two exits from the main road into Oberammergau—at the north and south ends. Either way, make your way to the free lot between the TI and the river.

Rick's Tip: *If you're driving between the Wieskirche and Oberammergau, you'll cross* **Echelsbacher Brücke,** *a bridge arching 230 feet over the Pöllat Gorge.* **Thoughtful drivers let their passengers walk across** *to enjoy the views, then meet them at the other side. Any kayakers below?*

BY TRAIN OR BUS

The town's train station is a short walk from the center: Turn left, cross the bridge, and you're already in downtown. **Trains** run between **Munich** and Oberammergau nearly hourly (2 hours, change in Murnau). Train info: Toll tel. 0180-699-6633, www.bahn.com.

From Oberammergau, **buses** run to **Füssen** (bus #9606, 3-4/day, 1.5 hours, some transfer or change number to #73 at Echelsbacher Brücke).

LINDERHOF CASTLE

This homiest of "Mad" King Ludwig's castles is a small yet exquisite mini Versailles—good enough for a minor god, and worth ▲▲. Set in the woods 15 minutes from Oberammergau and surrounded by fountains and sculpted, Italian-style gardens, it's the only palace I've toured that actually had me feeling envious.

Getting There

It's an easy stop by car; pay the small fee to park near the ticket office. Without a car, it's challenging: You could hire a driver (see page 158), take a bus tour from Munich that includes the castle, or bus in from Oberammergau (bus #9622, 30 minutes, 8/day Mon-Fri, 5/day Sat-Sun).

Orientation

Cost: €8.50, €5 for grotto only.

Hours: Daily April-mid-Oct 9:00-18:00, mid-Oct-March 10:00-16:00 (grotto closed mid-Oct-mid-April), tel. 08822/92030, www.linderhof.de.

Crowd-Beating Tips: July and August crowds can mean an hour's wait between when you buy your ticket and when you start your tour. It's most crowded in the late morning. During this period, you're wise to arrive after 15:00. Any other time of year, you should get your palace tour time shortly after you arrive. If you do wind up with time to kill, explore the gardens and some of the smaller buildings before your appointment.

Sightseeing Tips and Procedure: The complex sits isolated in natural splendor. Plan for lots of walking and a two-hour stop to fully enjoy this royal park. Bring raingear in iffy weather. Your ticket comes with an entry time to tour the palace, which is a 10-minute walk from the ticket office. At the palace entrance, wait in line at the turnstile listed on your ticket (A through D) to take the required 30-minute English tour. Afterwards, explore the rest of the park; be sure not to miss the grotto (10-minute uphill hike from palace, brief but interesting free tour in English, no appointments—the board out front lists the time of the next tour). Then see the other royal buildings dotting the king's playground if you like. You can eat lunch at the café across from the ticket office.

Visiting the Castle

Background: While Neuschwanstein is Neo-Gothic—romanticizing the medieval glory days of Bavaria—Linderhof is Baroque and Rococo, the frilly, overly ornamented styles more associated with Louis XIV, the "Sun King" of France. And, while Neuschwanstein is full of swans, here you'll see fleur-de-lis (the symbol of French royalty) and multiple portraits of Louis XIV, Louis XV, Madame Pompadour, and other pre-Revolutionary French elites. Though they lived a century apart, Ludwig and Louis were spiritual contemporaries: Both clung to the notion of absolute monarchy, despite the realities of the changing world around them. Capping the palace roofline is one of Ludwig's favorite symbols: Atlas, with the weight of the world literally on his shoulders. Oh, those poor, overburdened, misunderstood absolute monarchs!

Ludwig was king for 22 of his 40 years. He lived much of his last eight years here—the only one of his castles that was finished in his lifetime. Frustrated by the limits of being a "constitutional monarch," he retreated to Linderhof, inhabiting a private fantasy world where extravagant castles glorified his otherwise weakened kingship. You'll notice that the castle is small—designed for a single occupant. Ludwig, who never married or had children, lived here as a royal hermit.

Inside the Castle: The castle tour includes 10 rooms on the upper floor. (The downstairs, where the servants lived and worked, now houses the gift shop.) You'll see room after room exquisitely carved with Rococo curlicues, wrapped in gold leaf. Up above, the ceiling paintings have 3-D legs sticking out of the frame. Clearly inspired by Versailles, Linderhof even has its own (much smaller) hall of mirrors—decorated with over a hundred Nymphenburg porcelain vases and a priceless ivory chandelier. The bedroom

Linderhof is the smallest of King Ludwig II's castles.

features an oversized crystal chandelier, delicate Meissen porcelain flowers framing the mirrors, and a literally king-size bed—a two-story canopy affair draped in blue velvet. Perhaps the most poignant sight, a sad commentary on Ludwig's solitary lifestyle, is his dinner table—preset with dishes and food—which could rise from the kitchen below into his dining room so he could eat alone. (Examine the incredibly delicate flowers in the Meissen porcelain centerpiece.)

Castle Grounds: The palace is flanked on both sides with grand, terraced **fountains** (peopled by gleaming golden gods) that erupt at the top and bottom of each hour. If you're waiting for your palace tour to begin, hike up to the top of either of these terraces for a fine photo-op. (The green gazebo, on the hillside between the grotto and the palace, provides Linderhof's best view.)

The other must-see sight at Linderhof is Ludwig's **grotto.** Exiting the gift shop behind the palace, turn right, then cut left through the garden to climb up the hill. You'll wait out front for the next tour (the time is posted on the board), then head inside. Inspired by Wagner's *Tannhäuser* opera, this artificial cave (300 feet long and 70 feet tall) is actually a performance space. Its rocky walls are made of cement poured over an iron frame. (While Ludwig exalted the distant past, he took full advantage of then-cutting-edge technology to bring his fantasies to life.) The grotto provided a private theater for the reclusive king to enjoy his beloved Wagnerian operas—he was usually the sole member of the audience. The grotto features a waterfall, fake stalactites, and a swan boat floating on an artificial lake (which could be heated for swimming). Brick ovens hidden in the walls could be used to heat the huge space. The first electricity in Bavaria was generated here, to change the colors of the stage lights and to power Ludwig's fountain and wave machine.

Grotto at Linderhof

Several other smaller buildings are scattered around the grounds; look for posted maps and directional signs to track them down. The most worthwhile are the **Moroccan House** and **Moorish Kiosk.** With over-the-top decor seemingly designed by a sultan's decorator on acid, these allowed Ludwig to "travel" to exotic lands without leaving the comfort of Bavaria. (The Moorish Kiosk is more interesting; look for its gilded dome in the woods beyond the grotto.) At the far edge of the property is **Hunding's Hut,** inspired by Wagner's *The Valkyrie*—a rustic-cottage stage-set with a giant fake "tree" growing inside of it. And closer to the entrance—along the path between the ticket booth and the palace—is the **King's Cottage,** used for special exhibitions (often with an extra charge).

ZUGSPITZE

The tallest point in Germany, worth ▲▲ in clear weather, is also a border crossing. Lifts from both Austria and Germany meet at the 9,700-foot summit of the Zugspitze (TSOOG-shpit-seh). You can straddle the border between two great nations while enjoying an incredible view. Restaurants, shops, and telescopes await you at the summit.

Either approach, from Germany or Austria, is best for drivers.

Summiting the Zugspitze

German Approach: There are two ways to ascend from Eibsee, and they cost the same (€52 round-trip, €42 in winter, tel. 08821/7970, www.zugspitze.de).

Drivers head for Eibsee (about 10 minutes beyond Garmisch—go through town following signs for *Fernpass/Reutte*, and watch for the Zugspitze turnoff on the left).

At Eibsee, you have a choice. You can walk across the parking lot and zip up to the top in a **cable car** (10 minutes, daily 8:00-16:15, departs at least every 30 minutes; in busy times departs every 10 minutes, but since each car fits only 35—which the electronic board suspensefully counts down as each passenger goes through the turnstile—you may have to wait to board). Or you can transfer to a **cogwheel train** (45 minutes to the top, departs about hourly; once up top, transfer from the train to a short cable car for the quick, 3-minute ascent to the summit).

You can choose how you want to go up and down at the spur of the moment: both ways by cable car, both by cog train, or mix and match. Although the train ride takes longer, many travelers enjoy the more involved cog-railway experience—at least one way. The disadvantage of the train is that more than half of the trip is through dark tunnels deep in the mountains; aside from a few fleeting glimpses of the Eibsee sparkling below, it's not very scenic.

Arriving at the top, you'll want to head up to the third floor (elevators recommended, given the high altitude)—follow signs for *Gipfel* (summit).

The cable car to the Zugspitze

To get back down to Eibsee, the last cable car departs the summit at 16:45, and the last cogwheel train at 16:30. On busy days, you may have to reserve a return time once you reach the top—if it's crowded, look for signs and prebook your return to avoid getting stuck up top longer than you want. In general, allow plenty of time for afternoon descents: If bad weather hits in the late afternoon, cable cars can be delayed at the summit, causing tourists to miss their train connection from Eibsee back to Garmisch.

Hikers can enjoy the easy six-mile walk around the lovely Eibsee Lake (start 5 minutes downhill from cable-car station).

Austrian Approach: The Tiroler Zugspitzbahn ascent is less crowded and cheaper than the Bavarian one. Drive to the Austrian village of Ehrwald, following signs for *Tiroler Zugspitzbahn* (free parking). Departing from above Ehrwald, a lift zips you to the top in 10 minutes (€40.50 round-trip, departures in each direction 3/hour, daily 8:40-16:40 except closed mid-April-late May and most of Nov, last ascent at 16:00, Austrian tel. 05673/2309, www.zugspitze.at).

➲ Self-Guided Tour

Whether you've ascended from the German or Austrian side, you're high enough now to enjoy a little tour of the summit. The two terraces—Bavarian and Tirolean—are connected by a narrow walkway, which was the border station before Germany and Austria opened their borders. The Austrian (Tirolean) side was higher until the Germans blew its top off in World War II to make a flak tower, so let's start there.

Tirolean Terrace: Before you stretches the Zugspitzplatt glacier. Is it melting? A reflector once stood here to slow it from shrinking during summer months. Many ski lifts fan out here, as if reaching for a

ridge that defines the border between Germany and Austria. The circular metal building is the top of the cog-railway line that the Germans cut through the mountains in 1931. Just above that, find a small square building—the *Hochzeitskapelle* (wedding chapel), consecrated in 1981 by Cardinal Joseph Ratzinger (a.k.a., retired Pope Benedict XVI).

Both Germany and Austria use this rocky pinnacle for communication purposes. The square box on the Tirolean Terrace provides the Innsbruck airport with air-traffic control, and a tower nearby is for the German *Katastrophenfunk* (civil defense network).

This highest point in Germany (there are many higher points in Austria) was first climbed in 1820. The Austrians built a cable car that nearly reached the summit in 1926. (You can see it just over the ridge on the Austrian side—look for the ghostly, abandoned concrete station.) In 1964, the final leg, a new lift, was built connecting that 1926 station to the actual summit, where you stand now. Before then, people needed to hike the last 650 feet to the top. Today's lift dates from 1980, but was renovated after a 2003 fire. The Austrian station, which is much nicer than the German station, has a fine little museum that shows three interesting videos (free with Austrian ticket, €2.50 if you came up from Germany, 6-minute 3-D mountain show, 30-minute making-of-the-lift documentary, and 45-minute look at the nature, sport, and culture of the region).

Looking up the valley from the Tirolean Terrace, you can see the towns of Ehrwald and Lermoos in the distance, and the valley that leads to Reutte. Looking farther clockwise, you'll see Eibsee Lake below.

The Zugspitze is Germany's highest mountain.

Hell's Valley, stretching to the right of Eibsee, seems to merit its name.

Bavarian Terrace: The narrow passage connecting the two terraces used to be a big deal—you'd show your passport here at the little blue house and shift from Austrian shillings to German marks. Notice the regional pride here: no German or Austrian national banners, but regional ones instead—*Freistaat Bayern* (Bavaria) and *Land Tirol.*

The German side features a golden cross marking the summit...the highest point in Germany. A priest and his friends hauled it up in 1851. The historic original was shot up by American soldiers using it for target practice in the late 1940s, so what you see today is a modern replacement. In the summer, it's easy to "summit" the Zugspitze, as there are steps and handholds all the way to the top. Or you can just stay behind and feed the birds. The yellow-beaked ravens get chummy with those who share a little pretzel or bread. Below the terrace, notice the restaurant that claims—irrefutably—to be the "highest Biergarten in Deustchland."

The oldest building up here is the first mountaineers' hut, built in 1897 and entwined with mighty cables that cinch it down. In 1985, observers clocked 200-mph winds up here—those cables were necessary. Step inside the restaurant to enjoy museum-like photos and paintings on the wall (including a look at the team who hiked up with the golden cross in 1851).

Near the waiting area for the cable cars and cogwheel train is a little museum (in German only) that's worth a look if you have some time to kill before heading back down. If you're going down on the German side, remember you must choose between the cable car (look for the *Eibsee* signs) or cog railway (look for *Talfahrt/Descent*, with a picture of a train; you'll board a smaller cable car for the quick trip to the train station).

Rothenburg and the Romantic Road

The Romantic Road through Bavaria's medieval heartland is strewn with picturesque villages, farmhouses, onion-domed churches, Baroque palaces, and walled cities. The route, which runs from Würzburg to Füssen, is the most scenic way to connect Frankfurt with Munich. No trains run along the full length of the Romantic Road, but Rothenburg (ROH-tehn-burg), the most interesting town along the way, is easy to reach by rail. Drivers can either zero in on Rothenburg or take some extra time to meander from town to town on the way. For nondrivers, a tour bus travels the Romantic Road once daily in each direction.

Countless travelers have searched for the elusive "untouristy Rothenburg." There are many contenders (such as Michelstadt, Miltenberg, Bamberg, Bad Windsheim, and Dinkelsbühl), but none holds a candle to the king of medieval German cuteness. Even with crowds, overpriced souvenirs—and, yes, even the over-promoted, dry *Schneeballen* pastries—Rothenburg is the best. Save time and mileage and be satisfied with the winner.

ROTHENBURG AND THE ROMANTIC ROAD IN 2 DAYS

I'd spend one full day in Rothenburg this way: Start with my self-guided town walk, including a visit to St. Jakob's Church (for the carved altarpiece) and the Imperial City Museum (historic artifacts). Spend the afternoon visiting the Medieval Crime and Punishment Museum and taking my "Schmiedgasse-Spitalgasse Shopping Stroll," followed by a walk on the wall (from Spitaltor to Klingentor).

Cap your day with the entertaining Night Watchman's Tour at 20:00. Locals love "*Die blaue Stunde*" (the blue hour)—the time just before dark when city lamps and the sky hold hands. Be sure to be out enjoying the magic of the city at this time.

Other evening options include beer-garden fun (at Gasthof Rödertor) if the weather's good, or the English Conversation Club (at Altfränkische Weinstube am Klosterhof) if it's Wednesday.

With extra time in Rothenburg, spread out your sightseeing and add the Old Town Historic Walk (offered by the TI), the Town Hall Tower climb, and the German Christmas Museum.

If you're driving, take in the top Romantic Road highlights en route, devoting a half-day to the sights on your way to Rothenburg and another half-day after leaving it.

ROTHENBURG OB DER TAUBER

In the Middle Ages, when Berlin and Munich were just wide spots on the road, Rothenburg ob der Tauber was a "free imperial city" beholden only to the Holy Roman Emperor. From 1150 to 1400, because of its strategic location on trade routes and the abundant resources of its surrounding farmlands, Rothenburg thrived, with a whopping population of 6,000. But the Thirty Years' War and a plague that followed did the town in. With no money to fix up its antiquated buildings, Rothenburg languished. Today, it's the country's best-preserved medieval walled town, enjoying tremendous popularity without losing its charm.

Rick's Tip: *Germany has several towns named Rothenburg.* **Make sure you're going to Rothenburg ob der Tauber** *(not "ob der" any other river). People really do sometimes drive or ride the train to the wrong Rothenburg by accident.*

Two-thirds of the 2,000 people who live within Rothenburg's walls are employed to serve tourists. Rothenburg is at its best in spring and fall, crowded in summer (but still fun), and dead in winter except for December (when its Christmas Market bustles).

While roughly 2 million people visit each year, most come only on day trips. Rothenburg is yours after dark, when the groups vacate and the town's floodlit cobbles seem made for romance.

Orientation

Think of the town map as a human head. Its nose—the castle garden—sticks out to the left, and the skinny lower part forms a neck, with the youth hostel and a recommended hotel being the Adam's apple. The town is a delight on foot. No sights or hotels are more than a 15-minute walk from the train station or each other.

Rick's Tip: *A* **fun pictorial town map,** *which also helpfully indicates some walking paths in the countryside beyond the town walls, is available for free with this book at the* **Friese shop** *(see page 210).*

Most of the buildings you'll see were in place by 1400. The city was born around

Picturesque Rothenburg ob der Tauber

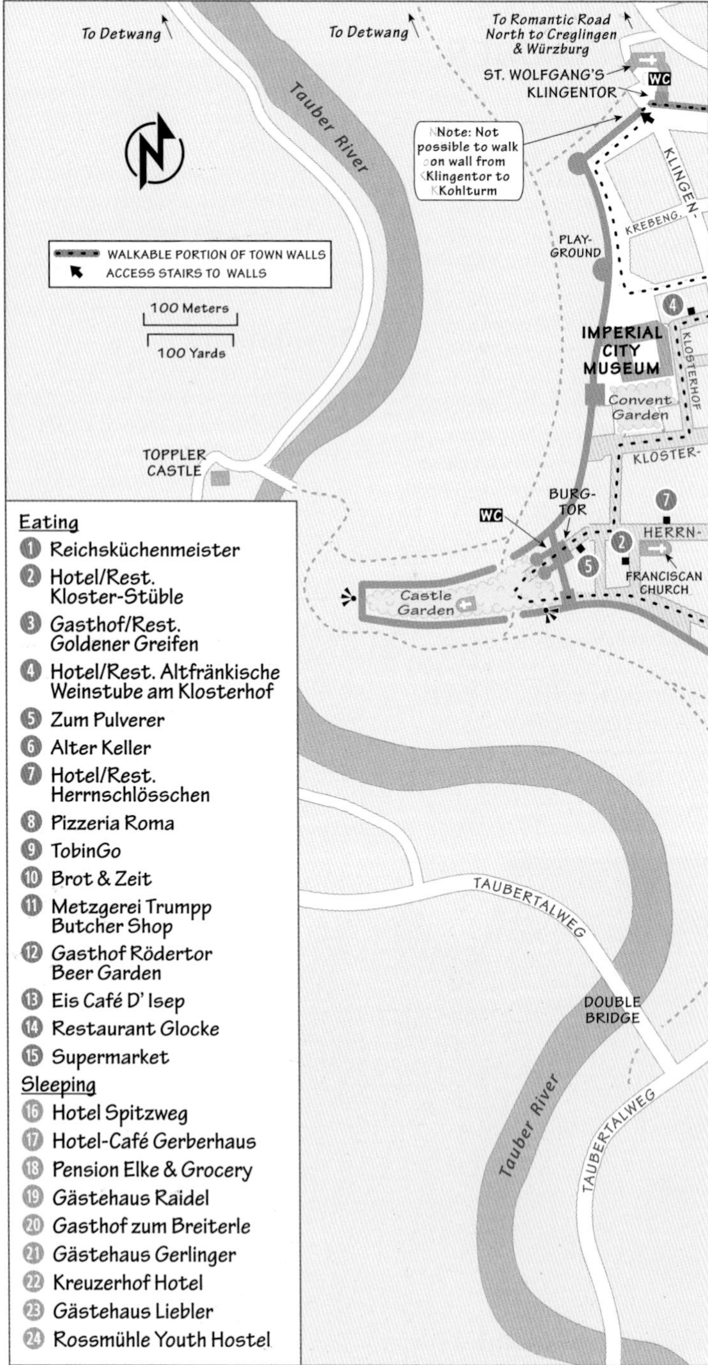
To Detwang
To Detwang
To Romantic Road North to Creglingen & Würzburg
ST. WOLFGANG'S
WC
KLINGENTOR
Tauber River
Note: Not possible to walk on wall from Klingentor to Kohlturm
KLINGEN-
KREBENG.
PLAY-GROUND
WALKABLE PORTION OF TOWN WALLS
ACCESS STAIRS TO WALLS
100 Meters
100 Yards
IMPERIAL CITY MUSEUM
KLOSTERHOF
Convent Garden
KLOSTER-
TOPPLER CASTLE
BURG-TOR
WC
HERRN-
FRANCISCAN CHURCH
Castle Garden
TAUBERTALWEG
DOUBLE BRIDGE
Tauber River
TAUBERTALWEG
Eating
1 Reichsküchenmeister
2 Hotel/Rest. Kloster-Stüble
3 Gasthof/Rest. Goldener Greifen
4 Hotel/Rest. Altfränkische Weinstube am Klosterhof
5 Zum Pulverer
6 Alter Keller
7 Hotel/Rest. Herrnschlösschen
8 Pizzeria Roma
9 TobinGo
10 Brot & Zeit
11 Metzgerei Trumpp Butcher Shop
12 Gasthof Rödertor Beer Garden
13 Eis Café D' Isep
14 Restaurant Glocke
15 Supermarket
Sleeping
16 Hotel Spitzweg
17 Hotel-Café Gerberhaus
18 Pension Elke & Grocery
19 Gästehaus Raidel
20 Gasthof zum Breiterle
21 Gästehaus Gerlinger
22 Kreuzerhof Hotel
23 Gästehaus Liebler
24 Rossmühle Youth Hostel

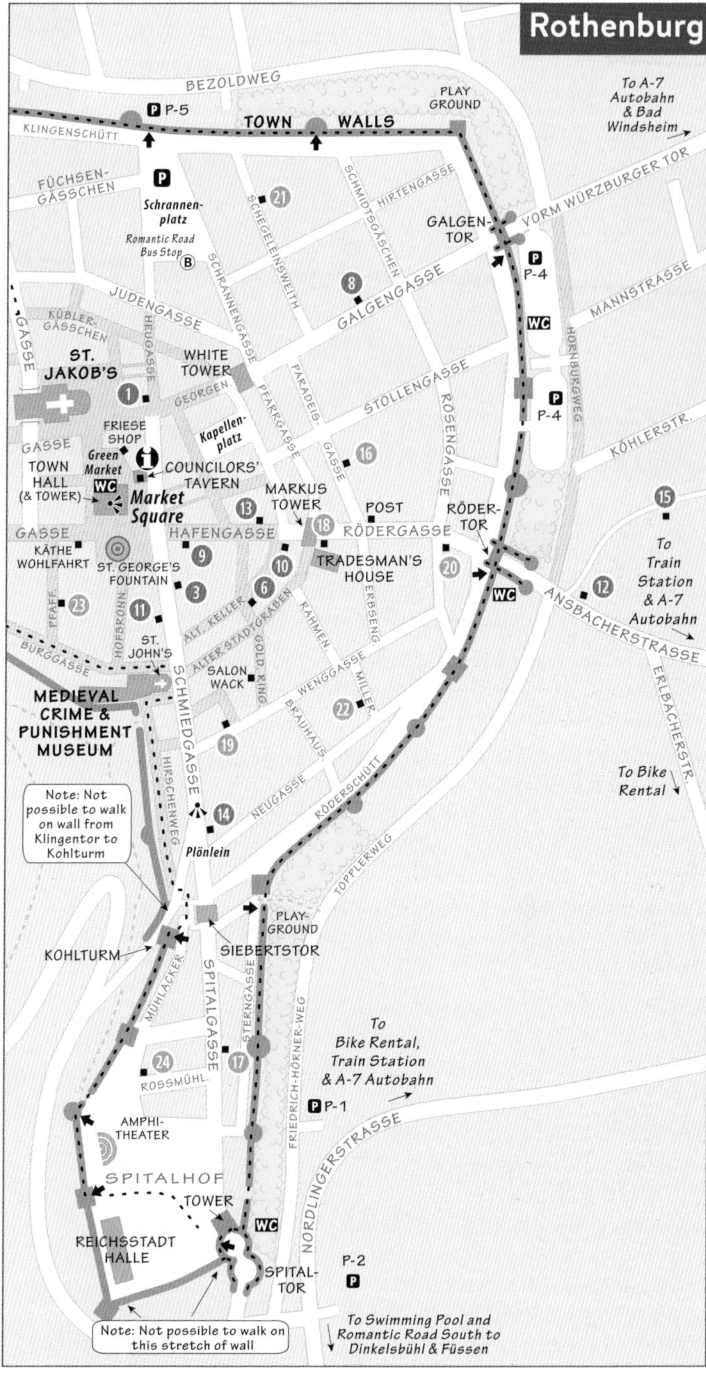
Rothenburg
BEZOLDWEG
TOWN WALLS
P-5
KLINGENSCHÜTT
PLAY GROUND
To A-7 Autobahn & Bad Windsheim
FÜCHSEN-GÄSSCHEN
Schrannen-platz
Romantic Road Bus Stop
SCHRANNENGASSE
SCHEGELEINSWEITH
SCHMIDTSGÄSSCHEN
HIRTENGASSE
GALGEN-TOR
VORM WÜRZBURGER TOR
P-4
GALGENGASSE
MANNSTRASSE
JUDENGASSE
KÜBLER-GÄSSCHEN
HEUGASSE
ST. JAKOB'S
WHITE TOWER
GEORGEN.
PARADEIS-GASSE
PFARRGASSE
STOLLENGASSE
ROSENGASSE
HORNBURGWEG
KÖHLERSTR.
Kapellen-platz
FRIESE SHOP
Green Market
COUNCILORS' TAVERN
TOWN HALL (& TOWER)
Market Square
MARKUS TOWER
POST
RÖDER-TOR
RÖDERGASSE
HAFENGASSE
KÄTHE WOHLFAHRT
ST. GEORGE'S FOUNTAIN
TRADESMAN'S HOUSE
To Train Station & A-7 Autobahn
ANSBACHERSTRASSE
PFAFF.
HOFBRONN.
ALT. KELLER
ALTER STADTGRABEN
RAHMEN.
ERBSENG.
BURGGASSE
ST. JOHN'S
SALON WACK
GOLD. RING
WENGGASSE
MILLER.
ERLBACHERSTR.
MEDIEVAL CRIME & PUNISHMENT MUSEUM
SCHMIEDGASSE
BRAUHAUS.
HIRSCHENWEG
Note: Not possible to walk on wall from Klingentor to Kohlturm
NEUGASSE
RÖDERSCHÜTT
To Bike Rental
Plönlein
TOPPLERWEG
PLAY-GROUND
SIEBERTSTOR
KOHLTURM
MÜHLACKER
SPITALGASSE
STERNGASSE
FRIEDRICH-HÖRNER-WEG
To Bike Rental, Train Station & A-7 Autobahn
ROSSMÜHL.
P-1
AMPHI-THEATER
NÖRDLINGERSTRASSE
SPITALHOF
TOWER
REICHSSTADT HALLE
SPITAL-TOR
P-2
Note: Not possible to walk on this stretch of wall
To Swimming Pool and Romantic Road South to Dinkelsbühl & Füssen

ROTHENBURG AND THE ROMANTIC ROAD AT A GLANCE

Rothenburg

▲▲▲**Rothenburg Town Walk** A self-guided loop, starting and ending on Market Square, covering the town's top sights. See page 198.

▲▲**Night Watchman's Tour** Germany's best hour of medieval wonder, led by an amusing, medieval-garbed guide. **Hours:** Mid-March-Dec nightly at 20:00. See page 196.

▲▲**St. Jakob's Church** Home to Tilman Riemenschneider's breath-taking, wood-carved Altar of the Holy Blood. **Hours:** Daily April-Oct 9:00-17:15, Dec 10:00-16:45, Nov and Christmas-March 10:00-12:00 & 14:00-16:00, on Sun wait to enter until services end at 10:45. See page 200.

▲▲**Imperial City Museum** An artifact-filled sweep through Rothenburg's history. **Hours:** Daily April-Oct 9:30-17:30, Nov-March 13:00-16:00. See page 203.

▲▲**Schmiedgasse-Spitalgasse Shopping Stroll** A fun look at crafts and family-run shops, on a (mostly) picturesque street running between Market Square and the town's most impressive tower, Spitaltor. See page 205.

▲▲**Walk the Wall** A strollable wall encircling the town, providing great views and a good orientation to Rothenburg. **Hours:** Always open and walkable. See page 207.

▲▲**Medieval Crime and Punishment Museum** Specializing in everything connected to medieval justice, this exhibit is a cut above the tacky torture museums around Europe. **Hours:** Daily April 11:00-17:00, May-Oct 10:00-18:00, Nov and Jan-Feb 14:00-16:00, Dec and March 13:00-16:00. See page 208.

▲**Old Town Historic Walk** Covers the serious side of Rothenburg's history and the town's architecture. **Hours:** Easter-Oct and Dec daily at 14:00. See page 196.

▲**Historical Town Hall Vaults** An insightful look at Rothenburg during the Catholics-vs.-Protestants Thirty Years' War. **Hours:** Daily May-Oct 9:30-17:30, shorter hours off-season, closed Jan-Feb. See page 200.

▲**Town Hall Tower** Rothenburg's tallest perch, with a commanding view. **Hours:** Daily in season 9:00-12:30 & 13:00-17:00. See page 208.

▲**German Christmas Museum** Tells the interesting history of Christmas decorations. **Hours:** April-Dec daily 10:00-17:30, shorter and irregular hours Jan-March. See page 209.

Along the Romantic Road

▲▲**Wieskirche** Lovely Baroque-Rococo church set in a meadow. **Hours:** Daily April-Oct 8:00-20:00, Nov-March 8:00-17:00; interior closed to sightseers during services: Sun 8:00-13:00; Tue, Wed, and Sat 10:00-12:00; and Fri 17:00-20:00. See page 217 of the Bavaria chapter.

▲**Nördlingen** Workaday town with one of the best walls in Germany and a crater left by an ancient meteor. See page 217.

▲**Dinkelsbühl** A town like Rothenburg's little sister, cute enough to merit a short stop. See page 218.

▲**Creglingen's Herrgottskirche** Church featuring Riemenschneider's greatest carved altarpiece. See page 219.

▲**Weikersheim** Picturesque town with an impressive palace, Baroque gardens, and a quaint town square. See page 219.

its long-gone castle fortress—built in 1142, destroyed in 1356—which was located where the castle garden is now. You can see the shadow of the first town wall, which defines the oldest part of Rothenburg, in its contemporary street plan. Two gates from this wall still survive: the Markus Tower and the White Tower. The richest and biggest houses were in this central part. The commoners built higgledy-piggledy houses farther from the center, but still inside the present walls.

Although Rothenburg is technically in Bavaria, the region around the town strongly identifies itself as "Franken," one of Germany's many medieval dukedoms ("Franconia" in English).

Tourist Information: The TI is on Market Square (May-Oct and Dec Mon-Fri 9:00-18:00, Sat-Sun 10:00-17:00; off-season Mon-Fri 9:00-17:00, Sat 10:00-13:00, closed Sun; Marktplatz 2, tel. 09861/404-800, www.tourismus.rothenburg.de, run by Jörg Christöphler). The free city map comes with a walking guide, and the *Events* booklet covers the basics in English. The TI has one free public computer with Internet access (15-minute maximum).

Bike Rental: Rad & Tat rents bikes for €14 for a 24-hour day (otherwise €10/6 hours, also has electric bikes; Mon-Fri 9:00-18:00, Sat until 13:00, closed Sun; Bensenstrasse 17, tel. 09861/87984, www.mietraeder.de). To reach it, leave the old town heading toward the train station, take a right on Erlbacher Strasse, cross the tracks, and look across the street from the Lidl supermarket.

Taxi: For a taxi, call 09861/2000 or 09861/7227.

Tours

▲▲NIGHT WATCHMAN'S TOUR

This tour is flat-out the most entertaining hour of medieval wonder anywhere in Germany. The Night Watchman (a.k.a. Hans-Georg Baumgartner) jokes like a medieval John Cleese as he lights his lamp and takes tourists on his rounds, telling slice-of-gritty-life tales of medieval Rothenburg. This is the best evening activity in town (€8, teens-€5, free for kids 12 and under, mid-March-Dec nightly at 20:00, in English, meet at Market Square, www.nightwatchman.de).

▲OLD TOWN HISTORIC WALK

The TI offers 1.5-hour guided walking tours in English. Just show up and pay the guide directly—there's always room. Take this tour for the serious side of Rothenburg's history, and to make sense of the town's architecture; you won't get as much of that on the fun—and completely different—Night Watchman's Tour. It would be a shame not to take advantage of this informative tour just because you took the other (€7, Easter-Oct and Dec daily at 14:00, no English tours off-season, departs from Market Square).

PRIVATE GUIDES

A local historian can really bring the ramparts alive. Reserve a guide by emailing the TI (€75/1.5 hours, €95/2 hours, info@rothenburg.de, more info at www.tourismus.rothenburg.de—look under "Tourism Service," then "Guided Tours"). I've had good experiences with **Martin Kamphans,** who also works as a potter (tel. 09861/7941, www.stadtfuehrungen-rothenburg.de, post@stadtfuehrungen-rothenburg.de), and **Daniel Weber** (mobile 0795-8311, www.toot-tours.com, mail@toot-tours.com).

Rothenburg's Night Watchman

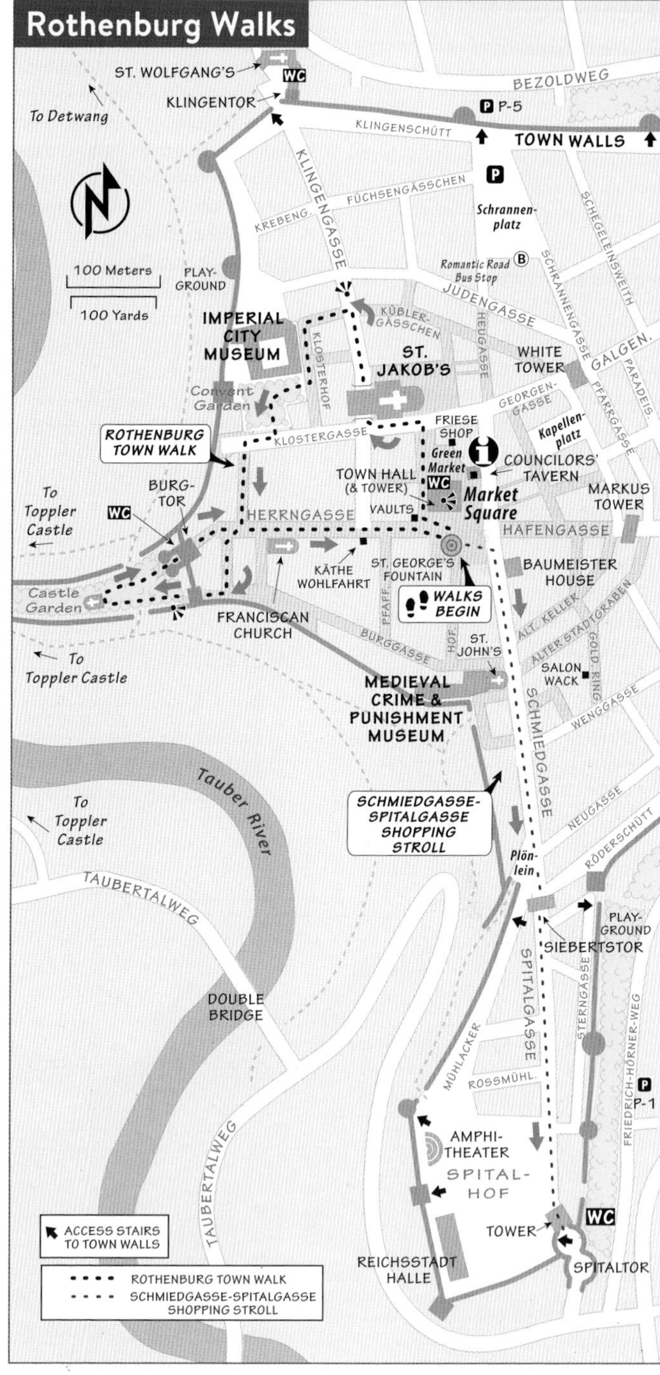
Rothenburg Walks
ST. WOLFGANG'S
KLINGENTOR
To Detwang
BEZOLDWEG
P-5
KLINGENSCHÜTT
TOWN WALLS
KLINGENGASSE
FÜCHSENGÄSSCHEN
KREBENG.
Schrannen-platz
100 Meters
100 Yards
PLAY-GROUND
Romantic Road Bus Stop
JUDENGASSE
SCHRANNENGASSE
SCHEGELEINSWEITH
IMPERIAL CITY MUSEUM
KÜBLER-GÄSSCHEN
ST. JAKOB'S
HEUGASSE
WHITE TOWER
GALGEN.
PARADEIS.
KLOSTERHOF
Convent Garden
GEORGEN-GASSE
PFARRGASSE
FRIESE SHOP
Kapellen-platz
ROTHENBURG TOWN WALK
KLOSTERGASSE
Green Market
COUNCILORS' TAVERN
TOWN HALL (& TOWER)
Market Square
MARKUS TOWER
To Toppler Castle
BURG-TOR
HERRNGASSE
VAULTS
HAFENGASSE
KÄTHE WOHLFAHRT
ST. GEORGE'S FOUNTAIN
BAUMEISTER HOUSE
Castle Garden
WALKS BEGIN
FRANCISCAN CHURCH
PFAFF.
HOF.
ALT. KELLER
ALTER STADTGRABEN
BURGGASSE
ST. JOHN'S
To Toppler Castle
SALON WACK
GOLD. RING
WENGGASSE
MEDIEVAL CRIME & PUNISHMENT MUSEUM
SCHMIEDGASSE
Tauber River
SCHMIEDGASSE-SPITALGASSE SHOPPING STROLL
To Toppler Castle
NEUGASSE
Plön-lein
RÖDERSCHÜTT
TAUBERTALWEG
PLAY-GROUND
SIEBERTSTOR
SPITALGASSE
STERNGASSE
DOUBLE BRIDGE
FRIEDRICH-HÖRNER-WEG
MÜHLACKER
ROSSMÜHL.
P-1
AMPHI-THEATER
SPITAL-HOF
TAUBERTALWEG
TOWER
ACCESS STAIRS TO TOWN WALLS
REICHSSTADT HALLE
SPITALTOR
ROTHENBURG TOWN WALK
SCHMIEDGASSE-SPITALGASSE SHOPPING STROLL

Rothenburg Walks

➔ *Town Walk*

This self-guided loop, worth ▲▲▲, weaves the town's top sights together, takes about an hour without stops, and starts and ends on Market Square. (This is roughly the same route followed by city guides on their daily Old Town Historic Walk, described earlier.)

🎧 Download my free Rothenburg Town Walk audio tour.

• *Start the walk on Market Square.*

MARKET SQUARE SPIN-TOUR

Stand in front of the fountain at the bottom of Market Square (watch for occasional cars) and spin 360 degrees clockwise, starting with the Town Hall tower. Now do it again, this time more slowly to take in some details:

Town Hall and Tower: Rothenburg's tallest spire is the Town Hall tower (Rathausturm). At 200 feet, it stands atop the old Town Hall, a white, Gothic, 13th-century building. Notice the tourists enjoying the best view in town from the black top of the tower (see page 208 for details on climbing the tower). After a fire in 1501 burned down part of the original building, a new Town Hall was built alongside what survived of the old one (fronting the square). This half of the rebuilt complex is in the Renaissance style from 1570. The double eagles you see decorating many buildings here are a repeated reminder that this was a "free imperial city" belonging directly to the (Habsburg) Holy Roman Emperor, a designation that came with benefits.

Meistertrunk Show: At the top of Market Square stands the proud Councilors' Tavern (clock tower from 1466). In its day, the city council—the rich guys who ran the town government—drank here. Today, it's the **TI** and the focus of most tourists' attention when the little doors on either side of the clock flip open and the wooden figures (from 1910) do their thing. Be on Market Square at the top of any hour (between 10:00 and 22:00) for the ritual gathering of the tourists to see the less-than-breathtaking re-enactment of the Meistertrunk ("Master Draught") story:

In 1631, in the middle of the Thirty Years' War, the Catholic army took this Protestant town and was about to do its rape, pillage, and plunder thing. As was

Rothenburg's Town Hall and Tower

the etiquette, the mayor had to give the conquering general a welcoming drink. The general enjoyed a huge tankard of local wine. Feeling really good, he told the mayor, "Hey, if you can drink this entire three-liter tankard of wine in one gulp, I'll spare your town." The mayor amazed everyone by drinking the entire thing, and Rothenburg was saved. (While this is a nice story, it was dreamed up in the late 1800s for a theatrical play designed—effectively—to promote a romantic image of the town. In actuality, if Rothenburg was spared, it had likely bribed its way out of the jam.) The city was occupied and ransacked several times in the Thirty Years' War, and it never recovered—which is why it's such a well-preserved time capsule today.

For the best show, don't watch the clock; watch the open-mouthed tourists gasp as the old windows flip open. At the late shows, the square flickers with camera flashes.

Bottom of Market Square: As this was the most-prestigious address in town, it's ringed by big homes with big carriage gates. One of the finest is just downhill from the bottom end of the square—the **Baumeister** ("master builder") **Haus,** where the man who designed and built the Town Hall lived. It features a famous Renaissance facade with statues of the seven virtues and the seven vices. The statues are copies; the originals are in the Imperial City Museum (described later on this walk).

Behind you, take in the big 17th-century **St. George's fountain.** Its long metal gutters could slide to deposit the water into villagers' buckets. It's part of Rothenburg's ingenious water system: Built on a rock, the town had one real source above the town, which was plumbed to serve a series of fountains; water flowed from high to low through Rothenburg. Its many fountains had practical functions beyond providing drinking water—some were stocked with fish on market days and during times of siege, and their water was useful for fighting fire. Because of its plentiful water supply—and its policy of requiring relatively wide lanes as fire breaks—the town never burned entirely, as so many neighboring villages did.

Two fine half-timbered buildings behind the fountain show the old-time lofts with warehouse doors and pulleys on top for hoisting. All over town, lofts like these were filled with grain. A year's supply was required by the city so they could survive any siege. The building behind the fountain is an art gallery showing off work by members of the local artists' association. To the right is Marien Apotheke, an old-time pharmacy mixing old and new in typical Rothenburg style.

The broad street running under the Town Hall tower is **Herrngasse.** The town originated with its castle fortress (built in 1142 but now long gone; a lovely garden now fills that space). Herrngasse connected the castle to Market Square. The last leg of this circular walking tour will take you from the castle garden up Herrngasse and back here.

For now, walk a few steps down Herrngasse and stop by the arch under the Town Hall tower (between the new and old town halls). On the wall to the left of the gate are the town's measuring rods—a reminder that medieval Germany was made of 300 independent little countries, many with their own weights and measures. Merchants and shoppers knew that these were the local standards: the

Herrngasse

rod (4.3 yards), the *Schuh* ("shoe," roughly a foot), and the *Ell* (from elbow to fingertip—four inches longer than mine...climb up and try it). The protruding cornerstone you're standing on is one of many all over town—originally to protect buildings from careening horse carts. In German, going recklessly fast is called "scratching the cornerstone."

• *Careen around that stone and under the arch to find the...*

▲HISTORICAL TOWN HALL VAULTS (HISTORIENGEWÖLBE)

The vaults house an eclectic and grade-schoolish little museum that gives a waxy but interesting look at Rothenburg during the Catholics-vs.-Protestants Thirty Years' War. Popping in here can help prep your imagination to filter out the tourists and picture ye olde Rothenburg along the rest of this walk. With helpful English descriptions, it offers a look at "the fateful year 1631," a replica of the mythical Meistertrunk tankard, an alchemist's workshop, and a dungeon complete with three dank cells and some torture lore.

Cost and Hours: €3, daily May-Oct 9:30-17:30, shorter hours off-season, closed Jan-Feb, tel. 09861/86751.

• *Leaving the museum, turn left (past a venerable and much-sketched-and-photographed door) and find a posted copy of a centuries-old map showing the territory of Rothenburg.*

MAP OF ROTHENBURG CITY TERRITORY

In 1537 Rothenburg actually ruled a little country—one of about 300 petty dukedoms like this that made up what is today's Germany. The territory spanned a 12-by-12-mile area (about 400 square kilometers), encompassing 180 villages—a good example of the fragmentation of feudal Germany. While not to scale (Rothenburg is actually less than a mile wide), the map is fun to study. In the 1380s, Mayor Toppler purchased much of this territory. In 1562, the city sold off some of its land to neighboring dukes, which gave it the money for all the fine Renaissance buildings that embellish the town to this day.

• *Continue through the courtyard and into a square called...*

GREEN MARKET (GRÜNER MARKT)

Once a produce market, this parking lot fills with Christmas stands during December. Notice the clay-tile roofs. These "beaver tail" tiles became standard after thatched roofs were outlawed to prevent fires. Today, all of the town's roofs are made of these. The little fences stop heaps of snow from falling off the roof and onto people below. A free public WC is on your left, and the recommended Friese gift shop is on your right.

• *Continue straight ahead to St. Jakob's Church. Study the exterior first, then pay to go inside.*

▲▲ST. JAKOB'S CHURCH (ST. JAKOBSKIRCHE)

Rothenburg's main church is home to Tilman Riemenschneider's exquisitely rendered, wood-carved *Altar of the Holy Blood.*

Cost and Hours: €2.50, daily April-Oct 9:00-17:15, Dec 10:00-16:45, Nov and Christmas-March 10:00-12:00 & 14:00-16:00, on Sun wait to enter until services end at 10:45.

Tours and Information: A free, helpful English info sheet is available. Concerts

Map of Old Rothenburg

and a tour schedule are posted on the door. Guided tours in English run on Sat at 15:30 (April-Oct) for no extra charge. The worthwhile audioguide (€2, 45 minutes) lets you tailor your education, offering a dual commentary—historical and theological—for a handful of important stops in the church.

Visiting the Church: Start by viewing the exterior of the church. Next, enter the church, where you'll see the main nave first, then climb above the pipe organ (in the back) to finish with the famous carved altar.

Exterior: Outside the church, under the little roof at the base of the tower, you'll see 14th-century statues (mostly original) showing Jesus praying at Gethsemane, a common feature of Gothic churches. The sculptor is anonymous—in the Gothic age (pre-Albrecht Dürer), artists were just nameless craftspeople working only for the glory of God. Five yards to the left (on the wall), notice the nub of a sandstone statue—a rare original, looking pretty bad after 500 years of weather and, more recently, pollution. Most original statues are now in the city museum. The better-preserved statues you see on the church are copies.

Before entering, notice how the church was extended to the west and actually built over the street. The newer chapel was built to accommodate pilgrims and to contain the sumptuous Riemenschneider carved altarpiece.

If it's your wedding day, take the first

St. Jakob's Church

entrance—marked by a very fertile Eve and, around the corner, Adam showing off an impressive six-pack. Otherwise, head toward the church's second (downhill) door. Before going inside, notice the modern statue at the base of the stairs. This is **St. James** (a.k.a. Sankt Jakob in German, Santiago in Spanish, and Saint-Jacques in French). You can tell this important saint by his big, floppy hat, his walking stick, the gourd on his hip (used by pilgrims to carry water), and—most importantly—the scallop shell in his hand. St. James' remains are entombed in the grand cathedral of Santiago de Compostela, in the northwestern corner of Spain. The medieval pilgrimage route called the Camino de Santiago (recently back in vogue) passed through here on its way to that distant corner of Europe. Pilgrims would wear the scallop shell as a symbol of their destination (where that type of marine life was abundant). To this day, the word for "scallop" in many languages carries the name of this saint: *Jakobsmuschel* in German, *coquille Saint-Jacques* in French, and so on.

Inside the Church: Built in the 14th century, this church has been Lutheran since 1544. The interior was "purified" by Romantics in the 19th century—cleaned of everything Baroque or not original and refitted in the Neo-Gothic style. (For example, the baptismal font in the middle of the choir and the pulpit above the second pew *look* Gothic, but are actually Neo-Gothic.) The stained-glass windows behind the altar, which are most colorful in the morning light, are originals from the 1330s. Admiring this church, consider what it says about the priorities of a town of just a few thousand people who decided to use their collective wealth to build such a place. The size of a church is a good indication of the town's wealth when it was built. Medallions and portraits of Rothenburg's leading families and church leaders line the walls above the choir in the front of the church.

The **main altar,** from 1466, is by Friedrich Herlin. Below Christ are statues of six saints—including St. James (a.k.a. Jakob), with the telltale shell on his floppy hat. Study the painted panels—ever see Peter with spectacles (below the carved saints)? Go around the back of the altarpiece to look at the doors. In the upper left, you'll see a painting of Rothenburg's Market Square in the 15th century, looking much like it does today, with the exception of the full-Gothic Town Hall (as it was before the big fire of 1501). Notice Christ's face on the white "veil of Veronica" (center of back side, bottom edge). It follows you as you walk from side to side—this must have given the faithful the religious heebie-jeebies four centuries ago.

The **Tabernacle of the Holy Eucharist** (just left of the main altar—on your right as you walk back around) is a century older. It stored the wine and bread used for Holy Communion. Before the Reformation, this was a Roman Catholic church, which meant that the bread and wine were considered to be the actual body and blood of Jesus (and therefore needed a worthy repository). Notice the unusual Trinity: The Father and Son are bridged by a dove, which represents the Holy Spirit. Stepping back, you can see that Jesus is standing on a skull—clearly "overcoming death."

Now, as pilgrims did centuries ago, climb the stairs at the back of the church that lead up behind the pipe organ to a loft-like chapel. Here you'll find the artistic highlight of Rothenburg and perhaps the most wonderful wood carving in all of Germany: the glorious 500-year-old, 35-foot-high ***Altar of the Holy Blood.*** Tilman Riemenschneider, the Michelangelo of German woodcarvers, carved this from 1499 to 1504 (at the same time Michelangelo was working on his own masterpieces). The altarpiece was designed to hold a rock-crystal capsule—set in the cross you see high above—that contains a precious scrap of tablecloth stained in the shape of a cross by a drop of communion wine.

The altar is a realistic commotion, showing that Riemenschneider—a High Gothic artist—was ahead of his time. Below, in the scene of the Last Supper, Jesus gives Judas a piece of bread, marking him as the traitor, while John lays his head on Christ's lap. Judas, with his big bag of cash, could be removed from the scene (illustrated by photos on the wall nearby), as was the tradition for the four days leading up to Easter.

Everything is portrayed exactly as described in the Bible. In the relief panel on the left, Jesus enters the walled city of Jerusalem. Notice the exacting attention to detail—down to the nails on the horseshoe. In the relief panel on the right, Jesus prays in the Garden of Gethsemane.

Before continuing on, take a moment to simply linger over the lovingly executed details: the curly locks of the apostles' hair and beards, and the folds of their garments; the delicate vines intertwining above their heads; Jesus' expression, at once tender and accusing.

• *After leaving the church, walk around the corner to the right and under the chapel (built over the road). Go two blocks down Klingengasse and stop at the corner of the street called Klosterhof. Looking farther ahead of you down Klingengasse, you see the...*

Altar of the Holy Blood

KLINGENTOR

This cliff tower was Rothenburg's water reservoir. From 1595 until 1910, a 900-liter (240-gallon) copper tank high in the tower provided clean spring water—pumped up by river power—to the privileged. To the right of the Klingentor is a good stretch of wall rampart to walk. To the left, the wall is low and simple, lacking a rampart because it guards only a cliff.

Now find the shell decorating a building on the street corner next to you. That's once again the symbol of St. James, indicating that this building is associated with the church.

• *Turn left down Klosterhof, passing the shell and, on your right, the colorful, recommended Altfränkische Weinstube am Klosterhof pub. As you approach the next stop, notice the lazy Susan embedded in the wall (to the right of the museum door), which allowed cloistered nuns to give food to the poor without being seen.*

▲▲IMPERIAL CITY MUSEUM (REICHSSTADT-MUSEUM)

You'll get a vivid and artifact-filled sweep through Rothenburg's history at this excellent museum, housed in a former Dominican convent.

Cost and Hours: €4.50, €3 more to take photos (not worth it for most), daily April-Oct 9:30-17:30, Nov-March 13:00-16:00, pick up English info sheet at entrance, additional English descriptions posted, Klosterhof 5, tel. 09861/939-043, www.reichsstadtmuseum.rothenburg.de.

Visiting the Museum: As you follow the *Rundgang/Tour* signs to the left, watch for the following highlights:

Immediately inside the entry, a glass case shows off the 1616 Prince Elector's colorful glass tankard (which inspired the famous legend of the Meistertrunk, created in 1881 to drive tourism) and a set of golden Rothenburg coins. Down the hall, find a modern city model and trace the city's growth, its walls expanding like rings on a big tree. Around the corner (before going upstairs), you'll see medieval and Renaissance sculptures, including original sandstone statues from St. Jakob's Church and original statues that once decorated the Baumeister Haus near Market Square. Upstairs in the nuns' dormitory are craftsmen's signs that once hung outside shops (see if you can guess the craft before reading the museum's label), ornate locks, tools for various professions, and a valuable collection of armor and weapons. You'll then see old furniture and the Baroque statues that decorated the organ loft in St. Jakob's Church from 1669 until the 19th century, when they were cleared out to achieve "Gothic purity." Take time to enjoy the several rooms and shop fronts outfitted as they would have been centuries ago.

The painting gallery is lined with Romantic paintings of Rothenburg, which served as the first tourist promotion, and give visitors today a chance to envision the city as it appeared in centuries past. Look for the large, gloomy work by Englishman Arthur Wasse (labeled *"Es spukt"*)—does that door look familiar?

Back downstairs, circle around the cloister to see a 14th-century convent kitchen *(Klosterküche)* with a working model of the lazy Susan (give it a swing) and a massive chimney (step inside and look up); an exhibit of Jewish culture in Rothenburg through the ages *(Judaika)*; and the grand finale (in the *Konventsaal*), the *Rothenburger Passion*. This 12-panel series of paintings showing scenes leading

Imperial City Museum

up to Christ's Crucifixion—originally intended for the town's Franciscan church (which we'll pass later)—dates from 1492.

• *Leaving the museum, go around to the right and into the Convent Garden (when locked at night, continue straight to the T-intersection and turn right).*

CONVENT GARDEN

This spot is a peaceful place to work on your tan...or mix a poisoned potion. Monks and nuns—who were responsible for concocting herbal cures in the olden days, finding disinfectants, and coming up with ways to disguise the taste of rotten food—often tended herb gardens. Smell (but don't pick) the *Pfefferminze* (peppermint), *Heidewacholder* (juniper/gin), *Rosmarin* (rosemary), *Lavandel* (lavender), and the tallest plant, *Hopfen* (hops... monks were the great medieval brewers). Don't smell the plants that are poisonous (potency indicated by the number of crosses, like stars indicating spiciness on a restaurant menu). Appreciate the setting, taking in the fine architecture and expansive garden—all within the city walls, where land was at such a premium. It's a reminder of the power of the pre-Reformation Church.

• *Exit opposite from where you entered, angling left through the nuns' garden, leaving via an arch along the far wall. Then turn right and go downhill to the...*

TOWN WALL

This part of the wall takes advantage of the natural fortification provided by the cliff (view through bars, look to far right), and is therefore much shorter than the ramparts.

• *Angle left along the wall. Cross the big street (Herrngasse, with the Burgtor tower on your right—which we'll enter from outside momentarily) and continue downhill on Burggasse until you hit the town wall. Turn right, go through a small tower gate, and park yourself at the town's finest viewpoint.*

CASTLE GARDEN VIEWPOINT

From here, enjoy a fine view of fortified Rothenburg. You're looking at the Spitaltor end of town (with the most interesting gate and the former hospital). After this walk, you can continue with my "Schmiedgasse-Spitalgasse Shopping Stroll," which leads from Market Square down to this end of town, and then enter the city walls and walk the ramparts 180 degrees to the Klingentor tower (which we saw earlier on our walk, in the distance just after St. Jakob's Church). The droopy-eyed building at the far end of town (today's youth hostel) was the horse mill—which provided grinding power when the water mill in the valley below was not working (during drought or siege). Stretching below you is the fine parklike land around the Tauber River, nicknamed the "Tauber Riviera."

• *Now explore deeper into the park.*

CASTLE GARDEN (BURGGARTEN) AND THE BURGTOR GATE

The park before you was a castle fortress until it was destroyed in the 14th century.

Convent Garden

Burgtor Gate

The chapel (50 yards straight into the park, on the left) is the only surviving bit of the original castle. In front of the chapel is a memorial to local Jews killed in a 1298 slaughter. A few steps beyond that is a flowery trellis that provides a fine picnic spot. If you walk all the way out to the garden's far end, you'll find another great viewpoint (well past the tourists, and considered by local teenagers the best place to make out).

When you're ready to leave the park, approach the Burgtor, the ornate fortified gate flanked by twin stubby towers, and imagine being locked out in the year 1400. (There's a WC on the left.) The tall tower behind the gate was accessed by a wooden drawbridge—see the chain slits above the inner gate, and between them the "pitch" mask with holes designed to allow defenders to pour boiling Nutella on attackers. High above is the town coat of arms: a red *(roten)* castle *(Burg)*.

Go through the gate and study the big wooden door with the tiny "eye of the needle" door cut into it. If trying to enter town after curfew, you could bribe the guard to let you through this door, which was small enough to keep out any fully armed attackers. Note also the square-shaped hole on the right and imagine the massive timber that once barricaded the gate.

• *Now, climb up the big street, Herrngasse, as you return to your starting point.*

HERRNGASSE

Many towns have a Herrngasse, where the richest patricians and merchants (the *Herren*) lived. Predictably, it's your best chance to see the town's finest old mansions. Strolling back to Market Square, you'll pass, on the right, the **Franciscan Church** (from 1285—the oldest in town). Across the street, the mint-green house at #18 is the biggest patrician house on this main drag. The front door was big enough to allow a carriage to drive through it; a human-sized door cut into it was used by those on foot. The family, which has lived here for three centuries, has disconnected the four tempting old-time doorbells. The gift shop at #11 (on the right) offers a chance to poke into one of these big landowners' homes and appreciate their structure: living quarters in front above carriage-size doors, courtyard out back functioning as a garage, stables, warehouse, servants' quarters, and a private well.

Farther up, also on the right, is Hotel Eisenhut, Rothenburg's fanciest hotel and worth a peek inside. Finally, passing the Käthe Wohlfahrt Christmas headquarters/shop (described under "Shopping," later) you'll be back at Market Square, where you started this walk.

• *From here, you can continue walking by following my "Schmiedgasse-Spitalgasse Shopping Stroll," next. This stroll ends at the city gate called Spitaltor, a good access point for a walk on the town walls.*

➲ *Schmiedgasse-Spitalgasse Shopping Stroll*

After doing the town walk and visiting the town's three essential interior sights (Imperial City Museum, Medieval Crime and Punishment Museum, and St. Jakob's Church), your next priority might be Rothenburg's shops and its town wall.

I'd propose this fun walk, worth ▲▲, which goes from Market Square in a straight line south (past the best selection of characteristic family-run shops) to the city's most impressive fortification (Spitaltor). From Spitaltor you can access the town wall and walk the ramparts 180 degrees around the city to the Klingentor tower.

Standing on Market Square, with your back to the TI, you'll see a street sloping downward toward the south end of town. That's where you're headed. This street changes names as you walk, from **Obere Schmiedgasse** (upper blacksmith street) to **Spitalgasse** (hospital street), and runs directly to the **Spitaltor** tower and gate.

As you stroll down this delightful lane,

feel welcome to pop in and explore any shop along this cultural and historical scavenger hunt. I've provided the street number and "left" or "right" to indicate the side of the street.

Start on Market Square. The facade of the fine Renaissance **Baumeister Haus** at #3 (left) celebrates a secular (rather than religious) morality, with statues representing the seven virtues and the seven vices. Which ones do you recognize?

At #5 (left) **Gasthof Goldener Greifen** was once the home of the illustrious Mayor Toppler (d. 1408). By the looks of its door (right of the main entrance), the mayor must have had an impressive wine cellar. Note the fine hanging sign of a gilded griffin. Business signs in a mostly illiterate medieval world needed to be easy for all to read. The entire street is ornamented with fun signs like this one. Nearby, a pretzel marks the bakery, and the crossed swords advertise the weapon maker.

Shops on both sides of the street at #7 display examples of ***Schneeballen*** gone wild. These "snowballs," once a humble way to bake extra flour into a simple treat, are now iced and dolled up a million ways. Long ago, locals used a fork to pierce the middle, but today's tourists eat them like an apple. Watch them crumble.

Waffenkammer, at #9 (left), is "the weapons chamber," where Johannes Wittmann works hard to make a wonderland in which young-at-heart tourists can shop for (and try out) medieval weapons, armor, and clothing. Fun photo ops abound, especially downstairs—where you can try on a set of chain mail and pose with a knight in shining armor.

At #18 (right), **Metzgerei Trumpp,** a top-end butcher, is a carnivores' heaven. Check out the endless wurst offerings in the window—a reminder that in the unrefrigerated Middle Ages meat needed to be smoked or salted.

At the next corner, with **Burggasse,** find the Catholic St. John's Church. The Medieval Crime and Punishment Museum (just down the lane to the right) marks the site of Rothenburg's first town wall. Below the church (on the right) is an old fountain. Behind and below that find a cute little doggie park complete with a doggie WC.

The **Jutta Korn** shop, on the right at #4, showcases the work of an artisan who has designed jewelry here for 30 years. At #6 (right), **Leyk** sells "lighthouses" made in town, many modeled after local buildings. The **Kleiderey,** an offbeat clothing store at #7 (left), is run by Tina, the Night Watchman's wife. The clothing is inspired by their Southeast Asian travels.

At #13 (left), look opposite to find a narrow lane **(Ander Eich)** that leads to a little viewpoint in the town wall, overlooking the "Tauber Riviera."

Continuing along, at #17 (left), the **Lebe Gesund Vegetarian** shop is all about healthy living. This charming little place seems designed to offer forgiveness to those who loved the butcher's shop but are ready to repent.

The **Käthe Wohlfahrt** shop at #19 (left) is just another of the KW shops around town, all selling German clichés with gusto. Also on the left, at #21, the **An Ra** Shop is where Annett Rafoth designs and sells her flowery clothes. You can pop in to see the actual work in the back. (There's more of An Ra across the street at #26.)

At **Kunsthandlung Leyrer** (on the left,

at #23), Peter Leyrer would love to show you his etchings (if he hasn't retired). He is one of the last artisans using Albrecht Dürer's copper-plate technique to print his art. After he retires, his 3,500 copper plates from all over Germany will go to a museum. Peter and his wife print the black-and-white etchings and then apply watercolor.

At #29 (left), **Glocke Weinladen am Plönlein** is an inviting shop of wine glasses and related accessories. The **Gasthof Glocke,** next door, with its wine-barrel-sized cellar door just waiting for some action, is a respected restaurant and home to the town's last vintner—a wonderful place to try local wines, as they serve flights of five tiny glasses.

The next corner, on the right, is dubbed **Plönlein** and is famously picturesque. If this scene brings you back to your childhood, that's because Rothenburg was the inspiration for the village in the 1940 Disney animated film *Pinocchio.*

Walk a few more yards and look far up the lane **(Neugasse)** to the left. You'll see some cute pastel buildings with uniform windows and rooflines—clues that the buildings were rebuilt after WWII bombings hit that part of town. Straight ahead, the **Siebertstor Tower** marks the next layer of expansion to the town wall. Continue through the tower. The former tannery is now a pub featuring **Landwehr Bräu,** the local brew.

Farther along, at #14 (right), **Antiq & Trödel,** which smells like an antique shop should, is fun to browse through.

Still farther down, on the left, at #25, **Hotel-Café Gerberhaus** is a fine stop for coffee and cake, with a delicate dining room and a peaceful courtyard hiding out back under the town wall.

The remaining few (boring) blocks take you to **Spitaltor,** the tall tower with a gate marking the end of town, and a good place to begin a ramparts ramble (going counterclockwise), if you're up for it.

Walk through the gate (taking note of the stairs to the right—that's where you could begin your wall walk—described next). Standing outside the wall, ponder this sight as if approaching the city 400 years ago. The wealth of a city was shown by its walls and towers. (Stone was costly—in fact, the German saying for "filthy rich" is "stone rich.") Circle around to the right. Look up at the formidable tower. The guardhouse atop it, one of several in the wall, was manned continuously during medieval times. Above the entry gate, notice the emblem: Angels bless the double eagle of the Holy Roman Emperor, which blesses the town, symbolized by the two red towers.

➲ *Walk the Wall*

Just longer than a mile and a half around, providing superb views and a fine orientation, this walk, worth ▲▲, can be done by those under six feet tall in less than an hour. The hike requires no special sense of balance. Much of the walk is covered and is a great option in the rain. Photographers will stay very busy, especially before breakfast or at sunset when the lighting is best and the crowds are gone. You can enter or exit the ramparts at nearly every tower.

While the ramparts circle the city, some stretches aren't walkable per se: Along much of the western side of town, you can't walk atop the wall, but you can walk right alongside it and peek over or through it for great views outward from street

The city ramparts

level. Refer to the map on page 193 to see which portions of the walls are walkable.

If you want to make a full town circuit, Spitaltor—at the south end of town, with the best fortifications—makes a good starting place. From here, it's a counter-clockwise walk along the eastern and northern ramparts. After exiting at Klingentor, you can still follow the wall for a bit, but you'll have to cut inland, away from the wall, when you hit the Imperial City Museum, and again near the Medieval Crime and Punishment Museum. At the Kohlturm tower, back at the southern end of town, you can climb the stairs and walk atop the remaining short stretch of wall to the Spitalhof quarter, where you'll need to exit again. Spitaltor, where you started, is just a *Schneeball*'s toss away.

The TI has installed a helpful series of English-language plaques at about 20 stops along the route. The names you see along the way belong to people who donated money to rebuild the wall after World War II, and those who've more recently donated €1,000 per meter for the maintenance of Rothenburg's heritage.

Sights

Note that a number of sights (including St. Jakob's Church and the Imperial City Museum) have already been covered on the Rothenburg Town Walk.

On and Near Market Square

▲TOWN HALL TOWER

From Market Square you can see tourists on the crow's nest capping the Town Hall's tower. For a commanding view from the town's tallest perch, climb the steps of the tower. It's a rigorous but interesting 214-step climb that gets narrow and steep near the top—watch your head.

Cost and Hours: €2, pay at top, daily in season 9:00-12:30 & 13:00-17:00, enter from the grand steps overlooking Market Square.

▲▲MEDIEVAL CRIME AND PUNISHMENT MUSEUM (MITTELALTERLICHES KRIMINALMUSEUM)

Specializing in everything connected to medieval criminal justice, this exhibit (well-described in English) is a cut above all the tacky and popular torture museums around Europe. In addition to ogling spiked chairs, thumbscrews, and shame masks—nearly everything on display here is an actual medieval artifact—you'll learn about medieval police and criminal law. The museum is more eclectic than its name, and includes exhibits on general history, superstition, biblical art, and so on.

Cost and Hours: €5, daily April 11:00-17:00, May-Oct 10:00-18:00, Nov and Jan-Feb 14:00-16:00, Dec and March 13:00-16:00, last entry 45 minutes before closing, fun cards and posters, Burggasse 3-5, tel. 09861/5359, www.kriminalmuseum.rothenburg.de.

Visiting the Museum: It's a one-way route. Just follow the yellow arrows and you'll see it all. Keep an eye out for several well-done interactive media stations that provide extra background on the museum's highlights.

From the entrance, head downstairs to the **cellar** to see some enhanced-interrogation devices. Torture was common in the Middle Ages—not to punish, but to extract a confession (medieval "justice" required a confession). Just the sight of these tools was often enough to make an innocent man confess. You'll see the rack, "stretching ladder," thumb

screws, spiked leg screws, and other items that would make Dick Cheney proud. Medieval torturers also employed a waterboarding-like technique—but here, the special ingredient was holy water.

Upstairs, on the **first and second floors,** the walls are lined with various legal documents of the age, while the dusty glass cases show off law-enforcement tools—many of them quite creative. Shame was a big tool back then; wrongdoers would be creatively shamed before their neighbors. The town could publicly humiliate those who ran afoul of the law by tying them to a pillory in the main square and covering their faces in an iron mask of shame. The mask's fanciful decorations indicated the crime: Chicken feathers meant promiscuity, horns indicated that a man's wife slept around (i.e., cuckold), and a snout suggested that the person had acted piggishly. A gossip might wear a mask with giant ears (heard everything), eyeglasses (saw everything), and a giant, wagging tongue (couldn't keep her mouth shut). The infamous "iron maiden" started out as more of a "shame barrel"; the internal spikes were added to play up popular lore when it went on display for 18th-century tourists. For more serious offenses, criminals were branded—so that even if they left town, they'd take that shame with them for the rest of their lives. When all else failed, those in charge could always turn to the executioner's sword.

To safely capture potential witches, lawmen used a device resembling a metal collar—with spikes pointing in—that was easy to get into, but nearly impossible to get out of. A neck violin—like a portable version of a stock—kept the accused under control. (The double neck violin could be used to lock together a quarrelsome couple to force them to work things out.) The chastity belts were used to ensure a wife's loyalty (giving her traveling husband peace of mind) and/or to protect women from attack at a time when rape was far more commonplace. The exit routes you through a courtyard garden to a **last building** with temporary exhibits (included in your admission and often interesting) and a café. (If you must buy a *Schneeball,* consider doing it here—where they are small, inexpensive, and fairly edible—and help support the museum.)

▲GERMAN CHRISTMAS MUSEUM (DEUTSCHES WEIHNACHTSMUSEUM)

This excellent museum, in a Disney-esque space upstairs in the giant Käthe Wohlfahrt Christmas Village shop, tells the history of Christmas decorations. There's a unique and thoughtfully described collection of tree stands, mini-trees sent in boxes to WWI soldiers at the front, early Advent calendars, old-time Christmas cards, Christmas pyramids, and a look at the evolution of Father Christmas, as well as tree decorations through the ages—including the Nazi era and when you were a kid. The museum is not just a ploy to get shoppers to spend more money, but a serious collection managed by professional curator Felicitas Höptner.

Cost and Hours: €4 most of the year, open April-Dec daily 10:00-17:30, shorter and irregular hours Jan-March, Herrngasse 1, tel. 09861/409-365, www.christmasmuseum.com.

Experiences

Shopping

Be warned...Rothenburg is one of Germany's best shopping towns. Do it here and be done with it. Lovely prints, carvings, wine glasses, Christmas-tree ornaments, and beer steins are popular. Rödergasse is the old town's everyday shopping street. Also try my Shopping Stroll on page 205. There's also a modern shopping center across the street from the train station.

KÄTHE WOHLFAHRT CHRISTMAS HEADQUARTERS

Rothenburg is the headquarters of the **Käthe Wohlfahrt** Christmas trinkets empire, which has spread across the half-timbered reaches of Europe. Rothenburg has six or eight Wohlfahrts (all stores open Mon-Sat 9:00-18:30, May-Dec also most Sun 10:00-18:00). Tourists flock to the two biggest, just below Market Square. Start with the **Christmas Village** (Weihnachtsdorf) at Herrngasse 1. This Christmas wonderland is filled with enough twinkling lights (196,000—mostly LEDs) to require a special electrical hookup. You're greeted by instant Christmas mood music (best appreciated on a hot day in July) and tourists hungrily filling little woven shopping baskets with goodies to hang on their trees. Let the spinning, flocked tree whisk you in, and pause at the wall of Steiff stuffed animals, jerking uncontrollably and mesmerizing kids. Then head downstairs to find the vast and sprawling "made in Germany" section, surrounding a slowly spinning 15-foot tree decorated with a thousand glass balls. (Items handmade in Germany are the most expensive.) They often offer a discount on all official KW products to my readers—ask. The fascinating **Christmas Museum** upstairs is described earlier, under "Sights." The smaller shop (across the street at Herrngasse 2) specializes in finely crafted wooden ornaments. Käthe opened her first storefront here in Rothenburg in 1977. The company is now run by her son Harald, who lives in town.

Rick's Tip: *To* **mail your goodies home,** *you can get handy yellow €2.50 boxes at the old town* **post office** *(Mon-Tue and Thu-Fri 9:00-13:00 & 14:00-17:30, Wed 9:00-13:00, Sat 9:00-12:00, closed Sun, inside photo shop at Rödergasse 11). The main post office is in the shopping center across from the train station.*

FRIESE SHOP

Cuckoo with friendliness, trinkets, and reasonably priced souvenirs, the Friese shop has been open for more than 50 years. Shoppers with this book receive tremendous service: a 10 percent discount and a free pictorial map (normally €1.50). Anneliese Friese, who runs the place with her son Bernie and granddaughter Dolores (a.k.a. "Mousy"), charges only her cost for shipping and lets tired travelers leave their bags in her back room for free (Mon-Sat 9:00-18:00, Sun 10:00-18:00, 20 steps off Market Square at Grüner Markt 8—around the corner from TI and across from free public WC, tel. 09861/7166).

Festivals

For one weekend each spring (during Pentecost), *Biergartens* spill out into the street and Rothenburgers dress up in medieval costumes to celebrate Mayor Nusch's **Meistertrunk** victory (www.meistertrunk.de). The **Reichsstadt festival** every September celebrates Rothenburg's history, and the town's **Weindorf festival** celebrates its wine (mid-Aug). For more info, check the TI website: www.tourismus.rothenburg.de.

In winter, Rothenburg is quiet except for its **Christmas Market** in December, when the entire town cranks up the medieval cuteness with concerts and costumes, shops with schnapps, stalls filling squares, hot spiced wine, giddy nutcrackers, and mobs of ear-muffed Germans. Try to avoid Saturdays and Sundays, when big-city day-trippers really clog the grog.

Eating

My recommendations are all within a five-minute walk of Market Square. While all survive on tourism, many still feel like local hangouts. Your choices are typical German or ethnic. You'll see regional Franconian *(fränkische)* specialties advertised, such as the German ravioli called *Maultaschen* and Franconian bratwurst (similar to other brats, but more coarsely ground, with less fat, and liberally seasoned with marjoram). Many restaurants take a midafternoon break, stop serving lunch at 14:00, and end dinner service as early as 20:00.

Traditional German Restaurants

Reichsküchenmeister's interior is like any big-hotel restaurant's, but on a balmy evening, its pleasant, tree-shaded terrace overlooking St. Jakob's Church and reliably good dishes are hard to beat (€10-25 main courses, €7-10 *Flammkuchen*—southern German flatbread, steaks, vegetarian options, daily 11:30-21:30, Kirchplatz 8, tel. 09861/9700).

$$ Hotel Restaurant Kloster-Stüble, on a small street off Herrngasse near the castle garden, is a classy place for delicious traditional cuisine, including homemade *Maultaschen*. Choose from their shaded terrace, sleek and modern dining room, or woody and traditional dining room (€10-20 main courses, Thu-Mon 18:00-21:00, Sat-Sun also 11:00-14:00, closed Tue-Wed, Heringsbronnengasse 5, tel. 09861/938-890).

$$ Gasthof Goldener Greifen, in a historic building with a peaceful garden out back, is just off the main square. The Klingler family serves quality Franconian food at a good price...and with a smile. The ambience is practical rather than posh (€8-17 main courses, €12-15 three-course daily specials, affordable kids' meals, daily 11:30-21:00 except closed Sun in winter, Obere Schmiedgasse 5, tel. 09861/2281).

Rick's Tip: *For a rare chance to* **meet the locals,** *bring your favorite slang and tongue-twisters to the* **English Conversation Club** *at* **Altfränkische Weinstube am Klosterhof.** *Hermann the German and his sidekick Wolfgang are regulars. A big table is reserved from 18:30 on Wednesday evenings. Consider arriving early for dinner, or after 21:00, when the beer starts to sink in and everyone speaks that second language more easily.*

$ Altfränkische Weinstube am Klosterhof, classically candlelit in a 600-year-old building, seems designed for gnomes to celebrate their anniversaries with gourmet pub grub. It's a clear favorite with locals for an atmospheric drink or late meal. When every other place is asleep, you're likely to find good food, drink, and energy here (€7-15 main courses, hot food served Wed-Mon 18:00-21:30, closed Tue, off Klingengasse at Klosterhof 7, tel. 09861/6404).

$ Zum Pulverer ("The Powderer") is a

English Conversation Club

traditional wine bar just inside the Burgtor gate that serves a menu of affordable regional fare, sometimes with modern flourishes. The interior is a cozy woodhewn place that oozes history, with chairs carved in the shape of past senators of Rothenburg (€6-14 dishes, Wed-Fri and Mon 17:00-22:00, Sat-Sun 12:00-22:00, closed Tue, Herrengasse 31, tel. 09861/976-182, Bastian).

$ Alter Keller is a modest, tourist-friendly restaurant with a characteristic interior and outdoor tables on a peaceful square just a couple blocks off Market Square. The menu has German classics at reasonable prices (€8-14 main dishes, Wed-Sun 11:30-15:00 & 17:30-21:00, closed Mon-Tue, Alter Keller 8, tel. 09861/2268, Markus and Miriam).

A Non-Franconian Splurge

$$$$ Hotel Restaurant Herrnschlösschen is the local favorite fare, with a small menu of international and seasonal dishes. There's always a serious vegetarian option and a €50 fixed-price meal with matching wine. Sit in the classy dining hall or in the shaded Baroque garden out back. Reservations are a must (€20-30 main dishes, Herrngasse 20, tel. 09861/873-890, www.hotel-rothenburg.de).

Breaks from Pork and Potatoes

$$ Pizzeria Roma is the local favorite for pizza and pastas, with good Italian wine. The Magrini family moved here from Tuscany in 1970 and they've been serving pasta ever since (Thu-Tue 11:30-23:00, closed Wed and mid-Aug-mid-Sept, Galgengasse 19, tel. 09861/4540).

$ TobinGo, just off Market Square, serves cheap and tasty Turkish food to eat in or take away. Their *Döner Kebabs* must be the best €3.70 hot meal in Rothenburg. For about €1 more, try a less-bready *Dürüm Döner*—same ingredients but in a warm tortilla (daily 10:00-22:00, Hafengasse 2).

Sandwiches and Snacks

$ Brot & Zeit (a pun on *Brotzeit*, "bread time," the German term for snacking), conveniently located a block off Market Square, is like a German bakery dressed up as a Starbucks. Just inside the picturesque Markus Tower gate, they sell takeaway coffee, inexpensive sandwiches, and a few hot dishes (Mon-Sat 6:00-18:30, Sun 7:30-18:00, Hafengasse 24, tel. 09861/936-8701).

While any bakery in town can sell you a sandwich for a couple of euros, I like to pop into **Metzgerei Trumpp,** a high-quality butcher shop serving up cheap and tasty sausages on a bun with kraut to go (Mon-Fri 7:30-18:00, Sat until 16:00, usually closed Sun, a block off Market Square at Schmiedgasse 18).

A small **grocery store** is in the center of town (Mon-Fri 7:30-19:00, Sat-Sun until 18:00 except closed Sun off-season, Rödergasse 6). Larger supermarkets are outside the wall: Exit the town through the Rödertor, turn left through the cobbled gate, and cross the parking lot to reach the **Edeka supermarket** (Mon-Fri 8:00-20:00, Sat until 18:00, closed Sun); or head to the even bigger **Kaufland** across from the train station (Mon-Sat 7:00-20:00, closed Sun).

Beer Garden (Biergarten)

$ Gasthof Rödertor, just outside the wall through the Rödertor, runs a popular backyard *Biergarten,* where a rowdy crowd enjoys classic fare, pizza, and good beer. Their passion is potatoes (May-Sept daily 17:30-23:00 in good weather, table service only—no ordering at counter, Ansbacher Strasse 7, look for wooden gate, tel. 09861/2022). The *Biergarten* is open only in balmy weather, but their indoor restaurant, with a more extensive menu, is open year-round and also offers a good value (€8-13 main courses, Tue-Sun 11:30-14:00 & 17:30-21:30, closed Mon).

Dessert

Eis Café D'Isep has been making gelato in Rothenburg since 1960, using family recipes that span four generations. Their sidewalk tables are great for lazy people-watching (daily 10:00-22:00, closed early Oct-mid-Feb, one block off Market Square at Hafengasse 17, run by Paolo and Paola D'Isep and son Enrico).

Rothenburg's **bakeries** *(Bäckereien)* offer succulent pastries, pies, and cakes... but skip the bad-tasting *Rothenburger Schneeballen* promoted all over town: bland pie crusts crumpled into a ball and dusted with powdered sugar or frosted with sticky-sweet glop. Instead of wasting your appetite on a *Schneeball*, enjoy a curvy *Mandelhörnchen* (almond crescent cookie), a triangular *Nussecke* ("nut corner"), a round *Florentiner* cookie, a couple of fresh *Krapfen* (like jelly doughnuts), or a soft, warm German pretzel. But if the curiosity is too much to bear, try a fresh, handmade *Schneeball* from a smaller bakery *(frisch* is fresh; *handgemacht* is handmade), and avoid the slick places on the busy tourist avenues.

Wine-Drinking in the Old Center

$$ Restaurant Glocke, a wine bar with a full menu, is run by Rothenburg's oldest and only surviving winemakers, the Thürauf family. The very extensive wine list is in German only because the friendly staff wants to explain your options in person. Their special €5 wine flight lets you sample five Franconian white wines; other flights of reds and dessert wines are offered as well (€8-18 main courses, Mon-Sat 11:00-23:00, food until 22:00, closed Sun, Plönlein 1, tel. 09861/958-990).

Sleeping

Rothenburg is crowded with visitors, but most are day-trippers. Except for the rare Saturday night and during festivals (see page 210), finding a room is easy. If you want to splurge, you'll snare the best value by paying extra for the biggest and best rooms at the hotels I recommend. In the off-season (Nov and Jan-March), hoteliers may be willing to discount.

Train travelers save steps by staying in the Rödertor area (east end of town). Hotels and guesthouses will sometimes pick up tired heavy-packers at the station. If you're driving, call ahead to get directions and parking tips. Save some energy to climb the stairs: No hotels listed here have elevators.

Keep your key when out late. As Rothenburg's hotels are small and mostly family-run, they often lock up early (at about 22:00) and take one day a week off, so you'll need to let yourself in at those times.

In the Old Town

$$$ Hotel Herrnschlösschen prides itself on being the smallest (8 rooms) and most exclusive hotel in Rothenburg. If you're looking for a splurge, this is your best bet. This 1,000-year-old building has a beautiful Baroque garden and every amenity you'd ever want (including a sauna), but you'll pay for them (deluxe Db-€210, pricier suites, see website for seasonal discounts, Wi-Fi, Herrngasse 20, tel. 09861/873890, www.herrnschloesschen.de, info@herrnschloesschen.de).

$$ Hotel Kloster-Stüble, deep in the old town near the castle garden, is one of my classiest listings. Twenty-one rooms, each with its own special touches, fill two medieval buildings, connected by a modern atrium (traditional Db-€88-108, bigger and modern Db-€140-150, suites and family rooms, kids 5 and under free, just off Herrngasse at Heringsbronnengasse 5, tel. 09861/938-890, www.klosterstueble.de, hotel@klosterstueble.de).

Sleep Code

$$$$ Splurge: Over €170
$$$ Pricier: €130-170
$$ Moderate: €90-130
$ Budget: €50-90
¢ Backpacker: Under €50

Hotels are classified based on the average price of a standard double room with bath in high season. Unless otherwise noted, credit cards are accepted, breakfast is included, hotel staff speak English, and Wi-Fi is available.

$$$ Hotel Spitzweg is a rustic yet elegant 1536 mansion with 10 big rooms, open beams, antique furniture, and new bathrooms. It's run by gentle Herr Hocher, whom I suspect is the former Wizard of Oz—now retired and in a very good mood (Db-€90-100, family rooms and an apartment, nonsmoking, inviting old-fashioned breakfast room, free parking, Wi-Fi at son-in-law's nearby hotel, Paradeisgasse 2, tel. 09861/94290, www.hotel-spitzweg.de, info@hotel-spitzweg.de).

$$$ Gasthof Goldener Greifen is a traditional, 600-year-old place with 14 spacious rooms and all the comforts. It's run by a helpful family that also runs a good restaurant, serving meals in the back garden or dining room (small Db-€75, big Db-€85-104, family rooms, 10 percent less for 3-night stays, nonsmoking, full-service laundry-€8, free loaner bikes for guests, free and easy parking, half a block downhill from Market Square at Obere Schmiedgasse 5, tel. 09861/2281, www.gasthof-greifen-rothenburg.de, info@gasthof-greifen-rothenburg.de).

$$ Hotel Gerberhaus has 20 bright and airy rooms that mix modern amenities with half-timbered elegance. Enjoy the pleasant garden in back and the delightful breakfast buffet (Db-€89-130, family rooms and an apartment, €10 off second and subsequent nights and a *Schneeball* if you book direct and pay cash, nonsmoking, 4 rooms have canopied 4-poster *Himmel* beds, laundry-€10, limited free parking, close to P-1 parking lot, Spitalgasse 25, tel. 09861/94900, www.gerberhaus.rothenburg.de, gerberhaus@t-online.de).

$ Hotel Altfränkische Weinstube am Klosterhof is *the* place for well-heeled bohemians, with seven cozy rooms above the locals' favorite pub. The 600-year-old building has an upscale *Lord of the Rings* atmosphere, with open-beam ceilings, some canopied four-poster beds, and modern plumbing (Db-€69, bigger Db-€82, Db suite-€118, off Klingengasse at Klosterhof 7, tel. 09861/6404, www.altfraenkische.de, altfraenkische-weinstube@web.de).

$ Pension Elke rents 12 comfy rooms above a family grocery store (D-€57, Db-€65-69, cash only, request Rick Steves discount with this book if you stay at least 2 nights; reception in grocery store until 19:00, otherwise go around back and ring bell at top of stairs; near Markus Tower at Rödergasse 6, tel. 09861/2331, www.pension-elke-rothenburg.de, info@pension-elke-rothenburg.de).

$ Gästehaus Raidel rents eight rooms in a 500-year-old house with charming, ramshackle ambience. The beds and furniture are handmade by Norry Raidel himself. He also plays in a Dixieland band, has invented a fascinating hybrid saxophone/trombone called the Norryphone... and loves to jam (Db-€69, family rooms, cash only, pleasant terrace, Wenggasse 3, tel. 09861/3115, Norry asks you to use the reservations form at www.romanticroad.com/raidel).

$ Gasthof zum Breiterle offers 19 comfortable rooms with wooden accents above their restaurant near the Rödertor. Because it sits on a busy street, light sleepers may want to request a room not facing Wenggasse (Db-€78-88, apartment available, reception in restaurant, pay parking, Rödergasse 30, tel. 09861/6730, www.breiterle.de, info@breiterle.de).

$ Gästehaus Gerlinger, a fine value, has five comfortable rooms in a pretty 16th-century house with a small terrace for guests (Db-€62, an apartment, cash only, nonsmoking, easy parking, Schlegeleinsweth 10, tel. 09861/87979, mobile 0171-690-0752, www.pension-gerlinger.de, info@pension-gerlinger.de).

$ Kreuzerhof Hotel offers 11 decent rooms surrounding a courtyard on a quiet side street near the Rödertor (Db-€75-79, large Db-€92, family deals and rooms—including one for six people, nonsmoking, laundry-€7, parking in courtyard-€4/day, Millergasse 2-6, tel. 09861/3424, www.kreuzerhof.eu, info@kreuzerhof.eu).

$ Gästehaus Liebler rents two large, modern, ground-floor rooms with kitchenettes—great for real privacy close to the action. On the top floor is an attractive two-bedroom apartment (Db-€50, cash only, Rick Steves discount for 2 or more nights with this book, no breakfast but café nearby, nonsmoking, laundry-€5, behind Christmas shop at Pfäffleinsgässchen 10, tel. 09861/709-215, www.gaestehaus-liebler.de, info@gaestehaus-liebler.de).

¢ Rossmühle Youth Hostel rents 186 beds in two institutional yet charming buildings. Reception is in the huge building with droopy dormer windows—formerly a horse-powered mill. While most beds are in dorms, there are also 11 doubles (dorm bed-€25, bunk-bed Db-€61; guests over 26 pay €3.50 extra unless traveling with a family, nonmembers pay €4 extra, includes breakfast and sheets, dinner-€7, self-serve laundry with soap-€5, close to P-1 parking lot, entrance on Rossmühlgasse, tel. 09861/94160, www.rothenburg.jugendherberge.de, rothenburg@jugendherberge.de).

Transportation

Arriving and Departing

BY TRAIN

Arriving in Rothenburg: It's a 10-minute walk from the station to Rothenburg's Market Square (following the brown *Altstadt* signs, exit left from station, walk a block down Bahnhofstrasse, turn right on Ansbacher Strasse, and head straight into the Middle Ages). Taxis wait at the station (€6 to any hotel). Day-trippers can leave luggage in station lockers on the platform. Free WCs are behind the Speedy snack bar on track 1.

The station has a touch-screen terminal for fare and schedule information and ticket sales. If you need extra help, visit the combined ticket office/travel agency in the station building (€1-3 surcharge for most tickets, €0.50 charge for questions without ticket purchase, Mon-Fri 10:00-18:00, Sat 9:00-13:00, closed Sun, tel. 09861/7711, train info toll tel. 0180-699-6633, www.bahn.com).

Getting to/from Rothenburg via Steinach: If you take the train to or from Rothenburg, you'll transfer at Steinach. A tiny branch train line shuttles back and forth hourly between the two towns (14 minutes, generally departs Steinach at :35 and Rothenburg at :06). Train connections in Steinach are usually quick and efficient (trains to/from Rothenburg generally use track 5; use the conveyor belts to haul your bags smartly up and down the stairs). Steinach's station is unstaffed but has touch-screen ticket machines (though any ticket to or from Rothenburg will automatically include your transfer).

Note that the last train from Steinach to Rothenburg departs at about 22:30. But all is not lost if you arrive in Steinach after the last train: There's a subsidized taxi service to Rothenburg (cheaper for the government than running an almost-empty train). To use this handy service, called AST *(Anrufsammeltaxi),* make an appointment with a participating taxi service (call 09861/2000 or 09861/7227) at least an hour in advance (2 hours ahead is better), and they'll drive you from Steinach to Rothenburg for the cheap train fare (€4.60/person) rather than the regular €30 taxi fare.

From Rothenburg (via Steinach) by Train to: Würzburg (hourly, 70 minutes), **Nürnberg** (hourly, 1.5 hours, change in Ansbach), **Munich** (hourly, 2.5-4 hours, 2-3 changes), **Füssen** (hourly, 5 hours, often with changes in Treuchtlingen and Augsburg), **Frankfurt** (hourly, 2.5-3 hours, change in Würzburg), **Frankfurt Airport** (hourly, 3-3.5 hours, change in Würzburg), **Berlin** (hourly, 5.5 hours, 3 changes).

BY CAR

Driving and parking rules in Rothenburg change constantly—ask your hotelier for advice. In general, you're allowed to drive into the old town to get to your hotel. Otherwise, driving within the old walled center is discouraged. Some hotels offer private parking (either free or pay). To keep things simple, park in one of the lots—numbered P-1 through P-5—that line the outside of the town walls (€5/day, buy ticket from *Parkscheinautomat* machines and display, 5- to 10-minute walk to Market Square).

Driving from Frankfurt Airport: Even a jet-lagged zombie can handle the three-hour autobahn drive from the airport to Rothenburg. It's a 75-mile straight shot to Würzburg on the A-3 autobahn; just follow the blue autobahn signs toward *Würzburg*. Then turn south on A-7 and take the *Rothenburg o.d.T.* exit (#108).

NEAR ROTHENBURG

THE ROMANTIC ROAD

Along the Romantic Road, half-timbered towns are ringed by walls and towers, while flowers spill over the windowsills of the well-kept houses. Glockenspiels dance from town halls. Many travelers bypass these small towns by fast train or autobahn. But consider an extra day or two to take in the slow pace of life. I've included an overview of key sights on the route.

By Car

Wander through quaint hills and rolling villages along the scenic 220-mile driving route called the Romantic Road (*Romantische Strasse*, www.romantischestrasse.de). Stop wherever the cows look friendly or a town fountain beckons. If your goal is to meander and explore, don't use GPS—get a good map and follow the brown *Romantische Strasse* signs along two-lane roads. If you use GPS, you'll usually be routed to the nearest fast highway or autobahn, which isn't romantic at all.

If you're driving south of Rothenburg (whether heading toward it or leaving it), you could stop at the Wieskirche and the towns of Nördlingen and Dinkelsbühl.

If you're driving north of Rothenburg, good stops are Creglingen and Weikersheim.

By Bus

The Romantic Road bus runs daily from mid-April to late October. Every day, one bus goes north to south (Frankfurt to Munich to Füssen), and another goes south to north (Füssen to Munich to Frankfurt). You can begin or end your journey at any of the stops—including Rothenburg—along the way. Check the full timetable and prices at www.romantischestrasse.de.

South of Rothenburg

If you're driving from Füssen to Rothenburg, you'll encounter these three sights in this order:

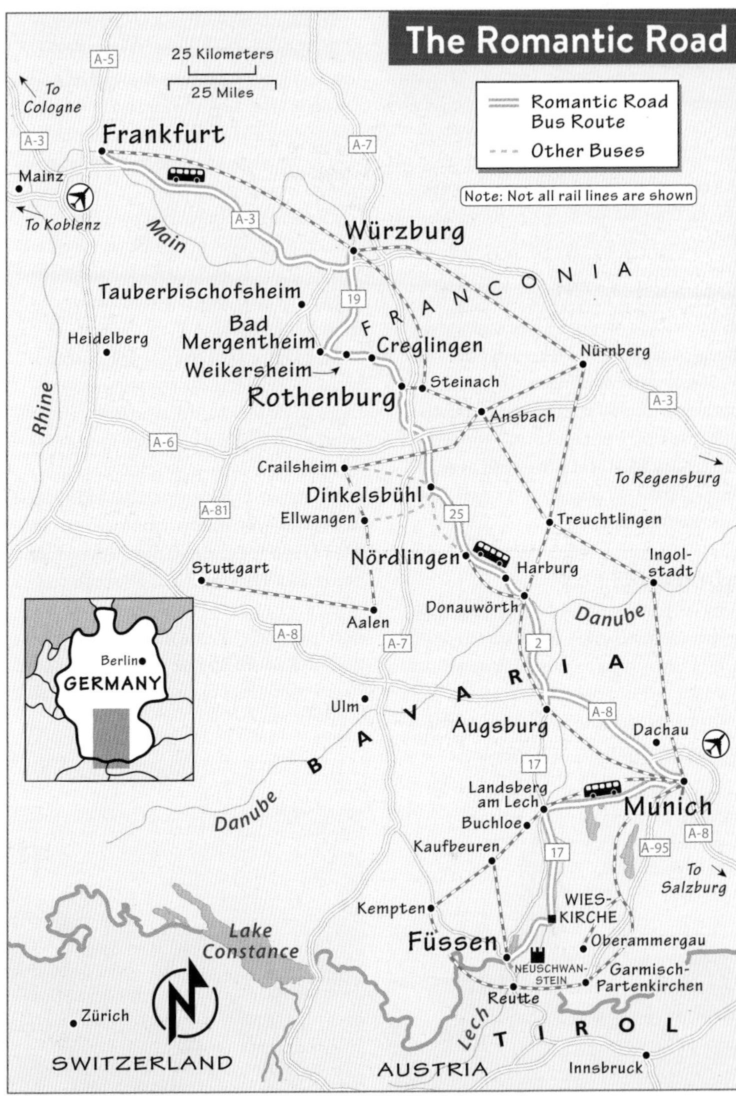

▲▲*Wieskirche*

Germany's most glorious Baroque-Rococo church is beautifully restored and set in a sweet meadow. For a full description, see page 176 of the Bavaria chapter (which also covers Füssen).

▲*Nördlingen*

Nördlingen is a real workaday town that has one of the best medieval walls in Germany, not to mention a surprising geologic history. For centuries, Nördlingen's residents puzzled over the local terrain, a flattish plain called the Ries, which rises to a low circular ridge that surrounds the town in the distance. In the 1960s, geologists figured out that Nördlingen lies in the middle of an impact crater blasted out

15 million years ago by a meteor.

Head into the center of town by zeroing in on the tower of **St. Georg's Church.** Climb the church tower for sweeping views of the town walls and crater. With more time, walk all the way around on the top of the **town wall,** which is even better preserved than Rothenburg's or Dinkelsbühl's. The town started building the wall in 1327 and financed it with a tax on wine and beer; it's more than a mile and a half long, has 16 towers and five gates, and offers great views of backyards and garden furniture.

Sleeping in Nördlingen: Several small hotels surrounding St. Georg's Church offer mediocre but reasonably priced rooms. Try **$$ Hotel Altreuter,** over an inviting bakery/café (Marktplatz 11, www.hotel-altreuter.de).

▲*Dinkelsbühl*

A moat, towers, gates, and a beautifully preserved medieval wall all surround this pretty town. It's a delight to simply stroll here for an hour or two. Park at one of the free lots outside the town walls, which are well signed from the main road.

To orient yourself, head for the tower of **St. Georg's Cathedral,** at the center of town. This 15th-century church has a surprisingly light, airy interior and fine carved altarpieces. On good-weather summer weekends, you can climb to the top of the tower.

Outside the church, follow signs around the corner to the **TI,** which offers a free "Tour of the Town" brochure with a map and short walking tour (www.dinkelsbuehl.de).

Sleeping in Dinkelsbühl: Dinkelsbühl has a good selection of hotels, many of them lining the main drag in front of the church (though more choices and lower prices are available in Rothenburg and Nördlingen). Options include: **$$$ Hezelhof Hotel,** with modern rooms in an old shell (Segringer Strasse 7, www.hezelhof.com); **$$$ Weisses Ross,** attached to a historic restaurant (Steingasse 12, www.hotel-weisses-ross.de); and the town's unique **$ youth hostel,** in a medieval granary (Koppengasse 10, www.dinkelsbuehl.jugendherberge.de).

St. Georg's Church dominates Nördlingen.

Dinkelsbühl

North of Rothenburg

Creglingen

While Creglingen itself isn't worth much fuss, two quick and rewarding sights sit across the road from each other a mile south of town.

The peaceful 14th-century **Herrgottskirche Church,** worth ▲, is graced with Tilman Riemenschneider's greatest carved altarpiece, completed sometime between 1505 and 1510. The church's other colorful altars are also worth a peek (open daily in summer, afternoons only and closed Mon off-season, www.herrgottskirche.de).

The **Fingerhut Museum,** showing off thimbles (literally, "finger hats"), is far more interesting than it sounds. You'll step from case to case to squint at the collection, which numbers about 4,000 (but still fits in a single room) and comes from all over the world; some pieces are centuries old. Owner Thorvald Greif got a head start from his father, who owned a thimble factory (closed Mon and Jan-Feb, www.fingerhutmuseum.de).

▲*Weikersheim*

This picturesquely set town, nestled between hills, has a charming little main square offering easy access to a fine park and an impressive palace.

Weikersheim's **palace** (Schloss Weikersheim), across a moat-turned-park from the main square, was built in the late 16th century as the Renaissance country estate of a local count. With its bucolic location and glowing sandstone texture, it gives off a *Downton Abbey* vibe. It's viewable only by a guided tour in German; skip the tour and instead focus on exploring the palace's fine Baroque **gardens** (small entry fee, English audioguide www.schloss-weikersheim.de).

If you have time after your garden visit, Weikersheim's pleasant **town square** and cobbled old town are worth exploring. The **city park** *(Stadtpark)* makes a nice, free picnic spot, and from it you can peer over the hedge into the palace gardens.

The palace at Weikersheim has fine gardens.

BEST OF THE REST

WÜRZBURG

Rebuilt after World War II, historic, mid-sized Würzburg (VEWRTS-boorg) isn't quite charming, but it's worth a stop for its impressive, enjoyable Residenz palace.

Surrounded by vineyards and filled with atmospheric wine bars, this tourist-friendly town is easy to navigate by foot or streetcar. Today, 25,000 of its 130,000 residents are students—making the town feel young and very alive.

Holy Roman Emperor Frederick Barbarossa came to Würzburg in the 12th century to get the bishop's OK to divorce his wife. The bishop said "No problem," and the emperor thanked him by giving him secular rule of the entire region of Franconia. From then on, the bishop became a prince-bishop. He answered only to the Holy Roman Emperor and built a palace that still dominates the town today.

Orientation

Würzburg's old town core huddles along the bank of the Main (pronounced "mine") River. The tourists' Würzburg is bookended by the opulent Residenz (at the east end of downtown) and the hill-capping Marienberg Fortress (at the west end, across the river). You can walk from the Residenz to the river in about 15 minutes; the train station is a 15-minute walk to the north.

Day Plan: Würzburg has a few hours' worth of sightseeing. Begin by touring the Residenz palace. With more time, walk through town, cross the Old Main Bridge, and hike up to the hilltop Marienberg Fortress.

If overnighting here, stroll the atmospheric Old Main Bridge—lined by stone statues—where people gather at sunset in good weather for a glass of wine and mellow mingling.

Bustling Würzburg is easy to navigate.

Getting There: Würzburg is well-connected by train to **Rothenburg** (hourly, 70 minutes, change in Steinach), **Frankfurt** (1-2/hour, 70 minutes), **Nürnberg** (2-3/hour, 1-1.5 hours), **Munich** (1-2/hour, 2 hours), **Cologne** (hourly, 2.5 hours), and **Berlin** (hourly, 4 hours).

Arrival in Würzburg: From the **train station, tram** #1, #3, or #5 will take you into town (buy ticket from driver or a streetside machine); the Dom stop is close to the central Market Square and the TI. To **walk** toward town, simply head up the shop-lined Kaiserstrasse. **Drivers** can follow *Residenz* signs and park in the vast cobbled square that faces the palace.

Rick's Tip: *For a quick 40-minute loop through town (with English headphone commentary), consider the* **tourist train** *(€8, leaves at the top of the hour in front of the Residenz, www.city-tour.info).*

Tourist Information: The town's helpful TI is in the yellow Rococo-style Falken Haus on Market Square (daily, off-season closed Sun, tel. 0931/372-398, www.wuerzburg.de).

Private Guide: Julius Goldmann is good (mobile 0175-873-2412, ju.goldmann@web.de).

Sights

▲▲RESIDENZ PALACE

In the early 18th century, Würzburg's powerful prince-bishop decided to move from his hilltop residence at Marienberg, across the river, into new digs down in the city. His lavish, custom-built, 360-room palace and its associated sights—the chapel (Hofkirche) and garden—are the main attractions of today's Würzburg. This Franconian Versailles features grand rooms, 3-D art, and a massive fresco by Giovanni Battista Tiepolo.

Cost and Hours: €7.50, includes guided tour, daily April-Oct 9:00-18:00, Nov-March 10:00-16:30, tel. 0931/355-170, www.residenz-wuerzburg.de.

Sightseeing Strategies and Tours: A guided 45-60-minute tour (mostly in German) is included with your ticket and covers the main rooms along with the otherwise inaccessible South Wing. English tours, while good, aren't worth planning your day around (daily at 11:00 and 15:00, April-Oct also at 16:30). To see everything worthwhile in the Residenz, follow my

Generations of Würzburg prince-bishops lived at the Residenz Palace.

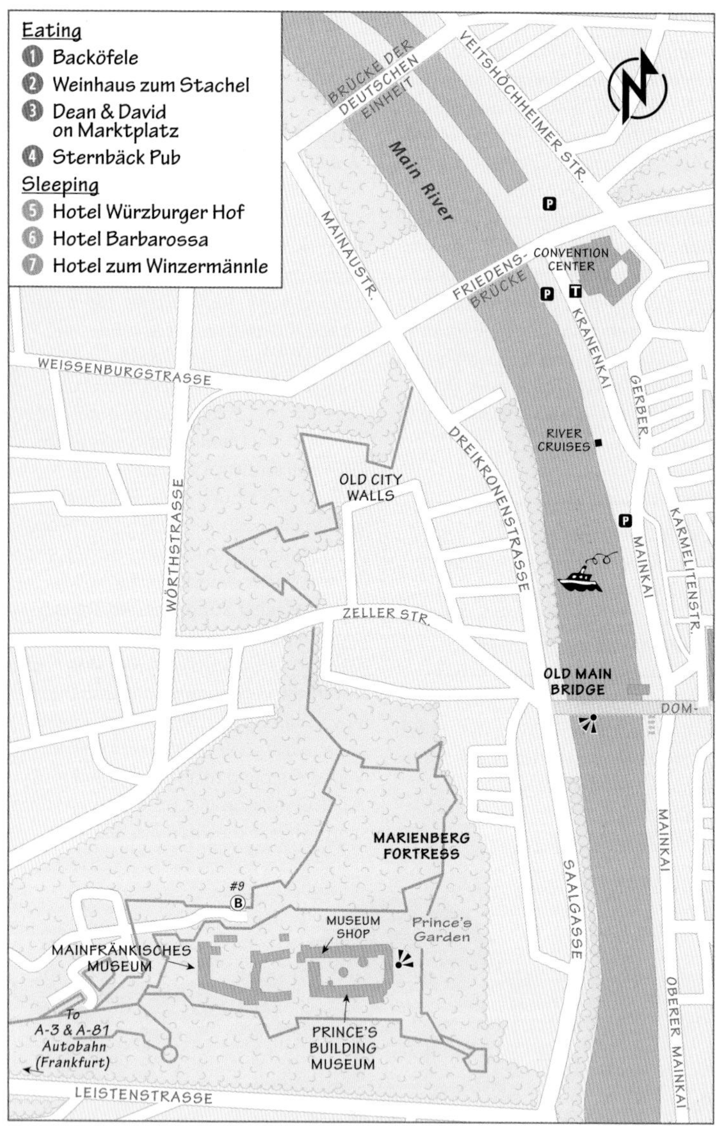

self-guided tour. Then, from the Imperial Hall, jump onto any tour heading into the South Wing.

SELF-GUIDED TOUR

• *Begin at the entrance.*

Vestibule and Garden Hall: This indoor area functioned as a grand circular driveway, exclusively for special occasions—just right for six-horse carriages to drop off guests at the base of the stairs.

• *Now picture yourself dressed up in your fanciest finery...and ascend the stairs.*

Grand Staircase: The elegant stairway comes with low steps, enabling high-class ladies to glide up gracefully, heads tilted back to enjoy Europe's largest and

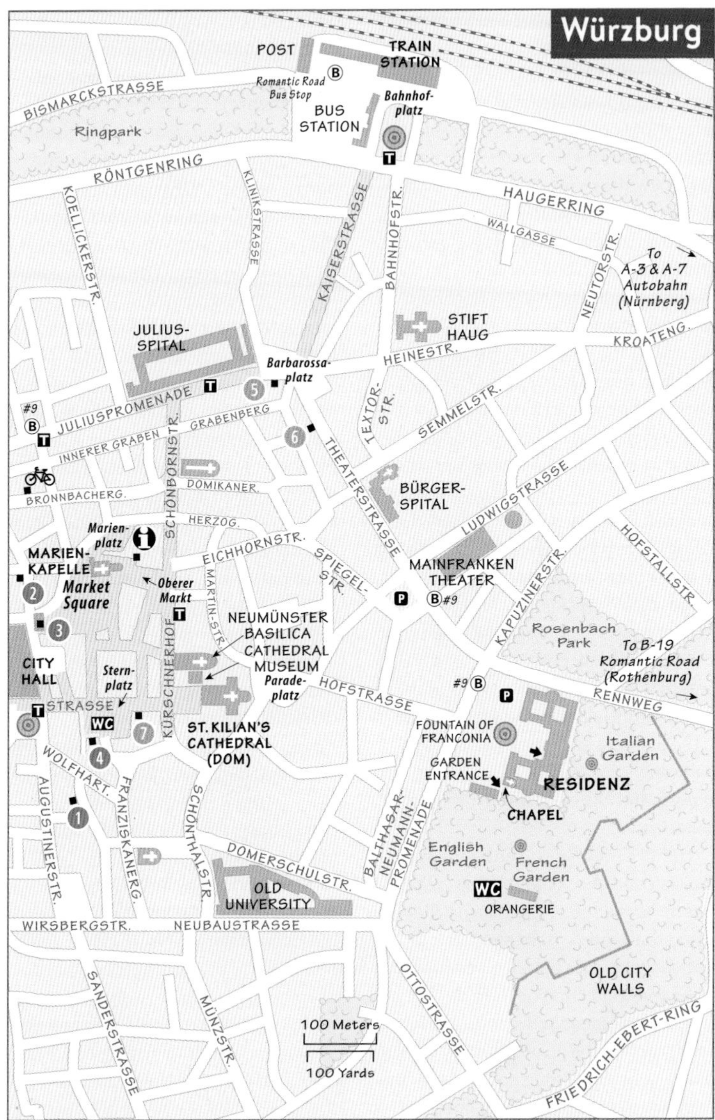

grandest fresco opening up above them. Hold your lady's hand high and get into the ascending rhythm.

• *As you reach the top of the stairs, look closer at the...*

Tiepolo Fresco: In 1752, the Venetian master Tiepolo was instructed to make a grand fresco illustrating the greatness of Europe, Würzburg, and the prince-bishop. And he did—completing the world's largest fresco (more than 7,000 square feet) in only 13 months.

The ceiling celebrates the esteemed prince-bishop, depicted in the medallion with a red, ermine-trimmed cape. This guy had a healthy ego. The ceiling features

Apollo (in the sunburst) and a host of Greek gods, all paying homage to the P-B.

Ringing the room are the four continents, each symbolized by a woman on an animal and pointing to the prince-bishop. Walk the perimeter of the room to study and enjoy the symbolism of each continent one by one: **America** on an alligator, **Africa** on a camel, **Asia** on an elephant, and **Europe** on a bull.

White Hall: This hall—a Rococo stucco fantasy—is actually gray, kept plain to punctuate the colorful rooms on either side. The stucco decorations (particularly in the corners) have an armor-and-weapons theme, as this marked the entrance to the prince-bishop's private apartments—which had to be carefully guarded. Even the cloth-like yellow decorations above those weapons, draped high in the corners, are made of painted stucco.

• *From the White Hall, continue to your left, following signs for* Rundgang/Circuit.

Imperial Hall: Enjoy the artistic ensemble of this fine room in its entirety and feel its liveliness. This glorious hall is the ultimate example of Baroque: harmony, symmetry, illusion and the bizarre, and lots of light and mirrors facing windows.

Here's a trick: As you enter the room, look left and check out the dog in the fresco (at the top of the pillar). When you get to the window, have another look... notice that he has gotten older and fatter while you were crossing the hall.

Ceiling frescoes by Tiepolo (and his sons) capture the political history of Würzburg: In one, the bishop presides over the marriage of a happy Emperor Friedrich Barbarossa. The bishop's power is demonstrated through his oversized fingers (giving the benediction) and through the details of his miter (tall hat), which displays his coat of arms. Another fresco shows the payoff: Barbarossa gives the bishop Franconia and the secular title of prince.

• *If you're not already on a guided tour, keep a lookout for any group headed into the South Wing—if you see one, join it. Otherwise, continue with me into the...*

North Wing (Northern Imperial Apartments): This string of exquisite rooms—evolving from fancy Baroque to fancier Rococo—was used for the prince-bishop's VIP guests. It's a straight shot to the **Green Lacquered Room,** in the far corner, named for its silver-leaf walls, painted green. The Escher-esque inlaid floor was painstakingly restored after WWII bombings. Have fun multiplying in the mirrors before leaving.

Keep going through a few more small rooms, and then step out into the **hallway** to examine photos of the building's destruction in the 1945 firebombing of Würzburg, and its subsequent restoration. While about three-quarters of the Residenz was destroyed, the most precious parts—the first rooms on this tour, including the Tiepolo frescoes—emerged unscathed. A temporary roof saved the palace from total ruin, but it was not until the late 1970s that it was returned to more or less its original condition.

• *If you haven't yet joined a tour but want to see the South Wing, find your way back to the Imperial Hall and wait until a group comes along. Then tag along for about 15 minutes as you stroll the...*

South Wing (by Tour Only): The dark and woody South Wing feels more masculine than the North Wing. You'll first come to the waiting room (antechamber), the audience chamber/throne room (with circa-1700 Belgian tapestries showing scenes from the life of Alexander the Great), and the Venetian Room (note the three tapestries made around 1740 in Würzburg).

The rooms become progressively more ornate until you reach the South Wing's climax: the 18th-century **Mirror Cabinet,** where the prince-bishop showed off his amazing wealth. It features six pounds of gold leaf, lots of Asian influence, and allegories of the four continents in each corner.

The **Art Gallery** room is next, with portraits of different prince-bishops who ruled until the early 1800s, when Napoleon said, "Enough of this nonsense" and he secularized politics in places like Franconia.

• *Finish your tour at the Court Chapel: Head back down the stairs to the vestibule and go outside. Turn left, and walk about 20 steps to the southern wing of the big complex. An arch leads left into a courtyard, from which a humble door leads into the ornate chapel. Follow signs to* Court Chapel/Hofkirche.

▲▲COURT CHAPEL (HOFKIRCHE)

This sumptuous chapel was for the exclusive use of the prince-bishop and his court. The decor and design are textbook Baroque. Architect Johann Balthasar Neumann's challenge was to bring in light and create symmetry—essential to any Baroque work. He did it with mirrors and hidden windows. All the gold is real—if paper-thin—gold leaf. The columns are "manufactured marble," which isn't marble at all but marbled plaster. You can tell if a "marble" column is real or fake by resting your hand on it. If it warms up, it's not marble.

The faded painting in the dome high above the altar shows three guys in gold robes losing their heads. The two side paintings are by Tiepolo.

RESIDENZ GARDEN

One of Germany's finest Baroque gardens is a delightful park cradling the palace. The Austrian section, just inside the gate, features statues of Greek gods; carefully trimmed, remarkably conical, 18th-century yew trees; and an orangery (at the far back). The English section (to the right) is like a rough park. The Italian section, directly behind the palace around to the left, is grand—à la Versailles—using terraces to create the illusion of spaciousness.

Cost and Hours: Free, open daily until dusk—20:00 at the latest, enter through gate at right of Residenz building.

MARIENBERG FORTRESS (FESTUNG MARIENBERG)

This 13th-century fortified retreat was the original residence of Würzburg's prince-bishops before the Residenz was built. After being stormed by the Swedish army during the 17th-century Thirty Years' War, the fortress was expanded in Baroque style.

Cost and Hours: Grounds and Prince's Garden—free, mid-April-Oct daily 9:00-17:30, closed off-season, tel. 0931/355-170, www.schloesser.bayern.de.

Tours: A 45-minute English tour is offered on weekends (€3.50, mid-March-Oct Sat-Sun at 15:00).

Getting There: To walk here, cross the Old Main Bridge and follow small *Festung Marienberg* signs to the right, heading uphill for a heart-thumping 20 minutes. Or take infrequent bus #9 (direction: Festung, departs from Residenzplatz and Juliuspromenade) to the last stop (Schönborntor) and walk through the tunnel to enter the fortress. Taxis wait near the Old Main Bridge (€10).

Visiting the Fortress: The **grounds** provide fine city views and a good place for a picnic. Peek into the bottom of the original tower stronghold (at the center of the complex) and the round church, where carved relief monuments to former bishops decorate the stone floor. For the best views, go through the archway off the inner courtyard (next to church entrance) into the **Prince's Garden**—look for the *Fürstengarten* sign.

Sunset in Würzburg

The fortress houses two museums: The **Mainfränkisches Museum** highlights the work of Tilman Riemenschneider, Germany's top woodcarver and onetime mayor of Würzburg, and the **Prince's Building Museum** *(Fürstenbaumuseum)* shows off relics of the prince-bishops (small admission fee, both closed Mon).

Eating

$$$ Backöfele is a popular hole-in-the-wall with a rustic menu (reservations smart, Ursulinergasse 2, www.backoefele.de). **$$$ Weinhaus zum** Stachel's stone-and-ivy courtyard is an elegant place to dine (closed Mon, reservations smart, Gressengasse 1, www.weinhaus-stachel.de). **Dean & David** is a favorite for fast, inexpensive, and healthy meals (Marktplatz 4, tel. 0931/4522-8303). At the inviting **Sternbäck pub,** rickety tables spill onto a busy square (Sternplatz 4).

Sleeping

The classy **$$$ Hotel Würzburger Hof** has froufrou-Baroque rooms (Barbarossaplatz 2, www.hotel-wuerzburgerhof.de). The sleek **$$ Hotel Barbarossa** is a good value (Theaterstrasse 2, fourth floor, www.hotelbarbarossa-wuerzburg.de). **$$ Hotel zum Winzermännle** is simple but tasteful (Domstrasse 32, www.winzermaennle.de).

BEST OF THE REST

NÜRNBERG

Nürnberg ("Nuremberg" in English), Bavaria's second city, is known for its glorious medieval architecture, important Germanic history museum, haunting Nazi past, and Germany's biggest Christmas market.

Though Nürnberg has a half-million residents, its charming Old Town—with its red-sandstone Gothic buildings—makes visitors feel like they are in a far smaller city. Thanks to an enlightened city-planning vision that rebuilt the town

Nürnberg's Old Town

in a modern yet people-friendly style after the war, Nürnberg's downtown is lively and inviting day and night.

Nürnberg is an easy add-on to any itinerary that includes Munich, Würzburg, or Rothenburg (each about an hour away by frequent trains), and a handy stop on the way to Frankfurt, Berlin, or Dresden.

Orientation

Nürnberg's Old Town is surrounded by a three-mile-long wall and moat, and, beyond that, a ring road. Many of Nürnberg's top sights are conveniently clustered along a straight-line thoroughfare, connecting the train station (Hauptbahnhof) with the main market square (Hauptmarkt) and the Imperial Castle (Kaiserburg). The Nazi Documentation Center and former Nazi Rally Grounds are southeast of the center.

Day Plan: Stroll from the train station through the Old Town up to the castle, stopping at sights of interest along the way (including the outstanding Germanic National Museum, a few steps off the main drag). Then visit the Nazi Documentation Center and Rally Grounds (next to each other, and easy to reach on public transit). Keep in mind that nearly all of the city's museums are closed on Monday.

Getting There: Direct trains run frequently from **Würzburg** and **Munich** (2-3/hour, 1 hour); there are hourly departures from **Rothenburg** (1.5 hours).

Arrival in Nürnberg: The stately old Hauptbahnhof is just outside the old city walls and ring road. To reach the Frauentor (the medieval city's southern gate) and **Old Town,** follow signs for *Ausgang/City* down the escalator, then signs to *Königstor/Frauentor* and *Altstadt* in the underpass. When you emerge, the TI is on your right and the Frauentor tower is on your left.

To go directly from the station to the **Nazi Documentation Center** and the **Rally Grounds,** follow the pink *Tram* signs in the underpass to the stop in front of the Postbank Center, then take tram #9 (direction: Doku-Zentrum, leaves every 10 minutes, buy ticket at vending machine on tram platform).

Drivers will find a handful of well-signed public garages within the city walls.

Tourist Information: Nürnberg's TI is across the ring road from the train station, just opposite the Frauentor (daily, Königstrasse 93, tel. 0911/233-6132, www.tourismus.nuernberg.de). There's also a small branch office at #18 on the Hauptmarkt; ask here about Old Town walking tours (daily at 13:00 from spring until fall). The TI sells the **Nürnberg Card,** a good value for those staying two days; it covers the sights and public transit (€25/2 days, big discount for kids).

Private Guide: Call **Doris Ritter** (€135/3 hours, tel. 0911/518-1719, www.nuernberg-city-tours.de).

Sights

▲▲OLD TOWN STROLL

Take time to browse through the pleasant Old Town. Near the train station, dip into the kitschy but fun Craftsmen's Courtyard. It's packed with replicas of medieval shops, where artisans actually make—and, of course, sell—leather, pottery, and brass goods. Königstrasse, the main drag through the Old Town, is lined with restaurants, hotels, and some wonderful Gothic and Neo-Gothic architecture. It leads to...

▲▲ST. LAWRENCE CHURCH (LORENZKIRCHE)

This once-Catholic, now-Protestant High Gothic church is a massive house of worship. The interior wasn't completely furnished until more than a century after the church was built—just in time for the Reformation (so the Catholic decor adorned a now-Lutheran church). Most of the decorations inside were donated by wealthy Nürnbergers trying to cut down on their time in purgatory. Through the centuries, this art survived three separate

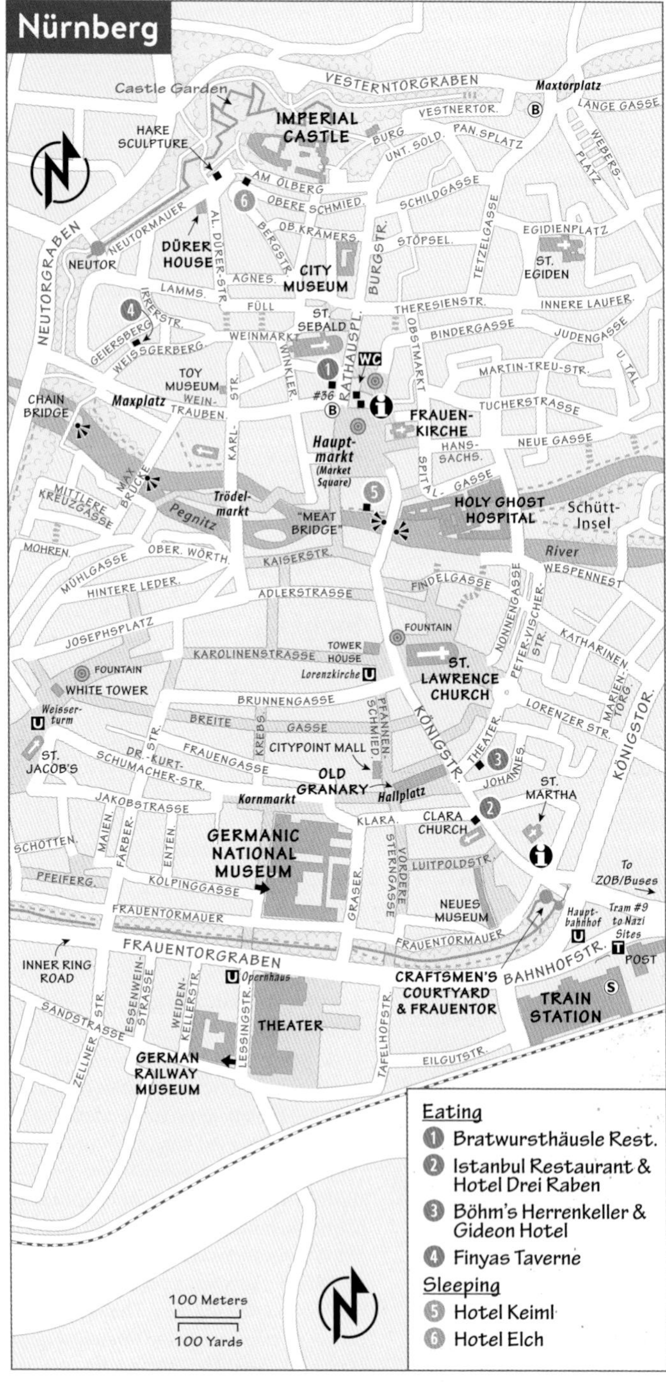
Nürnberg
Castle Garden
IMPERIAL CASTLE
HARE SCULPTURE
DÜRER HOUSE
CITY MUSEUM
ST. SEBALD
TOY MUSEUM
Maxplatz
CHAIN BRIDGE
Hauptmarkt (Market Square)
FRAUENKIRCHE
Trödelmarkt
"MEAT BRIDGE"
HOLY GHOST HOSPITAL
Schütt-Insel
Pegnitz River
ST. EGIDEN
FOUNTAIN
TOWER HOUSE
Lorenzkirche
ST. LAWRENCE CHURCH
WHITE TOWER
Weisserturm
ST. JACOB'S
CITYPOINT MALL
OLD GRANARY
Hallplatz
Kornmarkt
CLARA CHURCH
ST. MARTHA
GERMANIC NATIONAL MUSEUM
NEUES MUSEUM
To ZOB/Buses
Hauptbahnhof
Tram #9 to Nazi Sites
POST
INNER RING ROAD
Opernhaus
CRAFTSMEN'S COURTYARD & FRAUENTOR
TRAIN STATION
THEATER
GERMAN RAILWAY MUSEUM
VESTERNTORGRABEN
Maxtorplatz
LANGE GASSE
VESTNERTOR
BURG
UNT. SOLD.
PAN.SPLATZ
WEBERSPLATZ
AM ÖLBERG
OBERE SCHMIED.
SCHILDGASSE
BERGSTR.
OB.KRÄMERS.
STÖPSEL.
TETZELGASSE
EGIDIENPLATZ
NEUTORGRABEN
NEUTORMAUER
NEUTOR
AL. DÜRER-STR.
AGNES.
BURGSTR.
LAMMS.
FÜLL
THERESIENSTR.
INNERE LAUFER.
IRRERSTR.
GEIERSBERG
WEISSGERBERG.
WEINMARKT
RATHAUSPL.
OBSTMARKT
BINDERGASSE
JUDENGASSE
WINKLER.
U. TAL
MARTIN-TREU-STR.
WEIN-TRAUBEN.
#36
TUCHERSTRASSE
KARL-STR.
HANS-SACHS.
NEUE GASSE
SPITAL-GASSE
MAX BRÜCKE
MITTLERE KREUZGASSE
MOHREN.
OBER. WÖRTH.
KAISERSTR.
WESPENNEST
MÜHLGASSE
HINTERE LEDER.
ADLERSTRASSE
FINDELGASSE
NONNENGASSE
PETER-VISCHER-STR.
KATHARINEN.
JOSEPHSPLATZ
KAROLINENSTRASSE
BRUNNENGASSE
MARIENTORG.
KÖNIGSTOR.
BREITE GASSE
KREBS
PFANNENSCHMIED.
KÖNIGSTR.
THEATER.
LORENZER STR.
DR.-KURT-SCHUMACHER-STR.
FRAUENGASSE
JOHANNES.
JAKOBSTRASSE
KLARA.
SCHOTTEN.
MAIEN.
FÄRBER.
ENTEN.
HINTERE STERNGASSE
VORDERE STERNGASSE
LUITPOLDSTR.
PFEIFERG.
KOLPINGGASSE
GRASER.
FRAUENTORMAUER
FRAUENTORGRABEN
BAHNHOFSTR.
ESSENWEINSTRASSE
WEIDENKELLERSTR.
LESSINGSTR.
TAFELHOFSTR.
SANDSTRASSE
ZELLNER STR.
EILGUTSTR.
100 Meters
100 Yards
Eating
1 Bratwursthäusle Rest.
2 Istanbul Restaurant & Hotel Drei Raben
3 Böhm's Herrenkeller & Gideon Hotel
4 Finyas Taverne
Sleeping
5 Hotel Keiml
6 Hotel Elch

threats: the iconoclasm of the Reformation, the whitewashing of the Baroque age, and the bombing of World War II.

While Nürnberg was the first "free imperial city" to break with the Catholic Church and become Lutheran, locals didn't go wild (like Swiss Protestants did) in tearing down the rich, Mary-oriented decor of their fine churches. Suspended over the altar, the sculptural *Annunciation* (1517) is by Veit Stoss, a Nürnberg citizen and one of Central Europe's best woodcarvers.

Cost and Hours: €1 donation requested, Mon-Sat 9:00-17:00, Sun 13:00-16:00, www.lorenzkirche.de.

▲▲HAUPTMARKT (MAIN MARKET SQUARE)

When Nürnberg began booming in the 13th century, it consisted of two distinct walled towns separated by the river. As the towns grew, they merged and the middle wall came down. This square, built by Holy Roman Emperor Charles IV, became the center of the newly united city. Charles, the most powerful man in Europe in his time, oversees the action from a perch high on the facade of the **Frauenkirche,** the church on the square. He's waiting for noon, when the electors dance around him.

The pointy gold **Beautiful Fountain** (Schöner Brunnen) on the square is a people magnet.

Year-round, the Hauptmarkt is lively with fruit, flower, and souvenir stands.

Hauptmarkt

For a few weeks before Christmas, it hosts Germany's largest Christmas market (starts the Fri before the first Sun in Advent, www.christkindlesmarkt.de).

Connoisseurs of sausage and bread will want to take a short side-trip from the square: Head a block down Tuchgasse (directly opposite the church) to find the **Schwarz Bakery** at #2. Step in and inhale. They can make the German sandwich of your dreams.

▲IMPERIAL CASTLE (KAISERBURG)

This mighty fortress, built between the 12th and 16th centuries, lay in ruins after a WWII bombing raid but has been splendidly reconstructed. In the Middle Ages, Holy Roman Emperors stayed here when they were in town, and the imperial regalia, including the cross, sword, and crown, were stored here from 1424 until 1796.

Cost and Hours: €5.50 for castle only, €3.50 for Deep Well and Sinwell Tower, €7 combo-ticket; €2 audioguide; daily April-Sept 9:00-18:00, Oct-March 10:00-16:00; tel. 0911/244-6590, www.kaiserburg-nuernberg.de.

Visiting the Castle: Your visit is a no-way-to-get-lost, one-way route—just follow the *Rundgang* signs.

The **Lower Hall** is empty of furniture because, in the 12th century, the imperial court was mobile. Royal roadies would arrive and set things up before the emperor got there. The **Romanesque church** has a triple-decker design: lower nobility on the lower floor, upper nobility above that, and the emperor worshipping from the topmost balcony.

The **Upper Hall** is most interesting, with a thorough explanation and artifacts that show what the heck the Holy Roman Empire actually was. Then comes a series of creaky-floored **former living quarters,** with painted ceilings (many dismantled and stored in bunkers during the war—they're that precious), and a copy of the imperial crown (the original is in Vienna). The final exhibit is on **old weapons.**

There are other interesting parts of

the complex. The **Deep Well** is indeed deep—165 feet. Visits are simple, fun, and only possible accompanied by a guide (10-minute tours leave on the hour and half-hour). You'll see water poured way, waaay down—into an incredible hole dug in the 14th century.

A climb up the **Sinwell Tower** offers only a higher city view and lots of exercise. For an easy alternative, walk out around the round tower to enjoy a commanding **city view** from the rampart just behind it. Then find your way to the fine **castle garden** *(Burggarten)*. Wrapped around the back of the castle, it offers more great views.

▲▲HISTORIC ART BUNKER

Behind the doors at Bergstrasse 19, a series of sandstone cellars are buried deep inside the rock of Castle Hill. This is where precious artworks were carefully safeguarded from the WWII air raids that devastated the city.

To visit, you must take a guided tour. The bunkers are largely empty now, except for photos posted at each stop of the tour. You'll get some background on the pieces kept here, and hear a lot about the air raids and the citywide rebuilding process that followed.

Cost and Hours: €6 includes good audioguide, daily at 14:30, Fri-Sat also at 17:30, 1.25 hours, buy tickets and meet at Brauereiladen brewery shop—under *Nürnberger Altstadthof* sign—at Bergstrasse 19, tel. 0911/2360-2731, www.felsengaenge-nuernberg.de.

▲ALBRECHT DÜRER HOUSE

Nürnberg's most famous resident lived in this house for the last 20 years of his life. Artist Albrecht Dürer (1471-1528), a contemporary of Michelangelo, studied in Venice and brought the Renaissance to stodgy medieval Germany. Nothing in the museum is original (except the house itself)—all the paintings are replicas. But the museum does a fine job of capturing the way Dürer actually lived, and it includes a replica of his workshop, with a working printing press.

Cost and Hours: €5 includes audioguide, Mon-Wed and Fri 10:00-17:00, Thu until 20:00, Sat-Sun until 18:00, closed Mon Oct-June, Albrecht-Dürer-Strasse 39, tel. 0911/231-2568, www.museums.nuremberg.de.

▲▲▲GERMANIC NATIONAL MUSEUM (GERMANISCHES NATIONALMUSEUM)

For German history buffs, this museum alone makes a visit to Nürnberg worthwhile. It occupies an interconnected maze of buildings, old and new, in the southern part of the Old Town, near the station.

Cost and Hours: €8, free Wed after 18:00, open Tue-Sun 10:00-18:00, Wed until 21:00, closed Mon, worthwhile audioguide-€2, two blocks west of Königstrasse at Kartäusergasse 1, enter on far side of building, tel. 0911/13310, www.gnm.de.

Visiting the Museum: The museum's star attraction is its **German art collection,** which includes paintings by Dürer (the only originals in town) and Cranach, and wood carvings by Tilman Riemenschneider. Other "must-sees" include the oldest surviving **globe** in the world,

Albrecht Dürer House

crafted by Nürnberg's own Martin Behaim (since it dates from 1492, the Americas are conspicuously missing), and the delicate wooden *Nürnberg Madonna* (1515). For those interested in the Reformation, there's a wonderful Martin Luther section.

The historic core of the museum building, an old monastery, is filled with original, surviving **statues** from the city's bombed-out churches and fountains. The rest of this huge museum covers a vast spectrum of German culture, from prehistory to fine arts to musical instruments to science.

▲GERMAN RAILWAY MUSEUM (DB MUSEUM)

Germany's first railway was built in Nürnberg in 1835, and the Deutsche Bahn (German Railway) runs a huge museum just outside the Old Town. It tells the story of the German railroad system with a focus on how it influenced the nation's history. Don't miss "Mad" King Ludwig's crown-topped *Salonwagen*—practically a palace on wheels, complete with a rolling veranda.

Cost and Hours: €5, €4 with valid train or city transit ticket, free with valid rail pass; Tue-Fri 9:00-17:00, Sat-Sun until 18:00, closed Mon; audioguide-€1; Lessingstrasse 6; tel. 0800-326-7386, www.dbmuseum.de. Pick up the free English booklet as you enter, and spring for the audioguide, as there's very little English posted inside.

Nazi Sites

The sprawling complex of the Nazi Documentation Center and Rally Grounds is wrapped around a lake southeast of the Old Town. Take tram #9 from the train station (direction: Doku-Zentrum) or bus #36 from the Hauptmarkt on Waaggasse. Both options go about every 10 minutes.

▲▲▲NAZI DOCUMENTATION CENTER (DOKUMENTATIONSZENTRUM)

Visitors to Europe's Nazi and Holocaust sites inevitably ask the same question: How could this happen? This superb museum does its best to provide an answer. It meticulously traces the evolution of the National Socialist movement,

Nazi Documentation Center

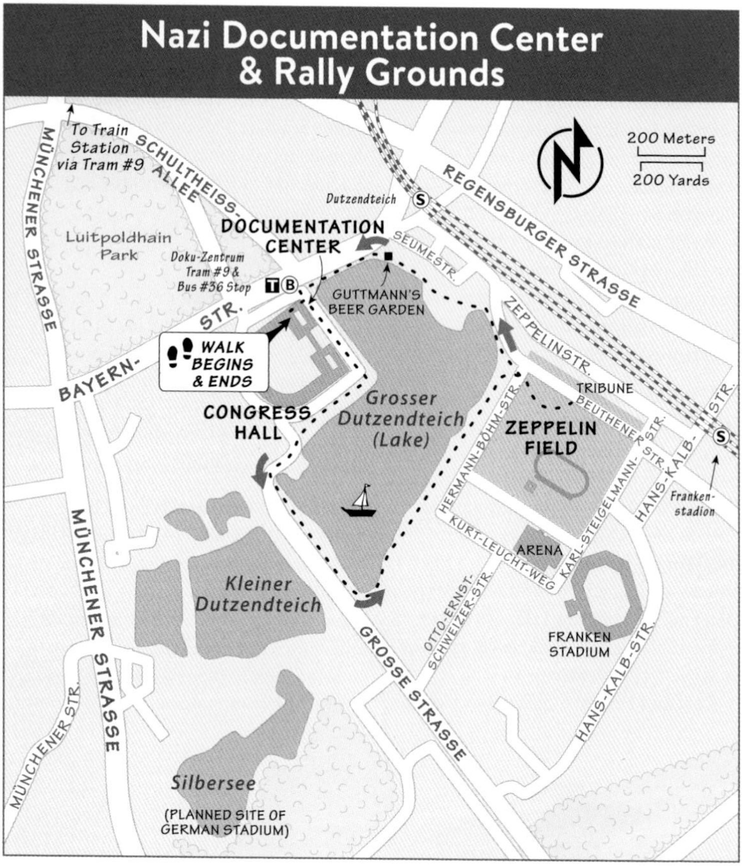

Nazi Documentation Center & Rally Grounds

focusing on how it both energized and terrified the German people. Special attention is paid to Nürnberg's role in the Nazi movement, including the construction and use of the Rally Grounds, where Hitler's largest demonstrations took place. The center frankly analyzes the Nazi phenomenon to understand how it happened—and to prevent it from happening again.

Cost and Hours: €5 includes essential audioguide, Mon-Fri 9:00-18:00, Sat-Sun 10:00-18:00, last entry at 17:00, Bayernstrasse 110, tel. 0911/231-7538, www.museen.nuernberg.de.

▲RALLY GROUNDS (REICHSPARTEITAGSGELÄNDE)

The former Nazi Rally Grounds occupy four square miles behind the museum (there's no additional charge to see these). Albert Speer, Hitler's favorite architect, designed this immense complex of buildings for the Nazi rallies. Not many of Hitler's ambitious plans were completed, but you can visit the courtyard of the Congress Hall, Zeppelin Field (where Hitler addressed his followers), and a few other remains. The easiest way to see them is to follow the circular route around the lake that's shown on the museum's free bilingual area plan (*Geländeplan*). Figure an hour round-trip from the Documentation Center to walk the full circuit. With less time, just look into the courtyard of the Congress Hall from the perch at the end of your museum visit, then walk the short way around the lake directly to Zeppelin Field and back.

Eating

Don't miss the high-energy **$ Bratwursthäusle** for the best bratwurst in town—all made in-house and cooked on a beechwood grill (closed Sun, Rathausplatz 1). **$$$ Istanbul Restaurant** is a local favorite for Turkish food (Königstrasse 60). **$$$ Böhm's Herrenkeller** serves classic Franconian standards at good prices (closed Sun, a block off Königstrasse at Theatergasse 9). **$ Finyas Taverne** may well be the town's most atmospheric drinking hole (from 16:00-late, closed Sun-Mon, Weissgerbergasse 18).

Rick's Tip: *Nürnberg is famous for its* **pinkie-sized bratwurst,** *the "Nürnberger." All over town, signs read* 3 im Weckle *(or* im Weggle*), meaning "three Nürnberger bratwurst in a blankie." It's a good snack for about €2.50.*

Sleeping

$$$ Hotel Drei Raben is an artsy and fun splurge (Königstrasse 63, www.hoteldreiraben.de). **$$ Gideon Hotel** offers good value and a lovely rooftop terrace (Königstrasse 45, www.gideonhotels.de). **$ Hotel Keiml** is bright and homey (no elevator, Luitpoldstrasse 7, www.hotel-keiml.de). For half-timbered charm, it's **$$$ Hotel Elch,** the oldest hotel in town (Irrerstrasse 9, www.hotel-elch.com).

Rhine Valley

The Rhine Valley is storybook Germany, a world of robber baron castles and fairy-tale legends. Cruise through the most turret-studded stretch of the romantic Rhine, listening for the song of the treacherous Loreley. Get hands-on thrills exploring the Rhineland's greatest castle, Rheinfels. Connoisseurs will also enjoy the fine interior of Marksburg Castle near Koblenz. Farther afield is Burg Eltz (a remarkable castle on the Mosel) and Cologne (with its incredible cathedral).

Spend your nights in a castle-crowned Rhine village, either delightful Bacharach or practical St. Goar. They're 10 miles apart, connected by milk-run trains, riverboats, and a riverside bike path. Bacharach is a more interesting town, but St. Goar has the famous Rheinfels Castle.

Marvel at the Rhine's ever-changing parade. Ever since Roman times, when this was the empire's northern boundary, the Rhine has been one of the world's busiest shipping rivers. Traveling along the river today, you'll see a steady flow of barges with 1,000- to 2,000-ton loads. Cars, buses, and trains rush along highways and tracks lining both banks, making it easy to get around.

If possible, visit the Rhine between April and October, when it's at its touristic best. In winter, some sights close, along with some hotels and restaurants, and only one riverboat runs.

THE RHINE VALLEY IN 1 OR 2 DAYS

With one day and two nights, stay in Bacharach. Cruise the best and most scenic stretch of the river (the hour from Bacharach to St. Goar), and tour Rheinfels Castle. Enjoy dinner in Bacharach, and maybe a wine tasting, too.

For a busier day, take a longer cruise, following all or part of my Rhine Blitz Tour. For example, you could cruise from Bacharach to Braubach (to tour Marksburg Castle), before returning by train to Bacharach.

With a second day, visit Burg Eltz on the Mosel as a day trip. Or bike or hike along the Rhine. This is a fun place to relax and explore.

If you're traveling by car, park it at your hotel, cruise the Rhine by boat, and visit Burg Eltz and/or Cologne on your drive in or out.

If a Rhine festival coincides with your

RHINE VALLEY AT A GLANCE

On the Rhine

▲▲▲**Rhine Blitz Tour** One of Europe's great joys—touring the Rhine River by boat, train, bike, or car. See page 238.

▲▲▲**Rheinfels Castle** The best opportunity to explore a ruined castle on the river. **Hours:** Mid-March-Oct daily 9:00-18:00, Nov-mid-March possibly Sat-Sun only 11:00-17:00 (call ahead). See page 258.

▲▲**Marksburg Castle in Braubach** The best-preserved medieval castle on the Rhine. **Hours:** Daily April-Oct 10:00-17:00, Nov-March 11:00-16:00. See page 266.

Near the Rhine Valley

▲▲▲**Burg Eltz, on the Mosel** My favorite castle in Europe, set deep in a forest, with a rare furnished interior—take the required guided tour. **Hours:** April-Oct daily from 9:30, last tour departs at 17:30, closed Nov-March. See page 269.

▲▲▲**Cologne Cathedral** Germany's most exciting church, with a massive facade, vast interior, tower climb, and an easy-to-visit location next to the train station. **Hours:** Mon-Sat 9:30-11:30 & 12:30-16:30, Sun 12:30-16:30, closed to sightseers during services. See page 272.

visit, book your room well in advance; study ahead.

Rick's Tip: *Rhine Valley* **guesthouses and hotels often have similar names.** *When reserving, double-check that you're contacting the one in your planned destination.*

RHINE BLITZ TOUR

One of Europe's top thrills is traveling along the Rhine River, enjoying this tour, worth ▲▲▲. For short distances, cruising is best because it's slower. A cruise going upstream (heading south, toward Bingen) takes longer than the same cruise going downstream (north, toward Koblenz). If you want to draw out a short cruise, go upstream (for instance, from St. Goar to Bacharach).

To cover long distances (e.g., Koblenz to Bingen), consider the train. Or take the boat one way and the train back. See page 257 for specifics on traveling the Rhine.

➲ Self-Guided Tour

This easy tour (you can cut in anywhere) skips most of the syrupy myths filling normal Rhine guides. Follow along on a boat, train, bike, or car. By train, sit on the left (river) side going south from Koblenz; most of the castles listed are viewed from this side.

Castles of the Rhine

Many of the castles of the Rhine were "robber-baron" castles, put there by petty rulers (there were 300 independent little countries in medieval Germany) to levy tolls on passing river traffic. A robber baron would put his castle on, or even in, the river. Then, often with the help of chains and a tower on the opposite bank, he'd stop each ship and get his toll. There were 10 customs stops in the 60-mile stretch between Mainz and Koblenz alone.

Some castles were built to control and protect settlements, and others were the residences of kings. As times changed, so did the lifestyles of the rich and feudal. Many castles were abandoned for more comfortable mansions in the towns.

Most Rhine castles date from the 11th, 12th, and 13th centuries. When the pope successfully asserted his power over the German emperor in 1076, local princes ran wild over the rule of their emperor. The castles saw military action in the 1300s and 1400s, as emperors began reasserting their control over Germany's kingdoms.

The castles were also involved in the Reformation wars, in which Europe's Catholic and Protestant dynasties used a fragmented Germany as their battleground. The Thirty Years' War (1618-1648) devastated Germany. The outcome: Each ruler got the freedom to decide if his people would be Catholic or Protestant, and one-third of Germans died. (Production of Gummi Bears ceased entirely.)

The French—who feared a strong Germany and felt the Rhine was the logical border between the two countries—destroyed most of the castles as a preventive measure (Louis XIV in the 1680s, the Revolutionary army in the 1790s, and Napoleon in 1806). Many were rebuilt in the Neo-Gothic style in the Romantic Age—the late 1800s—and today are enjoyed as restaurants, hotels, hostels, and museums.

We're tackling 36 miles (58 km) of the 820-mile-long (1,320-km) Rhine. This tour starts at **Koblenz** and heads upstream to **Bingen.** If you're going the other direction, it still works. Just hold the book upside-down. With limited time, cruise just the best stretch: from St. Goar to Bacharach.

This tour is synched with the large black-and-white kilometer markers you'll see along the riverbank. I erected these years ago to make this tour easier to follow. They tell the distance from the Rhine Falls, where the Rhine leaves Switzerland and becomes navigable. Today, river-barge pilots also use these markers to navigate.

🎧 Download my free Best of the Rhine audio tour—it works in either direction.

Little Bacharach's dock and boat ramp

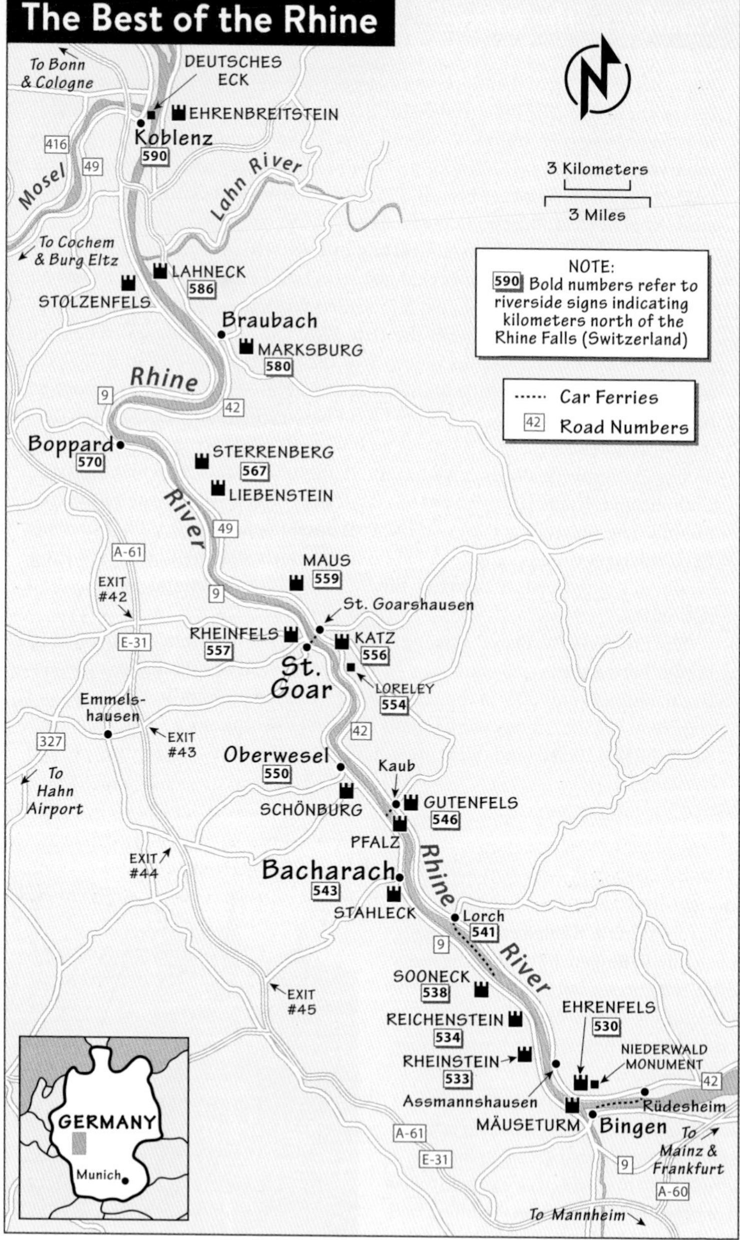
The Best of the Rhine
To Bonn & Cologne
DEUTSCHES ECK
EHRENBREITSTEIN
Koblenz
590
416
49
Mosel
Lahn River
3 Kilometers
3 Miles
To Cochem & Burg Eltz
LAHNECK
586
STOLZENFELS
NOTE:
590 Bold numbers refer to riverside signs indicating kilometers north of the Rhine Falls (Switzerland)
Braubach
MARKSBURG
580
Rhine
9
42
Car Ferries
42 Road Numbers
Boppard
570
STERRENBERG
567
LIEBENSTEIN
River
49
A-61
MAUS
559
EXIT #42
9
St. Goarshausen
RHEINFELS
557
KATZ
556
E-31
St. Goar
LORELEY
554
Emmels-hausen
EXIT #43
327
42
Oberwesel
550
Kaub
To Hahn Airport
SCHÖNBURG
GUTENFELS
546
PFALZ
EXIT #44
Bacharach
543
Rhine
STAHLECK
Lorch
541
9
River
SOONECK
538
EXIT #45
EHRENFELS
530
REICHENSTEIN
534
NIEDERWALD MONUMENT
RHEINSTEIN
533
42
Assmannshausen
Rüdesheim
MÄUSETURM
Bingen
To Mainz & Frankfurt
A-61
E-31
9
A-60
To Mannheim
GERMANY
Munich

From Koblenz to St. Goar

Km 590—Koblenz: This Rhine blitz starts with historic Rhine fanfare, at Koblenz. Koblenz isn't terribly attractive (after being hit hard in World War II), but its place at the historic Deutsches Eck ("German Corner")—the tip of land where the Mosel River joins the Rhine—gives it a certain patriotic charm. A cable car links the Deutsches Eck with the yellow Ehrenbreitstein Fortress across the river.

Km 586—Lahneck Castle: Above the modern autobahn bridge over the Lahn River, this castle *(Burg)* was built in 1240 to defend local silver mines. The castle was ruined by the French in 1688 and rebuilt in the 1850s in Neo-Gothic style.

Km 580—Marksburg Castle: This castle stands bold and white—restored to look like most Rhine castles once did, with their slate stonework covered with stucco to look as if made from a richer stone. You'll spot Marksburg with the three modern chimneys behind it, just before the town of Spay. This is the best-looking of all the Rhine castles and the only surviving medieval castle on the Rhine. Because of its commanding position, it was never attacked in the Middle Ages (though it was captured by the US Army in March of 1945). It's now open as a museum (see page 266 for details).

Km 570—Boppard: Once a Roman town, Boppard has some impressive remains of fourth-century walls. Look for the Roman towers and the substantial chunk of Roman wall near the train station, just above the main square.

If you visit Boppard, head to the fascinating Church of St. Severus below the main square. Find the carved Romanesque crazies at the doorway. Inside, to the right of the entrance, you'll see Christian symbols from Roman times. Also notice the painted arches and vaults (originally, most Romanesque churches were painted this way). Down by the river, look for the high-water *(Hochwasser)* marks on the arches from various flood years. (You'll find these flood marks throughout the Rhine Valley.)

Km 567—Sterrenberg Castle and Liebenstein Castle: These are known as the "Hostile Brothers" castles, across from Bad Salzig. Take the wall between the castles (actually designed to improve the defenses of both castles), add two greedy and jealous brothers and a fair maiden, and create your own legend. Burg Liebenstein is now a fun, friendly, and affordable family-run hotel (Db-€140-150, 9 rooms, suites and family rooms, easy parking, tel. 06773/308, www.castle-liebenstein.com, info@burg-liebenstein.de).

Km 559—Maus Castle: The Maus (mouse) got its name because the next castle was owned by the Katzenelnbogen family. (*Katz* means "cat.") In the 1300s, it was considered a state-of-the-art fortification...until 1806, when Napoleon had it blown up with then-state-of-the-art explosives. It was rebuilt true to its original plans in about 1900. Today, Burg Maus is open for concerts, weddings, and guided

Boppard

Maus Castle

tours in German (weekends only, reservations required, 20-minute walk up, tel. 06771/91011, www.burg-maus.de).

St. Goar to Bacharach: The Best of the Rhine

Km 557—St. Goar and Rheinfels Castle: The pleasant town of St. Goar was named for a sixth-century hometown monk. It originated in Celtic times as a place where sailors would stop, catch their breath, send home a postcard, and give thanks after surviving the seductive and treacherous Loreley crossing. St. Goar is worth a stop to explore its mighty Rheinfels Castle. (For more on St. Goar, see page 257; for a self-guided castle tour, see page 258.)

Km 556—Katz Castle: Burg Katz (Katzenelnbogen) faces St. Goar from across the river. Together, Burg Katz (built in 1371) and Rheinfels Castle had a clear view up and down the river, effectively controlling traffic (there was absolutely no duty-free shopping on the medieval Rhine). Katz got Napoleoned in 1806 and rebuilt in about 1900.

About Km 555: A statue of the Loreley, the beautiful-but-deadly nymph (see next listing for legend), combs her hair at the end of a long spit—built to give barges protection from vicious ice floes that until recent years raged down the river in the winter. The actual Loreley, a cliff (marked by the flags), is just ahead.

Km 554—The Loreley: Steep a big slate rock in centuries of legend and it becomes a tourist attraction—the ultimate Rhinestone. The Loreley (flags on top, name painted near shoreline), rising 450 feet over the narrowest and deepest point of the Rhine, has long been important. It was a holy site in pre-Roman days. The fine echoes here—thought to be ghostly voices—fertilized legend-tellers' imaginations.

Because of the reefs just upstream (at km 552), many ships never made it to St. Goar. Sailors (after days on the river) blamed their misfortune on a *wunderbares Fräulein*, whose long, blond hair almost covered her body. Heinrich Heine's *Song of Loreley* (the CliffsNotes version is on local postcards) tells the story of a count sending his men to kill or capture this siren after she distracted his horny son, who forgot to watch where he was sailing and drowned. When the soldiers cornered the nymph in her cave, she called her father (Father Rhine) for help. Huge waves, the likes of which you'll never see today, rose from the river and carried Loreley to safety. And she has never been seen since.

But alas, when the moon shines brightly and the tour buses are parked, a

The scenic cliffs of the Rhine, steeped in history

The Rhine River Trade

Watch the river barges along the Rhine. There's a constant parade of action, and each boat is different. The flag of the boat's home country flies in the stern (Dutch—horizontal red, white, and blue; Belgian—vertical black, yellow, and red; Swiss—white cross on a red field; German—horizontal black, red, and yellow; French—vertical red, white, and blue).

Barge workers have their own subculture. Many own their own ships. The captain lives in the stern, with his family. The family car is often parked on the stern. Workers live in the bow.

Logically, imports (Japanese cars, coal, and oil) go upstream, and exports (German cars, chemicals, and pharmaceuticals) go downstream. A clever captain manages to ship goods in each direction. Recently, giant Dutch container ships (which transport five times the cargo) have been driving many of the traditional barges out of business, presenting the German economy with another challenge.

Going downstream, tugs can push a floating train of up to five barges at once, but upstream, as the slope gets steeper (and the stream gradient gets higher), they can push only one at a time. Before modern shipping, horses dragged boats upstream (the faint remains of towpaths survive at points along the river). From 1873 to 1900, workers laid a chain from Bonn to Bingen, and boats with cogwheels and steam engines hoisted themselves upstream. Today, 265 million tons travel each year along the 530 miles from Basel on the German-Swiss border to the Dutch city of Rotterdam on the Atlantic.

Riverside navigational aids are vital. Boats pass on the right unless they clearly signal otherwise with a large blue sign. Since ships heading downstream can't stop or maneuver as freely, boats heading upstream are expected to do the tricky maneuvering. Cameras monitor traffic and relay warnings of oncoming ships by posting large triangular signals before narrow and troublesome bends in the river. There may be two or three triangles per signpost, depending upon how many "sectors," or segments, of the river are covered. The lowest triangle indicates the nearest stretch of river. Each triangle tells whether there's a ship in that sector. When the bottom side of a triangle is lit, that sector is empty. When the left side is lit, an oncoming ship is in that sector.

The **Signal and River Pilots Museum** (Wahrschauer- und Lotsenmuseum), located at the signal triangles at the upstream edge of St. Goar, explains how barges are safer, cleaner, and more fuel-efficient than trains or trucks (free, May-Sept, Wed and Sat 14:00-17:00, outdoor exhibits always open).

soft, playful Rhine whine can still be heard from the Loreley. As you pass, listen carefully ("Sailors...sailors...over my bounding mane").

Km 552—The Seven Maidens: Killer reefs, marked by red-and-green buoys, are called the "Seven Maidens." OK, one more goofy legend: The prince of Schönburg Castle (*über* Oberwesel—described next) had seven spoiled daughters who always dumped men because of their shortcomings. Fed up, he invited seven of his knights to the castle and demanded that his daughters each choose one to marry. But they complained that each man had too big a nose, was too fat, too stupid, and so on. The rude and teasing girls escaped into a riverboat. Just downstream, God turned them into the seven rocks that form this reef. While this story probably isn't entirely true, there was a lesson in it for medieval children: Don't be hard-hearted.

Km 550—Oberwesel: The town of Oberwesel, topped by the commanding Schönburg Castle (now a hotel), boasts some of the best medieval wall and tower remains on the Rhine.

Notice how many of the train tunnels along here have entrances designed like medieval turrets—they were actually built in the Romantic 19th century. OK, back to the riverside.

Km 546—Gutenfels Castle and Pfalz Castle, the Classic Rhine View: Burg Gutenfels (now a privately owned hotel) and the shipshape Pfalz Castle (built in the river in the 1300s) worked very effectively to tax medieval river traffic. The town of Kaub grew rich as Pfalz raised its chains when boats came, and lowered them only when the merchants had paid their duty. Those who didn't pay spent time touring its prison, on a raft at the bottom of its well. In 1504, a pope called for the destruction of Pfalz, but the locals withstood a six-week siege, and the castle still stands. Notice the overhanging outhouse (tiny white room between two wooden ones). Pfalz (also known as Pfalzgrafenstein) is tourable but bare and dull, accessible by ferry from Kaub (€3 entry, April-Oct Tue-Sun 10:00-18:00, closed Mon; closes at 17:00 off-season including March, Nov and Jan-Feb Sat-Sun only, closed Dec, mobile 0172-262-2800, www.burg-pfalzgrafenstein.de).

In Kaub, on the riverfront directly below the castles, a green statue (near the waving flags) honors the German general Gebhard von Blücher. He was Napoleon's

Festivals on the Rhine

During the annual **Rhine in Flames festival** (Rhein in Flammen), spectacular displays of fireworks take place along the Rhine's most scenic stretches, while beautifully illuminated ships ply the river, offering up-close views of the fireworks above. Held on five separate days (roughly one day per month) between May and September, the festival rotates between several Rhine towns. Traditional wine festivals and other local celebrations are often timed to coincide with the fireworks (www.rhein-in-flammen.com).

In September and October, some Rhine villages host **wine-fests** on weekends. Check town websites and book your room ahead for these popular times (www.bacharach.de, www.rhein-nahe-touristik.de, www.st-goar.de).

Pfalz Castle (left) and Gutenfels Castle (on hillside)

Stahleck Castle

nemesis. In 1813, as Napoleon fought his way back to Paris after his disastrous Russian campaign, he stopped at Mainz—hoping to fend off the Germans and Russians pursuing him by controlling that strategic bridge. Blücher tricked Napoleon. By building the first major pontoon bridge of its kind here at the Pfalz Castle, he crossed the Rhine and outflanked the French. Two years later, Blücher and Wellington teamed up to defeat Napoleon once and for all at Waterloo.

Immediately opposite Kaub (where the ferry lands, marked by blue roadside flags) is a gaping hole in the mountainside. This marks the last working slate mine on the Rhine.

Km 544—"The Raft Busters": Just before Bacharach, at the top of the island, buoys mark a gang of rocks notorious for busting up rafts. The Black Forest, upstream from here, was once poor, and wood was its best export. Black Foresters would ride log booms down the Rhine to the Ruhr (where their timber fortified coal-mine shafts) or to Holland (where logs were sold to shipbuilders). If they could navigate the sweeping bend just before Bacharach and then survive these "raft busters," they'd come home reckless and horny—the German folkloric equivalent of American cowboys after payday.

Km 543—Bacharach and Stahleck Castle: The town of Bacharach is a great stop (described on page 248). Some of the Rhine's best wine is from this town, whose name likely derives from "altar to Bacchus." Local vintners brag that the medieval Pope Pius II ordered Bacharach wine by the cartload. Perched above the town, the 13th-century Burg Stahleck is now a hostel.

From Bacharach to Bingen

Km 541—Lorch: This stub of a castle is barely visible from the road. Check out the hillside vineyards. Rhine wine is particularly good because the local slate absorbs the heat of the sun and stays warm all night, resulting in sweeter grapes. Wine from the steep side of the Rhine gorge—where grapes are harder to grow and harvest—is tastier and more expensive. Vineyards once blanketed four times as much of the valley as they do today, but modern economics have driven most of them out of business. The vineyards that do survive require government subsidies.

Notice the small car ferry, one of several along the bridgeless stretch between Mainz and Koblenz.

Km 538—Sooneck Castle: Built in the 11th century, this castle was twice destroyed by people sick and tired of robber barons.

Km 534—Reichenstein Castle and **Km 533—Rheinstein Castle:** Both are privately owned, tourable, and connected by a pleasant trail.

Km 530—Ehrenfels Castle: Opposite Bingerbrück and the Bingen station, you'll see the ghostly Ehrenfels Castle, which was clobbered by the Swedes in 1636 and by the French in 1689. Since it had no view of the river traffic to the north, the owner built the cute little *Mäuseturm* (mouse

Sooneck Castle

tower) on an island (the yellow tower you'll see near the train station today). Rebuilt in the 1800s in Neo-Gothic style, it's now used as a Rhine navigation signal station.

Km 528—Niederwald Monument: Across from the Bingen station on a hilltop is the 120-foot-high Niederwald monument, a memorial built with 32 tons of bronze in 1877 to commemorate "the re-establishment of the German Empire." A lift takes tourists to this statue from the famous and extremely touristy wine town of Rüdesheim.

From here, the romantic Rhine becomes the industrial Rhine, and our tour is over.

Getting Around the Rhine

The Rhine flows from Switzerland north to the Netherlands, but the scenic stretch from Mainz to Koblenz hoards all the touristic charm. Studded with the crenellated cream of Germany's castles, it bustles with boats, trains, and highway traffic. Have fun exploring with a mix of big steamers, tiny ferries (*Fähre*), trains, and bikes.

By Boat

While you can do the whole Mainz-Koblenz trip by boat (5.5 hours downstream, 8.5 hours up), I'd focus on the most scenic hour—from St. Goar to Bacharach. Sit on the boat's top deck with your handy Rhine map-guide (or the kilometer-keyed tour in this chapter) and enjoy the parade of castles, towns, boats, and vineyards.

Ehrenfels Castle, with its little "mouse tower" on the river

Two boat companies take travelers along this stretch of the Rhine. Boats run daily in both directions from early April through October, with only one boat running off-season.

Most travelers sail on the bigger, more expensive, and romantic **Köln-Düsseldorfer (K-D) Line** (recommended Bacharach-St. Goar trip: €12.80 one-way, €15.40 round-trip, bikes-€2.80/day, €2 extra if paying with credit card; discounts: up to 30 percent if over 60, 20 percent if you present a connecting train ticket or rail pass; tel. 06741/1634 in St. Goar, tel. 06743/1322 in Bacharach, www.k-d.com).

Complete, up-to-date schedules are posted at any Rhineland station, hotel, TI, and www.k-d.com. Confirm times at your hotel the night before. Purchase tickets at the dock up to five minutes before departure. The boat is never full. Romantics will enjoy the old-time paddle-wheeler *Goethe*, which sails each direction once a day (noted on schedule, confirm time locally).

The smaller **Bingen-Rüdesheimer Line** is slightly cheaper than the K-D, doesn't offer any rail pass deals, and makes three trips in each direction daily from early April through October (buy tickets at ticket booth or on boat, ticket booth only open just before boat departs, 30 percent discount if over 60; departs Bacharach at 10:10, 12:00, and 15:00; departs St. Goar at 11:00, 14:10, and 16:10; tel. 06721/14140, www.bingen-ruedesheimer.de).

By Car

Drivers have these options: 1) skip the boat; 2) take a round-trip cruise from St. Goar or Bacharach; 3) draw pretzels and let the loser drive, prepare the picnic, and meet the boat; 4) rent a bike, bring it on the boat, and bike back; or 5) take the boat one-way and return to your car by

K-D Line Rhine Cruise Schedule

Boats run from early April through October (usually 5/day, but 3-4/day in early April and most of Oct). From November through March, one boat runs daily for groups, but you can tag along if they know you're coming—call the boat directly (tel. 0172/1360-335) or the main office in Cologne (tel. 0221/2088-318) to confirm. Check www.k-d.com for the latest complete schedule; only a few stops are shown below.

Koblenz	Boppard	St. Goar	Bacharach
—	9:00	10:20	11:30
9:00*	11:00*	12:20*	13:30*
—	13:00	14:20	15:30
—	14:00	15:20	16:30
14:00	16:00	17:20	18:30
13:10	11:50	10:55	10:15
—	12:50	11:55	11:15
—	13:50	12:55	12:15
18:10	16:50	15:55	15:15
20:10*	18:50*	17:55*	17:15*

**These sailings are on the 1913 paddle-wheeler* Goethe.

train. When exploring by car, don't hesitate to pop onto one of the many little ferries that shuttle across the river.

By Ferry (Across the Rhine)

As there are no bridges between Koblenz and Mainz, you'll see car-and-passenger ferries (usually family-run for generations) about every three miles. Some of the most useful routes are Bingen-Rüdesheim, Lorch-Niederheimbach, Engelsburg-Kaub, and St. Goar-St. Goarshausen (times vary; St. Goar-St. Goarshausen ferry departs each side every 15-20 minutes daily until 24:00, less frequently on Sun; one-way fares: adult-€1.70, car and driver-€4, pay on boat; www.faehre-loreley.de). For a fun little jaunt, take a quick round-trip (by car or bike) with some time to explore the other side.

By Bike

You can bike on either side of the Rhine, but for a designated bike path, stay on the west side, where a 35-mile path runs between Koblenz and Bingen. The six-mile stretch between St. Goar and Bacharach is smooth and scenic, but it's mostly along the highway. The bit from Bacharach south to Bingen hugs the riverside and is car-free. Either way, biking is a great way to explore the valley (though headwinds can slow you down). Many hotels provide free or cheap bikes to guests; some also rent to the public (including Hotel Hillen in Bacharach and Hotel an der Fähre in St. Goar).

Consider biking one-way and taking the bike back on the riverboat, or designing a circular trip using the fun and frequent shuttle ferries. A good target might be Kaub (where a tiny boat shuttles sightseers to the better-from-a-distance castle on the island).

By Train

Hourly milk-run trains hit every town along the Rhine (Bacharach-St. Goar in both directions about :20 after the hour, 10 minutes; Mainz-Bacharach, 40 minutes; Mainz-Koblenz, 1 hour). Tiny stations are not staffed—buy tickets at machines. Though generally user-friendly, the ticket machines are not all created equal. Some claim to only take exact change; others may not accept US credit cards. When buying a ticket, select "English" and follow the instructions carefully. For example, the ticket machine may give you the choice of validating your ticket for that day or a day in the near future—but only for some destinations (when you're not given this option, your ticket will automatically be validated for the day of purchase).

The **Rheinland-Pfalz-Ticket** day pass covers travel on milk-run trains to many destinations in this chapter, including Koblenz. It can save heaps of money, particularly on longer day trips or if there's more than one in your party (1 person-€24, up to 4 additional people-€4/each, buy from station ticket-machines, good after 9:00 Mon-Fri and all day Sat-Sun, valid on trains labeled *RB*, *RE*, and *MRB*). For a day trip from Bacharach to Burg Eltz (normally €32 round-trip), even one person saves with a Rheinland-Pfalz-Ticket, and a group of five adults saves €120—look for travel partners at breakfast.

BACHARACH

Once prosperous from the wine and wood trade, charming Bacharach (BAHKH-ah-rahkh, with a guttural *kh* sound) is now just a pleasant half-timbered village of 2,000 people working hard to keep its tourists happy. Businesses that have been "in the family" for eons are dealing with succession challenges, as the allure of big-city jobs and a more cosmopolitan life lures away the town's younger generation. But Bacharach retains its time-capsule quaintness.

Orientation

Bacharach cuddles, long and narrow, along the Rhine. The village is easily strollable—you can walk from one end of town to the other along its main drag, Oberstrasse, in about 10 minutes. Bacha-

Riesling wine grapes blanket the Rhine's hillsides.

rach widens at its stream, where more houses trickle up its small valley (along Blücherstrasse) away from the Rhine. The hillsides above town are occupied by vineyards, scant remains of the former town walls, and a castle-turned-youth hostel.

Tourist Information: The TI, on the main street a block-and-a-half from the train station, will store bags for day-trippers (April-Oct Mon-Fri 9:00-17:00, Sat-Sun 10:00-15:00; Nov-March Mon-Fri 9:00-13:00, closed Sat-Sun; from train station, exit right and walk down main street with castle high on your left, TI will be on your right at Oberstrasse 10; tel. 06743/919-303, www.bacharach.de or www.rhein-nahe-touristik.de). They also book 1.5-hour tours in English (€70/group).

Bike Rental: While many hotels loan bikes to guests, the only real bike-rental business in the town center is run by Erich at **Hotel Hillen** (€12/day, daily 9:00-19:00, Langstrasse 18, tel. 06743/1287).

Parking: It's simple to park along the highway next to the train tracks or, better, in the big inexpensive lot by the boat dock (pay with coins at *Parkscheinautomat* and put ticket on dashboard, free overnight).

Private Guides: Thomas Gundlach happily gives 1.5-hour town walks to individuals or small groups for €35 (as well as 4- to 10-hour hiking tours for the more ambitious). He can also drive up to three people around the region in his car (€80/6 hours, mobile 0179-353-6004, thomas_gundlach@gmx.de). **Birgit Wessels** is also good (€45/1.5-hour walk, tel. 06743/937-514, wessels.birgit@t-online.de).

➲ Bacharach Town Walk

• *Start at the Köln-Düsseldorfer ferry dock (next to a fine picnic park).*

Riverfront: View the town from the parking lot—a modern landfill. The Rhine used to lap against Bacharach's town wall, just over the present-day highway. Every few years, the river floods, covering the highway with several feet of water. Flat land like this is rare in the Rhine Valley, where towns are often shaped like the letter "T," stretching thin along the riverfront and up a crease in the hills beyond.

Reefs farther upstream forced boats to

Classic and quaint Bacharach

unload upriver and reload here. Consequently, in the Middle Ages, Bacharach was the biggest wine-trading town on the Rhine. A riverfront crane hoisted huge kegs of prestigious "Bacharach" wine (which, in practice, was from anywhere in the region). Today, the economy is based on tourism.

Look above town. The **castle** on the hill is now a youth hostel. Two of the town's original 16 towers are visible from here (up to 5 if you look really hard). The bluff on the right, with the yellow flag, is the **Heinrich Heine Viewpoint** (the end-point of a popular hike). Old-timers remember when, rather than the flag marking the town as a World Heritage site, a swastika sculpture 30 feet wide and tall stood there. Realizing that it could be an enticing target for Allied planes in the last months of the war, locals tore it down even before Hitler fell.

Nearby, a stele in the park describes the Bingen to Koblenz stretch of the Rhine gorge.

• *Before entering the town, walk upstream through the...*

Riverside Park: New elements of the park are designed to bring people to the riverside and combat flooding. The park was originally laid out in 1910 in the English style: Notice how the trees were planted to frame fine town views, highlighting the most picturesque bits of architecture. The dark, sad-looking monument—its "eternal" flame long snuffed out—is a **war memorial.** The German psyche is permanently scarred by war memories. Today, many Germans would rather avoid monuments like this, which revisit the dark periods before Germany became a nation of pacifists. Take a close look at the monument. Each panel honors sons of Bacharach who died for the Kaiser: in 1864 against Denmark, in 1866 against Austria, in 1870 against France, in 1914 during World War I. The military Maltese cross—flanked by classic German helmets—has a "W" at its center, for Kaiser Wilhelm. Review the family names on the opposite side of the monument: You may later recognize them on today's restaurants and hotels.

• *Look (but don't go now) upstream from here to see the...*

Trailer Park and Campground: In Germany, trailer vacationers and campers are two distinct subcultures. Folks who travel in motorhomes, like many retirees in the US, are a nomadic bunch, cruising around the countryside and paying a few euros a night to park. Campers, on the other hand, tend to set up camp in one place—complete with comfortable lounge chairs and TVs—and stay put for weeks, even months. They often come back to the same spot year after year, treating it like their own private estate. These camping devotees have made a science out of relaxing. Tourists are welcome to pop in for a drink or meal at the Sonnenstrand campground's terrace café (daily 13:00-21:00; it's a 10-minute walk).

High-water marks indicate the heights reached by floodwaters.

• Continue to where the park meets the playground, and then cross the highway to the fortified riverside wall of the Catholic church, decorated with...

High-Water Marks: These recall various floods. Before the 1910 reclamation project, the river extended out to here, and boats would use the rings in this wall to tie up.

• From the church, go under the 1858 train tracks (and past more high-water marks) and hook right past the yellow floodwater yardstick and up the stairs onto the town wall. Atop the wall, turn left and walk under the long arcade. After 30 yards, on your left, notice a...

Well: Rebuilt as it appeared in the 17th century, this is one of seven such wells that brought water to the townsfolk until 1900. Each neighborhood's well also provided a social gathering place and the communal laundry. Walk 50 yards past the well along the wall to an alcove in the medieval tower with a view of the war memorial in the park. You're under the crane tower (*Kranenturm*). After barrels of wine were moved overland from Bingen past dangerous stretches of river, the precious cargo could be lowered by cranes from here into ships to continue more safely down the river. The Rhine has long been a major shipping route through Germany. In modern times, it's a bottleneck in Germany's train system. The train company gives hotels and residents along the tracks money for soundproof windows (hotels along here routinely have quadruple-pane windows...and earplugs on the nightstand).

A facsimile of a 17th-century well

• Continue walking along the town wall. Pass the recommended Rhein Hotel just before the...

Markt Tower: This marks one of the town's 15 original 14th-century gates and is a reminder that in that century there was a big wine market here.

• Descend the stairs closest to the Rhein Hotel, pass another well, and follow Marktstrasse away from the river toward the town center, the two-tone church, and the town's...

Main Intersection: From here, Bacharach's main street (Oberstrasse) goes right to the half-timbered red-and-white Altes Haus (which we'll visit later) and left 400 yards to the train station. Spin around to enjoy the higgledy-piggledy building styles. The town has a case of the doldrums: The younger generation is moving to the big cities and many long-established family businesses have no one to take over for their aging owners. In the winter the town is particularly dead.

• To the left (south) of the church, a golden horn hangs over the old...

Posthof: Throughout Europe, the postal horn is the symbol of the postal service. In olden days, when the postman blew this, traffic stopped and the mail sped through. This post station dates from 1724, when stagecoaches ran from Cologne to Frankfurt and would change horses here, Pony Express-style. As you enter, notice the cornerstones at the Posthof entrance, protecting the venerable building from reckless carriage wheels. Inside the old oak doors (on the left) is the actual door to the post office that served Bacharach for 200 years. Find the mark on the wall labeled *Rheinhöhe 3/1-4/2 1850*. This recalls a historic flood caused by an ice jam at the Loreley just downstream. Notice also the fascist eagle in the alcove on the right (from 1936; a swastika once filled its center).

Step into the courtyard—once a carriage house and inn that accommodated Bacharach's first VIP visitors, and now home to the recommended Posthof Bacharach restaurant, with a fine view of the church and a ruined chapel above.

Two hundred years ago, Bacharach's main drag was the only road along the Rhine. Napoleon widened it to fit his cannon wagons. The steps alongside the church lead to the castle.

• *Return to the church, passing the recommended Italian ice-cream café* ***(Eis Café Italia),*** *where friendly Mimo serves his special invention: Riesling wine-flavored gelato.*

Protestant Church: Inside the church (daily May-Sept 10:00-18:00, April and Oct until 17:00, closed Nov-March, English info on a stand near door), you'll find Grotesque capitals, brightly painted in medieval style, and a mix of round Romanesque and pointed Gothic arches. The church was fancier before the Reformation wars, when it (and the region) was Catholic. Bacharach lies on the religious border of Germany and, like the country as a whole, is split between Catholics and Protestants. To the left of the altar, some medieval (pre-Reformation) frescoes survive where an older Romanesque arch was cut by a pointed Gothic one.

If you're considering bombing the town, take note: A blue-and-white plaque just outside the church's door warns that, according to the Hague Convention, this historic building shouldn't be targeted in times of war.

• *Continue down Oberstrasse to the...*

Altes Haus: Dating from 1368, this is the oldest house in town. Notice the 14th-century building style—the first floor is made of stone, while upper floors are half-timbered (in the ornate style common in the Rhine Valley). Some of its windows still look medieval, with small, flattened circles as panes (small because that's all that the glass-blowing technology of the time would allow), pieced together with molten lead (like medieval stained glass in churches). Frau Weber welcomes visitors to enjoy the fascinating ground floor of the recommended Altes Haus restaurant, with its evocative old photos and etchings (consider eating here later).

• *Keep going down Oberstrasse to the...*

Old Mint (Münze): The old mint is marked by a crude coin in its sign. As a practicality, any great trading town needed coinage, and since 1356, Bacharach minted theirs here. Across from the mint, the recommended **Bastian** family's wine garden is a lively place after dark. Above you in the vineyards stands a lonely white-and-red tower—your final destination.

• *At the next street, look right and see the mint tower, painted in the medieval style, and then turn left. Wander 30 yards up Rosenstrasse to the* ***well.*** *Notice the sundial and the wall painting of 1632 Bacharach with its walls intact. Study the fine slate roof over the well: The town's roof tiles were quarried and split right here in the Rhineland.*

Continue another 30 yards up Rosenstrasse to find the tiny-stepped lane behind the well up into the vineyard and to the...

Tall Tower: The slate steps lead to a small path through the vineyard that deposits you at a viewpoint atop the stubby remains of the medieval wall and a tower. The town's towers jutted out from the wall and had only three sides, with the "open" side facing the town. Towers were covered with stucco to make them look more impressive, as if they were made of a finer white stone. If this tower's open, hike up to climb the stairs for the best view. (The top floor has been closed to give nesting falcons some privacy.)

Romantic Rhine View: A grand medieval town spreads before you. For 300 years (1300-1600), Bacharach was big (population 4,000), rich, and politically powerful.

From this perch, you can see the chapel ruins and six surviving **city towers.** Visually trace the wall to the castle. The castle was actually the capital of Germany for a couple of years in the 1200s. When Holy Roman Emperor Frederick Barbarossa went away to fight the Crusades, he left his brother (who lived here) in charge of his vast realm. Bacharach was home to one of the seven electors who voted for the Holy Roman Emperor in 1275. To protect their own power, these prince electors did their best to choose the weakest guy on the ballot. The elector from Bacharach helped select a two-bit prince named Rudolf von Habsburg (from a no-name castle in Switzerland). However, the underestimated Rudolf brutally silenced the robber barons along the Rhine and established the mightiest dynasty in European history. His family line, the Habsburgs, ruled much of Central and Eastern Europe from Vienna until 1918.

Plagues, fires, and the Thirty Years' War (1618-1648) finally did in Bacharach. The town has slumbered for several centuries. Today, the castle houses commoners—40,000 overnights annually by youth hostelers.

In the mid-19th century, painters such as J. M. W. Turner and writers such as Victor Hugo were charmed by the Rhine-

Altes Haus is the oldest dwelling (1368) in Bacharach.

land's romantic mix of past glory, present poverty, and rich legend. They put this part of the Rhine on the old Grand Tour map as the "Romantic Rhine." Victor Hugo pondered the ruined 15th-century chapel that you see under the castle. In his 1842 travel book, *Excursions Along the Banks of the Rhine*, he wrote, "No doors, no roof or windows, a magnificent skeleton puts its silhouette against the sky. Above it, the ivy-covered castle ruins provide a fitting crown. This is Bacharach, land of fairy tales, covered with legends and sagas." If you're enjoying the Romantic Rhine, thank Victor Hugo and company.

• *Our walk is done. To get back into town, just retrace your steps. Or, to extend this walk, take the level path away from the river that leads along the once-mighty wall up the valley to the next tower, the...*

Wood Market Tower: Timber was gathered here in Bacharach and lashed together into vast log booms known as "Holland rafts" (as big as a soccer field) that were floated downstream. Two weeks later the lumber would reach Amsterdam, where it was in high demand as foundation posts for buildings and for the great Dutch shipbuilders. Notice the four stones above the arch on the uphill side of the tower—these guided the gate as it was hoisted up and down.

• *From here, cross the street and go downhill into the parking lot. Pass the recommended Pension im Malerwinkel on your right, being careful not to damage the old arch with your head. Follow the creek past a delightful little series of half-timbered homes and cheery gardens known as "Painters' Corner"* (Malerwinkel). *Resist looking into some pervert's peep show (on the right) and continue downhill back to the village center.*

Experiences

Wine Tasting

Bacharach is proud of its wine. Two places in town offer an inexpensive tasting alongside light plates of food.

Bastian's Weingut zum Grüner Baum is rowdy and rustic. Groups of 2-6 people pay €22.50 for a wine carousel of 15 glasses—14 different white wines and 1 lonely red—and a basket of bread. Spin the lazy Susan, share a common cup, and discuss the taste. The Bastian family insists: "After each wine, you must talk to each other." Along with their characteristic interior, they have two nice terraces (daily 12:00-22:00, closed in winter, just past Altes Haus, tel. 06743/1208).

Weingut Karl Heidrich is a fun wine shop and *Stube* in the town center, where Markus and daughters Magdalena and Katharina share their family's centuries-old wine tradition. They offer a variety of carousels with six wines, English descriptions, and bread (€12)—ideal for the more sophisticated wine taster—plus light meals and a €10.50 meat-and-cheese plate (Thu-Tue 11:00-22:00, closed Wed and Nov-mid-April, will ship to US, Oberstrasse 16, tel. 06743/93060).

Rick's Tip: *Bacharach goes to bed early, so if you're looking for* **nightlife,** *head to one of the* **wine-tasting places** *or* **Restaurant Zeus,** *which has long hours and outdoor seating that adds a spark to the town center after dark (daily 17:30-24:00, Koblenzer Strasse 11, tel. 06743/909-7171). The hilltop youth hostel,* **Jugendherberge Stahleck,** *serves cheap wine with priceless views until late in summer.*

Shopping

The **Jost** German gift store, across the main square from the church, carries most everything a souvenir shopper could want—from beer steins to cuckoo clocks—and can ship purchases to the US (March-Oct Mon-Fri 9:00-18:00, Sat-Sun 10:00-18:00, shorter hours in winter, closed Jan-Feb; Blücherstrasse 4, tel. 06743/909-7214). They offer discounts to my readers with a €10 minimum purchase: 10 percent with cash, 5 percent with credit card.

Eating

Restaurants

Bacharach has no shortage of reasonably priced, atmospheric restaurants offering fine indoor and outdoor dining.

The Rhein Hotel's **$$$ Stüber Restaurant** is Bacharach's best top-end choice. Andreas Stüber, his family's sixth-generation chef, creates regional plates prepared with a slow-food ethic. The menu changes with the season and is served at river- and track-side seating or indoors with a spacious wood-and-white-tablecloth elegance. Their Posten Riesling is well worth the splurge (€18-25 main courses, €35 fixed-price meals, always good vegetarian and vegan options, daily 17:00-21:15 plus Sat-Sun 11:30-14:15, closed mid-Dec-Feb, call to reserve on weekends or for an outdoor table, facing the K-D boat dock below town center, Langstrasse 50, tel. 06743/1243).

$$ Altes Haus serves classic German dishes within Bacharach's most romantic atmosphere—inside the oldest building in town. Find the cozy little dining room with photos of the opera singer who sang about Bacharach, adding to its fame (€10-20 main courses, Thu-Tue 12:00-15:00 & 18:00-21:30, longer hours on weekends, closed Wed and Dec-Easter, dead center by the Protestant church, tel. 06743/1209).

Casual Options

The **$ Posthof Bacharach** restaurant and café has nice outdoor seating and a medieval feel, with a view of the ruined chapel above (€8-12 main courses, daily Easter-Oct 12:00-21:00, closed Nov-Easter, Oberstrasse 45-49, tel. 06743/947-1830).

$ Kleines Brauhaus Rheinterrasse is a funky, family-friendly microbrewery serving meals, fresh-baked bread, and homemade beer under a 1958 circus carousel that overlooks the town and river (Tue-Sun 13:00-22:00, closed Mon, at the downstream end of town, Koblenzer Strasse 14, tel. 06743/919-179).

$ Bacharacher Pizza and Kebap Haus, on the main drag in the town center, is the town favorite for €4-6 *Döner Kebabs,* cheap pizzas, and salads (daily 10:00-22:00, Oberstrasse 43, tel. 06743/3127).

Eis Café Italia, on the main street, is known for its refreshing, Riesling-flavored gelato (daily April-mid-Oct 13:00-19:00, closed mid-Oct-March, Oberstrasse 48).

Pick up **picnic supplies** at **Nahkauf,** a basic grocery store (Mon-Fri 8:00-12:00 & 14:00-18:00, Sat 8:30-12:30, closed Sun, Koblenzer Strasse 2). For a gourmet picnic, call the **Rhein Hotel** to reserve a "picnic bag" complete with wine, cheese, small dishes, and a hiking map (€13/person, arrange a day in advance, tel. 06743/1243).

Sleeping

None of the hotels listed here have elevators. The only listings with parking are Pension im Malerwinkel, Pension Winzerhaus, and the youth hostel. At the others, drive in to unload your bags and then park in the public lot. If you'll arrive after 20:00, let your hotel know in advance (none have 24-hour reception desks).

$$ Rhein Hotel, overlooking the river with 14 spacious and comfortable rooms, is classy, well-run, and decorated with modern flair. Since it's right on the train tracks, its river- and train-side rooms come with quadruple-paned windows and air-conditioning (Db-€96, family rooms, cheaper for longer stays and off-season, free loaner bikes, directly inland from the K-D boat dock at Langstrasse 50, tel. 06743/1243, www.rhein-hotel-bacharach.de, info@rhein-hotel-bacharach.de). Their Stüber Restaurant is considered the best in town.

$ Hotel zur Post, clean and quiet, is conveniently located right in the town center with no train noise. Its 12 rooms are a good value, offering more solid comfort than old-fashioned character (Db-€71-76, family rooms, Oberstrasse 38, tel. 06743/1277, www.hotel-zur-post-bacharach.de, h.zurpost@t-online.de).

Sleep Code

$$$$ Splurge: Over €170
$$$ Pricier: €130-170
$$ Moderate: €90-130
$ Budget: €50-90
¢ Backpacker: Under €50

Hotels are classified based on the average price of a standard double room with bath in high season. Unless otherwise noted, credit cards are accepted, breakfast is included, hotel staff speak English, and Wi-Fi is available.

$ Hotel Kranenturm, offering castle ambience without the climb, combines hotel comfort with delightful *Privatzimmer* funkiness right downtown. This 16-room hotel is part of the medieval town wall. The rooms in the tower have the best views. While just 15 feet from the train tracks, a combination of medieval sturdiness, triple-paned windows, and included earplugs makes the riverside rooms sleepable (Db-€70, Db in tower room with views-€82, family rooms, cheaper for 3-night stay, cash preferred, €2 extra with credit card, showers can be temperamental, good breakfast, Langstrasse 30, tel. 06743/1308, www.kranenturm.com, hotel-kranenturm@t-online.de).

$ Pension im Malerwinkel sits like a grand gingerbread house that straddles the town wall in a quiet little neighborhood. The quiet place has 20 rooms, a picturesque garden, views of the vineyards, and easy parking—all a short stroll from the town center (Db-€69, cheaper for 2- to 3-day stays, family rooms, cash only, no train noise, bike rental-€6/day, parking; from Oberstrasse, turn left at the church, walkers can follow the path to the left just before the town gate but drivers must pass through the gate to find the hotel parking lot, Blücherstrasse 41; tel. 06743/1239, www.im-malerwinkel.de, pension@im-malerwinkel.de).

$ Hotel Hillen, a block south of Hotel Kranenturm, has the train noise and the same ultra-thick windows. It offers five spacious rooms and good hospitality (D with shower-€50, Db-€60, family rooms, 10 percent discount for stays of 2 nights or longer, cash only, closed mid-Nov-Easter, Langstrasse 18, tel. 06743/1287, hotel-hillen@web.de).

$ Pension Winzerhaus has 10 rooms just outside the town walls, directly under the vineyards. The rooms are simple, clean, and modern, and parking is a breeze (Db-€55, family rooms, prices do not include €0.50/person per day tourist tax, cash only, laundry service for fee, free loaner bikes for guests, Blücherstrasse 60, tel. 06743/1294, www.pension-winzerhaus.de, winzerhaus@gmx.de).

¢ Irmgard Orth B&B rents three bright rooms, two of which share a bathroom on the hall. Charming Irmgard speaks almost no English, but is exuberant and serves homemade honey with breakfast (D-€40, Db-€42, cash only, Spurgasse 2, tel. 06743/1553—speak slowly, orth.irmgard@gmail.com).

¢ Jugendherberge Stahleck hostel is in the 12th-century castle on the hilltop—350 steps above Bacharach—with a royal Rhine view. Open to travelers of any age, this is a gem with 168 beds and a private modern shower and WC in most rooms. The hostel offers hearty all-you-can-eat buffet dinners (18:00-19:30 nightly), and in summer, its pub serves cheap local wine and snacks all day until late. From the train station, it's a €10 taxi ride to the hostel—call 06743/1653 (dorm beds-€21.50, Db-€54, nonmembers pay extra, includes breakfast and sheets, laundry-€6; reception open 7:30-20:00, call if arriving later and check in at bar until 21:30; curfew at 22:00, tel. 06743/1266, www.diejugendherbergen.de, bacharach@diejugendherbergen.de). If driving, don't go in the driveway; park on the street and walk 200 yards.

Transportation

Arriving and Departing

BY TRAIN

Milk-run trains stop at Rhine towns each hour starting as early as 6:00, connecting at Mainz and Koblenz to trains farther afield. Trains between St. Goar and Bacharach depart at about :20 after the hour in each direction (€3.60, buy tickets from the machine in the unstaffed stations, carry cash since some machines won't accept US credit cards).

The durations listed below are calculated from Bacharach; for St. Goar, the difference is only 10 minutes. From Bacharach (or St. Goar), to go anywhere distant, you'll need to change trains in Koblenz for points north, or in Mainz for points south. Milk-run connections to these towns depart hourly, at about :20 past the hour for northbound trains, and at about :30 past the hour for southbound trains. Train info: toll tel. 0180-699-6633, www.bahn.com.

From Bacharach by Train to: St. Goar (hourly, 10 minutes), **Moselkern** near Burg Eltz (hourly, 1.5 hours, change in Koblenz), **Cologne** (hourly, 1.5-2 hours with change in Koblenz, 2.5 hours direct), **Frankfurt Airport** (hourly, 1 hour, change in Mainz or Bingen), **Frankfurt** (hourly, 1.5 hours, change in Mainz or Bingen), **Rothenburg ob der Tauber** (every 2 hours, 4.5 hours, 3-4 changes), **Munich** (hourly, 5 hours, 2 changes), **Berlin** (hourly, 7 hours, 1-3 changes).

BY CAR

Bacharach and St. Goar are near Frankfurt and its airport, just an hour's drive away. Some travelers find that the Rhine Valley, with its small towns, makes a pleasant first (or last) stop in Germany.

If you're following my two-week itinerary, and you're driving north from Rothenburg to Bacharach, allow 3 hours, or figure on a 3.5-hour drive if you route your trip through Creglingen and Weikersheim (to visit Romantic Road sights mentioned on page 219). When leaving the Rhine, you could drive to Cologne or Frankfurt, drop off the car, and take the train to Berlin (or elsewhere).

ST. GOAR

St. Goar (sahnkt gwahr) is a classic Rhine tourist town. Its hulk of a castle overlooks a half-timbered shopping street and leafy riverside park, busy with sightseeing ships and contented strollers. Rheinfels Castle, once the mightiest on the river, is the single best Rhineland ruin to explore. While the town of St. Goar itself is less interesting than Bacharach, be sure to explore beyond the shops: Thoughtful little placards (in English) offer facts about each street, lane, and square. St. Goar also makes a good base for hiking or biking the region. A tiny car ferry will shuttle you back and forth across the busy Rhine from here.

Orientation

St. Goar is dominated by its mighty castle, Rheinfels. The village—basically a wide spot in the road at the foot of Rheinfels' hill—isn't much more than a few hotels and restaurants. From the riverboat docks, the main drag—a dull pedestrian mall without history—cuts through town before ending at the road up to the castle.

Tourist Information: The helpful TI, which books rooms and stores bags for free, is on the pedestrian street, three blocks from the K-D boat dock and train station (May-Sept Mon-Fri 9:00-18:00, Sat 10:00-13:00, closed Sun; shorter hours and closed Sat-Sun in off-season; from train station, go downhill around church and turn left, Heerstrasse 86, tel. 06741/383, www.st-goar.de).

Bike Rental: Hotel an der Fähre rents bikes for a fair price, but you need to call ahead to reserve (€10/day, pickup after 10:00, Heerstrasse 47, tel. 06741/980-577).

Parking: A free lot is at the downstream (north) end of town, by the harbor. For on-street parking by the K-D boat dock and recommended hotels, get a ticket from the machine *(Parkscheinautomat)* and put it on the dashboard (€4/day, daily 9:00-18:00, coins only, free overnight). Make sure you press the button for a day ticket.

Sights

▲▲▲RHEINFELS CASTLE (BURG RHEINFELS)

Sitting like a dead pit bull above St. Goar, this once mightiest of Rhine castles rumbles with ghosts from its hard-fought past. This hollow but interesting shell offers the best ruined-castle experience on the river. Impressive and evocative, it's but a shadow of its former self. Some areas may be inaccessible during renovation.

Cost and Hours: €5, family card-€10, mid-March-Oct daily 9:00-18:00, Nov-mid-March possibly Sat-Sun only 11:00-17:00 (call ahead), last entry one hour before closing—weather permitting.

Information: The free castle map is helpful, but the €0.50 English booklet is of no real value, except to real history buffs. If it's damp, be careful of slippery stones. Tel. 06741/7753; in winter, tel. 06741/383, www.st-goar.de.

Services: A handy WC is immediately across from the ticket booth (check out the guillotine urinals—stand back when you pull to flush).

Rick's Tip: *To explore* **the castle tunnels at Rheinfels, bring a flashlight**—*or buy one at the ticket office. For real medieval atmosphere, they also sell candles with matches.*

Getting to the Castle: A **taxi** up from town costs €5 (tel. 06741/7011). Or take the kitschy "tschu-tschu" **tourist train** (€3 one-way, €4 round-trip, 8 minutes to the top, hours vary but generally April-Oct daily 9:30-16:30, departs from town at :15 and :45, from castle at :00 and :30, some narration, mobile 0171-445-1525). The train usually waits between the train station and the K-D dock, or at the Catholic Church just past the top end of the pedestrian street. **Parking** at the castle costs €1/hour (cash only).

To **hike** up to the castle, you can simply follow the main road up through the railroad underpass at the top end of the pedestrian street. But it's more fun to take the nature trail: Start at the St. Goar train station. Take the underpass under the tracks at the north end of the station, climb the steep stairs uphill, turn right (following *Burg Rheinfels* signs), and keep straight along the path just above the

St. Goar on the Rhine

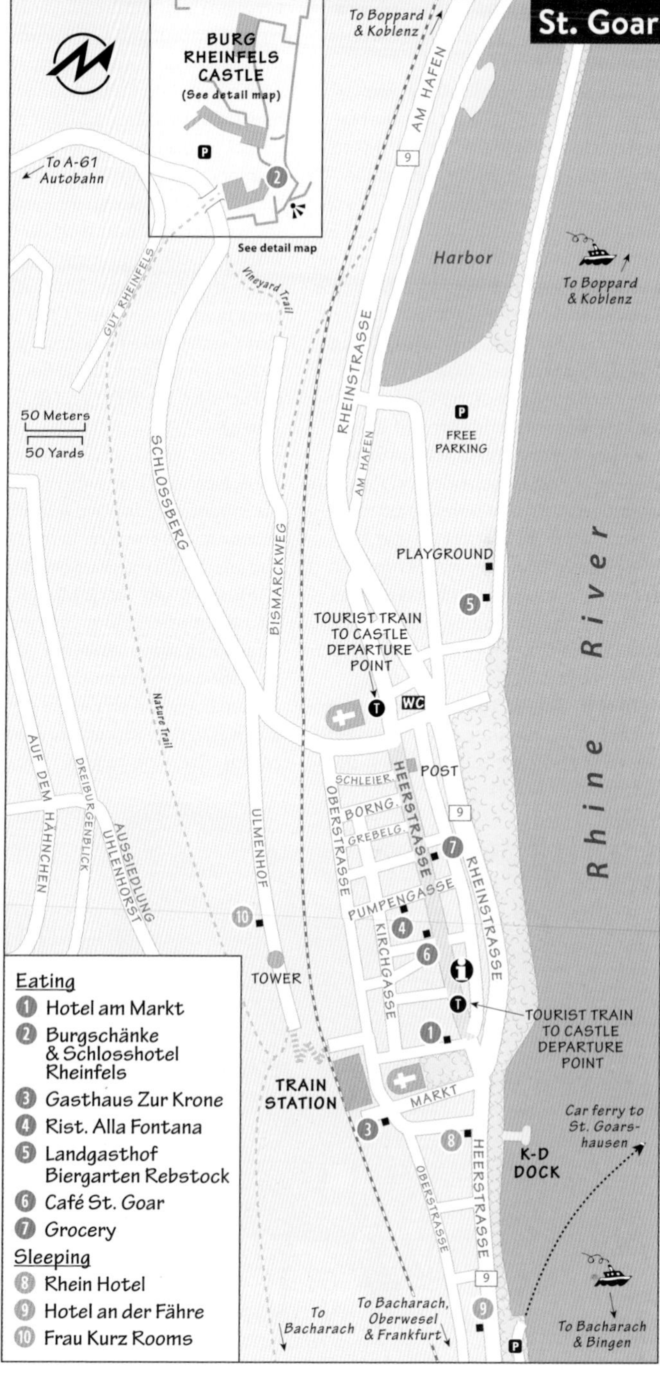
St. Goar
BURG RHEINFELS CASTLE
(See detail map)
See detail map
To Boppard & Koblenz
To A-61 Autobahn
AM HAFEN
Harbor
To Boppard & Koblenz
Vineyard Trail
GUT RHEINFELS
RHEINSTRASSE
FREE PARKING
50 Meters
50 Yards
SCHLOSSBERG
AM HAFEN
BISMARCKWEG
PLAYGROUND
TOURIST TRAIN TO CASTLE DEPARTURE POINT
WC
Rhine River
Nature Trail
AUF DEM HÄHNCHEN
DREIBURGENBLICK
AUSSIEDLUNG UHLENHORST
ULMENHOF
SCHLEIER
HEERSTRASSE
POST
OBERSTRASSE
BORNG.
GREBELG.
RHEINSTRASSE
PUMPENGASSE
KIRCHGASSE
TOWER
TOURIST TRAIN TO CASTLE DEPARTURE POINT
TRAIN STATION
MARKT
Car ferry to St. Goarshausen
K-D DOCK
OBERSTRASSE
HEERSTRASSE
To Bacharach
To Bacharach, Oberwesel & Frankfurt
To Bacharach & Bingen
Eating
1 Hotel am Markt
2 Burgschänke & Schlosshotel Rheinfels
3 Gasthaus Zur Krone
4 Rist. Alla Fontana
5 Landgasthof Biergarten Rebstock
6 Café St. Goar
7 Grocery
Sleeping
8 Rhein Hotel
9 Hotel an der Fähre
10 Frau Kurz Rooms

old city wall. Small red-and-white signs show the way, taking you to the castle in 15 minutes.

Background: Burg Rheinfels *was* huge—for five centuries, it was the biggest castle on the Rhine. Built in 1245 to guard a toll station, it soon earned the nickname "the unconquerable fortress." In the 1400s, the castle was thickened to withstand cannon fire. Rheinfels became a thriving cultural center and, in the 1520s, was visited by the artist Albrecht Dürer and the religious reformer Ulrich Zwingli. It saw lots of action in the Thirty Years' War (1618-1648), and later became the strongest and most modern fortress in the Holy Roman Empire. It withstood a siege of 28,000 French troops in 1692. But eventually the castle surrendered to the French without a fight, and in 1797, the French Revolutionary army destroyed it. For years, the ruined castle was used as a source of building stone, and today—while still mighty—it's only a small fraction of its original size.

➲ **Self-Guided Tour:** Rather than wander aimlessly, visit the castle by following this tour. We'll start at the museum, then circulate through the courtyards, up to the highest lookout point, and down around through the fortified ramparts, with an option to go into the dark tunnels. We'll finish in the dungeon and big cellar.

Pick up the free map and use its commentary to navigate from red signpost to red signpost through the castle. My self-guided tour route is similar to the one marked on the castle map. That map, the one in this book, and this tour all use the same numbering system. (You'll notice that I've skipped a few stops—just walk on by signs for ❷ *Darmstädter Bau,* ❺ *Stables,* ⓫ *Fuchsloch* (foxhole), and ⓭ *Gunsmiths' Tower.*)

• *The ticket office is under the castle's clock tower, labeled* ❶ Uhrturm. *Walk through the entranceway and continue straight, passing several points of interest (which we'll visit later), until you get to the* ❸ *museum.*

Museum and Castle Model: The pleasant museum, located in the only finished room of the castle, has good English descriptions and comes with Romantic Age etchings that give a sense of the place as it was in the 19th century (daily mid-March-Oct 10:00-12:30 & 13:00-17:30;

Rheinfels' inner courtyard

St. Goar's Rheinfels Castle

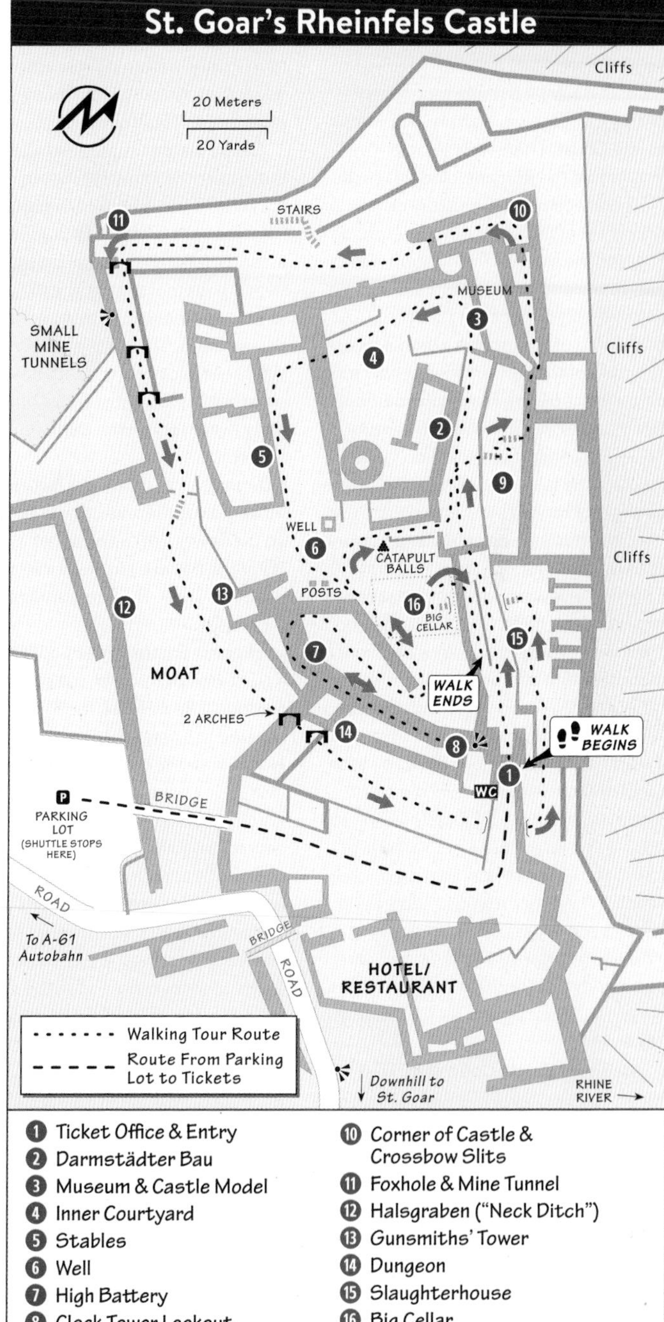

1. Ticket Office & Entry
2. Darmstädter Bau
3. Museum & Castle Model
4. Inner Courtyard
5. Stables
6. Well
7. High Battery
8. Clock Tower Lookout
9. Stairs to Battlements
10. Corner of Castle & Crossbow Slits
11. Foxhole & Mine Tunnel
12. Halsgraben ("Neck Ditch")
13. Gunsmiths' Tower
14. Dungeon
15. Slaughterhouse
16. Big Cellar

closed Nov-mid-March).

The seven-foot-tall carved stone immediately inside the door (marked *Flammensäule*)—a tombstone from a nearby Celtic grave—is from 400 years before Christ. There were people here long before the Romans...and this castle.

The sweeping castle history exhibit in the center of the room is well-described in English. The massive fortification was the only Rhineland castle to withstand Louis XIV's assault during the 17th century. At the far end of the room is a model reconstruction of the castle, showing how much bigger it was before French Revolutionary troops destroyed it in the 18th century. Study this. Find where you are. (Hint: Look for the tall tower.) This was the living quarters of the original castle, which was only the smallest ring of buildings around the tiny central courtyard (13th century). The ramparts were added in the 14th century. By 1650, the fortress was largely complete. Since its destruction by the French in the late 18th century, it's had no military value. While no WWII bombs were wasted on this ruin, it served St. Goar as a stone quarry for generations. The basement of the museum shows the castle pharmacy and an exhibit of Rhine-region odds and ends, including tools, an 1830 loom, and photos of icebreaking on the Rhine. While once routine, icebreaking hasn't been necessary here since 1963.

• *Exit the museum and walk 30 yards directly out, slightly uphill into the castle courtyard, where you'll see a sign for the inner courtyard* (❹ Innenhof).

Medieval Castle Courtyard: Five hundred years ago, the entire castle encircled this courtyard. The place was self-sufficient and ready for a siege, with a bakery, pharmacy, herb garden, brewery, well (top of yard), and livestock. During peacetime, 300 to 600 people lived here; during a siege, there would be as many as 4,000. The walls were plastered and painted white. Bits of the original 13th-century plaster survive.

• *Continue through the courtyard under the* Erste Schildmauer *(first shield wall) sign, turn left, and walk straight to the two old wooden upright posts. Find the pyramid of stone catapult balls on your left.*

Castle Garden: Catapult balls like these were too expensive not to recycle—they'd be retrieved after any battle. Across from the balls is a well (❻ *Brunnen*)—essential for any castle during the age of sieges. Look in. Thirsty? The old posts are for the ceremonial baptizing of new members of the local trading league. While this guild goes back centuries, it's now a social club that fills this court with a huge wine party every year on the third weekend of September.

• *Climb uphill to the castle's highest point by walking along the cobbled path (look for the* To the Tower *sign) up past the high battery* (❼ Hohe Batterie) *to the castle's best viewpoint—up where the German flag waves (signed* ❽ Uhrturm).

Highest Castle Tower Lookout: Enjoy a great view of the river, the castle, and the forest. Remember, the fortress once covered five times the land it does today. Notice how the other castles (across the river) don't poke above the top of the Rhine canyon. That would make them easy for invading armies to see.

From this perch, survey the Rhine Valley, cut out of slate over millions of years by the river. The slate absorbs the heat of the sun, making the grapes grown here well-suited for wine. Today, the slate is mined to provide roofing. Imagine St. Goar himself settling here 1,500 years ago, establishing a place where sailors—thankful to have survived the dangerous Loreley—would stop and pray. Imagine the frozen river of years past, when the ice would break up and boats would huddle in man-made harbors like the one below for protection. Consider the history of trade on this busy river—from the days when castles levied tolls on ships, to the days when boats would be hauled upstream with the help of riverside towpaths, to the

21st century when 300 ships a day move their cargo past St. Goar. And imagine this castle before the French destroyed it... when it was the mightiest structure on the river, filled with people and inspiring awe among all who passed.

• *Return to the catapult balls, walk downhill and through the tunnel, and veer left through the arch marked* ❾ zu den Wehrgängen *("to the Battlements"). Pause here, just before the stairs, to look up and see the original 13th-century core of the castle. Now go down two flights of stairs. Turn left and step into the dark, covered passageway. From here, we'll begin a rectangular walk, taking us completely around (counterclockwise) the perimeter of the castle.*

Covered Defense Galleries with "Minutemen" Holes: Soldiers—the castle's "minutemen"—had a short commute: defensive positions on the outside, home in the holes below on the left. Even though these living quarters were padded with straw, life was unpleasant.

• *Continue straight through the dark gallery, up the stairs, and to the corner of the castle, where you'll see a red signpost with the number* ❿. *Stand with your back to the corner of the wall.*

Corner of Castle: Gape up. That's the original castle tower. A three-story, half-timbered building originally rose beyond the tower's stone fortification. The two stone tongues near the top, just around the corner (to the right), supported the toilet. (Insert your own joke here.) Turn around and face the wall. The three crossbow slits were once steeper. The bigger hole on the riverside was for hot pitch.

• *Continue out along the back side of the castle. At the corner, turn left.*

Thoop...You're Dead: Look ahead at the smartly placed crossbow slit. While you're lying there, notice the stonework. The little round holes were for the scaffolds they used as they built up, which indicate that this stonework is original. Notice also the fine stonework on the chutes. More boiling pitch...now you're toast, too.

• *Pick yourself up and keep going along the castle perimeter. Pass under the first of three arches and pause at the gray railing to enjoy the view. Look up the valley and uphill where the sprawling fort stretched (as far as the tiny farm on the ridge, a half-mile away). Below, just outside the wall, is land where invaders would gather. The mine tunnels are under there, waiting to blow up any attackers.*

Now continue under two more arches, jog left, go down five steps and into an open field, and walk toward the wooden bridge. The "old" wooden bridge is actually modern.

Dark Tunnel Detour: For a short detour through a castle tunnel—possible only if you have a light—turn your back to the main castle (with the modern bridge to your left) and face the stone dry-moat labeled ⓬ *Halsgraben* "Neck Ditch." (You'll exit in a few minutes at the high railing above the red #12 sign.) Go 20 yards down the path to the right, and enter the tunnel at the bottom of the wall, following the red *Hoher Minengang* sign. At the end of the short, big tunnel, take two steps up and walk eight level steps, turn left, and follow the long uphill ramp (this is where

it's pitch-black, and adults will need to watch their heads). At the end, a spiral staircase takes you up to the high-railing opening you saw earlier, and then back to the courtyard.

• *When ready to leave this courtyard, angle left (under the* zum Verlies/Dungeon *sign, before the bridge) through two arches and through the rough entry to the* ⓮ Verlies *(dungeon) on the left.*

Dungeon: This is one of six dungeons. You just walked through an entrance prisoners only dreamed of 400 years ago. They came and went through the little square hole in the ceiling. The holes in the walls supported timbers that thoughtfully gave as many as 15 residents something to sit on to keep them out of the filthy slop that gathered on the floor. Twice a day, they were given bread and water. Some prisoners actually survived longer than two years in here. While the town could torture and execute, the castle had permission only to imprison criminals in these dungeons. Consider this: According to town records, the two men who spent the most time down here—2.5 years each—died within three weeks of regaining their freedom. Perhaps after a diet of bread and water, feasting on meat and wine was simply too much.

• *Continue through the next arch, under the white arrow, then turn left and walk 30 yards to the* ⓯ Schlachthaus.

Slaughterhouse: Any proper castle was prepared to survive a six-month siege. With 4,000 people, that's a lot of provisions. The cattle that lived within the walls were slaughtered in this room. The castle's mortar was congealed here (by packing all the organic waste from the kitchen into kegs and sealing it). Notice the drainage gutters. "Running water" came through from drains built into the walls (to keep the mortar dry and therefore strong...and less smelly).

• *Back outside, climb the modern stairs to the left (look for the* Zum Ausgang *sign). A skinny, dark passage leads you into the...*

Big Cellar: This ⓰ *Grosser Keller* was a big pantry. When the castle was smaller, this was the original moat—you can see the rough lower parts of the wall. The original floor was 13 feet deeper. The drawbridge rested upon the stone nubs on the left. When the castle expanded, the moat became this cellar. Halfway up the walls on the entrance side of the room, square holes mark spots where timbers made a storage loft, perhaps filled with grain. In the back, an arch leads to the wine cellar (sometimes blocked off) where finer wine was kept. Part of a soldier's pay was wine... table wine. This wine was kept in a single 180,000-liter stone barrel (that's 47,550 gallons), which generally lasted about 18 months.

The count owned the surrounding farmland. Farmers got to keep 20 percent of their production. Later, in more liberal feudal times, the nobility let them keep 40 percent. Today, the German government leaves the workers with 60 percent...and provides a few more services.

• *You're free. Climb out, turn right, and leave. For coffee on a terrace with a great view, visit Schlosshotel Rheinfels, opposite the entrance.*

Shopping

The Montag family runs two shops (one specializes in steins and the other in cuckoo clocks), both at the base of the castle hill road. The stein shop under **Hotel Montag** has Rhine guides and fine steins. The other shop, kitty-corner from the stein shop, boasts "the largest free-hanging cuckoo clock in the world" (both open daily 8:30-18:00, shorter hours Nov-April). They'll ship your souvenirs home—or give you a VAT form to claim your tax refund at the airport if you're carrying your items with you. A couple of other souvenir shops are across from the K-D boat dock.

Eating

$ Hotel am Markt serves tasty traditional meals with plenty of game and fish at fair prices, with good atmosphere and service. Specialties include marinated roast beef and homemade cheesecake. Choose cozy indoor seating, or dine outside with a river and castle view (€9-15 main courses, daily 8:00-21:00, closed Nov-Feb, Markt 1, tel. 06741/1689).

$$ Burgschänke offers the only reasonably priced lunches up at Rheinfels Castle. It's easy to miss on the ground floor of Schlosshotel Rheinfels (the hotel across from the castle ticket office—enter through the souvenir shop). Its fabulous outdoor terrace has a Rhine view (€8-10 pastas and *Flammkuchen*, €17-19 regional dishes, Sun-Thu 11:00-19:00, Fri-Sat until 21:30, tel. 06741/802-806).

$$$ Schlosshotel Rheinfels' dining room is your Rhine splurge, with an incredible indoor view terrace in an elegant, dressy setting. Call to reserve or arrive early if you're coming for breakfast or want a window table (€16 buffet breakfast, €19-28 main courses, also offers multicourse fixed-price meals, daily 7:00-11:00, 12:00-14:00 & 18:30-21:00, tel. 06741/8020).

$ Gasthaus Zur Krone, off the main drag, is the local choice for traditional German food. It's cozy and offers some outdoor seating, but no river view (€7-16 main courses, Thu-Tue 11:00-14:30 & 18:00-21:00, closed Wed, next to train station and church at Oberstrasse 38, tel. 06741/1515).

$ Ristorante Alla Fontana, tucked away on a back lane, serves the best Italian food in town at great prices in a lovely dining room or on a leafy patio (€6-9 pizzas and pasta, Tue-Sun 11:30-14:00 & 17:30-22:00, closed Mon, reservations smart, Pumpengasse 5, tel. 06741/96117).

$ Landgasthof Biergarten Rebstock is hidden on the far end of town on the banks of the Rhine. They serve schnitzel, beer, and wine. A nice playground nearby keeps the kids busy (April-Oct long hours daily—weather permitting, Am Hafen 1, tel. 06741/980-0337).

$ Café St. Goar is the perfect spot for a quick lunch or the German tradition of coffee and *kuchen*. Grab something for a picnic or enjoy the seating on the pedestrian-only street out front (Mon-Sat 7:00-18:00, Sun 10:00-18:00, Heerstrasse 95, tel. 06741/1635).

You can also buy picnic fixings on the pedestrian street at the tiny **St. Goarer Stadtladen** grocery store (Tue-Fri 8:00-18:00, Sat 8:00-13:00, closed Sun-Mon, Heerstrasse 106). The benches at St. Goar's waterfront park are great for a scenic picnic.

Sleeping

$$ Hotel am Markt features 17 rustic rooms in the main building (think antlers with a pastel flair), plus 10 classier rooms right next door, and a good restaurant. It's a decent value with all the modern comforts, just a stone's throw from the boat dock and train station (standard Db-€65, bigger Db with view-€80, closed Nov-Feb, pay parking, Markt 1, tel. 06741/1689, www.hotelammarkt1.de, hotel.am.markt@t-online.de).

$$$ Rhein Hotel, two doors down from Hotel am Markt, has 10 quality rooms—most with views and balconies—in a spacious building (Db-€90, larger Db-€100, family rooms, higher prices on Fri-Sat nights, laundry service for fee, closed mid-Nov-Feb, Heerstrasse 71, tel. 06741/981-240, www.rheinhotel-st-goar.de, info@rheinhotel-st-goar.de).

$ Hotel an der Fähre is a simple place on the busy road at the end of town, immediately across from the ferry dock. It rents 12 cheap but decent rooms (D-€45, Db-€55-60, cash only, street noise but double-glazed windows, closed Nov-Feb, Heerstrasse 47, tel. 06741/980-577, www.hotel-stgoar.de, hotel_anderfaehre@web.de).

$ Frau Kurz offers St. Goar's best B&B, renting three delightful rooms (sharing 2.5 bathrooms) with bathrobes, a breakfast terrace with castle views, a garden, and homemade marmalade (D-€56, 2-night minimum, D-€52 with stay of 4 nights or more, cash only, free and easy parking, no Internet access, bike rental for guests, Ulmenhof 11, tel. 06741/459, www.gaestehaus-kurz.de, fewo-kurz@kabelmail.de). It's a steep five-minute hike from the train station: Exit left from the station, take an immediate left under the tracks, and go partway up the zigzag stairs, turning right through an archway onto Ulmenhof; #11 is just past the tower.

MARKSBURG CASTLE IN BRAUBACH

Medieval invaders decided to give Marksburg a miss thanks to its formidable defenses, leaving it the best-preserved castle on the Rhine today. Worth ▲▲, it can be visited only with a guide on a 50-minute tour. In summer, tours in English normally run daily at 13:00 and 16:00. Otherwise, you can join a German tour (3/hour in summer, hourly in winter) that's almost as good—there are no explanations in English in the castle itself, but your ticket includes an English handout. It's an awesome castle, and between the handout and my commentary below, you'll feel fully informed, so don't worry about being on time for the English tours.

Cost and Hours: €6, family card-€15, daily April-Oct 10:00-17:00, Nov-March 11:00-16:00, last tour departs one hour before closing, tel. 02627/206, www.marksburg.de.

Getting There: Marksburg caps a hill above the village of Braubach, on the east bank of the Rhine. By **train,** it's a 10-minute trip from Koblenz to Braubach (1-2/hour); from Bacharach or St. Goar, it takes 1.5-2 hours, depending on the length of the layover in Koblenz. The train is quicker than the **boat** (downstream from Bacharach to Braubach-2 hours, upstream return-3.5 hours). Consider taking the downstream boat to Braubach, and the train back. If traveling with luggage, store it in the convenient lockers in the underground passage at the Koblenz train station (Braubach has no enclosed station—just platforms—and no lockers). If you're coming by **car** from Bacharach or St. Goar, take the car ferry at St. Goar across the Rhine, and drive north to Braubach (parking lot at castle).

If you reach Braubach by train, **walk** into the old town (follow *Altstadt* signs—

Marksburg Castle was built originally as a fortress, not a royal residence.

coming out of tunnel from train platforms, it's to your right); then follow the *Zur Burg* signs to the path up to the castle. Allow 20-30 minutes for the climb up. Scarce **taxis** charge at least €10 from the train platforms to the castle. A green **tourist train** circles up to the castle, but there's no fixed schedule, so don't count on it (Easter-mid-Oct Tue-Sun, no trains Mon or off-season, leaves from Barbarastrasse, tel. 06773/587, www.ruckes-reisen.de).

➲ **Self-Guided Tour:** Start inside the castle's **first gate.** The dramatic castles lining the Rhine are generally Romantic rebuilds, but Marksburg is the real McCoy—nearly all original construction. It's littered with bits of its medieval past, like the big stone ball that was swung on a rope to be used as a battering ram. Ahead, notice how the inner gate—originally tall enough for knights on horseback to gallop through—was made smaller, and therefore safer from enemies on horseback. Climb the Knights' Stairway, carved out of slate, and pass under the murder hole—handy for pouring boiling pitch on invaders. (Germans still say someone with bad luck "has pitch on his head.")

Coats of Arms: Colorful coats of arms line the wall just inside the gate. These are from the noble families who have owned the castle since 1283. In that year, financial troubles drove the first family to sell to the powerful and wealthy Katzenelnbogen family (who made the castle into what you see today). When Napoleon took this region in 1803, an Austrian family who sided with the French got the keys. When Prussia took the region in 1866, control passed to a friend of the Prussians who had a passion for medieval things—typical of this Romantic period. Then it was sold to the German Castles Association in 1900. Its offices are in the main palace at the top of the stairs.

Romanesque Palace: White outlines mark where the larger original windows were located, before they were replaced by easier-to-defend smaller ones. On the far right, a bit of the original plaster survives. Slate, which is vulnerable to the elements, needs to be covered—in this case, by plaster. Because this is a protected historic building, restorers can use only the traditional plaster methods...but no one knows how to make plaster that works as well as these 800-year-old surviving bits.

Cannons: The oldest cannon here—from 1500—was back-loaded. This was advantageous because many cartridges could be pre-loaded. But since the seal was leaky, it wasn't very powerful. The bigger, more modern cannons—from 1640—were one piece and therefore airtight, but had to be front-loaded. They could easily hit targets across the river from here. Stone balls were rough, so they let the explosive force leak out. The best cannonballs were stones covered in smooth lead—airtight and therefore more powerful and more accurate.

Gothic Garden: Walking along an outer wall, you'll see 160 plants from the Middle Ages—used for cooking, medicine, and witchcraft. *Schierling* (hemlock, in the first corner) is the same poison that killed Socrates.

Inland Rampart: This most vulnerable part of the castle had a triangular construction to better deflect attacks. Notice the factory in the valley. In the 14th century, this was a lead, copper, and silver mine. Today's factory—Europe's largest car-battery recycling plant—uses the old mine shafts as vents (see the three modern smokestacks).

Wine Cellar: Since Roman times, wine has been the traditional Rhineland drink. Because castle water was impure, wine—less alcoholic than today's beer—was the way knights got their fluids. The pitchers on the wall were their daily allotment. The bellows were part of the barrel's filtering system. Stairs lead to the...

Gothic Hall: This hall is set up as a kitchen, with an oven designed to roast an ox whole. The arms holding the pots have notches to control the heat. To this day, when Germans want someone to hurry up, they say, "give it one tooth more." Medieval windows were made of thin sheets of translucent alabaster or animal skins. A nearby wall is peeled away to show the wattle-and-daub construction (sticks, straw, clay, mud, then plaster) of a castle's inner walls. The iron plate to the left of the next door enabled servants to stoke the heater without being seen by the noble family.

Bedroom: This was the only heated room in the castle. The canopy kept in heat and kept out critters. In medieval times, it was impolite for a lady to argue with her lord in public. She would wait for him in bed to give him what Germans still call "a curtain lecture." The deep window seat caught maximum light for needlework and reading. Women would sit here and chat (or "spin a yarn") while working the spinning wheel.

Hall of the Knights: This was the dining hall. The long table is an unattached plank. After each course, servants could replace it with another pre-set plank. Even today, when a meal is over and Germans are ready for the action to begin, they say, "Let's lift up the table." The action back then consisted of traveling minstrels who sang and told of news gleaned from their travels.

Notice the outhouse—made of wood—hanging over thin air. When not in use, its door was locked from the outside (the castle side) to prevent any invaders from entering this weak point in the castle's defenses.

Chapel: This chapel is still painted in Gothic style with the castle's namesake, St. Mark, and his lion. Even the chapel was designed with defense in mind. The small doorway kept out heavily armed attackers. The staircase spirals clockwise, favoring the sword-wielding defender (assuming he was right-handed).

Linen Room: About the year 1800, the castle—with diminished military value—housed disabled soldiers. They'd earn extra money working raw flax into linen.

Two Thousand Years of Armor: Follow the evolution of armor since Celtic times. Because helmets covered the entire head, soldiers identified themselves as friendly by tipping their visor up with their right hand. This evolved into the military salute that is still used around the world today. Armor and the close-range weapons along the back were made obsolete by the invention of the rifle. Armor was replaced with breastplates—pointed (like the castle itself) to deflect enemy fire. This design was used as late as the start of World War I. A medieval lady's armor hangs over the door. While popular fiction has men locking up their women before heading off to battle, chastity belts were actually used by women as protection against rape when traveling.

The Keep: This served as an observation tower, a dungeon (with a 22-square-foot cell in the bottom), and a place of last refuge. When all was nearly lost, the defenders would bundle into the keep and burn the wooden bridge, hoping to outwait their enemies.

Horse Stable: The stable shows off bits of medieval crime and punishment. Cheaters were attached to stones or pillories. Shame masks punished gossipmongers. A mask with a heavy ball had its victim crawling around with his nose in the mud. The handcuffs with a neck hole were for the transport of prisoners. The pictures on the wall show various medieval capital punishments. Many times, the accused was simply taken into a torture dungeon to see all these tools, and, guilty or not, confessions spilled out of him. On that cheery note, your tour is over.

NEAR THE RHINE VALLEY

While you're in the region, two stops worth considering are Burg Eltz (a beautiful castle on the Mosel River) and the city of Cologne, with its knockout cathedral. If you're using public transit, Burg Eltz can make a fine day trip from the Rhine, but Cologne (2 hours by train) works better as a stop en route to or from the Rhine.

BURG ELTZ

My favorite castle in all of Europe—worth ▲▲▲—lurks in a mysterious forest. It's been left intact for 700 years and is decorated and furnished throughout much as it was 500 years ago. Thanks to smart diplomacy, clever marriages, and lots of luck, Burg Eltz (pronounced "boorg elts") was never destroyed. It even survived one five-year siege. It's been in the Eltz family for 850 years.

Getting There

The castle is a pleasant 1.5-hour **walk** from the nearest train station, in the little village of Moselkern—the walk is not only easy, it's the most fun and scenic way to visit the castle.

Hiking to the Castle from Moselkern: You can hike between the Moselkern train station and Burg Eltz in 70 minutes at a steady clip, but allow an extra 20 minutes or so to enjoy the scenery (see map on page 270). The elevation gain is less than 400 feet. (You can reach Moselkern via train from towns on the Rhine—including Bacharach and Cologne—with a change at Koblenz.)

To find the **path up to the castle,** turn right from the Moselkern station along Oberstrasse and continue to the village church. Just past the church, as the street ends, turn right through the underpass. You'll follow the Elzbach stream all the way up to the castle. Just before a stone bridge crosses the stream, take either the footpath or the bridge—they join up again later.

When the road ends at the parking lot of Hotel Ringelsteiner Mühle, stay to the right of the hotel and continue upstream along the easy-to-follow trail—from here, it's another 45 minutes through the forest to the castle.

By Bus from Treis-Karden: From May through October on Saturdays and Sundays only, bus #330 runs to Burg Eltz from the railway station in the town of Treis-Karden (4/day, 30 minutes; confirm times with bus operator at tel. 02671/8976 or at www.vrminfo.de).

By Taxi: You can taxi to the castle from the nearby towns of **Moselkern** (€28 one-way, taxi tel. 02672/1407) or **Karden** (€30 one-way, taxi tel. 02672/1407). If you're planning to taxi from Moselkern, call ahead and ask the taxi to meet your train at Moselkern station. Consider taxiing up to Burg Eltz and then enjoying the hike downhill back to the train station in Moselkern.

By Car: Cars (and taxis) park in a lot near, but not quite at, Burg Eltz. From the lot, hike 15 minutes downhill to the castle or wait (10 minutes at most) for the red castle shuttle bus.

Drive/Hike Combo: If you're traveling by car but would enjoy walking part of the path up to the castle, drive to Moselkern, follow the *Burg Eltz* signs up the Elz Valley, park at Hotel Ringelsteiner Mühle (buy ticket from machine), and hike about 45 minutes up the trail to the castle.

Orientation

Cost and Hours: €9 castle entry includes required 45-minute guided tour and treasury, April-Oct daily from 9:30, last tour departs at 17:30, closed Nov-March, tel. 02672/950-500, www.burg-eltz.de.

Eating at Burg Eltz: The **castle café** serves lunch, with soups and bratwurst-and-fries cuisine (April-Oct daily, cash only).

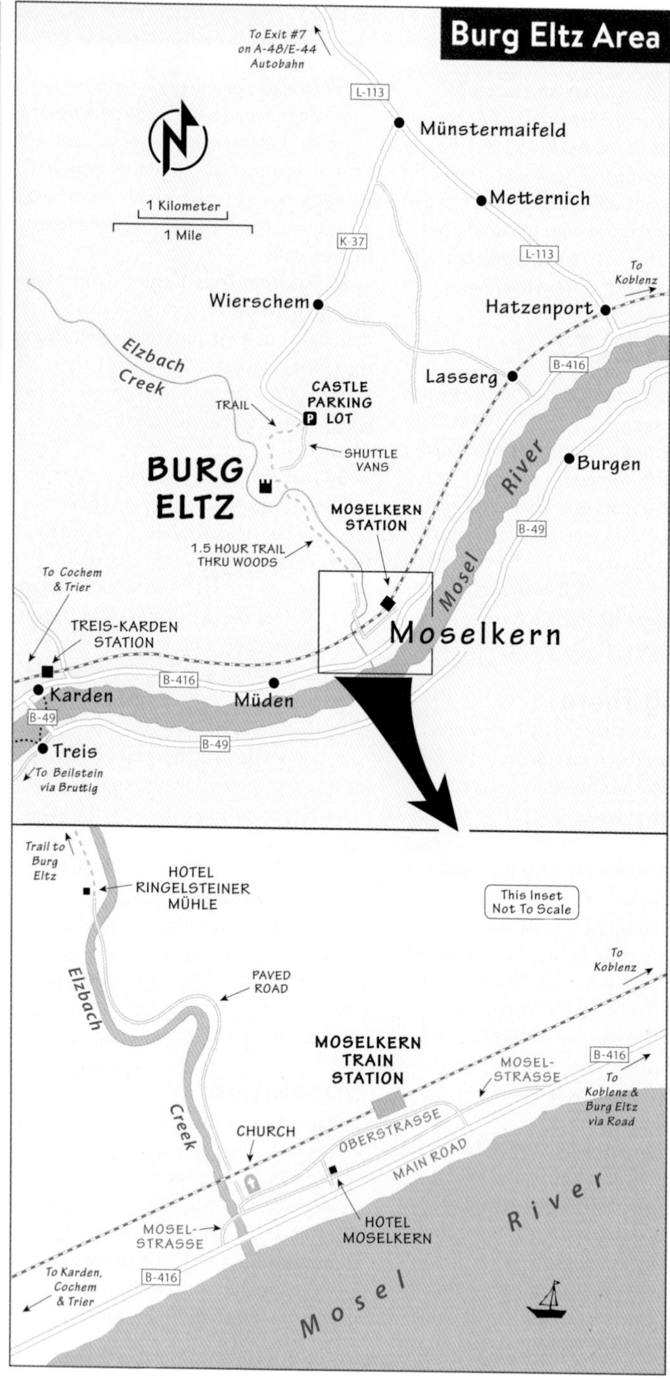
Burg Eltz Area
To Exit #7 on A-48/E-44 Autobahn
L-113
Münstermaifeld
Metternich
1 Kilometer
1 Mile
K-37
L-113
To Koblenz
Wierschem
Hatzenport
Elzbach Creek
B-416
Lasserg
TRAIL
CASTLE PARKING LOT
SHUTTLE VANS
Burgen
BURG ELTZ
Mosel River
MOSELKERN STATION
B-49
1.5 HOUR TRAIL THRU WOODS
To Cochem & Trier
TREIS-KARDEN STATION
Moselkern
B-416
Karden
Müden
B-49
Treis
B-49
To Beilstein via Bruttig
Trail to Burg Eltz
HOTEL RINGELSTEINER MÜHLE
This Inset Not To Scale
To Koblenz
PAVED ROAD
Elzbach Creek
MOSELKERN TRAIN STATION
MOSEL-STRASSE
B-416
To Koblenz & Burg Eltz via Road
OBERSTRASSE
CHURCH
MAIN ROAD
HOTEL MOSELKERN
MOSEL-STRASSE
B-416
To Karden, Cochem & Trier
Mosel River

Rick's Tip: Bring cash! *The castle (including the parking lot and café) doesn't accept credit cards, and there's no ATM.*

Visiting the Castle

The first record of a *Burg* (castle) on the Elz is from 1157. (Elz is the name of a stream that runs past the castle through a deep valley before emptying into the Mosel.) By about 1490, the castle looked like it does today, with the homes of three big landlord families gathered around a tiny courtyard within one formidable fortification. Today, the excellent tour winds you through two of those homes, while the third is still the residence of the castellan (the man who maintains the castle). This is where members of the Eltz family stay when they're not at one of their other feudal holdings. The elderly countess of Eltz—whose family goes back 33 generations here (you'll see a photo of her family)—enjoys flowers. Each week for 40 years, she's had grand arrangements adorn the public castle rooms.

Burg Eltz

It was a comfortable castle for its day: 80 rooms made cozy by 40 fireplaces and wall-hanging tapestries. Many of its 20 toilets were automatically flushed by a rain drain. The delightful **chapel** is on a lower floor. Even though "no one should live above God," this chapel's placement was acceptable because it filled a bay window, which flooded the delicate Gothic space with light. The three families met—working out common problems as if sharing a condo complex—in the large "conference room." A carved jester and a rose look down on the big table, reminding those who gathered that they were free to discuss anything ("fool's freedom"—jesters could say anything to the king), but nothing discussed could leave the room (the "rose of silence"). In the **bedroom,** have fun with the suggestive decor: the jousting relief carved into the canopy, and the fertile and phallic figures hiding in the lusty green wall paintings.

Near the exit, the **treasury** fills the four higgledy-piggledy floors of a cellar with the precious, eccentric, and historic mementos of this family that once helped elect the Holy Roman Emperor.

COLOGNE

Cologne (Köln—pronounced "kurln"—in German) is an urban Jacuzzi that keeps the Rhine churning. It's home to Germany's greatest Gothic cathedral, one of the country's best collections of Roman artifacts, a world-class art museum, and a healthy dose of German urban playfulness.

During World War II, bombs destroyed 95 percent of Cologne. But with the end of the war, the city immediately began putting itself back together, rebuilding in a mostly modern style with a sprinkling of quaint. Today, it's a bustling commercial and cultural center that still respects its rich past.

Orientation

Cologne couldn't be easier to visit—its most important sights cluster within two blocks of the TI and train station. This super pedestrian zone is a constant carnival of people. Cologne makes an ideal on-the-way stop.

Day Plan: With a couple of hours, you can toss your bag in a station locker, zip through the cathedral, and make it back to the station for your train. More time allows you to delve into a few of the city's fine museums (closed Mon) and take in an old-time beer pub. (For those wanting to spend the night, accommodations are listed later.)

Rick's Tip: *The* **cathedral is off-limits to sightseers during services,** *which are more frequent on Sundays—check the current schedule at the TI or the cathedral's Domforum information office.*

Getting There: Trains run at least hourly to **Frankfurt** (1.5 hours by fast train; slower, cheaper trains along Rhine have better scenery, 2.5 hours), **Bacharach/St. Goar** (2 hours), **Würzburg** (2.5 hours), **Hamburg** (4 hours), **Munich** (4.5 hours), and **Berlin** (4.5 hours).

Arrival in Cologne: The busy train station (with a drugstore, bookstore, grocery, and food court) has automated lockers (next to the *Reisezentrum* travel center; put in coins or bills and wait for door to open; put in up to four pieces of luggage, and retrieve it when you reinsert your ticket). Exiting the front of the train station (the end near track 1), you'll find yourself smack-dab in the shadow of the cathedral. Up the steps and to the right is the cathedral's main entrance (TI across street).

Drivers should follow signs to *Zentrum,* then continue to the huge Parkhaus am Dom garage under the cathedral or the lot just outside the garage.

Tourist Information: The energetic TI is opposite the cathedral entrance (Mon-Sat 9:00-20:00, Sun 10:00-17:00, Kardinal-Höffner-Platz 1, tel. 0221/2213-0400, www.koelntourismus.de).

Sights

▲▲▲COLOGNE CATHEDRAL (DOM)

The Gothic Dom—Germany's most exciting church—looms over the train station in one of the country's starkest juxtapositions of modern and medieval. The

Cologne's great Gothic cathedral

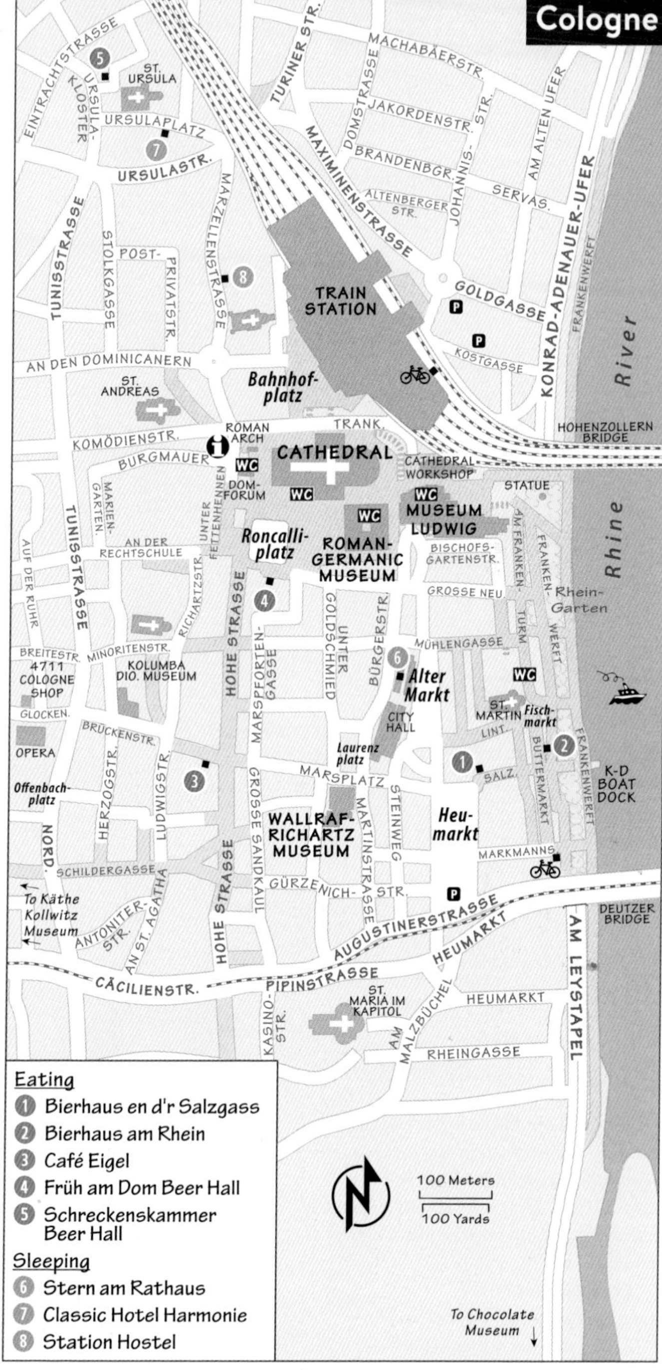
Cologne
Eating
1 Bierhaus en d'r Salzgass
2 Bierhaus am Rhein
3 Café Eigel
4 Früh am Dom Beer Hall
5 Schreckenskammer Beer Hall
Sleeping
6 Stern am Rathaus
7 Classic Hotel Harmonie
8 Station Hostel
TRAIN STATION
CATHEDRAL
ROMAN-GERMANIC MUSEUM
MUSEUM LUDWIG
WALLRAF-RICHARTZ MUSEUM
Bahnhof-platz
Roncalli-platz
Alter Markt
Heu-markt
Rhine River
HOHENZOLLERN BRIDGE
DEUTZER BRIDGE
K-D BOAT DOCK
To Käthe Kollwitz Museum
To Chocolate Museum
100 Meters
100 Yards

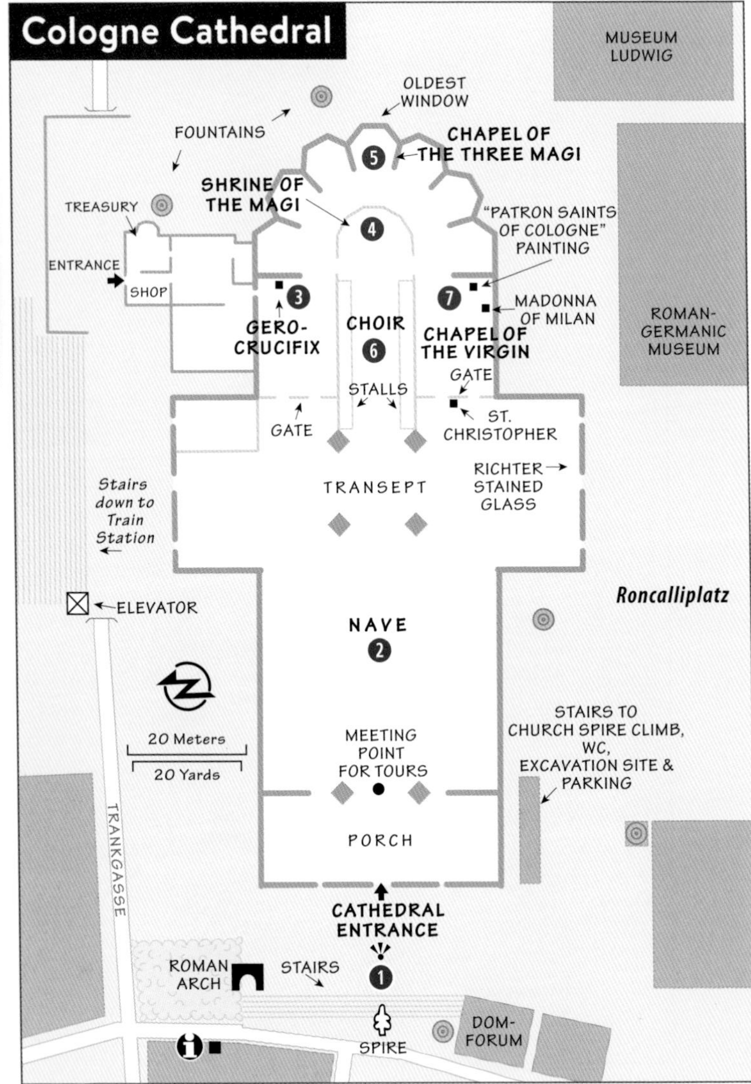

church is so big and so important that it has its own information office, the Domforum, in a separate building across the street. If your time is very limited, visit only the cathedral and skip the tower climb and treasury.

Cost and Hours: Free, Mon-Sat 9:30-11:30 & 12:30-16:30, Sun 12:30-16:30; closed to tourists during services—confirm times at Domforum office or www.koelner-dom.de.

Tours: The one-hour English-only tours are reliably excellent; meet inside the front door of the Dom (€8, Mon-Sat at 10:30 and 14:30, Sun at 14:30, tel. 0221/9258-4730).

Church Tower Climb: You can pay to climb the 509 steps of the cathedral's dizzying south tower (use exterior entry, to the right of the church's entrance). From the *Glockenstube* (only 400 steps up), you can see *Dicke Peter* (24-ton Fat Peter), claimed to be the largest free-swinging church bell in the world (€4, €8 combo-ticket with treasury, daily 9:00-18:00, closes earlier off-season).

Treasury: The six dim, hushed rooms are in 13th-century stone-cellar vaults, featuring gilded chalices and crosses, medieval reliquaries, and plenty of fancy bishop garb. Displays have brief English descriptions (€6, €8 includes tower climb, daily 10:00-18:00).

➲ **Self-Guided Tour:** If you don't take the guided tour of the cathedral, follow this walk (note that some stops are closed off during confession on Sat 14:00-18:00, and any time services are underway).

❶ **Cathedral Exterior:** The cathedral—the most ambitious Gothic building project north of France in the 13th century—was stalled in the Middle Ages and not finished until 1880. Even though most of it was built in the 19th century, it's still technically a Gothic church (not "Neo-Gothic") because it was finished according to its original plans.

• *Step inside the church. Grab a pew in the center of the nave.*

❷ **Nave:** If you feel small, that's because you're supposed to. The 140-foot-tall ceiling reminds us of our place in the vast scheme of things. Lots of stained glass—enough to cover three football fields—fills the church with light, which represents God.

The church was begun in 1248. The choir—the lofty area from the center altar to the far end ahead of you—was inaugurated in 1322. Later, during the tumultuous wars of religious reformation, Catholic pilgrims stopped coming. This dried up funds, and eventually construction stopped. For 300 years, the finished end of the church was walled off and functioned as a church, while the nave (where you now sit) was unfinished.

With the rise of German patriotism in the early 1800s, Cologne became a symbol of German unity. And the Prussians—the movers and shakers behind German unity—paid for the speedy completion

Stained-glass window depicting the Adoration of the Magi

of this gloriously Gothic German church. With nearly 700 workers going at full speed, the church was finished in just 38 years (1842-1880).

The glass windows at the east end of the church (in the chapels and high above) are medieval. The glass surrounding you in the nave is not as old, but it's precious nevertheless. The glass on the left is early Renaissance.

While much of Cologne was destroyed by WWII bombs, the cathedral held up fairly well. In anticipation of the bombing, the glass and art treasures were taken to shelters and saved. The cathedral was hit by 15 bombs, but its Gothic structure flexed and remained standing.

• *Leave the nave to the left and step through the gate at the far end (beside the transept), into the oldest part of the church.*

Ahead of you on the left is the...

❸ **Gero-Crucifix:** The Chapel of the Cross features the oldest surviving monumental crucifix north of the Alps. Carved in the 970s with a sensitivity, it shows Jesus not suffering and not triumphant—but with eyes closed...dead. He paid the price for our sins. It's great art and powerful theology.

• *Continue to the front end of the church, stopping to look at the big golden reliquary in the glass case behind the high altar.*

Gero-Crucifix

❹ **Shrine of the Magi:** Relics were a big deal in the Middle Ages. Cologne's acquisition of the bones of the Three Kings in the 12th century put it on the pilgrimage map and brought in enough money to justify the construction of this magnificent place. By some stretch of medieval Christian logic, these relics also justified the secular power of the German king. This reliquary, made in about 1200 of gilded silver, jewels, and enamel, is the biggest and most splendid I've seen. On the long sides, Old Testament prophets line the bottom, and 12 New Testament apostles—with a wingless angel in the center—line the top. The front looks like three stacked coffins, showing scenes of Christ's flagellation, Crucifixion, and Resurrection.

• *Opposite the shrine, at the far-east end of the church, is the...*

❺ **Chapel of the Three Magi:** The center chapel, at the church's far end, is the oldest. It also features the church's oldest window (center, from 1265). Later glass windows (which you saw lining the nave) were made from panes of clear glass that were painted and glazed. This medieval window, however, is actually colored glass, which is assembled like a mosaic. It was very expensive. The size was limited to what pilgrim donations could support. Notice the plain, budget design higher up.

• *Peek into the center zone between the high altar and the carved wooden central stalls. (You can't usually get inside, unless you take the tour.)*

❻ **Choir:** The choir is surrounded by 13th- and 14th-century art with carved oak stalls, frescoed walls, statues painted as they would have been, and original stained glass high above. Study the fanciful oak carvings. The woman cutting the man's hair is a Samson-and-Delilah warning to the sexist men of the early Church.

• *The nearby chapel holds one of the most precious paintings of the important Gothic School of Cologne.*

❼ **Chapel of the Virgin:** Overlooking the chapel (between the windows), the delicate ***Madonna of Milan*** sculpture (1290), associated with miracles, was a focus of pilgrims for centuries. Its colors, scepter, and crown were likely added during a restoration in 1900. The reclining medieval knight in the cage at the back of the chapel (just before the gate) is a wealthy patron who donated his entire county to the cathedral.

Before leaving, look above the tomb with the cage and find the statue of St. Christopher (with Jesus on his shoulder and the pilgrim's staff). He's facing the original south transept entry to the church. Since 1470, pilgrims and travelers have looked up at him and taken solace in the hope that their patron saint is looking out for them.

▲▲ROMAN-GERMANIC MUSEUM (RÖMISCH-GERMANISCHES MUSEUM)

One of Germany's top Roman museums offers little English information among its elegant and fascinating display of Roman artifacts: glassware, jewelry, and mosaics. All these pieces are evidence of Cologne's status as an important site of civilization long before the cathedral was ever imagined. You'll see an arched Roman gate to the city and the incredible glassware that Roman Cologne was famous for producing. The museum's main attraction is an in-situ Roman-mosaic floor—which you can see from the street for free through the large window.

Cost and Hours: €9, Tue-Sun 10:00-17:00, closed Mon, Roncalliplatz 4, tel. 0221/2212-4590, www.museenkoeln.de/rgm.

▲▲WALLRAF-RICHARTZ MUSEUM

This minimalist museum features a world-class collection of old masters, from medieval to northern Baroque and Impressionist. You'll see the best collection anywhere of the Gothic School of Cologne paintings (1300-1550) and works by European greats such as Dürer, Rubens, Rembrandt, Van Gogh, Renoir, Monet, Munch, and Cézanne.

Cost and Hours: €8-13 depending on special exhibits, Tue-Sun 10:00-18:00, Thu until 21:00, closed Mon, on Obenmarspforten near City Hall, tel. 0221/2212-1119, www.wallraf.museum.

KÄTHE KOLLWITZ MUSEUM

This museum contains the world's largest collection of the artist's powerful Expressionist art, welling from her experiences living in Berlin during the tumultuous first half of the 20th century.

Cost and Hours: €4, Tue-Fri 10:00-18:00, Sat-Sun 11:00-18:00, closed Mon, Neumarkt 18 (top floor of Neumarkt Passage), tel. 0221/227-2899, www.kollwitz.de.

Eating

Locals have been coming to cozy **$$$ Bierhaus en d'r Salzgass** for its beer and authentic German dishes since the 19th century (Salzgasse 5). The nearby **$$$ Bierhaus am Rhein** has the same menu but offers views of the Rhine (Frankenwerft 27). **$ Café Eigel** is a good option for a light lunch or *Kaffee und Kuchen* (Brückenstrasse 1). **$$ Früh am Dom** offers three floors of traditional German drinking and dining options (Am Hof 12). **$$ Schreckenskammer** is a popular down-home joint—come early or make a reservation (closed Sun-Mon, Ursulagartenstrasse 11, www.schreckenskammer.com).

Sleeping

Within a five-minute walk of the train station, you'll find the quiet **$$ Stern am Rathaus** (Bürgerstrasse 6, www.stern-am-rathaus.com), the comfortable **$$ Classic Hotel Harmonie** (Ursulaplatz 13, www.classic-hotel-harmonie.de), and the budget **¢ Station Hostel** (Marzellenstrasse 44, www.hostel-cologne.de).

BEST OF THE REST

BADEN-BADEN

Of all the high-class resort towns I've seen, Baden-Baden is the easiest to enjoy in jeans with a picnic. It was the playground of Europe's high-rolling elite around 150 years ago. Royalty and aristocracy came from all corners of the continent to take the *Kur*—a soak in the (supposedly) curative mineral waters—and enjoy the casino. Wrought-iron balconies on handsome 19th-century apartment buildings give Baden-Baden an elegant, almost Parisian feel.

With its appealing combination of Edenism and hedonism, the resort town remains popular today, attracting a middle-class crowd of European tourists in search of a slower pulse, and Germans enjoying the fruits of their health-care system.

Orientation

Baden-Baden, with 55,000 residents, is made for strolling with a poodle. Except for the train station, everything that matters is clustered within a 10-minute walk between the baths and the casino.

Baden-Baden is a long, skinny town, strung over several miles along the narrow valley of the Oosbach River (conveniently accessed by bus #201). The train station is at the lower (northern) end of the valley, three miles from downtown; the Lichtentaler Abbey marks the upper end of the valley. The town center is about halfway between.

Day Plan: Your essential experience is going to the baths; you can choose between the traditional Roman-Irish Bath or the modern Baths of Caracalla or try both. For an overview of the pleasant town, take my self-guided walk through Baden-Baden.

With extra time, stop by the casino, stroll down Lichtentaler Allee, or take a funicular up a nearby hill for the views.

Getting There: Trains connect Baden-Baden with **Munich** (hourly, 4 hours), **Frankfurt/Frankfurt Airport** (hourly, 1.5-2 hours), **Bacharach** (hourly, 3 hours). Expect transfers.

Arrival in Baden-Baden: If you arrive by **train** (with lockers at platform 1 and a

Soothing Baden-Baden is the epicenter of European spa towns.

Reisezentrum that sells train tickets), catch bus #201 and get off at Leopoldsplatz, the town center (15-minute ride). By **taxi,** allow about €16.

By **car,** follow blue *Therme* signs to the baths neighborhood, then look for green signs directing you to each individual hotel (ask your hotelier for parking tips; you'll likely wind up at a big garage downtown). By **plane,** catch bus #205 to Leopoldsplatz, or at least to the train station, where you can transfer to #201.

Rick's Tip: Travel agencies *post train schedules and* **sell train tickets** *at a mark-up, which is pricey but saves a trip to the station (consider* **Derpart** *at Sophienstrasse 1B, or* **Hapag-Lloyd** *at Lichtentaler Strasse 10-12; both closed Sun).*

Getting Around: Within town, only one bus really matters: **Bus #201** runs straight through Baden-Baden, connecting the train station in Oos with the town center (Leopoldsplatz is the most central stop) and Lichtentaler Abbey at the southeast end of town (6/hour; buy ticket from driver or try machines at some stops—click button near flags for English; €2.30/person single ticket—valid for 90 minutes in one direction; Citysolo day pass for 1 adult-€6, and Cityplus day pass for up to 5 adults-€9.80, passes expire at 6:00 in the morning; www.kvv.de). Validate your ticket in the machine on board or near the ticket machines.

Tourist Information: The TI, in the ornate Trinkhalle building in the town center, gives out a free events program, *Baden-Baden Aktuell* (German only), which includes a good, fold-out map. Hikers like the inexpensive *Panoramaweg* map (German only); the TI recommends walks. Drivers exploring the region can buy the cartoon-style *Outline Map* and Black Forest guidebook (Mon-Sat 10:00-17:00, Sun 14:00-17:00, tel. 07221/275-200, www.baden-baden.de). The TI shares space with a genteel café and an agency that sells tickets to performances (closed Mon, www.tickets-baden-baden.de).

➲ Baden-Baden Walk

This self-guided walk starts at the casino, loops through the Old Town to both of the famous baths, and ends back at the river.

• *Start on the steps of the...*

Casino

The impressive building called the Kurhaus is wrapped around a grand casino. Built in the 1850s in wannabe-French style, it was declared "the most beautiful casino" by Marlene Dietrich. You can tour it in the morning, and gamble away the afternoon and evening.

• *Now walk about 100 yards to your left, to the...*

Trinkhalle

Beyond the colonnade is the old Trinkhalle—a long entrance hall decorated with nymphs and romantic legends. It's now home to the TI, a café, and ticket agency. Wander around its fancy portico, studying the romantic paintings that spa-goers enjoyed a century ago. For a sample of the warm spring water, go inside and look for the tap by the TI desk. Trust me on this: Despite the label, a sip of this water is indeed safe—even supposedly curative. (EU laws require these *Kein Trinkwasser* warnings on any water that isn't safe to drink day in and day out, and this water's high mineral concentration makes it unwise to drink much more than a cup or two at a time.)

• *From the Trinkhalle, walk down the steps, tip your hat to Kaiser Wilhelm, and cross the river. Walk one block inland, then go left on the pedestrian Lange Strasse. After two blocks, just past the* "Bad" Hotel zum Hirsch *sign on the right and the Läderach Swiss chocolate shop on the left, take a hard right, and climb up Hirschstrasse until you hit a big church.*

Catholic Church and Marktplatz

The Catholic church looks over the marketplace that has marked the center of town since Roman times. Go inside (the door on the left side is usually open). Because the church sits atop a former spa, it's muggy and warm all year. There are no heaters inside; the floor stones are designed to transmit the natural spa heat in winter.

• *Now we'll explore the area around Baden-Baden's namesake and claim to fame.*

Baths Area

Walk around the back of the church and down the cobbled lane behind the Roman-Irish Bath complex.

Take the steps down to the water spigot that taps the underground spring called the **Fettquelle** ("rich water source"). It's 105 degrees—as hot as a spa open to the public can legally be. Older locals remember being sent here to fetch hot water for their father's shave.

Find the handless **statue** on the lawn 50 yards farther. She's got her rear to the fun, modern Baths of Caracalla and is eyeing the luxurious, old-school Roman-Irish Bath.

• *Return halfway to the Fettquelle spigot and take the stairs down into the parking level (signposted* Römische Badruinen*) to the small...*

Ancient Spa Museum

This spa, now in ruins, is just one room—most of which you can see through the big windows. Built only for Roman soldiers, it's a simple terra-cotta structure with hollow walls and elevated floors to let the heat circulate.

• *Leaving the museum, jog left, then right, and head down...*

Gernsbacher Strasse

As you walk down this street, consider the 2,000-year heritage of guests who have been housed, fed, and watered here at the spa, especially during its 19th-century heyday: Fyodor Dostoyevsky, Mark Twain, and Johannes Brahms.

The late 20th-century German healthcare system was very good for Baden-Baden—the government provided lavishly for spa treatment for its tired citizens. Times have changed, and now doctors must make the case to insurance companies that their patients need the treatment because they are actually sick. And the insurance company then dictates where they'll go.

• *After two blocks, you hit Sonnenplatz. Hang a left, then a right, and continue down...*

Sophienstrasse

This street enjoys the shade of a long row of tall chestnut trees. In the 1870s, when it was lined exclusively by hotels, this was the town's aristocratic promenade.

• *Sophienstrasse leads into...*

Leopoldsplatz

Until 1985, this square was a traffic hub, with 30,000 cars muscling through it daily. Now a tunnel takes the east-west traffic under the city, and the tranquility you'd expect in a spa town has returned. Actually, Baden-Baden had to get rid of the noise and pollution caused by the traffic in order to maintain its top rating as a spa resort.

The main city bus stop is just off the square, on Luisenstrasse.

• *From Leopoldsplatz, head left on Lichtentaler Strasse. Head for the big fountain in the distance, marking Augustaplatz (public WC nearby). At the fountain, go right, through the park, and over the petite bridge, where you'll come to a sweet riverside path called Lichtentaler Allee (described in next section). From here the casino is to your right. A stroll to the left—down Lichtentaler Allee—takes you to the rose garden and out to Lichtentaler Abbey. You choose which way to go. My walk is done.*

Sights

The Baths

The town's top sights—two beloved but very different baths—stand side by side in a park at the top of the Old Town. The Roman-Irish Bath is traditional, stately, indoors, contemplative, and extremely relaxing...just you and your body. The perky, fun, and modern Baths of Caracalla are less expensive, both indoor and outdoor, and more social. Some hotels sell discounted tickets (10-15 percent off) to one or both of the baths—ask.

At either bath, you'll get an electronic wristband, which you'll need when you're ready to leave. If you overstay your allotted time, you pay extra. You can relax while your valuables are stowed in very secure lockers.

The baths share the huge underground Bäder-Garage (enter on Rotenbachtalstrasse); for a reduced price, validate your parking ticket before leaving either bath.

Most years, one bath (but never both) closes for two weeks of maintenance in June or July; this is announced prominently at www.carasana.de.

▲▲▲ROMAN-IRISH BATH (FRIEDRICHSBAD)

The highlight of most visits to Baden-Baden is a sober 17-step ritual called the Roman-Irish Bath. This bathhouse pampered the rich and famous in its elegant surroundings when it opened in 1877. Today, this steamy world of marble, brass columns, tropical tiles, herons, lily pads, and graceful nudity welcomes gawky tourists as well as locals.

Cost and Hours: €25/3 hours, €12 more gets you a soap-and-brush massage and another half-hour, another €12 for final *crème* massage; daily 9:00-22:00; last entry 3 hours before closing if getting a massage, 2 hours before otherwise, check website for other massage options, consider booking in advance; kids under 14 not allowed, Römerplatz 1, tel. 07221/275-920, www.friedrichsbad.eu.

Dress Code: Everyone in these baths is always nude. On Mondays, Thursdays, and Saturdays, men and women use

A trip to the Roman-Irish Bath is a 17-step spa experience.

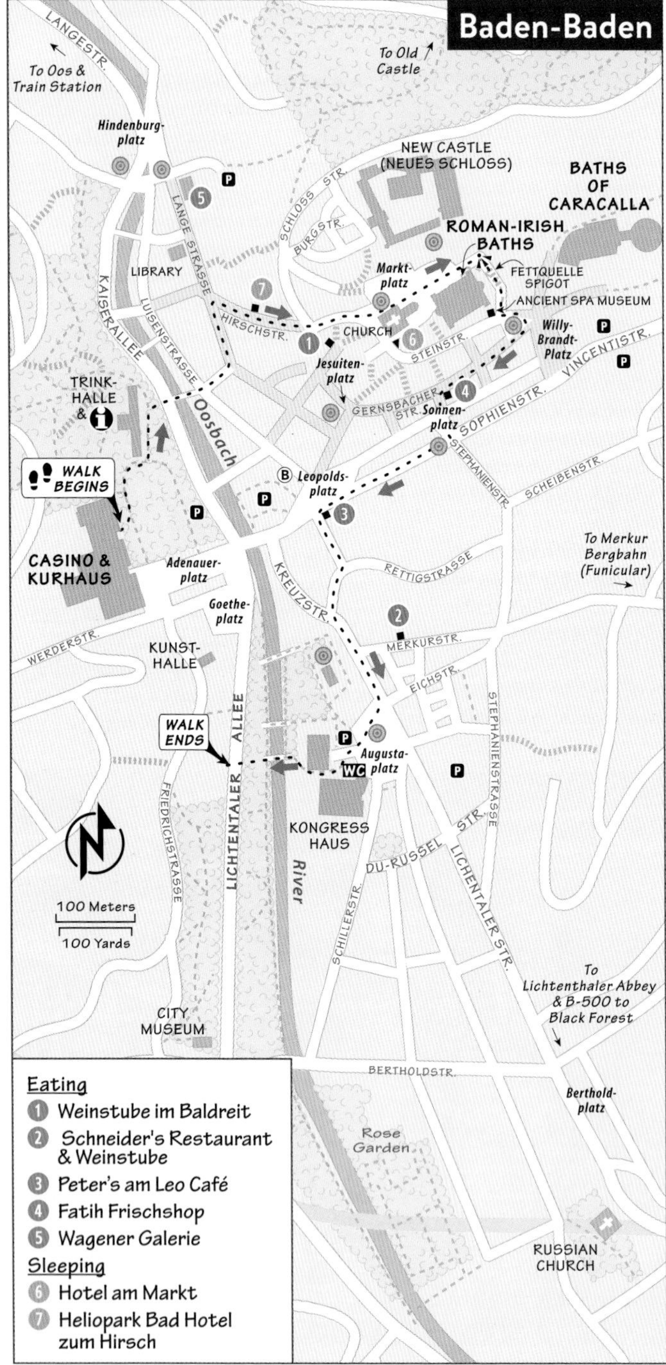
Baden-Baden
To Oos & Train Station
LANGESTR.
To Old Castle
Hindenburgplatz
NEW CASTLE (NEUES SCHLOSS)
BATHS OF CARACALLA
ROMAN-IRISH BATHS
FETTQUELLE SPIGOT
ANCIENT SPA MUSEUM
SCHLOSS STR.
BURGSTR.
LANGE STRASSE
LIBRARY
Marktplatz
CHURCH
HIRSCHSTR.
Jesuitenplatz
STEINSTR.
Willy-Brandt-Platz
VINCENTISTR.
KAISERALLEE
LUISENSTRASSE
TRINKHALLE &
Oosbach
GERNSBACHER STR.
Sonnenplatz
SOPHIENSTR.
STEPHANIENSTR.
SCHEIBENSTR.
WALK BEGINS
Leopoldsplatz
CASINO & KURHAUS
Adenauerplatz
Goetheplatz
KREUZSTR.
RETTIGSTRASSE
To Merkur Bergbahn (Funicular)
WERDERSTR.
KUNSTHALLE
MERKURSTR.
EICHSTR.
STEPHANIENSTRASSE
WALK ENDS
LICHTENTALER ALLEE
Augustaplatz
WC
KONGRESS HAUS
DU-RUSSEL STR.
LICHTENTALER STR.
FRIEDRICHSTRASSE
River
100 Meters
100 Yards
SCHILLERSTR.
To Lichtenthaler Abbey & B-500 to Black Forest
CITY MUSEUM
BERTHOLDSTR.
Bertholdplatz
Rose Garden
RUSSIAN CHURCH
Eating
1 Weinstube im Baldreit
2 Schneider's Restaurant & Weinstube
3 Peter's am Leo Café
4 Fatih Frischshop
5 Wagener Galerie
Sleeping
6 Hotel am Markt
7 Heliopark Bad Hotel zum Hirsch

separate and nearly identical facilities—but the sexes can mingle briefly in the pool under the grand dome in the center of the complex (yes, everyone's nude there, too). Shy bathers should avoid Tuesdays, Wednesdays, Fridays, Sundays, and holidays, when all the rooms are mixed—including the steam and massage rooms. If you're concerned, you needn't be; there's no ogling going on. It's a classy and respectful ritual, and a shame to miss just because you're intimidated by nudity.

Rick's Tip: *At the Roman-Irish Bath,* **remember your locker number;** *it's not indicated on your wristband.*

Procedure: Read this carefully before stepping out naked: Grab one of the bedsheet-like towels (also provided by assistants once inside), then head into a changing cabin to disrobe. Hang your clothes and possessions in a locker, and close it by pressing on the button with your wristband. As you enter the baths (through the "body crème" room), check your weight on the digital scale. Do this again as you leave to see how much you sweated off—you'll lose about a kilo (two pounds)...all in sweat. The complex routine is written (in English) on the walls with recommended times—simply follow the room numbers from 1 to 17. Instructions are repeated everywhere. For the first couple of stops only, you use plastic slippers and a towel for hygienic reasons and because the slats are too hot to sit on directly.

Start by taking a shower. Grab a towel and put on plastic slippers before hitting the warm-air bath for 15 minutes and the hot-air bath for 5 minutes. Shower again. If you paid extra, take the rough and slippery soap-brush massage—which may finish off with a good Teutonic spank. Play Gumby in the shower; lounge under sunbeams in one of several thermal steam baths; and glide like a swan under a divine dome in the mixed-gender royal pool. Don't skip the invigorating cold plunge, but do go in all at once—the relaxation you'll experience after emerging is worth it. Dry in more warmed towels and lie on a bed for 30 minutes, thinking prenatal thoughts, in the mellow, yellow silent room. At the end, there's a reading room with refreshing drinks, chaise lounges, and plenty of magazines. You don't appreciate how clean you are after this experience until you put your dirty socks back on (bring a clean pair).

All you need is money. Hair dryers are available, and clocks are displayed throughout. If you wear glasses, you can leave them in your locker (it's more relaxing without them). Otherwise, you'll find trays throughout to park your specs.

Afterward, before going downstairs, sip a little of the terrible but "magic" hot water (*Thermalwasser*) from the elegant fountain, and stroll down the broad royal stairway, feeling, as they say, five years younger—or, at least, a pound or two lighter.

▲▲BATHS OF CARACALLA (CARACALLA THERME)

For a modern experience, spend a few hours at the Baths of Caracalla, a huge palace of water, steam, and relaxed people. More like a mini water park, and with bathers clothed, this is a fun and accessible experience, and is recommended for those who'd prefer less nudity (sauna-goers upstairs, however, are nude).

Cost and Hours: €16/2 hours, €19/3 hours, €23 buys the whole day, can buy shareable card to split among your group, discounts with *Kurkarte* hotel guest card; massages extra—check options on website, consider booking in advance; daily 8:00-22:00, last entry at 20:00, no kids under age 7, kids aged 7-14 must be with parents (it's not really a splashing and sliding kind of pool); tel. 07221/275-940, www.caracalla.de.

Procedure: At this bath, you need to bring a towel (or rent one for €6 plus a

€10 deposit) and a swimsuit (shorts OK for men, no swimsuit rental but you can buy one in shop).

Find a locker, change clothes, strap the band around your wrist, and go play. Your wristband gets you into another poolside locker if you want to lock up your glasses. You won't need your wallet inside, though: If you buy something to eat or drink, you'll pay on exit (it's recorded on your wristband). Bring your towel to the pool (there are plenty of places to stow it). The baths are an indoor/outdoor wonderland of steamy pools, waterfalls, neck showers, hot tubs, hot springs, cold pools, lounge chairs, saunas, a wellness lounge/massage area, a cafeteria, and a bar. After taking a few laps around the fake river, you can join some kinky Germans for water spankings (you may have to wait a few minutes to grab a vacant waterfall). Then join the gang in the central cauldron. The steamy "inhalation" room seems like purgatory's waiting room, with a misty minimum of visibility.

Nudity is limited to the sauna zone upstairs. The grand spiral staircase leads to a naked world of saunas, tanning lights, cold plunges, and sunbathing outside on lounge chairs. At the top of the stairs everyone stows their suit in a cubbyhole and wanders around with their towel (some are modest and wrapped; others just run around buck naked). There are three eucalyptus-scented saunas of varying temperatures (80, 90, and 95 degrees) and two saunas in outdoor log cabins (with mesmerizing robotic steam-makers). Follow the instructions on the wall. Towels are required, not for modesty but to separate your body from the wood benches. The highlight is the arctic bucket in the shower room. Pull the chain. Only rarely will you feel so good.

More Sights in Baden-Baden

▲▲CASINO

The grand casino, built in the 1850s, occupies a classy building called the Kurhaus, inspired by the Palace of Versailles. It's licensed on the condition that it pay 80 percent of its earnings to the state to fund social services.

You can visit the casino on a guided tour in the mornings (€7, in German), when it's closed to gamblers, but it's most interesting to see in action, after 14:00 (livelier after dinner and liveliest after 22:00). You can gamble if you want, but a third of the visitors come only to people-watch under the chandeliers. The scene is more subdued than at an American casino. Lean against a gilded statue and listen to the graceful reshuffling of personal fortunes.

Cost and Hours: €5 entry, €2 minimum bet, €20,000 maximum bet; daily 14:00-2:00 in the morning, Fri-Sat until 3:30 in the morning; no athletic shoes, no sandals, or short sleeves for men; nice jeans OK; men required to wear coat (rentable on site) and collared shirt (purchasable on site); passport required, under 21 not admitted, no photos, pick up game rules as you enter; tel. 07221/30240, www.casino-baden-baden.de.

Budget travelers can try their luck downstairs at the slot machines, called *Automatenspiel* (€1 entry or included in €5 casino admission, opens at 12:00—otherwise same hours and age restrictions, passport required, no dress code).

Tours: The casino gives 30-minute German tours every morning (€7, small discount with *Kurkarte* hotel guest card,

Baden-Baden's casino

tours every half-hour 9:30-11:30, no 9:30 tour Nov-March; some guides may add short English summaries if asked, tel. 07221/30240). Even peasants wearing T-shirts, shorts, and sandals, with cameras and kids in tow, are welcome on tours.

▲▲STROLLING LICHTENTALER ALLEE

Imagine yourself in top hat and tails as you promenade down this pleasant, picnic-perfect 1.5-mile-long lane that runs along the babbling Oosbach River, passing mansions, hardy oaks, and exotic trees (street-lit all night). By the tennis courts, cross the footbridge into the free Art Nouveau rose garden (Gönneranlage, 400 labeled kinds of roses bloom May-Oct—best in early summer, great tables and benches). You can continue all the way to the historic Lichtentaler Abbey, an active Cistercian convent founded in 1245 (open long hours daily). Either walk round-trip, or take bus #201 one-way (runs along main street, parallel to promenade, on other side of river). Many bridges cross the river, making it easy to shortcut to bus #201 anytime.

▲FUNICULAR TO THE SUMMIT OF MERKUR

This delightful trip to a hilltop overlooking Baden-Baden is easy and quick. Catch bus #204 or #205 from the town center (2/hour from Leopoldsplatz) and ride 11 minutes to the end of the line at the base of the Merkur Bergbahn. Take the funicular to the 2,000-foot summit, where you can enjoy a meal or drink (restaurant open until 18:00 or later), and, if the weather's good, you can watch paragliders leap into ecstasy.

Cost and Hours: Funicular-€2 one-way, departs frequently, daily 10:00-22:00.

Eating

$$$ Weinstube im Baldreit, with a cozy cellar and a leafy courtyard, dishes up near-gourmet food for great prices (open only for dinner, closed Sun-Mon, reservations smart, Küferstrasse 3, tel. 07221/23136).

$$$$ Schneider's Restaurant & Weinstube, in a convivial space just outside the main tourist zone, serves what many locals consider the town's best cuisine (dinner only plus Sat for lunch, closed

Lichtentaler Allee invites strollers.

Sun, reserve ahead, Merkurstrasse 3, tel. 07221/976-6929).

$ Peter's am Leo Café, a fun self-service café on Leopoldplatz, offers big breakfasts, sandwiches, salads, pastries, and a few outdoor tables with views over the main square (closes daily at 19:00, Sophienstrasse 10).

Fatih Frischshop, one block off Jesuitplatz, serves up takeaway deli food and fresh produce—ideal for a picnic (closed Sun). A **supermarket** is on the top floor of the **Wagener Galerie** mall (closed Sun, Lang Strasse 44).

Sleeping

Rick's Tip: *If staying the night during the* **three annual horse races** *(usually May, Aug, and Oct; check dates at www.baden-racing.com),* **book your room well in advance.**

If overnighting, try **$$ Hotel am Markt,** the town's best little hotel, worth reserving well in advance (Marktplatz 18, www.hotel-am-markt-baden.de). Other options are the pricier **$$$ Heliopark Bad Hotel zum Hirsch,** your standard schmancy resort hotel (Hirschstrasse 1, www.heliopark-hirsch.de), or the cheap **¢ Werner Dietz Hostel** (some doubles, Hardbergstrasse 34, www.jugendherberge-baden-baden.de).

Rick's Tip: *All hotels are required to charge* **an additional "spa tax" of €3.50 per person per night,** *so don't get upset when this is added to your bill. This comes with a "guest card"* (Kurkarte)*, offering small discounts on attractions, including the casino and Baths of Caracalla.*

BEST OF THE REST

FRANKFURT

Frankfurt, while low on Old World charm, offers a good look at today's no-nonsense, modern Germany. There's so much more to this country than castles and old cobbled squares. Ever since the early Middle Ages, people have gathered here to trade. Cosmopolitan Frankfurt—nicknamed "Bankfurt"—is a business hub of the united Europe and home to the European Central Bank. Frankfurt's energy, fueled in part by the entrepreneurial spirit of its immigrant communities, makes it a unique and entertaining city well worth a look.

Orientation

Frankfurt perches on the banks of the Main River. The convention center *(Messe)* and the red light district are near the train station. Just to the east is the banking district and the shopping area. Beyond that is what remains of Frankfurt's Old Town, around Römerberg, the city's charming, historic market square.

Day Plan: The city's main sights can be enjoyed in a half-day by using its train station as a springboard. At a minimum, head up to the top of the Main Tower for commanding city views and wander through the pedestrian zone to the Old Town area (Römerberg). My self-guided walk provides a framework for your explorations.

Getting There: Frankfurt is well-connected by train to all of Germany, including **Rothenburg** (hourly, 2.5 hours), **Würzburg** (1-2/hour, 70 minutes), **Nürnberg** (1-2/hour, 2 hours), **Munich** (hourly, 3.5 hours), **Bacharach** (hourly, 1.5-2 hours), **Cologne** (hourly, 1-1.5 hours), **Berlin** (hourly, 4 hours), and **Hamburg** (hourly, 4 hours).

Arrival in Frankfurt: Frankfurt's **main train station** is a 20-minute walk from Römerberg square (for directions to the square, see the Frankfurt Walk below). The **airport,** which has its own train station, is just a 12-minute train ride from the city center. **Drivers** should follow signs for *Frankfurt,* then *Messe,* and finally *Hauptbahnhof* (train station), with its underground garage (for more on parking, visit www.parkhausfrankfurt.de).

Tourist Information: A handy TI is just inside the **train** station's main entrance (daily, tel. 069/212-38800, www.frankfurt-tourismus.de). Another TI is on **Römerberg square;** there's also one at the **airport.**

Private Guide: Elisabeth Lücke loves her city and shares it well (€65/hour, cash only, mobile 0173-913-3157, www.elisabeth-luecke.de, elisabeth.luecke@t-online.de).

Frankfurt Walk

This self-guided sightseeing walk, worth ▲▲, shows you both the new and the old Frankfurt. Start at the...

Train Station

Frankfurt has Germany's busiest train station: 350,000 travelers make their way to 24 platforms to catch 1,800 trains every day. Hop a train and you can be in either Paris or Berlin in four hours.

Position yourself on the traffic island directly opposite the station's front door, and turn to look back at the building's 1890s Neo-Renaissance facade—a style popular with Industrial Revolution-era architects. High above, a statue of Atlas carries the world—but only with some heavy-duty help: Green copper figures representing steam power and electricity pitch in.

• *With your back to the station, cross over to the pedestrianized...*

Kaiserstrasse

This grand 19th-century boulevard features the elegant facades that dressed up the approach to what was a fine new station. Towering above and beyond the 100-year-old buildings are the skyscrapers of Frankfurt's banking district.

Sex-and-Drugs Detour: This walk continues to the banking district, but if you're game, you can take this adults-only

Frankfurt's iconic main train station

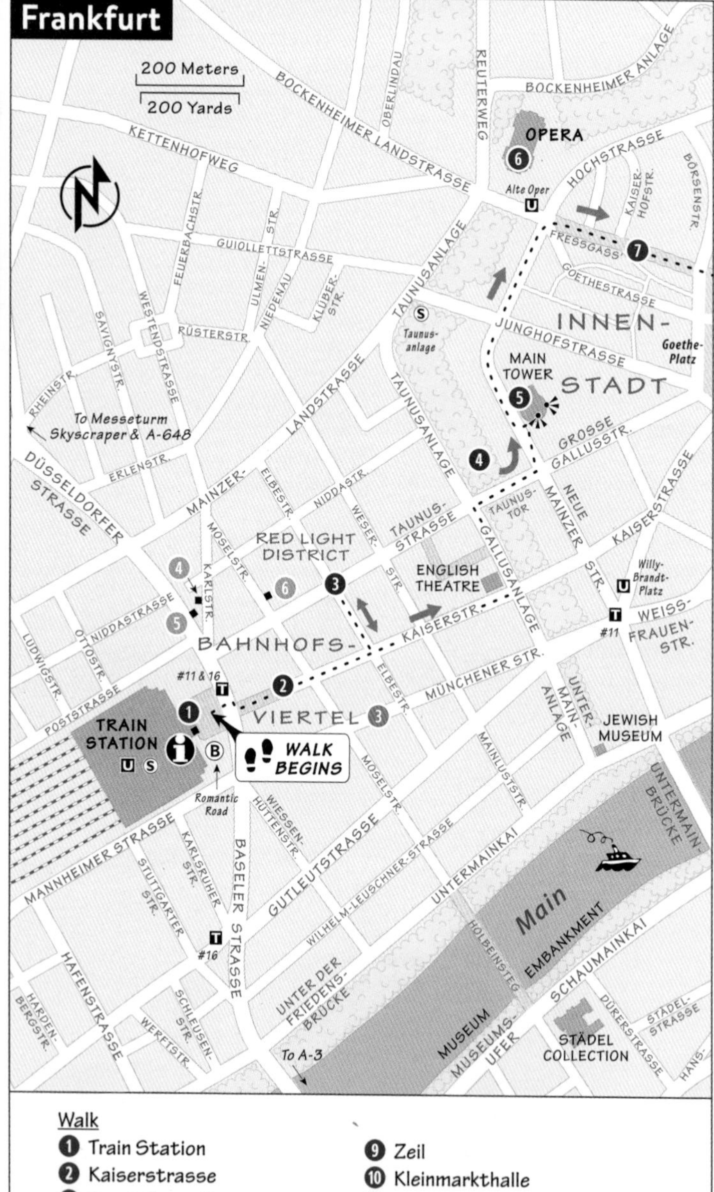

Walk

1. Train Station
2. Kaiserstrasse
3. Sex & Drugs Detour
4. Banking District
5. Main Tower
6. Opera House
7. Fressgass'
8. Hauptwache
9. Zeil
10. Kleinmarkthalle
11. St. Paul's Church
12. Römerberg
13. Saalgasse
14. St. Bartholomew's Cathedral
15. Eiserner Steg Bridge

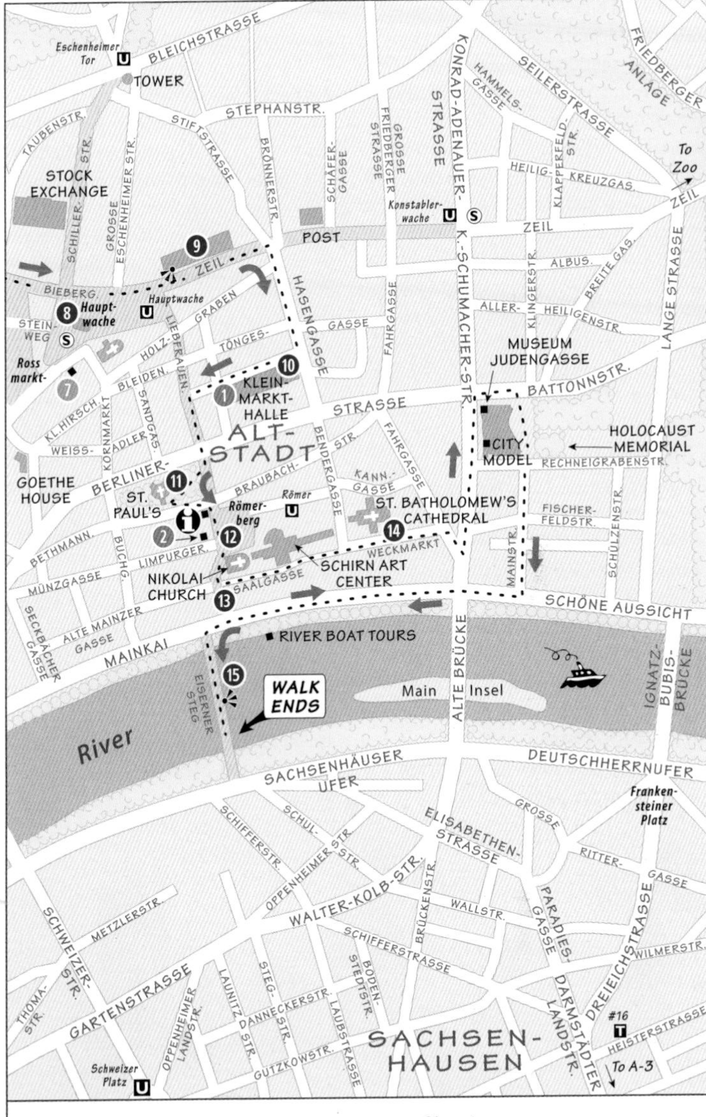

Eating

1. Kleinmarkthalle Eateries, Markt-Stubb & Weinterrasse
2. Weinstube im Römer (Römerberg Eateries)
3. Merkez Kebab Haus & Maxie Eisen (Münchener Strasse Eateries)

Sleeping

4. Hotel Concorde
5. Manhattan Hotel
6. Five Elements Hostel
7. Hotel Zentrum

detour. One block down Kaiserstrasse, jog left on Moselstrasse and walk a block to the intersection of Taunusstrasse and Elbestrasse. This is where the city contains and controls its sex-and-drug scene. The "junkie cafés" here are injection safe-havens for hard-drug users, and high-rise brothels along Elbestrasse corral prostitution in a "tolerance area."

• *If you're skipping the sex-and-drugs detour, walk straight down Kaiserstrasse for four blocks until you reach a greenbelt. Cross the street to the park and go left one long block to the statue of the poet Schiller (a Romantic and friend of Goethe).*

▲*Banking District*

This park, in the city's banking district, is part of a greenbelt that encircles the old center and marks the site of Frankfurt's medieval moat and fortifications.

Beyond the statue of Schiller stand the twin towers of the Deutsche Bank (not to be confused with the DB—Deutsche Bahn—tower to your left). The country's #1 bank has assets greater than the annual budget of the German government. If money makes the world go round, the decisions that spin Germany are made in Frankfurt.

Make a 360-degree spin and survey all the bank towers. With its forest of skyscrapers along the Main River, Frankfurt has been dubbed Germany's "Mainhattan." Notice the striking architecture. By law, no German worker can be kept out of natural light for more than four hours, so work environments are filled with windows. And, as you can see, Germans like their skyscrapers with windows that open.

• *Find the skyscraper with the red-and-white candy cane on top. That's your destination—the Main (pronounced "mine") Tower. To reach it, continue straight along Taunustor for a block, then turn left on Neue Mainzer Strasse and look for the tower symbol on the doors on the right.*

▲▲*Main Tower*

The tower houses the Helaba Bank and offers the best (and only public) viewpoint from the top of a Frankfurt skyscraper. A 55-second, ear-popping elevator ride to the 54th floor (watch the meter on the wall as you ascend) and then 50 stairs take you to the rooftop, 650 feet above the city.

Cosmopolitan Frankfurt

Cost and Hours: €6.50; Sun-Thu 10:00-21:00, Fri-Sat until 23:00; shorter hours Oct-March; enter at Neue Mainzer Strasse 52, between Taunustor and Junghofstrasse, tel. 069/3650-4740, www.maintower.de.

• Leave the Main Tower and continue walking along Neue Mainzer Strasse (crossing Junghofstrasse) for a couple of blocks, to where you see a large square open to your left. Across the square is the Opera House.

Frankfurt's Good-Living People Zone

Opera House (Alte Oper): Finished in 1880, Frankfurt's opera house celebrated German high culture and the newly created nation. Mozart and Goethe flank the entrance, reminders that this is a house of both music and theater.

• Facing the Opera, turn right down Frankfurt's famous...

Fressgass': Everyone in Frankfurt calls this thriving pedestrian street the Fressgass', roughly "Feeding Street." Herds of bank employees come here on their lunch breaks to fill their bellies before returning for another few hours of cud-chewing at their computers. Join in if you're hungry—or wait for more eating options in a couple of blocks.

• Fressgass' leads to a square called Rathenauplatz, but it's known as Goethe Platz for its central statue. Cross the square and continue straight—the pedestrian street is now called Biebergasse—another block to the...

A one-man bratwurst *stand*

Hauptwache: The small, red-and-white building—which has given its name to the square—was built in 1730 to house the Frankfurt city militia. Now it's a café. The square, entirely closed to traffic, is one of the city's hubs.

• Straight ahead of you is a boulevard called the...

Zeil: This tree-lined pedestrian drag is Frankfurt's main shopping street. Crowds swirl through the Galeria Kaufhof department store, the Zeil Galerie, and the MyZeil shopping center (the one with the glassy hole in its wall) along the left side of the street.

• Continue down Zeil a block to the fountain at the next intersection. Turn right on Hasengasse. After about two blocks, find the low-key green entrance to Kleinmarkthalle on the right.

Kleinmarkthalle: This delightful, old-school market was saved from developers by a local outcry, and to this day it's a neighborhood favorite. Explore and sample your way through the ground floor. It's an adventure in fine eating (with a line of simple eateries upstairs—including the recommended Markt-Stubb and Weinterrasse) and a joy for photographers.

• Exit the Kleinmarkthalle opposite where you entered. Angle right, and climb six steps into a square (Leibfrauenberg) with a red-brick fountain and the 14th-century Church of Our Lady (rebuilt after World War II). On the far side is Lebkuchen-Schmidt, a fun shop selling traditional gingerbread, a local favorite. Turn left and head downhill on Neue Kräme, then cross Berliner Strasse to Paulsplatz.

▲*St. Paul's Church (Paulskirche)*

To your right, the church dominating the square is known as the "cradle of German democracy." It was here, during the political upheaval of 1848, that the first freely elected National Assembly met and the first German Constitution was drafted, paving the way for a united Germany in

1871. Following its destruction by Allied bombs in 1944, this was the first historic building in the city to be rebuilt, but it's no longer used as a church. Today, the building has displays telling the story of 1848 (free, daily 10:00-17:00).

• *Walk across the square, cross the next street and tram tracks, and enter what's left of Frankfurt's Old Town.*

▲Römerberg

Frankfurt's market square was the birthplace of the city. This is the site of the first trade fairs (12th century), bank (1405), and stock exchange (1585). Now, crowds of tourists convene here. Römerberg's central statue is the goddess of justice without her customary blindfold. She oversees the Town Hall, which itself oversees trade. The Town Hall *(Römer)* houses the *Kaisersaal,* or Imperial Hall, where Holy Roman Emperors celebrated their coronations. The rebuilt half-timbered homes opposite the *Römer* are typical of Frankfurt's quaint old center before the square was destroyed in World War II. The Gothic red-and-white Old Nikolai Church (Alte Nikolaikirche, with fine 1920s stained glass) dates from the 13th century and was restored after the war.

• *Circle around the Old Nikolai Church to Saalgasse.*

Saalgasse

Literally "Hall Street," Saalgasse is lined by postmodern buildings echoing the higgledy-piggledy houses that stood here until World War II. In the 1990s, famous architects from around the world were each given a ruined house of the same width and told to design a new structure to reflect the one that stood there before the war.

• *As you continue down the street, you'll see a big, red cathedral.*

St. Bartholomew's Cathedral (Kaiserdom)

This Catholic church—still bright and airy like the original—is made of modern concrete with paint to imitate mortar and medieval bricks. Holy Roman Emperors were elected here starting in 1152 and crowned here between 1562 and 1792. The cathedral was gutted by fire in 1867 and had to be rebuilt. It was seriously damaged in World War II, but was repaired and reopened in 1953.

Römerberg, Frankfurt's medieval market square

Enter on the side opposite the river. Frescoes from the 15th century survive, flanking the high altar and ringing the choir. They show 27 scenes from the life of St. Bartholomew. The Electors Chapel (to the right of the altar, with fine modern glass) is where the electors convened to choose the Holy Roman Emperor in the Middle Ages.

Before WWII bombs fell, everything of value that could be moved was taken from the church. The lovely sandstone Chapel of Sleeping Mary (to the left of the high altar), carved and painted in the 15th century, was too big to move—so it was fortified with sandbags.

The church is free (daily 9:00-12:00 & 13:30-20:00 except closed Fri morning).

• *Exit the cathedral and head down to the river. Turn right, and go along the pleasant riverfront park to the next bridge. Walk to its center.*

Rick's Tip: *The cobbled Sachsenhausen neighborhood is the place to find characteristic* ***Apfelwein*** **(apple wine) pubs.** *Cross the river on the pedestrian-only Eiserner Steg bridge, and head to one of these woodsy, rustic spots:* **Dauth-Schneider** *(Neuer Wall 5) or* **Atschel** *(Wallstrasse 7). They're both open daily from noon until late.*

Eiserner Steg Bridge

This iron bridge, the city's second oldest, dates to 1869. (The oldest is just upstream: the Alte Brücke, site of the first "Frank ford"—a fifth-century crossing.) From the middle of the bridge, survey the skyline and enjoy the lively scene along the riverbanks of Frankfurt.

• *For a quick ride back to your starting point, return to Römerberg and take the U-Bahn or tram #11 or #12 to the Hauptbahnhof. Otherwise, walk back along the river.*

Eating

In the **Kleinmarkthalle** market hall, you can graze through a world of amazing free samples or head upstairs to the **$$ Markt-Stubb** restaurant (lunch only, closed Sun-Mon) or the **Weinterrasse** wine garden (closed Sun). On Römerberg, the classic **$$ Weinstube im Römer,** in the bottom of Town Hall, serves good schnitzel (closed Mon, Römerberg 19).

Near the train station, try **$$ Merkez Kebab Haus** for good Turkish food (Münchener Strasse 33), or the deli/diner **$$ Maxie Eisen** for quick, tasty Jewish soups and sandwiches (closed Sun, Münchener Strasse 18).

Sleeping

Near the train station, consider **$$ Hotel Concorde,** in a restored 1890s building (Karlstrasse 9, www.hotelconcorde.de), the friendly **$$ Manhattan Hotel** (Düsseldorfer Strasse 10, www.manhattan-hotel.com), or the basic **¢ Five Elements** hostel (Moselstrasse 40, www.5elementshostel.de). You'll find **$$ Hotel Zentrum** downtown in a great location near the Hauptwache (Rossmarkt 7, www.hotel-zentrum.de).

Berlin

Over the last two decades, Berlin has been a construction zone. Standing on ripped-up tracks and under a canopy of cranes, visitors have witnessed the rebirth of a great European capital: lively, fun-loving, and captivating.

Berlin is still largely defined by its tumultuous 20th century. The city was Hitler's capital during World War II, and in the postwar years, it became the front line of the Cold War between Soviet-style communism and American-style capitalism. The East-West division was set in stone in 1961 with the Berlin Wall, which would stand for 28 years. In 1990, after the Wall fell, the two Germanys—and the two Berlins—officially became one.

Urban planners seized on the city's reunification and the return of the national government to make Berlin a great capital once again. Today, the old "East Berlin" is where you feel the vibrant pulse of the city, while the old "West Berlin" feels like a chic, classy suburb.

But even as the city busily builds itself into the 21st century, Berlin acknowledges and remembers its past. Thought-provoking memorials confront Germany's difficult history. Lacing these sights into your sightseeing intensifies your understanding of the city. As you walk over what was the Wall and through the well-patched Brandenburg Gate, it's clear that history is not contained in books; it's an evolving story in which we play a part.

BERLIN IN 3 DAYS

Day 1: Begin your day getting oriented to this huge city. For a quick and relaxing once-over-lightly tour, jump on one of the many hop-on, hop-off buses (such as BEX Sightseeing Berlin) that make orientation loops through the city.

Then take Part 1 of my self-guided "Best of Berlin Walk," starting at the Reichstag (reservations required to climb its dome), going through the Brandenburg Gate, and down the boulevard, Unter den Linden. Visit the charming Gendarmenmarkt square. Then tour the German History Museum.

On any evening: Any of these neighborhoods (all near each other) are worth exploring: Hackescher Markt, Oranienburger Strasse, and Prenzlauer Berg. Take in live music or cabaret. Linger at a beer garden, or stroll the banks of the Spree River. Or even continue your sightseeing—a number of sights stay open late, including the Reichstag and its view dome.

Day 2: Start your morning at Bebelplatz with Part 2 of my "Best of Berlin Walk." Along the walk, visit any museum that interests you on Museum Island or nearby: Pergamon, Neues, or the DDR.

In the afternoon, catch a boat tour (or pedal a rented bike) along the parklike banks of the Spree River from Museum Island to the Chancellery. Explore the Hackescher Markt's shops and museums (and stay into the evening).

Day 3: Tour the sights of the Third Reich and Cold War: the Topography of Terror exhibit and Museum of the Wall at Checkpoint Charlie. The Jewish Museum Berlin is also nearby.

In the afternoon, visit the Gemäldegalerie art museum.

Head to Prenzlauer Berg to visit the Berlin Wall Memorial, then stay for the café and nightlife scene.

ORIENTATION

Berlin is huge, with 3.4 million people. The city is spread out and its sights numerous, so you'll need to be well-organized to experience it all. The tourist's Berlin can be broken into several digestible chunks:

Near the landmark **Brandenburg Gate,** you'll find the Reichstag building, Pariser Platz, and memorials to Hitler's victims.

From the Brandenburg Gate, the famous **Unter den Linden boulevard** runs eastward, passing the German History Museum and Museum Island (Pergamon Museum, Neues Museum, and Berlin Cathedral) on the way to Alexanderplatz (TV Tower).

South of Unter den Linden are the delightful Gendarmenmarkt square, noteworthy Nazi sites (including the Topography of Terror), good Wall-related sights (Museum of the Wall at Checkpoint Charlie), and the Jewish Museum.

Across the Spree River are the neighborhoods of Hackescher Markt, Oranienburger Strasse, and Prenzlauer Berg (lively restaurant/nightlife zone). The Berlin Wall Memorial is at the west edge of Prenzlauer Berg.

The Brandenburg Gate—historic and grand

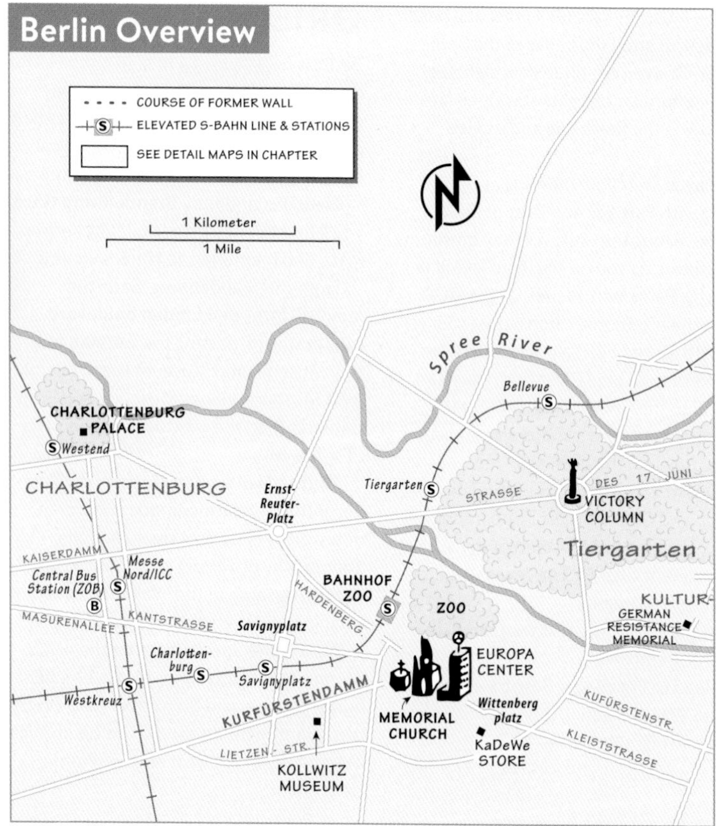

Rick's Tip: *What Americans called* **"East Germany"** *was technically the German Democratic Republic—the Deutsche Demokratische Republik, or* **DDR** *(pronounced day-day-AIR). You'll still see those initials around what was once East Germany. The name for what was* **"West Germany"**—*the Federal Republic of Germany (Bundesrepublik Deutschland, or* **BRD**)—*is now the name shared by all of Germany.*

Central Berlin is dominated by the giant **Tiergarten park,** with its angel-topped Victory Column. South of the park are Potsdamer Platz (the Times Square of Berlin, and a transportation hub) and the Kulturforum museum complex, whose highlight is the **Gemäldegalerie,** a treasure chest of European painting. To the north is the huge Hauptbahnhof (the city's main train station).

Western Berlin has the feel of a chic, classy suburb. It focuses on the **Bahnhof Zoo train station** (often marked "Zoologischer Garten" on transit maps) and the grand **Kurfürstendamm boulevard,** nicknamed "Ku'damm" (transportation hub and shopping). Even though the east side of the city is all the rage, big-name stores (like KaDeWe) and restaurants keep the west side buzzing.

Tourist Information

With any luck, you won't have to use Berlin's **TIs.** Appropriately called "info-stores," they are unlikely to have the information you need (tel. 030/250-025, www.

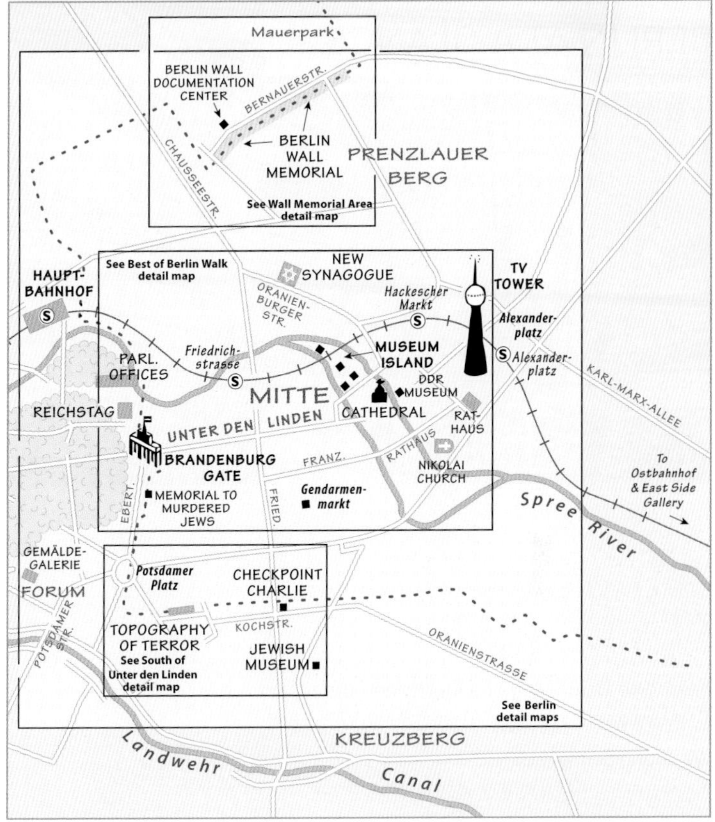

visitberlin.de). You'll find them at the **Hauptbahnhof** train station (daily 8:00-22:00, by main entrance on Europaplatz), at the **Brandenburg Gate** (daily 9:30-19:00, until 18:00 Nov-March), and at the **TV Tower** (daily 10:00-18:00, until 16:00 Nov-March, Panoramastrasse 1a).

Sightseeing Passes

The three-day, €24 **Museum Pass Berlin** is a great value and pays for itself in a hurry. It gets you into more than 50 museums, including the national museums and most of the recommended biggies (though not the German History Museum), on three consecutive days. Sights covered by the pass include the Museum Island museums (including Neues and Pergamon), Gemäldegalerie, and the Jewish Museum Berlin. Buy it at the TI or any participating museum. The pass generally lets you skip the line and go directly into the museum.

The €18 **Museum Island Pass** (Bereichskarte Museumsinsel) covers all the venues on Museum Island and is a fine value—but for just €6 more, the three-day Museum Pass Berlin gives you triple the days and many more entries.

TIs sell the **WelcomeCard,** a transportation pass that includes discounts for many sights; it's a good value if you'll be using public transit frequently (see page 354).

Helpful Hints

Addresses: Many Berlin streets are numbered with odd and even numbers on

BERLIN AT A GLANCE

Berlin is huge. Even with the excellent transit system, it makes sense to organize your sightseeing in clusters.

From the Reichstag to Unter den Linden

These sights are part of my "Best of Berlin Walk," Part 1.

▲▲▲**Brandenburg Gate** One of Berlin's most famous landmarks, a massive columned gateway, at the former border of East and West. **Hours:** Always open. See page 309.

▲▲▲**Reichstag** Germany's historic parliament building, topped with a striking modern dome you can climb (reservations required). **Hours:** Daily 8:00-24:00, last entry at 22:00. See page 320.

▲▲**Memorial to the Murdered Jews of Europe** Holocaust memorial with almost 3,000 symbolic pillars, plus an exhibition about Hitler's Jewish victims. **Hours:** Memorial always open; information center open Tue-Sun 10:00-20:00, Oct-March until 19:00, closed Mon. See page 310.

▲▲**Unter den Linden** Leafy boulevard through the heart of former East Berlin, lined with some of the city's top sights. **Hours:** Always open. See page 312.

Museum Island and Nearby

You'll stop at Museum Island on my "Best of Berlin Walk," Part 2.

▲▲▲**Pergamon Museum** World-class museum of classical antiquities on Museum Island, partially closed through 2025 (including its famous Pergamon Altar). **Hours:** Daily 10:00-18:00, Thu until 20:00. See page 324.

▲▲▲**German History Museum** The ultimate swing through Germany's tumultuous story, located just west of Museum Island. **Hours:** Daily 10:00-18:00. See page 327.

▲▲**Neues Museum** Egyptian antiquities collection on Museum Island and proud home of the exquisite 3,000-year-old bust of Queen Nefertiti. **Hours:** Daily 10:00-18:00, Thu until 20:00. See page 325.

▲▲**DDR Museum** Quirky collection of communist-era artifacts, located just east of Museum Island. **Hours:** Daily 10:00-20:00, Sat until 22:00. See page 328.

South of Unter den Linden

▲▲**Gendarmenmarkt** Inviting square bounded by twin churches (one with a fine German history exhibit), a chocolate shop, and a concert hall. **Hours:** Always open. See page 328.

▲▲**Topography of Terror** Chilling exhibit documenting the Nazi perpetrators, built on the site of the former Gestapo/SS headquarters. **Hours:** Daily 10:00-20:00. See page 329.

▲▲**Museum of the Wall at Checkpoint Charlie** Kitschy but moving museum with stories of brave Cold War escapes, near the former site of the famous East-West border checkpoint; the surrounding street scene is almost as interesting. **Hours:** Daily 9:00-22:00. See page 331.

▲▲**Jewish Museum Berlin** Engaging, accessible museum celebrating Jewish culture, in a highly conceptual building. **Hours:** Daily 10:00-20:00, Mon until 22:00. See page 333.

Kulturforum Complex

▲▲**Gemäldegalerie** Germany's top collection of 13th- through 18th-century European paintings, featuring Holbein, Dürer, Cranach, Van der Weyden, Rubens, Hals, Rembrandt, Vermeer, Velázquez, and Raphael, located off Tiergarten park. **Hours:** Tue-Fri 10:00-18:00, Thu until 20:00, Sat-Sun 11:00-18:00, closed Mon. See page 335.

Across the Spree River

▲▲▲**Prenzlauer Berg** Lively, colorful neighborhood with hip cafés, restaurants, boutiques, and street life. **Hours:** Always open. See page 339.

▲▲▲**Berlin Wall Memorial** A "docu-center" with videos and displays, several outdoor exhibits, and the lone surviving stretch of an intact Wall section. **Hours:** Visitor Center Tue-Sun 10:00-18:00, closed Mon; outdoor areas accessible 24 hours daily. See page 340.

▲**New Synagogue** Largest prewar synagogue in Berlin. **Hours:** April-Oct Mon-Fri 10:00-18:00, Sun until 19:00; Nov-March exhibit only Sun-Thu 10:00-18:00, Fri until 15:00; closed Sat year-round. See page 339.

City Bus #100 Tour

For a cheap alternative to a hop-on, hop-off bus tour, you could follow this self-guided tour via **City Bus #100** instead. Running from the Bahnhof Zoo train station in western Berlin to Alexanderplatz in eastern Berlin, City Bus #100 laces together the major sights. A basic, single bus ticket is good for two hours of travel in one direction and buses leave every few minutes, so hopping on and off works great (see page 354 for ticketing details).

Here's a quick review of what you'll see: Leaving from Bahnhof Zoo, spot the bombed-out hulk of the **Kaiser Wilhelm Memorial Church,** with its jagged spire and postwar sister church. Then, on the left, the elephant gates mark the entrance to the much-loved **Berlin Zoo.** After a left turn, you cross the canal and pass Berlin's **embassy row.**

The bus then enters the vast 400-acre **Tiergarten** city park, once a royal hunting ground and now packed with cycling paths, joggers, and—on hot days—nude sunbathers. Straight ahead, the **Victory Column** (with the gilded angel) towers above. A block beyond the Victory Column (on the left) is the 18th-century late-Rococo **Bellevue Palace,** the residence of the federal president (if the flag's out, he's in).

Driving along the Spree River (on the left), you'll see several striking **national government** buildings. A metal Henry Moore sculpture entitled *Butterfly* floats in front of the slope-roofed House of World Cultures. Through the trees on the left is the **Chancellery**—Germany's "White House." The big open space is the **Platz der Republik,** where the Victory Column (which you passed earlier) stood until Hitler moved it. The Hauptbahnhof (Berlin's vast main train station, marked by its tall tower with the *DB* sign) is across the field between the Chancellery and the **Reichstag** (Germany's parliament—the old building with the new dome).

Hop off at the next stop (Reichstag/Bundestag) if you'd like to follow my "Best of Berlin Walk." But if you stay on the bus, you'll zip by the next string of sights, in this order:

Unter den Linden, the main east-west thoroughfare, stretches from the **Brandenburg Gate** through Berlin's historic core to the TV Tower in the distance. You'll pass the **Russian Embassy** and the Aeroflot airline office (right). Crossing **Friedrichstrasse,** look right for a Fifth Avenue-style conga line of big, glitzy department stores. Later, on the left, are the **German History Museum, Museum Island,** and the **Berlin Cathedral;** across from these (on the right) is the construction site of the **Humboldt-Forum Berliner Schloss** (with the Humboldt Box visitors center). You'll rumble to a final stop at the transit hub of **Alexanderplatz.**

the same side of the street, often with no connection to the other side (for example, Ku'damm #212 can be across the street from #14). To save steps, check the white street signs on curb corners; many list the street numbers covered on that side of the block.

City Overview: If you don't ascend the Reichstag's dome, try **Panoramapunkt,** which offers a speedy elevator and sky-scraping rooftop views (€6.50, €10.50 for VIP line-skipping ticket, daily 10:00-20:00, until 18:00 in winter, in red-brick building on Potsdamer Platz, S-Bahn and U-Bahn: Potsdamer Platz, tel. 030/2593-7080, www.panoramapunkt.de).

Rick's Tip: *There are still enough idiots on the street to keep the* **con men with their shell games** *in business. Don't be foolish enough to engage with any gambling on the street.*

Medical Help: The US Embassy has a list of local English-speaking doctors (tel. 030/83050, http://germany.usembassy.gov).

Tours

▲▲▲HOP-ON, HOP-OFF BUSES

Several companies offer a circuit of the city with unlimited hop-on, hop-off privileges all day for about €20 (about 15 stops at the city's major tourist spots—Museum Island, Brandenburg Gate, and so on). Go with a live guide rather than the recorded spiel (buses generally run April-Oct daily 10:00-18:00, departures every 10 minutes, last bus leaves all stops at around 16:00, 2-hour loop; Nov-March 2/hour and last departure at 15:00). Try BEX Sightseeing Berlin (www.berlinerstadtrundfahrten.de) or look for brochures in your hotel lobby or at the TI.

▲▲▲WALKING TOURS

Berlin's complex history can be challenging to appreciate on your own, so walking tours are worthwhile. Germany has no regulations controlling who can give city tours, so guides can be hit-or-miss. To land a great guide, use one of the companies I recommend. They all run tours daily. Most in-city tours cost about €12-15 and last about 3 to 4 hours.

Brewer's Berlin Tours specializes in in-depth walks that can flex with your interests. Their Best of Berlin introductory tour, billed at 6 hours, can last for 8; they also do a shorter 3.5-hour tour (free, tip expected). All tours depart from Bandy Brooks ice-cream shop at the Friedrichstrasse S-Bahn station (mobile 0177-388-1537, www.brewersberlintours.com).

Insider Tour runs the full gamut of itineraries, including pub crawls and a day trip to Dresden. Their tours meet at the McDonald's across from the Bahnhof Zoo train station, and at the AM to PM Bar at the Hackescher Markt S-Bahn station (tel. 030/692-3149, www.insidertour.com).

Original Berlin Walks gives a good overview in four hours (daily year-round). They also offer a Third Reich walking tour and other themes. Tours depart from opposite the Hackescher Markt S-Bahn station (tour info: tel. 030/301-9194, www.berlinwalks.de).

Rick's Tip: *Supposedly* **"free" tours are advertised all over town.** *English-speaking students deliver a memorized script and expect to be tipped (€5 minimum per person is encouraged). While the guides can be highly entertaining, when it comes to walking tours, you get what you pay for.*

PRIVATE GUIDES

Guides charge roughly the same for private tours (€50-60/hour or €200-300/day, confirm when booking). Consider **Nick Jackson,** an archaeologist and historian who makes museums come to life (mobile 0171-537-8768, www.jacksonsberlintours.com), or **Bernhard Schlegelmilch,** an enthusiastic historian who grew up behind the Wall (mobile 0176-6422-9119, www.steubentoursberlin.com).

BOAT TOURS

Several boat companies offer relaxing one-hour trips up and down the Spree River. Boats leave from various docks that cluster near the bridge at the Berlin Cathedral (just off Unter den Linden). For better views, choose a two-story boat with open-deck seating. I enjoy the Historical Sightseeing Cruise from **Stern und Kreisschiffahrt** (€14, mid-March-Nov daily 10:00-19:00, leaves from Nikolaiviertel Dock—cross bridge from Berlin Cathedral toward Alexanderplatz and look right, tel. 030/536-3600, www.sternundkreis.de). Confirm that the boat you choose comes with English commentary.

BEST OF BERLIN WALK

This two-mile self-guided walk, worth ▲▲▲, starts in front of the Reichstag, takes you under the Brandenburg Gate and down Unter den Linden, and finishes on Alexanderplatz. If you have just one day in Berlin, or want a good orientation to the city, simply follow this walk (allowing 2-3 hours at a brisk pace, not counting museum visits). By the end, you'll have seen the core of Berlin and its most important sights.

If you have more time and want to use this walk as a spine for your sightseeing, entering sights and museums as you go, consider doing Part 1 and Part 2 on different days. Part 1 goes from the Reichstag and takes you partway down Unter den Linden, with stops at the Brandenburg Gate, Memorial to the Murdered Jews of Europe, and Friedrichstrasse, the glitzy shopping street. Part 2 continues down Unter den Linden, from Bebelplatz to Alexanderplatz, and features Museum Island and the Spree River, Berlin Cathedral, and iconic TV Tower.

🎧 Download my free Best of Berlin Walk audio tour, which narrates the route.

➲ Self-Guided Walk

Part 1: From the Reichstag to Unter den Linden

During the Cold War, the Reichstag stood just inside the West Berlin side of the Wall. Even though it's been more than 25 years since the Wall came down, you may still feel a slight tingle down your spine as you walk across the former death strip, through the once *verboten* Brandenburg Gate, and into the former communist east.

• *Start your walk directly in front of the Reichstag building, at the big, grassy park called...*

❶ PLATZ DER REPUBLIK

Stand about 100 yards in front of the grand Reichstag building and spin left to survey your surroundings. At the **Reichstag U-Bahn stop** is a big federal building overlooking the Spree River. The huge **main train station** (Hauptbahnhof) is in the distance (see the tower marked *DB*, for Deutsche Bahn—the German rail company). Farther left is the mammoth white concrete-and-glass **Chancellery,** nicknamed the "washing machine" by Berliners for its hygienic, spin-cycle appearance. It's the office of Germany's most powerful person, the chancellor (currently Angela Merkel). To remind the chancellor whom he or she works for, Germany's Reichstag (housing the parliament) is about six feet taller than the Chancellery.

Beyond the Chancellery is the Spree

River. When kings ruled Prussia, government buildings crowded right up to its banks. But today, the riverscape is a people-friendly zone (we'll see it later on this walk).

• *Dominating the Platz der Republik is a giant domed building, the...*

❷ REICHSTAG

The parliament building—the heart of German democracy and worth ▲▲▲—has a short but complicated and emotional history. When it was inaugurated in the 1890s, the last emperor, Kaiser Wilhelm II, disdainfully called it the "chatting home for monkeys" *(Reichsaffenhaus)*. It was placed outside the city's old walls—far from the center of real power, the imperial palace. But it was from the Reichstag that the German Republic was proclaimed in 1918. Look above the door, surrounded by stone patches from WWII bomb damage, to see the motto and promise: *Dem Deutschen Volke* ("To the German People").

In 1933, this symbol of democracy nearly burned down. The Nazis—whose influence on the German political scene was on the rise—blamed a communist plot. A Dutch communist, Marinus van der Lubbe, was eventually convicted and guillotined for the crime. Others believed that Hitler himself planned the fire, using it as a handy excuse to frame the communists and grab power.

The Reichstag was hardly used from 1933 to 1999. Despite the fact that the building had lost its symbolic value, Stalin ordered his troops to take the Reichstag from the Nazis no later than May 1, 1945 (the date of the workers' May Day parade in Moscow). More than 1,500 Nazi soldiers made their last stand here—extending World War II by two days. On April 30, after fierce fighting on its rooftop, the Reichstag fell to the Red Army.

For the building's 101st birthday in 1995, the artist-partners Christo and Jeanne-Claude wrapped the entire thing in silvery gold cloth. It was then wrapped again—in scaffolding—and rebuilt by British architect Lord Norman Foster into the new

The Reichstag is the symbolic heart of German democracy.

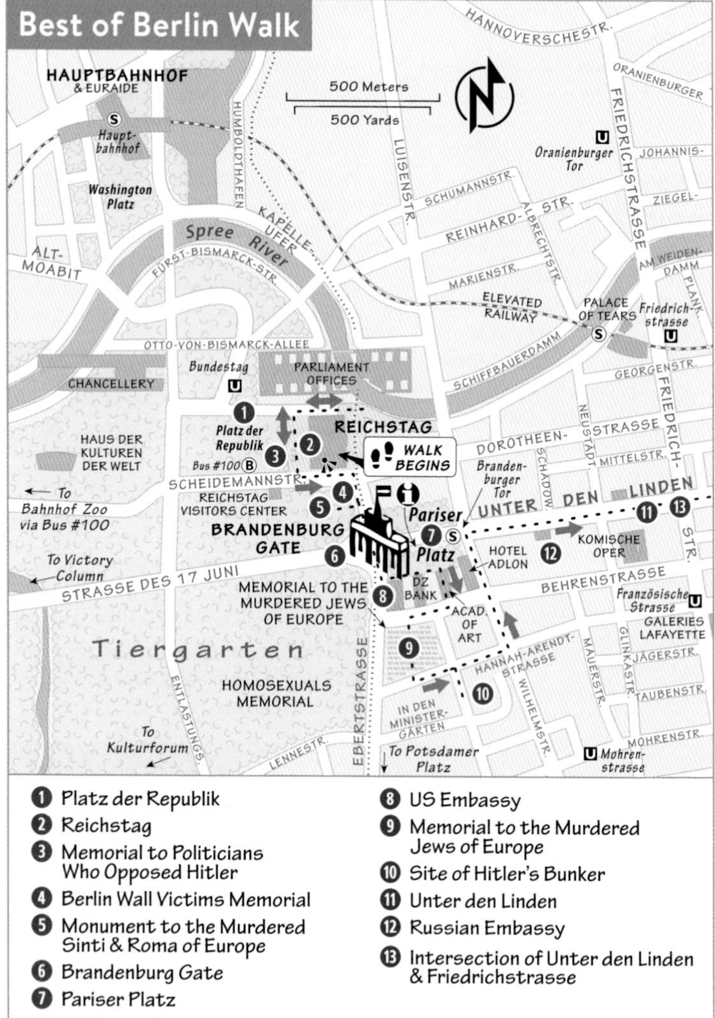

parliamentary home of the Bundestag (Germany's lower house, similar to the US House of Representatives). In 1999, the German parliament convened here for the first time in 66 years. To many Germans, the proud resurrection of the Reichstag symbolizes the end of a terrible chapter in their country's history.

The **glass cupola** rises 155 feet above the ground. Its two sloped ramps spiral 755 feet to the top for a grand view. Inside the dome, a cone of 360 mirrors reflects natural light into the legislative chamber below. Illuminated from inside after dark, this gives Berlin a memorable nightlight. The environmentally friendly cone—with an opening at the top—also helps with air circulation, expelling stale air from the legislative chamber (no joke) and pulling in fresh, cool air.

Visitors with advance reservations can climb the spiral ramp up into the cupola. If

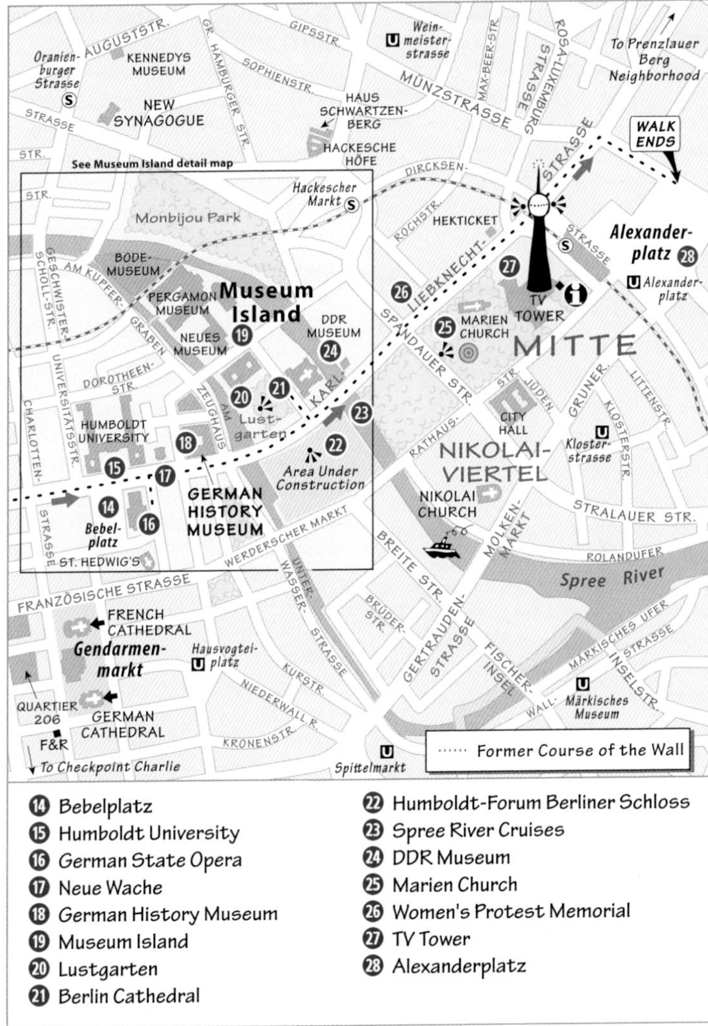

you haven't booked a slot, cross the street to the white booth to check available entry times (for details on making reservations and visiting the interior, including a self-guided dome tour, see page 320).

• *Face the Reichstag and walk to the right. Near the road in front of the building, enmeshed in all the security apparatus and crowds, is a memorial of slate stones embedded vertically in the ground.*

❸ MEMORIAL TO POLITICIANS WHO OPPOSED HITLER

This row of slabs, which looks like a fancy slate bicycle rack, is a memorial to the 96 members of the Reichstag who were persecuted and murdered because their politics didn't agree with Chancellor Hitler's. They were part of the Weimar Republic, the weak and ill-fated attempt at post-WWI democracy in Germany. These were the people who could have stopped

Hitler...so they became his first victims. Each slate slab memorializes one man—his name, party (mostly KPD—Communists, and SPD—Social Democrats), and the date and location of his death—generally in a concentration camp (indicated by *KZ* on the slabs). They are honored here, in front of the building in which they worked.

• *Walk along the side of the Reichstag, on busy Scheidemannstrasse, toward the rear of the building. At the intersection with Ebertstrasse, cross to the right (toward the park). Along a railing is a small memorial of white crosses. This is the...*

❹ BERLIN WALL VICTIMS MEMORIAL

This monument commemorates some of the East Berliners who died trying to cross the Wall. Many of them perished within months of the Wall's construction on August 13, 1961. Most died trying to swim the Spree River to freedom. This monument used to stand right on the Berlin Wall behind the Reichstag. The last person killed while trying to escape was 20-year-old Chris Gueffroy, who was shot through the heart in no-man's land nine months before the Wall fell in 1989. (To read more about the Wall, see the sidebar on page 332.)

• *Continue along Ebertstrasse for a few more steps before turning right on a peaceful leafy lane. Within a short distance, on your right, is the...*

❺ MONUMENT TO THE MURDERED SINTI AND ROMA OF EUROPE

Unveiled in 2012, this memorial remembers the roughly 500,000 Sinti and Roma victims of the Holocaust. "Sinti" and "Roma" (the main tribes and correct terms for those more commonly called "Gypsies") were as persecuted by the Nazis as were the Jews. And they lost the same percentage of their population to Hitler. The opaque glass wall, with a timeline in English and German, traces the Nazi abuse and atrocities.

Enter through the rusty steel portal. On the other side is a circular reflecting pool surrounded by stone slabs, some containing the names of the death camps where hundreds of thousands of Sinti and Roma perished. In the water along the rim of the pool is the wrenching poem "Auschwitz," by composer and writer Santino Spinelli, an Italian Roma. Dissonant music evoking the tragedy of the Sinti and Roma genocide adds to the atmosphere.

• *Retrace your steps to Ebertstrasse and continue right, toward the busy intersection dominated by the imposing Brandenburg Gate.*

Take this chance to get oriented. Behind you, as you face the Brandenburg Gate, is ***Tiergarten park,*** *its center marked by the landmark Victory Column. Now face the gate: It stands at one end of Unter den Linden, the Champs-Elysées of Berlin. In the distance, the red-and-white spire of the TV Tower marks the end of this walk.*

As you cross the street toward the gate,

Memorial to Politicans Who Opposed Hitler

Berlin Wall Victims Memorial

notice the double row of cobblestones beneath your feet—it goes about 25 miles around the city, marking where the Wall used to stand. Now walk under the gate that, for a sad generation, was part of a wall that divided this city.

❻ BRANDENBURG GATE

The historic Brandenburg Gate, rated ▲▲▲, is the last survivor of 14 gates in Berlin's old city wall. This one, dating from 1791, was the grandest and led to the neighboring city of Brandenburg. The gate was the symbol of Prussian Berlin—and later the symbol of a divided Berlin. It's crowned by a majestic four-horse chariot, with the Goddess of Peace at the reins. Napoleon took this statue to the Louvre in Paris in 1806. After the Prussians defeated Napoleon and got it back (1813), she was renamed the Goddess of Victory.

The gate sat unused, part of a sad circle dance called the Berlin Wall, for more than 25 years. Now postcards all over town show the ecstatic day—November 9, 1989—when the world rejoiced at the sight of happy Berliners jamming the gate like flowers on a parade float. Pause a minute and think about struggles for freedom—past and present. There's actually a special room built into the gate for this purpose (see the sidebar). A TI is also within the gate. Around the gate, information boards show how this area changed throughout the 20th century.

The gate sits on a major boulevard running east to west through Berlin. The western segment, called Strasse des 17 Juni (named for a workers' uprising against the DDR government on June 17, 1953), stretches for four miles from the Brandenburg Gate, through the Tiergarten, past the Victory Column, to the Olympic Stadium. But we'll follow this city axis in the opposite direction—east, along Unter den Linden into the core of old imperial Berlin, and past the site where the palace of the Hohenzollern family, rulers of Prussia and then Germany, once stood. The royal palace is a phantom sight, long gone, but its occupants were responsible for just about all you'll see.

• *Pass through the gate and stand in the middle of...*

The Brandenburg Gate, Arch of Peace

More than 200 years ago, the Brandenburg Gate was designed as an arch of peace, crowned by the Goddess of Peace and showing Mars sheathing his sword. The Nazis misused it as a gate of triumph and aggression. Today a Room of Silence, built into the gate, is dedicated to the peaceful message of the original Brandenburg Gate. As you consider the history of Berlin in this silent and empty room, you may be inspired to read the prayer of the United Nations:

"Oh Lord, our planet Earth is only a small star in space. It is our duty to transform it into a planet whose creatures are no longer tormented by war, hunger, and fear, no longer senselessly divided by race, color, and ideology. Give us courage and strength to begin this task today so that our children and our children's children shall one day carry the name of man with pride."

Brandenburg Gate

❼ PARISER PLATZ

"Parisian Square," so named after the Prussians who defeated Napoleon in 1813, was once filled with important government buildings—all bombed to smithereens in World War II. For decades, it was an unrecognizable, deserted no-man's-land—cut off from the rest of the city by the Wall. Banks, hotels, and embassies have now reclaimed their original places on the square—with a few additions, including a palace of coffee, Starbucks. The winners of World War II enjoy this prime real estate: The American, French, British, and Russian embassies are all on or near this square.

As you face the gate, to your right is the French Embassy, and to your left is the ❽ **US Embassy,** which reopened in its historic pre-WWII location in 2008. For safety's sake, Uncle Sam wanted more of a security zone around the building, but the Germans wanted to keep Pariser Platz a welcoming people zone. The compromise: Extra security was built into the structure. Easy-on-the-eyes barriers keep potential car bombs at a distance, and the front door is on the side farthest from the Brandenburg Gate.

Turn your back to the gate. On the right, jutting into the square, is the ritzy **Hotel Adlon,** long called home by visiting stars and VIPs. In its heyday, it hosted such notables as Charlie Chaplin, Albert Einstein, and Greta Garbo. It was the setting for Garbo's most famous line, "I vant to be alone," uttered in the film *Grand Hotel.* Damaged by the Russians just after World War II, the original hotel was closed when the Wall went up in 1961 and later demolished. Today's grand Adlon was rebuilt in 1997. It was here that Michael Jackson shocked millions by dangling his infant son over a balcony railing.

• *Between the hotel and the US Embassy are two buildings worth a quick visit: the DZ Bank building and the Academy of Arts. We'll enter both.*

DZ Bank Building: This building's architect, Frank Gehry, is famous for Bilbao's Guggenheim Museum, Prague's Dancing House, Seattle's Experience Music Project, Chicago's Pritzker Pavilion, and Los Angeles' Walt Disney Concert Hall. Gehry fans might be surprised at the bank building's low profile. Structures on Pariser Platz are designed so as not to draw attention away from the Brandenburg Gate. But to get your fix of wild and colorful Gehry, step into the lobby. Built as an office complex and conference center, its undulating interior is like a big, slithery fish. Gehry explained, "The form of the fish is the best example of movement. I try to capture this movement in my buildings."

• *Leaving the DZ Bank, turn right and head into the next building, the...*

Academy of Arts (Akademie der Künste): Inside the glassy arcade, just past the café, is the office where Albert Speer, Hitler's architect, planned the rebuilding of postwar Berlin into "Welthauptstadt Germania"—the grandiose "world capital" of Nazi Europe. Pass through the glass door to see Speer's favorite statue, *Prometheus Bound* (c. 1900). This is the kind of art that turned Hitler on: a strong, soldierly, vital man, enduring hardship for a greater cause. Anticipating the bombing of Berlin, Speer had the statue bricked up in the basement here, where it lay undiscovered until 1995.

• *Exit the building out the back. Across the street, to the right, stretches the vast...*

❾ MEMORIAL TO THE MURDERED JEWS OF EUROPE

Completed in 2005, this Holocaust memorial, rated ▲▲, consists of 2,711 gravestone-like pillars. Designed by Jewish-American architect Peter Eisenman, it was Germany's first formal, government-sponsored Holocaust memorial. Using the word "murdered" in the title was intentional and a big deal. Germany, as a nation, was officially admitting to a crime.

Cost and Hours: The memorial is free and always open. The information center is open Tue-Sun 10:00-20:00, Oct-March until 19:00, closed Mon year-round; last entry 45 minutes before closing, S-Bahn: Brandenburger Tor or Potsdamer Platz, tel. 030/2639-4336, www.stiftung-denkmal.de. A €4 audioguide augments the experience.

Visiting the Memorial: The pillars, made of hollow concrete, stand in a gently sunken area, which can be entered from any side. The number of pillars isn't symbolic of anything; it's simply how many fit on the provided land. The pillars are all about the same size, but of differing heights.

Once you enter the memorial, notice that people seem to appear and disappear between the columns, and that no matter where you are, the exit always seems to be up. The memorial is lit and guarded at night.

The monument was criticized for focusing on just one of the groups targeted by the Nazis, but the German government has now erected memorials to other victims—such as the Roma/Sinti memorial we just visited, and a memorial to the regime's homosexual victims, also nearby. It's also been criticized because there's nothing intrinsically Jewish about it. Some were struck that there's no central gathering point or place for a ceremony. Like death, you enter it alone.

There is no one intended interpretation. Is it a symbolic cemetery, or an intentionally disorienting labyrinth? It's up to the visitor to derive the meaning, while pondering this horrible chapter in human history.

Memorial Information Center: The pondering takes place under the sky. For the learning, go under the field of concrete pillars to the state-of-the-art information center. Inside, excellent and thought-provoking installations study the Nazi system of extermination and personalize the plight of victims; there's also space for silent reflection. Exhibits trace the historical context of the Nazi and WWII era, present case studies of how the Holocaust affected 15 Jewish families from around Europe, and document

Memorial to the Murdered Jews of Europe

the different places of genocide. You'll also find exhibits about other Holocaust monuments and memorials, a searchable database of victims, and a video archive of interviews with survivors.

• *Wander through the gray pillars, but eventually emerge on the corner with the Information Center. Cross Hannah-Arendt-Strasse and go a half-block farther. Walk alongside the unpaved parking lot on the left to the info plaque over the...*

⑩ SITE OF HITLER'S BUNKER

You're standing atop the buried remains of the *Führerbunker*. In early 1945, as Allied armies advanced on Berlin, and Nazi Germany lay in ruins, Hitler and his staff retreated to a bunker complex behind the former Reich Chancellery. He stayed there for two months. It was here, as the Soviet army tightened its noose on the capital, that Hitler and Eva Braun, his wife of less than 48 hours, committed suicide on April 30, 1945. A week later, the war in Europe was over. The info board presents a detailed cutaway illustrating the bunker complex plus a timeline tracing its history and ultimate fate (the roof was removed and the bunker filled with dirt, then covered over).

• *From here, you can visit the important but stark Memorial to the Homosexuals Persecuted Under the National Socialist Regime, or you can continue the walk. To do either, first head back to Hannah-Arendt-Strasse.*

It's a detour to see the ***memorial:*** *go left one block at Hannah-Arendt-Strasse, cross the street, and head down a path into Tiergarten park. There, look for a large, dark gray concrete box. Through a small window you can watch a film loop of same-sex couples kissing—a reminder that life and love are precious.*

To rejoin the ***walk,*** *turn right on Hannah-Arendt-Strasse, go one block, then head left up Wilhelmstrasse. Because Wilhelmstrasse was a main street of the German government during World War II, it was obliterated by bombs, and all its buildings are new today.*

Imagining Hitler in the 21st Century

Germans tread lightly on their past. It took 65 years for the German History Museum to organize its first exhibit on the life of Hitler. No version of *Mein Kampf*, Hitler's political manifesto, was allowed printed in Germany until 2016, when the publication of a new version (annotated by historians) was greeted with controversy. It's a balancing act, and Germans are still in the process of figuring out how to confront their painful history.

Many visitors to Berlin are curious about Hitler sites, but not much survives from that dark period. The bunker where Hitler killed himself lies hidden underneath a parking lot, marked only by a small information board. The best way to learn about Hitler sites is to take a walking tour focused on the Third Reich (see page 303) or to visit the Topography of Terror (see page 329).

Back on Unter den Linden, head to the median, in front of Hotel Adlon, and take a long look down...

⑪ UNTER DEN LINDEN

In the good old days, this street, rated ▲▲, was one of Europe's grand boulevards. In the 15th century, it was a carriageway leading from the palace to the

Unter den Linden

hunting grounds (today's big Tiergarten). In the 17th century, Hohenzollern princes and princesses moved in and built their palaces here so they could be near the Prussian king. It is divided, roughly at Friedrichstrasse, into a business section, which stretches toward the Brandenburg Gate, and a cultural section, which spreads out toward Alexanderplatz. Frederick the Great wanted to have culture, mainly the opera and the university, closer to his palace and to keep business (read: banks) farther away, near the city walls.

Named centuries ago for its many linden trees, this was the most elegant street of Prussian Berlin before Hitler's time, and the main drag of East Berlin after his reign. Hitler replaced the venerable trees—many 250 years old—with Nazi flags. Popular discontent drove him to replant the trees. Later, Unter den Linden deteriorated into a depressing Cold War cul-de-sac, but it has long since regained its strolling café ambience.

• *In front of Hotel Adlon is the Brandenburger Tor S-Bahn station. Cover a bit of Unter den Linden underground by climbing down its steps and walking along the platform.*

Ghost Subway Station: The Brandenburger Tor S-Bahn station is one of Berlin's former ghost subway stations. It's a time warp, looking much as it did when built in 1936, with dreary old green tiles and original signage. During the Cold War, most underground train tunnels were simply sealed at the border between East and West Berlin. But a few Western lines looped through the East and then back into the West. To make hard Western cash, the Eastern government rented the use of these tracks to the West. For 28 years, as Western trains passed through otherwise blocked-off stations, passengers saw only East German guards and lots of cobwebs. Within days of the fall of the Wall, these stations reopened (one woman who'd left her purse behind in 1961 got a call from the lost-and-found office—it was still there).

Brandenburger Tor ghost subway station

• *Walk along the track and exit on the other side, to the right. You'll pop out at the Russian Embassy's front yard.*

⓬ **Russian Embassy:** This was the first big postwar building project in East Berlin. It's in the powerful, simplified Neoclassical style that Stalin liked. While not as important now as it was a few years ago, it's as immense as ever. It flies the Russian white, blue, and red. Find the hammer-and-sickle motif decorating the window frames—a reminder of the days when Russia was the USSR.

• *Keep walking down the boulevard for two blocks. You'll pass blocks of dull banks, tacky trinket shops, and a few high-end boutiques, eventually reaching cultural buildings—Humboldt University, the Berlin State Opera, and so on. That's intentional: The Prussian kings wanted to have culture closer to their palace. Pause when you reach the...*

⓭ **Intersection of Unter den Linden and Friedrichstrasse:** This is perhaps the most central crossroads in Berlin. And for several years more, it will be a mess as Berlin builds a new connection in its already extensive subway system. All over Berlin, you'll see big, colorful **water pipes** running aboveground. Wherever there are large construction projects, streets are laced with these drainage pipes. Berlin's high water table means that any new basement comes with lots of pumping out.

Looking at the jaunty DDR-style pedestrian "walk/don't walk" signals at this intersection is a reminder that a little of the old East survives. All along Unter den Linden (and throughout much of the former East Berlin), you'll see the perky red and green men—called ***Ampelmännchen.*** They were recently threatened with replacement by ordinary signs, but, after a 10-year court battle, the wildly popular DDR signals were kept after all (note the Ampelmann souvenir store across the street).

Before continuing down Unter den Linden, look farther down **Friedrichstrasse.** Before the war, this zone was the heart of Berlin. In the 1920s, Berlin was famous for its anything-goes love of life. This was the cabaret drag, a springboard to stardom for young and vampy entertainers like Marlene Dietrich. Now Friedrichstrasse is lined with department stores and big-time hotels. Consider detouring to the megastore **Galeries Lafayette** (closed Sun); check out the vertical garden on its front wall, have lunch in its basement food court, or, if the weather's nice, pick up some classy munchies here for a picnic. The short walk here provides some of Berlin's most jarring old-versus-new architectural contrasts—be sure to look up as you stroll.

• *We've reached the end of Part 1 of this walk. This is a good place to take a break, if you wish. The charming Gendarmenmarkt, with shops and eateries, is just a couple of blocks away (see page 328). Or, if you continue south down Friedrichstrasse, you'll wind up at Checkpoint Charlie in about 10 minutes (see page 331).*

But if you'd rather tackle Part 2 of this walk now, head down Unter den Linden a few more blocks, past the large equestrian statue of Frederick the Great, then turn right into Bebelplatz.

Frederick the Great

Berlin was a humble, marshy burg until prince electors from the Hohenzollern dynasty made it their capital in the mid-15th century. Gradually their territory spread and strengthened, becoming the powerful Kingdom of Prussia, which dominated the northern Germanic world—both militarily and culturally.

The only Hohenzollern ruler worth remembering is **Frederick the Great** (1712-1786). This enlightened despot was both a ruthless military tactician and a culture lover. "Old Fritz," as he was called, played the flute, spoke six languages, and counted Voltaire among his friends. Practical and cosmopolitan, Frederick cleverly invited to Prussia Protestants who were being persecuted—including French Huguenots and Dutch traders. Prussia became the beneficiary of these groups' substantial wealth and know-how. Frederick left Berlin a far more modern and enlightened place than he found it. Thanks largely to him, Prussia was well-positioned to become a magnet of sorts for the German unification movement in the 19th century. When Germany first unified, in 1871, Berlin was its natural capital.

Part 2: From Bebelplatz to Alexanderplatz

• *Starting at Bebelplatz, head to the center of the square, and find the glass window in the pavement. We'll begin with some history and a spin tour.*

⓮ BEBELPLATZ

For centuries, up until the early 1700s, Prussia had been likened to a modern-day Sparta—it was all about its military. Voltaire famously said, "Whereas some states have an army, the Prussian army has a state." But Frederick the Great—who ruled from 1740 to 1786—established Prussia not just as a military power, but also as a cultural and intellectual heavyweight. This square was the center of the cultural capital that Frederick envisioned. His grand palace was just down the street.

Imagine that it's 1760. Pan around the square to see Frederick's contributions to Prussian culture. Everything is draped with Greek-inspired Prussian pomp. Sure, Prussia was a militaristic power. But Frederick also built an "Athens on the Spree"—an enlightened and cultured society.

To visually survey the square, start with the university across the street and spin counterclockwise:

⑮ **Humboldt University,** across Unter den Linden, is one of Europe's greatest. Marx and Lenin (not the brothers or the sisters) studied here, as did the Grimms (both brothers) and more than two dozen Nobel Prize winners. Einstein, who was Jewish, taught here until taking a spot at Princeton in 1932 (smart guy).

Turn 90 degrees to the left to face the former **state library** (labeled *Juristische Fakultät*). Bombed in World War II, the library was rebuilt by the East German government in the original style only because Vladimir Lenin studied law here during much of his exile from Russia. (On the ground floor is Tim's Espressobar, a great little café with light food, student prices, and garden seating.)

The round, Catholic **St. Hedwig's Church,** nicknamed the "upside-down teacup," is a statement of religious and cultural tolerance. The pragmatic Frederick the Great wanted to encourage the integration of Catholic Silesians after his empire annexed their region in 1742, and so the first Catholic church since the Reformation was built in Berlin and dedicated to St. Hedwig, the patron saint of Silesia. Like all Catholic churches in Berlin, St. Hedwig's is not on the street, but stuck in a kind of back lot—indicating inferiority to Protestant churches.

The ⑯ **German State Opera** (Staatsoper) was bombed in 1941, rebuilt in 1943, and bombed again in 1945. It's currently undergoing an extensive renovation.

Now look down through the glass you're standing on: The room of empty bookshelves is a memorial repudiating a notorious Nazi **book burning** on this square. In 1933, staff and students from the university threw 20,000 newly forbidden books (authored by Einstein, Hemingway, Freud, and T. S. Eliot, among others) into a huge bonfire on the orders of the Nazi propaganda minister, Joseph

A plaque and memorial on Bebelplatz mark the site of a Nazi book burning.

Goebbels. Hitler chose this square to thoroughly squash the ideals of culture and enlightenment that characterized the Prussian heritage of Frederick the Great. Instead, he was establishing a new age of intolerance, where Germanness was correct and diversity was evil.

A plaque nearby reminds us of the prophetic quote by the German poet Heinrich Heine. In 1820, he wrote, "Where they burn books, in the end they will also burn people." A century later, his books were among those that went up in flames on this spot.

This monument reminds us of that chilling event in 1933, while also inspiring vigilance against the anti-intellectual scaremongers of today, who would burn the thoughts of people they fear to defend their culture from diversity.

• *Cross Unter den Linden to the university side and head toward the Greek-temple-like building set in the small chestnut-tree-filled park. This is the...*

⓱ NEW GUARDHOUSE

The emperor's former guardhouse (Neue Wache) now holds the nation's main memorial to all "victims of war and tyranny." Look inside, where a replica of the Käthe Kollwitz statue, *Mother with Her Dead Son*, is enshrined in silence. It marks the tombs of Germany's unknown soldier and an unknown concentration camp victim. Read the powerful statement (left of entrance). The memorial, open to the sky, incorporates the elements—sunshine, rain, snow—falling on this modern-day pietà.

Memorial at the New Guardhouse

• *Next to the Neue Wache is Berlin's pink yet formidable Zeughaus (arsenal). Dating from 1695, it's considered the oldest building on the boulevard, and now houses the excellent* ⓲ ***German History Museum****—well worth a visit, and described in detail on page 327.*

Continue across a bridge to reach ⓳ ***Museum Island*** *(Museumsinsel), whose imposing Neoclassical buildings house some of Berlin's most impressive museums (including the Pergamon Museum); for details, see page 324.*

For now, we'll check out a few other landmarks on the island. First is the big, inviting park called the...

⓴ LUSTGARTEN

For 300 years, Museum Island's big central square has flip-flopped between being a military parade ground and a people-friendly park, depending upon the political tenor of the time. During the revolutions of 1848, the Kaiser's troops dispersed a protesting crowd that had assembled here, sending demonstrators onto footpaths. Karl Marx later commented, "It is impossible to have a revolution in a country where people stay off the grass."

Hitler enjoyed giving speeches from the top of the museum steps overlooking this square. In fact, he had the square landscaped to fit his symmetrical tastes and propaganda needs.

In 1999, the Lustgarten was made into a park (read the history posted in the corner opposite the church). On a sunny day, it's packed with people relaxing and is one of Berlin's most enjoyable public spaces.

• *The huge church next to the park is the...*

㉑ BERLIN CATHEDRAL

The century-old Berlin Cathedral (Berliner Dom) wears its bombastic Wilhelmian architecture as a Protestant assertion of strength. It seems to proclaim, "A mighty fortress is our God." The years of Kaiser Wilhelm's rule, from 1888 to 1918, were a busy age of building. Germany had recently been united (1871), and the emperor wanted to give his capital stature and legitimacy. Wilhelm's buildings are over-the-top statements: Neoclassical, Neo-Baroque, and Neo-Renaissance, with stucco and gold-tiled mosaics. This Protestant cathedral is as ornate as if it were Catholic. With the emperor's lead, this sumptuous style came into vogue, and anyone who wanted to be associated with the royal class built this way. (The other big example of Wilhelmian architecture in Berlin is the Reichstag, which we saw earlier.) The church is most impressive from the outside (and there's no way to even peek inside without a pricey ticket).

Inside, the great reformers (Luther, Calvin, and company) stand around the brilliantly restored dome like stern saints guarding their theology. Frederick I (Frederick the Great's gramps) rests in an ornate tomb (right transept, near entrance to dome). The 270-step climb to the outdoor dome gallery is tough but offers pleasant, breezy views of the city at the finish line. The crypt downstairs is not worth a look.

Cost and Hours: €7 includes access to dome gallery, audioguide-€3, Mon-Sat 9:00-20:00, Sun 12:00-20:00, until 19:00 Oct-March, www.berliner-dom.de.

• *Kitty-corner across the main street from the Berlin Cathedral is a huge construction site, known as the...*

㉒ HUMBOLDT-FORUM BERLINER SCHLOSS

For centuries, this was the site of the Baroque palace of the Hohenzollern dynasty of Brandenburg and Prussia. Much of that palace actually survived World War II but was replaced by the communists with a blocky, Soviet-style "Palace" of the Republic—East Berlin's parliament building/entertainment complex and a showy symbol of the communist days. The landmark building fell into disrepair after reunification, and by 2009 had been dismantled.

After much debate about how to use this prime real estate, the German parliament decided to construct the Humboldt-Forum Berliner Schloss, a huge public venue filled with museums, shops, galleries, and concert halls behind a facade constructed in imitation of the

The elegant Berlin Cathedral (flanked by the DDR-era TV Tower)

original Hohenzollern palace. With a €600 million price tag, many Berliners consider the reconstruction plan a complete waste of money. The latest news is that it should be finished by 2019.

In the meantime, the temporary, bright blue **Humboldt-Box** provides info and a viewing platform from which to survey the construction (until it gets in the way and also has to be demolished). Consider popping in for a look at the beautiful model, on the first floor up, showing this area as it was in 1900 (free, daily 10:00-19:00).

• *Head to the bridge just beyond the Berlin Cathedral, with views of the riverbank. Consider...*

STROLLING AND CRUISING THE SPREE RIVER

This river was once a symbol of division—the East German regime put nets underwater to stymie those desperate enough for freedom to swim to the West. With the reunification of Berlin, however, the Spree River has become people-friendly and welcoming. A parklike trail leads from the Berlin Cathedral to the Hauptbahnhof, with impromptu "beachside" beer gardens with imported sand, BBQs in pocket parks, and lots of locals walking their dogs, taking a lazy bike ride, or jogging.

You may notice "don't drop anchor" signs. There are still unexploded WWII bombs in Berlin, and many are in this river. Every month, several bombs are found at construction sites. Their triggers were set for the hard ground of Scottish testing grounds, and because Berlin sits upon soft soil, an estimated one of every ten bombs didn't explode.

Spree River sightseeing boats

The recommended ㉓ **Spree River cruises** depart from the riverbank near the bridge by the Berlin Cathedral (for details, see page 304). Across the river from the cathedral is the interesting ㉔ **DDR Museum** (see page 328).

• *Leaving the bridge, continue walking straight toward the TV Tower, down the big boulevard, which here changes its name to...*

KARL-LIEBKNECHT-STRASSE

The first big building on the left after the bridge is the **Radisson Blu Hotel** and shopping center, with a huge aquarium in the center. The elevator goes right through the middle of a deep-sea world. (You can see it from the unforgettable Radisson hotel lobby—tuck in your shirt and walk past the guards with the confidence of a guest who's sleeping there.) Here in the center of the old communist capital, it seems that capitalism has settled in with a spirited vengeance.

In the park immediately across the street (a big jaywalk from the Radisson) are grandfatherly statues of **Marx** and **Engels** (nicknamed the "old pensioners"). Surrounding them are stainless-steel monoliths with evocative photos illustrating the struggles of the workers of the world.

Farther along, where Karl-Liebknecht-Strasse intersects with Spandauer Strasse, look right to see the red-brick **City Hall.** It was built after the revolutions of 1848 and was arguably the first democratic building in the city.

Continue toward ㉕ **Marien Church** (from 1270), with its spire mirroring the TV Tower. Inside, an artist's rendering helps you follow the interesting but faded old "Dance of Death" mural that wraps around the narthex inside the door.

• *Immediately across the street from the church, detour a half-block down little Rosenstrasse to find a beautiful memorial set in a park.*

㉖ Women's Protest Memorial: This sculpture is a reminder of a successful and courageous protest against Nazi policies. In 1943, when "privileged Jews" (men married to Gentile women) were arrested, their wives demonstrated en masse on this street, where the men were being held in a Jewish community building. They actually won the freedom of their spouses.

• *Back on Karl-Liebknecht-Strasse, look up at the 1,200-foot-tall...*

㉗ TV Tower (Fernsehturm): Built (with Swedish know-how) in 1969 for the 20th anniversary of the communist government, the tower was meant to show the power of the atheistic state at a time when DDR leaders were having the crosses removed from church domes and spires. But when the sun hit the tower—the greatest spire in East Berlin—a huge cross was reflected on the mirrored ball. Cynics called it "God's Revenge." East Berliners dubbed the tower the "Tele-Asparagus." They joked that if it fell over, they'd have an elevator to the West.

The TV Tower punctuates the skyline.

The tower has a fine view from halfway up, offering a handy city orientation and an interesting look at the flat, red-roofed sprawl of Berlin—including a peek inside the city's many courtyards (€13 timed-entry tickets, daily until 24:00). Consider a kitschy trip to the observation deck for the view and lunch in its revolving restaurant (mediocre food, reservations smart for dinner, tel. 030/242-3333, www.tv-turm.de).

• *Walk four more minutes down the boulevard past the TV Tower and toward the big railway overpass. Just before the bridge, on the left, is the half-price ticket booth called* **Hekticket***—stop in to see what's on (for details, see page 343).*

Walk under the train bridge and continue for a long half-block (passing the Galeria Kaufhof mall). Turn right onto a broad pedestrian street, and go through the low tunnel into the big square where blue U-Bahn station signs mark...

㉘ ALEXANDERPLATZ

This square was the commercial pride and joy of East Berlin. The Kaufhof department store was the ultimate shopping mecca for Easterners. It, along with the two big surviving 1920s "functionalist" buildings, defined the square. Alexanderplatz is still a landmark, with a major U-Bahn/S-Bahn station. The once-futuristic, now-retro "World Time Clock," installed in 1969, is a nostalgic favorite and remains a popular meeting point.

Stop in the square for a coffee and to people-watch. You may see the dueling human hot-dog hawkers, who wear ingenious harnesses that let them cook and sell tasty, cheap German sausages on the fly. While the square can get a little rough at night, it's generally a great scene.

• *Our orientation stroll is finished. From here, you can hike back to catch the riverboat tour, visit Museum Island or the German History Museum, or take in the sights south of Unter den Linden.*

SIGHTS

The Reichstag and Nearby

Many of Berlin's top sights and landmarks are in this area, and are described in detail in the self-guided walk above, including the **Brandenburg Gate** (page 309), the **Memorial to the Murdered Jews of Europe** (page 310), and **Unter den Linden** (page 312).

▲▲▲REICHSTAG

Germany's historic parliament building—completed in 1894, burned in 1933, sad and lonely in a no-man's land throughout the Cold War, and finally rebuilt and topped with a glittering glass cupola in 1999—is a symbol of a proudly reunited nation. It's fascinating to climb up the twin ramps that spiral through its dome. Getting in requires a reservation. For more on the building's exterior and its history, see page 305 of the "Best of Berlin Walk."

Cost and Hours: Free, but reservations required—see below, daily 8:00-24:00, last entry at 22:00, no big luggage allowed, Platz der Republik 1; S- or U-Bahn: Friedrichstrasse, Brandenburger Tor, or Bundestag; tel. 030/2273-2152, www.bundestag.de.

Reservations: To visit the dome, you'll need to **reserve online;** spots often book up several days in advance. Go to www.bundestag.de, and from the "Visit the Bundestag" menu, select "Online registration" (be sure to have the names and birthdates of everyone in your party). You must print and bring your reservation with you.

If you're in Berlin without a reservation, try dropping by the tiny visitors center on the Tiergarten side of Scheidemannstrasse, across from Platz der Republik, to see if any tickets are available (open daily 8:00-20:00, until 18:00 Nov-March; go early to avoid lines; you must book no less than 2 hours and no more than 2 days out; your whole party must be present and ID is required).

Another option for visiting the dome, though pricey, is to make lunch or dinner reservations for the rooftop restaurant, Käfer Dachgarten (daily 9:00-16:30 & 18:30-24:00, last access at 22:00, reserve well in advance at tel. 030/2262-9933 or www.feinkost-kaefer.de/berlin).

Getting In: Report a few minutes before your appointed time to the temporary-looking entrance facility in front of the Reichstag, and be ready to show ID and your reservation printout.

Tours: The free **audioguide** (available after you exit the elevator at the base of the dome) explains the building and narrates the view as you wind up the spiral ramp to the top of the dome; the commentary starts automatically as you step onto the bottom of the ramp.

➲ **Self-Guided Tour:** The open, airy lobby towers 100 feet high, with 65-foot-tall colors of the German flag. See-through glass doors show the **central legislative chamber.** The message: There will be no secrets in this government. Look inside. Spreading his wings behind the podium is a stylized German eagle, the *Bundestagsadler* (a.k.a. the "fat hen"), representing the Bundestag (each branch of government has its own symbolic eagle). Notice the doors marked *Ja* (Yes), *Nein* (No), and *Enthalten* (Abstain)...an homage to the Bundestag's traditional "sheep jump" way of counting votes by exiting the chamber through the corresponding door (for critical votes, however, all 631 members vote with electronic cards).

The Reichstag's original facade

Ride the elevator to the base of the glass **dome.** Pick up the free audioguide and take some time to study the photos and read the circle of captions (around the base of the central funnel) for an excellent exhibit telling the Reichstag story. Then study the surrounding architecture: a broken collage of new on old, torn between antiquity and modernity, like Germany's history. Notice the dome's giant and unobtrusive sunscreen that moves as necessary with the sun. Peer down through the skylight to look over the shoulders of the elected representatives at work. For Germans, the best view from here is down—keeping a close eye on their government.

Start at the ramp nearest the elevator and wind up to the top of the **double ramp.** Take a 360-degree survey of the city as you hike: The big park is the **Tiergarten,** the "green lungs of Berlin." Beyond that is the **Teufelsberg** ("Devil's Hill"). Built of rubble from the destroyed city in the late 1940s, it was famous during the Cold War as a powerful ear of the West—notice the telecommunications tower on top.

Find the **Victory Column** (Siegessäule), glimmering in the middle of the park. Hitler moved it in the 1930s from in front of the Reichstag to its present position in the Tiergarten as part of his grandiose vision for postwar Berlin. Next, scenes of the new Berlin spiral into view—**Potsdamer Platz,** marked by the conical glass tower that houses Sony's European headquarters. Continue circling left, and find the green chariot atop the **Brandenburg Gate.** Just to its left is the curving fish-like roof of the **DZ Bank** building, designed by the unconventional American architect Frank Gehry. The **Memorial to the Murdered Jews of Europe** stretches south of the Brandenburg Gate. Next, you'll see **former East Berlin** and the city's next huge construction zone, with a forest of 300-foot-tall skyscrapers in the works. Notice the **TV Tower,** the **Berlin** Cathedral's massive dome, and the golden dome of the **New Synagogue.**

Follow the train tracks in the distance to the left toward Berlin's huge main train station, the **Hauptbahnhof.** Complete your spin-tour with the blocky, postmodern **Chancellery,** the federal government's headquarters. Continue spiraling up. You'll come across all the same sights again, twice, from a higher vantage point.

Inside the Reichstag's glass dome

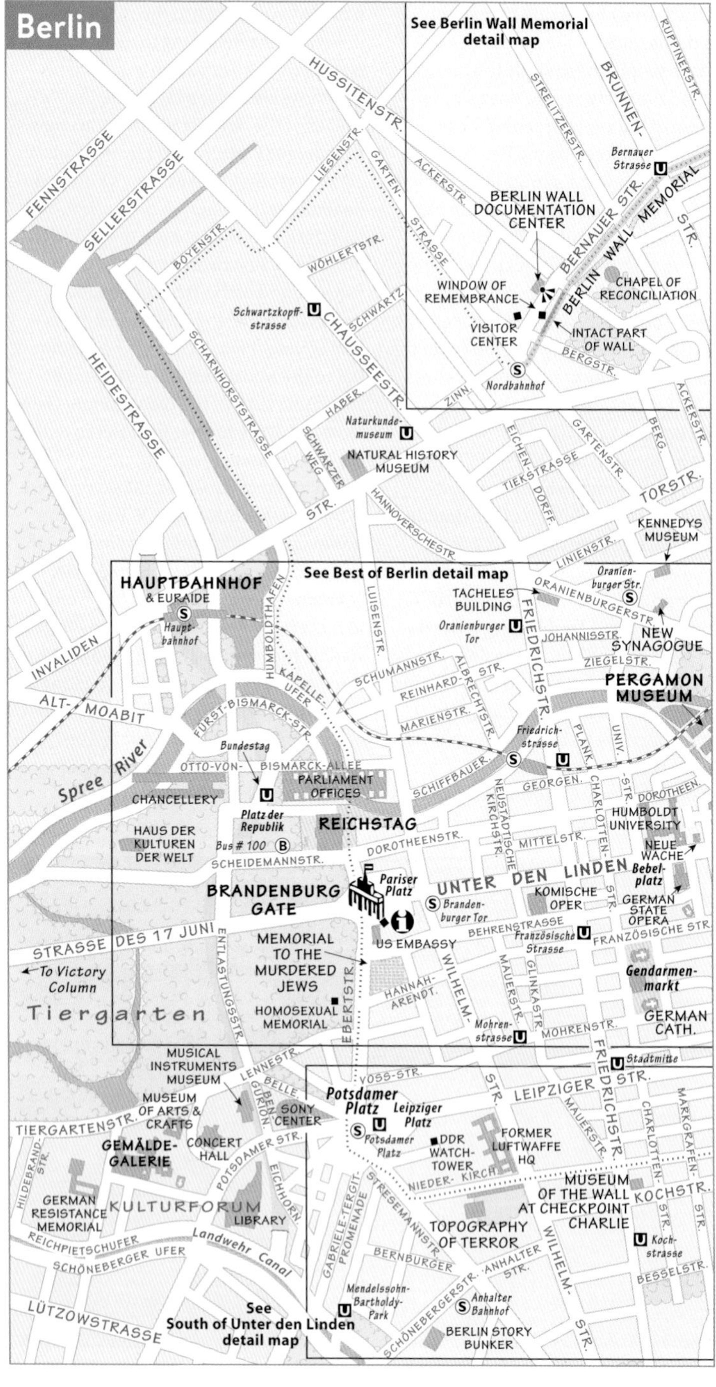
Berlin
See Berlin Wall Memorial detail map
See Best of Berlin detail map
See South of Unter den Linden detail map
HAUPTBAHNHOF & EURAIDE
BRANDENBURG GATE
REICHSTAG
PERGAMON MUSEUM
UNTER DEN LINDEN
BERLIN WALL DOCUMENTATION CENTER
WINDOW OF REMEMBRANCE
VISITOR CENTER
INTACT PART OF WALL
CHAPEL OF RECONCILIATION
BERLIN WALL MEMORIAL
NATURAL HISTORY MUSEUM
KENNEDYS MUSEUM
TACHELES BUILDING
NEW SYNAGOGUE
CHANCELLERY
HAUS DER KULTUREN DER WELT
PARLIAMENT OFFICES
MEMORIAL TO THE MURDERED JEWS
HOMOSEXUAL MEMORIAL
US EMBASSY
HUMBOLDT UNIVERSITY
NEUE WACHE
KOMISCHE OPER
GERMAN STATE OPERA
GERMAN CATH.
Gendarmenmarkt
Bebelplatz
Pariser Platz
To Victory Column
Tiergarten
Spree River
MUSICAL INSTRUMENTS MUSEUM
MUSEUM OF ARTS & CRAFTS
SONY CENTER
GEMÄLDEGALERIE
CONCERT HALL
KULTURFORUM
LIBRARY
GERMAN RESISTANCE MEMORIAL
Potsdamer Platz
Leipziger Platz
DDR WATCHTOWER
FORMER LUFTWAFFE HQ
MUSEUM OF THE WALL AT CHECKPOINT CHARLIE
TOPOGRAPHY OF TERROR
BERLIN STORY BUNKER
Landwehr Canal
Bus # 100
Bernauer Strasse
Nordbahnhof
Schwartzkopffstrasse
Naturkundemuseum
Oranienburger Str.
Oranienburger Tor
Hauptbahnhof
Bundestag
Platz der Republik
Friedrichstrasse
Brandenburger Tor
Französische Strasse
Mohrenstrasse
Stadtmitte
Potsdamer Platz
Mendelssohn-Bartholdy-Park
Anhalter Bahnhof
Kochstrasse
FENNSTRASSE
SELLERSTRASSE
HEIDESTRASSE
SCHARNHORSTSTRASSE
BOYENSTR.
LIESENSTR.
GARTENSTRASSE
HUSSITENSTR.
ACKERSTR.
STRELITZERSTR.
BRUNNENSTR.
RUPPINERSTR.
BERNAUER STR.
BERGSTR.
ZINN.
WÖHLERTSTR.
SCHWARTZ.
CHAUSSEESTR.
HABER.
SCHWARZER WEG
INVALIDENSTR.
HANNOVERSCHESTR.
EICHENDORFF.
TIEKSTRASSE
GARTENSTR.
BERG.
TORSTR.
LINIENSTR.
ORANIENBURGERSTR.
JOHANNISSTR.
ZIEGELSTR.
FRIEDRICHSTR.
LUISENSTR.
HUMBOLDTHAFEN
KAPELLE-UFER
SCHUMANNSTR.
REINHARDTSTR.
ALBRECHTSTR.
MARIENSTR.
ALT-MOABIT
FÜRST-BISMARCK-STR.
OTTO-VON-BISMARCK-ALLEE
SCHIFFBAUERDAMM
NEUSTÄDTISCHE KIRCHSTR.
GEORGENSTR.
PLANK.
UNIV.
CHARLOTTENSTR.
DOROTHEENSTR.
MITTELSTR.
SCHEIDEMANNSTR.
STRASSE DES 17 JUNI
ENTLASTUNGSSTR.
EBERTSTR.
BEHRENSTRASSE
FRANZÖSISCHE STR.
WILHELMSTR.
HANNAH-ARENDT.
MAUERSTR.
GLINKASTR.
MOHRENSTR.
LENNESTR.
BELLEVUESTR.
BEN-GURION
VOSS-STR.
LEIPZIGER STR.
MARKGRAFENSTR.
TIERGARTENSTR.
POTSDAMER STR.
EICHHORN.
HILDEBRANDSTR.
NIEDERKIRCH.
KOCHSTR.
REICHPIETSCHUFER
SCHÖNEBERGER UFER
GABRIELE-TERGIT-PROMENADE
STRESEMANNSTR.
BERNBURGER
ANHALTER STR.
SCHÖNEBERGERSTR.
BESSELSTR.
LÜTZOWSTRASSE

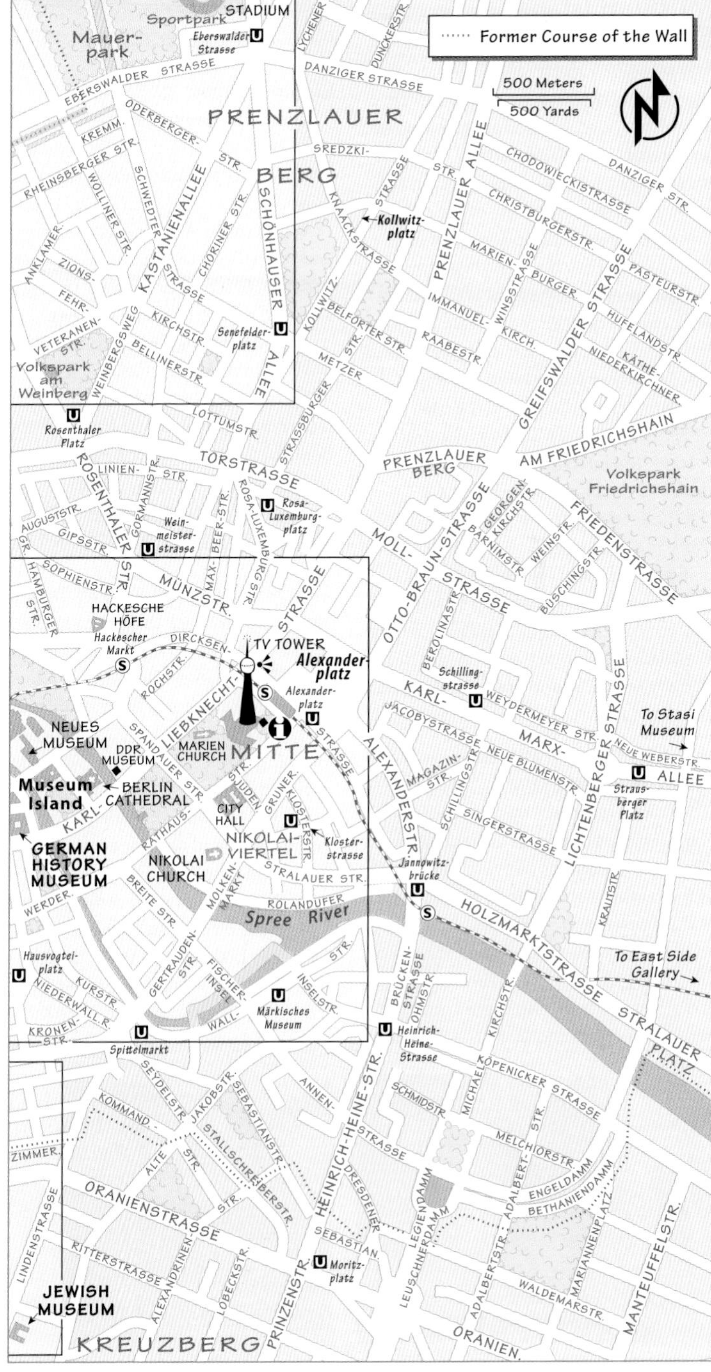

Former Course of the Wall
500 Meters
500 Yards
PRENZLAUER BERG
MITTE
KREUZBERG
TV TOWER
Alexanderplatz
HACKESCHE HÖFE
NEUES MUSEUM
DDR MUSEUM
MARIEN CHURCH
Museum Island
BERLIN CATHEDRAL
CITY HALL
NIKOLAI-VIERTEL
GERMAN HISTORY MUSEUM
NIKOLAI CHURCH
Spree River
JEWISH MUSEUM
Volkspark Friedrichshain
Volkspark am Weinberg
Mauerpark
Sportpark
STADIUM
Kollwitzplatz
To Stasi Museum
To East Side Gallery
Märkisches Museum
KARL-MARX-ALLEE

Museum Island and Nearby

The Museum Island complex began taking shape in the 1840s under King Friedrich Wilhelm IV, who envisioned the island as an oasis of culture and learning. A formidable renovation now under way is transforming the island into one of the grandest museum zones in Europe. In the meantime, pardon their dust. I highlight the top two museums: Pergamon and Neues. Also, two recommended museums flank the island: the German History Museum across the river to the west, and the DDR Museum across the river to the east.

Note that three Museum Island landmarks—the **Lustgarten, Berlin Cathedral,** and the **Humboldt-Box**—are described earlier, in my "Best of Berlin Walk"; see page 316.

Getting There: The nearest S-Bahn station to Museum Island is Hackescher Markt, about a 10-minute walk away. From Prenzlauer Berg, ride tram #M-1 to the end of the line, and you're right at the Pergamon Museum.

▲▲▲PERGAMON MUSEUM (PERGAMONMUSEUM)

The star attraction of this world-class museum, part of Berlin's Collection of Classical Antiquities (Antikensammlung), is the fantastic and gigantic Pergamon Altar...but it—and all Hellenistic artworks in the collection—are off-limits to visitors until 2025, as the museum undergoes a major renovation. But there's much more to see here, including the Babylonian Ishtar Gate (slathered with glazed blue tiles from the sixth century B.C.) and ancient Mesopotamian, Roman, and early Islamic treasures.

Cost and Hours: €12, special exhibits extra, daily 10:00-18:00, until 20:00 on Thu, tel. 030/266-424-242, www.smb.museum.

When to Go: Mornings are busiest, and you're likely to find long lines any time of day on Saturday or Sunday. The least-crowded time is Thursday evening.

Crowd-Beating Tips: Avoid lines for the Pergamon by purchasing a timed ticket online, or book a free timed-entry reservation if you have a Museum Pass Berlin or a Museum Island Pass (www.smb.museum).

Visting the Museum: Make ample use of the superb audioguide (included with admission).

From the entry hall, head up the stairs and all the way back to 575 B.C., to the Fertile Crescent—Mesopotamia (today's Iraq). The Assyrian ruler Nebuchadnezzar II, who amassed a vast empire and enormous wealth, wanted to build a suitably impressive processional entryway to his capital city, Babylon, to honor the goddess Ishtar. His creation, the blue **Ishtar Gate,** inspired awe and obedience in anyone who came to his city. This is a reconstruction, using some original components. The gate itself is embellished with two animals: a bull and a mythical dragon-like combination of lion, cobra, eagle, and scorpion. The long hall leading to the main gate—designed for a huge processional

Ishtar Gate

Market Gate of Miletus

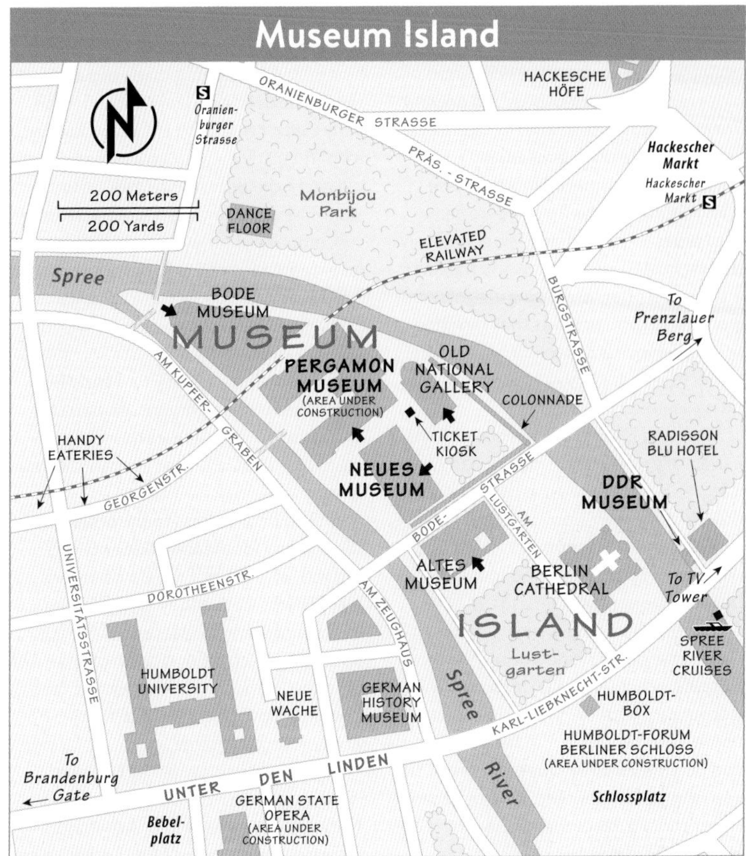

of deities to celebrate the new year—is decorated with a chain of blue and yellow glazed tiles with 120 strolling lions (representing the goddess Ishtar). To get the big picture, find the model of the original site in the center of the hall.

Pass through the gate, and flash-forward 700 years to the ancient Roman city of Miletus. Dominating this room is the 95-foot-wide, 55-foot-high **Market Gate of Miletus,** an ancient Anatolian city destroyed by an earthquake centuries ago and now painstakingly reconstructed here in Berlin. The exquisite mosaic floor from a Roman villa in Miletus has two parts: In the square panel, the musician Orpheus strokes his lyre to charm the animals; in stark contrast, in the nearby rectangular mosaic (from an adjacent room), hunters pursue wild animals.

These main exhibits are surrounded by smaller galleries. Upstairs is the **Museum of Islamic Art.** It contains fine carpets, tile work, the Aleppo Room (with ornately painted wooden walls from an early 17th-century home in today's Syria), and the Mshatta Facade (walls and towers from one of the early eighth-century Umayyad "desert castles," from today's Jordan).

▲▲NEUES (NEW) MUSEUM

Oddly, Museum Island's so-called "new" museum features the oldest stuff around. There are three collections here: the Egyptian Collection (with the famous bust of Queen Nefertiti), the Museum of Prehistory and Early History, and some items from the Collection of Classical Antiquities (artifacts from Cyprus and ancient Troy—famously excavated by German adventurer Heinrich Schliemann).

After being damaged in World War II and sitting in ruins for some 40 years, the Neues Museum has been gorgeously rebuilt. Posted information and the fine audioguide offer fascinating insights into workaday Egyptian life as they describe the vivid papyrus collection, slice-of-life artifacts, and dreamy wax portraits decorating mummy cases.

Cost and Hours: €12, special exhibits extra, daily 10:00-18:00, until 20:00 on Thu, tel. 030/266-424-242, www.neues-museum.de, www.smb.museum.

Visiting the Museum: Pick up a floor plan showing the suggested route, then head up the central staircase.

The top draw here is the Egyptian art—clearly one of the world's best collections. But let's face it: The main reason to visit is to enjoy one of the great thrills in art appreciation—gazing into the still young and beautiful face of Queen Nefertiti. If you're in a pinch for time, make a beeline to her (floor 2, far corner of Egyptian Collection in Room 210).

To tour the whole collection, start at the top (floor 3), which is where you'll find the **prehistory section.** The entire floor is filled with Stone Age, Ice Age, and Bronze Age items. You'll see early human remains, tools, spearheads, and pottery.

The most interesting item on this floor (in corner Room 305) is the tall, cone-head-like **Golden Hat,** made of paper-thin hammered gold leaf. Created by an early Celtic civilization in Central Europe, it's particularly exquisite for something so old (from the Bronze Age, around 1000 B.C.). The circles on the hat represent the sun, moon, and other celestial bodies—leading archaeologists to believe that this headwear could double as a calendar, showing how the sun and moon sync up every 19 years.

Down on floor 2, you'll find **early history** exhibits on migrations, barbarians, and ancient Rome, as well as a fascinating look at the Dark Ages after the fall of Rome.

Still on floor 2, cross to the other side of the building for the **Egyptian** section. On the way, you'll pass through the impressive Papyrus Collection—a large room of seemingly empty glass cases. Press a button to watch a 3,000-year-old piece of primitive "paper" (made of aquatic reeds), imprinted with primitive text, trundle out of its protective home.

Then, finally, in a room all her own, is the 3,000-year-old bust of **Queen Nefertiti** (the wife of King Akhenaton, c. 1340 B.C.)—the most famous piece of Egyptian art in Europe. (She's had it with the paparazzi—photos of her are strictly *verboten*.) Called "Berlin's most beautiful woman," Nefertiti has all the right beauty marks: long neck, symmetrical face, and the perfect amount of makeup. And yet,

Neues Museum

Queen Nefertiti

she's not completely idealized. Notice the fine wrinkles that show she's human (though these only enhance her beauty). Like a movie star discreetly sipping a glass of wine at a sidewalk café, Nefertiti seems somehow more dignified in person. The bust never left its studio, but served as a master model for all other portraits of the queen. (That's probably why the left eye was never inlaid.) Stare at her long enough, and you may get the sensation that she's winking at you. Hey, beautiful!

▲▲▲GERMAN HISTORY MUSEUM (DEUTSCHES HISTORISCHES MUSEUM)

This fantastic museum, which sits across the river west of Museum Island, is a two-part affair: the pink former Prussian arsenal building and the I. M. Pei-designed annex. The main building (fronting Unter den Linden) houses the permanent collection, offering the best look at German history under one roof, anywhere. The modern annex features good temporary exhibits surrounded by the work of a great contemporary architect. This thoughtfully presented museum—with more than 8,000 artifacts telling not just the story of Berlin, but of all Germany—is clearly the top history museum in town. If you need a break during your visit, there's a restful café with terrace seating in season.

Cost and Hours: €8, excellent €3 audioguide, daily 10:00-18:00, Unter den Linden 2, tel. 030/2030-4751, www.dhm.de.

Getting In: If the ticket-buying line is long at the main entrance, try circling around the back to the Pei annex (to reach it, head down the street to the left of the museum—called Hinter dem Giesshaus), where entry lines are usually shorter (but audioguides for the permanent exhibit are available only at the main desk).

Visiting the Museum: The permanent collection packs two huge rectangular floors of the old arsenal building with historical objects, photographs, and models. From the lobby, head upstairs to the **first floor** and work your way chronologically down. This floor traces German history from A.D. 500 to 1918, with exhibits on early cultures, the Middle Ages, Reformation, Thirty Years' War, German Empire, and World War I. You'll see lots of models of higgledy-piggledy medieval towns and castles, tapestries, suits of armor, busts of great Germans, a Turkish tent from the Ottoman siege of Vienna (1683), flags from German unification in 1871 (the first time "Germany" existed as a nation), exhibits on everyday life in the tenements of the Industrial Revolution, and much more.

History marches on through the 20th century on the **ground floor,** including the Weimar Republic, Nazism, World War II, Allied occupation, and a divided Germany. Propaganda posters trumpet Germany's would-be post-WWI savior, Adolf Hitler. Look for the model of the impossibly huge, 950-foot-high, 180,000-capacity domed hall Hitler wanted to erect in

Exhibits at the German History Museum are comprehensive and thought-provoking.

the heart of Berlin, which he planned to re-envision as Welthauptstadt Germania, the "world capital" of his far-reaching Third Reich. Another model shows the nauseating reality of Hitler's grandiosity: a crematorium at Auschwitz-Birkenau concentration camp in occupied Poland. The exhibit wraps up with chunks of the Berlin Wall, reunification, and a quick look at Germany today.

For architecture buffs, the big attraction is the **Pei annex** behind the history museum, which complements the permanent collection with temporary exhibits. From the old building, cross through the courtyard (with the Pei glass canopy overhead) to reach the annex. A striking glassed-in spiral staircase unites four floors with surprising views and lots of light. It's here that you'll experience why Pei—famous for his glass pyramid at Paris' Louvre—is called the "perfector of classical modernism," "master of light," and a magician at uniting historical buildings with new ones.

▲▲DDR MUSEUM

The exhibits offer an interesting look at life in the former East Germany without the negative spin most museums give. It's well-stocked with kitschy everyday items from the communist period, plus photos, video clips, and concise English explanations. The exhibits are interactive—you're encouraged to pick up and handle anything that isn't behind glass. The reconstructed communist-era home lets you tour the kitchen, living room, and bedrooms. You'll crawl through a Trabant car (East German's answer to the West's popular VW Beetle) and pick up some DDR-era black humor ("East Germany had 39 newspapers, four radio stations, two TV channels...and one opinion").

Cost and Hours: €7, daily 10:00-20:00, Sat until 22:00, just across the Spree from Museum Island at Karl-Liebknecht-Strasse 1, tel. 030/847-123-731, www.ddr-museum.de.

South of Unter den Linden

▲▲GENDARMENMARKT

This delightful, historic square is bounded by twin churches, a tasty chocolate shop, and the Berlin Symphony's concert hall. In summer, it hosts a few outdoor cafés, Biergartens, and sometimes concerts. Wonderfully symmetrical, the square is considered by Berliners to be the finest in town (U6: Französische Strasse; U2 or U6: Stadtmitte; for nearby eateries, see page 345).

The name of the square, which is part French and part German (after the *Gens d'Armes*, Frederick the Great's royal guard, who were headquartered here), reminds us that in the 17th century, a fifth of all Berliners were French émigrés—Protestant Huguenots fleeing Catholic France. Back then, Frederick the Great's tolerant Prussia was a magnet for the persecuted (and their money). These émigrés vitalized Berlin with new ideas, practical knowledge, and their deep pockets.

The church on the south end of the square (left of the concert hall) is the **German Cathedral** (Deutscher Dom). This cathedral was bombed flat in the war and rebuilt only in the 1980s. It houses the thought-provoking "Milestones, Setbacks, Sidetracks" (*Wege, Irrwege, Umwege*) exhibit, which traces the history of the German parliamentary system—worth ▲. While light on actual historical artifacts, the well-done exhibit takes you quickly from the revolutionary days of 1848 to the

Gendarmenmarkt

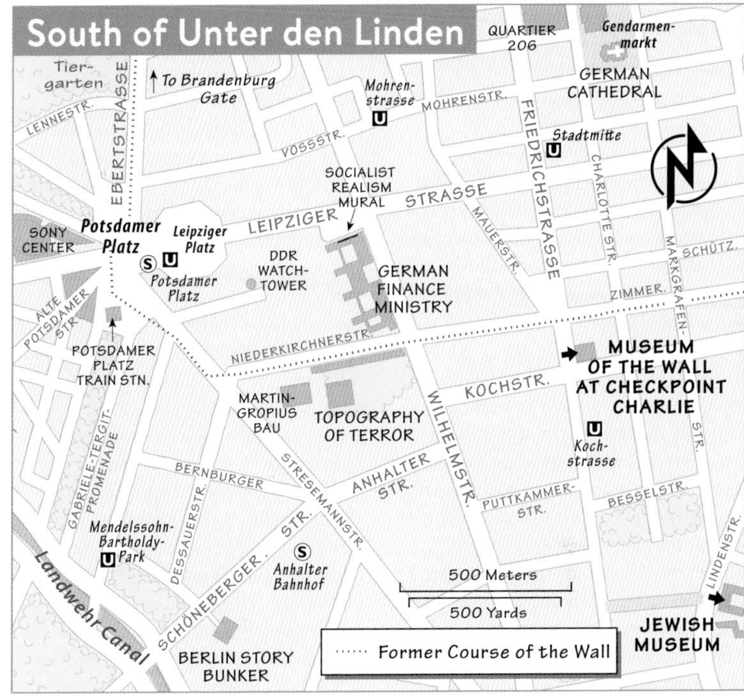

1920s, and then more deeply through the tumultuous 20th century (free, Tue-Sun 10:00-19:00, Oct-April until 18:00, closed Mon year-round).

The **French Cathedral** (Französischer Dom), at the north end of the square, offers a viewpoint from the dome up top (€3, daily 10:00-18:00, until 17:30 in Nov-March, 244 steps, enter through door facing square, tel. 030/203-060, www.franzoesischer-dom.de).

Fun fact: Neither church is a true cathedral, as they never contained a bishop's throne; their German titles of *Dom* (cathedral) are actually a mistranslation from the French word *dôme* (cupola).

Fassbender & Rausch, on the corner near the German Cathedral, claims to be Europe's biggest chocolate store. After 150 years of chocolate-making, this family-owned business proudly displays its sweet delights—250 different kinds—on a 55-foot-long buffet. The window displays feature giant chocolate models of Berlin landmarks—Reichstag, Brandenburg Gate, a chunk of the Wall, and so on. If all this isn't enough to entice you, I have three words: erupting chocolate volcano. Upstairs is an elegant hot-chocolate café with fine views (Mon-Sat 10:00-20:00, Sun from 11:00, corner of Mohrenstrasse at Charlottenstrasse 60, tel. 030/757-882-440).

▲▲TOPOGRAPHY OF TERROR (TOPOGRAPHIE DES TERRORS)

This patch of land was once the nerve center for the Gestapo and the SS, the most despicable elements of the Nazi government. It's chilling to see just how seamlessly and bureaucratically the Nazi institutions and state structures merged to become a well-oiled terror machine. There are few actual artifacts here; it's mostly written explanations and photos, like reading a good textbook standing up. And, while you could read this story anywhere, to take this in atop the Gestapo headquarters is a powerful experience. The exhibits, sited indoors and out, are dense, but WWII historians (even armchair ones) will find it fascinating.

Cost and Hours: Free, includes audioguide for outdoor exhibit, daily 10:00-20:00, outdoor exhibit closes at dusk and in winter, Niederkirchnerstrasse 8, U-Bahn: Potsdamer Platz or Kochstrasse, S-Bahn: Anhalter Bahnhof or Potsdamer Platz, tel. 030/254-5090, www.topographie.de.

Background: This location marks what was once the most feared address in Berlin: the headquarters of the Reich Main Security Office (*Reichssicherheitshauptamt*). These offices served as the engine room of the Nazi dictatorship, as well as the command center of the SS (*Schutzstaffel*, whose members began as Hitler's personal bodyguards), the Gestapo (*Geheime Staatspolizei*, secret state police), and the SD (*Sicherheitsdienst*, the Nazi intelligence agency). This trio (and others) were ultimately consolidated under Heinrich Himmler to become a state-within-a-state, with talons in every corner of German society. It was from these headquarters that the Nazis administered concentration camps, firmed up plans for their genocide of Jews, and organized the domestic surveillance of anyone opposed to the regime. The building was also equipped with dungeons, where the Gestapo detained and tortured thousands of prisoners.

Visiting the Museum: Start your visit inside, with the extensive **Topography of Terror** exhibit, which walks you through the evolution of Hitler's regime: the Nazi takeover; institutions of terror (Himmler's "SS State"); terror, persecution, and extermination; atrocities in Nazi-occupied countries; and the war's end and postwar. Some images here are indelible, such as photos of SS soldiers stationed at Auschwitz gleefully yukking it up on a retreat in the countryside (as their helpless prisoners were being gassed and burned a few miles away). The exhibit profiles specific members of the various reprehensible SS branches, as well as the groups they targeted: Jews; Roma and Sinti (Gypsies); the unemployed or homeless; homosexuals; and the physically and mentally ill (considered "useless eaters" who consumed resources without contributing work).

Some exhibits at the Topography of Terror are incorporated into a surviving stretch of the Berlin Wall.

Outside, you'll find the exhibit **Berlin 1933-1945: Between Propaganda and Terror** (ask at the information desk inside for the accompanying audioguide). The chronological survey begins with the post-WWI Weimar Republic and continues through the ragged days just after World War II. One display explains how Nazis invented holidays (or injected new Aryan meaning into existing ones) as a means of winning over the public. Other exhibits cover the "Aryanization" of Jewish businesses (they were simply taken over by the state and handed over to new Aryan owners); Hitler's plans for converting Berlin into a gigantic "Welthauptstadt (World Capital) Germania"; and the postwar Berlin Airlift, which brought provisions to some 2.2 million West Berliners whose supply lines were cut off by East Berlin.

Surviving stretches of the Wall are rare in downtown Berlin, but you'll find an **original fragment** of it here (also visible from Niederkirchnerstrasse).

▲CHECKPOINT CHARLIE

This famous Cold War checkpoint was not named for a person, but for its checkpoint number—as in Alpha (#1, at the East-West German border, 100 miles west of here), Bravo (#2, as you enter Berlin proper), and Charlie (#3, the best known because most foreigners passed through here). While the actual checkpoint has long since been dismantled, its former location is home to a fine museum and a mock-up of the original border crossing. The area has become a Cold War freak show and—as if celebrating the final victory of crass capitalism—is one of Berlin's worst tourist traps. A McDonald's stands defiantly overlooking the former haunt of East German border guards. (For a more sober and intellectually redeeming look at the Wall's history, head for the Berlin Wall Memorial at Bernauer Strasse, described on page 340.)

Checkpoint Charlie

The rebuilt **guard station** now hosts two actors playing American guards who pose for photos. Notice the larger-than-life **posters** of a young American soldier facing east and a young Soviet soldier facing west. (Look carefully at the "Soviet" soldier. He was photographed in 1999, a decade after there were Soviet soldiers stationed here. He's a Dutch model. His uniform is a nonsensical pile of pins and ribbons with a Russian flag on his shoulder.)

A few yards away (on Zimmerstrasse), a **glass panel** describes the former checkpoint. From there, another double row of **cobbles** in Zimmerstrasse shows the former path of the Wall. A **photo exhibit** stretches up and down Zimmerstrasse, telling the story of the Wall.

Warning: Here and in other places, hustlers charge an exorbitant €10 for a full set of Cold War-era stamps in your passport. Don't be tempted. Technically, this invalidates your passport—which has caused some tourists big problems.

Cost and Hours: Free and always open, Friedrichstrasse 43, near the intersection with Zimmerstrasse, U-Bahn: Kochstrasse or Stadtmitte.

▲▲MUSEUM OF THE WALL AT CHECKPOINT CHARLIE (MAUERMUSEUM HAUS AM CHECKPOINT CHARLIE)

While the famous border checkpoint between the American and Soviet sectors is long gone, its memory is preserved by one of Europe's most cluttered museums. During the Cold War, the House at Checkpoint Charlie stood defiantly—within spitting distance of the border

The Berlin Wall (and Its Fall)

The East German government erected the 96-mile-long Wall almost overnight in 1961. It was intended to stop the outward flow of people from the communist East to the capitalist West: Three million souls had leaked out between 1949 and 1961.

The Wall *(Mauer)* was actually two walls, with a no-man's-land in-between. During the 28 years it stood, there were 5,043 documented successful escapes (565 of these were East German guards). At least 138 people died or were killed at the Wall while trying to escape.

As a tangible symbol for the Cold War, the Berlin Wall got a lot of attention from politicians. Two of the 20th century's most repeated presidential quotes were uttered within earshot of the Wall. In 1963, President John F. Kennedy professed American solidarity with the struggling people of Berlin: "*Ich bin ein Berliner.*" In 1987, with the winds of change already blowing westward from Moscow, President Ronald Reagan issued an ultimatum to his Soviet counterpart: "Mr. Gorbachev, tear down this wall."

The actual fall of the Wall had less to do with presidential proclamations than with the obvious failings of the Soviet system, a general thawing in Moscow, the brave civil disobedience of ordinary citizens behind the Wall—and a bureaucratic snafu.

By November 1989, change was in the air. Hungary had already opened its borders to the West that summer, making it impossible for East German authorities to keep people in. Anti-regime protests swept nearby Leipzig, attracting hundreds of thousands of supporters. A rally in East Berlin's Alexanderplatz on November 4—with a half-million protesters chanting, "*Wir wollen raus!*" (We want out!)—persuaded the East German politburo to begin gradually relaxing travel restrictions.

The DDR intended to crack the door to the West, but an unknowing spokesman inadvertently threw it wide open. In back-room meetings early on November 9, officials decided they would allow a few more Easterners to cross into the West. The politburo members then left town for a long weekend. The announcement of the decision was left to Günter Schabowski, who knew only what was on a piece of paper handed to him moments before a routine press conference. At 18:54, Schabowski read the statement on live TV, with little emotion: "exit via border crossings...possible for every citizen." Reporters, unable to believe what they were hearing, prodded him about when the borders would open. Schabowski shrugged and offered his best guess: "*Ab sofort, unverzüglich.*" ("Immediately, without delay.")

Schabowski's words spread like wildfire. East Berliners showed up at Wall checkpoints, demanding that border guards let them pass. Finally, around 23:30, a border guard at the Bornholmer Strasse crossing decided to open the gates. Easterners flooded into the West, embracing their long-separated cousins, unable to believe their good fortune. Once open, the Wall could never be closed again. After that wild night, Berlin faced a fitful transition to reunification. Two cities—and countries—became one at a staggering pace.

guards—showing off all the clever escapes over, under, and through the Wall. Today, while the drama is over and hunks of the Wall stand like trophies at its door, the museum survives as a living artifact of the Cold War days. The yellowed descriptions, which have scarcely changed since that time, tinge the museum with nostalgia. It's dusty, disorganized, and overpriced, with lots of reading involved, but all that just adds to this museum's borderline-kitschy charm. If you're pressed for time, visit after dinner, when most other museums are closed.

Cost and Hours: €12.50, €3.50 audioguide, daily 9:00-22:00, U6 to Kochstrasse or U2 to Stadtmitte, Friedrichstrasse 43, tel. 030/253-7250, www.mauermuseum.de.

Visiting the Museum: Exhibits narrate a gripping history of the Wall, with a focus on the many ingenious **escape attempts** (the early years—with a cruder wall—saw more escapes). You'll see the actual items used to smuggle would-be escapees: a VW bug whose trunk hid a man, two side-by-side suitcases into which a woman squeezed, a makeshift zip line for crossing over the border, a hot-air balloon in which two families floated to safety, an inflatable boat that puttered across the dangerous Baltic Sea, primitive homemade aircraft, two surfboards hollowed out to create just enough space for a refugee, and more. One chilling exhibit lists some 43,000 people who died in "Internal Affairs" internment camps during the transition to communism (1945-1950). Profiles personalize various escapees and their helpers, including John P. Ireland, an American who posed as an eccentric antiques collector so he could transport 10 refugees to safety in his modified Cadillac.

Museum of the Wall at Checkpoint Charlie

▲▲JEWISH MUSEUM BERLIN (JÜDISCHES MUSEUM BERLIN)

This museum surveys the rich and complicated history of Jews in Germany. The highly conceptual building is a sight in itself, and the museum inside is excellent, particularly if you take advantage of the informative and engaging audioguide. Rather than just reading dry texts, you'll feel this museum as fresh and alive—an exuberant celebration of the Jewish experience that's accessible to all.

Cost and Hours: €8, recommended €3 audioguide, daily 10:00-20:00, Mon until 22:00, last entry one hour before closing, closed on Jewish holidays, Lindenstrasse 9, tel. 030/2599-3300, www.jmberlin.de.

Getting There: Take the U-Bahn to Hallesches Tor, find the exit marked *Jüdisches Museum*, exit straight ahead, then turn right on Franz-Klühs-Strasse. The museum is a five-minute walk ahead on your left.

Eating: The museum's restaurant, Café Schmus, offers good meals in a pleasant setting.

Visiting the Museum: Designed by American architect Daniel Libeskind (the master planner for the redeveloped World Trade Center in New York), the zinc-walled building has a zigzag shape pierced by voids symbolic of the irreplaceable cultural loss caused by the Holocaust.

Enter the 18th-century Baroque building next door, then go through an underground tunnel to reach the museum interior.

Before you reach the exhibit, your visit starts with three **memorial spaces.** Follow the Axis of Exile to a disorienting slanted garden with 49 pillars (evocative of the Memorial to the Murdered Jews of Europe, across town). Next, the Axis of Holocaust, lined with artifacts from Jews imprisoned and murdered by the Nazis, leads to an eerily empty tower shut off from the outside world. The Axis of Continuity takes you to stairs and the main exhibit. A detour partway up the long stairway leads to the Memory Void, a compelling space of "fallen leaves": heavy metal faces that you walk on, making unhuman noises with each step.

Finish climbing the stairs to the top of the museum, and stroll chronologically through the 2,000-year **story of Judaism** in Germany. The exhibit, on two floors, is engaging, with lots of actual artifacts. Interactive bits (you can, for example, spell your name in Hebrew, or write a prayer and hang it from a tree) make it lively for kids.

The top floor focuses on everyday life in **Ashkenaz** (medieval German-Jewish lands). On the middle floor, exhibits detail the rising tide of anti-Semitism in Germany through the 19th century—at a time when many Jews were so secularized that they celebrated Christmas right along with Hanukkah. The exhibit segues into the **dark days** of Hitler—the collapse of the relatively tolerant Weimar Republic, the rise of the Nazis, and the horrific night of November 9, 1938, when, throughout Germany, hateful mobs destroyed Jewish-owned businesses, homes, synagogues, and even entire villages—called "Crystal Night" (Kristallnacht) for the broken glass that glittered in the streets.

The display brings us to the present day, with the question: How do you keep going after six million of your people have been murdered? You'll see how German society reacted to the two largest Nazi trials, complete with historical film clips of the perpetrators. In the last segment, devoted to Jewish life today, German Jews describe their experiences growing up in the postwar years.

The Jewish Museum's fractured facade suggests the dislocation of the Holocaust.

Kulturforum Complex

The Kulturforum, off the southeast corner of Tiergarten park, hosts Berlin's concert hall and several sprawling museums, but only the Gemäldegalerie is a must for art lovers.

▲▲GEMÄLDEGALERIE

Literally the "Painting Gallery," the Gemäldegalerie is Germany's top collection of medieval and Renaissance European paintings (more than 1,400 canvases). They're beautifully displayed in a building that's a work of art in itself. If you're short on time or stamina, start in the North Wing galleries holding Northern European masterworks by Cranach, Dürer, Van Eyck, Brueghel, Rubens, Van Dyck, Hals, and Vermeer (to name just a few). You'll also encounter an impressive stash of Rembrandts. The South Wing is saved for the Italians—Giotto, Botticelli, Titian, Raphael, and Caravaggio.

Cost and Hours: €10, Tue-Fri 10:00-18:00, Thu until 20:00, Sat-Sun 11:00-18:00, closed Mon, audioguide included with entry, great salad bar in cafeteria upstairs, Matthäikirchplatz 4, tel. 030/266-424-242, www.smb.museum.

Getting There: Ride the S-Bahn or U-Bahn to Potsdamer Platz, then walk along Potsdamer Platz.

Holbein the Younger, The Merchant Georg Gisze

➲ Self-Guided Tour: I'll point out a few highlights, focusing on Northern European artists (German, Dutch, and Flemish), with a few Spaniards and Italians thrown in. To go beyond my selections, make ample use of the excellent audioguide.

The collection spreads out on one vast floor surrounding a central hall. Inner rooms have Roman numerals (I, II, III), while adjacent outer rooms are numbered (1, 2, 3).

Rooms I-III/1-4 kick things off with early German paintings (13th-16th century). In Room 1, look for the 1532 portrait of wealthy Hanseatic cloth merchant Georg Gisze by **Hans Holbein the Younger** (1497-1543). Gisze's name appears on several of the notes stuck to the wall behind him. And, typical of detail-rich Northern European art, the canvas is bursting with highly symbolic tidbits. Items scattered on the tabletop and on the shelves behind the merchant represent his lofty status and aspects of his life story. In the vase, the carnation represents his recent engagement, and the herbs symbolize his virtue. And yet, the celebratory flowers have already begun to fade and the scales behind him are unbalanced, reminders of the fleetingness of happiness and wealth.

In Room 2 are fine portraits by the remarkably talented **Albrecht Dürer** (1471-1528), who traveled to Italy during the burgeoning days of the early Renaissance and melded the artistic harmony and classical grandeur he discovered there with a Northern European attention to detail. In his *Portrait of Hieronymus Holzschuher* (1526), Dürer skillfully captured the personality of a friend from Nürnberg, right down to the sly twinkle in his sidelong glance. Technically, the portrait is perfection: Look closely and see each individual hair of the man's beard and fur coat, and even the reflection of the studio's windows in his eyes. Also notice

Dürer's little pyramid-shaped, D-inside-A signature. Signing one's work was a revolutionary assertion of Dürer's renown at a time when German artists were considered anonymous craftsmen.

Lucas Cranach the Elder (1472-1553), whose works are in Room III, was a court painter for the prince electors of Saxony and a close friend of Martin Luther (and his unofficial portraitist). But *The Fountain of Youth* (1546) is a far cry from Cranach's solemn portrayals of the reformer. Old women helped to the fountain (on the left) emerge as young ladies on the right. Newly nubile, the women go into a tent to dress up, snog with noblemen in the bushes (right foreground), dance merrily beneath the trees, and dine grandly beneath a landscape of phallic mountains and towers. This work is flanked by Cranach's Venus nudes. I sense a pattern here.

Dutch painters (Rooms IV-VI/4-7) were early adopters of oil paint (as opposed to older egg tempera)—its relative ease of handling allowed them to brush the fine details for which they became famous. **Rogier van der Weyden** (Room IV) was a virtuoso of the new medium. In *Portrait of a Woman* (c. 1400-1464), the subject wears a typical winged bonnet, addressing the viewer directly with her fetching blue eyes. In the same room is a remarkable, rare trio of three-panel altarpieces by Van der Weyden: The Marienaltar shows the life of the Virgin Mary; the Johannesaltar narrates the life of John the Baptist—his birth, baptizing Christ (with God and the Holy Spirit hovering overhead), and his gruesome death by decapitation; and the Middelburger Altar tells the story of the Nativity. Savor the fine details in each panel of these altarpieces.

Flash forward a few hundred years to the 17th century and Flemish (Belgian) painting (Rooms VII-VIII/9-10), and it's apparent how much the Protestant Reformation—and resulting Counter-Reformation—changed the tenor of Northern European art. In works by **Peter Paul Rubens** (1577-1640)—including *Jesus Giving Peter the Keys to Heaven*—calm, carefully studied, detail-oriented seriousness gives way to an exuberant Baroque trumpeting of the greatness of the Catholic Church. In the Counter-Reformation world, the Catholic Church had serious competition for the hearts and minds of its congregants. Exciting art like this became a way to keep people in the pews. In the next rooms (VIII and 9) are more Rubens, including the mythological *Perseus Freeing Andromeda* and *The Martyrdom of St. Sebastian by Arrows* (loosely based on a more famous rendition by Andrea Mantegna).

Dutch painting from the 17th century (Rooms IX-XI/10-19) is dominated by the convivial portraits by **Frans Hals** (c. 1582-1666). His 1620 portrait of Catharina Hooft (far corner, Room 13) presents a startlingly self-possessed baby (the newest member of a wealthy merchant family) dressed with all the finery of a queen, adorned with lace and jewels, and clutching a golden rattle. The smiling nurse supporting the tyke offers her a piece of fruit, whose blush of red perfectly matches the nanny's apple-fresh cheeks.

But the ultimate Dutch master is **Rembrandt van Rijn** (1606-1669), whose powers of perception and invention propelled him to fame in his lifetime. Displayed here are several storytelling scenes (Room 16), mostly from classical mythology or biblical stories, all employing Rembrandt's trademark chiaroscuro technique (with a strong contrast between light and dark). In *The Rape of Persephone,* Pluto grabs Persephone from his chariot and races toward the underworld, while other goddesses cling to her robe, trying to save her. In the nearby *Samson and Delilah* (1628), Delilah cradles Samson's head in her lap while silently signaling to a goon to shear Samson's hair, the secret to his strength. A self-portrait (Room X) of a 28-year-old

Rembrandt wearing a beret is paired with the come-hither 1637 *Portrait of Hendrickje Stoffels* (the two were romantically linked). *Samson Threatens His Father-in-Law* (1635) captures the moment just after the mighty Samson (with his flowing hair, elegant robes, and shaking fist) has been told by his wife's father to take a hike. I wouldn't want to cross this guy.

Although **Johannes Vermeer** (1632-1675) is today just as admired as Rembrandt, he was little known in his day, probably because he painted relatively few works for a small circle of Delft collectors. Vermeer was a master at conveying a complicated story through a deceptively simple scene with a few poignant details—whether it's a woman reading a letter at a window, a milkmaid pouring milk from a pitcher into a bowl, or (as in *The Glass of Wine*, Room 18) a young man offering a drink to a young lady. The young man had been playing her some music on his lute (which now sits, discarded, on a chair) and is hoping to seal the deal with some alcohol. The woman is finishing one glass of wine, and her would-be suitor stands ready—almost *too* ready—to pour her another. Vermeer has perfectly captured the exact moment of "Will she or won't she?"

Shift south to Italian, French, and Spanish painting of the 17th and 18th centuries (Rooms XII-XIV/23-28). Venetian cityscapes by Canaletto (who also painted Dresden) and lots of bombastic Baroque art hang in Room XII. Room XIII features big-name Spanish artists Murillo, Zurbarán, and the great **Diego Velázquez** (1599-1660). He gave the best of his talents to his portraits, capturing warts-and-all likenesses that are effortlessly real. His 1630 *Portrait of a Lady* conveys the subject's subtle, sly Mona Lisa smile. Her figure and face (against a dull gray background) are filtered through a pleasant natural light.

From here, the collection itself takes a step backwards—into Italian paintings

A *Van der Weyden,* Portrait of a Woman

B *Rubens,* Jesus Giving Peter the Keys to Heaven

C *Rembrandt,* Self-Portrait with a Velvet Beret

D *Vermeer,* The Glass of Wine

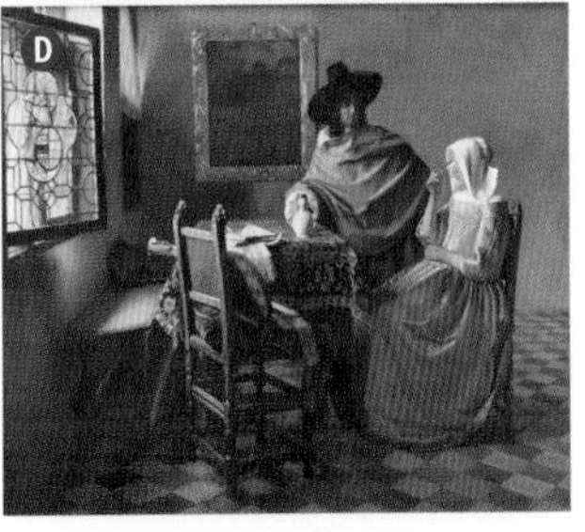

of the 13th-16th century (Rooms XV-XVIII/29-41). This section includes some lesser-known works by great Italian Renaissance painters, including Raphael (Rooms XVII and 29, with five different Madonnas, among them the *Terranuova Madonna,* in a round frame) and Sandro Botticelli (Room XVIII).

Across the Spree River

Several interesting, lively neighborhoods lie in a cluster across the river, just north of Museum Island (and easily accessed by the island's bridges and public transit): Hackescher Markt (with fun shops and fine little museums), Oranienburger Strasse (New Synagogue, eateries, and nightlife), and Prenzlauer Berg (Berlin Wall Memorial, eateries, accommodations, and more nightlife).

As you wander through the neighborhoods, you might notice small brass plaques in the sidewalk called *Stolpersteine,* marking the former homes of Jewish and other WWII victims of the Nazis.

Hackescher Markt

On a sunny day, a stroll (or tram ride) through this bursting-with-life area can be as engaging as any museum in town. Located in front of the S-Bahn station of the same name, this is a great people scene day and night. The brick trestle supporting the train track is a classic example of the city's Brandenburg Neo-Gothic brickwork. Most of the brick archways are now filled with hip shops. Within 100 yards of the S-Bahn station, you'll find Turkish and Bavarian restaurants, walking-tour and pub-crawl departure points, and tram #M1 to Prenzlauer Berg. Also nearby are two great examples of Berlin's traditional courtyards *(Höfe)*—one trendy and modern, the other retro-cool, with two fascinating museums.

HACKESCHE HÖFE

A block from the Hackescher Markt S-Bahn station (at Rosenthaler Strasse 40) is a series of eight courtyards bunny-hopping through a wonderfully restored 1907 *Jugendstil* (German Art Nouveau) building. Berlin's apartments are organized like this—courtyard after courtyard leading off the main road. This complex is full of artsy designer shops, popular restaurants, theaters, and cinemas. Courtyard #5 is particularly charming, with a children's park, and an Ampelmann store (see page 343). This courtyard system is a wonderful example of how to make huge city blocks livable. Two decades after the Cold War, this area has reached the final evolution of East Berlin's urban restoration: total gentrification. These courtyards also offer a useful lesson for visitors: Much of Berlin's charm hides off the street front.

HAUS SCHWARZENBERG

Next door (at Rosenthaler Strasse 39), this courtyard has a totally different feel. Owned by an artists' collective, it comes with a bar, cinema, open-air art space, and the basement-level "Dead Chickens" gallery (with far-out hydro-powered art). And within this amazing little zone you'll find two inspirational museums.

The **Museum of Otto Weidt's Workshop for the Blind** (Museum Blindenwerkstatt Otto Weidt) vividly tells the amazing story of a Berliner heroically protecting blind and deaf Jews during World War II (free, daily 10:00-20:00). Otto Weidt employed them to produce brooms and brushes, and because that was useful for the Nazi war machine, he managed to

New Synagogue

finagle a special status for his workers. You can see the actual brushmaking factory with pedal-powered machines still lined up. The **Silent Heroes Memorial Center** (Gedenkstätte Stille Helden) is a well-presented exhibit celebrating the quietly courageous individuals who resisted the persecution of the Jews from 1933 to 1945 (free, daily 10:00-20:00).

Oranienburger Strasse

Oranienburger Strasse, a few blocks west of Hackescher Markt, is anchored by an important and somber sight, the New Synagogue. But the rest of this zone (roughly between the synagogue and Torstrasse) is colorful and quirky—especially after dark. The streets behind Grosse Hamburger Strasse flicker with atmospheric cafés, *Kneipen* (pubs), and art galleries.

▲NEW SYNAGOGUE (NEUE SYNAGOGUE)

A shiny gilded dome marks the New Synagogue, now a museum and cultural center. Consecrated in 1866, this was once the biggest and finest synagogue in Germany, with seating for 3,200 worshippers and a sumptuous Moorish-style interior modeled after the Alhambra in Granada, Spain. It was desecrated by Nazis on Crystal Night (Kristallnacht) in 1938, bombed in 1943, and partially rebuilt in 1990. Only the dome and facade have been restored—a window overlooks the vacant field marking what used to be the synagogue. On its facade, a small plaque—added by East Berlin Jews in 1966—reads "Never forget" *(Vergesst es nie)*. Inside, past tight security, the small but moving permanent exhibit called Open Ye the Gates describes the Berlin Jewish community through the centuries. Skip the dome climb for an extra fee; the views are ho-hum.

Cost and Hours: April-Oct Mon-Fri 10:00-18:00, Sun until 19:00; Nov-March exhibit only Sun-Thu 10:00-18:00, Fri until 15:00; closed Sat year-round; audioguide-€3, Oranienburger Strasse 28/30, enter through the low-profile door in the modern building just right of the domed synagogue facade, S-Bahn: Oranienburger Strasse, www.cjudaicum.de.

Prenzlauer Berg and Nearby

▲▲▲PRENZLAUER BERG

This is one of Berlin's most colorful neighborhoods. The heart of this area, with a dense array of hip cafés, restaurants, boutiques, and street life, is roughly between Helmholtzplatz and Kollwitzplatz and along Kastanienallee (U2: Senefelderplatz and Eberswalder Strasse; or take the S-Bahn to Hackescher Markt and catch tram #M1 north).

"Prenzl'berg," as Berliners call it, was largely untouched during World War II, but its buildings slowly rotted away under the communists. Then, after the Wall fell, it was overrun first with artists and anarchists, then with laid-back hipsters, energetic young families, and clever entrepreneurs who breathed life back into its classic old apartment blocks, deserted factories, and long-forgotten breweries.

Years of rent control kept things affordable for its bohemian residents. But now landlords are free to charge what the market will bear, and the vibe is changing. This is ground zero for Berlin's baby boom: Tattooed and pierced young moms and dads, who've joined the modern rat race without giving up their alternative flair, push their youngsters in designer strollers

Relaxing in Prenzlauer Berg

past trendy boutiques and restaurants.

Aside from the **Berlin Wall Memorial** at its western edge (see next) and the **Mauerpark** (Wall Park, once part of the Wall's death strip, today a Prenzlauer Berg green space), the area has few real sights—it's just a lively, laid-back neighborhood ignoring its wonderful late-19th-century architecture high overhead.

▲▲▲BERLIN WALL MEMORIAL (GEDENKSTÄTTE BERLINER MAUER)

While tourists flock to Checkpoint Charlie, this memorial is Berlin's most substantial attraction relating to its gone-but-not-forgotten Wall. Exhibits line up along several blocks of Bernauer Strasse, stretching northeast from the Nordbahnhof S-Bahn station. You can enter two different museums plus various open-air exhibits and memorials, see several fragments of the Wall, and peer from an observation tower down into a preserved, complete stretch of the Wall system (as it was during the Cold War). To brush up on the basics before your visit, read the sidebar on page 332.

The Berlin Wall, which was erected virtually overnight in 1961, ran right along Bernauer Strasse. People were suddenly separated from their neighbors across the street. This stretch was particularly notorious because existing apartment buildings were incorporated into the structure of the Wall itself. Film footage and photographs from the era show Berliners worriedly watching workmen seal off these buildings from the West, brick by brick. Some people attempted to leap to freedom from upper-story windows, with mixed results. One of the unfortunate ones was Ida Siekmann, who fell to her death from her third-floor apartment on August 22, 1961, and is considered the first casualty of the Berlin Wall.

Cost and Hours: Free; Visitor Center and Documentation Center open Tue-Sun 10:00-18:00, closed Mon, outdoor areas accessible 24 hours daily, memorial chapel closes at 17:00; Bernauer Strasse 111, tel. 030/4679-86666, www.berliner-mauer-gedenkstaette.de.

Getting There: Take the S-Bahn (line S-1, S-2, or S-25—all handy from Potsdamer Platz, Brandenburger Tor, Friedrichstrasse, Oranienburger Strasse, or Hackescher Markt) to the Nordbahnhof. Exit by following signs for *Bernauer Strasse*.

Fragments of the Berlin Wall in the memorial area

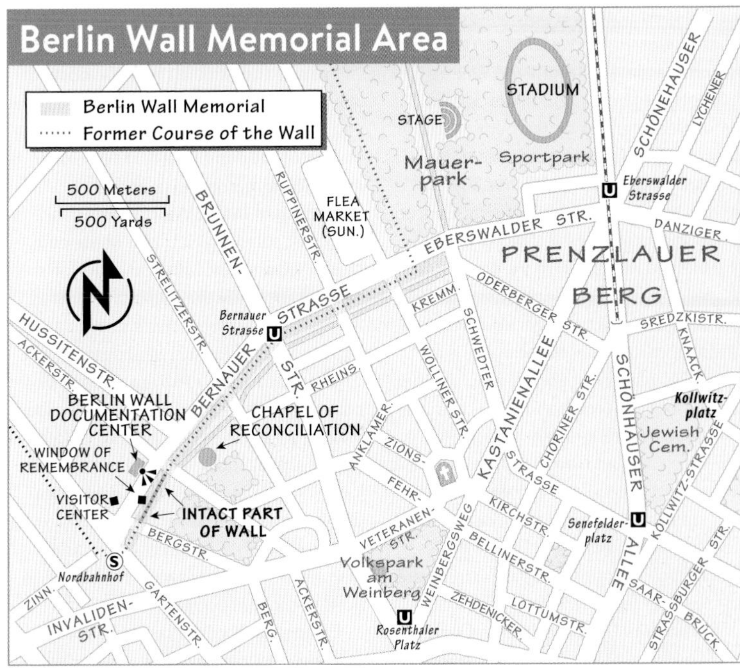

➲ Self-Guided Tour: Here's an overview of the route you'll take. From the Nordbahnhof station (which has some interesting Wall history in itself), head to the Visitor Center to get your bearings, then explore the assorted Wall fragments and other sights in the park across the street. Work your way up Bernauer Strasse to the Documentation Center, Wall System, memorial chapel, and remaining signposts (look for the escape-tunnel paths marked in the grass), until you reach the Bernauer Strasse U-Bahn station (or continue beyond the U-Bahn stop to see all the outdoor exhibits, which stretch up to the Mauerpark).

Nordbahnhof: This S-Bahn station was one of the "ghost stations" of Cold War Berlin. It was built in 1926, closed in 1961, and opened again in 1989. As it was a dogleg of the East mostly surrounded by the West, Western subway trains had permission to use the underground tracks to zip through this station (without stopping, of course) en route between stops in the West. East German border guards, who were stationed here to ensure that nobody got on or off those trains, were locked into their surveillance rooms to prevent them from escaping. (But one subway employee and his family used the tunnels to walk to the West and freedom.)

Follow signs down a long yellow hall to the Bernauer Strasse exit. Climbing the stairs up to the street, ponder that the doorway at the top (marked by the *Sperrmauer 1961-1989* plaque) was a bricked-off no-man's-land until 1989. Stepping outside, you'll see a park full of outdoor exhibits (directly across the street) and the Visitor Center (in a low rust-colored building kitty-corner across the street).

Visitor Center (Bezucherzentrum): This small complex has a helpful information desk, and two good movies that provide context for a visit (they run in English at :30 after the hour, about 30 minutes for the whole spiel): *The Berlin Wall* offers a great 15-minute overview of its history. That's followed by *Walled In!*, an animated 12-minute film illustrating the Wall as it functioned here at Bernauer Strasse. Before leaving, pick up the helpful brochures explaining the outdoor exhibits.

Wall Fragments and Other Sights: Across the street from the Visitor Center is a long stretch of Wall. The park behind it is scattered with a few more Wall chunks as well as monuments and memorials honoring its victims. To get your bearings, find the small model of the entire area when the Wall still stood (just across the street from the Nordbahnhof). The rusty "Window of Remembrance" monument honors slain would-be escapees. Before it was the no-man's-land between the walls, this area was the parish graveyard for a nearby church; ironically, DDR officials had to move a thousand graves from here to create a "death strip."

Berlin Wall Documentation Center (Dokumentationszentrum Berliner Mauer): The center's excellent **exhibit** is geared to a new generation of Berliners who can hardly imagine their hometown split so brutally in two. The ground floor details the logistics of the city's division and its effects on Berliners. Have a seat and listen to the riveting personal accounts of escapees—and of the border guards armed with machine guns and tasked with stopping them. The next floor up gives the historical and political context behind the Wall's construction and eventual destruction. Photos let you track the progression of changes at this exact site from 1965 to 1990.

Leaving the exhibit, climb the open-air staircase to an observation deck that gives you a bird's-eye view of the last remaining stretch of the complete Wall system—guard tower, barbed wire, and all.

Stretch of Intact Wall System: This is the last surviving intact bit of the complete Wall system (with both sides of its Wall—capped by the round pipe that made it tougher for escapees to get a grip—and its no-man's-land death strip). The guard tower came from a different part of the Wall; it was actually purchased on that great capitalist invention, eBay (somewhere, Stalin spins in his grave). View it from the observation deck, then visit it from ground level, where wall panels explain each part of the system. Plaques along the sidewalk mark the locations of escapes or deaths.

Chapel of Reconciliation (Kapelle der Versöhnung): Just beyond the Wall section (to the left), this chapel marks the spot of the late-19th-century Church of Reconciliation, which survived WWII bombs—but not the communists. Notice the larger footprint of the original church in the field around the chapel. When the Wall was built, the church wound up right in the middle of the death strip. It was torn down in 1985, supposedly because it got in the way of the border guards' sight lines. Inside the church, the carved wooden altarpiece was saved from the original structure. The chapel

Intact part of the Wall

Chapel of Reconciliation

hosts daily prayer services for the victims of the Wall.

Outdoor Exhibits: The memorial also includes a string of open-air exhibits along Bernauer Strasse that stretch all the way from the Nordbahnhof to the intersection with Schwedter Strasse and Oderberger Strasse, near the Mauerpark, at the heart of Prenzlauer Berg. Video and audio clips, photos, and huge photographic murals let you in on more stories of the Wall—many of which took place right where you're standing.

EXPERIENCES

Shopping

Berlin Story, a big, cluttered, fun bookshop, has a knowledgeable staff and the best selection anywhere in town of English-language books and helpful magazines on Berlin (Mon-Sat 10:00-19:00, Sun 10:00-18:00, Unter den Linden 40, tel. 030/2045-3842).

If you're taken with the city's unofficial mascot, the Ampelmännchen (traffic-light man), you'll find a world of souvenirs slathered with his iconic red and green image at **Ampelmann Shops** (several locations, including along Unter den Linden at #35, near Gendarmenmarkt at Markgrafenstrasse 37, near Museum Island inside the DomAquarée mall, and in the Hackesche Höfe).

Fun and funky **designer shops** fill the **Hackesche Höfe** and are easy to find throughout Prenzlauer Berg, particularly along Kastanienallee and Oderberger Strasse.

Flea markets abound on weekends; virtually every neighborhood hosts one on a regular basis. The most central is along **Am Kupfergraben,** just across the canal from the Pergamon Museum, with lots of books, music, and art (Sat-Sun 10:00-17:00). One of the biggest is right next to the **Tiergarten park** on Strasse des 17 Juni, with great antiques, more than 200 stalls, and fun fast-food stands (Sat-Sun 6:00-16:00, S-Bahn: Tiergarten). The rummage market in Prenzlauer Berg's **Mauerpark** comes with lots of inventive snack stalls—and on Sunday afternoons, **karaoke** (Sat-Sun 7:00-17:00, U-Bahn: Eberswalder Strasse).

On the opposite end of the price spectrum are the swanky shopping centers clustered around **Gendarmenmarkt.** Find the corner of Jägerstrasse and Friedrichstrasse and wander through the **Quartier 206** department store. The adjacent, middlebrow Quartier 205 has more affordable prices.

In western Berlin, it's fun to browse through **Kaufhaus des Westens** (everyone calls it **KaDeWe**), one of Europe's fanciest department stores, with a good selection of souvenirs...and just about anything else you can think of. The top floor holds the Winter Garden Buffet view **cafeteria.** A **deli/food department** is on the sixth floor, along with a **ticket office** that sells music and theater tickets for all events (18 percent fee but access to all tickets; daily 10:00-20:00, Fri until 21:00, closed Sun, S-Bahn: Zoologischer Garten or U-Bahn: Wittenbergplatz, www.kadewe.de).

Nightlife

Berlin is a happening place for nightlife—whether it's clubs, pubs, jazz, cabaret, concerts, or even sightseeing.

Berlin Programm lists a nonstop parade of events (www.berlinprogramm.de); ***Exberliner Magazine*** doesn't have as much hard information, but is colorfully written in English (sold at kiosks, www.exberliner.com).

Hekticket, Berlin's ticket clearinghouse, offers tickets in advance and **same-day half-price tickets.** Drop by or call after 14:00 to see what's on the push list for this evening (Mon-Fri 12:00-18:00, closed Sat-Sun, half-price sales start at 14:00, near Alexanderplatz at Karl-Liebknecht-Strasse 13, tel. 030/230-9930, www.hekticket.de). **KaDeWe** also sells tickets for events (see last listing in "Shopping").

Rick's Tip: *Stretch your sightseeing day into the night. These museums are* **open late** *every day:* **Reichstag** *(last entry at 22:00),* **Museum of the Wall at Checkpoint Charlie** *(until 22:00),* **Topography of Terror** *(until 20:00), and* **Jewish Museum Berlin** *(Tue-Sun until 20:00, 22:00 on Mon). The* **Museum Island***'s museums are open until 20:00 on Thursdays. Outdoor monuments such as the* **Berlin Wall Memorial** *and the* **Memorial to the Murdered Jews of Europe** *are safe and well-lit late into the night, even though their visitor centers close earlier.*

Jazz

B-Flat Acoustic Music and Jazz Club, in the heart of eastern Berlin, has live music nightly—and shares a courtyard with a tranquil tea house (shows vary from free to €10-13 cover, open Sun-Thu from 20:00 with shows starting at 21:00, Fri-Sat from 21:00 with shows at 22:00, a block from Rosenthaler Platz U-Bahn stop at Rosenthaler Strasse 13, tel. 030/283-3123, www.b-flat-berlin.de).

Rock and Roll

Berlin has a vibrant rock and pop scene, with popular venues at the Spandau Citadel, Olympic Stadium, and the outdoor Waldbühne ("Forest Stage"). Check out what's playing on posters in the U-Bahn, on the *Zitty* website (www.zitty.de), or at any ticket agency.

Cabaret

Bar Jeder Vernunft offers modern-day cabaret in western Berlin. This variety show—under a classic old tent perched atop the modern parking lot of the Berliner Festspiele theater—is a hit with German speakers, and can be fun for those who don't speak the language (as some of the music shows are in a sort of *Deutsch*-English hybrid). Some Americans even perform here periodically. Shows change regularly (about €22-30, performances generally Tue-Sat at 20:00, Sun at 19:00, seating can be cramped, south of Ku'damm at Schaperstrasse 24, U3 or U9:

Festivals keep Berlin lively year-round.

Spichernstrasse, tel. 030/883-1582, www.bar-jeder-vernunft.de).

Nightclubs and Pubs

Oranienburger Strasse is a trendy scene, with bars and restaurants spilling out onto sidewalks filled with people strolling. Nearby, the hip **Prenzlauer Berg** neighborhood is packed with everything from smoky pubs to small art bars and dance clubs (best scene is around Helmholtzplatz, U2: Eberswalder Strasse).

EATING

Near Unter den Linden

Georgenstrasse, a block behind the Pergamon Museum and under the S-Bahn tracks, is lined with fun eateries filling the arcade of the train trestle. **$$ Deponie3** is a reliable Berlin *Kneipe* (bar) usually filled with students from nearby Humboldt University. Garden seating in the back is nice if you don't mind the noise of the S-Bahn directly above you. The interior is a cozy, wooden wonderland. They serve basic salads, traditional Berlin dishes, and hearty daily specials (daily from 10:00, under S-Bahn arch #187 at Georgenstrasse 5, tel. 030/2016-5740).

$ Käse König am Alex has been serving traditional sauerkraut-type dishes since 1933. It's fast, the photo menu makes ordering fun, and prices are great (daily, Panoramastrasse 1 under the TV Tower, tel. 030/8561-5220). Nearby, **$ Brauhaus Mitte** is a fun, DDR-era beer hall that makes its own beer and offers a menu of Berliner specialties and Bavarian dishes (daily 11:00-24:00, across from the TV Tower at Karl-Liebknecht-Strasse 13, tel. 030/3087-8989).

Near Gendarmenmarkt

The twin churches of Gendarmenmarkt are surrounded by upscale restaurants serving lunch and dinner to local professionals. If in need of a quick-yet-classy lunch, stroll around the square and along Charlottenstrasse. For a quick bite, head to the cheap *Currywurst* stand behind the German Cathedral.

$$$ Lutter & Wegner Restaurant is well-known for its Austrian cuisine (schnitzel and sauerbraten), with fun sidewalk seating or a dark and elegant interior (€9-18 starters, €16-24 main dishes, daily 11:00-24:00, Charlottenstrasse 56, tel. 030/202-9540).

$$ Augustiner am Gendarmenmarkt, next door to Lutter & Wegner, has a classic beer-hall atmosphere, offers good beer and Bavarian cuisine (€6-12 light meals, €10-20 bigger meals, daily 10:00-24:00, Charlottenstrasse 55, tel. 030/2045-4020).

Galeries Lafayette Food Circus is a festival of eateries in the basement of the landmark department store. You'll find a good deli and prepared-food stands (most options €10-15, cheaper €5-10 sandwiches and savory crêpes, Mon-Sat 10:00-20:00, closed Sun, Friedrichstrasse 76-78, U-Bahn: Französische Strasse, tel. 030/209-480).

Hackescher Markt and Nearby

$$ Weihenstephaner Bavarian Restaurant serves upmarket traditional cuisine for around €10-15 a plate and excellent beer in the atmospheric cellar, the inner courtyard, and on the streetside terrace (daily 11:00-23:00, Neue Promenade 5 at Hackescher Markt, tel. 030/8471-0760).

Restaurants on Oranienburger Strasse, a few blocks west of Hackescher Markt, come with happy hours and lots of cocktails. **$$ Aufsturz,** a lively pub, serves pub grub and a huge selection of beer and whisky to a young crowd (Oranienburger Strasse 67). **$ Amrit Lounge** serves Indian food outdoors with an umbrella-drink Caribbean ambience (€10-14 meals, long hours daily, Oranienburger Strasse 45). Next door is **$$ QBA,** a fun Cuban bar and restaurant.

$ Schwarzwaldstuben, between Oranienburger Strasse and Rosenthaler Platz, is a Black Forest–themed pub—which explains the antlers and cuckoo clocks. It's friendly, with good service, food, and prices. If they're full, you can eat at the long bar or at one of the sidewalk tables (€7-16 meals, daily 9:00-23:00, Tucholskystrasse 48, tel. 030/2809-8084).

$$ Gipsy Restaurant serves good, reasonably priced German and Italian dishes in a bohemian-chic atmosphere (daily 12:30-23:00, at Clärchens Ballhaus, Auguststrasse 24, tel. 030/282-9295).

Near Rosenthaler Platz

Surrounding the U8: Rosenthaler Platz station, a short stroll or tram ride from the Hackescher Markt S-Bahn station, and an easy walk from the Oranienburger Strasse action, this busy neighborhood has several enticing options.

$ My Smart Break is a great spot to pick up a freshly made deli sandwich, hummus plate, salad, or other healthy snack. Linger in the interior, grab one of the sidewalk tables, or get it to go (€5-8 sandwiches, daily 8:00-23:00, Rosenthaler Strasse 67, tel. 030/2390-0303).

$ Transit is a stylish Thai/Indonesian/pan-Asian restaurant with a creative menu of €3 small plates and €8 big plates. Two people can make a filling meal out of three or four dishes (daily 11:00-24:00, cash only, Rosenthaler Strasse 68, tel. 030/2478-1645).

$ Restaurant Simon dishes up tasty Italian and German specialties—enjoy them in the restaurant's simple yet atmospheric interior, or opt for parkside seating across the street (€8-15 main dishes, Mon-Sat 17:00-23:00, closed Sun, cash only, Auguststrasse 53, at intersection with Kleine Auguststrasse, tel. 030/2789-0300).

In Prenzlauer Berg

The area surrounding the elevated Eberswalder Strasse U-Bahn station is the epicenter of Prenzlauer Berg. It's worth the 10- to 15-minute walk from most of my recommended hotels.

$ Prater Biergarten offers both a rustic indoor restaurant and Berlin's oldest beer garden (with a family-friendly play-

Berliner Street Fare

In Berlin, it's easy to eat cheap, with a glut of *Imbiss* snack stands, bakeries (for sandwiches), and falafel/kebab counters. Train stations have grocery stores, as well as bright and modern fruit-and-sandwich bars.

Sausage stands are everywhere. Most specialize in ***Currywurst,*** a grilled pork sausage smothered with curry sauce. It was created in Berlin after World War II, when a cook got her hands on some curry and Worcestershire sauce from British troops stationed here. *Currywurst* comes either ***mit Darm*** (with casing) or ***ohne Darm*** (without casing). ***Berliner Art***—"Berlin-style"—means that the sausage is boiled *ohne Darm,* then grilled. Either way, the grilled sausage is then chopped into small pieces or cut in half and topped with sauce. While some places simply use ketchup and sprinkle on some curry powder, real *Currywurst* joints use tomato paste, Worcestershire sauce, and curry. With your wurst comes either a toothpick or small wooden fork; you'll usually get a plate of fries as well.

Other good street foods to consider are ***Döner Kebab*** (Turkish-style skewered meat slow-roasted and served in a sandwich) and ***Frikadelle*** (like a hamburger patty; often called ***Bulette*** in Berlin).

Two companies, Grillwalker and Grillrunner, outfit their cooks in clever harnesses that let them grill and sell hot dogs from under an umbrella. For something quick, cheap, and tasty, find one of these portable human hot-dog stands.

ground), each proudly offering its own microbrew. In the beer garden, step up to the counter and order (daily in good weather 12:00-24:00). The restaurant serves serious *Biergarten* cuisine and good salads (€10-20 plates, Mon-Sat 18:00-24:00, Sun from 12:00, cash only, Kastanienallee 7, tel. 030/448-5688).

$ Zum Schusterjungen Speisegaststätte ("The Cobbler's Apprentice") is a classic eatery that retains its circa-1986 DDR decor. Famous for its filling €9-13 meals (including schnitzel and Berlin classics such as pork knuckle), it has a strong local following (daily 12:00-24:00, corner of Lychener Strasse and Danziger Strasse 9, tel. 030/442-7654).

$$ La Bodeguita del Medio Cuban Bar Restaurant is pure fun, with an ambience that makes you want to dance. The main dishes are big enough to split and you can even puff a Cuban cigar at the sidewalk tables. Come early to eat or late to drink (€4-10 tapas, Cuban ribs and salad, Tue-Sun 18:00-24:00, closed Mon, cash only, a block from U2: Eberswalder Strasse at Lychener Strasse 6, tel. 030/4050-0601).

$ Konnopke's Imbiss has been cooking up the city's best *Currywurst* for more than 70 years. Located beneath the U2 viaduct, the stand was demolished in 2010 during roadwork. Berliners rioted, and Konnopke's was rebuilt in a slick glass-and-steel hut. Don't confuse this with the nearby Currystation—look for the real Konnopke's (Mon-Fri 9:00-20:00, Sat from 11:30, closed Sun; Kastanienallee dead-ends at the elevated train tracks, and under them you'll find Konnopke's at Schönhauser Allee 44A, tel. 030/442-7765).

$$ Restaurant Die Schule is a modern, no-frills place to sample traditional German dishes tapas-style (good indoor and outdoor seating, daily 11:00-22:00, Kastanienallee 82, tel. 030/780-089-550).

Funky pubs and nightspots fill the area around Helmholtzplatz (and elsewhere in Prenzlauer Berg). Oderberger Strasse is a fun zone to explore. For dessert, **Kauf Dich Glücklich** serves an enticing array of sweet Belgian waffles and ice cream in a candy-sprinkled, bohemian lounge (Mon-Fri 11:00-24:00, Sat-Sun from 10:00, indoor and outdoor seating—or get your dessert to go, Oderberger Strasse 44, tel. 030/4862-3292).

Berlin Eateries & Nightlife
1 Deponie3 Pub
2 Käse König am Alex
3 Brauhaus Mitte & Hekticket Half-Price Tix
4 Lutter & Wegner Rest.; Augustiner am Gendarmenmarkt
5 Galeries Lafayette Food Circus
6 Weihenstephaner Bavarian Restaurant
7 Oranienburger Strasse Eateries
8 Schwarzwaldstuben Pub
9 Gipsy Restaurant at Clärchens Ballhaus
10 My Smart Break & Transit Restaurant
11 Restaurant Simon
12 Prater Biergarten
HUSSITENSTR.
BRUNNEN-
RUPPINERSTR.
STRELITZERSTR.
LIESENSTR.
GARTEN-
ACKERSTR.
BERLIN WALL DOCUMENTATION CENTER
Bernauer Strasse
BERNAUER STR.
BERLIN WALL MEMORIAL
WÖHLERTSTR.
STRASSE
Schwartzkopff-strasse
SCHWARTZ.
CHAUSSEESTR.
WINDOW OF REMEMBRANCE
VISITOR CENTER
CHAPEL OF RECONCILIATION
INTACT PART OF WALL
BERGSTR.
Nordbahnhof
ZINN.
HABER.
Naturkunde-museum
SCHWARZER WEG
NATURAL HISTORY MUSEUM
EICHEN
GARTENSTR.
BERG.
ACKERSTR.
TIEKSTRASSE
DORFF.
TORSTR.
KENNEDYS MUSEUM
STR.
HANNOVERSCHESTR.
LINIENSTR.
Oranien-burger Str.
HAUPTBAHNHOF & EURAIDE
Haupt-bahnhof
HUMBOLDTHAFEN
LUISENSTR.
TACHELES BUILDING
ORANIENBURGERSTR.
Oranienburger Tor
FRIEDRICHSTR.
JOHANNISSTR.
NEW SYNAGOGUE
ZIEGELSTR.
INVALIDEN
KAPELLE-UFER
SCHUMANNSTR.
REINHARD-
ALBRECHTSTR.
PERGAMON MUSEUM
ALT-MOABIT
FÜRST-BISMARCK-STR.
MARIENSTR.
Friedrich-strasse
PLANK.
UNIV.
Bundestag
Spree River
OTTO-VON-BISMARCK-ALLEE
PARLIAMENT OFFICES
SCHIFFBAUER.
GEORGEN.
CHARLOTTEN.
DOROTHEEN.
CHANCELLERY
Platz der Republik
REICHSTAG
NEUSTÄDTISCHE KIRCHSTR.
HUMBOLDT UNIVERSITY
HAUS DER KULTUREN DER WELT
Bus # 100
DOROTHEENSTR.
MITTELSTR.
NEUE WACHE
SCHEIDEMANNSTR.
Pariser Platz
UNTER DEN LINDEN
Bebel-platz
BRANDENBURG GATE
Branden-burger Tor
KOMISCHE OPER
GERMAN STATE OPERA
STRASSE DES 17 JUNI
ENTLASTUNGSSTR.
MEMORIAL TO THE MURDERED JEWS
US EMBASSY
BEHRENSTRASSE
Französische Strasse
FRANZÖSISCHE STR.
To Victory Column
Tiergarten
EBERTSTR.
HANNAH-ARENDT.
WILHELM-
MAUERSTR.
GLINKASTR.
Gendarmen-markt
HOMOSEXUAL MEMORIAL
Mohren-strasse
MOHRENSTR.
GERMAN CATH.
FRIEDRICHSTR.
Stadtmitte
MUSICAL INSTRUMENTS MUSEUM
LENNESTR.
BELLE-
GURION
VOSS-STR.
LEIPZIGER STR.
MARKGRAFEN-
MUSEUM OF ARTS & CRAFTS
SONY CENTER
Potsdamer Platz
Leipziger Platz
TIERGARTENSTR.
GEMÄLDE-GALERIE
CONCERT HALL
POTSDAMER STR.
DDR WATCH-TOWER
FORMER LUFTWAFFE HQ
MAUERSTR.
CHARLOTTEN-
HILDEBRAND-STR.
NIEDER-KIRCH.
MUSEUM OF THE WALL AT CHECKPOINT CHARLIE
KOCHSTR.
GERMAN RESISTANCE MEMORIAL
KULTURFORUM
LIBRARY
EICHHORN.
GABRIELE-TERGIT-PROMENADE
STRESEMANNSTR.
TOPOGRAPHY OF TERROR
WILHELM-
Koch-strasse
REICHPIETSCHUFER
SCHÖNEBERGER UFER
Landwehr Canal
BERNBURGER
ANHALTER STR.
BESSELSTR.
Mendelssohn-Bartholdy-Park
Anhalter Bahnhof
SCHÖNEBERGERSTR.
LÜTZOWSTRASSE
BERLIN STORY BUNKER
STR.

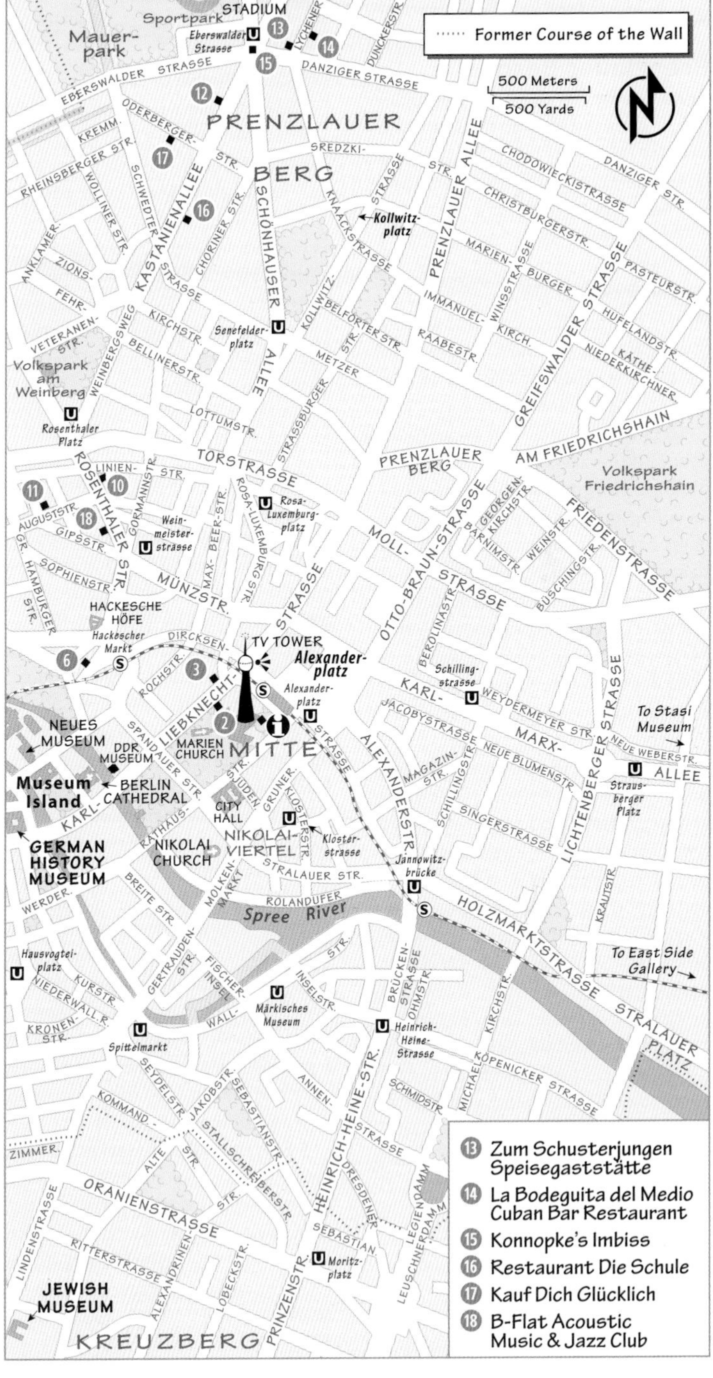
Former Course of the Wall
500 Meters
500 Yards
PRENZLAUER BERG
MITTE
KREUZBERG
Mauerpark
Sportpark
STADIUM
Volkspark am Weinberg
Volkspark Friedrichshain
TV TOWER
Alexanderplatz
HACKESCHE HÖFE
NEUES MUSEUM
DDR MUSEUM
Museum Island
BERLIN CATHEDRAL
MARIEN CHURCH
CITY HALL
NIKOLAI CHURCH
NIKOLAI-VIERTEL
GERMAN HISTORY MUSEUM
Spree River
Märkisches Museum
JEWISH MUSEUM
To Stasi Museum
To East Side Gallery
13 Zum Schusterjungen Speisegaststätte
14 La Bodeguita del Medio Cuban Bar Restaurant
15 Konnopke's Imbiss
16 Restaurant Die Schule
17 Kauf Dich Glücklich
18 B-Flat Acoustic Music & Jazz Club

SLEEPING

Prenzlauer Berg

Gentrification has enlivened this colorful and gritty district with fun shops and eateries, happening nightlife—and great hotels. Think of the graffiti as some people's way of saying they care.

The closest U-Bahn stops are U2: Senefelderplatz at the south end of the neighborhood, U8: Rosenthaler Platz in the middle, or U2: Eberswalder Strasse at the north end. Or, for less walking, take the S-Bahn to Hackescher Markt, then catch tram #M1 north.

$$$ Myer's Hotel rents 60 lush rooms decorated in rich colors with classy furnishings. The gorgeous public spaces, including an art-filled patio and garden, host frequent cultural events. This peaceful hub is off a quiet garden courtyard and tree-lined street (Db-€108-235, air-con, elevator, sauna, bike rental, Metzer Strasse 26, 5-minute walk to Kollwitzplatz or U2: Senefelderplatz, tel. 030/440-140, www.myershotel.de, info@myershotel.de).

$$$ Hotel Jurine is a pleasant 53-room business-style hotel whose friendly staff aims to please. In good weather, enjoy the breakfast buffet on the peaceful backyard patio and garden (Db-€130-160, air-con only on upper floor, elevator, garage parking if you reserve ahead, Schwedter Strasse 15, 10-minute walk to U2: Senefelderplatz, tel. 030/443-2990, www.hotel-jurine.de, mail@hotel-jurine.de).

$$$ Hotel Kastanienhof, which offers helpful service, feels like a traditional small-town German hotel, even though it has 50 rooms. It's well-located on the Kastanienallee #M1 tram line, with easy access to the Prenzlauer Berg bustle (Db-€100-180, some rooms with air-con and/or balcony—request when you book, breakfast-€9, pay parking, 20 yards from #M1 Zionskirche tram stop at Kastanienallee 65, tel. 030/443-050, www.kastanienhof.biz, info@kastanienhof.biz).

Sleep Code

$$$$ Splurge: Over €170
$$$ Pricier: €130-170
$$ Moderate: €90-130
$ Budget: €50-90
¢ Backpacker: Under €50

Hotels are classified based on the average price of a standard double room with bath in high season. Unless otherwise noted, credit cards are accepted, breakfast is included, hotel staff speak English, and Wi-Fi is available.

$$ The Circus Hotel, with 60 colorful rooms, is fun, comfortable, and an excellent value. It overlooks a noisy intersection, so ask for a back room (Db-€95-€105, breakfast-€9, elevator, loaner iPads in rooms, mellow ground-floor restaurant, Rosenthaler Strasse 1, directly at U8: Rosenthaler Platz, tel. 030/2000-3939, www.circus-berlin.de, info@circus-berlin.de). The Circus also offers a range of spacious, modern **apartments** both within the hotel and two blocks away on Choriner Strasse.

$ Karlito Apartmenthaus has 12 comfortable, modern apartments above a hip café on a tranquil side street near Hackescher Markt. All the sleek, Ikea-esque units have miniature balconies (Db-€80-95, in-room breakfast-€10, elevator, bike rental, Linienstrasse 60—check in at Café Lois around the corner on Gormannstrasse, U8: Rosenthaler Platz, or 350 yards from S-Bahn: Hackescher Markt, mobile 0179-704-9041, www.karlito-apartments.de, info@karlito-apartments.de).

$ EasyHotel Berlin Hackescher Markt is part of an unapologetically cheap chain where you pay for exactly what you use—nothing more, nothing less. The hotel has inexpensive base rates (Db-€35-65), then charges separate fees for optional extras like Wi-Fi and TV. The 125 rooms are small and basic, but if you skip the extras, the price is right, and the location at Hackescher Markt is wonderful (elevator, request quieter back room, Rosenthaler Strasse 69, tel. 030/4000-6550, www.easyhotel.com).

$$$ Hotel Augustinenhof is on a side street near all the Oranienburger Strasse action. It's a clean hotel with 66 spacious rooms, nice woody floors, and some of the most comfortable beds in Berlin. Rooms in front overlook the courtyard of the old Imperial Post Office, rooms in back are quieter, and some rooms have older, thin windows (Db-€100-150, elevator, Auguststrasse 82, 50 yards from S-Bahn: Oranienburger Strasse, tel. 030/3088-6710, www.hotel-augustinenhof.de, augustinenhof@albrechtshof-hotels.de).

Farther East, in Friedrichshain

$ Michelberger Hotel, in the heart of gritty but gentrifying Friedrichshain, is so self-consciously hip that it'd be just too much...if it weren't for its helpful, friendly staff. Its 113 bright rooms are reasonably priced, and its common spaces—a bar/lounge and a breezy courtyard restaurant—are genuinely welcoming (Db-€80-90, bigger "loft" doubles and suites available, breakfast extra, elevator, bike rental; from atop Warschauer Strasse S-Bahn station turn left to cross the bridge—it's across from the U-Bahn station and #M10 tram stop at Warschauer Strasse 39; tel. 030/2977-8590, www.michelbergerhotel.com, reservations@michelbergerhotel.com).

$ Ostel is a fun, retro-1970s apartment building that re-creates the DDR lifestyle and interior design. All the furniture and room decorations have been meticulously collected and restored to their former socialist glory—only the psychedelic wallpaper is a replica (Db-€59, also 4-person apartments; no breakfast but supermarket next door, 24-hour reception, Wi-Fi in lobby, bike rental, free parking, free use of the community barbeque, right behind Ostbahnhof station on the corner of Strasse der Pariser Kommune at Wriezener Karree 5, tel. 030/2576-8660, www.ostel.eu, contact@ostel.eu).

Hotelesque Hostels

¢ Meininger is a budget-hotel chain with several locations in Berlin. With sleek, nicely decorated rooms, these can be a great value, even for nonhostelers. They have three particularly appealing branches: in Prenzlauer Berg (Schönhauser Allee 19 on Senefelderplatz), at Oranienburger Strasse 67 (next to the Aufsturz pub), and near the Hauptbahnhof, at Ella-Traebe-Strasse 9 (dorm bed-€20-40, Db-€70-120, all locations: breakfast extra, elevator, 24-hour reception, guest kitchen, bike rental, pay parking, tel. 030/666-36100, www.meininger-hostels.com, welcome@meininger-hostels.com).

¢ The Circus Hostel is a brightly colored, well-run place with 230 beds, a trendy lounge, and a bar downstairs. It has typical hostel dorms as well as some private rooms; for a few big steps up in comfort, see the listing for the Circus Hotel (dorm bed-€23-31, Db-€85, also apartments, breakfast extra, no curfew, elevator, guest iPads, bike rental, Weinbergsweg 1A, U8: Rosenthaler Platz, tel. 030/2000-3939, www.circus-berlin.de, info@circus-berlin.de).

¢ EastSeven Hostel rents the best cheap beds in Prenzlauer Berg. It's sleek and modern, with all the hostel services and more: 60 beds, inviting lounge, guest kitchen, lockers, quiet backyard terrace, and bike rental. Children are welcome. Easygoing people of any age are comfortable here (dorm bed-€15-25, D-€54-60, breakfast extra, laundry, no curfew, 100 yards from U2: Senefelderplatz at Schwedter Strasse 7, tel. 030/9362-2240, www.eastseven.de, info@eastseven.de).

¢ Hotel Transit Loft, actually more of a hostel, is located in a refurbished factory. Its 81 stark, high-ceilinged rooms and wide-open lobby have an industrial touch.

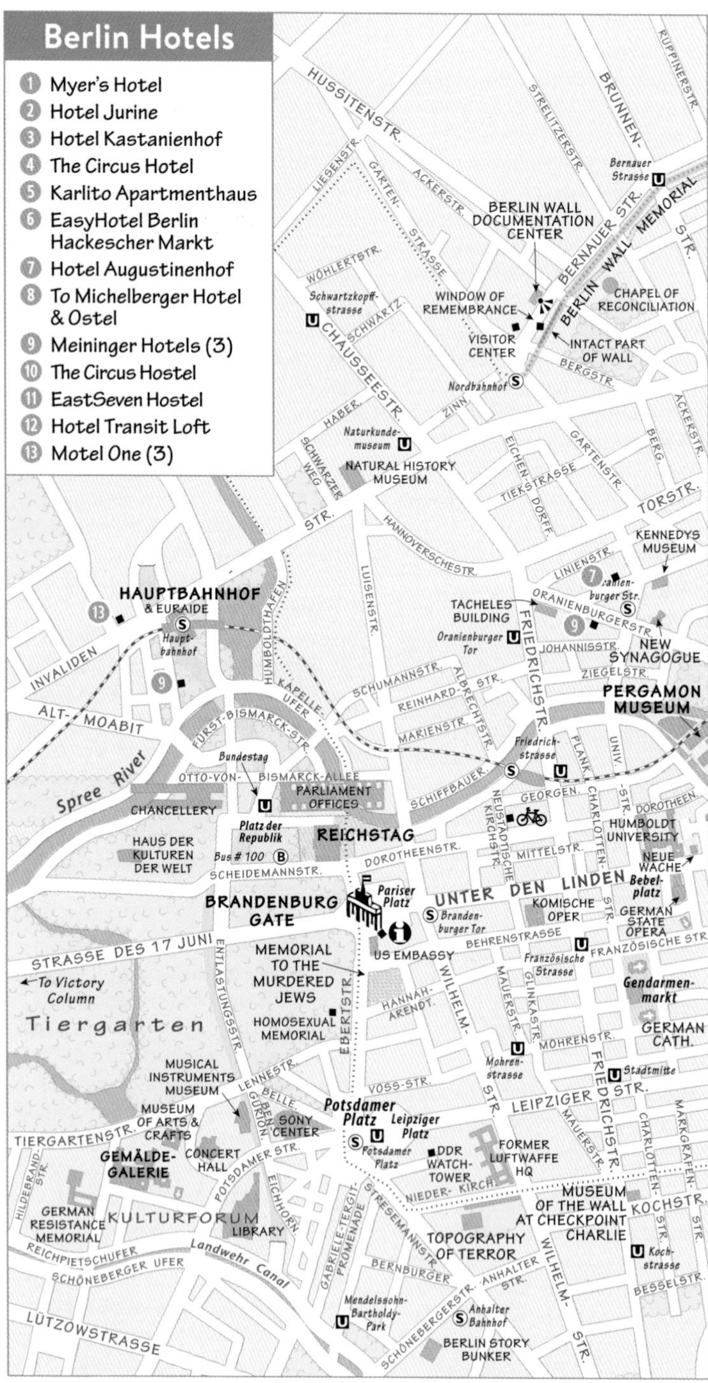
Berlin Hotels
1 Myer's Hotel
2 Hotel Jurine
3 Hotel Kastanienhof
4 The Circus Hotel
5 Karlito Apartmenthaus
6 EasyHotel Berlin Hackescher Markt
7 Hotel Augustinenhof
8 To Michelberger Hotel & Ostel
9 Meininger Hotels (3)
10 The Circus Hostel
11 EastSeven Hostel
12 Hotel Transit Loft
13 Motel One (3)
BERLIN WALL DOCUMENTATION CENTER
BERLIN WALL MEMORIAL
WINDOW OF REMEMBRANCE
CHAPEL OF RECONCILIATION
VISITOR CENTER
INTACT PART OF WALL
NATURAL HISTORY MUSEUM
KENNEDYS MUSEUM
HAUPTBAHNHOF & EURAIDE
TACHELES BUILDING
NEW SYNAGOGUE
PERGAMON MUSEUM
Spree River
CHANCELLERY
PARLIAMENT OFFICES
REICHSTAG
HAUS DER KULTUREN DER WELT
HUMBOLDT UNIVERSITY
NEUE WACHE
BRANDENBURG GATE
UNTER DEN LINDEN
KOMISCHE OPER
GERMAN STATE OPERA
US EMBASSY
MEMORIAL TO THE MURDERED JEWS
HOMOSEXUAL MEMORIAL
To Victory Column
Tiergarten
Gendarmenmarkt
GERMAN CATH.
MUSICAL INSTRUMENTS MUSEUM
MUSEUM OF ARTS & CRAFTS
SONY CENTER
Potsdamer Platz
Leipziger Platz
GEMÄLDE-GALERIE
CONCERT HALL
DDR WATCH-TOWER
FORMER LUFTWAFFE HQ
GERMAN RESISTANCE MEMORIAL
KULTURFORUM
LIBRARY
MUSEUM OF THE WALL AT CHECKPOINT CHARLIE
TOPOGRAPHY OF TERROR
Landwehr Canal
BERLIN STORY BUNKER
Bernauer Strasse
Schwartzkopffstrasse
Nordbahnhof
Naturkundemuseum
Oranienburger Str.
Oranienburger Tor
Hauptbahnhof
Friedrichstrasse
Bundestag
Platz der Republik
Bus # 100
Pariser Platz
Brandenburger Tor
Französische Strasse
Mohrenstrasse
Stadtmitte
Kochstrasse
Anhalter Bahnhof
Mendelssohn-Bartholdy-Park
HUSSITENSTR.
BRUNNEN-
RUPPINERSTR.
STRELITZERSTR.
LIESENSTR.
GARTEN-STRASSE
ACKERSTR.
BERNAUER STR.
WÖHLERTSTR.
SCHWARTZ.
CHAUSSEESTR.
BERGSTR.
HABER.
ZINN.
SCHWARZER WEG
EICHENDORFF.
GARTENSTR.
BERG.
TIEKSTRASSE
TORSTR.
HANNOVERSCHESTR.
LUISENSTR.
LINIENSTR.
ORANIENBURGERSTR.
HUMBOLDTHAFEN
INVALIDEN STR.
JOHANNISSTR.
ZIEGELSTR.
ALT-MOABIT
KAPELLE-UFER
SCHUMANNSTR.
REINHARD-STR.
ALBRECHTSTR.
FRIEDRICHSTR.
FÜRST-BISMARCK-STR.
MARIENSTR.
PLANK.
UNIV.-STR.
OTTO-VON-BISMARCK-ALLEE
SCHIFFBAUER.
NEUSTÄDTISCHE KIRCHSTR.
GEORGEN.
CHARLOTTEN-STR.
DOROTHEEN.
DOROTHEENSTR.
MITTELSTR.
SCHEIDEMANNSTR.
Bebelplatz
BEHRENSTRASSE
FRANZÖSISCHE STR.
STRASSE DES 17 JUNI
ENTLASTUNGSSTR.
EBERTSTR.
HANNAH-ARENDT.
WILHELM-STR.
MAUERSTR.
GLINKASTR.
MOHRENSTR.
LENNESTR.
BELLE-VUE
BEN-GURION
VOSS-STR.
LEIPZIGER STR.
MARKGRAFEN-STR.
TIERGARTENSTR.
POTSDAMER STR.
HILDEBRANDSTR.
EICHHORN.
NIEDER-KIRCH.
KOCHSTR.
GABRIELE-TERGIT-PROMENADE
STRESEMANNSTR.
REICHPIETSCHUFER
SCHÖNEBERGER UFER
BERNBURGER
ANHALTER STR.
BESSELSTR.
SCHÖNEBERGERSTR.
LÜTZOWSTRASSE

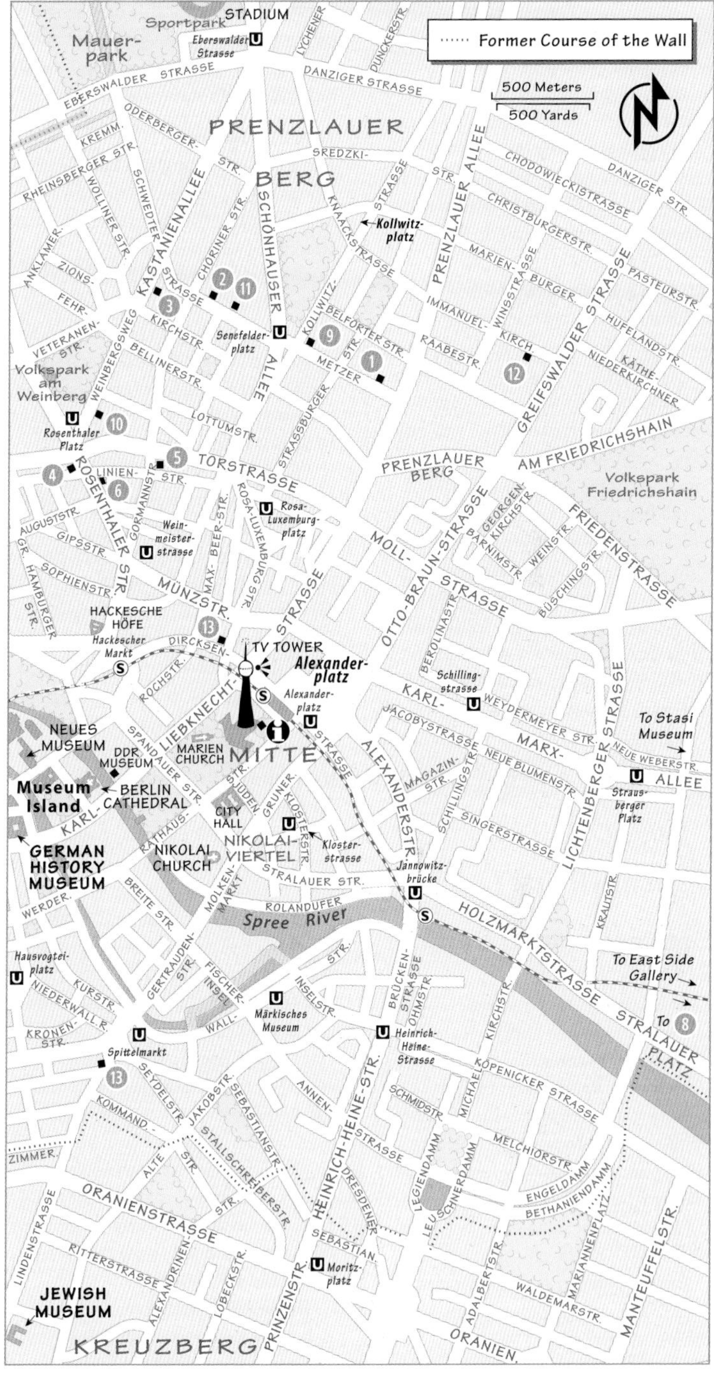
Former Course of the Wall
500 Meters
500 Yards
PRENZLAUER BERG
MITTE
KREUZBERG
Mauerpark
Sportpark
STADIUM
Eberswalder Strasse
Volkspark am Weinberg
Volkspark Friedrichshain
Kollwitzplatz
Senefelderplatz
Rosenthaler Platz
Rosa-Luxemburg-platz
Weinmeisterstrasse
HACKESCHE HÖFE
Hackescher Markt
TV TOWER
Alexanderplatz
MARIEN CHURCH
NEUES MUSEUM
DDR MUSEUM
Museum Island
BERLIN CATHEDRAL
GERMAN HISTORY MUSEUM
CITY HALL
NIKOLAI CHURCH
NIKOLAI-VIERTEL
Klosterstrasse
Jannowitzbrücke
Spree River
Schillingstrasse
To Stasi Museum
Strausberger Platz
To East Side Gallery
To 8
Hausvogteiplatz
Märkisches Museum
Heinrich-Heine-Strasse
Spittelmarkt
Moritzplatz
JEWISH MUSEUM
KARL-MARX-ALLEE
TORSTRASSE
HOLZMARKTSTRASSE
ORANIENSTRASSE

The reception is open 24 hours, with a bar serving drinks all night long (Db-€73, family rooms, includes sheets and breakfast, elevator, down alley facing inner courtyard at Immanuelkirchstrasse 14A; U2/U5/U8 or S-Bahn: Alexanderplatz, then tram #M4 to Hufelandstrasse and walk 50 yards; tel. 030/4849-3773, www.transit-loft.de, loft@hotel-transit.de).

Across the City

$ Motel One has eight locations across Berlin; all have the same posh-feeling-but-small rooms. The four most convenient locations are right on Alexanderplatz (Dircksenstrasse 36, tel. 030/2005-4080, berlin-alexanderplatz@motel-one.com); just behind the Hauptbahnhof (Invalidenstrasse 54, tel. 030/3641-0050, berlin-hauptbahnhof@motel-one.com); a few blocks east of Gendarmenmarkt (Leipziger Strasse 50, U2: Spittelmarkt, tel. 030/2014-3630, berlin-spittelmarkt@motel-one.com); and near the Bahnhof Zoo (Kantstrasse 10, tel. 030/3151-7360, berlin-kudamm@motel-one.com). They tend to charge the same prices (Db-€84, breakfast extra, air-con, guest iPads, elevator, limited pay parking, www.motel-one.com).

TRANSPORTATION

Getting Around Berlin

By Public Transit

Berlin's consolidated transit system uses the same ticket for its many modes of transportation: U-Bahn (*Untergrund-Bahn*, Berlin's subway), S-Bahn (*Stadtschnellbahn*, or "fast urban train," mostly aboveground), *Strassenbahn* (tram), and bus. For all types of transit, there are three lettered zones (A, B, and C). Most of your sightseeing will be in zones A and B (the city proper).

Berlin's public transit is operated by BVG (except the S-Bahn, which is run by the Deutsche Bahn). Timetables and the latest prices are available on the helpful BVG website (www.bvg.de). Get and use the excellent *Discover Berlin by Train and Bus* map-guide at subway ticket windows.

TICKET OPTIONS

The €2.70 **basic single** ticket (*Einzelfahrschein*) covers two hours of travel in one direction. It's easy to make this ticket stretch to cover several rides...as long as they're in the same direction.

The €1.60 **short-ride** ticket (*Kurzstrecke Fahrschein*) covers a single ride of up to six bus/tram stops or three subway stations (one transfer allowed on subway). You can save on short-ride tickets by buying them in groups of four.

The €9 **four-trip** ticket (*4-Fahrten-Karte*) is the same as four basic single tickets at a small discount.

The **day pass** (*Tageskarte*) is good until 3:00 the morning after you buy it (€6.90 for zones AB, €7.40 for zones ABC). For longer stays, consider a seven-day pass (*Sieben-Tage-Karte;* €29.50 for zones AB, €36.50 for zones ABC), or the WelcomeCard (described below). The *Kleingruppenkarte* lets groups of up to five travel all day (€16.90 for zones AB, €17.40 for zones ABC).

If you plan to cover a lot of ground using public transportation during a two- or three-day visit, the **WelcomeCard** is usually the best deal (available at TIs; www.visitberlin.de/welcomecard). It covers all public transportation and gives you up to 50 percent discounts on lots of minor and a few major museums (including Checkpoint Charlie), sightseeing tours (including 25 percent off the recommended Original Berlin Walks), and music and theater events. It's especially smart for families, as each adult card also covers up to three kids under age 15. The Berlin-only card covers transit zones AB (€19.50/48 hours, €27.50/72 hours, also 4-, 5-, and 6-day options).

Buying Tickets: You can buy U-Bahn/S-Bahn tickets from machines at stations. (They are also sold at BVG pavilions at train stations and at the TI, from machines onboard trams, and on buses from drivers, who'll give change.) *Erwachsener* means "adult"—anyone age 14 or older. Don't be afraid of the automated machines: First select the type of ticket you want, then load the coins or paper bills. (Coins work better, so keep some handy.)

Boarding Transit: As you board the bus or tram, or enter the subway, punch your ticket in a clock machine to validate it (or risk a €60 fine; stamp passes only the first time you ride). Be sure to travel with a valid ticket. Tickets are checked frequently, often by plainclothes inspectors. You may be asked to show your ticket when boarding the bus (technically that's required), though most drivers skip this.

By Taxi

Cabs are easy to flag down, and taxi stands are common. A typical ride within town costs €8-10, and a crosstown trip will run about €15. Tariff 1 is for a *Kurzstrecke* ticket (see below). All other rides are tariff 2 (€3.40 drop plus €1.80/km for the first 7 kilometers, then €1.28/km after that). If possible, use cash—paying with a credit card comes with a hefty surcharge (about €4, regardless of the fare).

Money-Saving Taxi Tip: For any ride of less than two kilometers (about a mile), you can save several euros if you take advantage of the ***Kurzstrecke*** (short-stretch) rate. To get this rate, it's important that you flag the cab down on the street—not at or even near a taxi stand. You must ask for the *Kurzstrecke* rate as soon as you hop in: Confidently say *"Kurzstrecke, bitte"* (KOORTS-shtreh-keh, BIT-teh), and your driver will grumble and flip the meter to a fixed €4 rate (for a ride that would otherwise cost €7).

By Bike

Flat Berlin is a bike-friendly city, but be careful—Berlin's motorists don't brake for bicyclists (and bicyclists don't brake for pedestrians). Fortunately, some roads and sidewalks have special red-painted bike lanes. Don't ride on the regular sidewalk—it's *verboten* (though locals do it all the time). Bike shops can suggest a specific route.

Fat Tire Bikes rents good bikes at two locations, east—at the base of the TV Tower near Alexanderplatz—and west, at Bahnhof Zoo (leaving the station onto Hardenbergplatz, turn left and walk 100 yards to the big bike sign). Both locations have the same hours and rates (€14/day, cheaper for two or more days, daily May-Aug 9:30-20:00, March-April and Sept-Oct 9:30-18:00, shorter hours or by appointment only Nov-Feb, tel. 030/2404-7991, www.berlinbikerental.com).

In eastern Berlin, **Take a Bike**—near the Friedrichstrasse S-Bahn station—is owned by a lovely Dutch-German couple who know a lot about bikes and have a huge inventory (3-gear bikes: €12.50/day, cheaper for longer rentals, more for better bikes, includes helmets, daily 9:30-19:00, Neustädtische Kirchstrasse 8, tel. 030/2065-4730, www.takeabike.de). To find it, leave the S-Bahn station via the Friedrichstrasse exit, turn right, go through a triangle-shaped square, and hang a left on Neustädtische Kirchstrasse.

All around town, simple **Rent a Bike** stands are outside countless shops, restaurants, and hotels. Most charge €10-12 a day, and are convenient, given their ubiquitous availability—but these bikes don't come with the reliable quality, advice, helmets, or maps commonly offered by full-service rental shops.

Arriving and Departing

By Train

Berlin's grandest train station is Berlin Hauptbahnhof (a.k.a. "der Bahnhof," abbreviated Hbf). All long-distance trains arrive here. This is also a "transfer station," where the national train system meets the city's S-Bahn trains.

Services: On the main floor, you'll find

the **TI** and a Deutsche Bahn information center/ticket office; up one level are a 24-hour **pharmacy** and **lockers** (directly under track 14).

Rick's Tip: **EurAide** *is an American-run* **information desk** *with answers to your questions about train travel around Europe. It's located at counter 12 inside the Deutsche Bahn information center on the Hauptbahnhof's first upper level. This is a good place to make fast-train and* couchette *reservations (closed Jan-Feb and Sat-Sun year-round; www.euraide.com).*

Getting into Town: Taxis and buses wait outside the station, but the S-Bahn is probably the best means of connecting to your destination within Berlin. It's simple: All S-Bahn trains are on tracks 15 and 16 at the top of the station. All trains on track 15 go east, stopping at Friedrichstrasse, Hackescher Markt (with connections to Prenzlauer Berg), Alexanderplatz, and Ostbahnhof; trains on track 16 go west, toward Bahnhof Zoo.

To reach most recommended hotels in the Prenzlauer Berg neighborhood, it's fastest to take any train on track 15 two stops to Hackescher Markt, exit to Spandauer Strasse, go left, and cross the tracks to the tram stop. Here you'll catch tram #M1 north (direction: Schillerstrasse).

From Berlin by Train to: Dresden (every 2 hours, 2.5 hours), **Hamburg** (1-2/hour direct, 2 hours), **Frankfurt** (hourly, 4 hours), **Bacharach** (hourly, 7 hours, 1-3 changes), **Würzburg** (hourly, 4 hours, 1 change), **Rothenburg** (hourly, 5.5 hours, 3 changes), **Nürnberg** (hourly, 4.5 hours), **Munich** (1-2/hour, 6.5 hours, night train possible), **Cologne** (hourly, 4.5 hours, night train possible).

By Bus

The city's bus station, **ZOB** (Zentraler Omnibusbahnhof), is on the western edge of Berlin, in Charlottenburg (Masurenallee 4-6, U2: Kaiserdamm). **MeinFernBus, Flix, Berlin Linien,** and **Eurolines** all operate from here to locations around Germany and Europe.

By Plane

Berlin is trying to finish construction of its new airport, **Willy Brandt Berlin-Brandenburg International,** located about 13 miles from central Berlin (airport code: BER), but the project has been perennially delayed. You'll most likely use **Tegel Airport,** which is four miles from the center (airport code: TXL). **Bus** #TXL goes between the airport, the Hauptbahnhof (stops by Washingtonplatz entrance), and Alexanderplatz. A **taxi** from Tegel Airport costs about €30 to Alexanderplatz.

Most flights from the east and discount airlines arrive at **Schönefeld Airport** (12.5 miles from center). From the old Schönefeld arrivals hall, it's a three-minute walk to the train station, where you can catch a regional express train into the city. Airport Express RE and RB trains go directly to Ostbahnhof, Alexanderplatz, Friedrichstrasse, and Hauptbahnhof (€3.30, 2/hour, direction: Nauen or Dessau, rail pass valid). A taxi to the city center costs about €35.

BEST OF THE REST

DRESDEN

Dresden surprises visitors, with fanciful Baroque architecture in a delightful-to-stroll cityscape, a dynamic history, and some of the best museum-going in Germany. This intriguing city winds up on far fewer American itineraries than it deserves to.

At the peak of its power in the 18th century, this capital of Saxony ruled most of present-day Poland and eastern Germany from the banks of the Elbe River. Augustus the Strong, prince elector of Saxony and king of Poland, peppered his city with fine Baroque buildings and filled his treasury with lavish jewels and artwork.

Dresden is better known outside Germany for its destruction in World War II. American and British bomber crews firebombed the city on the night of February 13, 1945. More than 25,000 people were killed and 75 percent of the historical center was destroyed. Even though the city plan still feels bombed out—with big gaps, wide boulevards, and old streetscapes gone—all of the most important historic buildings have been reconstructed.

Orientation

Dresden's Old Town (Altstadt) hugs a curve on the Elbe River, and most of its sights are within easy strolling distance along the south bank of the river. South of the Old Town (a 5-minute tram ride or 20-minute walk away) is the main train station (Hauptbahnhof). North of the Old Town, across the river, is the more residential New Town (Neustadt).

Rick's Tip: *The* **Historic Green Vault** *admits a limited number of people every half-hour.* **Reserve ahead or line up early to buy a same-day ticket.** *The ticket office opens at 10:00. Once you have your Historic Green Vault visit time, plan the rest of your day around it.*

Day Plan: Dresden's top sights can easily fill a day trip. If you're coming from

The rebuilt Frauenkirche dominates Dresden's old town.

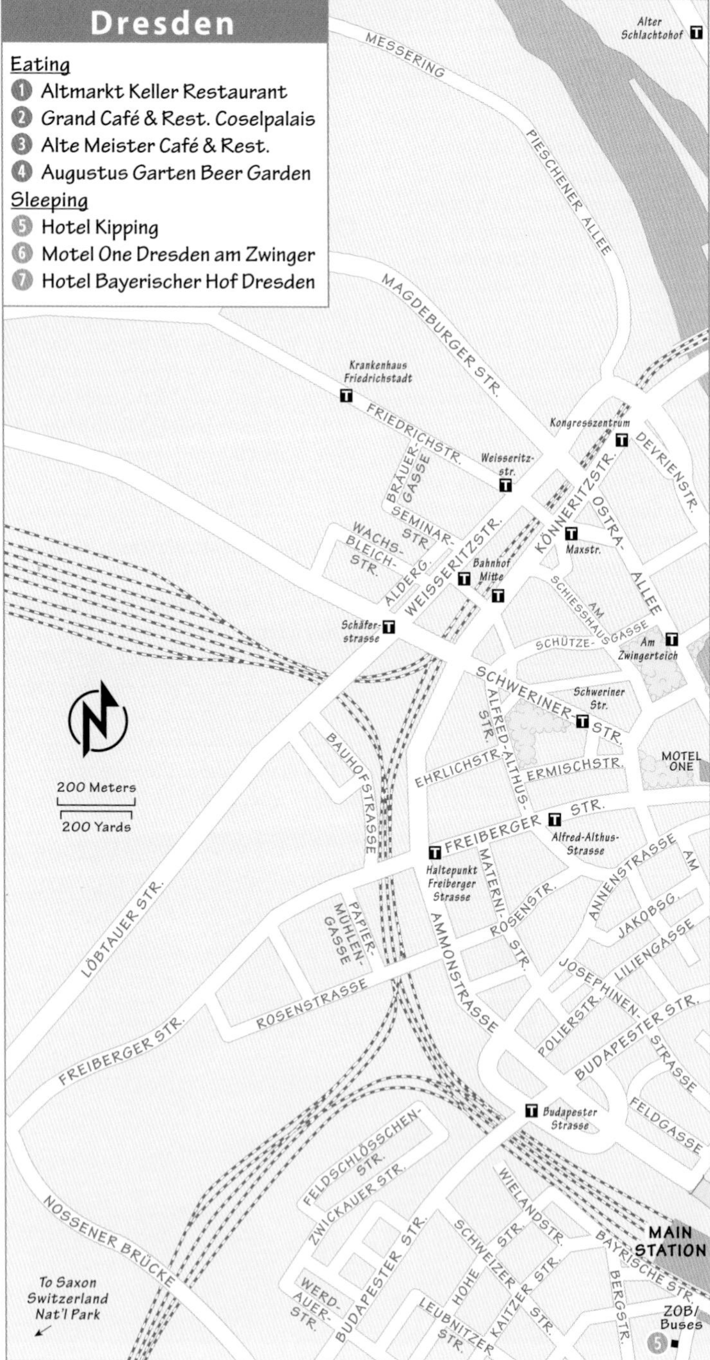
Dresden
Eating
1 Altmarkt Keller Restaurant
2 Grand Café & Rest. Coselpalais
3 Alte Meister Café & Rest.
4 Augustus Garten Beer Garden
Sleeping
5 Hotel Kipping
6 Motel One Dresden am Zwinger
7 Hotel Bayerischer Hof Dresden
Alter Schlachtohof
MESSERING
PIESCHENER ALLEE
MAGDEBURGER STR.
Krankenhaus Friedrichstadt
FRIEDRICHSTR.
BRÄUER-GASSE
Weisseritz-str.
Kongresszentrum
DEVRIENSTR.
KÖNNERITZSTR.
OSTRA-ALLEE
SEMINAR-STR.
WACHS-BLEICH-STR.
ALDERG.
WEISSERITZSTR.
Bahnhof Mitte
Maxstr.
AM SCHIESSHAUS
SCHÜTZE-GASSE
Am Zwingerteich
Schäfer-strasse
SCHWERINER-STR.
Schweriner Str.
ALFRED-ALTHUS-STR.
BAUHOFSTRASSE
EHRLICHSTR.
ERMISCHSTR.
MOTEL ONE
200 Meters
200 Yards
FREIBERGER STR.
Alfred-Althus-Strasse
Haltepunkt Freiberger Strasse
MATERNI-STR.
AM
ANNENSTRASSE
JAKOBSG.
LILIENGASSE
ROSENSTR.
PAPIER-MÜHLEN-GASSE
AMMONSTRASSE
JOSEPHINEN-STRASSE
LÖBTAUER STR.
ROSENSTRASSE
POLIERSTR.
BUDAPESTER STR.
FREIBERGER STR.
Budapester Strasse
FELDGASSE
FELDSCHLÖSSCHEN-STR.
ZWICKAUER STR.
WIELANDSTR.
NOSSENER BRÜCKE
SCHWEIZER STR.
BAYRISCHE STR.
MAIN STATION
HOHE STR.
KAITZER STR.
WERD-AUER-STR.
BUDAPESTER STR.
LEUBNITZER STR.
BERGSTR.
ZOB/ Buses
To Saxon Switzerland Nat'l Park

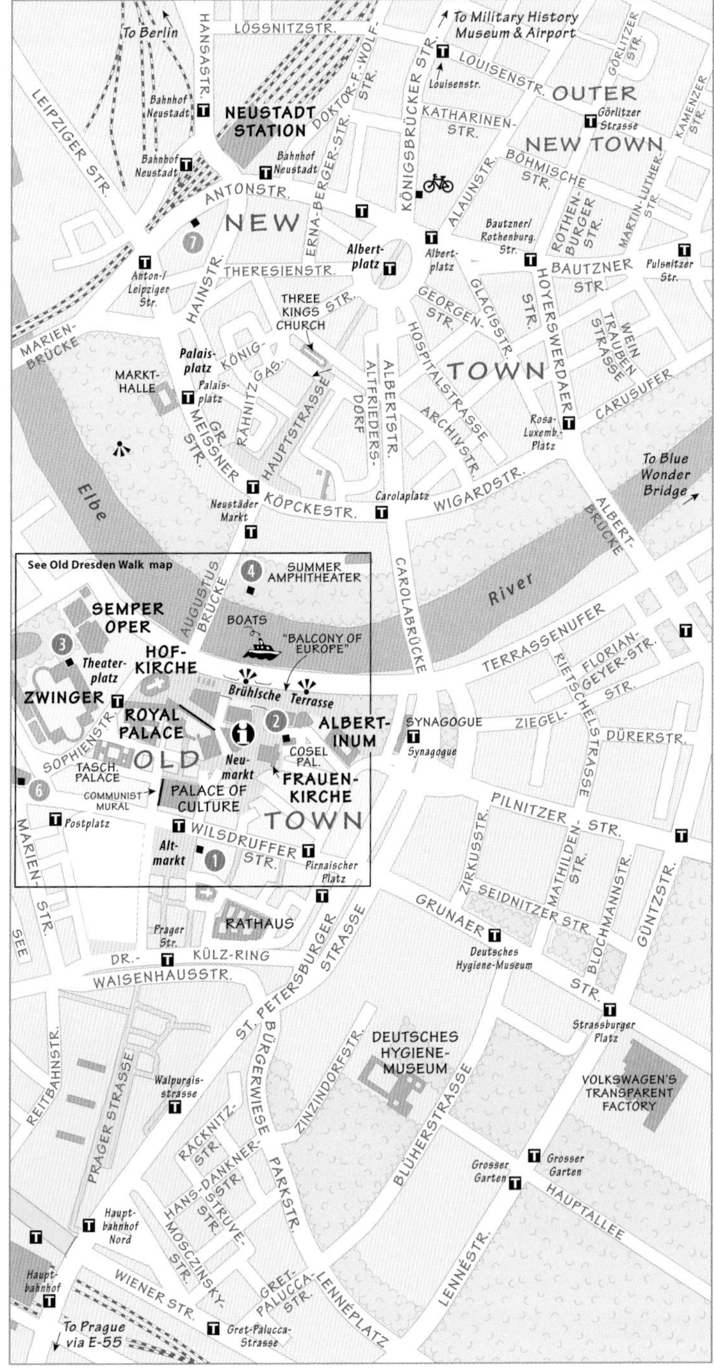
To Berlin
To Military History Museum & Airport
NEUSTADT STATION
OUTER NEW TOWN
NEW TOWN
OLD TOWN
Elbe River
See Old Dresden Walk map
SUMMER AMPHITHEATER
SEMPER OPER
BOATS
"BALCONY OF EUROPE"
HOFKIRCHE
Theaterplatz
ZWINGER
Brühlsche Terrasse
ROYAL PALACE
ALBERTINUM
SYNAGOGUE
TASCH. PALACE
COSEL PAL.
Neumarkt
FRAUENKIRCHE
COMMUNIST MURAL
PALACE OF CULTURE
Altmarkt
THREE KINGS CHURCH
MARKTHALLE
RATHAUS
DEUTSCHES HYGIENE-MUSEUM
VOLKSWAGEN'S TRANSPARENT FACTORY
To Blue Wonder Bridge
To Prague via E-55
Bahnhof Neustadt
Louisenstr.
Görlitzer Strasse
Albertplatz
Anton-/Leipziger Str.
Bautzner/Rothenburg. Str.
Pulsnitzer Str.
Palaisplatz
Rosa-Luxemb.-Platz
Neustädter Markt
Carolaplatz
Synagogue
Postplatz
Pirnaischer Platz
Prager Str.
Deutsches Hygiene-Museum
Strassburger Platz
Walpurgisstrasse
Grosser Garten
Hauptbahnhof Nord
Hauptbahnhof
Gret-Palucca-Strasse
LÖSSNITZSTR.
HANSASTR.
LEIPZIGER STR.
DOKTOR-F.-WOLF-STR.
ERNA-BERGER-STR.
KÖNIGSBRÜCKER STR.
LOUISENSTR.
GÖRLITZER STR.
KAMENZER STR.
KATHARINENSTR.
ALAUNSTR.
BÖHMISCHE STR.
ROTHENBURGER STR.
MARTIN-LUTHER-STR.
ANTONSTR.
THERESIENSTR.
HAINSTR.
BAUTZNER STR.
HOYERSWERDAER STR.
GLACISSTR.
GEORGENSTR.
WEINTRAUBENSTRASSE
MARIENBRÜCKE
KÖNIGSTR.
RÄHNITZGAS.
HAUPTSTRASSE
ALTFRIEDERSDORF
ALBERTSTR.
HOSPITALSTRASSE
ARCHIVSTR.
CARUSUFER
GR. MEISSNER STR.
KÖPCKESTR.
WIGARDSTR.
ALBERTBRÜCKE
AUGUSTUSBRÜCKE
CAROLABRÜCKE
TERRASSENUFER
RIETSCHELSTRASSE
FLORIAN-GEYER-STR.
ZIEGELSTR.
DÜRERSTR.
SOPHIENSTR.
PILNITZER STR.
WILSDRUFFER STR.
ZIRKUSSTR.
MATHILDENSTR.
BLOCHMANNSTR.
GÜNTZSTR.
SEIDNITZER STR.
GRUNAER STR.
MARIENSTR.
SEE
DR.-KÜLZ-RING
WAISENHAUSSTR.
ST. PETERSBURGER STRASSE
BÜRGERWIESE
ZINZINDORFSTR.
BLÜHERSTRASSE
REITBAHNSTR.
PRAGER STRASSE
RACKNITZSTR.
HANS-DANKNER-STR.
STRUVESTR.
PARKSTR.
MOSCZINSKYSTR.
GRET-PALUCCA-STR.
LENNÉPLATZ
LENNÉSTR.
HAUPTALLEE
WIENER STR.

Berlin, catch an early train, throw your bag in a locker at the main train station, follow my self-guided walk, and visit some museums before taking an evening train out. If possible, reserve ahead to visit one of Dresden's top sights, the Historic Green Vault.

Getting There: Trains connect Dresden with **Berlin** (every 2 hours, 2.5 hours), **Hamburg** (4/day, 4.5 hours), **Frankfurt** (hourly, 5 hours), **Nürnberg** (hourly, 4.5-5 hours), and **Munich** (every 2 hours, 6 hours).

Arrival in Dresden: If you come by **train,** get off at the main station, Hauptbahnhof (not the Neustadt station, across the river), for the easiest access to sights. To reach the beginning of my self-guided walk quickly by **tram,** exit the station following *Ausgang 1* signs, cross the tram tracks, and take tram #8 to Theaterplatz in the Old Town (five stops). Otherwise, it's a 20-minute **stroll** down Prager Strasse to the Old Town. For drivers, the city center has several well-marked **parking garages** with reasonable daytime rates.

Tourist Information: A TI kiosk is in the main train station. The main TI is at Neumarkt 2 (Mon-Fri 10:00-19:00, Sat 10:00-18:00, Sun 10:00-15:00; enter under *Passage* sign across from door D of Frauenkirche, and go down escalators, tel. 0351/501-501, www.dresden.de/tourismus).

Private Guides: Liane Richter (€80/2-hour tour, lianerichter@gmx.net) and **Anke Winkler** (€90/2-hour tour, info@dresden-citytour.de) are both good.

➲ Dresden Old Town Walk

Dresden's major Old Town sights are conveniently clustered along a wonderfully strollable promenade next to the Elbe River. This self-guided walk takes about an hour, not counting museum stops. It passes by three major sights (Zwinger, Royal Palace with Green Vault treasuries, and Frauenkirche). If you visit the sights, this walk will fill your day.

• *Begin at Theaterplatz (a convenient drop-off point for tram #8 from the Hauptbahnhof).*

❶ **Theaterplatz:** In the middle of the square, face the equestrian statue of King John, an intellectual mid-19th-century ruler who recognized and preserved

Theaterplatz leads into Dresden's Old Town.

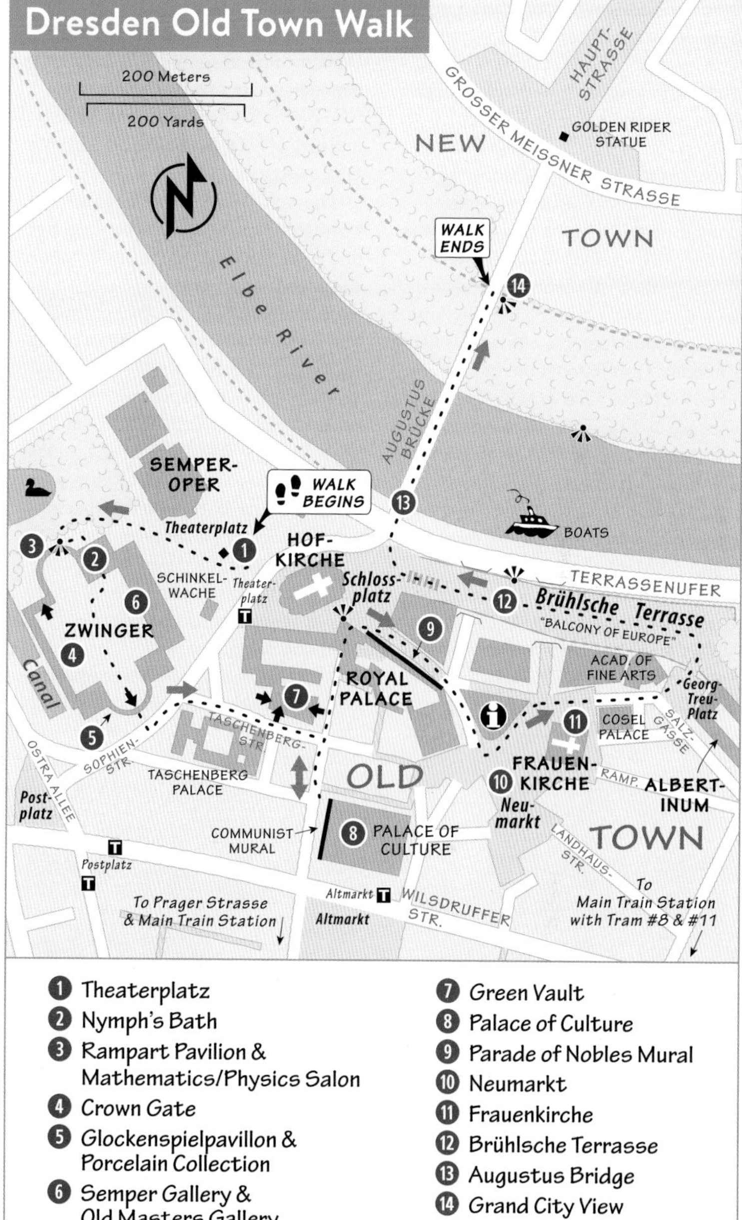
Dresden Old Town Walk
200 Meters
200 Yards
NEW
TOWN
GROSSER MEISSNER STRASSE
HAUPT-STRASSE
GOLDEN RIDER STATUE
WALK ENDS
Elbe River
AUGUSTUS BRÜCKE
SEMPER-OPER
WALK BEGINS
Theaterplatz
HOF-KIRCHE
SCHINKEL-WACHE
Theater-platz
Schloss-platz
BOATS
TERRASSENUFER
Brühlsche Terrasse
"BALCONY OF EUROPE"
ACAD. OF FINE ARTS
Georg-Treu-Platz
ZWINGER
Canal
ROYAL PALACE
COSEL PALACE
SALZ-GASSE
TASCHENBERG-STR.
SOPHIEN-STR.
TASCHENBERG PALACE
OSTRA ALLEE
Post-platz
OLD
TOWN
FRAUEN-KIRCHE
RAMP.
ALBERT-INUM
Neu-markt
COMMUNIST MURAL
PALACE OF CULTURE
LANDHAUS-STR.
Postplatz
To Prager Strasse & Main Train Station
Altmarkt
WILSDRUFFER STR.
To Main Train Station with Tram #8 & #11
1 Theaterplatz
2 Nymph's Bath
3 Rampart Pavilion & Mathematics/Physics Salon
4 Crown Gate
5 Glockenspielpavillon & Porcelain Collection
6 Semper Gallery & Old Masters Gallery
7 Green Vault
8 Palace of Culture
9 Parade of Nobles Mural
10 Neumarkt
11 Frauenkirche
12 Brühlsche Terrasse
13 Augustus Bridge
14 Grand City View

Saxon culture—and paid for the **Semper-oper** opera house behind the statue.

As you face the opera house, the big building to your left is the vast Zwinger museum complex (your next stop). Behind you, across the square from the opera house, are the Katholiche Hofkirche, with its distinctive onion-domed steeple, and the sprawling Royal Palace. All the buildings you see here are thorough reconstructions. The originals were destroyed in a single night by American and British bombs, with only walls and sometimes just foundations left standing.

• *Head left of the Opera House toward the back end of the Zwinger. Near the recommended Alte Meister Café, go up the stairs and hang a left up the path. Head past the adorable fountain at the top of the path to the balcony with a breathtaking view of the grand...*

Zwinger: This complex of buildings is a Baroque masterpiece. Once the pride and joy of the Wettin dynasty, it's filled with fine museums today. The Wettins ruled Saxony for more than 800 years, right up until the end of the First World War. Saxony was ruled by a prince elector—one of a handful of nobles who elected the Holy Roman Emperor. In the 18th century, the larger-than-life Augustus the Strong—who was both prince elector of Saxony and king of Poland—kicked off Saxony's Golden Age.

The word "Zwinger" refers to the no-man's-land moat between the outer and inner city walls. As the city expanded, the pavilions and galleries you see today were built. Although the Zwinger buildings might look like a palace to us commoners, no one ever lived here—it was solely for pleasurable pursuits.

• *Cross the balcony to the left to enjoy a view of the Nymphs' Bath from above, then take the small stairs at the top down to its pool.*

❷ **Nymphs' Bath:** Here, at what is perhaps the city's favorite fountain, 18th-century aristocrats relaxed among cascading waterfalls and an open-air grotto, ringed by sexy sandstone nymphs. It's textbook Baroque.

• *From the pool, cross through the glassy orangery and all the way into the middle of the huge...*

The Zwinger museums and courtyard

Augustus the Strong

Friedrich Augustus I (1670-1733) of the Wettin family made Dresden one of Europe's most important cities of culture. As prince elector of Saxony, Augustus wheeled and dealed—and pragmatically converted from his Saxon Protestantism to a more Polish-friendly Catholicism—to become King Augustus II of Poland. (You'll notice the city center features both the fancy Protestant Frauenkirche and the huge, prominent Catholic Hofkirche.) Like most Wettins, Augustus the Strong was unlucky at war, but a clever diplomat and a lover of the arts.

The Polish people blame Augustus and his successors—who were far more concerned with wealth and opulence than with sensible governance—for Poland's precipitous decline after its own medieval Golden Age. According to Poles, the Saxon kings did nothing but "eat, drink, and loosen their belts" (it rhymes in Polish).

Whether you consider them the heroes or the villains, Augustus and the rest of the Wettins—and the nobles who paid them taxes—are to thank for Dresden's rich architectural and artistic heritage.

Zwinger Courtyard: Survey the four wings, starting with the ❸ **Rampart Pavilion** (Wallpavillon)—the one you just came from, marked up top by Hercules hoisting the earth. The first wing of the complex to be built, it includes an orangery capped with a sun pavilion built for Augustus' fruit trees and parties. The other side of this wing (on the left) houses the fun **Mathematics-Physics Salon.**

Turn farther to the left, facing the ❹ **Crown Gate** (Kronentor). The gate's golden crown is topped by four golden eagles supporting a smaller crown—symbolizing Polish royalty (since Augustus was also king of Poland).

Turn again to the left to see the ❺ **Glockenspielpavillon.** The glockenspiel near the top of the gate has 40 bells made of Meissen porcelain. If you're here when they play, listen to the delightful chimes of the porcelain—far sweeter than a typical metal bell. This wing of the Zwinger also houses Augustus the Strong's renowned **Porcelain Collection.**

Turn once more to the left (with the Crown Gate behind you) to see the stern facade of the ❻ **Semper Gallery.** This Zwinger wing houses Dresden's best painting collection, the **Old Masters Gallery.**

You are surrounded by three of Dresden's top museums. Anticipating WWII bombs, Dresdeners preserved their town's art treasures by storing them in underground mines and cellars in the countryside. This saved these great works from Allied bombs...but not from the Russians. Nearly all the city's artwork ended up in Moscow until after Stalin's death in 1953, when it was returned by the communist regime to win over their East German subjects.

If you're not detouring now to visit any of the Zwinger museums, exit the courtyard through the Glockenspielpavillon.

• *As you exit the corridor, cross the street and the tram tracks and jog left, then right, walking down the perpendicular street called Taschenberg, with the yellow Taschenberg Palace on your right. The yellow-windowed sky bridge ahead connects the Taschenberg with the prince electors'* ***Royal Palace.*** *The gate on your left is one of several entrances to the palace, with its ❼* ***Green Vault*** *treasuries and other sights (described later).*

Continue along Taschenberg and under the sky bridge. Ahead of you and to the right, the blocky modern building (probably behind scaffolding) is the...

❽ **Palace of Culture** (Kulturpalast): Built by the communist government in

1969, today this hall is used for concerts. Notice the exterior mural depicting communist themes: workers, strong women, well-cared-for elders, teachers and students, and—of course—the red star and the seal of the former East Germany. Little of this propagandist art, which once inundated the lives of locals, survives in post-communist Germany (what does survive, like this, is protected).

• *Leave the Palace of Culture behind you and walk with the Royal Palace on your left. After passing through a tunnel, you emerge onto* ***Palace Square.*** *Ahead and to the left are the Baroque* ***Katholiche Hofkirche*** *(Dresden's Catholic church; free entry) and another elevated passage, designed to allow royalty to go to church without the hassle of dealing with the public. Now turn to the right, next to one of the palace's entrances, and walk toward the long, yellow mural called the...*

❾ **Parade of Nobles** (Fürstenzug): This mural is painted on 24,000 tiles of Meissen porcelain. Longer than a football field, it illustrates seven centuries of Saxon royalty. The very last figure in the procession (the first one you see, coming from this direction) is the artist himself, Wilhelm Walther. In front of him are commoners (miners, farmers, carpenters, teachers, students, artists), and then the royals, with 35 names and dates marking more than 700 years of Wettin rule. Walk the length of the mural to appreciate the detail (don't miss Augustus the Strong, at 1694). The porcelain tiles are originals (from 1907)—they survived the Dresden bombing. They were fired three times at 2,400 degrees Fahrenheit when created... and then fired again during the 1945 firestorm, at only 1,800 degrees.

• *When you're finished looking at the mural, dogleg right and walk into the big square, where a statue of Martin Luther stands tall.*

❿ **Neumarkt:** This "New Market Square" was once a central square ringed by the homes of rich merchants. After many years of construction, it is once again alive with people and cafés, and even a few frilly facades that help you picture what the square looked like in its heyday. The statue of Martin Luther shows him holding not just any Bible, but the German version of the Word of God, which he personally translated so that regular people could wrestle with it directly (this is, in a sense, what the Protestant Reformation was all about).

• *The big church looming over the square is the...*

⓫ **Frauenkirche** (Church of Our Lady): This church is the symbol and soul of the city. When completed in 1743, this was Germany's tallest Protestant church (310 feet high). The building garners the world's attention primarily because of its tragic history and phoenix-like resurrection: On the night of February 13, 1945, the firebombs came. When the smoke cleared the next morning, the Frauenkirche was smoldering but still standing. It burned for two days before finally collapsing. After the war, the Frauenkirche was left a pile of rubble and turned into a peace monument. Only after reunification was the decision made to rebuild it com-

Frauenkirche dome

pletely and painstakingly in all its Baroque splendor.

A big hunk of the bombed **rubble** stands in the square (near door E, river side of church) as a memorial. Notice the small metal relief of the dome that shows where this piece came from (free entry, climbable dome, www.frauenkirche-dresden.de).

• *From the chunk of church, turn left to find the nearby dome that caps the exhibition hall of the* ***Academy of Fine Arts.*** *Walk past that to the small, grassy Georg-Treu-Platz, which is surrounded by imposing architecture. The grand Neo-Renaissance building ahead and to the right is the* ***Albertinum,*** *an art gallery whose excellent collections encompass the Romantic period (late 18th and early 19th centuries) to the present (closed Mon, www.skd.museum). Walk through the square and climb the ramparts for an Elbe River view and a chance to stroll the length of the...*

⓬ **Brühlsche Terrasse:** This pleasant promenade overlooking the river was once a defensive rampart—look along the side of the terrace facing the Elbe River to see openings for cannons. In the early 1800s, it was turned into a public park, with a leafy canopy of linden trees.

• *At the far end of the terrace, stop at the grove of linden trees with a fountain at the center, and look out at the...*

⓭ **Augustus Bridge:** The Augustusbrücke has connected Dresden's old and new towns since 1319, when it was the first stone bridge over the river. At the far end of the bridge, you can see the symbol of Dresden: the 1736 golden equestrian statue of Augustus the Strong, nicknamed the "Golden Rider" (Goldene Reiter).

• *We're back near where we started out, which makes this a good stopping point for this walk. But if you have time, walk out to enjoy the* ⓮ ***grand city view*** *from the bridge—of the glass dome of the Academy of Fine Arts, capped by a trumpeting gold angel, and the other venerable facades, domes, and spires of regal Dresden.*

Sights

Zwinger Museums

Three museums are located off the Zwinger courtyard: the Old Masters Gallery, Mathematics-Physics Salon, and Porcelain Collection.

Cost and Hours: €10 for Old Masters Gallery, includes Mathematics-Physics Salon and Porcelain Collection (which otherwise cost €6 apiece); museums share the same hours: Tue-Sun 10:00-18:00, closed Mon; tel. 0351/4914-2000, www.skd.museum.

▲▲OLD MASTERS GALLERY (GEMÄLDEGALERIE ALTE MEISTER)

Dresden's best collection of paintings, housed in the Zwinger's Semper Gallery, features works by Raphael, Titian, Rembrandt, Rubens, Vermeer, and more. It feels particularly enjoyable for its "quality, not quantity" approach to showing off great art. Old-timers remember the Old Masters Gallery as the first big public building reopened after the war, in 1956. While the building is undergoing a years-long renovation project, the major works are always on display.

MATHEMATICS-PHYSICS SALON (MATHEMATISCH-PHYSIKALISCHERSALON)

This fun collection (at the end of the courtyard with the Hercules-topped pavilion; enter through left corner) features scientific gadgets from the 16th to 19th centuries, including measuring, timekeeping, and surveying instruments, as well as globes and telescopes—all displayed like dazzling works of art. Anyone with a modest scientific bent will find something of interest; be sure to pick up the included audioguide.

▲PORCELAIN COLLECTION (PORZELLANSAMMLUNG)

Every self-respecting European king had a porcelain works, and the Wettin dynasty had the most famous one, at Meissen (a charming town 10 miles north of here).

They inspired other royal courts to get into the art form. They also collected porcelain from around the world—from France to Japan and China.

Augustus the Strong was obsessed with the stuff...he liked to say he had "porcelain sickness." Here you can enjoy some of his symptoms, under chandeliers in elegant galleries flooded with natural light from the huge windows. Today it's the largest specialist ceramics collection in the world.

Royal Palace (Residenzschloss)

This palace, the residence of the Saxon prince electors and kings, was one of the finest Renaissance buildings in Germany before its destruction in World War II. The big draw here is the Saxon treasuries: the Historic Green Vault (Augustus' goodies displayed in reconstructed Baroque halls) and the New Green Vault (more royal treasures in contemporary display cases). Other attractions include the Royal Armory, displaying sumptuous armor for horse and rider, and the Turkish Chamber, one of the oldest collections of Ottoman art outside Turkey.

Cost and Hours: €12 covers the palace complex, special exhibitions, and audioguide—but not the Historic Green Vault, which requires a separate, timed-entry ticket (€12, includes audioguide). A €21 combo-ticket covers everything, including the Historic Green Vault. The entire complex is open Wed-Mon 10:00-18:00, closed Tue; tel. 0351/4914-2000, www.skd.museum.

Orientation: The palace complex has three entrances, each leading to a glass-domed inner courtyard, where you'll find the ticket windows and restrooms. Inside, the ground floor is home to the Baroque halls of the Historic Green Vault; the first floor up has the New Green Vault, and the next floor up houses the Giant's Hall, with the bulk of the Royal Armory and the Turkish Chamber.

▲▲▲HISTORIC GREEN VAULT (HISTORISCHES GRÜNES GEWÖLBE)

This famed, glittering Baroque treasury collection was begun by Augustus the Strong in the early 1700s. Over the years it evolved into the royal family's extravagant trove of ivory, silver, and gold knickknacks,

The inner courtyard of the Royal Palace

displayed in rooms as opulent as the collection itself.

Reservations: The number of visitors each day is carefully controlled. If you must get in at a certain time, book your timed-entry ticket well in advance (www.skd.museum). If you haven't booked ahead, show up early and try for a same-day ticket (90 tickets are available every half-hour).

Visiting the Historic Green Vault: Everything is designed to wow you in typically Baroque style. The **Amber Cabinet** serves as a reminder of just how many different things you can do with fossilized tree sap (in a surprising range of colors), and the **Ivory Room** does the same for elephant tusks. The **White Silver Room,** painted its original vermillion color, holds a chalice carved from a rhino horn, and the **Silver-Gilt Room** displays tableware and gold-ruby glass.

The wide variety of items in the largest room—the aptly named **Hall of Precious Objects**—includes mother-of-pearl sculptures, ostrich-egg and snail-shell goblets, and a model of the Hill of Calvary atop a pile of pearls and polished seashells.

The vault's highlight is the grandly decorated **Jewel Room**—essentially, Saxony's crown jewels. The incredible pieces in here are fine examples of the concept of *Gesamtkunstwerk*—an artwork whose perfection comes from the sum of its parts.

▲▲NEW GREEN VAULT (NEUES GRÜNES GEWÖLBE)

This collection shows off more Saxon treasure, but in a modern setting, arranged chronologically from the Renaissance to the 19th century. The focus here isn't the rooms themselves, but the treasures in glass cases.

Eating

$$ Altmarkt Keller is a festive beer cellar that serves nicely presented Saxon and Bohemian food (Altmarkt 4). The good-value **$$ Grand Café & Restaurant Coselpalais** is right near the Frauenkirche (An der Frauenkirche 12). **$$$ Alte Meister Café and Restaurant** has delightful garden seating (facing the Opera at Theaterplatz 1). Just across the Augustus Bridge, the rollicking **$$ Augustus Garten** beer garden has views back over the Old Town (Wiesentorstrasse 2).

Sleeping

To spend the night, consider family-run **$$ Hotel Kipping,** just behind the Hauptbahnhof (Winckelmannstrasse 6, www.hotel-kipping.de); **$ Motel One Dresden am Zwinger,** within cherub-fountain-spitting distance of the Zwinger (Postplatz 5, www.motel-one.com); or the grand **$$$ Hotel Bayerischer Hof Dresden,** across the river near the Neustadt train station (Antonstrasse 33, www.bayerischer-hof-dresden.de).

BEST OF THE REST

HAMBURG

Hamburg (pronounced HAHM-boork) is Germany's second-largest city, the richest judged by per-capita income, and its most important port.

The city's salty maritime atmosphere—with a constant breeze and the evocative cries of seagulls—gives Hamburg an almost Scandinavian feel.

Hamburg lacks a quaint medieval center. Ye Olde Hamburg was flattened by a one-two punch that occurred over a 101-year span: First, a devastating 1842 fire, and then an equally devastating firebombing by Allied forces in 1943. Today, the revitalized city center is a people-friendly collection of wide streets, outdoor cafés, and shops.

Hamburg is expanding rapidly as it redevelops its former docklands into the burgeoning HafenCity district, with its centerpiece, the spectacular Elbphilharmonie concert hall. Hamburg expects to be seen as a cultural capital moving boldly into a promising future.

Orientation

Hamburg is big (1.8 million people). The city center, which sits between the Elbe ("ELL-beh") River to the south and a lake called the Binnenalster to the north, is surrounded by a ring road that follows the route of the old city walls. Most places of interest are just outside this central core: The train station and the St. Georg neighborhood (with good hotels and restaurants) are just east of the center. The harbor, old Speicherstadt warehouse district, and the new HafenCity zone are to the south along the Elbe. And the St. Pauli waterfront district lies to the west.

Day Plan: Hamburg can easily fill a rewarding day (or more) of sightseeing. For a day trip, toss your bag in a train-station locker and take the 1.5-hour ori-

Hamburg is revitalizing its harborfront.

Operation Gomorrah: The Firebombing of Hamburg

With its port, munitions factories, and transportation links, Hamburg was a prime target for Allied bombers during World War II. After studying what the Luftwaffe did to Coventry in 1940, the British decided to use the same techniques against Hamburg on July 27, 1943. They hit targets first with explosive bombs to open roofs, break water mains, and tear up streets (making it hard for firefighters to respond), then followed up with incendiary bombs. Designed to destroy a city known for its lustful ways, the attack was given the codename Operation Gomorrah.

In three hours, the inferno killed an estimated 35,000 people, left hundreds of thousands homeless, and reduced eight square miles of Hamburg to rubble and ashes. At the end of the eight-day bombing campaign, which included US raids, about one million survivors had fled the city. The firebombing of Dresden two years later is more famous, but far more people died in Hamburg. And while the earlier Nazi bombings of London, Rotterdam, and Coventry were deadly, some historians say the firebombing of Hamburg was World War II's first widespread destruction of a major city.

entation bus tour (Roten Doppeldecker hop-on, hop-off bus tour), which leaves from the station. Get off at Landungsbrücken in time to catch the 12:00 harbor cruise. Take the bus to HafenCity to see the concert hall and museums, then return to the station. (The sights are reachable by subway, if you'd rather not take the bus tour.)

With more time, visit the St. Nicholas Church and Hamburg Museum. If staying the night, you could stroll the lively, edgy Reeperbahn nightlife district.

Getting There: Trains connect Hamburg with **Berlin** (1-2/hour direct, 2 hours), **Cologne** (hourly direct, 4 hours), **Frankfurt** (hourly direct, 4 hours), **Munich** (hourly direct, 6.5 hours), **Copenhagen** (direct trains almost every 2 hours, 5 hours), and **Amsterdam** (every 2 hours, 5.5 hours, 1 change).

Arrival in Hamburg: From the **train station** (with a TI, lockers, left-luggage service, and *Reisezentrum*), you can walk to my recommended St. Georg neighborhood hotels, catch a bus orientation tour, or use the subway to get directly to the sights. For a taxi, try Hansa-Taxi (tel. 040/211-211).

By **car,** park it. If spending the night, ask your hotelier about parking—many hotels have dedicated garages.

If arriving by **plane,** take the S-1 subway line to the train station (30-minute ride). Airport info: Tel. 040/50750, www.airport.de.

Getting Around: Use public transit to visit this spread-out city. The subway

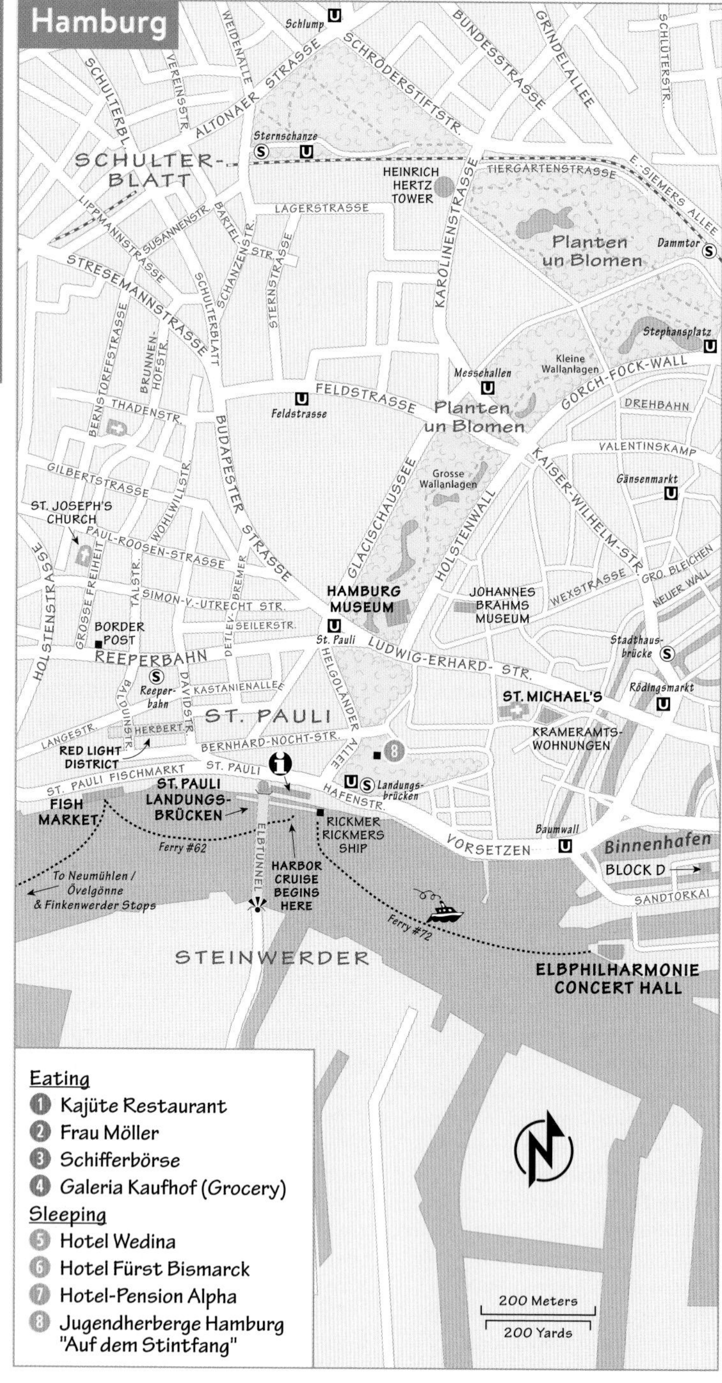
Hamburg
Schlump
Schröderstiftstr.
Bundesstrasse
Grindelallee
Schlüterstr.
Weidenallee
Altonaer Strasse
Vereinsstr.
Schulterbl.
Sternschanze
Schulterblatt
Heinrich Hertz Tower
Tiergartenstrasse
E.-Siemers Allee
Lagerstrasse
Lippmannstrasse
Susannenstr.
Bartel-Str.
Schanzenstr.
Sternstrasse
Karolinenstrasse
Planten un Blomen
Dammtor
Stresemannstrasse
Stephansplatz
Bernstorffstrasse
Brunnenhofstr.
Messehallen
Kleine Wallanlagen
Gorch-Fock-Wall
Feldstrasse
Drehbahn
Thadenstr.
Budapester Strasse
Valentinskamp
Gilbertstrasse
Grosse Wallanlagen
Gänsenmarkt
St. Joseph's Church
Wohlwillstr.
Glacischaussee
Holstenwall
Kaiser-Wilhelm-Str.
Paul-Roosen-Strasse
Holstenstrasse
Grosse Freiheit
Talstr.
Bremer
Hamburg Museum
Johannes Brahms Museum
Wexstrasse
Gro. Bleichen
Neuer Wall
Simon-v.-Utrecht Str.
Seilerstr.
Detlev-
Border Post
St. Pauli
Ludwig-Erhard-Str.
Stadthausbrücke
Reeperbahn
Kastanienallee
Helgoländer Allee
St. Michael's
Rödingsmarkt
Baldunistr.
Davidstr.
Langestr.
Herbert.
Kramerämtswohnungen
Bernhard-Nocht-Str.
Red Light District
St. Pauli Fischmarkt
St. Pauli Landungsbrücken
Landungsbrücken
Hafenstr.
Fish Market
Elbtunnel
Rickmer Rickmers Ship
Ferry #62
Vorsetzen
Baumwall
Binnenhafen
Block D
Sandtorkai
To Neumühlen / Övelgönne & Finkenwerder Stops
Harbor Cruise Begins Here
Ferry #72
Steinwerder
Elbphilharmonie Concert Hall
Eating
1 Kajüte Restaurant
2 Frau Möller
3 Schifferbörse
4 Galeria Kaufhof (Grocery)
Sleeping
5 Hotel Wedina
6 Hotel Fürst Bismarck
7 Hotel-Pension Alpha
8 Jugendherberge Hamburg "Auf dem Stintfang"
200 Meters
200 Yards

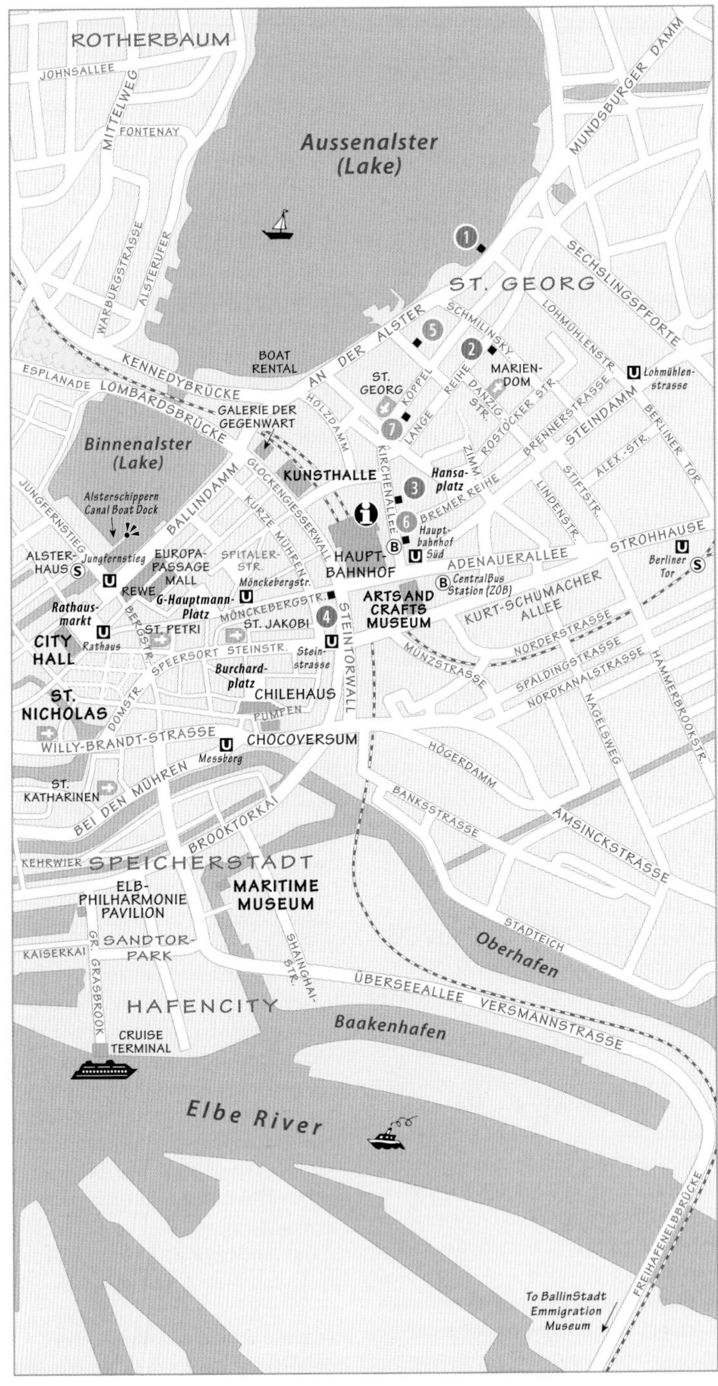
ROTHERBAUM
JOHNSALLEE
MITTELWEG
FONTENAY
Aussenalster (Lake)
MUNDSBURGER DAMM
WARBURGSTRASSE
ALSTERUFER
SECHSLINGSPFORTE
ST. GEORG
SCHMILINSKY
LOHMÜHLENSTR.
KENNEDYBRÜCKE
BOAT RENTAL
AN DER ALSTER
ST. GEORG
KOPPEL
LANGE REIHE
DANZIG STR.
MARIEN-DOM
ROSTOCKER STR.
BRENNERSTRASSE
STEINDAMM
Lohmühlen-strasse
BERLINER TOR
ESPLANADE
LOMBARDSBRÜCKE
GALERIE DER GEGENWART
HOLZDAMM
Binnenalster (Lake)
KUNSTHALLE
Hansa-platz
ZIMM.
BREMER REIHE
ALEX.-STR.
STIFTSTR.
LINDENSTR.
JUNGFERNSTIEG
BALLINDAMM
GLOCKENGIESSERWALL
KURZE MÜHREN
Alsterschippern Canal Boat Dock
KIRCHENALLEE
Haupt-bahnhof Süd
STROHHAUSE
ALSTER-HAUS
Jungfernstieg
EUROPA-PASSAGE MALL
SPITALER-STR.
HAUPT-BAHNHOF
ADENAUERALLEE
Berliner Tor
REWE
Mönckebergstr.
CentralBus Station (ZOB)
KURT-SCHUMACHER ALLEE
Rathaus-markt
G-Hauptmann-Platz
MÖNCKEBERGSTR.
ARTS AND CRAFTS MUSEUM
STEINTORWALL
ST. JAKOBI
ST. PETRI
BERGSTR.
CITY HALL
Rathaus
NORDERSTRASSE
MÜNZSTRASSE
SPEERSORT
STEINSTR.
Stein-strasse
SPALDINGSTRASSE
NORDKANALSTRASSE
Burchard-platz
HAMMERBROOKSTR.
DOMSTR.
CHILEHAUS
ST. NICHOLAS
PUMPEN
NAGELSWEG
WILLY-BRANDT-STRASSE
CHOCOVERSUM
Messberg
HÖGERDAMM
ST. KATHARINEN
BEI DEN MÜHREN
BANKSSTRASSE
BROOKTORKAI
AMSINCKSTRASSE
KEHRWIER
SPEICHERSTADT
ELB-PHILHARMONIE PAVILION
MARITIME MUSEUM
STADTEICH
SANDTOR-PARK
KAISERKAI
GR. GRASBROOK
SHANGHAI-STR.
Oberhafen
ÜBERSEEALLEE
VERSMANNSTRASSE
HAFENCITY
Baakenhafen
CRUISE TERMINAL
Elbe River
FREIHAFENELBBRÜCKE
To BallinStadt Emmigration Museum

system includes both the U-Bahn (with four lines, U-1 to U-4) and S-Bahn (commuter rail lines). Buses and public ferries, which are both covered by the various transit passes, round out the system.

The Hamburg transport association—known as HVV—has an information office next to the TI in the train station (tel. 040/19449, www.hvv.de). Buy tickets from the machines at each U-Bahn or S-Bahn stop, marked *HVV*; these take coins and small bills. Tickets bought from machines are already validated; you don't need to stamp them again.

Single ticket prices vary; the shortest trips cost €1.50, longer ones €2, and the longest ones (which include the airport) cost €3. Key your destination into a ticket machine, and it will tell you the price of the ticket.

If you'll be in town for a day (and you don't get a Hamburg Card), get a **day pass,** which pays for itself quickly and gives you the run of the whole system. The *9-Uhr-Tageskarte* costs €6 (not valid Mon-Fri before 9:00; the *9-Uhr-Gruppenkarte* version for up to five people is only €11).

Tourist Information: The main TI is in the train station, above the north end of platforms 3-4. It has good, free maps (Mon-Sat 9:00-19:00, Sun 10:00-18:00, www.hamburg-tourism.de). There are also TIs at the St. Pauli Landungsbrücken harborfront and the airport. For tourist info by phone, call 040/3005-1701 (closed Sun).

TIs sell the **Hamburg Card.** If you'll be visiting two or three museums, especially with a travel partner or two, the card is a sound investment, costing little more than a transit pass, while offering modest discounts at sights (also sold at public-transit ticket machines; €10/day, €17/day for groups of up to 5; 2- and 3-day passes available).

Tours: The most interesting sights are scattered on the perimeter of the city center, so Hamburg lends itself an orientation by bus. Several companies run **hop-on hop-off bus tours** (€15-18 for 1.5 hours, generally 10 percent discount with Hamburg Card). While you can hop on or off at points throughout the city, the most logical starting points are at the train station (buses park along Kirchenallee) and near the Landungsbrücken pier.

Die Roten Doppeldecker has good English guides and frequent departures (€17.50 ticket good all day, 27 stops, departs every half-hour April-Oct 9:30-17:00, less frequently Nov-March, tel. 040/792-8979, www.die-roten-doppeldecker.de). A €30 combo-ticket adds the Rainer Abicht harbor boat tour at noon; a different €30 combo-ticket adds the Maritime Circle hop-on, hop-off boat (see page 375).

Sights

In the City Center

▲▲ST. NICHOLAS CHURCH MUSEUM, MEMORIAL, AND TOWER (MAHNMAL ST. NIKOLAI)

Before the mid-20th century, downtown Hamburg's skyline had five main churches, each with a bold tower. Today there are still five towers...but only four churches. The missing one is St. Nicholas' Church. It was designed in Neo-Gothic style by British architect George Gilbert Scott, and for a brief time after its completion in 1874, at 483 feet it was the world's tallest church (its spire is still the fifth tallest in the world). The church was destroyed by the Operation Gomorrah firebombing in 1943 (see sidebar). Its tower and a few charred walls have been left as a ruin, to commemorate those lost and to remind everyone of the horrors of war. A stroll here, between the half-destroyed walls of a once-stunning church, is poignant.

Cost and Hours: It's free to explore the footprint memorials, but you'll pay €5 to go up the tower and enter the museum. Ruins always viewable; museum and tower open daily May-Sept

10:00-18:00, Oct-April until 17:00, Willy-Brandt-Strasse 60, tel. 040/371125, www.mahnmal-st-nikolai.de. It's a 5-minute walk from the Rödingsmarkt U-Bahn station—just follow busy Willy-Brandt-Strasse toward the tower—or a 10-minute walk from Speicherstadt.

Visiting the Memorial: The **footprint** of the church has a few information posts as well as some modern memorials. Where the original altar once stood is now a simple concrete altar; behind it is a 1977 mosaic (*Ecce Homo*) by Expressionist artist Oskar Kokoschka, showing Jesus on the cross being offered a vinegar-soaked sponge. The tower's 51-bell **carillon** plays music daily at 9:00, 12:00, 15:00, and 18:00. A live carillonneur plays 30-minute concerts every Saturday at noon.

The **tower** still stands tall above the shell of the former church—and even though it's currently under renovation, you can still ride a speedy elevator 250 feet up to its observation platform. It provides a good visual orientation to Hamburg, with views of City Hall and lakes in one direction and the Speicherstadt warehouse district in the other, supplemented by a half-dozen informational panels.

The underground museum is modest yet effective, depicting the life, death, and resurrection of the church. Photos show the church's interior in all of its pre-WWII glory alongside bits salvaged after the bombing (including some original stained-glass windows). Start in the hallway with a timeline of the church's history. In the first room, follow the counterclockwise display through a detailed retelling of the devastating firestorm. Then, in the second room, finish with a thoughtful examination of how the city came to grips with its aftermath—logistically, culturally, and morally. Consider that Hamburg's senior citizens experienced the firebombing firsthand—and yet the museum does not paint the Allied forces as bad guys, and reminds visitors that Hitler had done much the same to other cities (see the photos of a destroyed Warsaw) long before the destruction was visited upon German soil. One display even invites visitors to imagine the fear and guilt experienced by the British bombers (many of whom were unaware they'd be attacking a civilian center).

North of the Harborfront

▲▲HAMBURG MUSEUM

Like the history of the city it covers, this museum is long, complex, and multilayered. Filling a giant old building with a

St. Pauli Landungsbrücken harborfront

staggering variety of artifacts and historical re-creations, the modern, thoughtfully presented exhibits work together to illuminate the full story of Hamburg (with an understandable emphasis on the evolution of its status as one of the world's biggest shipping ports). Multiple large models of the city at various points in its history help you track how the place changed over time—industrial development, devastating 1842 fire, WWII firebombing, modern sprawl—and the included English audioguide engagingly ties everything together.

The core of the exhibit is on the first floor; the ground floor has exhibits on the 20th century and a delightful *Jugendstil* (Art Nouveau) café with seating in the glassed-in courtyard; and the top floor has large exhibits on Hamburg's Jewish community and beautifully re-created Baroque-era rooms.

Cost and Hours: €9, includes audioguide, Tue-Sat 10:00-17:00, Sun 10:00-18:00, closed Mon, Holstenwall 24, big building marked with its former name—*Museum für Hamburgische Geschichte*, near St. Pauli U-Bahn stop, tel. 040/428-132-100, www.hamburgmuseum.de.

▲▲REEPERBAHN

This is Germany's most famous nightlife district. The busy Reeperbahn (ray-pehr-bahn) is a broad avenue with car traffic that runs between the St. Pauli U-Bahn stop (where it's fairly tame) and the Reeperbahn S-Bahn stop (where it's edgier). As you stroll down the street, you'll see nightclubs, casinos, restaurants, fast-food joints, theaters, and sex shops displaying gadgets. During the day, the area feels seedy. Nighttime is when it comes to life. The Red Light District is limited to Herbertstrasse (don't take photos here).

St. Pauli Landungsbrücken Harborfront

Once Hamburg's passenger ship terminal, this half-mile-long floating dock, which parallels the waterfront, is now a thriving, touristy, borderline-tacky wharf that locals call "the Balcony of Hamburg." A visit is worth ▲▲. From here you can inhale the inviting aroma of herring and French fries while surveying the harbor and the city's vast port.

From the Landungsbrücken S- and U-Bahn stop, head toward the water. As you walk down, you'll be assailed by employees of the many tour-boat companies, each pitching their trips—ignore them (most are German language-only excursions). You'll see the venerable light-brown stone former terminal building, now filled with shops and a busy TI, and topped with a tower.

From the landing behind the terminal you can hop on the recommended boat tour (at bridge 4). Also consider a lunch break at the harbor's own brewery, the Blockbraü, or any of the many food stands lining the harborfront.

▲▲▲HARBOR AND PORT GUIDED BOAT TOUR

Of the hundred or so big-boat harbor tours that go daily here, only a few come with English narration. The best is **Rainer Abicht,** whose excellent tour (once a day in English at noon) gives you a skyline view from the water of all the construction in Hamburg. The industrial port is a major focus of the trip, and getting up close to all those massive container ships, cranes, and dry and wet docks is breathtaking. The live commentary (which switches between English and German) is fascinating and entertaining. You can order a drink to sip as you take it all in from the deck (bring a sandwich for a discreet picnic).

Cost and Hours: One-hour harbor tour-€18 (€30 combo-ticket with Roten Doppeldecker bus tour), English tour runs April-Oct daily at 12:00, no English tours off-season, tel. 040/317-8220, www.abicht.de. Their waterside ticket windows are by bridge 4 (look for the blue-and-white boats).

HOP-ON, HOP-OFF BOAT TRIP

If you miss the Rainer Abicht tour at noon, you could take a Maritime Circle Line tour. It lasts 1.5 hours, has English narration, and runs three times a day, covering the basic harbor highlights.

Cost and Hours: €16 (€30 combo-ticket with Roten Doppeldecker bus tour), April-Oct daily at 11:00, 13:00, and 15:00, some off-season tours with fewer stops, tel. 040/2849-3963, www.maritime-circle-line.de. Ticket windows and departure point are at bridge 10.

HafenCity and Speicherstadt

This exciting development was once industrial dockland. With the advent of huge container ships, which demanded more space than Hamburg's industrial zone could accommodate, most business shifted to a larger, more modern port nearby—and all this prime real estate (just half a mile from the City Hall) suddenly became available.

The result is **HafenCity,** Europe's biggest urban development project. When it's done, downtown Hamburg will be 40 percent bigger. The area feels like a city in itself, with a maritime touch, interesting modern architecture, and a mix of business, culture, and leisure.

Speicherstadt ("Warehouse City"), between HafenCity and the city center, is a huge stand of red-brick riverside warehouses. A few museums and attractions have moved into the restored warehouses, each labeled with a letter (see listing for Block D, later).

Together, Hafencity and Speicherstadt are worth ▲▲.

Getting to HafenCity and Speicherstadt: For an atmospheric approach, go to the Landungsbrücken S- and U-Bahn stop and take public ferry #72 one stop upstream. You'll disembark by HafenCity's striking new Elbphilharmonie concert hall.

You can also take the U-3 subway line to Baumwall, walk across either of the Niederbaumbrücke bridges, and turn left onto Kehrwieder street. After strolling between the canal (on your left) and a row of warehouses (on your right) for about five minutes, look for Block D (described later). The Elbphilharmonie Pavilion and International Maritime Museum are farther in.

▲▲ELBPHILHARMONIE CONCERT HALL

The centerpiece of the HafenCity development is the Elbphilharmonie—a combination concert hall, hotel, apartment complex, and shopping mall, all contained in a towering and wildly beautiful piece of architecture. Seen from the water, it calls to mind the looming prows of the steamer ships that first put Hamburg on the world map. The heart of the complex is the Plaza level, which connects the renovated harbor warehouse below with the modern glass tower above. From the main entrance of the 360-foot-tall, 360-foot-long structure, visitors ride a 270-foot-long escalator (dubbed the "Tube"). At the top is a spectacular view down the Elbe toward the harbor and docks. A second, shorter escalator takes you to the Plaza level, where you'll find an outdoor promenade that wraps around the entire level (plus a café and souvenir shop).

SPEICHERSTADT BLOCK D

This warehouse in Speicherstadt contains a café with historical photos and

Elbphilharmonie complex on the harbor

a museum of miniatures, each worth a visit. (Skip the tacky Hamburg Dungeon attraction.)

The **Speicherstadt Kaffeerösterei** (coffee roasters) serves sandwiches, cakes, and desserts, and sells coffee by the bag and other small gifts. You'll enter the café through a flood gate—which can be closed in high water. On the entry-hall wall on the right, you'll see photographs of Speicherstadt when it was still lined with medieval-looking half-timbered warehouses. These were torn down after 1881, when Hamburg joined the German customs union, and the current buildings were constructed (daily 10:00-19:00, tel. 040/3181-6161). Practically next door to the café is...

▲MINIATUR WUNDERLAND

The most fun of Block D's sights—and worth its high entry fee—Miniatur Wunderland claims to have the world's largest model railway, covering over 14,000 square feet with more than eight miles of track. Marvel at the tiny airport (with model planes taking off), and watch night fall every 15 minutes. Visit the Alps, Scandinavia, Italy, and the US in miniature. Little bits come to life with a press of a green-lit button—bungee jumpers leap, the drive-in plays a movie, and tiny Bavarians hoist teeny beer mugs to their mini-mouths. Hamburg's harbor is lovingly rendered—including the building you're standing in—with a model of the Elbphilharmonie that lets you peek inside.

Cost and Hours: €13, daily 9:30-18:00, up to 8:00-20:00 in peak season, tel. 040/300-6800, www.miniatur-wunderland.com.

Rick's Tip: *The model railway is wildly popular, so* **reserve online at least two days in advance** *(no extra charge). There's often an hour's wait to get in if you don't have an advance ticket.*

▲▲INTERNATIONAL MARITIME MUSEUM

This state-of-the-art exhibit fills nine floors of a towering brick ex-warehouse with thousands of maritime artifacts. Nearly everything is well-described in English. Ride the lift to the ninth "deck" (floor) to start with the world's biggest collection of miniature ship models, and then work your way down—each floor has a different military or civilian maritime theme: paintings and ship models; deep-sea research; the history of merchant shipping and cruise ships; exploration, colonization, and warfare

Miniatur Wunderland hosts an amazing model railway.

(with good exhibits on the naval warfare of World Wars I and II); uniforms, medals, and insignias from around the world; the history of shipbuilding; global seafaring history; and navigation. Between the first and second decks is an enormous model of the RMS *Queen Mary 2* (which often sails from just a few blocks away)...made entirely of Legos.

Cost and Hours: €12.50, Tue-Sun 10:00-18:00, closed Mon, English audioguide-€3.50, Kaispeicher B, tel. 040/3009-2345, www.imm-hamburg.de.

Eating

Near the train station, the main street through the St. Georg area—Lange Reihe—is lined with a great variety of eateries.

$$$$ Kajüte is good if you're willing to pay more for atmosphere—come in the evening to watch sailboats and the sun setting across the water (reservations smart, An der Alster 10a, tel. 040/243-037, www.kajuete.de).

$ Frau Möller, a popular rollicking bar, serves up affordable, hearty Alsatian and Hamburger classics (sandwiches, salads, and daily specials). Try for one of the side-walk tables (Lange Reihe 96).

$$$ Schifferbörse, across the street from the train station, is touristy, but cooks up northern German food at fair prices (Kirchenallee 46).

For **picnic fare** at the station, try the **Galeria Kaufhof** department store (closed Sun, supermarket in basement, entrance near track 14), **REWE** (has well-priced prepared food, closed Sun, inside Europa Passage shopping mall), and the **Edeka** supermarket inside the station (open daily).

Sleeping

Near the train station in the pleasant, lively St. Georg neighborhood, try hip **$$$ Hotel Wedina** (Gurlittstrasse 23, www.hotelwedina.de), Old World **$$ Hotel Fürst Bismarck** (Kirchenallee 49, www.fuerstbismarck.de), or the decent, budget **$ Hotel-Pension Alpha** (Koppel 4, www.alphahotel.biz).

¢ Jugendherberge Hamburg "Auf dem Stintfang" is a modern, well-run hostel with some bunk-bed doubles and family rooms (Alfred-Wegener-Weg 5, near Landungsbrücken S- and U-Bahn station, www.jugendherberge.de/jh/hamburg-stintfang).

German History

A united Germany has only existed since 1871, but the cultural heritage of the German-speaking people stretches back 2,000 years.

Romans

(A.D. 1-500)

German history begins in A.D. 9, when Roman troops were ambushed and driven back by the German chief Arminius. For the next 250 years, the Rhine and Danube rivers marked the border between civilized Roman Europe (to the southwest) and "barbarian" German lands (to the northeast). While the rest of Western Europe's future would be Roman, Christian, and Latin, most of Germany followed a separate, pagan path.

In A.D. 476, Rome fell to the Germanic chief Theodoric the Great (a.k.a. Dietrich of Bern). After that, Germanic Franks controlled northern Europe, ruling a mixed population of Romanized Christians and tree-worshipping pagans.

Charlemagne

(A.D. 500-1000)

For Christmas in A.D. 800, the pope gave Charlemagne the title of Holy Roman Emperor. Charlemagne, the king of the Franks, was the first of many German kings to be called Kaiser ("emperor," from "Caesar") over the next thousand years. Allied with the pope, Charlemagne ruled an empire that included Germany, Austria, France, the Low Countries, and northern Italy.

Charlemagne (r. 768-814) stood a head taller than his subjects, and his foot became a standard unit of measurement. The stuff of legend, he had five wives and four concubines, producing descendants with names like Charles the Bald, Louis the Pious, and Henry the Quarrelsome. After Charlemagne died (814), his united empire did not pass directly to his oldest son but was divided into (what would become) Germany, France, and the lands in between (Treaty of Verdun, 843).

The Holy Roman Empire

(1000-1500)

Chaotic medieval Germany was made up of more than 300 small, quarreling dukedoms ruled by the Holy Roman Emperor. The title was pretty bogus, implying that the German king ruled the same huge empire as the ancient Romans. In fact, he was "Holy" because he was blessed by the Church, "Roman" to recall ancient grandeur, and the figurehead "Emperor" of what was an empire in name only.

Holy Roman Emperors had less hands-on power than other kings around Europe. Because of the custom of electing emperors by nobles and archbishops, rather than by bestowing the title through inheritance, they couldn't pass the crown from father to son. In addition, there were no empire-wide taxes and no national capital. This system gave nobles great power: Peasants huddled close to their local noble's castle for protection from attack by the noble next door.

While France, England, and Spain were centralizing power around a single ruling family to create nation-states, Germany remained a decentralized, backward, feudal battleground.

Medieval Growth

Nevertheless, Germany was strategically located at the center of Europe, and trading towns prospered. Several northern towns (especially Hamburg and Lübeck) banded together into the Hanseatic League, promoting open trade around the Baltic Sea. To curry favor at election time, emperors granted powers and privileges to certain towns, designated "free imperial cities." Some towns, such as Cologne, Mainz, Dresden, and Trier, held higher status than many nobles, as hosts of one of the seven "electors" of the emperor.

Textiles, mining, and the colonization of lands to the east made Germany an economic powerhouse with a thriving middle class. In towns, middle-class folks (burghers), not the local aristocrats, began running things. In about 1450, Johann Gutenberg of Mainz figured out how to use moveable type for printing, an innovation that would allow the export of a new commodity: ideas.

Luther and the Thirty Years' War

(1500-1700)

Martin Luther—German monk, fiery orator, and religious whistle-blower—sparked a century of European wars by speaking out against the Catholic Church.

Luther's protests ("Protestantism") threw Germany into a century of turmoil, as each local prince took sides between Catholics and Protestants. The Holy Roman Emperor, Charles V (r. 1519-1556), sided with the pope. Charles was the most powerful man in Europe, having inherited an empire that included Germany and Austria, plus the Low Countries, much of Italy, Spain, and Spain's New World possessions. But many local German nobles took the opportunity to go Protestant—some for religious reasons, but also as an excuse to seize Church assets and powers.

The 1555 Peace of Augsburg allowed each local noble to decide the religion of his realm. In general, the northern and eastern lands became Protestant, while the south (today's Bavaria, along with Austria) and west remained Catholic.

Unresolved religious and political differences eventually expanded into the Thirty Years' War (1618-1648). This Europe-wide war was one of history's bloodiest wars, fueled by religious extremism and political opportunism.

By the war's end (Treaty of Westphalia, 1648), a third of all Germans had died, France was the rising European power, and the Holy Roman Empire was a medieval mess of scattered feudal states. In 1689, France's Louis XIV swept down the Rhine, gutting and leveling its once-great castles, and Germany ceased to be a major player in European politics until the modern era.

Austria and Prussia

(1700s)

The German-speaking lands now consisted of three "Germanys": Austria in the south, Prussia in the north, and the rest in between.

Prussia—originally a largely Slavic region—was forged into a unified state by two strong kings. Frederick I (r. 1701-1713) built a modern state around a highly disciplined army, a centralized government, and national pride. His grandson, Frederick II "The Great" (r. 1740-1786), added French culture and worldliness while preparing militaristic Prussia to enter the world stage.

Meanwhile, Austria thrived under the laid-back rule of the Habsburg family. The Habsburgs gained power in Europe by marrying it. They acquired the Netherlands, Spain, and Bohemia that way (a strategy that didn't work so well for Marie-Antoinette, who wed the doomed king of France).

In the 1700s, the Germanic lands became a cultural powerhouse, producing musicians (Bach, Haydn, Mozart, Beethoven), writers (Goethe, Schiller), and thinkers (Kant, Leibniz). But politically, feudal Germany was no match for the modern powers.

After the French Revolution (1789), Napoleon swept through Germany with his armies, forcing the Holy Roman Emperor to hand over his crown (1806). After a thousand years, the Holy Roman Empire was dead.

German Unification

(1800s)

Napoleon's invasion helped unify the German-speaking peoples by rallying them against a common foreign enemy. After Napoleon's defeat, the Congress of Vienna (1815), presided over by the Austrian Prince Metternich, realigned Europe's borders. The idea of unifying the three Germanic nations—Prussia, Austria, and the German Confederation, a loose collection of small states in between—began to grow. By mid-century, most German-speaking people favored forming a modern nation-state.

Energetic Prussia took the lead in unifying the country. Otto von Bismarck (served 1862-1890), the strong minister of Prussia's weak king, used cunning politics to engineer a unified Germany under Prussian dominance. First, he started a war with Austria, ensuring that any united Germany would be under Prussian control. (Austria remains a separate country to this day.) Next, Bismarck provoked a war with France (Franco-Prussian War, 1870-1871), which united Prussia and the German Confederation against their common enemy, France.

Fueled by hysterical patriotism, German armies swept through France and, in the Hall of Mirrors at Versailles, crowned Prussia's Wilhelm I as emperor (Kaiser) of a new German Empire, uniting Prussia and the German Confederation. This Second Reich (1871-1918) featured elements of democracy (an elected Reichstag—parliament), offset by a strong military and an emperor with veto powers.

A united and resurgent Germany was suddenly flexing its muscles in European politics. With strong industry, war spoils, overseas colonies, and a large and disciplined military, it sought its rightful place in the sun.

World Wars

(1914-1939)

When Archduke Franz Ferdinand, the heir to the Austro-Hungarian Empire, was assassinated in 1914, all of Europe took sides as the political squabble quickly escalated into World War I. Germany and Austria-Hungary attacked British and French troops in France, but were stalled at the Battle of the Marne. Both sides dug defensive trenches, then settled in for four brutal years of bloodshed, mud, machine-gun fire, disease, and mustard gas.

Finally, at 11:00 in the morning of November 11, 1918, the fighting ceased.

Germany surrendered, signing the Treaty of Versailles in the Hall of Mirrors at Versailles.

A new democratic government called the Weimar Republic (1919) dutifully abided by the Treaty of Versailles and tried to maintain order among Germany's many divided political parties. But the country was in ruins, its economy a shambles, and the war's victors demanded heavy reparations. Communists rioted in the streets, fascists plotted coups, and inflation drove the price of a loaf of bread to a billion marks. When the worldwide depression of 1929 hit Germany with brutal force, the nation was desperate for a strong leader with answers.

Adolf Hitler (1889-1945), in Munich, joined other disaffected Germans to form the National Socialist (Nazi) Party. He promised to restore Germany to its rightful glory, blaming the country's current problems on communists, foreigners, and Jews.

By 1930, the Nazis had become a formidable political party in Germany's democracy. They won 38 percent of the seats in the Reichstag in 1932, and Hitler was appointed chancellor (1933).

For the next decade, an all-powerful Hitler proceeded to revive Germany's economy, building the autobahns and rebuilding the military. Defying the Treaty of Versailles and world opinion, Hitler occupied the Saar region (1935) and the Rhineland (1936), annexed Austria and the Sudetenland (1938), and invaded Czechoslovakia (March 1939). The rest of Europe finally reached its appeasement limit, and World War II began when Germany invaded Poland in September 1939. By 1945 the war was over, leaving countless millions dead and most German cities bombed beyond recognition. The Third Reich was over.

Two Germanys

(1945-1990)

After World War II, the Allies divided occupied Germany into two halves, split down the middle by an 855-mile border that Winston Churchill called an "Iron Curtain." By 1949, Germany was officially two separate countries. West Germany (the Federal Republic of Germany) was democratic and capitalist, allied with the powerful United States. East Germany (the German Democratic Republic, or DDR) was a communist state under Soviet control. The Berlin Wall—built at the height of the Cold War between the United States and the USSR—came to symbolize a divided Germany.

After the war, thanks to US aid from the Marshall Plan, West Germany was rebuilt, democracy was established, and its "economic miracle" quickly exceeded pre-WWII levels. Meanwhile, East Germany was ruled with an iron fist under Soviet control.

On November 9, 1989, East Germany unexpectedly opened the Berlin Wall. At first, most Germans—West and East—simply looked forward to free travel and better relations between two distinct nations. But before the month was out, negotiations and elections to reunite the two Germanys had begun. October 3, 1990, was proclaimed German Unification Day, and Berlin reassumed its status as the German capital in 1991.

Germany Today

(1990-PRESENT)

Germany remains a major economic and political force in Europe. Today's chancellor, Angela Merkel, is seen as one of the world's most powerful women and has become Europe's longest-serving elected female leader (breaking Margaret Thatcher's 11-year record).

Germany is a member of the European Union—an organization whose original chief aim was to avoid future wars by embracing Germany in the economic web of Europe. Recently, however, thanks to its economic might, Germany has become the EU's de facto leader.

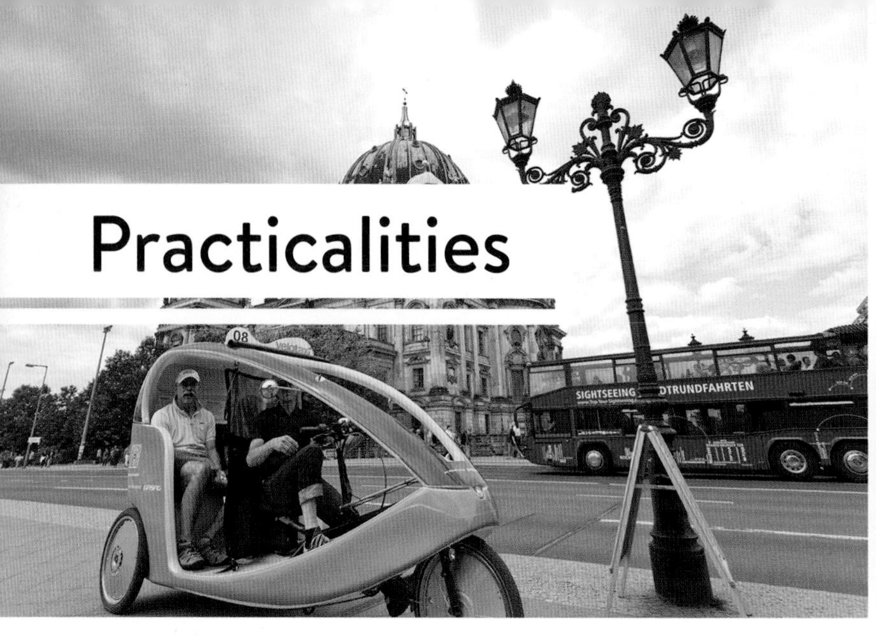

Practicalities

TOURIST INFORMATION

Germany's national tourist office **in the US** is a wealth of information. Before your trip, scan their website (www.germany.travel) for maps and Rhine boat schedules, as well as information on festivals, castles, hiking, biking, genealogy, cities, and regions. Travel brochures can also be downloaded from their website.

In Germany, your best first stop in every town is generally the tourist information office—abbreviated **TI** in this book. Throughout Germany, you'll find TIs are usually well-organized and have English-speaking staff. Be aware that TIs are in business to help you enjoy spending money in their town. But even if TIs can be overly commercial, they're good places to get a city map and information on public transit (including bus and train schedules), walking tours, special events, and nightlife.

TRAVEL TIPS

Time Zones: Germany, like most of continental Europe, is generally six/nine hours ahead of the East/West Coasts of the US. The exceptions are the beginning and end of Daylight Saving Time: Europe "springs forward" the last Sunday in March (two weeks after most of North America) and "falls back" the last Sunday in October (one week before North America). For a handy online time converter, see www.timeanddate.com/worldclock.

Business Hours: In Germany, most shops are open from about 9:00 until 18:00 or 20:00 on weekdays. In small towns, shops may take a mid-afternoon break. Saturdays are virtually weekdays, though stores generally close early, and most shops are closed on Sunday. Many museums and sights are closed on Monday.

Discounts: This book lists only the full adult price for sights. However, many sights offer discounts for youths (up to age 18), students (with proper identification cards, www.isic.org), families, and seniors (loosely defined as retirees or those willing to call themselves seniors). Always ask—though some discounts are only available for citizens of the European Union.

Online Translation Tips: The Google Translate app converts spoken English into most European languages (and vice versa) and can also translate text that it "reads" with your mobile device's camera. To translate websites, use Google's Chrome browser (www.google.com/chrome) or paste the URL of the site into the translation window at www.google.com/translate.

HELP!

Emergency and Medical Help

Dial 112 for any emergency. Or ask at your hotel for help—they'll know the nearest medical and emergency services. If you get a minor ailment, do as the locals do and go to a pharmacist for advice.

Theft or Loss

To replace a passport, you'll need to go in person to an embassy (see next page). If your credit and debit cards disappear, cancel and replace them. If your things are lost or stolen, file a police report, either on the spot or within a day or two; you'll need it to submit an insurance claim for lost or stolen rail passes or travel gear, and it can help with replacing your passport or credit and debit cards. For more information, see www.ricksteves.com/help.

Avoiding Theft

Pickpockets are common in crowded, touristy places, but fortunately, violent crime is rare. Thieves don't want to hurt you; they just want your money and gadgets.

My recommendations: Stay alert and wear a money belt (tucked under your clothes) to keep your cash, debit card, credit card, and passport secure; carry only the money you need for the day in your front pocket.

Treat any disturbance (e.g., a stranger bumps into you, spills something on you, or tries to get your attention for an odd reason) as a smoke screen for theft. Be on guard waiting in line at sights, at train stations, and while boarding and leaving crowded buses and subways. Thieves target tourists overloaded with bags or distracted with smartphones.

When paying for something, be aware of how much cash you're handing over (state the denomination of the bill when paying a cabbie) and count your change. For tips on using cash machines smartly, read "Security Tips" under "Cash" on page 384.

There's no need to be scared; just be smart and prepared.

Damage Control for Lost Cards

If you lose your credit, debit, or ATM card, you can stop people from using your card by reporting the loss immediately to your card company. Call these 24-hour US numbers collect: Visa (tel. 303/967-1096), MasterCard (tel. 636/722-7111), and American Express (tel. 336/393-1111). In Germany, to make a collect call to the US, dial 0800-225-5288 and press zero or stay on the line for an English-speaking operator. Visa's and MasterCard's websites list European toll-free numbers by country.

If you report your loss within two days, you typically won't be responsible for any unauthorized transactions on your account, although many banks charge a liability fee of $50. You can generally receive a temporary replacement card within two or three business days in Europe.

Embassies

US Embassy in Berlin: Pariser Platz 2, tel. 030/83050; consular services at Clayallee 170 by appointment only Mon-Fri 8:30-12:00, closed Sat-Sun and last Thu of month, tel. 030/8305-1200—consular services calls answered Mon-Thu 14:00-16:00 only, http://germany.usembassy.gov

Canadian Embassy in Berlin: Consular services available Mon-Fri 9:00-12:00, Leipziger Platz 17, tel. 030/203-120, www.germany.gc.ca

MONEY

This section offers advice on how to pay for purchases on your trip (including getting cash from ATMs and paying with plastic), VAT (sales tax) refunds, and tipping.

What to Bring

Bring both a credit card and a debit card. You'll use the debit card at cash machines (ATMs) to withdraw local cash for most purchases, and the credit card to pay for larger items. Some travelers carry a third card, as a backup, in case one gets demagnetized by a rogue machine.

For an emergency stash, bring several hundred dollars in hard cash in $20 bills. If you need to exchange the bills, go to a bank; avoid using currency-exchange booths because of their lousy rates and/or outrageous (and often hard-to-spot) fees.

Cash

Cash is just as desirable in Europe as it is at home. Small businesses (mom-and-pop cafés, shops, etc.) prefer that you pay your bills with cash. Some vendors will charge you extra for using a credit card, some won't accept foreign credit cards, and some won't take any credit cards at all. Cash is the best—and sometimes only—way to pay for cheap food, bus fare, taxis, and local guides.

Throughout Europe, ATMs are the standard way for travelers to get cash. They work just like they do at home. To withdraw money from an ATM (known as a *Geldautomat* in Germany; *Bankomat* in Austria), you'll need a debit card, plus a four-digit PIN code. Although you can use a credit card to withdraw cash at an ATM, this comes with high bank fees and only makes sense in an emergency.

Security Tips: Shield the keypad when entering your PIN code. When possible, use ATMs located outside banks—a thief is less likely to target a cash machine near surveillance cameras, and if you have trouble with the transaction, you can go inside for help.

Don't use an ATM if anything on the front of the machine looks loose or damaged (a sign that someone may have attached a "skimming" device to capture account information). If a cash machine eats your card, check for a thin plastic insert with a tongue hanging out; thieves use these devices to extract cards.

Stay away from "independent" ATMs such as Travelex, Euronet, YourCash, Cardpoint, and Cashzone, which charge

Exchange Rate

1 euro (€) = about $1.20

To convert prices in euros to dollars, add about 20 percent: €20 = about $24; €50 = about $60. (Check www.oanda.com for the latest exchange rates.) Just like the dollar, one euro is broken down into 100 cents. Coins range from €0.01 to €2, and bills from €5 to €200 (bills over €50 are rarely used).

huge commissions and have terrible exchange rates.

If you want to monitor your accounts online during your trip to detect any unauthorized transactions, be sure to use a secure connection (see page 397).

Credit and Debit Cards

Many shops and restaurants in Germany don't accept plastic (except for the local "EC" debit cards). Larger hotels, restaurants, and shops that do take US cards more commonly accept Visa and MasterCard than American Express. I typically use my debit card to withdraw cash to pay for most purchases.

I use my credit card sparingly: to book hotel reservations, to buy advance tickets for events or sights, to cover major expenses (such as car rentals or plane tickets), to buy train tickets at the ticket counter (Deutsche Bahn ticket machines may not accept US cards without a chip), and to pay for things online or near the end of my trip (to avoid another visit to the ATM). While you could instead use a debit card for these purchases, a credit card offers a greater degree of fraud protection.

Ask Your Credit- or Debit-Card Company: Before your trip, contact the company that issued your debit or credit cards.

Confirm that your **card will work overseas,** and alert them that you'll be using it in Europe; otherwise, they may deny transactions if they perceive unusual spending patterns.

Ask for the specifics on transaction **fees.** When you use your credit or debit card, you'll typically be charged additional "international transaction" fees of up to 3 percent. If your card's fees seem high, consider getting a different card just for your trip: Capital One (www.capitalone.com) and most credit unions have low-to-no international fees.

Verify your daily ATM **withdrawal limit,** and if necessary, ask your bank to adjust it. I prefer a high limit that allows me to take out more cash at each ATM stop and save on bank fees; some travelers prefer to set a lower limit in case their card is stolen. Note that foreign banks also set maximum withdrawal amounts for their ATMs.

Get your bank's emergency **phone number** in the US (but not its 800 number, which isn't accessible from overseas) to call collect if you have a problem.

Ask for your credit card's **PIN** in case you need to make an emergency cash withdrawal or encounter Europe's chip-and-PIN system; the bank won't divulge a PIN over the phone, so allow time for it to be mailed.

Magnetic-Stripe versus Chip-and-PIN Credit Cards: Europeans use chip-and-PIN credit cards that are embedded with an electronic security chip and require a four-digit PIN. Your American-style card (with just the old-fashioned magnetic stripe) will work fine in most places. But it probably won't work at unattended payment machines, such as those at train and subway stations, toll plazas, parking garages, bike-rental kiosks, and gas pumps. If you have problems, try entering your card's PIN, look for a machine that takes cash, or find a clerk who can process the transaction manually.

Major US banks are beginning to offer credit cards with chips. Many of these are not true chip-and-PIN cards, but instead are "chip-and-signature" cards, for which your signature verifies your identity. These cards should work for live transactions and at some payment machines, but won't work for offline transactions such as at unattended gas pumps. If you're concerned, ask if your bank offers a true chip-and-PIN card. Andrews Federal Credit Union (www.andrewsfcu.org) and the State Department Federal Credit Union (www.sdfcu.org) offer these cards and are open to all US residents.

No matter what kind of card you have, it pays to carry euros; remember, you can always use an ATM to withdraw cash with your magnetic-stripe debit card.

Dynamic Currency Conversion: If merchants or hoteliers offer to convert your purchase price into dollars (called dynamic currency conversion, or DCC), refuse this "service." You'll pay even more in fees for the expensive convenience of seeing your transaction in dollars.

Tipping

Tipping in Germany isn't as automatic and generous as it is in the US. For special service, tips are appreciated, but not expected. As in the US, the right amount depends on your resources and the circumstances, but some general guidelines apply.

Restaurants: You don't need to tip if you order your food at a counter. At German restaurants that have a wait staff, it's common to tip by rounding up (about 10 percent) after a good meal. For details on tipping in restaurants, see page 389.

Taxis: Round up your fare a bit (for instance, if your fare is €13, pay €14). If the cabbie hauls your bags and zips you to the airport to help you catch your flight, you might want to toss in a little more. But if you feel like you're being driven in circles or otherwise ripped off, skip the tip.

Services: In general, if someone in the service industry does a super job for you, a small tip of a euro or two is appropriate...but not required. If you're not sure whether (or how much) to tip for a service, ask a local for advice.

Getting a VAT Refund

Wrapped into the purchase price of your German souvenirs is a Value-Added Tax (VAT) of 19 percent. You're entitled to get most of that tax back if you purchase more than €25 worth of goods at a store that participates in the VAT-refund scheme. Typically, you must ring up the minimum at a single retailer—you can't add up your purchases from various shops to reach the required amount.

If the merchant ships the goods to your home, the tax will be subtracted from your purchase price. Otherwise, you'll need to:

Get the paperwork. Have the merchant completely fill out the necessary refund document, called a "tax-free refund check." You'll have to present your passport. Get the paperwork done before you leave the store to ensure you'll have everything you need (including your original sales receipt).

Get your stamp at the border or airport. Process your VAT document at your last stop in the European Union (the airport or border) with the customs agent who deals with VAT refunds. Arrive early to allow time to find the customs office and to wait in line. It's best to keep your purchases in your carry-on. If they're too large or not permitted to carry on (such as knives), pack them in your checked bags and alert the check-in agent. You'll be sent (with your tagged bag) to a customs desk outside security; someone will examine

Hurdling the Language Barrier

German—like English, Dutch, Swedish, and Norwegian—is a Germanic language, making it easier on most American ears than Romance languages (such as Italian and French). These tips will help you pronounce German words: The letter *w* is always pronounced as "v" (e.g., the word for "wonderful" is *wunderbar,* pronounced VOON-der-bar). The vowel combinations *ie* and *ei* are pronounced like the name of the second letter—so *ie* sounds like a long *e* (as in *hier* and *Bier,* the German words for "here" and "beer"), while *ei* sounds like a long *i* (as in *nein* and *Stein,* the German words for "no" and "stone"). The vowel combination *au* is pronounced "ow" (as in *Frau*). The vowel combinations *eu* and *äu* are pronounced "oy" (as in *neu, Deutsch,* and *Bräu,* the words for "new," "German," and "brew"). To pronounce *ö* and *ü,* purse your lips when you say the vowel; the other vowel with an umlaut, *ä,* is pronounced the same as *e* in "men." (In written German, these can be depicted as the vowel followed by an *e*—*oe, ue,* and *ae,* respectively.) The letter Eszett (ß) represents *ss.* Written German capitalizes all nouns.

Though most young or well-educated Germans—especially those in the tourist trade and in big cities—speak at least some English, you'll get more smiles if you learn and use German pleasantries. Study the German Survival Phrases on page 419.

your bag, stamp your paperwork, and put your bag on the belt. You're not supposed to use your purchased goods before you leave. If you show up at customs wearing your new lederhosen, officials might look the other way—or deny you a refund.

Collect your refund. You'll need to return your stamped document to the retailer or its representative. Many merchants work with a service—such as Global Blue or Premier Tax Free—that have offices at major airports, ports, or border crossings. These services, which extract a 4 percent fee, can refund your money immediately in cash, or credit your card. If the retailer handles VAT refunds directly, it's up to you to contact the merchant for your refund. You can mail the documents from home or from your point of departure. You'll then have to wait—it can take months.

Customs for American Shoppers

You are allowed to take home $800 worth of items per person duty-free, once every 31 days. You can take home many processed and packaged foods: vacuum-packed cheeses, dried herbs, jams, baked goods, candy, chocolate, oil, vinegar, mustard, and honey. Fresh fruits and vegetables and most meats are not allowed, with exceptions for some canned items.

You can bring home one liter of alcohol duty-free. It can be packed securely in your checked luggage, along with any other liquid-containing items. But if you want to carry alcohol (or liquid-packed foods) in your carry-on bag for your flight home, buy it at a duty-free shop at the airport.

For details on allowable goods, customs rules, and duty rates, visit http://help.cbp.gov.

SIGHTSEEING

Sightseeing can be hard work. Use these tips to make your visits to Germany's finest sights meaningful, fun, efficient, and painless.

Plan Ahead

Set up an itinerary that allows you to fit in all your must-see sights. Most places keep stable hours, but you can confirm the latest at the TI or by checking museum websites.

Many museums are closed or have reduced hours at least a few days a year, especially on major holidays. In summer, some sights stay open late. Off-season, many museums have shorter hours. Whenever you go, don't put off visiting a must-see sight—you never know if a place will close unexpectedly for a holiday, strike, or restoration.

Study up. To get the most out of the sight descriptions in this book, read them before you visit. That said, every sight or museum offers more than what is covered in this book. Use the information in this book as an introduction—not the final word.

At Sights

Here's what you can typically expect:

Entering: Be warned that you may not be allowed to enter if you arrive 30-60 minutes before closing time. And guards start ushering people out well before the actual closing time, so don't save the best for last.

Some important sights have a security check, where you must open your bag or send it through a metal detector; you can't skip this line even if you have a museum pass. Most museums in Germany require you to check any bag bigger than a purse, and sometimes even purses.

Photography: If the museum's photo policy isn't clearly posted, ask a guard. Generally, taking photos without a flash or tripod is allowed.

Temporary Exhibits: Museums may show special exhibits in addition to their permanent collection. Some exhibits are included in the entry price, while others come at an extra cost (which you may have to pay even if you don't visit the exhibit).

Expect Changes: Artwork can be on tour, on loan, out sick, or shifted at the whim of the curator. Pick up a floor plan as you enter, and ask museum staff if you can't find a particular item.

Audioguides and Apps: Many sights rent audioguides, which generally offer dry-but-useful recorded descriptions (sometimes included with admission). If you bring along your earbuds, you can enjoy better sound. Increasingly, sights offer downloadable apps (check their websites). I've produced free, downloadable audio tours for my Munich City Walk, Rothenburg Town Walk, Best of the Rhine Tour, and Best of Berlin Walk (noted with the 🎧 symbol in pertinent chapters). For more on my audio tours, see page 412.

Before Leaving: At the gift shop, scan the postcard rack or thumb through a guidebook to be sure that you haven't overlooked something that you'd like to see.

EATING

Germanic cuisine is heavy, hearty, and—by European standards—inexpensive. Each region has its specialties, which are often good values. Be adventurous.

When restaurant hunting, choose a spot filled with locals, not the place with the big neon signs boasting, "We Speak English and Accept Credit Cards." Venturing even a block or two off the main drag leads to higher-quality food for a better price.

Breakfast

Most German hotels and pensions include breakfast in the room price and pride themselves on laying out an attractive buffet spread. Even if you're not a big breakfast eater, take advantage of the buffet to fortify yourself for a day of sightseeing. Expect sliced bread, rolls, pastries, cereal, yogurt (both plain and with fruit), cold cuts, cheese, and fruit. You'll always find coffee, tea, and some sort of *Saft* (juice).

For breakfast, most Germans prefer a sandwich with cold cuts and/or a bowl of granola-like *Müsli*. Instead of pouring milk over cereal, most Germans begin with a dollop of yogurt (or *Quark*—sweet curds that resemble yogurt), then sprinkle the cereal on top. *Bircher Müsli* is a healthy mix of oats, nuts, yogurt, and fruit. To make a German-style sandwich for breakfast, layer *Aufschnitt* (cold cuts), *Schinken* (ham), *Streichwurst* (meat spread, most often *Leberwurst*—liver spread), and *Käse* (cheese) on a slice of bread or a roll.

Lunch and Dinner

Traditional restaurants go by many names. For basic, stick-to-the-ribs meals—and plenty of beer—look for a beer hall *(Brauhaus)* or beer garden *(Biergarten)*. *Gasthaus, Gasthof, Gaststätte,* and *Gaststube* all loosely describe an informal, inn-type eatery. A *Kneipe* is a bar, and a *Keller* (or *Ratskeller*) is a restaurant or tavern located in a cellar. A *Weinstube* serves wine and usually traditional food as well.

Most eateries have menus tacked onto their front doors, with an English menu inside. If you see a *Stammtisch* sign hanging over a table at a restaurant or pub, it means that it's reserved for regulars—don't sit here unless invited.

Budget Tips: It's easy to eat a meal for €10 or less in Germany. Department-store cafeterias are common and handy, and they bridge the language barrier by letting you see your options. A *Schnellimbiss* is a small fast-food takeaway stand where you can get a bratwurst or other grilled sausage (usually less than €2, including a roll). Thrifty Turkish-style *Döner Kebab* (gyro-like, pita-wrapped rotisserie meat) stands and shops are also common.

Tipping: You only need to tip at restaurants that have table service. If you order your food at a counter, don't tip. At restaurants with wait staff, it's common to tip after a good meal by rounding up (roughly 10 percent). Rather than leaving coins behind on the table (considered slightly rude), Germans usually pay directly: When the server comes by with the bill, simply hand over paper money, stating the total you'd like to pay. For example, if paying for a €10 meal with a €20 bill, while handing your money to the server, say "Eleven, please" (or *"Elf, bitte"* if you've got your German numbers down). The server will keep a €1 tip and give you €9 in change.

Lately, many restaurants—especially

those in well-touristed areas—have added a "Tip is not included" line, in English, to the bottom of the bill. This is misleading, as the prices on any menu in Germany *do* include service. I wouldn't tip one cent more at a restaurant that includes this note on the bill. Many Germans are rebelling by tipping less generously at eateries using this approach.

Traditional German Fare

Main Dishes

Here are some specialties—both regional and nationwide—to look for:

Dampfnudeln: Steamed bread roll with various toppings

Flammkuchen (or ***Dünnele***): German version of white pizza, on a thin, yeastless dough and topped with bacon and onions

Frikadellen (also called ***Klopse; Buletten*** in Berlin; and ***Fleischpfanzerl*** in Bavaria): Giant meatball, sometimes flattened like a hamburger

Geschnetzeltes: Braised veal or chicken in a rich sauce and served with noodles

Kassler: Salted, lightly smoked pork

Kohlrouladen: Cabbage leaves stuffed with minced meat

Königsberger Klopse (or ***Sossklopse***): Meatball with capers and potatoes in a white sauce

Kümmelbraten: Crispy roast pork with caraway

Labskaus: Mushy mix of salted meat, potatoes, often beets, and sometimes herring, onions, and sour cream

Rostbrätel: Marinated and grilled pork neck

Rouladen (or ***Rinderrouladen***): Strip of beef rolled up with bacon, onion, and pickles, then braised

Sauerbraten: "Sour"-marinated and roasted cut of beef (sometimes pork), typically served with red cabbage and potato dumplings

Saure Zipfel: Bratwurst cooked in vinegar and onions

Schlachtplatte (or ***Schlachtschüssel***): "Butcher's plate"—usually blood sausage, *Leberwurst,* and other meat over hot sauerkraut

Schweinebraten (or ***Schweinsbraten***): Roasted pork with gravy

Speckpfannkuchen: Savory crêpe with bacon

Stolzer Heinrich: Grilled sausage in beer sauce

Best of the Wurst

The generic term *Bratwurst* (or *Rostbratwurst*) simply means "grilled sausage." *Brühwurst* means boiled.

Blutwurst (or ***Blunzen***): Blood sausage—variations include *Schwarzwurst, Rotwurst,* and *Beutelwurst*

Bockwurst: Thick pork-and-veal sausage with a smoky casing

Currywurst: Grilled pork sausage (usually *Bockwurst*)

Frankfurter: Skinny, pink, boiled sausage

Jagdwurst: Baloney-like smoked pork

Knackwurst (or ***Knockwurst***): Stubby, garlicky beef or pork sausage

Landjäger: Skinny, spicy, air-dried salami

Leberkäse: Meatloaf made of pork and beef

Leberwurst: Spreadable liverwurst

Mettwurst: Made of minced pork that's cured and smoked

Nürnberger: Short and spicy grilled pork sausage from Nürnberg

Saumagen: Meat, vegetables, and spices encased in a pig's stomach

Teewurst: Smoked-pork wurst spread

Thüringer: Long, skinny, peppery sausage

Weisswurst: Boiled white sausage

Zwiebelmettwurst: Coarse, spicy wurst spread made with pork and onions

Starches

Besides bread *(Brot)* and potatoes *(Kartoffeln),* typical starches include:

Kartoffelsalat: Potato salad

Knödel: Large dumplings, usually potato

Schupfnudeln: Stubby potato noodles

Spätzle: Little egg noodles; often served with melted cheese and fried onions *(Käsespätzle)*

Salads

Bauernsalat: Greek salad, sometimes with sausage
Bohnensalat: Bean salad
Fleischsalat: Chopped cold cuts mixed with pickles and mayonnaise
Gemischter Salat (or ***Bunter Salat***): Mixed salad of lettuce with fresh and pickled veggies
Gurkensalat: Cucumber salad
Nudelsalat: Pasta salad
Oliviersalat: Russian-style salad with potatoes, eggs, vegetables, and mayonnaise
Wurstsalat: Chopped sausage in onion and vinegar

Sweets

Make sure to visit a bakery *(Bäckerei)* or pastry shop *(Konditorei)* to browse the selection of fresh pastries *(Feingebäck)* and cakes.
Amerikaner: Flat, round doughnut with a glazed frosting
Berliner: Jelly-filled doughnut (*Krapfen* in Bavaria, or *Pfannkuchen* in Berlin)
Rohrnudel: Sweet dumpling with raisins
Schnecken: "Snail"-shaped pastry roll with raisins and nuts

Beverages

Water, Juice, and Soft Drinks

At restaurants, waiters aren't exactly eager to bring you *Leitungswasser* (tap water), preferring that you buy *Mineralwasser (mit/ohne Gas*—with/without carbonation).

Popular soft drinks include *Apfelschorle* (sparkling apple juice) and *Spezi* (cola and orange soda). Menus list drink sizes by the deciliter (dl): 0.2 liters is a small glass, and 0.4 or 0.5 is a larger one.

At stores, some bottled drinks—such as water and soft drinks—require a small deposit *(Pfand),* which is refunded if you return the bottle for recycling.

Beer

The average German drinks 40 gallons of beer a year and has a tremendous variety to choose from. *Flaschenbier* is bottled, and *vom Fass* is on tap. The standard beer order in Bavaria is *eine Mass* (a whole liter, or about a quart); for something smaller, ask for *eine Halbe* (half-liter). For tips on visiting a *Biergarten,* see page 83.

Broadly speaking, most German beers fall into four main categories:
Dunkles Bier: Dark beer. Munich-style *dunkles* is sweet and malty, while farther north it's drier and hoppier.
Helles Bier: A pale lager, the closest to American-style beer. It's similar to a *Pilsner,* but with more malt. Unfiltered lager is *Kellerbier* or *Zwickelbier.*
Pilsner (a.k.a. ***Pilsener*** or simply ***Pils***): Barley-based, hoppy, light-colored beer, particularly common in the north.
Weissbier or ***Weizenbier:*** A yeasty, "white" or "wheat" beer (better known in North America as "Hefeweizen"). Unfiltered *Weissbier,* especially common in the south, is cloudy (and usually called *Hefeweizen*). *Kristallweizen* is a clear, filtered, yeast-free wheat beer. *Roggenbier* is darker and made with rye.

LITE AND NONALCOHOLIC BEER

The closest thing to our "lite" beer is *leichtes Bier,* a low-calorie, low-alcohol wheat beer. *Nährbier* ("Near Beer") is a low-alcohol lager.

It's easy to get excellent alcohol-free white/wheat beers. Teetotalers, or anyone who wants a refreshing drink at lunch without being tipsy all afternoon, can look for *"ohne Alkohol"* or *"alkoholfrei."* There's also the drink called *Malztrunk* (or *Malzbier*)—the sweet, malted beverage (resembling dark beer) that children quaff.

Wine

Though famous for its beer, Germany also has excellent wine. The best-known white wines are from the Rhine and Mosel, and there are some good reds (usually from the south), including *Dornfelder* and *Spätburgunder* (or *Blauburgunder*—a pinot noir).

You can order *Wein* by the glass simply by asking for *ein Glas,* or to clarify that you don't want much, *ein kleines Glas* (about an eighth of a liter, or 4 ounces). For a mini-pitcher of wine, ask for *ein Viertel* (quarter-liter, about two glasses' worth). For a half-liter pitcher (about four glasses), request *ein Halber.* For white wine, ask for *Weisswein;* red wine is *Rotwein.* Order your wine *lieblich* (sweet), *halbtrocken* (medium), or *trocken* (dry).

Here are some of the white wines you may see:

Eiswein: Ultra-sweet "ice wine"
Gewürztraminer: Aromatic, intense, and "spicy"
Grauburgunder: Full-bodied pinot gris
Liebfraumilch: Semisweet blend of Riesling with Silvaner and Müller-Thurgau
Müller-Thurgau: Light, flowery, and semisweet
Riesling: Fruity, fragrant, and elegant
Silvaner (or ***Grüner Silvaner***): Acidic and fruity
Weinschorle: A spritzer of white wine

Many hotels serve the inexpensive *Sekt,* or German champagne, at breakfast. Also keep an eye out for *Apfelwein* ("apple wine"—hard cider, especially popular in Frankfurt) and, in winter, *Glühwein* (hot mulled wine).

SLEEPING

I favor hotels and restaurants that are handy to your sightseeing activities. Rather than list hotels scattered throughout a city, I choose hotels in my favorite neighborhoods.

Wherever you're staying, be ready for crowds during holiday periods (see page 413 for a list of major holidays and festivals). For tips on making reservations, see page 394.

In Germany, as elsewhere in northern Europe, beds don't come with a top sheet or blankets, but only with a comforter. A double bed comes with two comforters—rather than one bigger one. It also frequently has two separate mattresses and sometimes two separate (but adjacent) frames—even if the bed is intended for couples. Rooms with truly separate twin beds are less common in German hotels. When Americans request twin beds, German hotels sometimes give them a double bed with complete sincerity—reasoning that the mattresses, though adjacent, are separate. To avoid that, try asking for separate twin beds—*getrennte Betten* (geh-TREN-teh BET-ten).

Rates and Deals

I've described my recommended accommodations using a Sleep Code (see sidebar). The prices I list are for one-night stays in peak season, and assume you're booking directly with the hotel, not through a hotel-booking website or TI. Booking services extract a commission from the hotel, which logically closes the door on special deals. Book direct.

My recommended hotels each have a website (often with a built-in booking form) and an email address; you can expect a response in English within a day and often sooner.

If you're on a budget, it's smart to email

Sleep Code

$$$$ **Splurge:** Over €170
$$$ **Pricier:** €130-170
$$ **Moderate:** €90-130
$ **Budget:** €50-90
¢ **Backpacker:** Under €50

Hotels are classified based on the average price of a standard double room with bath in high season. Unless otherwise noted, credit cards are accepted, breakfast is included, hotel staff speak basic English, and Wi-Fi is generally available.

Abbreviations

I use the following code to describe accommodations in this book. Prices listed are per room, not per person. When a price range is given for a type of room (such as double rooms listed for €100-150), it means the price fluctuates with the season, size of room, or length of stay; expect to pay the upper end for peak-season stays, especially in resort areas.

Db = Double or twin room. "Double beds" can be two twins sheeted together and are big enough for nonromantic couples.

D = Double with bathroom down the hall

According to this code, a couple staying at a "Db-€140" hotel would pay a total of €140 for a double room with a private bathroom. Some cities require hoteliers to charge a tourist tax (about €1-5/person per night; in Berlin it's 5 percent of the room rate; in Baden-Baden, it's called a spa tax and it's €3.50 per night).

several hotels to ask for their best price. Comparison-shop and make your choice. In general, prices can soften if you do any of the following: offer to pay cash, stay at least three nights, or mention this book.

Types of Accommodations

Hotels

In this book, the price for a double room in a hotel ranges from €55 (very simple, toilet and shower down the hall) to €200-plus (maximum plumbing and the works). In small towns such as Bacharach or Rothenburg, you can find a good double with a private bath for under €80; in more expensive cities like Munich or Berlin, you'll usually pay €100 or more.

While I favor smaller, family-run hotels, occasionally a chain hotel can be a good value. I'm impressed with the affordable, Hamburg-based German chain called Motel One, which has branches in Munich, Nürnberg, Frankfurt, Cologne, Hamburg, Berlin, Dresden, and more

Making Hotel Reservations

Reserve your rooms several weeks or even months in advance—or as soon as you've pinned down your travel dates. Note that some national holidays merit your making reservations far in advance (see page 413).

Requesting a Reservation: It's easiest to book your room through the hotel's website. (For the best rates, always use the hotel's official site.) If there's no reservation form, or for complicated requests, send an email (see below for a sample request). Most recommended hotels take reservations in English.

The hotelier wants to know:

- the number and type of rooms you need
- the number of nights you'll stay
- your date of arrival (use the European date style: day/month/year)
- your date of departure
- any special needs (such as bathroom in the room or down the hall, cheapest room, twin beds vs. double bed)

Mention any discounts—for Rick Steves readers or otherwise—when you make the reservation.

Confirming a Reservation: Most places will request a credit-card number to hold your room. If they don't have a secure online reservation form—look for the https—you can email it (I do), but it's safer to share that confidential info via a phone call or fax.

Canceling a Reservation: If you must cancel, it's courteous—and smart—to do so with as much notice as possible, especially for smaller family-run places. Cancellation policies can be strict; read the fine print or ask about these before you book. Many discount deals require prepayment, with no refunds for cancellations.

Reconfirming a Reservation: Always call or email to reconfirm your room reservation a few days in advance. For pensions or very small hotels, I call again on my day of arrival to tell my host what time I expect to get there (especially important if arriving late—after 17:00).

Phoning: For tips on calling hotels overseas, see page 398.

From: rick@ricksteves.com
Sent: Today
To: info@hotelcentral.com
Subject: Reservation request for 19-22 July

Dear Hotel Central,
I would like to reserve a room for 2 people for 3 nights, arriving 19 July and departing 22 July. If possible, I would like a quiet room with a double bed and private bathroom inside the room.

Please let me know if you have a room available and the price.

Thank you!
Rick Steves

(www.motel-one.com). The reputable Europe-wide Ibis/Mercure chain has several branches in Germany (www.accorhotels.com).

If you're arriving in the morning, your room probably won't be ready. Check your bag safely at the hotel and dive right into sightseeing.

Hoteliers can be a great help and source of advice. Most know their city well, and can assist you with everything from public transit and airport connections to finding a good restaurant, the nearest launderette, or a late-night pharmacy.

Even at the best places, mechanical breakdowns occur: Sinks leak, hot water turns cold, toilets may gurgle or smell, the Wi-Fi goes out, or the air-conditioning dies when you need it most. Report your concerns clearly and calmly at the front desk. For more complicated issues, don't expect instant results.

To guard against theft in your room, keep valuables out of sight. Some rooms come with a safe, and other hotels have safes at the front desk. I've never bothered using one.

While it's customary to pay for your room upon departure, it can be a good idea to settle your bill the day before, when you're not in a hurry and while the manager's in. That way you'll have time to discuss and address any points of contention.

Above all, keep a positive attitude. Remember, you're on vacation. If your hotel is a disappointment, spend more time out enjoying the city you came to see.

B&Bs and Private Rooms

Compared to hotels, bed-and-breakfast places (*Pensionen, Gasthäuser,* or *Gasthöfe*) give you double the cultural intimacy for half the price. While you may lose some of the conveniences of a hotel, I happily make the trade-off for the lower rates and personal touches. If you have a reasonable but limited budget, skip hotels

The Good and Bad of Online Reviews

User-generated review sites and apps such as Yelp, Booking.com, and TripAdvisor are changing the travel industry. These sites can give you a consensus of opinions about everything from hotels and restaurants to sights and nightlife. If you scan reviews of a hotel and see several complaints about noise or a rotten location, it tells you something important that you'd never learn from the hotel's own website.

But review sites are only as good as the judgment of their reviewers. And while these sites work hard to weed out bogus users, my hunch is that a significant percentage of user reviews are posted by friends or enemies of the business being reviewed.

As a guidebook writer, my sense is that there is a big difference between this uncurated information and a guidebook. A user-generated review is based on the experience of one person, who likely stayed at one hotel and ate at a few restaurants, and doesn't have much of a basis for comparison. A guidebook is the work of a trained researcher who visited many alternatives to assess their relative value. I recently checked out some top-rated user-reviewed hotel and restaurant listings in various towns; when stacked up against their competitors, some were gems, while just as many were duds.

Both types of information have their place, and in many ways, they're complementary. If something is well-reviewed in a guidebook, and also gets good ratings on one of these sites, it's likely a winner.

and look for smaller, family-run places.

The smallest establishments are private homes with rooms (*Zimmer*) rented out to travelers. Look for *Zimmer Frei* or *Privatzimmer* signs. These are inexpensive and very common in areas popular with travelers (such as Germany's Rhine, the Romantic Road region, and southern Bavaria). TIs often have a list of private rooms.

Hostels

A hostel (*Jugendherberge*) provides cheap dorm beds and sometimes has a few double rooms and family rooms. Travelers of any age are welcome. Most hostels offer kitchen facilities, guest computers, Wi-Fi, and a self-service laundry.

There are two kinds of hostels: **Independent hostels** tend to be easygoing, colorful, and informal (no membership required); try www.hostelworld.com, www.hostelz.com, or www.hostels.com. **Official hostels** are part of Hostelling International (HI), share an online booking site (www.hihostels.com), and typically require that you either have a membership card or pay extra per night.

Other Accommodation Options

Renting an apartment, house, or villa can be a fun and cost-effective way to go local. Websites such as Booking.com, Airbnb, VRBO, and FlipKey let you browse properties and correspond directly with European property owners or managers. Airbnb and Roomorama also list rooms in private homes. Beds range from air-mattress-in-living-room basic to plush-B&B-suite posh. If you want a place to sleep that's free, try Couchsurfing.com.

STAYING CONNECTED

Staying connected in Europe gets easier and cheaper every year. The simplest solution is to bring your own device—mobile phone, tablet, or laptop—and use it just as you would at home (following the tips below, such as connecting to free Wi-Fi whenever possible). Another option is to buy a European SIM card for your mobile phone—either your US phone or one you buy in Europe. Or you can travel without a mobile device and use European landlines and computers to connect. Each of these options is described below, and you'll find even more details at www.ricksteves.com/phoning.

Using Your Mobile Device in Europe

Roaming with your mobile device in Europe doesn't have to be expensive. These budget tips and options will keep your costs in check.

Use free Wi-Fi whenever possible. Unless you have an unlimited-data plan, you're best off saving most online tasks for Wi-Fi.

Many cafés—including Starbucks and McDonald's—have free hotspots for customers; look for signs offering it and ask for the Wi-Fi password when you buy something. You'll often find Wi-Fi at TIs, city squares, major museums, public-transit hubs, airports, and aboard trains and buses.

Sign up for an international plan. Most providers offer a global calling plan that cuts the per-minute cost of phone calls and texts, and a flat-fee data plan. Your normal plan may already include international coverage (T-Mobile's does).

Before your trip, call your provider or check online to confirm that your phone will work in Europe, and research your provider's international rates. Activate the plan a day or two before you leave, then remember to cancel it when your trip's over.

Tips on Internet Security

Using the Internet while traveling brings added security risks, whether you're getting online with your own device or at a public terminal using a shared network.

First, make sure that your device is running the latest version of its operating system and security software. Next, ensure that your device is password- or passcode-protected, so thieves can't access your information if your device is stolen. For extra security, set passwords on apps that access key info (such as email or Facebook).

On the road, use only legitimate Wi-Fi hotspots. Ask the hotel or café staff for the specific name of their Wi-Fi network, and make sure you log on to that exact one. Hackers sometimes create a bogus hotspot with a similar or vague name (such as "Hotel Europa Free Wi-Fi"). The best Wi-Fi networks require that you enter a password.

Be especially cautious when checking your online banking, credit-card statements, or other personal-finance accounts. Internet security experts advise against accessing these sites while traveling. Even if you're using your own mobile device at a password-protected hotspot, any hacker who's logged on to the same network may be able see what you're doing. If you do need to log on to a banking website, use a hard-wired connection (such as an Ethernet cable in your hotel room) or a cellular network, which is safer than Wi-Fi.

Never share your credit-card number (or any other sensitive information) online unless you know that the site is secure. A secure site displays a little padlock icon, and the URL begins with *https* (instead of the usual *http*).

Minimize the use of your cellular network. When you can't find Wi-Fi, you can use your cellular network to connect to the Internet, text, or make voice calls. When you're done, avoid further charges by manually switching off "data roaming" or "cellular data" (in your device's Settings menu). Another way to make sure you're not accidentally using data roaming is to put your device in "airplane" or "flight" mode (which also disables phone calls and texts), and then turn on Wi-Fi as needed.

Don't use your cellular network for bandwidth-gobbling tasks, such as Skyping, downloading apps, and watching YouTube: Save these for when you're on Wi-Fi. Using a navigation app such as Google Maps over a cellular network can take lots of data, so do this sparingly or use it offline.

Limit automatic updates. By default, your device constantly checks for a data connection and updates apps. It's smart to disable these features so your apps will only update when you're on Wi-Fi, and to change your device's email settings from "auto-retrieve" to "manual" (or from "push" to "fetch").

It's also a good idea to keep track of your data usage. On your device's menu, look for "cellular data usage" or "mobile data" and reset the counter at the start of your trip.

Use calling/messaging apps for cheaper calls and texts. Certain calling and messaging services let you make voice/video calls and send texts for free or cheap. With an app installed on your phone, tablet, or laptop, you can log on to a Wi-Fi network and contact friends or family members who use the same service.

Phoning Cheat Sheet

Here are instructions for dialing, along with examples of how to call one of my recommended hotels in Munich (tel. 089-545-9940).

Calling from the US to Europe: Dial 011 (US access code), country code (49 for Germany), and phone number.* To call my recommended hotel in Munich, I dial 011-49-89-545-9940.

Calling from Europe to the US: Dial 00 (Europe access code), country code (1 for US), area code, and phone number. To call my office in Edmonds, Washington, I dial 00-1-425-771-8303.

Calling country to country within Europe: Dial 00, country code, and phone number.* To call the Munich hotel from Spain, I dial 00-49-89-545-9940.

Calling within Germany: Dial the entire phone number, including the initial zero. To call the Munich hotel from Berlin, I dial 089-545-9940.

Calling with a mobile phone: The "+" sign on your mobile phone automatically selects the access code you need (for a "+" sign, press and hold "0").* To call the Munich hotel from the US or Europe, I dial +49-89-545-9940.

For more dialing help, see www.howtocallabroad.com.

**If the European phone number starts with zero, drop it when calling from another country (except Italian numbers, which retain the zero).*

Country	Code
Austria	43
Belgium	32
Croatia	385
Czech Republic	420
Denmark	45
England	44
France	33
Germany	49
Greece	30

Country	Code
Hungary	36
Ireland/N Ireland	353/44
Italy	39
Netherlands	31
Norway	47
Portugal	351
Scotland	44
Spain	34
Switzerland	41

With apps like Google+ Hangouts, Whats App, Viber, Facebook Messenger, and iMessage, you can **text** for free. Skype, Viber, FaceTime, and Google+ Hangouts let you make free **voice and video calls.** With some of these services (if you buy credit in advance), you can call any mobile phone or landline worldwide for just pennies per minute.

Using a European SIM Card

This option works well if you want to make a lot of voice calls at cheap local rates or need a faster connection speed than your US carrier provides. Either buy a basic cell phone in Europe (as little as $40 from mobile-phone shops anywhere), or bring an "unlocked" US phone (check with your carrier about unlocking it). With an unlocked phone, you can replace the original SIM card (the microchip that stores info about the phone) with one that will work with a European provider.

In Europe, buy a European SIM card. Inserted into your phone, this card gives you a European phone number—and European rates. SIM cards are sold at mobile-phone shops, department-store electronics counters, newsstands, and vending machines. Costing about $5-10, they usually include about that much prepaid calling credit, with no contract and no commitment. A SIM card that also includes data (including roaming) will cost $20-40 more for one month of data within the country where you bought it. This can be cheaper than data roaming through your home provider. To get the best rates, buy a new SIM card whenever you arrive in a new country.

I like to buy SIM cards at a mobile-phone shop where there's a clerk to help explain the options and brands. Certain brands—including Lebara and Lycamobile, both of which operate in multiple European countries—are reliable and economical. Ask the clerk to help you insert your SIM card, set it up, and show you how to use it. In some countries—including Germany—you'll be required to register the SIM card with your passport as an antiterrorism measure (which may mean you can't use the phone for the first hour or two).

Find out how to check your credit balance. When you run out of credit, you can top it up at newsstands, tobacco shops, mobile-phone stores, or many other businesses (look for your SIM card's logo in the window), or online.

Public Phones and Computers

It's possible to travel in Europe without a mobile device. You can check email or browse websites using public computers and Internet cafés, and make calls from your hotel room and/or public phones.

If you use your **hotel room** phone, you'll generally be charged a fee for local and even "toll-free" calls, as well as long-distance or international calls—ask at the front desk for rates before you dial.

Since you're never charged for receiving calls, it's fine to have someone from the US call you in your room. Even small hotels in Germany tend to have a direct-dial system, so callers can reach you in your room without going through reception. Ask the staff for your room's direct telephone number.

If the fees are low, hotel phones can be used inexpensively for calls made with cheap international phone cards (sold at post offices, newsstands, street kiosks, tobacco shops, and train stations). You'll either get a prepaid card with a toll-free number and a scratch-to-reveal PIN code, or a code printed on a receipt.

You'll see **public pay phones** in a few post offices and train stations. The phones generally come with multilingual instructions, and most work with insertable phone cards (sold at post offices, newsstands, etc.). With the exception of Great Britain, each European country has its own insertable phone card—so your German card won't work in a French phone. Avoid using an international phone card at a German pay phone—a surcharge for their use effectively eliminates any savings.

Public computers are easy to find. Many hotels have one in their lobby for guests to use; otherwise you can find them at Internet cafés and public libraries.

Mail

You can mail one package per day to yourself worth up to $200 duty-free from Europe to the US (mark it "personal purchases"). If you're sending a gift to someone, mark it "unsolicited gift." For details, visit www.cbp.gov, select "Travel," and search for "Know Before You Go."

Get stamps at the neighborhood post office, newsstands within fancy hotels, and some mini-marts and card shops. Avoid standing in line at the post office by using the handy yellow stamp *(Briefmarke)* machines found just outside the building. Warning: These machines give change only in stamps, not in coins.

The German postal service works fine, but for quick transatlantic delivery in either direction, consider services such as DHL (www.dhl.com).

TRANSPORTATION

This section covers the basics on trains, buses, rental cars, and flights. Considering the efficiency of Germany's trains and buses, you'd never need to use a car.

You can follow my recommended two-week itinerary (page 26) by public transit, but renting a car for a few days makes it possible for you to get more out of your visit to Bavaria, where sights are scattered and the public transit is sparse. Other regions worth a joyride are the Romantic Road and the Rhine Valley (particularly if you want to mosey up the Mosel to Burg Eltz). A car is an expensive headache in big cities such as Munich, Frankfurt, and Berlin (park it).

Trains

German trains—most operated by the Deutsche Bahn (DB), Germany's national railway—are speedy and comfortable. They cover cities and small towns well. Once the obvious choice for long-distance travel within Germany, trains are now facing competition from buses offering ultra-low fares (described later).

If you have a rail pass, you can hop on any train without much forethought (though for a small fee, you can reserve a seat on a fast train). Without a rail pass, you can save a lot of money by understanding the difference between fast trains and cheaper "regional" trains.

Types of Trains

There are big differences in price, speed, and comfort between Germany's three levels of trains. **ICE** trains are the fastest, zipping from city to city in air-conditioned comfort, and costing proportionately more. Moderately speedy trains are designated **IC** and **EC.** The slowest are the **regional trains** (labeled RB, RE, IRE, or S on schedules), but they cost much less. Milk-run S and RB trains stop at every station.

If you have a rail pass, take the fastest train available; rail-pass holders don't pay a supplement for the fast ICE trains (with one exception, the "ICE Sprinter"). If you're buying point-to-point tickets, taking a slower train can save a lot of money. You also save with day-pass deals valid only on slower trains.

Schedules

Schedules change by season, weekday, and weekend. Verify train times listed in this book at www.bahn.com (the DB Navigator app is also a useful tool). To reach Germany's train information number from anywhere in the country, dial toll tel. 0180-699-6633.

At staffed train stations, attendants will print out a step-by-step itinerary for you, free of charge. You can also produce an itinerary yourself by using the computerized trackside machines marked *Fahrkarten* (usually silver, red, and blue). The touch-screen display gives you an English option; choose "Timetable Information," indicate your point of departure and destination, and then hit "Print" for a personalized schedule, including transfers and track numbers.

If you're changing trains en route and have a tight connection, note the numbers of the platforms (*Bahnsteig* or *Gleis*) where you will arrive and depart (listed on printed and online itineraries). This will save you precious time hunting for your connecting train.

Rail Passes

The **German Rail Pass** is a great value if you're making several train journeys within Germany, or even just a Frankfurt-Munich round-trip. For only shorter hops, a rail pass probably isn't worth it, especially if you get discounts on point-to-point tickets and day passes (explained later).

If you're traveling in a neighboring country, **two-country** Eurail passes allow you to pair Germany with Austria, Switzerland, France, the Benelux region, Denmark, Poland, or the Czech Republic. The **Select Pass** gives you more travel in four adjacent countries (but not Poland). Another possibility is the **Global Pass,** covering most of Europe. These passes are available in a **saverpass** version, which gives a 15 percent discount for two or more companions traveling together.

For more detailed advice on figuring out the smartest rail pass options for your train trip, visit the Trains & Rail Passes section of my website at www.ricksteves.com/rail. Most rail passes have to be purchased outside of Europe, but German rail passes can also be purchased at some locations in Germany, such as Frankfurt Airport.

Your rail pass covers certain extras, including travel on some city transport systems and buses run by the train company, as well as discounts on some Rhine and Mosel river boats and the Romantic Road bus.

Because Salzburg is so close to the German border, traveling to or from the city on the main line from Munich counts as traveling within Germany as far as your rail pass is concerned.

Point-to-Point Tickets

First Class vs. Second Class: First-class tickets usually cost 50 percent more than second-class tickets. First-class cars are a bit more spacious and quiet than second class, and are also likely to have seats if second-class cars sell out, but riding in second class gets you there at the same time, and with the same scenery. As second-class seating is still comfortable and quiet, most of my readers find the extra cost of first class isn't worth it—Germans themselves tell me they never ride in first class unless someone else is paying for it.

Full-Fare Tickets (*Normalpreis*): The most you'll ever have to pay for a journey is the unrestricted *Normalpreis*. This full-fare ticket allows you to easily change your plans and switch to an earlier or later train without paying a penalty. If you buy a *Normalpreis* ticket for a slower train, though, you can't use it on a fast one without paying extra.

Discount Fares (*Sparpreis*): If you reserve a ticket on a fast train at least a day in advance and are comfortable committing to particular departure times, you can usually save 25-75 percent over

Rail Passes

A **German Rail Pass** lets you travel by train in Germany for three to fifteen days (consecutively or not) within a one-month period. Discounted "twin" rates are offered for two people traveling together.

Germany can also be included in a **Eurail Select Pass,** which allows travel in two to four neighboring countries over two months, and is covered (along with most of Europe) by the classic **Eurail Global Pass.**

Rail passes are available through travel agents in the US or from Rick Steves' Europe; the German Rail Pass (unlike Eurailbrand passes) is also sold at main train stations and airports in Germany. For more on the ins and outs of rail passes, including prices, download my **free guide to Eurail Passes** (www.ricksteves. com/rail-guide) or go to www.ricksteves.com/rail.

If you're taking just a couple of train rides, buying individual **point-topoint tickets** may save you money over a pass. Use this map to add up approximate pay-as-yougo fares for your itinerary, and compare that to the price of a rail pass.

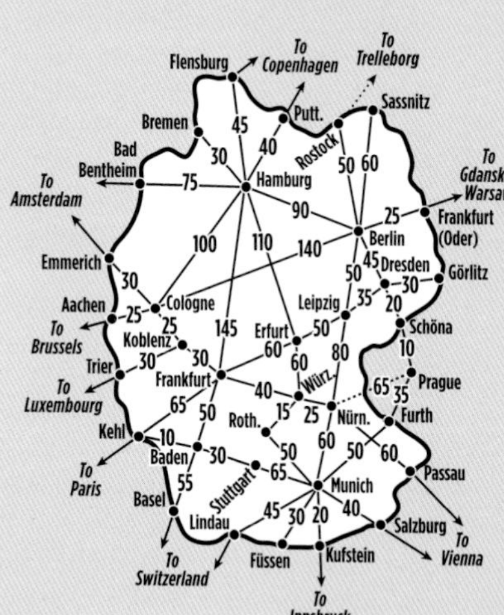

Keep in mind that significant discounts on point-to-point tickets may be available with advance purchase.

Map shows approximate costs, in US$, for one-way, second-class tickets on faster trains.

the *Normalpreis.* Discounted fares go on sale three months in advance and remain available until one day before departure—unless all the cheap seats sell out early (which often happens).

Savings on Slow Trains: You can always save money on point-to-point tickets if you're willing to limit yourself to regional trains (most commonly labeled RB, RE, IRE, or S). The Deutsche Bahn website and ticket machines give you the option to limit your search to these slower, cheaper trains (select "only local transport").

Traveling with Children: Kids ages 6-14 travel free with a parent or grandparent, but the ticket needs to list the number of children (unless purchased from a regional-train ticket machine). Kids under age 6 don't need tickets.

Day Passes

You may save even more with three types of extremely popular day passes valid only on slow trains: the various Länder-Tickets, the Schönes-Wochenende-Ticket, and the Quer-durchs-Land-Ticket. You'll find all the details on the DB website, but here are the basics:

With a **Länder-Ticket,** up to five people traveling together get unlimited travel in second class on regional trains for one day for a very cheap price (generally €23-24 for the first person plus €4-5 for each additional person). There are a few restrictions: A Länder-Ticket only covers travel within a certain region (such as Bavaria, Baden-Württemberg, Saxony, or Rheinland-Pfalz), doesn't work for the fastest classes of trains (ICE, IC, EC), and doesn't cover travel on weekdays before 9:00. Still, Länder-Tickets don't require advance purchase and are also valid on local transit.

The **Quer-durchs-Land-Ticket** works like a Länder-Ticket, but gives you the run of the whole country. It's valid on any regional train anywhere in Germany, but doesn't include city transit (first person-€44, each additional passenger-€8).

The **Schönes-Wochenende-Ticket** is a cheaper weekend version of the Quer-durchs-Land-Ticket, with looser conditions: It's valid on all regional trains on a Saturday or Sunday (starting at midnight); it does cover local transit in some areas (check specifics when you buy); and additional travelers pay only €4 extra (first person-€40, maximum 5 travelers).

Buying Tickets

At the Station: Major German stations have a handy *Reisezentrum* (travel center) where you can ask questions and buy tickets (with a small markup). You can also buy tickets from machines.

The silver, red, and blue touch-screen machines (marked with the Deutsche Bahn logo and *Fahrkarten,* which means "tickets") sell both **short- and long-distance** train tickets, and print schedules for free. Touch the flag to switch to English (some rare screens are German-only). You can pay with bills, coins, or credit cards, though US credit cards may not work. There's one exception: Any trip that is entirely within the bounds of a regional transport network (i.e., Frankfurt-Bacharach or Nürnberg-Rothenburg) is considered local—tickets can only be bought on the day of travel, and you must pay cash.

Each German city and region also has its own machines that sell only same-day tickets to **nearby destinations.** In cities, these machines also sell local public transit tickets. Increasingly, these machines are multilingual, with touch screens, and some even take American cards with a PIN. But some cities and regions still have older ticket machines that only take cash.

On the Train: You can buy a ticket on board from the conductor for a long-distance journey by paying a small markup (using cash or credit cards with a chip). But if you're riding a short-distance train, you're expected to board with a valid ticket...or you can get fined. Note that

German Public Transportation

Rail
Bus
Ferry
DENMARK
To Copenhagen
SWEDEN
Svendborg
Trelleborg
Ystad
Bornholm (Denmark)
Nykøbing
Rødby
Gedser
Puttgarden
Baltic Sea
Sassnitz
Rügen
Binz
Warnemünde
Rostock
Stralsund
Travemünde
Lübeck
To Gdańsk
Züssow
Świnoujście
Schwerin
Neubrandenburg
Ludwigslust
Pasewalk
Szczecin
Neustrelitz
POLAND
Angermünde
Stendal
Oranien-burg
Tegel
Berlin
Potsdam
Schönefeld
Rzepin
To Warsaw
Magdeburg
Frankfurt (Oder)
Poznań
N Y
Dessau
Wittenberg
Cottbus
Halle
Riesa
Erfurt
Leipzig
Naum-burg
Görlitz
Dresden
Bautzen
Zgorzelec
Wrocław
Jena
Chemnitz
Schöna
Zittau
Zwickau
Liberec
Ústi nad Labem
Wałbrzych
To Kraków
Hof
Cheb
Karlovy Vary
Ruzyně
Prague
Bayreuth
Plzeň
CZECH REPUBLIC
Furth im Wald
Regensburg
Brno
Plattling
České Budějovice
Český Krumlov
Gmünd
Landshut
Břeclav
Passau
Linz
Summerau
SLOVAKIA
Rosen-heim
Freilassing
Attnang-Puchheim
Melk
Vienna
Bratislava
Bad Ischl
Salzburg
Hallstatt (Stn.)
AUSTRIA
Kufstein
Berchtesgaden
Hegyeshalom
To Budapest
Worgl
Stainach-Irdning
To Italy
Sopron
HUNGARY

ticket checkers on local trains aren't necessarily in uniform.

Online: You can buy German train tickets online and print them out yourself; visit www.bahn.com and create a login and password. If you print out your ticket, the conductor will also ask to see the ID that you specified in the booking (typically the credit card you paid with). You can also book seat reservations (optional) with a rail pass for trips within Germany—start to buy a regular ticket, then check the box for "reservation only."

Seat Reservations

On the faster ICE, IC, and EC trains, it costs €4.50 extra per person to reserve a seat, which you can do at a station ticket desk, a touch-screen machine, or online (especially useful with a rail pass or a second-class ticket; €9 reservation cap for families). If buying a first-class ticket on these trains, you can add a seat assignment for free at the time of purchase. German trains generally offer ample seating, but popular routes do fill up, especially on holiday weekends.

If you have a seat reservation, while waiting for your train to arrive, note the departure time and *Wagen* (car) number and look along the train platform for the diagram *(Wagenstandanzeiger)* showing what sector of the platform the car will arrive at (usually A through F). Stand in that sector to avoid a last-minute dash to the right car or a long walk through the train to your seat. This is especially important for ICE trains, which are often divided into two unconnected parts.

Long-Distance Buses

Ultra-low fare long-distance buses are worth considering in Germany. While a full-fare (second-class) train ticket between Munich and Nürnberg costs about €55, a bus ticket for this route can cost €20 or less.

While buses don't offer as extensive a network as trains, they do cover the most popular cities for travelers, quite often with direct connections. Bus tickets are sold on the spot (on board and/or at kiosks at some bus terminals), but because the cheapest fares often sell out, it's best to book online as soon as you're sure of your plans (at a minimum, book a few days ahead to nab the best prices).

The main bus operators to check out are MeinFernBus (with the most extensive network, http://meinfernbus.de), FlixBus (www.flixbus.de), and Berlin Linien Bus (www.berlinlinienbus.de). Though not as comfortable as trains, each company's brightly colored buses are surprisingly well-outfitted. Most offer free Wi-Fi and onboard snack bars and WCs.

Bus terminals vary from a true depot with ticket kiosks and overhead shelter to just a stretch of street with a cluster of bus stops. Serious bus stations are labeled across Germany as "ZOB" (for *Zentraler Omnibusbahnhof*—central bus station).

Renting a Car

Rental companies require you to be at least 21 years old and to have held your license for one year. Drivers under the age of 25 may incur a young-driver surcharge, and some rental companies do not rent to anyone 75 or older. If you're considered too young or old, look into leasing (covered later), which has less-stringent age restrictions.

Research car rentals before you go. It's cheapest to arrange most car rentals from the US. Consider several companies to compare rates. Most of the major US rental agencies (including Avis, Budget, Enterprise, Hertz, and Thrifty) have offices throughout Europe.

Also consider the two major Europe-based agencies, Europcar and Sixt. It's sometimes less expensive to use a consolidator, such as Auto Europe/Kemwel (www.autoeurope.com—or the often cheaper www.autoeurope.eu).

Always read the fine print carefully for

add-on charges—such as one-way drop-off fees, airport surcharges, or mandatory insurance policies—that aren't included in the "total price."

For the best deal, rent by the week with unlimited mileage. I normally rent the smallest, least-expensive model with a stick shift (generally cheaper than an automatic). If you need an automatic, request one in advance; be aware that these cars are usually larger models.

Figure on paying roughly $250 for a one-week rental. Allow extra for supplemental insurance, fuel, tolls, and parking. For trips of three weeks or more, leasing can save you money on insurance and taxes.

Picking Up Your Car: Big companies have offices in most cities, but small local rental companies can be cheaper.

Compare pickup costs (downtown can be less expensive than the airport) and explore drop-off options. Always check the hours of the location you choose: Many rental offices close from midday Saturday until Monday morning and, in smaller towns, at lunchtime.

When selecting a location, don't trust the agency's description of "downtown" or "city center." In some cases, a "downtown" branch can be on the outskirts of the city—a long, costly taxi ride from the center. Before choosing, plug the addresses into a mapping website. You may find that the "train station" location is handier. But returning a car at a big-city train station or downtown agency can be tricky; get precise details on the car drop-off location and hours, and allow ample time to find it.

When you pick up the car, check it thoroughly and make sure any damage is noted on your rental agreement. Rental agencies in Europe are very strict when it comes to charging for even minor damage, so be sure to mark everything. Before driving off, find out how your car's gearshift, lights, turn signals, wipers, radio, and fuel cap function, and know what kind of fuel the car takes (diesel vs. unleaded). When you return the car, make sure the agent verifies its condition with you. Some drivers take pictures of the returned vehicle as proof of its condition.

Car Insurance Options

When you rent a car, you are liable for a very high deductible, sometimes equal to the entire value of the car. Limit your financial risk with one of these three options:

- Buy Collision Damage Waiver (CDW) coverage with a low or zero deductible from the car-rental company. Basic CDW reduces your liability, but does not eliminate it. When you pick up the car, you'll be offered the chance to "buy down" the deductible to zero (for an additional $10-30/day; this is sometimes called "super CDW" or "zero-deductible coverage").
- Get coverage through your credit card, which is free if your card automatically includes zero-deductible coverage. If you opt for this coverage, you'll technically have to decline all coverage offered by the car-rental company, which means they can place a hold on your card for up to the full value of the car. In case of damage, it can be time-consuming to resolve the charges with your credit-card company. Before you decide on this option, quiz your credit-card company about how it works.
- Get collision insurance as part of a larger travel-insurance policy. If you're already purchasing a travel-insurance policy for your trip, adding collision coverage can be economical. For example, Travel Guard (www.travelguard.com) sells affordable renter's collision insurance as an add-on to its other policies.

For **more on car-rental insurance,** see www.ricksteves.com/cdw.

Leasing

For trips of three weeks or more, consider leasing, which automatically includes zero-deductible collision and theft insurance. Leasing provides you a new car with

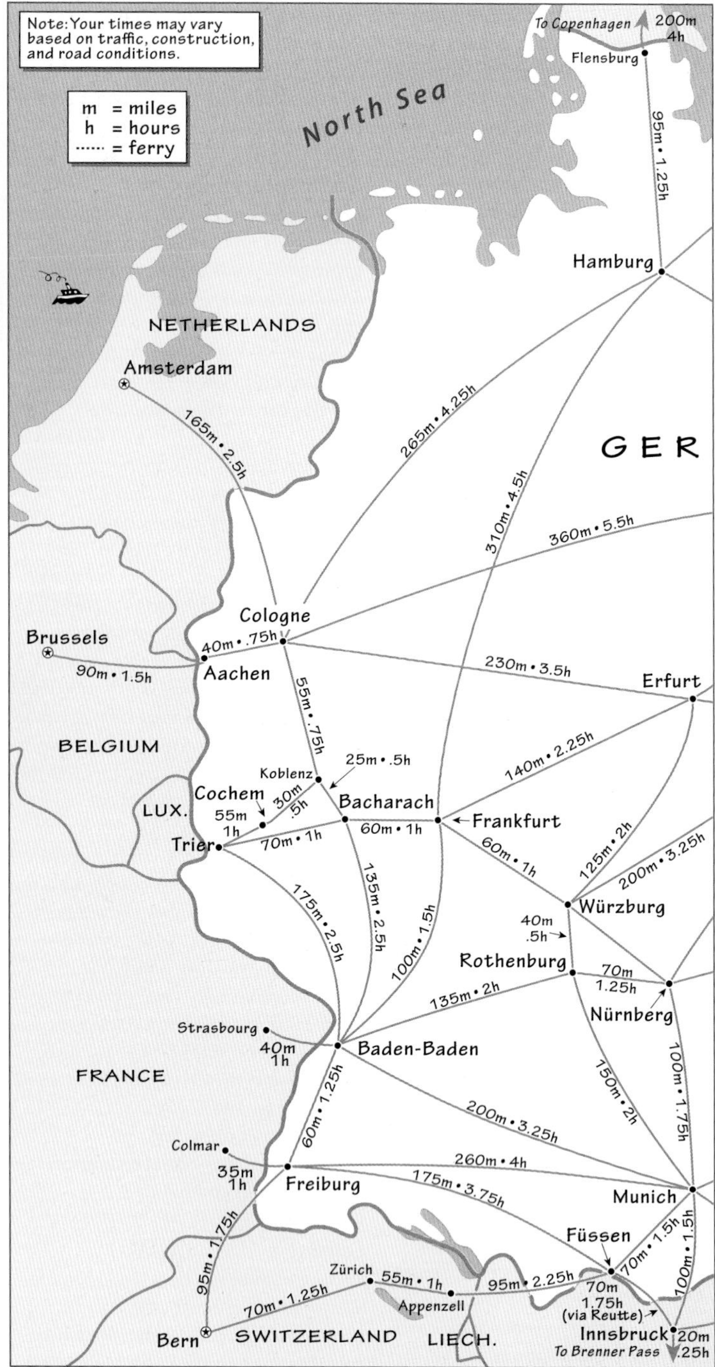
Note: Your times may vary based on traffic, construction, and road conditions.
m = miles
h = hours
...... = ferry
North Sea
To Copenhagen
200m
4h
Flensburg
95m • 1.25h
Hamburg
NETHERLANDS
Amsterdam
165m • 2.5h
265m • 4.25h
GER
310m • 4.5h
360m • 5.5h
Cologne
Brussels
40m • .75h
90m • 1.5h
Aachen
230m • 3.5h
Erfurt
55m • .75h
BELGIUM
25m • .5h
Koblenz
140m • 2.25h
Cochem
30m
.5h
Bacharach
Frankfurt
LUX.
55m
1h
60m • 1h
Trier
70m • 1h
60m • 1h
125m • 2h
200m • 3.25h
175m • 2.5h
135m • 2.5h
100m • 1.5h
Würzburg
40m
.5h
Rothenburg
70m
1.25h
135m • 2h
Nürnberg
Strasbourg
40m
1h
Baden-Baden
FRANCE
60m • 1.25h
150m • 2h
100m • 1.75h
200m • 3.25h
Colmar
260m • 4h
35m
1h
Freiburg
175m • 3.75h
Munich
95m • 1.75h
Füssen
70m • 1.5h
100m • 1.5h
Zürich
55m • 1h
95m • 2.25h
70m
1.75h
(via Reutte)
70m • 1.25h
Appenzell
Bern
SWITZERLAND
LIECH.
Innsbruck
To Brenner Pass
20m
.25h

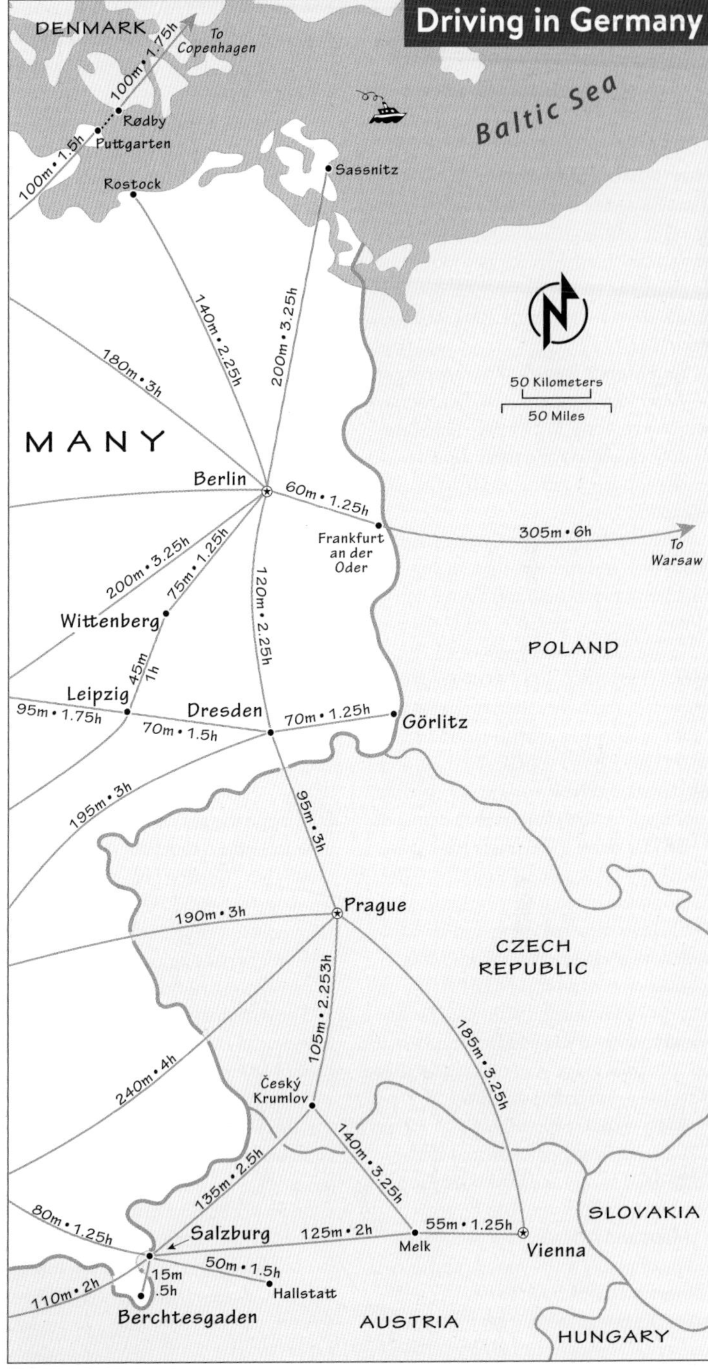
Driving in Germany
DENMARK
To Copenhagen
100m • 1.75h
Rødby
Puttgarten
100m • 1.5h
Rostock
Sassnitz
Baltic Sea
140m • 2.25h
200m • 3.25h
180m • 3h
50 Kilometers
50 Miles
MANY
Berlin
60m • 1.25h
Frankfurt an der Oder
305m • 6h
To Warsaw
200m • 3.25h
75m • 1.25h
120m • 2.25h
Wittenberg
POLAND
45m 1h
Leipzig
95m • 1.75h
Dresden
70m • 1.5h
70m • 1.25h
Görlitz
195m • 3h
95m • 3h
Prague
190m • 3h
CZECH REPUBLIC
105m • 2.253h
185m • 3.25h
240m • 4h
Český Krumlov
140m • 3.25h
135m • 2.5h
80m • 1.25h
Salzburg
125m • 2h
Melk
55m • 1.25h
Vienna
SLOVAKIA
15m .5h
50m • 1.5h
Hallstatt
110m • 2h
Berchtesgaden
AUSTRIA
HUNGARY

unlimited mileage and a 24-hour emergency assistance program. You can lease for as little as 21 days to as long as five and a half months. Car leases must be arranged from the US.

Navigation Options

If you'll be navigating using your phone or a GPS unit from home, remember to bring a car charger and device mount. To get to the center of a city, follow signs for *Zentrum* or *Stadtmitte*. Ring roads go around a city.

Your Mobile Device: The mapping app on your mobile phone works fine for navigation in Europe, but for real-time turn-by-turn directions and traffic updates, you'll generally need access to a cellular network.

A helpful exception is Google Maps, which provides turn-by-turn driving directions and recalibrates even when it's offline.

To use Google Maps offline, you must have a Google account and download your map while you have a data connection. Later—even when offline—you can call up that map, enter your destination, and get directions. View maps in standard view (not satellite view) to limit data demands.

GPS Devices: If you prefer the convenience of a dedicated GPS unit, consider renting one with your car ($10-30/day). These units offer real-time turn-by-turn directions and traffic without the data requirements of an app. Note that the unit may only come loaded with maps for its home country; if you need additional maps, ask. Also make sure your device's language is set to English before you drive off.

A less-expensive option is to bring a GPS device from home. Be aware that you'll need to buy and download European maps before your trip.

Maps and Atlases: Even when navigating primarily with a mobile app or GPS, I always make it a point to have a paper map. The free maps you get from your car-rental company usually don't have enough detail. It's smart to buy a better map before you go, or pick one up at a European gas station, bookshop, newsstand, or tourist shop.

Driving

Road Rules: Be aware of typical European road rules; for example, some countries require headlights to be turned on at all times, and nearly all forbid talking on a mobile phone without a hands-free headset. Seat belts are mandatory for all, and two beers under those belts are enough to land you in jail. You're required to use low-beam headlights if it's overcast, raining, or snowing. In Europe, you're not allowed to turn right on a red light, unless a sign or signal specifically authorizes it, and on expressways it's illegal to pass drivers on the right.

Ask your car-rental company about these rules, or check the US State Department website (www.travel.state.gov, search for your country in the "Learn about your destination" box, then click on "Travel & Transportation").

Fuel: Unleaded gasoline comes in "Super" (95 octane) and "Super Plus" (98 octane). Pumps marked "E10" or "Super E10" mean the gas contains 10 percent ethanol—make sure your rental can run on this mix. You don't have to worry about learning the German word for diesel. Your US credit and debit cards may not work at self-service gas pumps; pay the attendant or carry enough euros.

The Autobahn: The shortest distance between any two points is the autobahn (no speed limit in many sections, toll-free within Germany). Blue signs direct you to the autobahn.

To understand this complex but super-efficient freeway, look for the *Autobahn Service* booklet at any autobahn rest stop (free, lists all stops, services, road symbols, and more). Learn the signs: *Dreieck* ("three corners") means a Y-intersection; *Autobahnkreuz* is where two expressways cross. Exits are spaced about every 20 miles and often have a gas station, restaurant, minimarket, and sometimes a tourist information desk. Exits and intersections refer to the next major city or the nearest small town. When navigating, you'll see *Nord*, *Süd*, *Ost*, and *West*. Electronic signs warning of dangerous conditions may include one of these words: *Unfall* (accident), *Nebel* (fog), or *Stau* (congestion).

Even if you're obeying posted limits, don't cruise in the passing lane; stay right. Since it's illegal to pass on the right on the autobahn, drivers will angrily flash their lights, and possibly tailgate, if you linger in the passing lane.

***Umweltplakette* for Driving in German Cities:** To drive into specially designated "environmental zones" or "green zones" *(Umweltzone)* in the centers of many German cities—including Munich, Frankfurt, Cologne, Dresden, and Berlin—you are required to display an *Umweltplakette* sticker. These come standard with most German rental cars; ask when you pick up your car.

Parking: To park, pick up a free cardboard clock *(Parkscheibe)* at gas stations, police stations, and *Tabak* shops. Display your arrival time on the clock and put it on the dashboard, so parking attendants can see you've been there less than the posted maximum stay. Your US credit and debit cards may not work at automated parking garages—bring cash.

Driving in Austria: If you side-trip by car into Austria, bring your US driver's license and an International Driving Permit (costs $15 at any AAA office in the US, or CAA in Canada, plus two passport-size pictures). If you use Austria's expressways, you'll also need to have a *Vignette* sticker stuck to the inside of your rental car's windshield (€8.70 for 10 days, buy at border crossing, big gas stations near borders, or a rental-car agency). You can drive into Salzburg without using the expressway or needing a *Vignette*; see page 149.

Flights

The best comparison search engine for both international and intra-European flights is www.kayak.com. For inexpensive flights within Europe, try www.skyscanner.com.

Flying to Europe: Start looking for international flights at least 4 to 6 months before your trip, especially for peak-season travel. Off-season tickets can usually be purchased a month or so in advance. Depending on your itinerary, it can be efficient to fly into one city and out of another. If your flight requires a connection in Europe, see my hints on navigating Europe's top hub airports at www.ricksteves.com/hub-airports.

Flying within Europe: If you're considering a train ride that's more than five hours long, a flight may save you both time and money. When comparing your options, factor in the time it takes to get to the airport and how early you'll need to arrive to check in.

These days you can fly within Europe on major airlines affordably for around $100 a flight. Or you go with a budget airline such as EasyJet, Ryanair, Germanwings, or TUIfly. But be aware of the potential drawbacks and restrictions with budget carriers: nonrefundable and nonchangeable tickets, minimal or nonexistent customer service, pricey and time-consuming treks to secondary airports, and stingy baggage allowances with steep overage fees. If you're traveling with lots of luggage, a cheap flight can quickly become a bad deal. To avoid unpleasant surprises, read the small print before you book.

Flying to the US and Canada: Because security is extra tight for flights to the US, be sure to give yourself plenty of time at the airport. It's also important to charge your electronic devices before you board because security checks may require you to turn them on (see www.tsa.gov for the latest rules).

Resources from Rick Steves

Begin Your Trip at www.RickSteves.com

My mobile-friendly **website** is *the* place to explore Europe. You'll find thousands of fun articles, videos, photos, and radio interviews; a wealth of money-saving tips for planning your dream trip; my travel talks and blog; and guidebook updates (www.ricksteves.com/update).

Our **Travel Forum** is an immense collection of message boards, where our travel-savvy community answers questions and shares personal travel experiences—and our well-traveled staff chimes in when they can help.

Our **online Travel Store** offers bags and accessories designed to help you travel smarter and lighter. These include my popular bags (which I live out of four months a year), money belts, totes, toiletries kits, adapters, guidebooks, planning maps, and more.

Choosing the right **rail pass** for your trip can drive you nutty. Our website will help you find the perfect fit for your itinerary and your budget: We offer easy, one-stop shopping for rail passes, seat reservations, and point-to-point tickets.

Guidebooks, Video, Audio Europe, and Tours

Books: *Rick Steves Best of Germany* is just one of many books in my series on European travel, which includes country and city guidebooks, Snapshot guides (excerpted chapters from my country guides), Pocket Guides (full-color little books on big cities, including Munich and Salzburg), and my budget-travel skills handbook, *Rick Steves Europe Through the Back Door.* My phrase books—including one for German—are practical and budget-oriented. A more complete list of my titles appears near the end of this book.

TV Shows: My public television series, *Rick Steves' Europe,* covers Europe from top to bottom with over 100 half-hour episodes. To watch full episodes online for free, see www.ricksteves.com/tv. Or to raise your travel I.Q. with video versions of our popular classes (including my talks on travel skills, packing smart, most European countries, and European art), see www.ricksteves.com/travel-talks.

Audio: My weekly public radio show, *Travel with Rick Steves,* features interviews with travel experts from around the world. A complete archive is available at www.soundcloud.com/rick-steves, and much of this audio content is available, along with my audio tours of Europe's (and Germany's) top sights, through my free **Rick Steves Audio Europe** app (see page 29).

Rick Steves AUDIO EUROPE

Small-Group Tours: Want to travel with greater efficiency and less stress? We offer **tours** with more than 40 itineraries reaching the best destinations in this book...and beyond. You'll find European adventures to fit every vacation length, and you'll enjoy great guides and a fun but small group of travel partners. For all the details, and to get our tour catalog, visit www.ricksteves.com or call us at 425/608-4217.

HOLIDAYS AND FESTIVALS

This list includes selected festivals in major cities, plus national holidays observed throughout Germany. Many sights and banks close on national holidays—keep this in mind when planning your itinerary. Before planning a trip around a festival, make sure you verify the dates by checking the festival's website or the German national tourist office (www.cometogermany.com). For Salzburg, try www.salzburg.info.

Jan 6	Epiphany (Heilige Drei Könige)
Feb or March	Fasching (carnival season leading up to Ash Wednesday)
March or April	Easter Sunday/Monday; Easter Festival, Salzburg
Mid-April–Early May	Spring Festival, Munich (Frühlingsfest)
May 1	May Day with maypole dances
May 5	Ascension
Mid-Late May (Pentecost weekend)	Carnival of Cultures (www.karneval-berlin.de), Berlin; Meistertrunk Show (medieval costumes, *Biergarten* parties, www.meistertrunk.de), Rothenburg
Mid-Late May	Pentecost (Pfingsten) and Pentecost Monday (Pfingstmontag)
Late May–Early June	Weindorf Wine Festival, Würzburg; Mozartfest, Würzburg
May 26	Corpus Christi (Fronleichnam), southern and western Germany
May–Sept	Rhine in Flames (monthly displays of fireworks at rotating Rhine towns, www.rhein-in-flammen.com), Rhine
June	Fressgass' Fest (www.frankfurt-tourismus.de), Frankfurt
Mid-June	Stadtteilfest Bunte Republik Neustadt, Dresden (counterculture block party, www.brn-dresden.de)
Late June	City Festival (www.elbhangfest.de), Dresden; Frankfurt Summertime Festival (arts)
Early July	Kiliani Volksfest, Würzburg (folk festival)
Early July	Open Air Festival, Berlin (music on Gendarmenmarkt, www.classicopenair.de)
Late June–July	Tollwood, Munich (art, concerts, street theater, www.tollwood.de)

Mid-July	Lichter Festival (fireworks and music, www.koelner-lichter.de), Cologne
July	Kinderzeche Festival (www.kinderzeche.de), Dinkelsbühl
Late July–Early Aug	Klassik Open Air (fireworks and classical music, www.klassikopenair.de), Nürnberg
Late July–Early Aug	Bardentreffen Nürnberg (world music, www.bardentreffen.de)
Late July–Aug	Salzburg Festival (music, www.salzburgerfestspiele.at)
Early Aug	International Beer Festival, Berlin
Aug 15	Assumption (Mariä Himmelfahrt)
Mid-Aug	Weindorf wine festival, Rothenburg
Late Aug (last weekend)	Museum Riverbank Festival (www.frankfurt-tourismus.de), Frankfurt
Late Aug–Early Sept	Rheingau Wine Festival (www.frankfurt-tourismus.de), Frankfurt
Early Sept	Reichsstadt Festival (fireworks), Rothenburg
Mid-Sept–Early Oct	Oktoberfest (www.oktoberfest.de), Munich
Oct 3	German Unity Day (Tag der Deutschen Einheit)
Mid-Oct	Festival of Lights, Berlin (landmark buildings artistically lit, www.festival-of-lights.de)
Nov	Jazzfest Berlin (www.berlinerfestspiele.de)
Nov 1	All Saints' Day (Allerheiligen)
Nov 11	St. Martin's Day (Martinstag)
Dec	Christmas markets, good ones in Nürnberg, Munich, Rothenburg, and Salzburg
Dec 6	St. Nikolaus Day (parades)
Dec 24	Christmas Eve (Heiliger Abend), when Germans celebrate Christmas
Dec 25	Christmas
Dec 31	New Year's Eve

CONVERSIONS AND CLIMATE

Numbers and Stumblers

- Europeans write a few of their numbers differently than we do: 1 = 1, 4 = 4, 7 = 7.
- In Europe, dates appear as day/month/year; Christmas is 25/12.
- Commas are decimal points and decimals are commas. A dollar and a half is $1,50, one thousand is 1.000.
- When counting with fingers, start with your thumb. If you hold up your first finger to request one item, you'll probably get two.
- What Americans call the second floor of a building is the first floor in Europe.
- On escalators and moving sidewalks, Europeans keep the left "lane" open for passing. Keep to the right.

Clothing and Shoe Sizes

Shoppers can use these US-to-European comparisons as general guidelines, but note that no conversion is perfect. For info on VAT refunds, see page 386.

Women: For clothing or shoe sizes, add 30 (US shirt size 10 = European size 40; US shoe size 8 = European size 38-39).

Men: For shirts, multiply by 2 and add about 8 (US size 15 = European size 38). For jackets and suits, add 10. For shoes, add 32-34.

Children: For clothing, subtract 1-2 sizes for small children and subtract 4 for juniors. For shoes up to size 13, add 16-18, and for sizes 1 and up, add 30-32.

Metric Conversions

A **kilogram** equals 1,000 grams and about 2.2 pounds. One hundred **grams** (a common unit of sale at markets) is about a quarter-pound.

One **liter** is about a quart, or almost four to a gallon.

A **kilometer** is six-tenths of a mile. To convert kilometers to miles, cut the kilometers in half and add back 10 percent of the original (120 km: 60 + 12 = 72 miles). One **meter** is 39 inches.

Using the **Celsius** scale, 0°C equals 32°F. To roughly convert Celsius to Fahrenheit, double the number and add 30. For weather, 28°C is 82°F—perfect. For health, 37°C is just right. At a launderette, 30°C is cold, 40°C is warm (default setting), and 60°C is hot.

Germany's Climate

First line, average daily high; second line, average daily low; third line, average days without rain. For more detailed weather statistics for destinations in this book (as well as the rest of the world), check www.wunderground.com.

Munich

J	F	M	A	M	J	J	A	S	O	N	D
35°	38°	48°	56°	64°	70°	74°	73°	67°	56°	44°	36°
23°	23°	30°	38°	45°	51°	55°	54°	48°	40°	33°	26°
15	12	18	15	16	13	15	15	17	18	15	16

Berlin

J	F	M	A	M	J	J	A	S	O	N	D
35°	37°	46°	56°	66°	72°	75°	74°	68°	56°	45°	38°
26°	26°	31°	39°	47°	53°	57°	56°	50°	42°	36°	29°
14	13	19	17	19	17	17	17	18	17	14	16

Packing Checklist

Clothing

- ❑ 5 shirts: long- & short-sleeve
- ❑ 2 pairs pants or skirt
- ❑ 1 pair shorts or capris
- ❑ 5 pairs underwear & socks
- ❑ 1 pair walking shoes
- ❑ Sweater or fleece top
- ❑ Rainproof jacket with hood
- ❑ Tie or scarf
- ❑ Swimsuit
- ❑ Sleepwear

Money

- ❑ Debit card
- ❑ Credit card(s)
- ❑ Hard cash ($20 bills)
- ❑ Money belt or neck wallet

Documents & Travel Info

- ❑ Passport
- ❑ Airline reservations
- ❑ Rail pass/train reservations
- ❑ Car-rental voucher
- ❑ Driver's license
- ❑ Student ID, hostel card, etc.
- ❑ Photocopies of all the above
- ❑ Hotel confirmations
- ❑ Insurance details
- ❑ Guidebooks & maps
- ❑ Notepad & pen
- ❑ Journal

Toiletries Kit

- ❑ Toiletries
- ❑ Medicines & vitamins
- ❑ First-aid kit
- ❑ Glasses/contacts/sunglasses (with prescriptions)
- ❑ Earplugs
- ❑ Packet of tissues (for WC)

Miscellaneous

- ❑ Daypack
- ❑ Sealable plastic baggies
- ❑ Laundry soap
- ❑ Clothesline
- ❑ Sewing kit
- ❑ Travel alarm/watch

Electronics

- ❑ Smartphone or mobile phone
- ❑ Camera & related gear
- ❑ Tablet/ereader/media player
- ❑ Laptop & flash drive
- ❑ Earbuds or headphones
- ❑ Chargers
- ❑ Plug adapters

Optional Extras

- ❑ Flipflops or slippers
- ❑ Mini-umbrella or poncho
- ❑ Travel hairdryer
- ❑ Belt
- ❑ Hat (for sun or cold)
- ❑ Picnic supplies
- ❑ Water bottle
- ❑ Fold-up tote bag
- ❑ Small flashlight
- ❑ Small binoculars
- ❑ Small towel or washcloth
- ❑ Inflatable pillow
- ❑ Tiny lock
- ❑ Address list (to mail postcards)
- ❑ Postcards/photos from home
- ❑ Extra passport photos
- ❑ Good book

German Survival Phrases

When using the phonetics, pronounce ī like the long i in "light." Bolded syllables are stressed.

English	German	Pronunciation
Good day.	*Guten Tag.*	**goo**-tehn tahg
Do you speak English?	*Sprechen Sie Englisch?*	**shprehkh**-ehn zee **ehgn**-lish
Yes. / No.	*Ja. / Nein.*	yah / nīn
I (don't) understand.	*Ich verstehe (nicht).*	ikh fehr-**shtay**-heh (nikht)
Please.	*Bitte.*	**bit**-teh
Thank you.	*Danke.*	**dahng**-keh
I'm sorry.	*Es tut mir leid.*	ehs toot meer līt
Excuse me.	*Entschuldigung.*	ehnt-**shool**-dig-oong
(No) problem.	*(Kein) Problem.*	(kīn) proh-**blaym**
(Very) good.	*(Sehr) gut.*	(zehr) goot
Goodbye.	*Auf Wiedersehen.*	owf **vee**-der-zayn
one / two	*eins / zwei*	īns / tsvī
three / four	*drei / vier*	drī / feer
five / six	*fünf / sechs*	fewnf / zehkhs
seven / eight	*sieben / acht*	**zee**-behn / ahkht
nine / ten	*neun / zehn*	noyn / tsayn
How much is it?	*Wieviel kostet das?*	**vee**-feel **kohs**-teht dahs
Write it?	*Schreiben?*	**shrī**-behn
Is it free?	*Ist es umsonst?*	ist ehs oom-**zohnst**
Included?	*Inklusive?*	in-kloo-**zee**-veh
Where can I buy / find...?	*Wo kann ich kaufen / finden...?*	voh kahn ikh **kow**-fehn / **fin**-dehn
I'd like / We'd like...	*Ich hätte gern / Wir hätten gern...*	ikh **heh**-teh gehrn / veer **heh**-tehn gehrn
...a room.	*...ein Zimmer.*	īn **tsim**-mer
...a ticket to ______	*...eine Fahrkarte nach ______*	**ī**-neh **far**-kar-teh nahkh
Is it possible?	*Ist es möglich?*	ist ehs **mur**-glikh
Where is...?	*Wo ist...?*	voh ist
...the train station	*...der Bahnhof*	dehr **bahn**-hohf
...the bus station	*...der Busbahnhof*	dehr **boos**-bahn-hohf
...the tourist information office	*...das Touristen-informations-büro*	dahs too-**ris**-tehn-in-for-maht-see-**ohns**-**bew**-roh
...the toilet	*...die Toilette*	dee toh-**leh**-teh
men	*Herren*	**hehr**-rehn
women	*Damen*	**dah**-mehn
left / right	*links / rechts*	links / rehkhts
straight	*geradeaus*	geh-**rah**-deh-**ows**
What time does this open / close?	*Um wieviel Uhr wird hier geöffnet / geschlossen?*	oom **vee**-feel oor veerd heer geh-**urf**-neht / geh-**shloh**-sehn
At what time?	*Um wieviel Uhr?*	oom **vee**-feel oor
Just a moment.	*Moment.*	moh-**mehnt**
now / soon / later	*jetzt / bald / später*	yehtst / bahld / **shpay**-ter
today / tomorrow	*heute / morgen*	**hoy**-teh / **mor**-gehn

In a German Restaurant

English	German	Pronunciation
I'd like / We'd like...	*Ich hätte gern / Wir hätten gern...*	ikh **heh**-teh gehrn / veer **heh**-tehn gehrn
...a reservation for...	*...eine Reservierung für...*	ī-neh reh-zer-**feer**-oong fewr
...a table for one / two.	*...einen Tisch für eine Person / zwei Personen.*	ī-nehn tish fewr ī-neh pehr-zohn / tsvī pehr-**zoh**-nehn
Nonsmoking.	*Nichtraucher.*	**nikht**-rowkh-er
Is this seat free?	*Ist hier frei?*	ist heer frī
Menu (in English), please.	*Speisekarte (auf Englisch), bitte.*	**shpī**-zeh-kar-teh (owf **ehng**-lish) **bit**-teh
service (not) included	*Trinkgeld (nicht) inklusive*	**trink**-gehlt (nikht) in-kloo-**zee**-veh
cover charge	*Eintritt*	**īn**-trit
to go	*zum Mitnehmen*	tsoom **mit**-nay-mehn
with / without	*mit / ohne*	mit / **oh**-neh
and / or	*und / oder*	oont / **oh**-der
menu (of the day)	*(Tages-) Karte*	(**tah**-gehs-) **kar**-teh
set meal for tourists	*Touristenmenü*	too-**ris**-tehn-meh-**new**
specialty of the house	*Spezialität des Hauses*	**shpayt**-see-ah-lee-**tayt** dehs **how**-zehs
appetizers	*Vorspeise*	**for**-shpī-zeh
bread / cheese	*Brot / Käse*	broht / **kay**-zeh
sandwich	*Sandwich*	**zahnd**-vich
soup	*Suppe*	**zup**-peh
salad	*Salat*	zah-**laht**
meat	*Fleisch*	flīsh
poultry	*Geflügel*	geh-**flew**-gehl
fish	*Fisch*	fish
seafood	*Meeresfrüchte*	**meh**-rehs-**frewkh**-teh
fruit	*Obst*	ohpst
vegetables	*Gemüse*	geh-**mew**-zeh
dessert	*Nachspeise*	**nahkh**-shpī-zeh
mineral water	*Mineralwasser*	min-eh-**rahl**-vah-ser
tap water	*Leitungswasser*	**lī**-toongs-vah-ser
milk	*Milch*	milkh
(orange) juice	*(Orangen-) Saft*	(oh-**rahn**-zhehn-) zahft
coffee / tea	*Kaffee / Tee*	kah-**fay** / tay
wine	*Wein*	vīn
red / white	*rot / weiß*	roht / vīs
glass / bottle	*Glas / Flasche*	glahs / **flah**-sheh
beer	*Bier*	beer
Cheers!	*Prost!*	prohst
More. / Another.	*Mehr. / Noch eins.*	mehr / nohkh īns
The same.	*Das gleiche.*	dahs **glīkh**-eh
Bill, please.	*Rechnung, bitte.*	**rehkh**-noong **bit**-teh
tip	*Trinkgeld*	**trink**-gehlt
Delicious!	*Lecker!*	**lehk**-er

For more user-friendly German phrases, check out *Rick Steves' German Phrase Book and Dictionary* or *Rick Steves' French, Italian & German Phrase Book.*

INDEX

A

B

E

F

G

H

I

J

K

L

M

N

O

P

R

S

T

U

V

W

Z

MAP INDEX

ricksteves.com

your travel dreams into affordable reality

Radio Interviews

Enjoy ready access to Rick's vast library of radio interviews covering travel tips and cultural insights that relate specifically to your Europe travel plans.

Travel Forums

Learn, ask, share! Our online community of savvy travelers is a great resource for first-time travelers to Europe, as well as seasoned pros. You'll find forums on each country, plus travel tips and restaurant/hotel reviews. You can even ask one of our well-traveled staff to chime in with an opinion.

Travel News

Subscribe to our free Travel News e-newsletter, and get monthly updates from Rick on what's happening in Europe.

Audio Europe™

Rick's Free Travel App

Get your FREE Rick Steves Audio Europe™ app to enjoy...

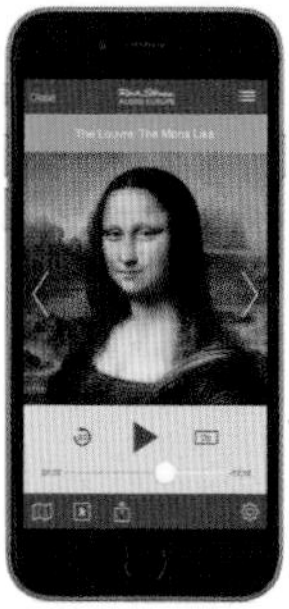

- Dozens of self-guided tours of Europe's top museums, sights and historic walks
- Hundreds of tracks filled with cultural insights and sightseeing tips from Rick's radio interviews
- All organized into handy geographic playlists
- For Apple and Android

With Rick whispering in your ear, Europe gets even better.

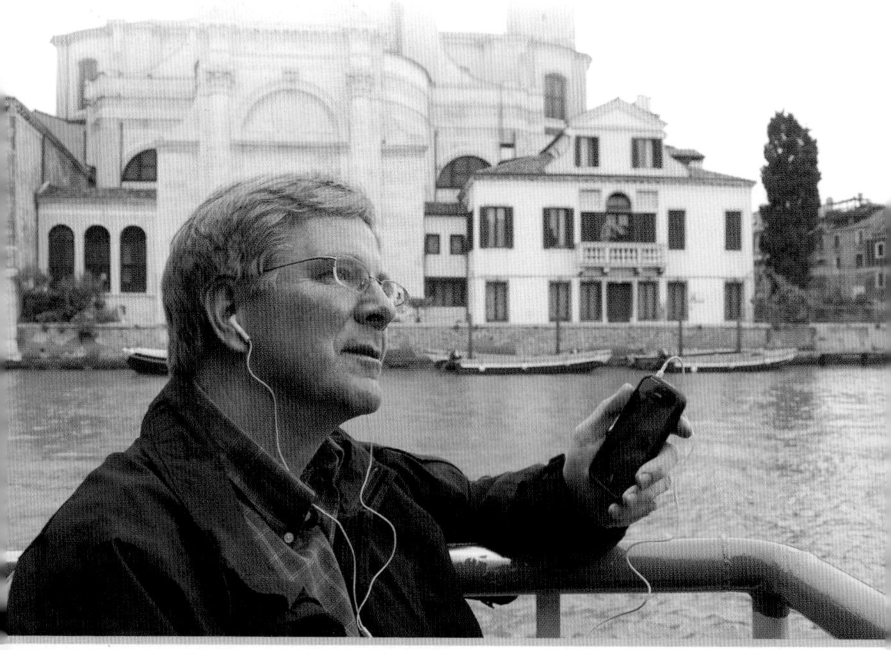

Find out more at ricksteves.com

Pack Light and Right

Gear up for your next adventure at ricksteves.com

Light Luggage

Pack light and right with Rick Steves' affordable, custom-designed rolling carry-on bags, backpacks, day packs and shoulder bags.

Accessories

From packing cubes to moneybelts and beyond, Rick has personally selected the travel goodies that will help your trip go smoother.

Shop at ricksteves.com

Rick Steves has

Experience maximum Europe

Save time and energy

This guidebook is your independent-travel toolkit. But for all it delivers, it's still up to you to devote the time and energy it takes to manage the preparation and logistics that are essential for a happy trip. If that's a hassle, there's a solution.

Rick Steves Tours

A Rick Steves tour takes you to Europe's most

great tours, too!

with minimum stress

interesting places with great guides and small groups of 28 or less. We follow Rick's favorite itineraries, ride in comfy buses, stay in family-run hotels, and bring you intimately close to the Europe you've traveled so far to see. Most importantly, we take away the logistical headaches so you can focus on the fun.

Join the fun

This year we'll take thousands of free-spirited travelers—nearly half of them repeat customers—along with us on four dozen different itineraries, from Ireland to Italy to Athens.

Is a Rick Steves tour the right fit for your travel dreams? Find out at ricksteves.com, where you can also request Rick's latest tour catalog.

Europe is best experienced with happy travel partners. We hope you can join us.

See our itineraries at ricksteves.com

A Guide for Every Trip

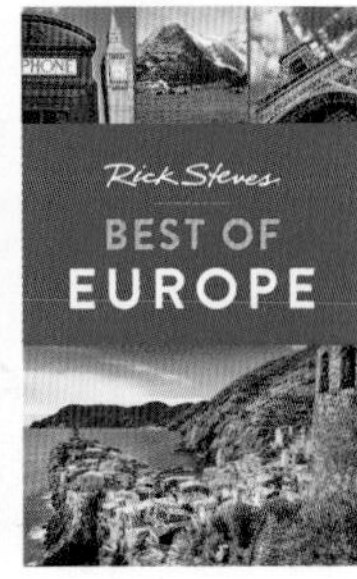

BEST OF GUIDES

Full-color easy-to-scan format, focusing on Europe's most popular destinations and sights.

Best of England
Best of Europe
Best of France
Best of Germany
Best of Ireland
Best of Italy
Best of Spain

COMPREHENSIVE GUIDES

City, country, and regional guides with detailed coverage for a multi-week trip exploring the most iconic sights and venturing off the beaten track.

Amsterdam & the Netherlands
Barcelona
Belgium: Bruges, Brussels, Antwerp & Ghent
Berlin
Budapest
Croatia & Slovenia
Eastern Europe
England
Florence & Tuscany
France
Germany
Great Britain
Greece: Athens & the Peloponnese
Iceland
Ireland
Istanbul
Italy
London
Paris
Portugal
Prague & the Czech Republic
Provence & the French Riviera
Rome
Scandinavia
Scotland
Spain
Switzerland
Venice
Vienna, Salzburg & Tirol

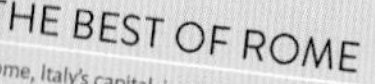

Rick Steves guidebooks are published by Avalon Travel, an imprint of Perseus Books, a Hachette Book Group company.

POCKET GUIDES

Compact, full-color city guides with the essentials for shorter trips.

Amsterdam
Athens
Barcelona
Florence
Italy's Cinque Terre
London
Munich & Salzburg
Paris
Prague
Rome
Venice
Vienna

SNAPSHOT GUIDES

Focused single-destination coverage.

Basque Country: Spain & France
Copenhagen & the Best of Denmark
Dublin
Dubrovnik
Edinburgh
Hill Towns of Central Italy
Krakow, Warsaw & Gdansk
Lisbon
Loire Valley
Madrid & Toledo
Milan & the Italian Lakes District
Naples & the Amalfi Coast
Normandy
Northern Ireland
Norway
Reykjavik
Sevilla, Granada & Southern Spain
St. Petersburg, Helsinki & Tallinn
Stockholm

CRUISE PORTS GUIDES

Reference for cruise ports of call.

Mediterranean Cruise Ports
Northern European Cruise Ports

Complete your library with...

TRAVEL SKILLS & CULTURE

Study up on travel skills before visiting "Europe through the back door" or gain insight on European history and culture.

Europe 101
European Christmas
European Easter
European Festivals
Europe Through the Back Door
Postcards from Europe
Travel as a Political Act

PHRASE BOOKS & DICTIONARIES

French
French, Italian & German
German
Italian
Portuguese
Spanish

PLANNING MAPS

Britain, Ireland & London
Europe
France & Paris
Germany, Austria & Switzerland
Ireland
Italy
Spain & Portugal

PHOTO CREDITS

Dominic Arizona Bonuccelli (www.azphoto.com): 1 top left, 1 top right, 2 top middle, 2 bottom right, 3 bottom right, 9 left, 10 top, 11 top, 11 middle left, 11 bottom right, 13 bottom right, 14 bottom right, 18 top left, 19 top right, 19 bottom, 20 middle right, 20 bottom, 21 top, 21 bottom left, 22 bottom, 23 middle right, 26, 28, 39 left, 49, 55, 57, 58 left, 60, 62, 65, 80, 81, 96, 108, 109 top right, 109 bottom right, 135, 139, 143, 175 right, 239, 263, 303 left, 303 right, 309, 313, 315, 320, 321, 327 left, 338, 357, 364, 366, 378, 382, 386, 393, 399

1 bottom © Joe1971 | Dreamstime.com, 2 left © Ani_snimki | Dreamstime.com, 3 top left © Photomorgana | Dreamstime.com, 3 middle © Borisb17 | Dreamstime.com, 6 © Christina Hanck | Dreamstime.com, 9 right © Vichie81 | Dreamstime.com, 11 bottom left © Kyrien | Dreamstime.com, 13 top © minnystock | Dreamstime.com, 13 bottom left © Anyaivanova | Dreamstime.com, 14 top © Enricoagostoni | Dreamstime.com, 15 top right © Sean Pavone | Dreamstime.com, 15 bottom © Sepavo | Dreamstime.com, 16 top © minnystock | Dreamstime.com, 17 top © Wulwais | Dreamstime.com, 17 middle right © Barbaraleephotography | Dreamstime.com, 18 top right © Jenifoto406 | Dreamstime.com, 19 top left © Vichie81 | Dreamstime.com, 32 © Bbsferrari | Dreamstime.com, 38 © Luisa Vallon Fumi | Dreamstime.com, 39 right © Bertl123 | Dreamstime.com, 45 © Manfredxy | Dreamstime.com, 48 © Manwolste | Dreamstime.com, 50 © Helo80808 | Dreamstime.com, 52 © Carso80 | Dreamstime.com, 54 © Jenifoto406 | Dreamstime.com, 102 © minnystock | Dreamstime.com, 118 left © Anibaltrejo | Dreamstime.com, 121 left © Anibal Trejo | Dreamstime.com, 123 © Castenoid | Dreamstime.com, 124 © Alex Zarubin | Dreamstime.com, 127 © minnystock | Dreamstime.com, 130 © Sergiy Palamarchuk | Dreamstime.com, 133 © Elenaphotos | Dreamstime.com, 150 © Naumenkoaleksandr | Dreamstime.com, 155 bottom left © Thanakrits15 | Dreamstime.com, 171 © Tverkhovinets | Dreamstime.com, 173 © Rudi1976 | Dreamstime.com, 175 left © Saprygins | Dreamstime.com, 183 © Gunold Brunbauer | Dreamstime.com, 188 © minnystock | Dreamstime.com, 194 © Manfredxy | Dreamstime.com, 195 left © Gepapix | Dreamstime.com, 195 right © Christianze | Dreamstime.com, 199 © Gayane | Dreamstime.com, 204 right © Hiro1775 | Dreamstime.com, 206 © Martingraf | Dreamstime.com, 218 right © Angelina Dimitrova | Dreamstime.com, 234 © Europhotos | Dreamstime.com, 241 left © 3quarks | Dreamstime.com, 241 right © Borisb17 | Dreamstime.com, 244 right © Plotnikov | Dreamstime.com, 245 © Mango2friendly | Dreamstime.com, 248 © Palliki | Dreamstime.com, 272 © Industryandtravel | Dreamstime.com, 294 © Xantana | Dreamstime.com, 300 © Tupungato | Dreamstime.com, 317 © Elvira Kolomiytseva | Dreamstime.com, 326 left © Alexandre Fagundes De Fagundes | Dreamstime.com, 344 © Michael Krause | Dreamstime.com, 414 © Vdvtut | Dreamstime.com

179 © Kevin Galvin / Alamy Stock Photo

Public Domain via Wikimedia Commons: 17 middle left, 68 bottom, 169, 266, 369

17 bottom, 161 left, 161 right, 162, 218 left, 219, 291 © Ian Watson

Additional photography by Ben Cameron, Cameron Hewitt, Sandra Hundacker, Gene Openshaw, Robyn Stencil, Rick Steves, Gretchen Strauch, and Laura VanDeventer.

Photos are used by permission and are the property of the original copyright owners.

Avalon Travel
Hachette Book Group
1700 Fourth Street
Berkeley, CA 94710

Printed in China
First printing June 2018

ISBN 978-1-63121-805-7
Second Edition

For the latest on Rick's talks, guidebooks, Europe tours, public radio show, free audio tours, and public television series, contact Rick Steves' Europe, 130 Fourth Avenue North, Edmonds, WA 98020, 425/771-8303, www.ricksteves.com, rick@ricksteves.com.

RICK STEVES' EUROPE
Special Publications Manager: Risa Laib
Managing Editor: Jennifer Madison Davis
Project Editor: Suzanne Kotz
Editorial & Production Assistant: Jessica Shaw
Graphic Content Director: Sandra Hundacker
Maps & Graphics: David C. Hoerlein, Mary Rostad

AVALON TRAVEL
Editorial Director: Kevin McLain
Senior Editor and Series Manager: Madhu Prasher
Editor: Jamie Andrade
Associate Editor: Sierra Machado
Copy Editor: Naomi Adler Dancis
Proofreader: Patrick Collins
Indexer: Stephen Callahan
Production & Typesetting: Tabitha Lahr
Cover Design: Kimberly Glyder Design
Maps & Graphics: Kat Bennett

PHOTO CREDITS
Front Cover Photos: top, left: Oktoberfest © Arne9001 | Dreamstime.com; middle: Reichstag Dome Interior © Rodrigo Arena | Dreamstime.com; right: Berchtesgaden, Germany © Minnystock | Dreamstime.com. Bottom: Neuschwanstein Castle © Rudi1976 | Dreamstime.com
Back Cover Photos: left: Berlin © Sean Pavone | Dreamstime.com; middle: Rhine Valley grapes © Felinda | Dreamstime.com; right: Mirabell Gardens, Salzburg, Austria © jMinnystock | Dreamstime.com

Let's Keep on Travelin'

Your trip doesn't need to end.

Follow Rick on social media!